2004 Edition

# Tourism Market Trends

# Europe

World Tourism Organization
Capitán Haya 42, 28020 Madrid, Spain
Tel: (+34) 915678100; Fax: (+34) 915713733
E-mail: omt@world-tourism.org
Web: www.world-tourism.org

**Tourism Market Trends – Europe 2004 Ed.**
ISBN 92-844-0800-8

Published and printed by the World Tourism Organization, Madrid, Spain
First printing in 2005




World Tourism Organization
Calle Capitán Haya, 42
28020 Madrid, Spain
Tel.: (+34) 915 678 100
Fax: (+34) 915 713 733
Web site: www.world-tourism.org
Email: omt@world-tourism.org

# Foreword

This report has been prepared by the WTO Market Intelligence and Promotion Section. Chapter I, *Main Features*, was drafted by Tourism Consultant Mr. Tim Bartlett, Director of TRI Hospitality Consulting Spain. Mr. Luigi Cabrini, WTO Regional Representative for Europe, also made a valuable contribution.

Except where otherwise indicated, data used was collected by the WTO Secretariat from the official institutions of the countries and territories. Quantitative data has been reported by National Tourism Administrations (NTAs), National Tourism Organizations (NTOs), statistical offices or national banks and a few international organizations. The *Survey* sections for the various countries and territories included in Chapter III were contributed by the tourism institutions that replied to the corresponding questionnaire sent by the WTO Secretariat.

The World Tourism Organization wishes to express its sincere gratitude to all who have participated in the elaboration of this report for their valuable and decisive cooperation, in particular to the organizations and persons involved from the various countries and territories.

**Explanation of symbols and conventions used**

| | | |
|---|---|---|
| * | = | provisional figure or data |
| .. | = | figure or data not (yet) available |
| 0 | = | rounded figure where the original figure is less than 0.5 (-0 when rounding a negative figure) |
| 0.0 | = | rounded figure where the original figure is less than 0.05 (-0.0 when rounding a negative figure) |
| (000) | = | thousand |
| mn | = | million (1,000,000) |
| bn | = | billion (1,000,000,000) |

Due to rounding, some totals may not correspond exactly with the sum of the separate figures.

# Table of Contents

Pages

**Annex**

# The *Tourism Market Trends, 2004 Edition* series

*Tourism Market Trends* is WTO's regular series of reports whose objective is to present international tourism trends in the world as well as in each region, subregion and country. The full series consists of one volume providing an overview of the tourism trends in the world and five regional volumes highlighting the international tourism trends in each of the regions.

The structure of the series introduced in the 2001 edition, and further developed in the 2002 and 2003 editions, has been maintained in the *Tourism Market Trends, 2004 Edition,* namely:

- The analysis of the evolution of international tourism worldwide and the accompanying aggregated data is presented in a separate volume *World Overview and Tourism Topics.*
- Detailed information on the various regions of the world, and on the individual countries and territories they are composed of, is included in five regional volumes covering Africa, Americas, Asia and the Pacific (integrating the WTO regions of East Asia and the Pacific and South Asia), Europe and the Middle East.
- Each regional volume opens with a first chapter *Main Features* containing an overview of the tourism development in the region based on the information provided by the National Tourism Administrations or National Tourism Organisations of the various countries in response to the survey conducted by the Market Intelligence and Promotion Department.
- Chapter II includes a more in-depth quantitative analysis of tourism trends in terms of tourism arrivals and receipts, as well as a breakdown of inbound by regions of origin, means of transport and purpose of visit. Concerning outbound tourism, data is also included on international tourism expenditure and outbound trips taken.
- Chapter III includes results for the individual countries or territories of the region. For each country the following information is included (to the extent that data has been made available):
    - A Profile table including the following data series:
        - International Arrivals: different categories of inbound tourism;
        - Tourism accommodation: number of rooms and nights spent (inbound tourism and domestic tourism);
        - Trips abroad (outbound tourism);
        - Receipts and Expenditure for International Tourism;
        - various indicators of economic or general nature.
    - The full response to the survey conducted by the WTO Secretariat for each individual country or territory that replied. The survey encompasses an evaluation of the past year (2003) as well as an outlook on the year 2004.
    - Detailed tables on arrivals and nights broken down by country of origin.
- Each of the six volumes is concluded with an annex comprising overview tables of data on international tourist arrivals and international tourism receipts for all countries for which data are available, methodological notes on concepts and definitions, sources of the data used, and sources of information.

The WTO Secretariat is constantly striving to extend and enhance the content of the Tourism Market Trends series. Some of the changes and additions introduced in the 2004 edition are:

- Data on International Tourism Receipts and International Tourism Expenditure is reported according to the International Monetary Fund (IMF) methodology for the Balance of Payments. International Tourism Receipts refers to the "Credit" side while International Tourism Expenditure refers to the "Debit" side (see for more information, the methodological notes in the annex).
- In the survey section for the individual countries in Chapter III, except for the regular questions on tourism development, a set of questions has been included paying special attention to the Meetings industry.

When using the reports the following considerations should be borne in mind:

- In accordance with the nature of the data provided by the countries and territories, the focus is on inbound tourism. When referring to outbound tourism trends, it should be taken into account that this information is largely derived from the same inbound-oriented data. The Secretariat covers outbound tourism in a separate series of reports (see the annex for more information).
- The emphasis in the analysis and the tables is on medium-term rather than on short-term development. For the short-term evolution of tourism please refer to the *WTO World Tourism Barometer*. The *WTO World Tourism Barometer* is published three times a year (January, June and October) and contains an overview of short-term tourism data; a retrospective and prospective evaluation of tourism performance by the WTO Panel of Tourism Experts and selected economic data relevant for tourism (see the annex or the WTO website at www.world-tourism.org/facts/menu.html for more information).
- The reports generally reflect data as collected by the WTO Secretariat up to September 2004 (see the foot of each table). Data is often still provisional and can be updated or revised by the reporting countries in a later stage without further notice. When making references it is preferable always to attempt using the latest published data.
- In the world and (sub)regional aggregates (totals, subtotals), estimates are included to make allowance for the countries and territories with data still missing based upon data available for a part of the year or the general trend for the region. The data presented for the individual countries, however, reflect what has been reported for each country and does not include estimates of the WTO Secretariat.
- The Secretariat of the World Tourism Organization is aware of the limitations of the available statistical information on tourism. Despite the considerable progress made in recent decades, tourism statistics are often not uniform, because definitions and methods of data collection tend to differ. Every user of this information should bear in mind that the international comparability of statistical data is still not optimal.

The contents of this report are prepared under the responsibility of the WTO Market Intelligence and Promotion Department. Except where otherwise indicated, the quantitative and qualitative information in this report is based on data supplied by the official institutions of the various countries and territories.

The WTO Secretariat wishes to express its sincere gratitude for the reception given to this publication and for the cooperation it received in preparing this report. It welcomes the active involvement of countries, as well as their comments and suggestions on the design and contents of this series.

# I

# Main Features: Europe

# I Main Features: Europe

## I.1 Summary

Is a "two-speed Europe" developing in tourism? Once again in 2003, with growth of 0.4 per cent in arrivals, Europe confirmed its resilience by outperforming the world, which declined by 1.7 per cent. But this relatively positive result was largely due to a good performance from "new" destinations in the Central and Eastern Europe subregion, which grew by 3.7 per cent. Northern Europe, after some very difficult years, showed a limited bounce-back, increasing by 2.1 per cent, but the areas which concentrate Europe's most important "mature" destinations had an indifferent 2003 –Southern/Mediterranean Europe remained virtually static and Western Europe declined by 1.4 per cent.

There were plenty of negative factors overhanging Europe's –and indeed the world's– tourism markets in 2003, notably the Iraq war, terrorism, SARS, weak global economic performance, and, for the countries inside the Eurozone, currency appreciation. But in Central and Eastern Europe, the euphoria surrounding European Union (EU) enlargement, plus favourable exchange rates against the euro, created a much more positive environment for tourism.

**Europe: International Tourist Arrivals (ITA) and International Tourism Receipts (ITR)**

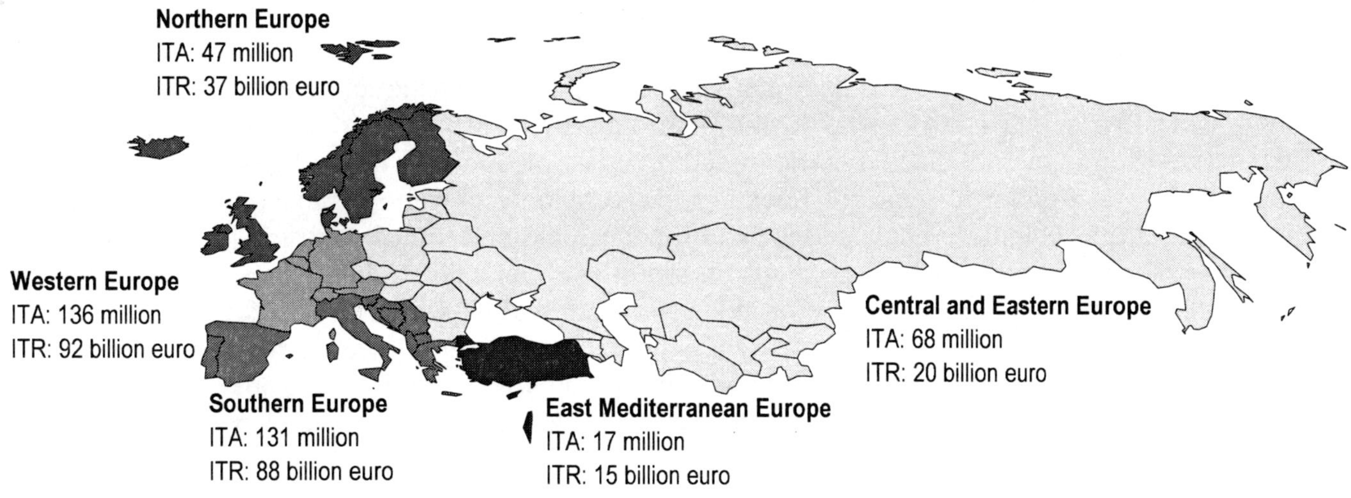


A factor, which in 2003 played a more significant role than usual in Europe, was the weather. There was a good early ski season, but ice paralysed sea travel in the North, especially in the Gulf of Finland. Then there was a remarkably sunny and hot summer in northern countries, a double-edged sword which had some detrimental impact on travel to sun and sea destinations in the south and which led to negative publicity regarding low water levels in Europe's rivers and lakes. The hot weather's impact was compounded by increased efforts to promote domestic tourism. Fires in Portugal and France not only affected tourism in those countries, but also had an impact on motoring traffic to Spain. The oil slick incident with Prestige in the Galician coast of Spain also created significant negative publicity.

There was continuing evidence of long-haul weakness, especially from Japan and the United States of America. France attributes much of its 2.6 per cent decline in 2003 to poor performances from these markets, and Italy continued to be suffered from loss of US and Japanese spending power. The Netherlands reported a decline of 15 per cent in arrivals from the United States of America and of 9 per cent from Asia. Belgium also saw decreases from the United States of America and Japan of 9 per cent and 26 per cent respectively. However green shoots of optimism regarding the US market started to appear in Spain, in the United Kingdom, and in Ireland.

There was less euphoria about growth from China than in the previous year, and more emphasis on neighbouring markets and on signs of regeneration in German outbound travel. Central and Eastern Europe, especially the European Union enlargement countries, is clearly producing growth both in inbound and outbound. Intraregional travel remains a very strong feature in Europe –it accounts for 96 per cent of arrivals in Cyprus, for example, and the European Union provides 70 per cent of foreign bed nights in Hungary. The post 11th September trend towards shorter and closer trips, preferably by land transport, is still apparent, and some European destinations feel they have been adversely impacted by this, for example Malta. Ireland has noticed a reduction in British length of stay. Generally revenue has suffered more than arrivals, and this was compounded in 2003 by continued weakness in the business travel market. In Luxembourg, for example, business and congress visits decreased, while Monaco suffered a 31 per cent decline in business overnights. Serbia and Montenegro attributes its decrease in domestic tourism partly to a weakening business travel market.

Proportionally leisure traffic increased, and the tendency towards independent travel continued. San Marino suffered a major decline in coach tours, due in part to growing customer disenchantment with this type of product and, for the second year running, independent visitors to Spain outnumbered packages. This tendency is clearly linked to increasing use of the Internet and to the extraordinary growth in budget airline services, passenger numbers on which have increased to Spain at a rate of over 40 per cent for the last two years. Budget airlines are boosting the popularity of hitherto unknown cities and regions, not only in mature destinations like France, Spain and the United Kingdom, but also for example in Hungary. New air competition to Estonia has also caused prices on Estonian Air to decrease substantially. Since the budget airline business model is based on trips of under three hours, their success is clearly compounding the trend towards short-haul travel. Another rapidly growing form of tourism, which does little for overnights, is cruising. 43 per cent more cruise ships visited Estonia in 2003 and 45 per cent more cruise passengers visited Croatia.

High profile products, which came on stream in 2003, include in Spain the Picasso Museum in Málaga and the Es Baluard Contemporary Art Museum in Palma de Mallorca, a Mystery Park in Switzerland, a new museum in Liechtenstein, a large thermal aquapark in Slovakia and a new conference centre in San Marino. There is a large aquacentrum under construction in the Czech Republic, a new waterpark that opened in March 2004 in Estonia, and also in 2004 Madrid's three top museums were being refurbished and expanded. Moreover there is continuing major investment in transport infrastructure, especially in Central and Eastern Europe, but also in Spain, Portugal and Italy.

There has been increasing emphasis on sporting products, for example a cycle route round Lake Balaton in Hungary, rafting and cycling in Serbia and Montenegro, and golf in Spain and Portugal, and major investment throughout the whole of Europe in wellness facilities and products. Events have also been a continuing theme, not just sports but also cultural and special interest events like Simenon and Brel Years in Belgium, and an Aviation Exhibition in San Marino to celebrate the 100th anniversary of motor powered flight.

Migration control affected to some extent tourist flows in Europe; for example traffic to Poland from Eastern Europe was constrained by visa problems and similarly traffic from Russia and Ukraine to Slovakia suffered from the cost of entry visas. However positive steps taken include Latvia's negotiation of a visa free regime with 60 countries, Cyprus' new consular offices in Russia and in the Commonwealth of Independent States (CIS), and a special law in Italy, which has facilitated the provision of 28 extra staff in overseas consulates. Moreover most new European Union entrants believe that membership will greatly streamline entry procedures –indeed Estonia believes that it will lead to shorter sea crossing times.

There have been several important structural changes in Government Tourism Organisations. For example, a Portuguese Tourism Institute was created to concentrate responsibilities for promotion, financial support and investment. The British Tourist Authority merged with the English Tourist Board to form VisitBritain, which will have more focus on marketing both overseas and domestic. Failte Ireland was formed by merging two state agencies, Bord Failte and CERT. Latvia transferred responsibility for tourism from the Ministry of Environmental Protection and Regional Development to the Ministry of Economics, which promptly set up a Tourism Department. Norway came up with a very original new structure by merging its Trade Council, Governmental Consultative Office for Inventors, Tourist Board, and Industrial and Regional Development Fund to form a new company, Innovation Norway. In response to 2003's difficult tourism conditions, Italy formed crisis units, dynamic structures which monitored international developments and promoted communication, spreading a series of positive and persuasive images of Italy and its regions.

Another major theme in 2003 was regional devolution. Regions in the Czech Republic and in Greece developed their own tourism plan, Italy aimed regional aid particularly at the south, and Portugal set up a new contractual relationship between the centre and the regional tourist boards. The emphasis continued on public/private partnerships and many Governments offered grants or incentives to encourage investment. Special VAT (value added tax) deals were a feature of the year. Latvia reduced VAT on tourist accommodation from 18 per cent in 2002 to 9 per cent in 2003 and 5 per cent in 2004, while Armenia abolished VAT on tourism altogether. European Union funds continued to play a major role in tourism development, for example financing investment incentives in Belgium and training in Portugal, and the new entrants started to work on their funding applications. Malta alone is submitting tourism bids totalling 8 million euro. Some individual countries also gave assistance to less developed ones for tourism projects –for example the Netherlands helped Slovenia with training, and the US Trade and Development Association funded Azerbaijan's Tourism Strategy.

Other key activities in 2003 were quality and labelling, for example museums, attractions and a scheme for physical accessibility in Denmark and the "Q Mark" in Spain, and the improvement of research and statistics, with progress towards the Tourism Satellite Account (TSA) being made in countries like Hungary and Estonia.

Marketing focus was very much on the short-haul with some increased domestic activity: For example Estonia's first domestic market campaign, and England's first co-ordinated domestic campaign in 10 years. The more mature markets increasingly concentrated on niches and affinity groups, which are normally more resilient in difficult times. Austria targeted classical music lovers. 'Luxembourg for Kids' was launched to take advantage of the growth in family holidays. Spain developed routes and special brands, for example the "Pilgrimage route to Santiago", "Heritage Cities", and "Green Spain". There were national umbrella brand building exercises, for example in Portugal and Slovenia. Not surprising there was increasing emphasis on security –the Czech Republic organised a conference branding itself as the Safe Tourist Destination.

There was also an interesting example of co-operative marketing across frontiers from the Visegrád countries – the Czech Republic, Hungary, Poland and Slovakia. However, in the more mature markets the most striking development was the rapid push towards technological tourism. Spain for example set up the State Organisation for the Technological Development of Tourism (SEDETTUR), which focuses not only on Information Technology (IT), but also on energy conservation, design, new materials, security, health and quality. Liechtenstein set up live web cameras, while Club France was relaunched with membership only available by Internet. The United Kingdom reported a fundamental shift in distribution methods with the Internet and direct marketing replacing walk in centres and telephone calls as the main point of customer contact. Switzerland continued to invest in its "Inno Tour Programme" and is launching an exciting Customer Relation Management (CRM) project in two modules, which will run from 1st June 2006 to 31st December 2010. Module 1 is e-Marketing and Module 2 Electronic Communication and Customercard. The basic aim is to create one-to-one communication with the customer. The technology tool will be the web.

Most countries have moderate expectations for 2004 and beyond, with growth between 3 and 6 per cent. The most pessimistic are Andorra, which expects a continuing decline in overnights, Malta, which predicts a flat 2004 but some growth subsequently, and Switzerland and Norway, which expect marginal growth. The optimists are Lithuania, Estonia, Romania and the Czech Republic, all in the 10 per cent range, topped by Latvia which is predicting an increase of 10 to 15 per cent, Turkey which expects to exceed 20 per cent for two years in a row, and Serbia and Montenegro, which anticipates a 50 per cent increase in tourism receipts.

Important events in 2004 include Hans Christian Andersen's 200th Anniversary in Denmark; Rock-in-Rio Lisbon in Portugal; and the Forum of the Cultures, the Centenary of Salvador Dali's birth, and the Xacobeo Holy Year Celebration in Spain, plus of course the two mega sporting events –the Football Eurocup 2004 in Portugal and the Olympic Games in Greece. Looking further forward, 2005 is the 200th Anniversary of Schiller's death in Germany, 250 years of Mozart will be celebrated in 2006, and so too will various sporting events ranging from the World Ice Hockey Championship in Latvia to the FIFA World Cup in Germany.

Western Europe, along with North America, is one of the best-organised world areas with regard to the Meeting, Incentives, Conferences and Exhibitions (MICE) sector. Germany for many years has dominated the exhibitions industry. Four of Germany's six largest trade and exhibition centres are among the top five in Europe, and all six are among the top 12 cities. France is exceptionally strong in meetings facilities. It has 120 convention centres of differing sizes, with 36 per cent of total European capacity. Spain, which is in the second position on the International Congress and Convention Association (ICCA) list of top convention countries, has more than 40 suitable cities with over 50 convention centres. The United Kingdom is in the third position on both the ICCA and Union of International Associations (UIA) lists. Europe is of course rich in historic buildings and in activities from golf to gastronomy and theatre, suitable not only for delegates to meetings but also for incentive trips and teambuilding events. Moreover, Europe provides the widest possible range of hotels, from Sweden's Ice Hotel through to major internationally branded properties with extraordinary convention facilities. The vast majority of venues are hotel based – for example of Italy's 5,231 meeting rooms, 3,602 are in hotels. Most countries in Europe, especially those within the EU, can provide good convention and exhibition facilities, but Brussels is constrained by the closure of its Convention Centre and by the lack of a permanent venue which can hold more than 5 thousand delegates.

Though the figures are not strictly comparable due to different research methods, the normal range of business travel as a proportion of overall tourism is from around 8 per cent in Malta, for example, to 30 per cent in France, Hungary and San Marino. The meetings industry alone ranges from around 2-4 per cent in Slovakia and Finland through to 10-15 per cent in Belgium and Norway, though Poland estimates it much higher at 40 per cent. Most countries handle the international promotion of MICE tourism through a specialised section within their National Tourist Office (NTO). Austria for example recently set up the Austrian Business and Convention Network as a new dedicated department of the NTO. Many countries also have city and regional convention bureaux, which bring together private sector members, but normally in collaboration with, or sometimes within, the structure of regional and city tourism organisations. Some countries also have a national convention bureau with predominantly private sector membership. The Maison de la France has formed a Business Tourism Club, which groups together the main inbound operators in the sector.

There is much optimism about the future growth potential of the MICE sector. Luxembourg will open a new convention centre in 2005. Spain expects its MICE profile to be greatly raised by hosting EIBTM (Exhibition for the Incentive, Business Travel & Meetings Industry) for the next 5 years in Barcelona, and Croatia is investing in four high capacity multi-purpose convention and exhibition facilities. Although shortage of accommodation remains a constraint in Serbia and Montenegro, in 2005 several important conferences and sporting events will be held in Belgrade. These are expected to draw more than 25 thousand participants. Hungary points out that, when Austria, Sweden and Finland joined the European Union in 1995, their MICE industries grew by between 20 and 50 per cent. However, although enlargement is expected to create new business, it is also providing more competition for established meetings destinations like the Netherlands. Switzerland only expects a slight increase in 2004, but Poland is predicting 15 to 20 per cent growth per annum over the next three years. Even Israel, which does not expect any growth in the current situation, is convinced that, with an improvement in the security situation, its meetings industry would return to robust activity over a period of time.

# I.2 Tourism Development and Outlook

## I.2.1 Overall Performance

In Northern Europe there were heartening signs from the **United Kingdom**. Inbound arrivals grew 2.2 per cent, a good performance in the context of reduced travel from the United States of America (because of the Iraq situation) and from the Far East (the SARS outbreak). The last quarter showed real recovery with arrivals up 8 per cent. Arrivals from Europe were stronger through most of the year, particularly from Eastern Europe. There was a small reduction in Europeans' length of stay. Arrivals on business trips saw a small decline, while holiday, and especially visits to friends and relatives (VFR), increased. Official statistics for domestic tourism show a decline in volume with a small growth in value, but this conflicts with most anecdotal evidence, which suggests a good year. There was also good news from **Ireland**. Overall arrivals increased by 5 per cent to 6.4 million and foreign earnings from tourism by 5 per cent to 3.4 billion euro. Holiday tourism grew by 2 per cent to 3.3 million visits. Britain remains the largest market at 3.6 million, but the strongest growth was recorded from mainland Europe and from North America, which continued its recovery. However North America has still not matched the record numbers achieved in 2000. The Iraq war slowed down the recovery in the United States of America and other long-haul markets and impacted on the type of holiday visitor from the United States of America, for example less coach tours. There was a continuing trend towards shorter holidays from Britain. Increases in costs, particularly for insurance, continued to put pressure on business margins. Attracting and retaining skilled staff remained a key challenge for the industry. The continuing appreciation of the euro impacted on performance from the United States of America and the United Kingdom, particularly in terms of perceived value for money. Tourism to **Denmark** also performed well in 2003 with an overall 2.7 per cent increase in bednights, the highest growth for more than a decade. There was positive development in both domestic (2.4%) and international (3.1%) tourism. Foreign visitor numbers increased by 0.3 per cent, with a 1 per cent increase from the United States of America, but growth in international tourism was mainly generated by neighbouring/near markets, particularly Germany, Norway and the Netherlands. Tourism related to camping and holiday houses performed particularly well, whereas tourism related to hotels, holiday centres and hostels declined. Preliminary estimates of tourism spending indicate a moderate growth of approximately one per cent in commercial tourism (i.e. excluding same-day visitors and tourists in private accommodation). A structural shift has moderated growth. The nationality and accommodation mix in 2003 shifted towards lower spending types of visitor. Coastal tourism saw the highest growth rate, but city breaks also recorded progress. The MICE segment appears to have declined slightly. On 1st October Denmark lowered its excises on alcohol and other items sensitive to border trade. This reduction has increased shopping visits from Norway and Sweden, and may also have stimulated more day trips. A 16 per cent increase in the Kroner against the US dollar made Denmark less competitive in non-euro markets. In **Sweden** the erosion of revenue was even more marked. There was an increase of 3 per cent in overall holiday arrivals. There was also an increase in the volume of nights spent of 2.7 per cent. Inbound tourism increase by 2 per cent while domestic nights increased by 4 per cent. However revenues for all types of commercial accommodation did not mirror these numbers, decreasing by 2.2 per cent. This above all reflects a shift in demand, with a reduction of the MICE market and an increase in the leisure/private market. An unstable domestic and international economic situation contributed to the reduction of inbound tourism to Sweden. According to official TSA calculations, total tourist consumption decreased by 0.5 per cent to 166.9 billion SEK (2,5% of total GDP) in 2003. Domestic private consumption increased by 2.9 per cent to 82.4 billion SEK and the export value of inbound tourism decreased by 6.2 per cent to 47.3 billion SEK. Employment in travel increased by 1.4 per cent to 127 thousand. Over the period 1995 to 2003 employment in the industry has increased by 35 per cent. The total number of visitors to attractions in Sweden increased by approximately 1.2 per cent. **Norway** reported an increase of 3 per cent in overall holiday arrivals, with growth from all major markets, and significant increases from Spain, France and Italy. Total inbound tourists numbers grew by 5.1 per cent. There was a decrease of 2 per cent in domestic overnights. Inbound results for **Finland** were less positive. Foreign arrival numbers decreased by 9.5 per cent. There was a sharp drop of 10 per cent in Russian overnights (the high exchange rate of the euro against the US dollar was unfavourable for tourism from Russia to Finland) and quite large decreases also in Norwegian and American overnights. On the other hand, very good overnight growth figures were achieved from the United Kingdom, the Netherlands, France, Italy, Switzerland and Spain. **Iceland** had a good 2003 with a 9.5 per cent increase in arrivals.

In Western Europe, as we have seen, the picture was less positive. Foreign arrivals in **France** suffered a decline of around 2.6 per cent, mainly due to poor results from long-haul markets, in particular the United States of America and Japan. These long-haul visitors are higher spenders, so in revenue terms the decline was greater –5.4 per cent. In addition to the long list of negative factors which affected tourism in 2003 – Iraq, SARS, terrorism, and economic problems, including the strengthening of the euro against the dollar and the pound sterling – France's image as a destination was undermined by the difficult relations with the United States of America prior to the Iraq war, and by press coverage of the Var forest fires, of the cancellation of festivals, of the heat wave, and of pollution on the Aquitaine coast following the sinking of the Prestige. In **Monaco** the tourism trend in 2003 was down for all types of tourism and all source markets. The business travel sector was particularly badly hit with a 31 per cent decline (in terms of hotel overnights). Leisure tourism was also down but far less –its decline was 4 per cent, which is less worrying considering the difficult international tourism climate. Overnights in **Switzerland**'s hotels decreased by 2.4 per cent, but there was an increase in day visitors due to the excellent summer weather. Mountain and wellness resorts registered marginally positive figures (+0.4% and +0.5% respectively). **The Netherlands** also reported a difficult year, due to SARS, the war in Iraq and the economic slowdown, the number of international arrivals declined by 4 per cent to 9.2 million. Long-haul markets performed particularly badly, with visitors from Asia and America declining by 15 per cent and 9 per cent respectively. The picture for European countries was more diverse. The number of tourists from neighbouring Germany and Belgium increased by 2 per cent and 11 per cent respectively. However, the number of British tourists declined by 11 per cent, mainly due to the more expensive euro. **Belgium, Flanders** was less badly affected with overnights down by just 0.2 per cent, inbound tourism up by 0.2 per cent, and domestic tourism down by 0.7 per cent. Incoming overnights to Brussels increased by 2.3 per cent in 2003 and many key markets for Belgium strengthened, for example the Netherlands +4.5 per cent, France +4.9 per cent, Italy +10.2 per cent, and Spain +2.3 per cent. However overnights from the United Kingdom, the United States of America and Japan decreased (-5.1%, -8.8% and -24.8% respectively). **Belgium, Wallonia** commented on the increase of business visits to Brussels, boosted by the preparations of the ten new entrants. The British stay-at-home campaign had a negative impact on Belgium. Tourism to **Luxembourg** registered a small decrease in foreign arrivals (-2%) and overnights. The city of Luxembourg performed worse but camping produced very good results. There was an increase in incoming tourism from the Netherlands and Denmark, and a decrease from the United Kingdom, the United States of America and Asia. Like Monaco, Luxembourg commented on the weakness of business and congress tourism in comparison with previous years. Belgium's new federal tax policy is probably discouraging some visits from that country. **Liechtenstein** reported a static year, but **Germany** bucked the subregional trend, achieving relatively good results. The number of arrivals from abroad increased in 2003 by 2.4 per cent and overnights by an encouraging 2.7 per cent. Europe, which is responsible for around three quarters of the overnight stays, expanded its market share by 2 percentage points in 2003. This increase came mainly from the Netherlands, Germany's most important source market, with +4 per cent. Other important source countries showing growth were: Switzerland (+10.5%), Belgium (+9%), Italy (+6.6%), France (+5.8%) and Denmark (+6%). There was a 1.6 per cent overall increase in the number of overnights stays in Germany by visitors from Eastern Europe. The Baltic States recorded a 6.6 per cent increase, while the number of overnight stays from Hungary and the Czech Republic rose by 3.8 per cent and 3.4 per cent respectively. However, the most important overseas market for Germany, the United States of America, recorded a 5.7 per cent decrease in 2003. China, on the other hand, fared well with a slight increase of 0.9 per cent to a total of around 580 thousand overnight stays. The number of overnight stays by visitors from Japan fell by 9.8 per cent. The Arab Gulf States recorded a significant increase with 11 per cent more overnight stays. There was also a 0.6 per cent increase in the number of domestic arrivals, though their number of overnights fell by 0.4 per cent. However, in 2003 Germany increased its market share of all holidays taken by Germans by 2 percentage points to 60 per cent. The survey "Reasons for booking a holiday in Germany" showed that, for 64 per cent of the Germans surveyed, their country still holds a number of unexplored regions. One of the main reasons for taking a holiday in Germany is that it is close to home. The holiday regions are easily accessible by car (51%), by rail (23%) and by coach (17%). Sixty per cent were satisfied with their holiday in Germany and 41 per cent were regular visitors. For 40 per cent, good value for money and the ease of organising the holiday were behind their decision to take a holiday in Germany. 2003 brought an increase in foreign arrivals (+2.5%) to **Austria**. Particularly large was the increase from the adhesion countries, especially Hungary, the Czech Republic, Slovenia and Slovakia. However arrivals and overnights from Asia and the United States of America declined.

Central and Eastern Europe was the best performing subregion in 2003, but the two largest destinations –Hungary and Poland– both registered slight declines. Visitor arrivals at **Hungary**'s frontiers decreased by one per cent to 31.4 million. Foreign arrivals at public accommodation establishments were down by 2.2 per cent and foreign bed-nights down 0.9 per cent. The top five inbound markets (visitor arrivals at frontiers) were Romania (+5.6%), Austria (+2.9%), Slovakia (+9.2%), Serbia and Montenegro (-14.4%) and Germany (+5%). Other important markets for Hungary are Italy (+11.5%), France (+6.9%) and Switzerland (+24.1%). The European Union provides 70 per cent of foreign bed-nights. Bed-nights increased in 2003 from Denmark (+12.4%); France (+8.1%); Italy (+5.9%); and the United States of America (+3.8%). They declined from Germany (-12.7%); Austria (-6.4%); the Netherlands (-2,8%); and the United Kingdom (-2.4%). The fast and significant decrease in value of the national currency (the Hungarian Forint - HUF) favoured inbound tourism, but economic problems within the largest European tourism generating markets kept many potential tourists at home in 2003. There were some other factors connected with this issue, for example shorter paid holidays in Germany and a new type of contribution to employees' holidays in Poland, which can be spent only on domestic holidays. Press coverage about the low water lever of Europe's rivers (e.g. in Hungary, the Danube and Tisza) and lakes (e.g.

Lake Balaton) had a negative impact. However the last phase of the European Union enlargement process gave a good opportunity to Hungary to improve its image. In 2003 domestic tourism in Hungary performed better than international. Domestic arrivals at public accommodation establishments rose by 2.6 per cent to 3.2 million and domestic bed-nights by 6 per cent to 8.6 million. Foreign arrivals in **Poland** decreased by 1.9 per cent. The strong euro helped to maintain visitor numbers, but impacted negatively on revenues. The first half of the year was rather poor but there was a substantial improvement in the summer season with more guests in hotels, more air-passengers and more tourists from the European Union. In the last quarter Eastern European markets declined (due to visa problems), but there were more shopping visits from western and southern neighbours (due to weakening local currency) and the growth in air traffic continued. 2003 was not a good year for domestic travel. In 2003, the tourism activity of Polish residents generally decreased. The number of holiday trips fell by 0.8 million to 17 million. The number of trips abroad dropped too, owing to the unfavourable impact of exchange rates. Compared with 2002, there were 11 per cent more tourist arrivals to the **Czech Republic** in 2003. Inbound tourism income grew 20 per cent in US dollar terms, but this is of course partly due to dollar depreciation (+0.3 % as expressed in euro terms). In 2003, 8.9 per cent more tourists (domestic and foreign) used the accommodation facilities. The number of foreign visitors to **Romania** in 2003 registered a growth of 17 per cent while domestic tourists increased by 2.7 per cent. These good results can be partly attributed to the completion of the privatisation programme in 2002, the improving quality of service and facilities, and increases in supply. In 2003, the number of foreign visitors to **Estonia** increased by 7 per cent to 1.5 million, the highest level ever. For a few consecutive years now, arrival flows from neighbouring Finland, Latvia and Russia have increased modestly or even decreased while arrivals from more distant countries, especially Germany, Norway and Poland, but also the United Kingdom, Italy, and France, have increased substantially. Visitor arrivals by plane increased 15 per cent (by almost 24 thousand people), thanks to new air capacity and pricing policies. Cruise passenger arrivals increased by more than 50 per cent with growth coming above all from the United States of America, Germany, the United Kingdom, Italy, Spain and France. Severe ice conditions in the Gulf of Finland in early 2003 hindered ferry traffic and postponed the start of the sea jet navigation season between Helsinki and Tallinn by a month and a half. This negatively affected visitor arrivals from Estonia's biggest market, Finland, but also slightly affected transit traffic from the Baltic to the Nordic countries. The decrease from Finland continued in June and July, partly due to the late start of summer, but arrivals started to increase in August, with the result that visitor arrivals by regular ships for the whole year decreased by only 1 per cent. Tourism stagnated in **Slovakia** in 2003. In US dollar terms income increased and there was a growth of foreign expenditure per day and per capita with more tourists coming from the most important feeder markets (the Czech Republic, Poland and Hungary). However, there was a decrease of 5.5 per cent in the total number of visitors; a decrease of 2.1 per cent of guests in accommodation facilities; a decrease of 1.6 per cent in the number of overnights of foreign guests; a decrease in foreign arrivals from Germany, Austria and the Ukraine; and a low ratio of new clients (7%). The overall number of inbound tourists to **Lithuania** in 2003 was 1.5 million, 4.4 per cent more than in 2002. 417 thousand of these came from Russia (-1.7%); 376 thousand came from other CIS countries (-6.1%); 140 thousand came from Latvia (+18%); 91 thousand from Estonia, (+64%) and 107 thousand from Germany (+27%). From other European countries (excluding Poland) there were 224 thousand inbound visitors (+6.4%). It is clear that the Lithuanian tourism market is gradually shifting from East to West. In Vilnius the number of cultural weekend tours increased rapidly and there was an overall increase in MICE activities country-wide. **Belarus** received 64 thousand foreign tourists in 2003, a rise of 7.2 per cent from the year 2000. Outbound tourist numbers were much larger at 1,1 million. Tourism receipts for 2003 are estimated at euro 236 million. **Latvia** had a very good year, with 971 million international arrivals and an increase of 15 per cent. There were 415 thousand foreign arrivals in hotels and similar accommodation establishments, producing 963 thousand overnights. The total expenditure of international visitors rose 30 per cent to 124 million LVL. The most important source markets were Lithuania with 31 per cent; Estonia (26%); Russia (8%); Finland (7%); Germany (8%); and Poland (4%). Outgoing tourism showed a slight decline of 0.5 per cent. Despite **Armenia**'s geo-political situation which tends to constrain tourism, arrival numbers continued to increase dramatically, albeit from a small base, growing by 27 per cent in 2003 following two previous years of massive increases (173% in 2001 and 32% in 2002). **Bulgaria** and the **Republic of Moldova** also showed good inbound arrival increases of 18 per cent and 17 per cent respectively, but **Uzbekistan** suffered a 30 per cent decline. **Azerbaijan** and **Kazakhstan** both reported an improved economic situation in 2003.

**Spain** in 2003 received 51.8 million tourists and consolidated its position as the world's second most important tourism destination. This represented a decrease of 1 per cent. The income from international tourism grew to 36.9 billion euro, a 3.4 per cent increase compared with the previous year. Spain has become Britain's favourite destination, and it is beginning to win back markets affected by the 11th September and by economic recession, for example the United States of America and Germany. Spain has also become Germany's top destination in respect of spend. 82 per cent of foreign tourists who arrived in 2003 had been to Spain before, and of these 75 per cent had visited four or more times. More than one and a half million jobs are tourism-related; 10 per cent of total employment. For the second year running, independent visitors outnumbered those on packaged tours. This phenomenon is closely linked to increased use of the Internet and of budget airlines. In 2003 more than 18 million tourists used the Internet to make enquiries about their trip to Spain, an increase of 51 per cent over the previous year. More than 7.4 million made a reservation, an increase of 72 per cent, while the number paying by Internet more than doubled to 7.6 million. In 2003, 6.4 million visitors to Spain used budget airlines, 45 per cent more than in 2002, which itself showed an increase of 42 per cent over 2001. The growth of budget airlines boosts short distance tourism –their business model is based on flights of under three hours. Spain also noted the increasing fragmentation of the market, tending towards more, but shorter trips, with widely and rapidly diversifying motives. The fires in France had a temporary negative impact on motoring traffic to Spain. With regard to outbound tourism, between January and September 2003, Spaniards took 38.3 million tourist trips, 3.8 per cent more than in the same period of the previous year. Of these 3.2 million went overseas, an increase of 5.2 per cent. In 2003, the total number of international arrivals (tourists, same-day visitors and cruise passengers) to **Portugal** amounted to 27.5 million, which represents an increase of 1.2 per cent over 2002. Of the total number of visitors, 43 per cent were tourists, 56 per cent same-day visitors and 1.1 per cent cruise passengers. By source market, 93 per cent of overall international arrivals originated from European countries and around 84 per cent from just six countries: Spain, the United Kingdom, Germany, France, the Netherlands and Italy, with Spain particularly strong, representing around 46 per cent of all arrivals and 98 per cent of same-day visitors. The number of overnight stays in hotels and similar establishments amounted to 33 million, a decrease of 0.7 per cent. This was mainly determined by the 1.3 per cent decline in foreign overnight stays, while nationals' overnight stays increased by 0.7 per cent. There was a decrease in room and bed occupancy rates, which in 2003 were 56 per cent and 48 per cent respectively, compared with 59 per cent and 50 per cent in 2002. Tourism receipts amounted to 6.1 billion euro, according to preliminary results from the Bank of Portugal, or 0.7 per cent more than in 2002. The net value of the tourism balance reached

3.7 billion euro, representing a 1.8 per cent growth. Average tourist expenditure per day grew slightly to 119.5 euro. This indicator has been increasing since 1990. Average visitor expenditure per day, though showing a more unstable behaviour in the period 1990-2003, grew in 2003 to 57.5 euro. There was a slight decrease in domestic tourism. Internally, the Portuguese economy went through a difficult phase due to the necessarily restrained budgetary policy, which inevitably affected tourism. The fires that occurred in several areas of the country during the summer months also affected tourism. On the positive side, it is clear that Portugal was perceived as a safe destination in an increasingly uncertain world. In **Andorra,** tourism continued to be the main motor of the economy. There were 11.6 million visitor arrivals, 0.8 per cent more than in 2002. Of these 8.1 million were day visitors, an increase of 4.2 per cent, and 3.1 million were tourists who spent a total of 8.4 million overnights in Andorra, a decrease of 14 per cent. The spending power of visitors to Andorra is weakening. Arrivals to **Italy** declined marginally in 2003 (-0,5%). ISTAT (Istituto Nazionale di Statistica) data confirms positive trends the United Kingdom (+8,7%). The German and Japanese markets showed weakness, but tourism officials feel that, since both these nationalities are great lovers of Italy, they are unlikely to stop choosing it as a destination, although they might experiment with new places for a short period. This is demonstrated by the figures for arrivals and overnights over the previous three years 2000-2002, which were, on the whole, stable. The North American market continued to be badly affected by security concerns and the strong euro, but some emerging countries performed well, for example Russia and the Republic of Korea. The increase of tourists from emerging markets has in part compensated for the drop in tourism to Italy's art and heritage cities. No country can fill the gap left by the Japanese, the German and the Americans, but, by aiming at new markets, Italy has been able to mitigate the damage. Group tours to **San Marino** decreased progressively in 2003, with 2 thousand less coach arrivals than in the previous year. This was due to several factors, including a general trend away from group tours; competition from new destinations; higher prices following conversion to the euro; and excessive heat. It is estimated that the political and economic situation, including the Iraq war and terrorism, has caused overall tourism activity to shrink by 7.9 per cent. However overnights increased substantially. Foreign arrivals in **Greece** decreased by 1.5 per cent. Some destinations performed positively, but the overall result was slightly negative, including on the domestic tourism front. The main reasons for this were Iraq, SARS, the strong euro, and economic stagnation in some important generating markets, for example Germany and Sweden. **Croatia** on the other hand enjoyed "new" destination status in 2003, with a 6.7 per cent increase in total tourist arrivals and a 4 per cent increase in overnights. In National Parks and areas of natural beauty, the increase in visitors was even higher at 9 per cent. Good growth was recorded from the majority of markets, for example Germany, France, United Kingdom, and the Netherlands. This has enabled Croatia to come closer to matching its pre-war results. The recession in many generating markets did have some negative effects, for example from Poland, but these were not significant on the whole, partly because Croatian prices are relatively low. Croatia also recorded exceptional growth in cruises (38% in number of ship visits and 45% in passenger numbers). While Croatia benefited from a stabilised political situation and **Bosnia and Herzegovina** reported a positive change of image and an increase in arrivals of 3.6 per cent due to enhanced promotion, the **Former Yugoslav Republic of Macedonia** continued to be perceived as less stable. Despite this, there was increased foreign demand for niche tourism products, cultural events, attractions and meetings facilities, and a remarkable 28 per cent increase in arrivals was achieved, albeit from a very low base. Domestic tourism demand also increased. In **Serbia and Montenegro**, domestic tourist numbers decreased by a substantial 13 per cent, but inbound continued to prosper, with international arrivals increasing by 7.4 per cent to 481 thousand and their overnights by 4 per cent to 1.7 million. Of all these international arrivals, 64 per cent visited Belgrade and Novi Sad, and the majority came from the former Yugoslavia, Germany, Italy, the United Kingdom, Greece, Russia and Austria. Their main purpose of visit was business and conferences, but leisure travellers are increasing, especially young ones, for example taking cruises on the Danube. In **Slovenia** tourist arrivals increased 4 per cent to 2.2 millions, 61 per cent of these were foreigners, a total of 1.4 million, and an increase of 5.5 per cent over the previous year. Overnight stays increased less rapidly –overall by 2 per cent, and for foreigners by 4 per cent. Foreign overnights represent 56 per cent of the total. More than 59 per cent of these came from the following four countries: Germany (20%), Italy (17%), Austria (16%), and Croatia (6%), but the German and other top generating markets tended to stay fewer nights. The larger emerging markets in terms of overnight stays (more than 30 thousand) were Ireland, which grew 33 per cent in 2003, the Netherlands and Israel, which both grew 30 per cent, and France, which grew by 20 per cent. There were also more tourist arrivals from Italy, Austria, Hungary and the United Kingdom. The most successful products in 2003 were spas, wellness centres, active and touring holidays, and city breaks. **Malta** experienced a decline in total tourist arrival figures of 0.6 per cent. It was affected by the post 11th September trends towards: more familiar and close to home destinations; more car, train and coach travel in preference to plane (Malta is mainly accessible by air); and late booking resulting from a 'wait and see' attitude. Decreases were registered from its principal source markets (Germany, Italy, France and the Netherlands) with the exception of the United Kingdom, whose arrivals increased by 3.4 per cent. Secondary markets like Scandinavia, Austria and Switzerland registered increases.

Results in East Mediterranean Europe were mixed. **Cyprus** reported a decline of 4.8 per cent in arrivals and an increase of 6.3 per cent in revenue as expressed in US$ (-11% in euro terms). By far the largest market share of arrivals was from Europe (95%). The average length of stay was estimated at 10.9 days. **Turkey** achieved an increase of 4.3 per cent, attaining a total of 13.3 million international tourist arrivals. The number of Turkish citizens going abroad grew even faster at 15.5 per cent, and amounted to 6 million. A decrease of 3.8 per cent was observed in the number of visitors coming from the Organisation for Economic Co-operation and Development (OECD) countries, while a 28 per cent increase occurred in foreign visitors from the Commonwealth of Independent States (CIS), which provided 56 per cent of total visitors in 2003. Tourism receipts in 2003 amounted to euro 11.7 billion –an decrease of 7 per cent (in US$ and in view of the exchange rate factor revenues increased by 11% to a total of US$ 13.2 million). Tourism expenditure during the same period declined to reach euro 1.7 billion. Tourism's share of GNP increased by 28 per cent. **Israel** reported a massive increase of over 23 per cent in inbound arrivals but a small 1 per cent decline in domestic tourism. The security situation improved.

## I.2.2 Supply and Access

The tourism industry in **Denmark,** of which 90 per cent consists of small businesses with less than 10 employees, has adapted to growing international competition by increasing its focus on product development, efficient and cost-saving production systems and by forming voluntary partnerships and alliances in marketing and distribution. A number of initiatives were undertaken to improve the variety and quality of the tourism product. Total accommodation capacity increased by 1.6 per cent in **Sweden**, but the bed occupancy rate stayed at the same level of 33 per cent. According to TSA calculations the production value for rail, bus, sea and air transport decreased by 1.9 per cent, but employment in the sector increased by 5.2 per cent. In **Norway** there was a shift in supply from hotel to self-catering accommodation and an increase in sale-leaseback arrangements. Additional direct flights to Norway were initiated. There was also an increase in the supply of wellness products. The main impact on supply in the **United Kingdom** came from the rapid growth of low-cost flight operators and budget hotels. There is some evidence of a contraction in supply of bed and breakfast and guesthouse accommodation as owners convert to residential use and sell up, taking advantage of high house prices. In the last quarter the electrification of the railway line in South East England reduced journey times on Eurostar. In **Ireland** the number of beds and rooms available in registered hotels increased by almost 3 per cent; however, beds and rooms in less formal accommodation declined, resulting in an overall increase of less than 1 per cent in paid, serviced accommodation capacity. There was growth in air supply. Weekly capacity on scheduled air services between the United States of America and Ireland increased by 22 per cent. New air route development continued on mainland European routes with non-stop scheduled capacity up by 5 per cent. Capacity on Britain-Ireland routes increased by 4 per cent.

Budget airline growth was a positive factor for **France**, boosting the popularity of some hitherto lesser known towns and regions. Additional capacity from Moscow and the new Canton route also bode well for future growth in foreign visitors. In **Monaco** most four-star and luxury four-star hotels underwent renovation, expansion and modernisation in 2003. A new hotel opened. By 2007 it is estimated that hotel capacity will increase by 30 per cent, reaching close to 2,900 rooms. Spas are increasingly a feature in most good hotels. The port was expanded to provide more cruise capacity. In May, **Switzerland** saw the opening of a new Mystery Park in the Berner Oberland. There were reductions in air capacity with the new SWISS Airline cancelling some direct flights (for example Beijing, Delhi, St. Petersburg, and Buenos Aires). **Belgium, Wallonia** reported improvements in high-speed train services to Germany and the United Kingdom, and growth in the regional airports of Charleroi and Liège. After the shock of the disappearance of Sabena, Brussels International Airport has started to grow again, with the arrival of new airlines. However some air routes to Japan and the United States of America were reduced or abolished. Rural tourism offer increased, and quality control was introduced for all accommodation and attractions. The year's big events –Brel in Brussels and Simenon in Liège– were successful. The promotional theme for the year was architecture in a cultural and local context. The Luxembourg-Saarbrücken motorway was opened. A new museum was inaugurated –the Landesmuseum Liechtenstein. The number of hotel and similar rooms available in **Germany** reached 892 thousand, offering around 1.6 million bed spaces. The capacity utilisation of the 500 thousand room main visitor stock is 60 per cent. 4-5 star hotels in **Austria** increased by 3.5 per cent. The "Destination Management Monitoring" and "Well-being Tourism" strategic programmes were further developed. So too were sports, city tourism (for example, Graz Cultural Capital 2003), cultural, and MICE (Meetings, Incentives, Conventions and Exhibitions) products.

The most positive factor in **Hungary** was the improvement in access, due to the development of regional airports, the appearance of budget airlines and decreasing prices on the Hungarian flag carrier. Hotel capacity also increased, mainly in the 4-5 star category. New conference and incentive venues were developed outside Budapest. In the Lake Balaton area, new products were created to spread demand over the year, a bicycle route round the lake was established, and new higher category hotels and congress centres were constructed. Traditional events continued to attract visitors and some new events and programmes proved to be successful as well. Spa and wellness products were further developed and improved. A growing number of tour operators are programming Hungary. However some of Hungary's main tourism generators, for example the Ukraine and Russia, suffered from more complicated entry processes. Transport capacity in the **Czech Republic** was enlarged. There are new tunnels, a new bypass around big cities (Pilsen), and a new motorway from Olomouc to the border with Poland. Additional terminals are under construction at the Prague airport. Almost all the most important foreign hotel chains are already represented in the Czech market, and new Czech hotel chains have started to emerge. A multifunctional Sazka arena was completed in Prague and a large aquacentrum in Pruhonice is under construction. Among the product development priorities of the tourism authorities are spa tourism, agro tourism and cycling. Much effort was also put into the organisation of folklore, music, theatre and film festivals. Health centres were set up primarily catering to foreign visitors and residents. In **Romania,** 231 new accommodation establishments were developed. Hotel bed capacity increased in 2003 by 0.5 per cent. A major positive factor for **Estonia** was the opening of five new direct air routes to Tallinn (from Prague, Paris, Berlin, Amsterdam and Oslo) during 2003 as well as the new pricing policy and substantially lower rates offered by the national carrier, Estonian Air. The number of cruise ships calling at the port of Tallinn increased from 165 in 2002 to 236 in 2003 (an increase of 43%). One new catamaran and one new ferry started to sail between Tallinn and Helsinki. Tallinn hotels continued to join international hotel chains. Choice Hotels Scandinavia, Design Hotels, and Sokos Hotels entered the Estonian hotel market in 2003. Tallinn's hotel capacity increased by 11 per cent in 2003 and bed capacity at Estonia's health spas increased by 15 per cent. The total number of bed spaces recorded by the statistical office in **Slovakia** was 121 thousand, which is a 2.6 per cent increase over 2002. Establishments of higher quality level increased their share. Within accommodation facilities many new leisure services were developed such as swimming pools, saunas, fitness centres, and meeting rooms. The first big aquapark based on thermal water was opened in the Liptov region. More MICE facilities were developed, mainly in response to healthy domestic demand. Besides new facilities, a great deal of reconstruction and refurbishment of existing establishments was undertaken in order to improve the standard and quality of service. Some new regular direct flights were launched from Bratislava to European cities (London, Paris, Brussels, Munich, and Stuttgart). Transport capacity for winter sports was improved significantly with many new ski lifts and chairlifts (chairlifts are increasingly more popular than ski lifts in medium and large resorts). The duty on the entry visa for Russia and the Ukraine was an obstacle. In **Lithuania** the number of accommodation establishments in 2003 reached 321, a 16 per cent increase over 2002. The total number of rooms in all accommodation establishments was 8.3 thousand, an increase of 17 per cent providing a total number of 17 thousand beds. Many hotels in the Druskinankai resort were renovated for spa and wellness tourism. In **Belarus** the number of accommodation units increased to 285. There were also 318 organisations offering sanatorium and health resort services. The capital of **Latvia**, Riga, suffered a shortage of accommodation capacity in the holiday season. A visa-free regime with 60 countries was negotiated. Efforts were made to improve information systems and signage. Following the opening in **Armenia** of 16 new high quality hotels in 2001 and 2002, a further two were opened in 2003: the hotel Europe in Yerevan and the Tsapatagh in Gegharkunik. The rail route from Yerevan to Tbilisi (Georgia) was opened but those to Turkey and Azerbaijan are still closed. An extensive programme for the reconstruction and improvement of roads was completed. Zvartnots international airport has undergone an expansion and reconstruction programme. The number of private buses operating in the tourism sphere doubled in 2003. In **Azerbaijan** the quantity and quality of accommodation has improved. Travel agencies and tour operators introduced new routes and types of tourism. Highways and roads are being improved. An airport, which meets world standards, has recently been constructed. "Air Astana" introduced a new scheduled flight from Almaty in **Kazakhstan** to London, and the airport infrastructure was rebuilt and improved. Visa formalities for tourists from the main generating markets were streamlined. Inter-urban, urban and rural roads were improved. **Turkmenistan** continued to develop its tourism infrastructures. A new hotel was constructed in the town of Turkmenbashi.

Especially worthy of note is the diversification of **Spain**'s tourism over recent years, not only as an alternative, but also as a complement, to its traditional sun and beach product. The cultural offer was enriched with the opening of the Picasso Museum in Málaga and of the Es Baluard Contemporary Art Museum in Palma de Mallorca. The product offer for nature, sport and health/beauty continued to expand. Spain consolidated its leadership position in the holiday golf market, of which it captures around 35 per cent, worth nearly one billion euro. Nautical tourism is growing steadily – Spain now offers more than 80 thousand moorings. Spain continued to implement its 'Infrastructure Plan 2000-2006', with total investment of more than 18 billion euro in roads, nearly 12 billion in high-speed rail travel, and nearly 2 billion in airports. Moreover during the same period 5.1 billion euro have been allocated to tourism related environmental projects, including improvements to water treatment, seafronts, beaches, nature reserves and park visitor centres. According to the National Institute of Statistics (INE), accommodation capacity in **Portugal** amounted to 246 thousand beds in 2003, which represents an increase of 2.4 per cent over 2002. The latest available data (INE, 2002) regarding the Portuguese road network indicate that total road extension in the mainland reached 12,399 km, of which 1,835 km are high-way. This is an area in which there has been significant development over recent years, making it possible to say that today the country possesses a modern and adequate road network. Portugal also has significantly good golf infrastructures, including a total of 62 golf courses, 57 of which are on the mainland. In 2003 there was reinforcement of air capacity, in particular to Lisbon, Faro and Ponta Delgada (the Azores), originating from some of the main generating markets to Portugal, such as the United Kingdom, France, Germany and Scandinavia. **Andorra** reported growth in accommodation capacity, especially at four star level. Access routes were improved. High levels of investment were maintained in mountain resorts (both for winter and summer). The commercial union between the Pas de la Casa – Grau Roig and Soldeu el Tarter ski stations, and the subsequent creation of GrandValira has generated very positive expectations. The cultural offer was improved but shopping remains the main motivation for 49 per cent of visitors. Trading up continued in the **Italian** hotel industry. There was a marked fall in capacity at one and two star level, and a considerable increase at three and four star level. Three-star properties now predominate, making up 44 per cent of hotels and 52 per cent of rooms. A special law was finalised to speed up the issuing of visas. The Government made ENIT (Ente Nazionale Italiano per el Turismo) responsible for this task, and specific funds were allocated to pay for new employees to work in understaffed consular offices. Using these funds, ENIT, in collaboration with the diplomatic offices, has hired 28 new staff on fixed term contracts for consulates in New Delhi, Mumbai, Moscow, St. Petersburg, Kiev, Beijing, Shanghai and Canton. Road access was improved to **San Marino** and the historic centre was illuminated. Several important events were organised, for example the San Marino Festival, the investiture ceremonies of the Capitaines Régent, the Libertatis Fundador Cultural Exhibition, and the San Marino Ethnic Festival. Sporting events also proved very successful, especially the Grand Prix Superbike, the Formula One Grand Prix, the aviation exhibition celebrating the 100$^{th}$ Anniversary of motor-powered flight, and the ATP Challenger Tennis Tournament. **Greece** improved its air, road and metro transportation infrastructure, and more high-speed ferries to the islands were provided. New conference centres and marinas were developed. Accommodation facilities in Athens and other destinations were modernised, in preparation for the Athens 2004 Olympic Games. In **Croatia**, based on international standards adopted in 2002, a total of 136 hotels were upgraded and a further 113 are in the process of being upgraded (most of them at least to 3-star or above). In 2003, some 300 million euro were invested in reconstruction, modernisation and refurbishing of accommodation facilities. The frequency and capacity of ferry and ship lines connecting the mainland with the islands were increased and the number of transferred passengers/cars rose by 8 per cent. The total of airline seats from the key generating markets (Germany, United Kingdom, the Netherlands, Sweden and Denmark) increased by some 14 per cent. The national carrier put on 14 per cent more charter flights. Seasonal tourist trains were introduced to take passengers and cars from Prague to Split. 191 kilometres of new highways to the Adriatic coast were constructed, and other roads repaired or renewed. A large number of swimming pools were constructed, 18 additional beaches were awarded «blue flags» and the number of restaurants, sports grounds and other entertainment and recreational offers has increased. **The Former Yugoslav Republic of Macedonia** reported the development of specific new cultural, rural and ecotourism products, improved quality of services due to tourism licensing, transport improvements, improved entry formalities and increased frequency on border crossings. **Serbia and Montenegro** added to its accommodation stock, especially in rural areas, and developed a number of new products, for example wine tours, cycling, rafting, youth packages, and Danube cruises, plus ethno and music events. In **Slovenia** there were investments in modern spas, thermal pools and wellness services, congress centres, MICE facilities and ski resorts. Three new authentic hostels were opened and a tourism information centre was inaugurated in the capital, Ljubljana. A couple of airlines started operations to **Malta**. Hotel beds in the five star category increased by 1,302. A "VisitMalta" bus service was set up to link tourist resorts with the most important visitor attractions, and some cultural sites were improved.

In **Cyprus** efforts continued to develop special interest products to attract each targeted segment. These included routes and thematic parks based on the island's rich cultural and natural heritage, information and interpretation centres, state-of-the-art museums, conference and incentive facilities, sports facilities (particularly for cycling, boating, water sports, hiking, and golf), events, exhibitions and workshops, and wellness and pampering facilities. Cyprus has developed the necessary infrastructure in Lemesos and Larnaka to become the cruise hub of the region. Entry formalities for Russian and CIS visitors were facilitated by the setting up of consular offices there. In **Israel** there was a 6 per cent decrease in travel agencies and tour operators, and a small decrease in specific products. **Turkey** reported an increase in the number of accommodation establishments and in bed capacity of 5.5 per cent and 6.2 per cent respectively.

## I.2.3 Tourism Policy

In 2003 **Denmark**'s tourism policy focused on implementing the Government's Action Plan on Tourism launched in May 2002. Initiatives in the plan which have already been carried out include: a quality labelling scheme for Danish attractions and museums; a new concept for meeting planning; a quality labelling scheme for physical accessibility; a new common concept for developing and marketing city breaks in Denmark; five active holiday quality labels –golf, wellness, fishing, gastronomy and cycling; stronger marketing co-operation on the branding of Denmark in specific foreign markets; and a co-ordinated effort to professionalise cultural events. Furthermore, the Danish Tourist Board launched a general debate with the industry, relevant organisations, politicians etc. on a new vision of Danish tourism for 2010. The debate was launched at the board's annual Tourism Conference in November 2003 where different future scenarios were discussed. **Sweden** continued to implement its strategic programme for tourism, produced in 2001, and involving several hundred organisations, companies and government authorities linked to tourism. The programme consists of more than one hundred separate projects. The **Norwegian** Trade Council (NTC), the Governmental Consultative Office for Inventors (SVO), the Norwegian Tourist Board (NTB) and the Norwegian Industrial and Regional Development Fund (SND) merged into a new company called "Innovation Norway" on 1st January 2004. Tourism will be one of its main areas of focus. The principal development last year in the **United Kingdom** was the changed role of the National Tourism Organisation (NTO). On 1st April 2003 a new structure came into effect to allow a greater focus on marketing activity. The British Tourist Authority merged with the English Tourism Council to form VisitBritain. The role of the new organisation is to promote England within Britain and Britain to the rest of the world. A new Licensing Act was passed on 10th July 2003 controlling the sale of alcohol. Key measures contained in the Act include: more flexible opening hours for premises, potentially up to 24 hours, seven days a week; a single premises licence which permit premises to be used to supply alcohol, to provide regulated entertainment and to provide refreshment late at night, bringing together the six existing licensing regimes (alcohol, public entertainment, cinemas, theatres, late-night refreshment houses and night cafes) thereby cutting down on red tape; and a new system of personal licences relating to the supply of alcohol which will enable holders to move more freely between premises subject to police scrutiny. A draft Gambling Bill was published. The proposed changes are aimed at achieving a managed relaxation of outdated restrictions and greater choice for adult gamblers, balanced by greater emphasis on social responsibility and protection of the vulnerable, particularly children. The Bill will allow for the establishment of a new regulator, the Gambling Commission, transforming the existing Gaming Board for Great Britain into a new body with wider functions, greater flexibility to act and stronger enforcement powers. There have also been government consultations on the future development of air transport in the United Kingdom to further the development of a sustainable airport policy for the next 30 years. In **Ireland** the Government published a major report by the Tourism Policy Review Group, which includes representatives from the state tourism agencies and from the private sector, entitled "New Horizons for Irish Tourism - An Agenda for Action", providing a framework for the development of Irish Tourism to 2012. Failte Ireland, the new development authority for Irish tourism, was established by the Government through the merger of two state agencies, Bord Failte and CERT. The new agency provides strategic and practical support to develop and sustain a high quality and competitive tourist destination in partnership with the tourism industry. Tourism Ireland is responsible for marketing the island of Ireland overseas.

There was also restructuring at the **Monaco** Tourism and Convention Directorate, with some functions being merged and some new ones created, for example Communications and a Convention Bureau. **Switzerland** renewed two tourism programmes focusing on the improvement of supply: 60 million swiss francs were allocated to the Swiss Hotel Credit Association for the period 2003 to 2007; and 35 million swiss francs were allocated for the same period to the Inno Tour Programme, to promote innovation and co-operation. In October 2003, the **Netherlands** Ministry of Economic Affairs presented a new Tourism Policy Plan. In this plan, the Ministry describes its policy for the coming years. The Ministry sees the stimulation of incoming tourism as its main objective. Besides more general policy making, the Ministry will focus especially on four important segments, namely the coast, cities/culture, events and MICE. In the year 2003 preparations were made to reorganise the structure of the Ministries in **Belgium's Flanders** Region. The Tourist Office for Flanders is one of the first "internal autonomous agencies", with no Board of Directors and more decision-making power for the Head of the Agency. **Belgium, Wallonia** reported investment incentives using European and regional co-financing funds, and the creation of tourism bodies bringing together several communities. In **Luxembourg** a new five-year Plan was introduced by the Tourism Ministry giving subsidies for tourism infrastructures. Discussions took place with regard to a possible Quality Management Study and to the introduction of a visitors' tax. In **Liechtenstein** various co-operation agreements were made and a number of workshops organised. **Austria** concentrated on improving its statistics, launching the "e-Gästeblatt" to record tourist data in accommodation establishments, and developing "T-Mona" (Tourism Monitor Austria) to collect regular data from surveys. Information services were improved and a new tourism development centre was opened in Berlin. The **German** government supports the German National Tourist Board (GNTB) via the Federal Ministry of Economics and Labour (BMWA). The GNTB budget has been continuously increased over recent years and places special emphasis on medium-sized tourism enterprises in Germany, helping them to offer their tourism products in international markets. It also supports general domestic tourism promotion. The main ongoing goals of the BMWA tourism policy are: to improve the quality of tourism products; to increase the number of employees in the German tourism industry; to research and evaluate the economic potential of specific segments of demand; and to increase sustainability in tourism.

In 2003 **Hungary**'s budget for tourism was 19 billion HUF (79.1 million euro as at January 2003), but this can be increased up to 32.3 billion HUF (134.5 million euro) by provisional decisions over the next two years. There are also some other resources, which are not allocated directly to the Tourism Secretariat, for example a budget for holiday vouchers (nearly 25 million euro) as an incentive for domestic tourism or for the inactive, and a budget for health spa treatments (22.9 million euro). The successful mid-term development plan has continued with new incentives and with a clearer evaluation process. The two main focus points are the development of Hungary's image as a tourism destination, and the development of the supply side. A regular survey of domestic and foreign tourists was started in 2003 and on the basis of this the Hungarian Central Statistical Office (HCSO) will develop a TSA. The State Secretariat in charge of tourism and the Hungarian National Tourist Office are working with HCSO on the tourism surveys and on the TSA project. The most important feature of the present State Tourism Policy is the promotion of the **Czech Republic** abroad as a peaceful destination. Various training and education programmes are being prepared with the support of European Union financial grants. Each region has prepared its own long-term tourism development plan, and public/private partnerships are being formed to carry these out. There is a strong emphasis on sustainability. **Romania** focused on improving its tourism institutional structure; on training and human resource development; on local and foreign investment; and on public/private partnerships. For the first time in 2003, the Statistical Office of **Estonia** analysed the contribution of tourism to GDP and employment in the period 1997 to 2000, using TSA methodology. According to this analysis, tourism in the year 2000 contributed 8.2 per cent of GDP and also employed 8.2 per cent of the total workforce. The Ministry of Economy in **Slovakia** finalised a Sectoral Operation Programme for European Union Structural Funds under the European Regional Development Fund (ERDF) and a Programme Complement for Industry and Services, of which one of the two priorities is the tourism sector, both private and public. These documents are valid for the whole territory of Slovakia except the Bratislava region. The Ministry of Construction and Regional Development also prepared a Single Programming Document for European Union Objective 2 Structural Funds valid for the Bratislava region. Tourism is one of its priorities. The Ministry of Economy has ordered a study on "Regionalisation of Tourism in the Slovak Republic" to assess the medium and long term potential of the regions for particular tourist activities. This document will be used in many ways, for example as a basis for the allocation of public funds, promotion, land planning, stimulation of private sector investments and motivation for regional co-operation. In **Lithuania** amendments to the tourism law came into force on 1st April 2003. The third National Tourism Development Programme was adopted for four years. The accommodation service tax was reduced from 18 per cent to 5 per cent. **Belarus** has a Ministry of Sports and Tourism. Investment planning is handled on the basis of co-operation and joint international projects with the Russian Federation, Poland, and Lithuania. Tourism zones are being set up, to be supported by tax incentives. In 2003 the Ministry certified tourist guides and group leaders (an obligatory requirement). There was also emphasis on specialised training. In **Latvia** the Cabinet of Ministers and Saeima (Parliament) decided to assign the responsibility for tourism policy and its implementation to the Ministry of Economics (moved from the Ministry of Environmental Protection and Regional Development with effect from the 1st of March, 2003). This gave more recognition to tourism as an important sector of the national economy. The Ministry of Economics set up in May 2003 a Tourism Department, which is under the supervision of the Deputy State Secretary, and started to work on the Latvian Tourism Development Guidelines which will constitute the basic mid-term policy-planning document. To increase the competitiveness of the industry, the Parliament adopted amendments to the Law on Value Added Tax, reducing VAT on tourism accommodation services from 18 per cent to 9 per cent in 2003, and to 5 per cent from 1st May, 2004. In **Armenia** the National Assembly approved the abolition of VAT on tourism. A law on tourism and tourism activity was passed on 17th December 2003. A State programme for health resort and summer house development was passed on 10th October. The Tourism Master Plan is currently being developed. Some human resources programmes were undertaken in collaboration with various partners (for example Egypt, Japan, Germany, Greece, and Cyprus). The Ministry of Trade and Economic Development together with the International Executive Service Corps (IESC) and the United States Agency for International Development (USAID) organised a Pilot Project in Dilijan and Ijevan under the scope of the "Tourism Development Project in Communities of the Republic of Armenia". The Tourism Development in the Provinces Programme was evaluated and is now being implemented. In **Azerbaijan** the United States Trade and Development Association (USTDA) approved funding to the Ministry of Youth, Sport and Tourism for technical assistance to develop a tourism strategy. **Kazakhstan** adopted a Tourism Industry Development Programme for 2003-2005. A law was passed to establish the insurance for civil law responsibility of travel agents and tour operators. There was improved co-operation with the Ministry of Foreign Affairs, for example in the facilitation of visas for tourists from the main generating countries. There was close co-operation with the World Tourism Organization, for example, by organising WTO seminars and participating in its events.

The tourism authorities in **Spain** are developing strategies to help the industry adapt to the new demands of the marketplace. The aim is to improve competitivity, controlling costs and increasing management efficiency with the aid of new technologies. The emphasis on technological progress led in 2003 to the creation of SEDETTUR (the State Organisation for the Technological Development of Tourism). Its areas of activity include amongst others the conservation of energy, the environment, architectural design and the use of new materials, communication and information technologies, security, health and quality. Plans are being made to renovate and recuperate tourism zones, adapting them to the principles of sustainability. Work continued, in close co-operation with the private sector, on the Spanish Tourism Quality System. Three thousand companies participate voluntarily. The system awards a "Q" mark to companies which make quality their principal management objective. In 2003 the **Portuguese** Government approved the "Tourism Development Plan", which includes 40 priority measures. On the supply side, there is emphasis on protected areas, licensing, quality evaluation, training, education and legal reforms. On the demand side, a new public/private model for tourism promotion co-ordination is planned, with increased decentralisation based on a contractual relationship between the central and the regional tourism boards, and reinforcement of the tourism promotion budget abroad and in Portugal. A Portuguese Tourism Institute was created to concentrate responsibilities for tourism promotion, financial support and investment; the role of the Directorate General for Tourism will be revised; and so too will the Basic Law regarding Regional Tourism Boards. There are also plans to redefine the system of statistical intelligence, to incentive tourism studies and research, and to reformulate the web portal. There was a boost to the political recognition of tourism as an important economic and social sector following the acceptance of the Portuguese Tourism Confederation in the Permanent Commission for Social Co-ordination. In 2003 tourism continued to benefit from a significant number of financial incentives: for example the Programme of Incentives to the Modernisation of the Economy and the National Training Programme "Better Tourism", both integrated in the III Community Support Framework, and the Programme of Interventions for the Qualification of Tourism. **Andorra** emphasised close collaboration between the public and private sectors, with joint planning of promotions. **Italy** responded rapidly to 2003's difficult tourism conditions by establishing "crisis units", dynamic structures that monitored international developments and promoted communication, spreading a series of positive and persuasive images of Italy and its regions. At the same time, ENIT intensified its activity to aid the worst affected regions with programme agreements and special communication campaigns aimed mainly at promoting specific products. ENIT also put greater emphasis on co-ordination and consultation with the regions and with members of the tourism industry. The Council of Ministers approved a bill aimed at reorganising support for tourism. This will create single information desks abroad, harmonise and co-ordinate promotional activities, and provide for the training of staff. The single information desks will lead to greater efficiency, by linking together activities carried out by the commercial offices of the diplomatic-consular networks, by ICE (the Italian Commerce Institute), by ENIT, by the Chambers of Commerce and by the regional authorities. **San Marino** concentrated on the development of investment incentives; public/private partnerships; collaboration with the Hotel Consortium; and research. Other priorities were sports tourism, training, new information points, regulation and liberalisation, and the opening a conference centre. The National Tourism Office of **Greece** elaborated Master Plans for the tourism development of the Greek Regions. New legislation was introduced for tourism education. Incentives were given to private investors to modernise accommodation establishments and to create new facilities, for example conference centres, marinas, spas, and golf courses. The **Former Yugoslav Republic of Macedonia** worked on the drafting of a tourism and catering law in which European Union directives will be included. A Master Plan was proposed to encourage better organisation and more investment in tourism. The Government espoused public/private partnership principles. **Bosnia and Herzegovina** co-operated with international organisations on projects relating to protected areas, sustainable tourism and poverty reduction. It also worked on policy making and on a tourism law. **Serbia and Montenegro** concentrated on encouraging public/private partnerships and private investment in accommodation supply. **Slovenia** continued to implement the "Slovenian Tourism Strategy 2002-2006". The Ministry of the Economy and its Tourism Section prepared a draft of a new Tourism Promotion Act and submitted it, in the latter part of 2003, to the Government and to the National Assembly. It was adopted in December 2003 and is valid with effect from January 2004. The Ministry of the Economy also prepared changes to the Mountain Guides Act in order to harmonise it with European Union regulations. In addition to this work on tourism legislation, the Ministry of the Economy prepared other proposals for amending acts and regulations, which create obstacles to entrepreneurship, as part of its campaign to encourage investment. The Ministry of the Economy started to implement TSA methodology in order to arrive at a more realistic evaluation of the impact of tourism and its importance in the national economy and to obtain internationally comparable data. Much emphasis was placed on the development of human resources and the improvement of the quality of intellectual capital, with steps being taken to: improve the quality and adaptability of educational and training programmes to the needs of the tourism industry and to European Union standards; improve the system of practical training by developing a network of hotels, catering establishments and tourist agencies for practical training purposes; encourage tourism companies to undertake larger investments in the development of modern management of intellectual capital; promote the development of a tourist culture among the population; and motivate young people for employment in the tourist sector. Of particular significance was the implementation of the project: “Closing the gap” prepared on the initiative of the Ministry of the Economy in co-operation with the Ministry of Education, Science, and Sport, the Ministry of Labour, Family and Social Affairs and the Centre of the Republic of Slovenia for vocational education, within a programme of bilateral assistance from the Netherlands. This project aims at the development of a flexible and practically oriented system of education and training for middle management and for the management of tourist destinations. The project is based on co-operation between the tourism industry and schools as well as other educational institutions in Slovenia and the Netherlands. In **Malta**, the Ministry of Tourism, in close collaboration with the Malta Tourism Authority, participated very actively in the preparation for the absorption of European Union Structural and Cohesion Funds, which will amount to Lm90 million for the period 2004-2006. This was been done through their contribution to the National Development Plan (December 2001-July 2002), followed by the drafting of the Single Programming Document and the Programme Complement (September 2002-March 2003). The Malta Tourism Authority submitted proposals of a value of around 8 million euro for projects, which have been identified and refined (through a wide ranging consultation process) during the last twenty-four months.

**Cyprus** drafted a long-term strategy to the year 2010. This Strategy aims to ensure the sustainability and quality of tourism development on the island, reinforce the destination's ability to compete successfully in a European environment, and enable it to grasp all opportunities arising from accession to the EU. In order to encourage the development of the special interest products specified in the Strategic Plan, the Government is currently revising the incentive scheme for ancillary tourism projects, upgrading the incentives offered to investors for the creation of the priority products. The Government is also examining the potential of developing casinos in Cyprus.

## I.2.4 Marketing and Promotion

**Sweden** continued to focus on major and new markets in Europe as well as on the development of some highly interesting markets in Asia. **Norway**'s new strategic markets are Russia and China. A branding programme started in 2001, and they are still following the same strategy. **Finland** launched a major campaign with the aim of increasing summer tourism to Finland from its main markets. The growth of summer tourism to Finland has stagnated. In response, the Finnish Tourist Board decided to concentrate funds on a big consumer campaign with wide media coverage, including TV spots. Product development was also an essential part of this project. Tourism **Ireland** developed a marketing strategy for the island of Ireland for the period 2004 to 2006 and published an Operating Plan for 2004. Failte Ireland produced operational plans for 2004 in respect of niche tourism products. **The United Kingdom** published its International Marketing Strategy "Leading the World to Britain" providing a strategic framework for VisitBritain's international marketing. This aims to boost inbound tourism to every part of England, Scotland and Wales in the longer term by working with all parts of the tourism industry. The United Kingdom in 2003 also ran a very successful European short-break campaign in response to the difficult market conditions, held the first Royal Tourism Day in June, and launched the first co-ordinated domestic marketing strategy for England in 10 years - Enjoy England. The Maison de la **France** carried out 208 overseas publicity campaigns, an increase of 17 per cent over 2002. The use of Internet grew markedly –there were 32 online campaigns. France participated in 119 trade or public tourism shows. A destination recovery plan was launched in the third quarter in many European and long-haul markets, comprising publicity campaigns and promotional events, for example a ski campaign in Belgium with Liberty Television, a poster campaign in Times Square (New York), and a France event in Australia to publicise the cities that will host the next Rugby World Cup in 2007. A new promotion club –the Club Outremer– was set up to promote France's overseas territories to the French market and to selected foreign markets. A campaign was held with theme "the France of the Three Oceans". The Club France for overseas clients was relaunched in several test markets. The membership card, which gives special offers and advantages, is only sold by Internet. Following the Prestige disaster a recovery campaign for the Aquitaine coast was carried out in the domestic and in some nearby overseas markets. A national promotion was launched for rural tourism. Poster campaigns promoted off-season coastal tourism in the French market and in relevant overseas markets. Work was carried out on the effective use of search engines to increase website hits. At the end of 2003, the Maison de la France undertook research in its main source markets to assess France's tourism image and positioning with respect to its competitors. **Monaco** produced a five year strategic tourism plan (up until 2008), which will be regularly updated by stakeholders on a partnership basis.

A new tourism policy and a serious budget cut from the Ministry of Economic Affairs had significant consequences for the national tourism organisation in the **Netherlands**. In June 2004, the Ministry and the Netherlands Board of Tourism and Conventions (NBTC) agreed a new contract for the period 2004-2006. In **Belgium, Flanders** the main marketing activities were focused on press, trade and the (potential) consumer. Markets are divided into three major areas: domestic, neighbouring and long-haul. Promotional activities were conducted in 11 key foreign markets. Event marketing also proved very successful (Beaufort 2003,

Khnopff, etc.). **Belgium, Wallonia** undertook targeted marketing based on product/segment fit. Its 2003 annual theme was architecture. An image campaign was carried out in the Walloon region. The Internet site was further developed. In **Luxembourg** increased focus was put on cultural tourism and joint promotion with the hotel and holiday apartment sector was encouraged to promote special thematic offers. A new family tourism publication ("Luxembourg for Kids") was released. Poster advertisements promoted the tourist pass (Luxembourg Card) and agenda. A tram in Brussels was decorated for 2 months in order to promote cycling in Luxembourg. Activities in **Liechtenstein** included: a new travel market; Internet development with promotion on the website and Live-Cams in Malbun and Vaduz; roadshows and Public Relations (PR) campaigns; and a "Gastronomy and Wine" route. MICE, cultural, wellness and sports tourism were targeted and new promotional material and packages were produced. **Austria** focused on three key values: intensive, civilised and straight. The major markets targeted were Austria, Germany, Italy, the Netherlands and the United Kingdom. A modern information service centre was inaugurated and a new advertising campaign developed. Affinity groups were targeted, for example classical music lovers. The Austrian image was boosted by a number of co-operative activities in commerce, sport and marketing. Market analysis was the basis of the **German** National Tourist Board's (GNTB) activities. The GNTB continued to focus on city breaks and health and fitness holidays. Spain, Italy and Sweden, in particular, offer hidden potential for growth. The GNTB also aimed to take advantage of opportunities created by the eastward expansion of the European Union and to develop new target groups for business travel and holidays. China, South Korea, and the Arab Emirates were additional markets in which the GNTB sought to secure and develop a competitive advantage. Attempts were also made to consolidate and continue previous growth in traditional markets, for example the United States of America and Japan.

The **Hungarian** National Tourist Office's total budget increased by nearly 21 per cent in 2003. The allocation for marketing increased by 25 per cent. Highlights in 2003 included: the year of Hungarian Culture in the United Kingdom; billboard campaigns in the Rome, Milan and London undergrounds; bus advertisements in London and Tokyo; a TV campaign on international channels in June and another in Autumn for spas; the establishment of a new representative office in Dublin and a new information office in Copenhagen; a joint campaign with the Budapest Tourism Office in Germany, France, Italy and the Scandinavian countries in May-June; and promotion of the Island Festival (Sziget Fesztivál). There was strong emphasis on co-operation and consultation with the travel trade and with other relevant bodies, including the Hungarian Investment and Trade Development Public Benefit Company. There was successful collaboration between the four Visegrád countries (Czech Republic, Hungary, Poland and Slovakia). Hungary also organised study tours and participated in many events, including 136 travel fairs and exhibitions. Domestically it participated in: Utazás (Travel) 2003, the Conference of Event Organisers, the $12^{th}$ Welcome to Hungary inbound workshop, the Wellness Expo, the II Sport and Activity Conference and Fair, Spa Hungary and the Business Travel Show. **Poland** continued to implement its marketing programme using such classic promotional tools in 2003 as: a national stand in 87 international tourist fairs with almost one thousand Polish exhibitors; 36 workshops for foreign and Polish tour operators; study tours for 364 foreign journalist, 160 VIPs and 772 tour operators; and the editing of 18 new brochures in 9 languages. Two of the most important target markets for the Polish Tourist Office (PTO) were Russia and the Ukraine. A branch office was opened in Moscow. Regionalisation of tourism promotion continued. Five new regional tourist offices and over fifteen new local tourist promotion centres were established in 2003. Work on the national tourism website was finished by the end of the year. Co-operation with the Commercial Department of Polish embassies in countries where the PTO does not have a branch office was considerably enlarged in 2003. **Czech** Tourism focused on five principal themes: the beauty of the country's castles, stately homes, historic towns and cities; a healthy and active vacation; Golden Prague (three aspects: a city of history, a city of culture, a city for the young); health spas as places of relaxation and enjoyment; and ecclesiastical monuments and places of pilgrimage. A TV spot targeting European Union neighbours was shown on four prestigious channels (BBC World Europe, CNN, Discovery Europe and Eurosport). The promotion strategy defines the basic features of a holiday in the Czech Republic as comfortable, peaceful, unchallenging, calm, pleasant and accessible. In January 2003 a conference was held in Prague entitled "Czech Republic – the Safe Tourist Destination". The main elements in the **Romanian** marketing and promotion plan were: participating at major international tourism fairs; adapting the form and content of advertising material; organising familiarisation visits for mass media and tour operators; developing special tourist areas of international standard; creating special promotional events in different countries all over Europe; and modernising the tourism base. **Estonia** organised in autumn 2003 a successful international workshop and familiarisation trip, aimed especially at tour operators not yet selling Estonia. Its first advertising campaign in Latvia took place in the summer. At the same time, it also organised its first domestic advertising campaign. The National Tourist Office in **Slovakia** carried out a detailed marketing analysis of products and segments. Plans were made to promote the historical heritage but implementation is still slow. Unified regional promotional brochures were completed, and new videocassettes focused on culture. Promotional brochures featuring caves and ecotourism were produced. An information campaign was initiated at border crossings. Slovakia participated in 31 international tourism fairs and organised ten workshops abroad, promoting mainly mountains and spa resorts. 54 presentations were made abroad, for example in Slovak embassies and at international conferences or events. **Lithuania** developed its 2003 marketing plan, which included fairs, visits for journalists, and new publications. For the first time, workshops for foreign tour operators were held in Lithuania. The main 2003 activities in **Latvia** were the participation in international tourism fairs, the opening of tourist information offices, and the publishing of promotional materials. The Latvian Tourist Bureau in Helsinki and the Baltic Bureau in Munster were maintained, and a new Latvian Tourist Bureau was opened in London. **Belarus** also co-ordinated a national stand at the top overseas tourism fairs, developed international tourism events in Belarus, organised familiarisation visits for the media and travel trade, advertised in key source markets, operated a website, and produced a range of promotional material including photo albums and an historic architectural itinerary. Plans were initiated to set up regional tourism information centres. The **Armenian** Tourism Development Agency (ATDA) was set up and a new three-year marketing plan was developed. This plan identified new target markets –Russia and the Middle East– and new distribution channels, in particular advertising on CNN and the BBC. Armenia joined the American Society of Travel Agents (ASTA) and participated in its convention. It also participated in international exhibitions, such as ITB in Berlin, WTM in London and the Silk Route of Tbilisi and Kiev, and in the "Sustainable Tourism in the Caucasian Region" seminar in Georgia. The Kenats Festival was organised under the umbrella of ATDA in September 2003. It is now planned to hold the festival annually, featuring Armenian culture, history, churches and monuments. **Azerbaijan** produced promotional materials, created new websites and participated in local and international fairs. **Kazakhstan** also exhibited at the main international trade fairs, for example FITUR in Madrid, ITB, WTM and MITT in Moscow, with increased participation from regional tourism administrations, and it developed domestic fairs, for example Otdykh Leisure in Astana and

KITF in Almaty. **Turkmenistan** continued to participate at the annual "Ashgabat is white stone" exhibition.

**Spain**'s principal marketing objectives in 2003 were to: consolidate Spain's holiday tourism leadership position, through a differentiation strategy based on quality; to position Spain as a front rank cultural destination; to increase MICE, sporting, and nature tourism, and thus achieve greater regional and seasonal spread; to maximise the value added to the promotion of products by the Spain brand, with focus on quality and innovation; and to lead the country's tourism marketing through increasing use of new information and communication technologies. Five supra-regional agreements were signed to promote brands or routes (the Pilgrimage Route to Santiago, the Silver Route, Heritage Cities, Green Spain and the Pyrenees). Another six agreements were signed with Autonomous Communities to carry out joint promotional campaigns. In **Portugal** major responsibilities were devolved to public and private regional agents, stimulating partnerships in the form of "Regional Tourism Promotion Agencies". The development of these regional plans was made possible by central administration financing, supported under a 3-year contractual system. The central tourism board remained responsible for the promotion on the brand "Portugal". In this context a thorough study on the advantages and values associated with the destination was carried out to develop a new positioning for Portugal. The output of this study was the design and implementation of a coherent communication strategy (the Portuguese Identity System). Marketing focus was intensified on 14 key generating markets out of the 22 where Portugal is active promotionally, with budgetary allocations as follows: Spain (strategic market): 19 per cent; the United Kingdom and Germany (priority markets): 48 per cent; the Netherlands, France, Scandinavia, Italy, Ireland, Belgium, the United States of America and Brazil: 25 per cent; other international markets: 8 per cent. Special attention was given to nearby markets, considered less vulnerable to safety factors and more responsive to consumer oriented promotional activities. International communication campaigns were carried out in the main markets during the first half of 2003 and a Euro 2004 Football Cup campaign during the last quarter. The 2003 promotional plan also included intensive public relations and trade activities, attendance at 63 international tourism fairs, and the targeting of a new segment - the Portuguese residing abroad. **Andorra** made further efforts to adapt its campaigns to specific target markets. Its first activities aimed at promoting business travel were undertaken. There were also more promotions involving sport. In 2003, **Italy** launched new plans and strategies to boost tourism, especially in the South. The Ministry of Productive Activities co-financed 34 interregional/intraregional projects aimed at developing Local Tourism Systems in the regions. Emphasis was placed on cultural activities, for example helping to organise creative Italian events, which were received with great enthusiasm by foreign tour operators and travel agents. The lion's share of these went to the United States of America, where Italian destinations are traded by 45 per cent of travel agencies and where visitors' prime interests are art, Italian life-style, design, fashion, music and food. **San Marino**'s marketing in 2003 focused on trade liaison, commercial participation, tourism conferences, and new strategies. Key activities included specialised international tourism fairs, campaigns, events, Internet and new technologies. The **Croatian** National Tourist Office continued to implement the agreed "Strategic Marketing Plan of Croatian Tourism to the Year 2005". Most important activities were: study tours for journalists and agents; special presentations; travel and tourism fairs; press conferences; advertising, including spots on TV and joint ads in the printed media; and national evenings presenting cuisine and culture. **Bosnia and Herzegovina** organised special promotions and activities, including a campaign in five world capital cities. **The Former Yugoslav Republic of Macedonia**'s General Promotion Program included brochures, fairs, journalist visits, and cultural events. **Serbia**

**and Montenegro** emphasised research in source markets and special offers. It increased its focus on the United Kingdom and Germany. The **Slovenian** Tourist Board (STB) concentrated on five key markets (Germany, Austria, Italy, Croatia and Slovenia itself) and carried out additional promotions in partnership with the industry in prospective/emerging markets (Great Britain, Ireland, Scandinavia, the Russian Federation, France and Israel). The touring campaign "Byways are more attractive than highways - Next Exit" was improved, and more wellness and convention products were developed. The STB created a Slovenian Tourist Internet Portal. An umbrella brand and the use of modern methods/technologies were key features of the marketing strategy. Much emphasis was placed on market intelligence, co-operation, assessment of results, research and statistical analysis. A new marketing consortium representing low cost airlines in Slovenia was set up, and a Regional Tourist Board was created for the Julian Alps –one of Slovenia's most important destinations. **Malta** continued its efforts to build on the United Kingdom market while trying to recover substantial losses from Germany and the Netherlands and achieve growth from other markets. The long-term objective for each source market remained that of projecting the Malta brand image and increasing recognition, customer trust and loyalty based on added value. The marketing and promotion plan for 2003 included the operation of an international network of offices and representatives, advertising campaigns, a public relations programme, tour operator support, the promotion of special incentive packages, participation in fairs and the promotion of the conference and incentive travel and special interest travel segments.

The **Cyprus** Tourism Organisation (CTO) revised and updated its 10-year Strategic Plan for tourism, the implementation of which began in 2000, in line with new conditions and trends evolving in the international tourism market. Consequently, the overall Marketing Strategy was modified. Within the framework of the Strategic Plan, the CTO is implementing an integral communication strategy, based on the systematic promotion of a single and unique image of Cyprus. Marketing activities in 2003 included promotional events; familiarisation trips for tourism professionals, journalists and other personalities; and tourism fairs. The generic summer advertising campaign "Cyprus the island for four seasons" ran from January to March in 14 source markets. It was subsequently boosted with additional funds, allowing its extension to July and to six more markets. The campaign consisted predominantly of press and outdoor advertising. Television advertising was carried out in the United Kingdom and German markets. A parallel campaign was scheduled in support using the international TV networks CNN International and Eurosport. This was of special importance in markets for which limited or no advertising funds were available. CTO promotional activities were geared towards the consumer, the travel trade and organised groups dealing within special interest market segments, as these have been determined in the modified Marketing Strategy. **Israel** continued to focus on niche segments. In 2003, the Ministry of Culture and Tourism in **Turkey** spent US$ 47 million on campaigns in over 50 countries, using press, media, posters, cinemas, Internet, VCD/DVD production, bulletins, and brochures. The focus was on promoting alternatives to mass (sun-sea) tourism with the aim of improving seasonal spread and sustainability. In addition to its traditional range of source markets, Turkey widened its promotional activities to Iran, Syria and Egypt.

## I.2.5 Outlook 2004

**Sweden** predicts slow and steady growth during the coming years, but this will be highly dependent on the evolution of the world economy. **Norway**, based on its Tourist Barometer, expects a slight increase from most markets in summer 2004. Most uncertain are the Danish and German markets. **Finland** is estimating growth of 3-4 per cent in incoming tourism for the years 2004 and 2005. The growth markets are likely to be Central and Southern Europe, the United States of America and Japan. **Denmark**'s outlook for 2004 is positive. Based on a Government initiative, the Danish Tourist Board on 1st January 2004 established "Event Denmark", a unit with the objective of developing more cultural events with appeal to an international audience. The prime target group is the city break segment. In 2004, the Royal Wedding, though of little direct tourism benefit, is very effective from the point of view of press coverage. In 2005 the celebration of Hans Christian Andersen's 200th anniversary will be followed by hundreds of cultural events, new attractions etc., that are expected to increase tourism demand, mainly from Europe, Japan and from the new Chinese market. Long-term expectations are generally positive based on a continuation of growth from the important established markets, but also on considerable potential from emerging tourism markets in East Europe and Asia. In February 2004, an agreement between Denmark and China was signed giving Denmark "Approved Destination Status" (ADS). The debate on a new vision for Danish tourism 2010 which was launched at the Danish Tourist Board's Annual Tourism Conference in November 2003 continued into 2004 at national, regional and local levels. The agreed common vision has now been launched. **Ireland's** target for 2004 is to increase foreign visitors by 4 per cent, then by almost 6 per cent per annum through to 2006, while increasing "promotable" visitors (holiday, conference, incentive, language learning) by almost 7 per cent per annum. The Government has set a target of doubling foreign visitor spending by 2012. Failte Ireland is implementing 2004 operational plans for home holidays and regional development, and also for niche tourism products such as walking, cycling, golf, equestrian pursuits, heritage and gardens, angling, language learning and business tourism. Tourism Ireland's marketing strategy for the whole island covering the period 2004 to 2006 will focus the bulk of resources on the United Kingdom, the United States of America, France and Germany. Almost two-thirds of allocated funds will be spent on advertising with the balance on below-the-line activities such as promotion, direct marketing, print, distribution and trade support. The **United Kingdom** is forecasting 3 per cent growth in 2004 for inbound visitors, assuming no further major disasters. Similar growth rates are anticipated for domestic tourism. Visit Britain is implementing its "Leading the World to Britain" international marketing strategy. Highlights of this include: sharpening the brand position of Britain in relation to the nations and regions of the United Kingdom; honing marketing skills and exploiting the potential of new media; engaging public and private stakeholders in the marketing of Britain; and aligning the organisation and its culture to deliver these objectives. International operations are being restructured into regional 'hubs' or centres of excellence to monitor and respond to opportunities throughout the region, not just in core markets. Clear priorities have been set in areas such as Customer Relationship Management (CRM), business tourism, Internet marketing and 'new' market development as well as development of a strong brand for Britain. Visit Britain will also continue its fundamental shift in distribution methods, with the Internet and direct marketing replacing walk-in centres and telephone calls as the main point of customer contact.

**France** experienced an excellent winter sports season (2003/2004), but trends for the spring varied by source market. Late reservations and direct booking, especially by Internet, are making medium term forecasting more difficult. Some markets, especially long-haul ones like the United States of America and Japan, are predicted to pick up in 2004. The strong new markets of Russia and China will continue to grow, the latter boosted still further by the fact that the Schengen countries have recently been attributed ADS. European Union markets will depend on the economic situation country by country, but France's biggest producers, the United Kingdom and Germany, are both expected to exceed their 2003 figures. The Maison de la France published a new Marketing Strategy based on image and positioning research done at the end of 2003. Looking forward, a major event for French tourism will be the Rugby World Cup in 2007. **Monaco** reports a good first five months, with hotel occupancy levels up. Nevertheless there is a hangover from the difficult conditions of 2003. Traffic from the United States of America is still very depressed and other markets remain sensitive to economic and political developments. **Switzerland** Tourism believes there will be a turnaround this year with an increase of 0.4 per cent in total visits; of 0.6 per cent in foreigners; but a decline of 0.7 per cent in the domestic market. The equivalent figures for the summer season are predicted to be: +1 per cent; +2.3 per cent; and -0.5 per cent, and for the whole of 2005: +1.4 per cent; +0.8 per cent and +1.8 per cent. Switzerland achieved approved destination status from China in 2004. 300 thousand Chinese overnights are forecast for 2006, compared with 106 thousand in 2003. **The Netherlands** expects 2.5 per cent growth in 2004 arrivals. The main objective for the Netherlands Board of Tourism and Conventions (NBTC) will be to gain market share from its competitors in North-West Europe. In 2003, the Netherlands' market share amounted to 14 per cent; in 2006, the target is set at 14.3 per cent. In order to reach this objective the NBTC has developed a new marketing strategy, in which choices are made on product-market combinations. In the coming years the NBTA will concentrate on the following products: Holland classics, city trips, the coast and the rest of Holland. On the promotion side, NBTC will develop some large campaigns directed primarily at neighbouring countries. Theme years and international events will also play an important promotional role. **Belgium, Flanders** is predicting improved economic stability, growth in Chinese travellers to Europe and Belgium, and a positive impact from increased activity by SN-Brussels Airlines. **Belgium, Wallonia** will concentrate on maintaining growth from the Dutch market, and increasing German and British market share by emphasising three key factors: quality of life style, quality of services, and price. With respect to the key domestic market, Belgium, Wallonia will attempt to arrest the decline in long holidays, short holidays and excursions by using a mix of promotional and pricing tools. **Luxembourg** is hoping that the US and Chinese markets will regain strength in 2004, and that levels of traffic from Denmark and the Netherlands can be maintained. It aims to increase tourism through a range of strategies, for example the extension of promotional campaigns to Eastern Europe; stronger emphasis on Belgium, the United Kingdom, Scandinavia and Asia; increased promotion in the professional press; new gardens, parks and cycling publications; and more co-operation with the national airline, Luxair, especially in the United Kingdom and Hungary. Events will be a key feature, for example the Garden Show and the $60^{th}$ Anniversary of the Battle of the Bulge. Luxembourg will hold the European Union Presidency in 2005, and increasing focus will be put on cultural tourism in the lead up to Cultural Year 2007. **Liechtenstein** will launch a summer campaign in Germany. A new Goethe theme ("Mit Gothe durch Vaduz") has been developed and there are plans to undertake hotel classification. In **Austria** overnight stays during the winter season (November 2003 to March 2004) grew by 1.7 per cent, with domestic nights up by 3 per cent and foreign by 1.3 per cent. Turnover in the same period increased by 3.6 per cent, and for the whole winter season this figure is expected to improve to 4 per cent. The Austrian Institute for Economic Research (WIFO) expects an increase of about 4.5 per cent in the summer season. A new advertising campaign has been launched. 2006 will be Mozart Year.

In 2004, the **German** National Tourist Board (GNTB) is expecting an increase of more than 2 per cent in overnight stays by visitors from abroad and an increase of 1 per cent in the number of overnight stays by German nationals. For the first time, GNTB is publishing a collection of important market data on incoming tourism to Germany in time for the ITB. Based on the GNTB's own market research, a core potential of 5.6 million trips could be generated from the East European Union accession countries alone by 2005. China also has massive potential - the number of overnight stays it generates is expected to reach the one million mark by 2009. The GNTB is expecting four million overnight stays per annum by visitors from the Far East. The GNTB aims to contribute to this with a "Germany in Japan" campaign in 2005/2006 (initiated by the German Government). With regard to the domestic market, a recent GNTB survey revealed that 90 per cent of travel agency managers in Germany anticipate growth in travel within Germany in 2004. The areas of health/wellness (86%) and city breaks/event-related travel (85%) were identified as having the greatest potential for growth. Thirty-seven per cent of travel agency managers forecast growth in demand for domestic holidays in 2004 and 33 per cent had already registered this effect in 2003. The GNTB is aiming to consolidate and strengthen domestic tourism in Germany based on three main approaches: co-operative projects with traditional nation-wide media, information management on the Germany portal, and sales and promotional campaigns for the travel industry. In international markets, Germany will continue to focus on the two mega-trends –culture and health– on which both the "City Tours/Events" and "Health and Fitness Holidays" product lines are based. From 2006 on, the GNTB will concentrate on one central theme per year. In addition to this, it will also feature each year anniversaries and major events with market-specific campaigns, for example the 200$^{th}$ Anniversary of Schiller's death in 2005, as well as the re-consecration of the Church of Our Lady in Dresden. Cologne is expecting up to 800 thousand visitors in August 2005 for the XX World Youth Day. For 2005, additional campaigns will be: "Vibrant Towns and Cities" and "Family Holidays". The following year will of course be a massive one for sport. The 2006 FIFA Football World Cup Germany™ represents an excellent opportunity for promoting the country all over the world. For 2006 as a whole, the GNTB is expecting an additional increase in the number of overnight stays of around 1.7 per cent as a direct result of this sporting event. The theme "250 Years of Mozart" will offer a cultural counterpoint. With new web areas, an e-book in 30 languages and additional online services, the GNTB is continuing to expand and improve its central marketing platform, the Germany web. A new, dedicated section of the GNTB website for the 2006 FIFA World Cup Germany™ came online in March 2004. Basic training for the GNTB's new e-learning programme has been successfully concluded; advanced training will be started in autumn 2004. 2,500 travel agents have already taken part in the course entitled "Expedition Germany - The Seminar for Explorers". The objective is to enhance the quality of travel advice and to increase the number of holiday bookings for Germany.

The **Hungarian** National Tourist Office's official forecast for 2004 is an increase of 3 per cent in foreign bed-nights at public accommodation establishments and an increase of 4 per cent in domestic bed-nights. This optimism is due to a higher marketing budget, more intensive marketing activity, European Union enlargement, improved accessibility, a more favourable exchange rate, and general recovery in the tourism market, both international and domestic. Special events will help boost visits, especially European Union accession, the 15$^{th}$ anniversary of the opening-up of borders between Austria and Hungary, and the year of Hungarian Culture in the United Kingdom (Magyar Magic). Moreover the traditional events, which took place successfully in 2003 and in previous years, will be organised in 2004 as well. Great emphasis will be placed in 2004 on the following products and markets: Budapest; Lake Balaton in nearby European markets; health/spas; conferences and incentives mainly in Western Europe; activities, mainly sports; culture; youth and seniors; and domestic tourism. Hungary joined the European Union on 1st May 2004 and has thus become eligible for support from the European Union Structural Funds and Cohesion Fund. **Poland** also expects tourism benefits from joining the EU. Increases in both leisure and business tourism are predicted. The exchange rate has not changed substantially in 2004, so Poland remains relatively inexpensive (except in high-class hotels). Surveys show that customers' opinions on safety in Poland have changed for the better. Polish GDP is growing considerably now, so domestic and outbound tourism may start to increase. The **Czech Republic** predicts that foreign tourist arrivals will grow by more than 10 per cent, to reach a total of 7.1 million in 2004. Events planned include a Regional Seminar on Tourism Sustainability Certification and a Film Festival. The Czech Republic will be represented at 53 tourism fairs all around the world. Two of these (GO+Regiontour and Holiday World) are held in the Czech Republic. In addition "Czech Days" will be organised in various countries. Preparations are underway for the ASTA Conference which will be held in Prague in 2006. Following entrance to the EU, immigration formalities with the most important European countries have been simplified. **Romania** also predicts that international arrivals will grow at a rate of approximately 10 per cent per annum. Promotional efforts will be intensified in the United States of America, Japan, Germany, Italy, Spain, France, the United Kingdom and China. Romania will continue to invite foreign mass media representatives to promote the different tourism regions. More domestic cultural events will be organised. Foreign overnights at accommodation establishments in **Estonia** are expected to increase by 10 per cent in 2004. The top growth markets are expected to be those European source markets that have shown good rates of increase over the past few years: Germany, the United Kingdom, Norway, Italy, and to a lesser extent Poland, France and Spain. In 2004, the total budget of the Estonian Tourist Board for promoting Estonia abroad has increased by 2.6 times in comparison with 2003. The Marketing Action Plan for 2004-2006 was completed at the beginning of the year. Joining the European Union on 1st May 2004 is an image boost for Estonia and will facilitate entry for citizens of other European Union countries. This should also lead to shorter border crossing times when travelling through the Baltic countries. This is important as Estonia and the Baltic countries are increasingly popular among car and bus tourists from Central Europe, especially from Germany. In the near future, European Union citizens will be able to travel to Estonia showing only their identification cards, not passports. Another advantage of membership is that additional European Union funds for the development of tourism infrastructure and tourism products will become available in Estonia, thus facilitating further investments from the private sector as well. Major increases in hotel room supply are already planned for 2004 –in Tallinn alone capacity will increase by over 20 per cent, mainly at two and three star level. A big water park and a hotel with 250 beds were opened in March 2004 and a new spa hotel with 91 rooms in May 2004. There will also be significant improvements in sea and air access and capacity. Many new investments are being completed in **Slovakia,** and the positive trends in tourism are expected to continue, especially the improvement of quality, increased visitor satisfaction, and growth of tourist expenditure. The entry of Slovakia into the European Union will create a short-term wave of interest in member states. The continuing strength of the Slovak crown may negatively influence the tourist flow from Poland but only slightly from the Czech Republic (the Polish zloty is fixed to the United States dollar and the Czech crown to the euro). Some problems of occupancy may occur in spa resorts because of the new approach of the Social and Health Insurance Organisations. Spa resorts will need to concentrate on new markets and clients. The National Tourism Office has launched a promotional campaign to develop domestic tourism but the motivation to spend holidays abroad (above all seaside holidays) is very strong. According to an Oxford Economic Forecasting Report, **Lithuania**'s travel and tourism industry is expected to generate 1.9 per cent of GDP and 26 thousand jobs, while the broader travel and tourism economy is expected to generate 10 per cent of GDP and 131 thousand jobs. Real travel and tourism demand growth is expected to be 9.3 per cent in 2004, and 6.8 per cent per annum between 2005 and 2014. Emphasis on tourism in **Latvia** increased dramatically in 2004. The Ministry of Economics multiplied the state budget for tourism by 2.3 times, which will lead to a significant increase in marketing activities. Further steady annual budget increases are planned together with more emphasis on the attraction of investment. As result of this active policy, significant progress is anticipated in key indicators, with 10-15 per cent annual growth in tourism service exports and a 5-7 per cent increase in tourism's share of GDP over the next 4 years. Public-private partnership will be strengthened by the establishment in 2004 of the Tourism Industry Expert Board. A key event looking forward will be the World Ice-Hockey Championship in 2006. **Belarus** aims to increase exports of tourism service by 18 per cent between 2000 and 2005. Emphasis will be on quality through the grading of tourism services, on research, on active co-operation with international tourism bodies including becoming a member of the World Tourism Organization, on revision of the tourism law, and on creating the Republican Tourism Development Foundation. The major generating markets for tourism to **Armenia** in 2004 are the United States of America and Western Europe. New emerging markets are visitors from South America, Japan and South-East Asia. The main niche market is based on regional tourism (the Silk Road); many visitors travel to Armenia from neighbouring Georgia and Iran. The principal target groups are visitors for cultural, historical and rural tourism, ecotourism and religious tourism. There are plans to arrange intensive courses on theme "How tourism works", to expand the annual Kenats Festival to the regions, and to organise an itinerant Wine and Cheese Festival. **Turkmenistan** and **Kazakhstan** both anticipate tourism growth. Kazakhstan plans to create a tourism research institute in 2006.

Early 2004 results in **Spain** permit moderate optimism, but the international situation remains uncertain. Major cultural happenings are scheduled this year –the Forum of the Cultures in Barcelona; the centenary of Salvador Dalí's birth; the fifth centenary of the death of Isabel la Católica; the celebration of the Xacobeo Holy Year; and the expansion of Madrid's three top museums. In **Portugal** of course the highlight of 2004 was the Euro Football Cup. Other important events include the Rock-in-Rio Festival and the Laureus Awards Ceremony. At the beginning of 2004, a pan European Contact Centre was set up to handle information requests and a new Internet portal will be activated towards the end of the year. Improving economic conditions are predicted, with Portugal benefiting from a more favourable external context and from the expected European and world economic recovery. In 2004, a new Government has been established, which includes, for the first time, a Ministry of Tourism, recognising thus the importance of the sector in the national economy. **Andorra** predicts a continuing decline in overnights. In an attempt to counteract this, it will be undertaking special promotions in the United Kingdom, France and Spain. It will also carry out a major MICE promotion. An initial analysis of international tourism receipts in **Italy** for the period January to March 2004 shows that receipts went up to 4.8 billion euro, 11 per cent more than in the previous year –a demonstration that travel confidence is improving after a very difficult period. The strategies pinpointed in the 2004/2006 three-year ENIT plan also give grounds for optimism. They should lead to: the rationalisation of promotional investments, with increased effectiveness and efficiency; a strong unitary image of Italy backed by strong regional identities; the development of total quality in accommodation; the opening of new markets by developing innovative cultural, nature and niche products; the introduction of new professionals responsible for pinpointing new market niches anywhere in the world; improved capacity and capability of tourism promotion institutions; and reciprocal agreements with other European national tourist boards to undertake special marketing programmes overseas. Many infrastructure improvements are also planned or underway. Strategic projects identified in the Government's General Transport Plan include the Frèjus Tunnel, the Simpon Rail Tunnel, the Brenner Rail Tunnel, the Mo.Se project to save the Venice Lagoon, the Romea road link from Rome to Eastern Europe, the Rome integrated transport node, the Salerno-Reggio-Calabria- Palermo-Catania-Siracusa-Gela road rail link, and the straits of Messina Bridge. Italy has also launched plans and strategies aimed at tourism product development, especially in the South. At present, projects centre on Calabria, Sicily and Puglia, where 770 million euro will be invested in five new tourist areas –7,770 rooms and 9 golf courses will be built, catering for 2.4 million tourists and creating 11,700 jobs. **San Marino**, due to its geographical location, depends essentially on tourists coming from Italy. It expects an increase in Italian visitors, as well as growth from the Eastern European and Russian markets. **Greece** is celebrating the success of the summer Olympic Games in Athens. In successive years, it is confident that tourism flows will continue to increase, as a result of the expected improvement of economic conditions in generating markets, of enhanced tourist supply and infrastructure, of the impact of the Olympic Games, and of intensified promotional activity. The nomination of the city of Patras as cultural capital of Europe for 2006 and an eventual nomination of Thessaloniki for the international "World Expo 2008" will also have a positive effect. **Croatia** predicts that foreign tourist traffic will grow at a moderate 3 to 5 per cent in 2004 and for the next few years. Further growth of traffic from all the West European generating markets, especially Germany, Italy, France, Great Britain and the Scandinavian countries, is expected. **Serbia and Montenegro** is much more optimistic, predicting an increase in tourism receipts of 50 per cent in 2004. However the decline in domestic tourism is expected to continue. **The Former Yugoslav Republic of Macedonia** will focus its promotional activities for the current and next year on neighbouring countries and on its key generating markets (the Netherlands, the United Kingdom, and Germany). Familiarisation trips will be arranged for specialised journalists and tour-operators. In 2004 **Bosnia and Herzegovina** will cooperage on a common promotion with the other ex-Yugoslavia countries. **Slovenia** is predicting 3 per cent growth in tourism arrivals, with particularly good performances from the United Kingdom (+5%), Hungary (+5%), Benelux (+6%) and Switzerland (+6%). Domestic tourism is expected to remain static. The Tourist Board's approach will be based on research and strategic partnership. It continued with its "Slovenia invigorates" advertising campaign in key markets (Germany, Italy and Austria) to coincide with European Union entrance in May 2004. Priority will be given to products with the best-developed Unique Selling Propositions. Traditional promotional activities will be supplemented by increased use of electronic media. There will be less emphasis on public fairs. A national on-line reservation system will be set up. In **Malta,** indications look good from certain markets, such as Italy and Sweden, and constant for other markets, such as the United Kingdom, Germany and France. The current year should end up level with 2003, but the situation is expected to improve from 2005 onwards. European Union structural funds should give a boost to product development. Tourism proposals costing around 8 million euro are being submitted.

On 1st May 2004, **Cyprus** became a full European Union member. The resulting lower airfares will stimulate tourism from the majority of European source markets. It is worth noting that the overwhelming majority of the island's visitors (around 83%) source from the enlarged European Union. Simplified entry formalities will also be a plus, but it is feared that new European tax regulations coming into force during 2004 will adversely affect competitiveness. The opening in 2004 of two new CTO Offices, one in Dubai and one in Finland, will further stimulate tourist traffic from these countries. To complement mainstream advertising, during 2004 a series of mega-events (concerts, ballet and opera etc.) will take place. In the light of the Olympic Games 2004 and within the framework of the development of sports tourism, the CTO entered into an agreement with the British Olympic Association to highlight the fact that Britain selected Cyprus for their Olympics preparation training. Furthermore, the CTO provided hospitality for the Olympic and Para-Olympic Committee from Ireland and supported the promotion of the Cyprus World Rally. Cyprus will also be investing heavily in the training and development of its human resources, in the promotion of quality and environmental systems in the industry, and in the modernisation and technological advancement of its tourist enterprises, which are mainly of small to medium size. **Israel** hopes that the current positive trend will continue and that inbound tourism as well as domestic tourism will increase. Tourists to **Turkey** increased by a massive 33 per cent between January and August of 2004, to reach a total of 11.4 million. There was a 29 per cent increase in the number of OECD visitors (62% of the total) and a 35 per cent increase in the number of visitors coming from East European countries (28% of the total). There were 2.6 million visitors from Germany (+22%); 1.2 million from Russia (+10%); and nearly one million from the United Kingdom (+8%). The next most important markets were: the Netherlands, Bulgaria, France, Iran, Austria, Belgium, Greece, Italy, Israel, Azerbaijan, Ukraine and Sweden. 14 million visitors are predicted by the end of the year, an increase of over 20 per cent. A similar percentage increase is also expected in 2005.

# I.3 International Meetings Industry

## I.3.1 Supply

**Denmark** has a large variety of meeting and conference facilities ranging from graceful castles and manor houses to modern hotels. Copenhagen in particular has a wide selection of centrally located hotels. International, state-of-the-art congress centres are located in Copenhagen, Aalborg, Århus, Herning and Odense. There is a hotel and conference facility rating system ranging from 1-5 stars. A wide range of teambuilding possibilities is also available from treasure hunts, fishing and golf to cultural/historical incentive programmes. **Finland** has very good facilities for congresses, not only in the major cities like Helsinki and Tampere, but also in most provincial capitals. In **Norway** the largest hotel chains, airlines and cities cooperate to offer MICE products. **Sweden's** main destinations for big events, conventions and meetings are Stockholm, Göteborg and Malmö. For small and medium sized events, meetings and incentives, Sweden offers a wide range of different and unique regions, for example Northern Sweden with its Ice Hotel, motor coach safaris and virgin nature, and the Stockholm area with its Archipelago. Sweden's offer is based on: professionalism and excellent organisational skills; direct daily flights from major European hubs; a wide range of centrally located congress centres; a friendly, welcoming environment in a country where English is widely spoken; novel and exotic meeting/incentive products; and value for money. In **Ireland** there has been a 5 billion euro investment in hotel and venue facilities over the last few years. Ireland has an experienced team of professional conference organisers to assist associations and corporations with their meetings. The range of four and five-star properties, creative Destination Management Companies, and variety of activities offered also make Ireland an ideal incentive travel destination. The **United Kingdom** can boast meetings, congress, conference and convention supply country-wide. Key international conference destinations with purpose built venues include: Aberdeen, Belfast, Birmingham, Bournemouth, Brighton, Cardiff, Edinburgh, Glasgow, Harrogate, Liverpool, London, Manchester, Newcastle and Gateshead. Incentive and exhibitions/fairs product supply also covers a wide geographic spread. For incentives, the emphasis is on luxury products particularly in London and Scotland, outdoor activities and increasingly spa products. Key international exhibition venues with purpose built facilities (single venue with over 10 thousand square metres) include: Birmingham, Belfast, Manchester, Glasgow and London.

According to the Association of the **German** Trade Fair Industry (AUMA), the six largest trade fair and exhibition centres in Germany in 2003 were: Hanover, Frankfurt/Main, Cologne, Düsseldorf, Munich and Berlin. The importance of these six locations alone is shown by the fact that four of them are among the top five locations within Europe and all six are among the top 12 cities. **France's** MICE offer is very diverse, with some 2000 establishments having the capacity to host professional events for at least 200 persons. The supply environment is also highly competitive due to the diversity and number of players in the market. Three large French regions alone account for 40 per cent of supply in the business tourism segment in France: Paris-Île-de-France, Rhône-Alpes and Provence-Alpes-Côte d'Azur. Some 1,500 hotels in France have developed "business" services in their establishments. They offer services tailored to the needs of business clients, as well as large-capacity conference halls with specialised equipment. There are currently 120 convention centres of different sizes in France. This makes France the top European country in terms of such facilities, with 36 per cent of capacity, which can be broken down as follows: around 15 centres with a capacity of over 4 thousand persons in major cities serving the regional, national and international markets; some 30 centres with capacities between 2 thousand and 4 thousand persons in large cities, also catering to the same markets; and the rest which are either in regional capitals or resort towns. With regard to exhibition centres, France has areas totalling over 1.6 million square metres. The offer is very diverse, with only two exhibition centres of over 100 thousand square metres –Paris Expo and Paris Nord. In **Belgium,** Brussels as the capital of Europe and headquarters city for many multinationals has naturally developed a wide range of MICE products to handle its high level of demand. However there are two major problems: the closure of the Convention Centre and the lack of a large permanent venue for congresses with more than five thousand delegates. Brussels is developing incentive traffic based on its mid range hotels. Belgium, Wallonia is focusing on three products for meetings and incentives: small hotels or large internationally branded ones; gastronomy; and specialised services. **The Netherlands** has excellent infrastructure with a balanced price/quality ratio, a wide offer of hotels, and many multifunctional conference centres. The main congress destinations are: Amsterdam, The Hague, Rotterdam, Noordwijk, Maastricht, Utrecht, Groningen and Eindhoven. Numerous places of interest are located in easy reach of each other, offering a wide range of possibilities for social programmes. The Dutch MICE industry prides itself of creativity, co-operative thinking and flexibility. **Liechtenstein** has an excellent central location in Europe and good infrastructure, while **Luxembourg** has a range of meeting venues, for example the Kirchberg Conference Centre, plus Lux Expo for exhibitions and the New Spirit and Destination Luxembourg products for incentives. The main MICE destinations in **Switzerland** are Basel, Bern, Crans-Montana, Davos, Flims, Fribourg, Geneva, Interlaken, Lausanne, Lugano, Luzern, Montreux, Pontresina, St. Gallen, St. Moritz and Zürich. **Monaco** has been a business travel destination since 1972, and its hotel and meeting facilities are ideally suited to this role, particularly with regard to congresses, seminars, product launches, exhibitions and fairs.

In the **Czech Republic**, central Prague in particular has high capacity, including its own Convention Centre, and a high level of technical services, both for congresses and incentives. Events can also be organised in historic buildings. There are large areas for Exhibitions and Fairs in Prague and Brno. **Hungary** has a range of unusual meeting places as well as new hotels. There are good Professional Congress Organisers (PCOs) which conference co-ordinators from overseas are advised to use in order to avoid problems of organisation. There has been a rapid increase of 4 and 5 star hotels in **Poland.** In 2002, their total grew by 11 per cent and of these over 13 per cent are 5 star. There are new exhibition and trade fair centres in Warsaw and Poznan. There has also been an increase in incentive travel organisers. The best facilities for meetings in **Slovakia** are mainly in Bratislava and some other cities such as Kosice, Zilina, Nitra, Banska Bystrica and Trencin. Historic towns, spas and mountain resorts, and some castles can also provide interesting venues, especially for smaller meetings. The most suitable facilities for exhibitions and trade fairs are located in Bratislava, Nitra and Trencin. Smaller exhibitions can be organised in places like Zilina, Banska Bystrica and Presov. There are a number of specialised event, exhibition and incentive organisers. In **Estonia** the main destination for international conferences and seminars is the capital Tallinn, which captures 78 per cent of foreign conference tourists staying in accommodation establishments, followed by the university town Tartu with 8 per cent and the resort town Pärnu with 5 per cent. In October 2003, Sokos Hotel Viru in Tallinn opened its new conference and banqueting centre. Together, the new multifunctional seminar rooms can seat up to 900 delegates, with the largest seating up to 400. Most meeting rooms in Estonia offer capacity of up to 300 participants –the size of the majority of conferences and seminars. There are a few larger conference halls, suitable for up to one thousand delegates, and one arena, which can seat up to 6 thousand. **Latvia**'s main meetings destination is Riga. Its good accessibility and value for money have earned it a place on the ICCA (International Congress & Convention Association) list. **Lithuania**'s exhibitions and fairs are concentrated in Vilnius, but there are also suitable facilities to organise meetings and incentives in other towns and in rural areas.

**Spain**'s MICE supply has been transformed and modernised over recent years. Today there are more than 40 suitable cities with over 50 Convention Centres, plus a large range of four and five star hotels. In recent years the facilities available for the meetings industry in **Portugal** have been growing in a sustained manner. There has been a simultaneous increase in the number and quality of accommodation establishments (4 and 5 star) and of specialised service providers in the main MICE destinations (Lisbon, Porto, Algarve and Madeira). Lisbon, the main national destination in terms of meetings and conventions, has excellent facilities for medium-size meetings (500 participants) and a growing capacity for larger meetings, as proven by the increasing number of events with over 5 thousand delegates being hosted. With regard to incentive travel, national supply is based firstly on diversity of experiences and landscapes in a concentrated geographic area, and secondly on the growing professionalism of specialised incentive travel enterprises and Convention Bureaux. The regulation and strict licensing of such enterprises has contributed to the quality of service and to enhanced recognition in the international market. Venues for sports and cultural events in Portugal have seen major expansion and improvement in the lead up to the Euro 2004 Football Cup and to “Rock in Rio Lisboa”. **Andorra** has some public centres in which meetings and congresses are organised. It also has more than 15 hotels which specialise in business tourism, and numerous Professional Congress Organizers (PCO's) offering a wide range of services. Meetings and conferences are a very important part of **Italy**'s tourism industry. The major art and business cities, as well as the lake resorts and spas, have a wide range of facilities. According to a recent survey for the Tourism Directorate of the Ministry of Productive Activities, there are 2,830 congress centres in Italy. Most of these are attached to hotels (1,979). Another 560 are in historic buildings and 291 are in other locations, such as dedicated convention centres, trade fair buildings and theatres. There are 5,231 meeting rooms. Most are in hotels (3,602). There are 736 in historic buildings and 893 in other types of facilities. In addition, there are 2,072 congress organisers, 1,314 incentive firms or travel agencies specialising in incentive travel, 786 firms specialising in the necessary equipment (stands, etc.), 630 catering and banquet firms, 562 businesses providing technical and audio-visual services, 228 performing arts companies providing services for conferences, and 338 interpretation and translation firms. In **Greece** there are fifteen conference centres spread throughout the country. There are also modern conference facilities in two hundred hotels, with various capacities. Important incentives, for example grants and tax breaks, are offered both in mainland Greece and on the islands to the private sector in order to encourage the creation of new facilities or increases in capacity. **Croatia** has MICE facilities country-wide. The most important is the Zagreb Fair and Congress Centre. There are 500 thousand square metres for exhibitions. **Malta** offers conference and meetings facilities of a very high standard in prime locations, with support from dedicated and professional Destination Management Companies. **Slovenia** has built new congress infrastructure. Its main congress destinations are: Portorož, Bled, Ljubljana, Maribor, Rogaška Slatina, Radenci, and Nova Gorica. A new conference centre opened in **San Marino.** It has a reasonable supply of meeting facilities, but hardly any areas suitable for exhibitions. In the **Former Yugoslav Republic of Macedonia,** investments have been made in meetings facilities, mainly in the enhancement of existing hotel capacities in the Ohrid Lake area.

The proximity of **Cyprus** to both European and Middle Eastern markets makes it an ideal regional centre. The Cyprus International Conference Centre, Lefkosia, offers three thousand square metres for international conferences, product launches, exhibitions and television shows. It can easily accommodate functions of up to 1,600 delegates. Located at the juncture of Europe and Asia, **Turkey** is an accessible venue for motivational meetings and conventions. It has a wealth of first-class hotel accommodation and conference facilities, fully equipped to handle meetings, incentives and conferences of all sorts and sizes in comfort and style. The MICE segment in Turkey, especially in Istanbul and Antalya, has developed strongly over recent years. The opening of Lutfi Kirdar Istanbul International Conference Centre doubled the capacity of congress facilities in that city. Moreover there are many alternative choices ranging from Mediterranean, thermal or ski resorts to the sophistication of Turkey's capital city, Ankara.

## I.3.2 Demand

Preliminary estimates of the MICE segment in **Denmark** indicate an estimated turnover of approximately 0.5 billion euro in 2003. This is around one fifth of commercial tourism (i.e. excluding same-day visitors and tourists in private accommodation). The **Finland** Convention Bureau (FCB) regularly carries out surveys and collects data on international congresses in Finland. These surveys include interviews with congress participants and organisers. At present the FCB is carrying out an extensive study of the entire Finnish meeting market. The objective is to determine the number of domestic and international meetings held in Finland and their impact on the economy and employment. Data on the number of foreign visitors taking part in congresses or seminars is also collected as part of the Finnish Tourist Board/Statistics Finland Border Survey. Some 300 international congresses with a total of 60 thousand delegates are held in Finland each year. Congress tourists account for around 2.3 per cent of total overnight visitors (2.6 million in 2003). In 2001, the expenditure of foreign congress participants totalled 42 million euro, which was approximately 2.6 per cent of the total expenditure of foreign tourists. Incentive visits to Finland are estimated at 80 thousand annually. Finland is number 15 on the list of the world's leading congress countries. **Norway** estimates that fifteen per cent of guest nights in hotels are related to meetings. There are no regular demand statistics for **Sweden**, so the evolution over recent years is difficult to estimate. An estimate for 2002 shows a turnover of SEK 32 billion for the meetings industry. Based on the Tourism Satellite Account there has been a noticeable decrease in domestic business consumption since 2002 and it is reasonable to assume that this decrease has also affected the meetings industry. On the other hand, there has been a notable focus on this segment by regions, cities, and the travel industry itself. The International Conference/Corporate Meetings sector to **Ireland** has grown by 11 per cent per annum over the past 10 years, despite a slowdown in recent years due to the unprecedented international turmoil. Ireland collects data through its international visitor survey conducted at points of departure from the country. Business trips are identified as association conference or convention, corporate event or seminar, trade fair or exhibition, or other business reasons. The number of international conference and corporate meeting visitors in 2002 was estimated at 122 thousand; worth some 146 million euro in visitor spend. Data for the **United Kingdom** is collected through the International Passenger Survey (IPS), an ongoing outbound visitor survey covering reason for visit, duration of visit, expenditure, etc. According to IPS figures for 2002: international travellers to Britain whose purpose of visit was to attend a conference accounted for a total of 682 thousand visits, 2.8 million nights and 441 million pound in direct expenditure; those whose purpose was to attend an exhibition accounted for 254 thousand visits, one million nights and 173 million pound in direct expenditure; and those whose purpose was other business accounted for 6.2 million visits, 25 million nights and 2,959 million pound in direct expenditure. According to ICCA statistics, the United Kingdom held the third highest number of international meetings in the world during 2002 (149 according to ICCA criteria). In the same year, the United Kingdom also came third in the Union of International Associations' (UIA) statistics (5.5% of all meetings according to UIA measurement criteria). There is also a range of other research available on the United Kingdom MICE industry, including surveys of conference buyers, of conference suppliers, and of exhibition venues, plus ICCA members' feedback on confirmed conferences, and various levels of business conversion analysis amongst destination marketing organisations for their stakeholders' interest.

According to the European Travel Monitor, of the 7.7 million business trips from Europe to **Germany** in 2003, 56 per cent were non-promotable or traditional business trips, 22 per cent were trips to trade fairs and exhibitions, 19 per cent were trips to conferences and congresses, and 3 per cent were incentive trips. With a total of 70 billion euro gross added value from Germany and abroad, the trade fair and conference travel sectors are clearly of great economic importance. Germany's MICE business is currently dominated by domestic travel. Available estimates indicate that business tourism accounted for around 30 per cent of **France**'s tourism receipts. The segment experienced difficulties and a considerable slowdown following the events of 11$^{th}$ September 2001, and the war in Iraq. Inbound MICE tourism accounts for 15 per cent of overnight stays in **Belgium** and domestic MICE tourism for 5 per cent. An estimated 60 per cent of overnights in Brussels are for business reasons and 12 per cent in Wallonia. The National Institute for Statistics (NIS) collects monthly data on arrivals and overnights in all commercial establishments. These data (only for staying tourists) are differentiated by motive of stay e.g. leisure, MICE and other business purposes. It is possible to extract the specific data of MICE visitors (period of stay, length of stay, region of origin, region of stay, type of accommodation) from the global database. Supplementary supplier and market studies are undertaken. In 2004, a market research project was commissioned to analyse MICE tourism in the Flanders and Brussels Region (supply analysis, demand, trends, etc.); supply data became available mid-2004 with the final report expected at the beginning of 2005. **The Netherlands** Board of Tourism and Conventions (NBTC) registers the number of international congresses on a yearly basis. Various criteria are applied by the NBTC to define international conventions and business meetings, for example the event must last at least two days, with one overnight stay; the number of participants on the first day must be at least 40; at least one third of all participants must reside outside the Netherlands; and the meeting must take place at external accommodation, including universities and academic medical centres. There were 998 international conventions and business meetings in 2002, with an average duration of 4 days and an average number of delegates of 222. These figures are based on data collected from the Regional Convention Bureaux, from organisers and from accommodation providers. Moreover, the NBTC recently undertook research on the expenditures of international non-corporate congress participants to gain insights into the economic importance of this specific market segment. The research established that in 2002, 360 international non-corporate congresses were held in the Netherlands, making up approximately one-third of the total international congress market. The foreign non-corporate congress participant spends on average 344 euro per day. More than two-thirds of this benefits the "local economy of the congress accommodation". The research also shows that total expenditure by foreign participants in non-corporate congresses in 2002 was 116 million euro. **Switzerland** captures an estimated 6 per cent share of the European outbound meetings market. This segment's share of all tourism overnights is 5 per cent. There are an estimated 30 thousand meetings visitors to Basel, 26 thousand to Geneva, 69 thousand to Zurich, 43 thousand to Bern, and 27 thousand to St-Gall. Their average length of stay is 3 nights. Switzerland has attracted no less than 14 tourism fairs, including Ferienmesse in Basel; Salons Vacances, Sports et Loisirs, Geneva; FESPO, Zurich; Ferien-und Gesundheitsmesse, Bern; and Ferienmesse + Touristiertag, St.-Gall. According to the ranking of the Union of International Associations (UIA) for 2002, **Austria** is listed as the 12th most popular convention destination world-wide, while according to ICCA's city ranking, Vienna is number four. At the present time, Austria does not collect detailed meetings statistics, though this is planned for the future. However Vienna does assemble data on international meetings with a minimum of half the delegates from a foreign country. The data comes directly from the organisers, is checked with meeting suppliers, and is published on a yearly basis. Total overnights in the meeting and conference segment have nearly tripled over the past 15 years and now represent approximately 4 per cent (4 million overnights) of total overnight stays. The congress industry leads to an Austrian employment rate of 21,700 to 26,800 employees. Business tourism accounts for 30 per cent of arrivals to **Monaco**, compared with 10 per cent in 1972. Detailed statistics have been gathered since 2000, including delegate numbers, overnights, sector of activity and nationality of the organiser. Moreover, a common database for the tourism and congress authorities is currently under construction. Some 600 event organisation requests are received each year. In **Luxembourg** there was a significant rise in MICE business until 2003, when there was a sudden decrease. The Luxembourg Convention Bureau and Luxembourg Congrès together produce an average of about 15 thousand overnights per year. No collective statistics are available from other organisations in the congress, conference and incentives field. **Liechtenstein** only counts the numbers of meetings co-organised by its tourist office.

**Czech** Tourism has started to research its MICE market this year. An estimate based on ICCA statistics indicates a total of 180 thousand conference delegates in 2003, and 630 thousand delegate days. The Czech Republic hosted the International Monetary Fund (IMF) Annual Meeting in 2003. In addition to the data published by the **Hungarian** Central Statistical Office, the Hungarian Convention Bureau collects statistical information, sending out 220 questionnaires quarterly to venues, organisers, and associations. In 2003, about 30 per cent of visitors came for business purposes, including conferences. 351 international conferences were held with a total of 83 thousand participants from 73 countries. The average length of stay was 3.2 days. March was the busiest period, with the number of meetings doubling compared with the previous year. Most of the delegates came from Germany, United Kingdom, Austria and France. In Hungary, scientific congresses have the highest participation rate. About 25 per cent of these are organised in the field of medical sciences. There has also been a rapid growth in corporate meetings, and increased demand for trade shows. The **Polish** Tourist Organisation estimates the MICE share of incoming tourism to Poland at around 40 per cent. The MICE sector in 2003 grew at a rate of 25 per cent. Conference tourism in **Estonia** has been increasing due to enhanced facility supply and promotion (for example participation in specialised travel trade fairs like EIBTM and IMEX), but due to the lack of statistics or surveys it is hard to assess its development over recent years accurately. However, in 2002 the Statistical Office of Estonia started to collect monthly data on domestic and foreign tourists staying at accommodation establishments with the purpose of participating in conferences or seminars of any size. In 2003, these amounted to 39 thousand domestic tourists (9% of the total) and 49 thousand foreign tourists (5% of the total). In **Slovakia,** there has been rapid growth over recent years, especially in small and medium-sized meetings for the domestic market. Slovakia estimates the contribution of international meetings at a very approximate 2 per cent of hotel guests and 3-4 per cent of hotel income, while **Armenia's** overall estimate is around 5 per cent of arrivals. Armenia held several successful meetings in 2003, including the first Armenia-Diaspora Economic Forum and an International Seminar on "Tendencies and Methods of World Tourism Development". **Kazakhstan** estimates that the share of the meeting industry in its tourism could be as high as 20 per cent. Due to its strategic geopolitical location and current economic boom, MICE demand has been increasing strongly. Moreover, some important events are held annually, for example the Eurasian Media Forum, the Congress of World and Traditional-National Religions, the Oil and Gas Exhibition and the Kazakhstan International Tourism Fair. For similar reasons to Kazakhstan, **Azerbaijan** is also benefiting from strong conference and meetings traffic.

Since the year 2000, Turespaña has conducted and published annual research on meetings tourism in **Spain**. The latest available figures (2003) show more than 17 thousand meetings which fit the research methodology, with a total of more than 3 million delegates, and with direct economic benefit to Spain of more than 3 billion euro. The overall weight of meetings as a part of total tourism is estimated at around 10 per cent. The sector has grown steadily over recent years, transforming Spain into a top meetings destination. It is now second on ICCA's international league table. In **Portugal,** there are no available statistics on the MICE industry, but new research is scheduled for 2005. Lisbon, which is the main national destination for MICE, was positioned 5th in ICCA's 2003 ranking of international destinations, with a volume of 63 meetings and a 20 per cent growth rate over 2002. No MICE statistics are available for **Greece**. The major tourism fair "Philoxenia" in Thessaloniki, along with other sectoral fairs and exhibitions in major cities, contribute to enhancing tourism flows. At present congress tourism is not recorded separately by the **Italian** Statistics Office. Business tourism represents 30 per cent of arrivals in **San Marino**. The **Croatian** Convention and Incentive Bureau is collecting information from regional Convention Bureaux and Tourist Boards. Although this process has not yet been completed, preliminary estimates indicate that approximately one thousand meetings and incentives were organised in 2003. In **Serbia and Montenegro** the main purpose of visit for international tourists is business and conferences. An estimated 14 thousand to 18 thousand visitors came to attend meetings. **The Former Yugoslav Republic of Macedonia** has no official data but estimates that approximately 90 per cent of foreign overnights in the capital Skopje can be attributed to the meetings segment. **Slovenia** also does not have statistics, but they hope to rectify this within the next few years. Their MICE industry has been growing strongly. In **Malta**, following the events of 11th September, this sector immediately suffered. However, in 2003 recovery began. The overall business purposes market accounts for 8 per cent of arrivals. It is estimated that just the conference & incentive travel segments account for 4 per cent. The Malta Tourism Authority regularly conducts research on this market segment.

In **Cyprus** MICE data is not available but the CTO recently carried out research and the results are being examined. In **Israel** the meetings industry was growing significantly until October 2000 when the security situation in the country changed. This was aggravated further by the growing tension in the Persian Gulf. However during the period 2001 to 2004 there have been a few international conferences initiated by local organising committees, which have managed to attract small numbers of some 30 to 80 foreign delegates. The meetings industry currently represents somewhere between 2 and 3 per cent of incoming tourism. Israel collects meetings data as part of the Ministry's on-going sample survey of incoming tourists –this contains several questions about conferences/conventions– and also direct from professional congress organisers, tour operators, educational and health institutions, hotels, convention centres and other relevant organisations. Israel's annual statistical report includes a summary table of the data. According to the State Institute of Statistics, approximately 10 per cent of foreign visitors to **Turkey** are attending meetings, congresses, seminars, fairs or exhibitions.

### I.3.3 Organisation and Promotion

**Denmark**'s international promotion of MICE tourism is organised through the Danish Tourist Board which has specialised MICE staff at its offices in Sweden, Norway, the United Kingdom/Ireland, Germany, the United States of America, Belgium and at the head office in Copenhagen. There are Regional Convention Bureaux in Copenhagen, Aalborg, Århus South East, Jutland, and Funen. The main organisation in charge of promoting congresses and conferences to **Finland** is the national Convention Bureau. The Helsinki City Tourist Office also has a congress department. The Finnish Tourist Board handles the promotion of incentive travel and event tourism. The **Norwegian** Convention Bureau (NCB) is responsible for promoting the meetings industry. The Bureau has been newly organised with a privately funded secretariat. In addition to the NCB, there are several events and travel bureaux, which offer MICE products. In 2004, Innovation Norway included a MICE project for the domestic market. **Sweden**'s meetings promotion at the national level is handled by the Swedish Travel & Tourism Council. There are a number of Regional Convention Bureaux, for example in Stockholm, Göteborg and Malmo. Professional Congress Organisers also do their own international promotion, for example Congress Stockholm. In **Ireland** MICE tourism is primarily handled by the Business Tourism Section of the National Tourism Authority and through its overseas marketing offices. Significant promotion is carried out by individual trade partners and City Convention Bureaux. International MICE industry destination promotion in the **United Kingdom** is organised on national, regional and city levels. With regard to international marketing, the key players are: the Visit Britain Business Tourism Department, responsible for marketing the United Kingdom-wide MICE product; the Visit Scotland Business Tourism Unit, responsible for marketing the Scottish MICE product; the Wales Tourist Board, responsible for marketing the Welsh MICE product; and Visit London Business and Conventions, responsible for marketing the London MICE product. There are also Regional and City Convention Bureaux, normally divisions within tourist boards. Budgets and levels of activity differ greatly and these organisations are variously funded by Regional Development Agencies, local authorities, membership fees and conference sales lead commissions. The British Association of Conference Destinations is also very active.

The Maison de la **France** handles the promotion of business tourism in foreign markets, in particular, through the Tourisme d'Affaires Club, which groups together the main inbound operators in the sector. With 160 members (convention centres, Convention Bureaux, hotels and hotel chains, organisers, etc.) the Club puts together an annual plan of action according to the targets and priority markets it establishes. Other bodies also take part in the international promotion of business tourism, for example Convention Bureaux in the major cities (in collaboration with Tourist Offices) and the Association France Congrès, which bring together the mayors of convention towns and cities. **Monaco's** MICE promotion is handled through its six overseas offices in Düsseldorf, London, Milan, New York, Paris and Tokyo;

through participation in specialised trade shows; through advertising and direct marketing; and through partnerships with specialised entities, including the Maison de la France. The **German** National Tourist Board has long-established co-operation with the German Convention Bureau. Priority activities are: the integration of unusual conference venues; presentations at trade fairs, workshops and site inspections; mailshots; and specific business development activities. The **Austrian** Business and Convention Network (ABCN) is a new dedicated department of the National Tourist Office. ABCN, through Austria's world-wide network of offices, provides a quick and efficient service to the industry. Other organisations active in the MICE market include the Austrian Convention Bureau, the Conference Hotels Round Table, and 14 provincial, regional and city Convention Bureaux or Tourist Boards. In **Belgium,** the Tourist Office for Flanders is responsible for the MICE promotion of the Flanders and Brussels Region. Activities are managed by the "Flanders-Brussels Convention Bureau" –a service within the Tourist Office for Flanders– in collaboration with 11 overseas offices. Several important major cities have their own Congress Bureau. Also recently some sub-regional authorities have become active in the field of MICE promotion. Teambuilding incentive initiatives are proving very successful in Brussels and Wallonia. The latter focuses its MICE marketing on Belgium, the Netherlands, Germany, the United Kingdom, and the North of France. **The Netherlands** Board of Tourism and Conventions (NBTC) has been given the exclusive task by the Government of promoting the country as an international congress destination. Regional Convention Bureaux (RCB) are partners of the NBTC and take part in the activities it organises. The NBTC supports and stimulates the MICE sector to secure the current position of the Netherlands as an important international congress destination and, where possible, to improve it. **Switzerland** has a National Convention Bureau operating within the structure of the National Tourist Office, plus a similar set up of Regional and City Bureaux within the appropriate Tourist Boards. There are also some independent organisations acting at regional level. In **Luxembourg** the MICE industry is organised in specialised structures under the aegis of the National Convention Bureau. **Liechtenstein**'s main MICE promotion tools are flyers, the Internet, and initiatives with private companies.

Since 1st January 2000, the **Hungarian** Convention Bureau (HCB) has been working as a division of the National Tourist Office. Its aim is to provide free and neutral information on Hungary as a MICE destination. The Bureau is operating with public funds and is a member of several international organisations such as UIA and ICCA. New brochures and a CD-ROM have been created for the MICE market. In the **Czech Republic,** international marketing is the responsibility of CzechTourism, but MICE promotion is still handled regionally or directly at city level. However a strategic White Paper for congress tourism has been produced and a Prague Convention Bureau is being established. The Ministry for Regional Development and the City of Prague will cooperate on the implementation of this White Paper. Promotion of the MICE segment is organised by the Convention Bureau of **Poland**, which is a part of the Polish Tourist Organisation. Promotion is also carried out by local Convention Bureaux in Warsaw, by Wroclaw in Cracow and by local entities in Poznan. In **Estonia** MICE promotion is organised at the national (Estonian Tourist Board) and city level (town governments of Tallinn, Tartu and Pärnu) in co-operation with private enterprises. Tallinn and Pärnu also promote themselves via membership in the European Federation of Conference Towns. Tallinn City Tourist Office and Convention Bureau employs one convention project manager. The **Latvian** Tourism Development Agency co-ordinates at the national level, supplemented by the convention and destination marketing organisation "Inspiration Riga". In **Lithuania** MICE promotion is also organised on national, regional and city levels, in **Belarus** the National Tourism Agency is responsible, while in **Romania** the most important company for organising conventions is the Romanian Conventions Bureau. In **Slovakia** a new department for MICE was set up in 1995 within the National Tourism Office. This department will be the core of the future National Convention Bureau. It was set up by the Ministry of Economy and it is still financed by this Ministry with more than 90 per cent of the total budget of the National Tourism Office. The department is currently preparing a catalogue of the facilities available for this kind of tourism in Slovakia. In 2001, travel agencies and tour operators dealing with MICE established the “Slovak Association of Congress and Motivation of Tourism (SAKOM)”. This year SAKOM will participate at IMEX in Frankfurt. In **Armenia,** international promotion is organised by the Tourism Development Agency.

**Spain** has within Turespaña a specialised MICE department, which has the responsibility for overseas promotion in collaboration with Spain’s 31 overseas offices. Turespaña co-ordinates joint promotions with the Autonomous Communities and with the various local and regional Convention Bureaux through an agreement signed in 2002 with the Spain Convention Bureau. There is also a specialised organisation for the promotion and management of meetings tourism. MICE promotion in **Portugal** is based at regional level on Convention Bureaux in Lisbon, Estoril, Sintra, the Algarve and Porto. Their activities are co-ordinated with the Regional Agencies for Tourism Promotion and with the National Agency responsible for tourism promotion, the Portuguese Tourism Institute. In **Andorra** at present each Congress Centre handles its own promotional activities, but work is underway to create a specialised National Convention Bureau type structure. In an attempt to arrest its steady decline in overnights, it plans to undertake a major MICE promotion. In **Italy** the promotion of the meetings industry is organised at the regional level. In 2003 **San Marino**’s international meetings promotion activity was handled by a private sector company, ACX, complemented by the initiatives taken by the Kursall Convention Centre. The **Greek** National Tourism Organisation (GNTO) promotes the MICE industry abroad, either specifically or integrated with more general promotion activities. The GNTO has also recently created a dedicated Conference and Incentives Office based in London. There are also two Conventions and Visitors Bureaux, in Athens and Thessaloniki. These were created by the private sector but are supported by public entities. The **Malta** Tourism Authority (MTA) has a Conference & Incentive Travel Division. MTA’s overseas network of offices actively promotes Malta as a MICE destination. In **Croatia** international promotion of the MICE industry is handled by the Croatian Convention and Incentive Bureau and by Regional and City Convention Bureaux. The main tasks of the Croatian Convention and Incentive Bureau are the development and improvement of the existing offer and building the image of Croatia as a high-quality congress and incentive destination. It offers a wide range of services, most of them complimentary or at a minimal charge, including site visits, familiarisation tours, contacts, promotional assistance, co-ordination of tours, planning of special events and other organisational assistance. In **Serbia and Montenegro** promotion of the meetings industry is the responsibility of the City Tourism Organisations and of the City Convention Bureaux. **Bosnia and Herzegovina** and the **Former Yugoslav Republic of Macedonia** both co-ordinate this activity at the national level through the relevant Ministry, the latter with input from industry and regional representatives. This year **Slovenia** has established its first National Convention Bureau or congress cluster. This is going to be the top marketing and strategic organisation for the development of the Slovenian meetings industry.

In **Cyprus** international MICE, promotion is organised in a specialised area within the structure of the National/Regional Tourism Organisation. The Cyprus State Fairs Authority (CSFA) organises the annual Cyprus International Fair and other specialised exhibitions, aiming at the promotion of products and services of Cypriot and foreign exhibitors in Cyprus and in the neighbouring countries. Alongside the exhibitions, the CSFA organises associated conferences. In **Israel,** promotion is handled by the National Convention Bureau and Regional Convention Bureaux. **Turkey's** Ministry of Culture and Tourism promotes this segment using PR, Internet, VCD/DVD production, and brochures. Also promotionally active are the Istanbul Convention and Visitors Bureau, the Antalya Convention Bureau, and the Istanbul Convention & Exhibition Centre.

## I.3.4 Prospects

The development of congress tourism in **Finland** has been stable and the future outlook is excellent. In 2006, Finland will again assume the Presidency of the European Union, and 2006 and 2007 also look like being extremely good congress years. In **Norway** the MICE share of the market is holding steady. **Sweden** believes that the segment has great future growth potential. The most important factor is economic - the spending of a meeting/convention attendee is much higher than that of a leisure traveller. **Ireland** is also optimistic, provided that the international economic situation remains strong and the environment stable.

Service providers in **France** have a great deal of faith in the future growth of the MICE segment, which remains very lucrative. The **German** trade fair and conference travel sectors are already very strong domestically, but there is clearly potential for future growth from abroad, especially as a result of the EU's eastward expansion. That is why, in addition to promoting holiday travel, the GNTB in Frankfurt is focusing more attention on the trade fair, congress and conference sector. The 2006 Football World Cup in Germany will greatly raise the country's profile. **The Netherlands** points out that more destinations are now competing with more traditional congress destinations, especially following the enlargement of the EU. The NBTC will place more emphasis on promoting the country as a congress destination through specific Product-Market-Partner-Combinations. In Brussels, the major MICE destination in **Belgium**, the closure of the Convention Centre is constraining the sector. However new European Union member state employees will clearly make a positive impact. **Switzerland,** after several stable years, is predicting a slight increase. Thanks to its strong business traffic, **Monaco's** tourism does not suffer from peaks or low seasons. The future strategy will be to promote business tourism even more strongly, particularly with the launch in autumn 2004 of the Monaco Convention Bureau. In this context business tourism could eventually grow to represent 50 per cent of arrivals. The Meetings Industry has been an important factor in **Liechtenstein's** overall tourism in the past and will continue to be so in the future. **Luxembourg's** infrastructure is not adequate but this will improve when the new Congress Centre opens in 2005.

**Poland** estimates that the increase of the MICE sector over the next 3 years will reach 15-20 per cent per annum. The number of conferences in the **Czech Republic** has been growing since it successfully hosted IMF Annual Meeting in 2003. The vision for the future is to be regularly among the five top European destinations for association meetings by 2008 and to be the leading European destination for small and medium sized association meetings by 2010. The most important factor for **Hungary** this year was European Union accession. When Austria, Sweden and Finland joined in 1995, their MICE industries grew by between 20 and 50 per cent. Hungary hopes to achieve similar growth. **Latvia** and **Lithuania** both see MICE as an important industry with good growth potential. **Kazakhstan** assumes that the meetings industry will develop fast in line with their anticipated economic growth. **Slovakia**

expects economic growth to stimulate continued increases in demand for small meetings from the domestic market. It also expects to generate more international, mainly medium-sized, events in the near future.

**Spain** expects the MICE growth it has achieved over recent years to continue. From 2004 and for a period of five years, Barcelona will host EIBTM. This should give a further boost to Spain's profile in the MICE market. The number of meetings programmed to be held in **Portugal** and the reports available indicate sustained future growth in the sector. New on-going research will provide, in the near future, a more consistent evaluation of MICE's impact on tourism and on the economy. Two factors are seen as important to maintaining growth – a competitive tourism product and an improved promotional structure. **Andorra** reports rapid growth and expects a good performance in the short term. The MICE sector is also growing in **Greece**. Increasing capacity, supported by public policies, is providing more modern facilities, but these are able to cover only part of the growing demand. In **Italy** the industry has been expanding fast, and more attention is now being given to MICE as a fully-fledged and major component of overall tourism and as a key product in its own right. **San Marino** plans to build up its congress business over the next five years, and **Malta** is planning further investment and innovation. Shortage of accommodation remains the main constraint in **Serbia and Montenegro.** Nevertheless in 2005 Belgrade will host several important conferences and sporting events, which are expected to attract more than 25 thousand participants. The development of meetings and incentives is a specific aim in **Croatia's** tourist policy through to 2010. Investments are planned in so-called "smart centres", multi-purpose convention and exhibition centres in Zagreb with a capacity of 4 thousand seats and in Dubrovnik, Opatija, and Istra with capacities of 1,500 seats. Growing numbers of Destination Management Companies and Professional Conference Organisers are also being established, especially in Zagreb, Dubrovnik, Opatija, Istra, and Dalmatia. **Slovenia** sees international meetings as one of its most important future segments, while the **Former Yugoslav Republic of Macedonia** reports continuing rapid growth in meetings, especially in its main tourism resort, Ohrid Lake.

**Cyprus** expects growth to continue, and will focus considerable effort on developing the necessary products to maintain the momentum. At the same time it will invest in the enhancement of the quality of services offered, improvement of the quality-value relationship and strengthening of the tourist industry's ability to compete effectively in a European, open market, modern and technologically advanced environment. Cyprus expects MICE product development to be undertaken using both public and private funds, and through the building of partnerships. Operating in a free market economy, the Government of Cyprus will focus on the creation of a favourable entrepreneurial climate and the provision of incentives to encourage investment by European Union residents and others in the priority areas specified in its Strategy, including MICE. A number of projects are expected to attract funding from European Union programmes and structural funds. In the current situation, **Israel** does not expect growth in the MICE segment. However it believes that, with an improvement in the security situation, the meetings industry would return to robust activity over a period of time. The Government in **Turkey** believes that it has all the necessary ingredients to become a top meetings destination within the next few years, especially in Istanbul and Antalya. Recent events held very successfully in Turkey, for example the NATO Summit and the Eurovision Song Contest, constitute good references for the future.

# II

# Quantitative Analysis of Tourism Results

# II Quantitative Analysis of Tourism Results

## II.1 Tourism Trends in the Region

The economic situation in some of the major generating markets of Europe, together with the belligerent conflict in Iraq, determined tourism performance in Europe during 2003. The region, which just maintained the results obtained in 2002 in term of tourist arrivals (+0.4%), saw, however, tourism receipts, as expressed in local currencies and constant prices, decrease by some 3 per cent under an overall pressure on prices.

Some important destinations were particularly affected by the decline in long-haul traffic caused by the war in Iraq, but also by the emergence of SARS in Asia and the Pacific, and by the increasingly weaker US dollar. Trends of short distance travel were reinforced, benefiting countries in Central and Eastern Europe (+3.7% in terms of tourist arrivals) as well as domestic tourism, which in some cases proved to be essential to compensate for the losses in inbound tourism. The exchange rates US dollar/euro and Great Britain pound/euro also contributed to the distribution of flows within Europe, with euro zone countries losing competitiveness to other destinations given their comparatively higher prices resulting from the continuous appreciation of the euro. Countries that benefited from this redistribution were among others Croatia (+7%), Slovenia (+6%), Turkey (+4%) and the United Kingdom (+2%), while traditional holiday destinations such as France (-3%), Italy (-0.5%), Spain (-1%) and Portugal (+0.5%) posted comparatively modest results.

Europe: Inbound tourism
International Tourist Arrivals (million)

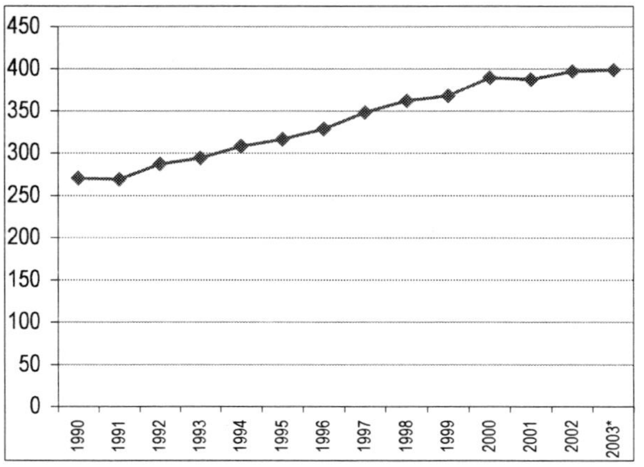


Source: World Tourism Organization (WTO) ©

Europe: Inbound tourism
International Tourist Arrivals (change over previous year, %)

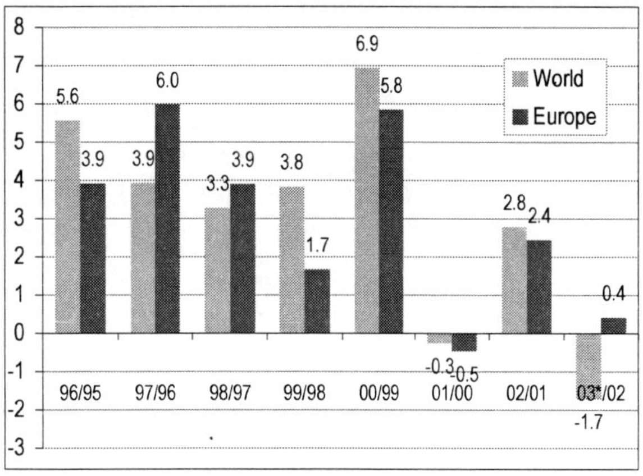


Source: World Tourism Organization (WTO) ©

## II.1.1 Inbound Tourism

*International tourist arrivals*

In 2003 the growth of international tourist arrivals to Europe slowed down to a slight 0.4 per cent after the 2.4 per cent increase experienced in 2002. The region received almost 400 million tourist arrivals, which corresponds to a 58 per cent market share of the world's international tourist arrivals. Although during the last decade Europe's market share has decreased from 61 per cent in 1990 to 57 per cent between 2000 and 2002, the region managed to maintain its share in the last years due essentially to the significant decrease in the share of the Americas in world tourism (from 18.7% in 2000 to 16.4% in 2003). In 2003, due to the significant decrease of tourist arrivals to Asia and the Pacific under the impact of SARS, and to the continued negative performance of the Americas, Europe reinforced its market share by one percentage point in spite of its relatively weak results.

Regarding the subregional distribution of tourist arrivals to Europe, Western Europe continues to lead, with a 34 per cent market share, followed by Southern Europe, with 33 per cent. Both regions are, together, responsible for almost 70 per cent of inbound tourism in Europe. In a second line are Central and Eastern Europe (17%) and Northern Europe (12%), representing together a 28 per cent market share, while East Mediterranean Europe accounts for slightly over 4 per cent. In terms of evolution, whereas the market share of Northern Europe has been mostly stable since 2000, gains have been obtained in Central and Eastern Europe and in Southern and East Mediterranean Europe at the expenses of Western Europe's share, which decreased by almost 2 percentage points from 36 per cent in 2000 to 34 per cent in 2003.

In 2003 all European subregions, except Western and Southern Europe, achieved positive results. The best performances occurred in East Mediterranean Europe with a 4 per cent increase due in particular to the good results of Turkey (+4%) once the country holds a 80 per cent share of all tourist arrivals in the subregion, and in Central and Eastern Europe (+3.7%). Northern Europe went up by 2.1 per cent, while tourist arrivals to Western Europe decreased by 1.4 per cent, due particularly to the 2.6 per cent drop in France, destination which receives more than half of all tourist arrivals in the subregion, and to the negative performances of the Netherlands (-4%) and Switzerland (-5%). In Southern Europe, and in spite of the good results obtained by "emerging destinations", the performance was just negative (-0.4%) as all major destinations performed rather weakly.

World and regions: Inbound tourism
International Tourist Arrivals (change 03*/02, %)

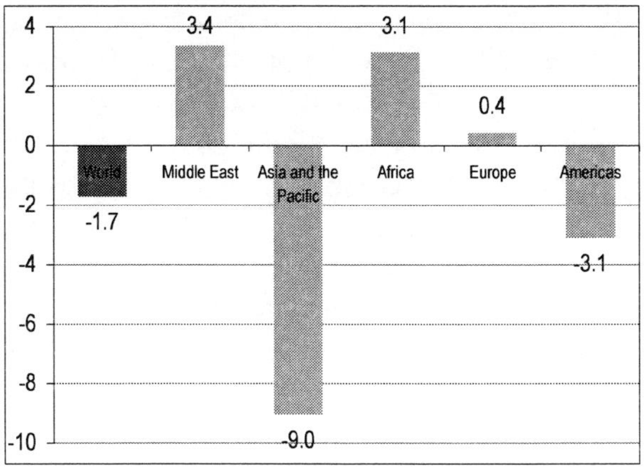


Source: World Tourism Organization (WTO) ©

Europe: Inbound tourism
International Tourist Arrivals (share in world total, %)

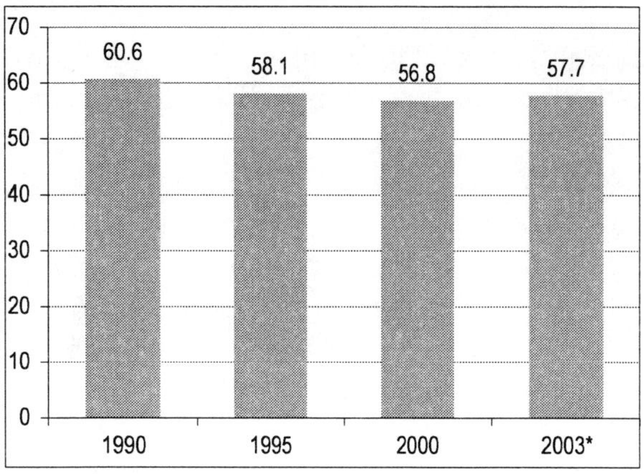


Source: World Tourism Organization (WTO) ©

Europe and subregions: Inbound tourism
International Tourist Arrivals, 2003* (share, %)

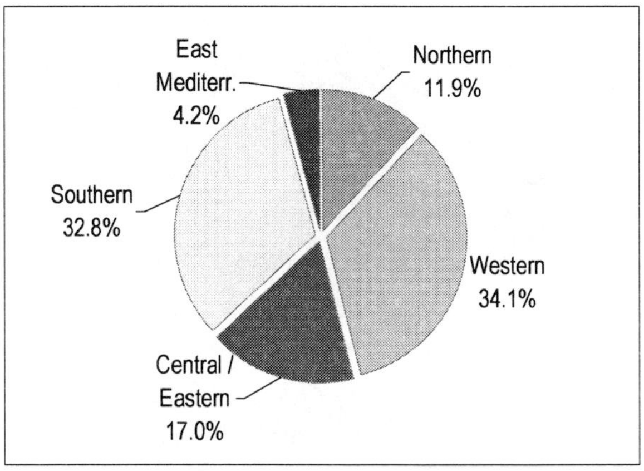


Source: World Tourism Organization (WTO) ©

Europe and subregions: Inbound tourism
International Tourist Arrivals (change 03*/02, %)

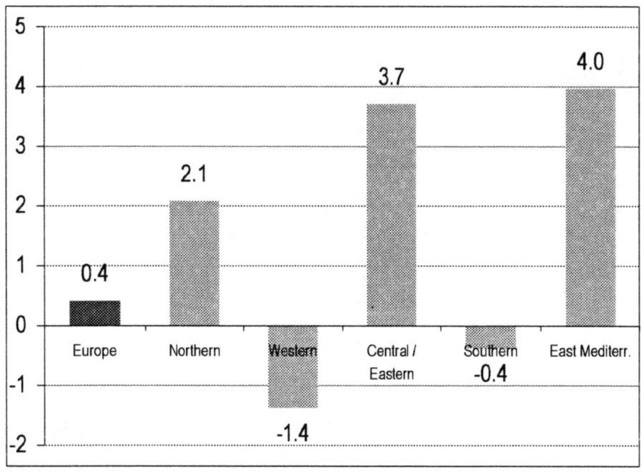


Source: World Tourism Organization (WTO) ©

**International Tourist Arrivals by (Sub)region**

| | International Tourist Arrivals (million) | | | | | Market share (%) | | Growth rate (%) | | Average annual growth (%) | |
|---|---|---|---|---|---|---|---|---|---|---|---|
| | 1990 | 1995 | 2000 | 2002 | 2003* | 1995 | 2003* | 02/01 | 03*/02 | '90-'95 | '95-'00 |
| **World** | **445.8** | **544.9** | **685.5** | **702.8** | **690.9** | **100** | **100** | **2.8** | **-1.7** | **4.1** | **4.7** |
| ***Europe*** | ***270.4*** | ***316.4*** | ***389.6*** | ***397.3*** | ***399.0*** | ***58.1*** | ***57.7*** | ***2.4*** | ***0.4*** | ***3.2*** | ***4.2*** |
| Northern Europe | 32.0 | 41.6 | 46.9 | 46.4 | 47.4 | 7.6 | 6.9 | 3.5 | 2.1 | 5.4 | 2.4 |
| Western Europe | 108.6 | 112.2 | 139.7 | 138.0 | 136.1 | 20.6 | 19.7 | 1.6 | -1.4 | 0.6 | 4.5 |
| Central/Eastern Europe | 35.9 | 60.0 | 62.3 | 65.3 | 67.8 | 11.0 | 9.8 | 3.0 | 3.7 | 10.8 | 0.8 |
| Southern Europe | 86.5 | 91.3 | 126.1 | 131.5 | 131.0 | 16.8 | 19.0 | 2.0 | -0.4 | 1.1 | 6.7 |
| East Mediterranean Eu. | 7.4 | 11.4 | 14.7 | 16.1 | 16.7 | 2.1 | 2.4 | 9.5 | 4.0 | 9.0 | 5.2 |

Source: World Tourism Organization (WTO) © (Data as collected by WTO December 2004)

*International tourism receipts*

In 2003, Europe earned 252 billion euro (or US$ 285 billion) from international tourism, representing a significant 5.2 billion euro decline over 2002. It is important to note that for financial data it is always difficult to correctly interpret trends as the figures are usually expressed in US dollar or euro at current prices (not taking account of inflation) and are subject to fluctuations in exchange rate versus local currencies. Expressed in (weighted) local currencies in constant prices (i.e. deflated), international tourism receipts for Europe decreased by almost 3 per cent in 2003, while international tourism receipts for the world as a whole declined by 1.9 per cent. Europe, where receipts per arrival amount to 632 euro, is responsible for almost 55 per cent of worldwide international tourism receipts.

Europe: Inbound tourism
International Tourism Receipts (euro billion, current prices)

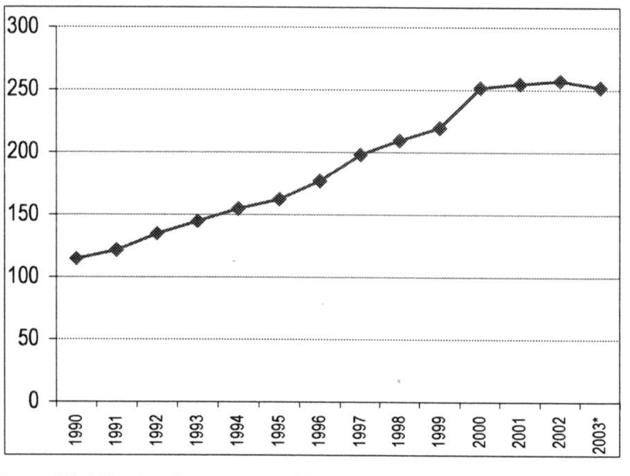


Source: World Tourism Organization (WTO) ©

Europe: Inbound tourism
International Tourism Receipts (share in world total, %)

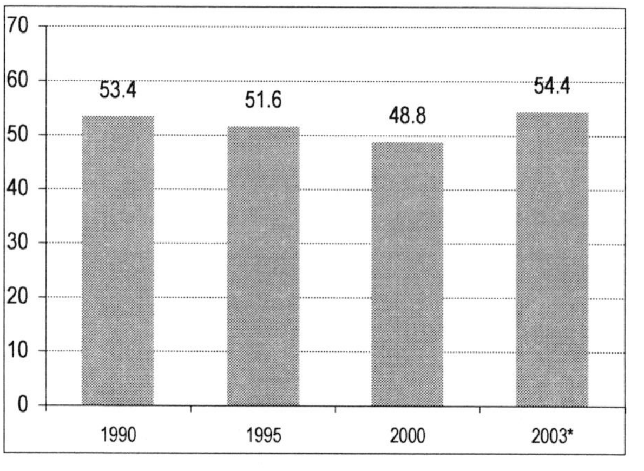


Source: World Tourism Organization (WTO) ©

In terms of subregional distribution, more than 70 per cent of tourism receipts were generated in countries of Western and Southern Europe (36% and 35% respectively), while Northern Europe destinations accounted for a 15 per cent share, and countries in Central and Eastern Europe and in East Mediterranean Europe for 8 and 6 per cent respectively.

In 2003, the increased pressure on prices, as well as the strength of the euro, led to the drop of international tourism receipts (as measured in local currencies, constant prices) in all subregions. Declines ranged from 1.2 per cent in Southern Europe to a significant -11 per cent in East Mediterranean Europe, where Turkey's negative results draw back the performance of the subregion as the country holds an 80 per cent share of the overall receipts. In Western and in Central and Eastern Europe receipts felt by 2.5 and 4 per cent respectively, while Northern Europe registered a 2 per cent negative rate.

Europe and subregions: Inbound tourism
International Tourism Receipts, 2003* (share, %)

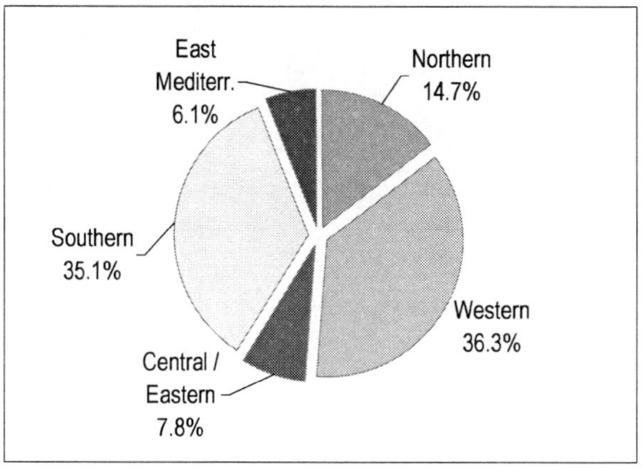


Source: World Tourism Organization (WTO) ©

Europe and subregions: Inbound tourism
Receipts per Arrival, 2003* (euro)

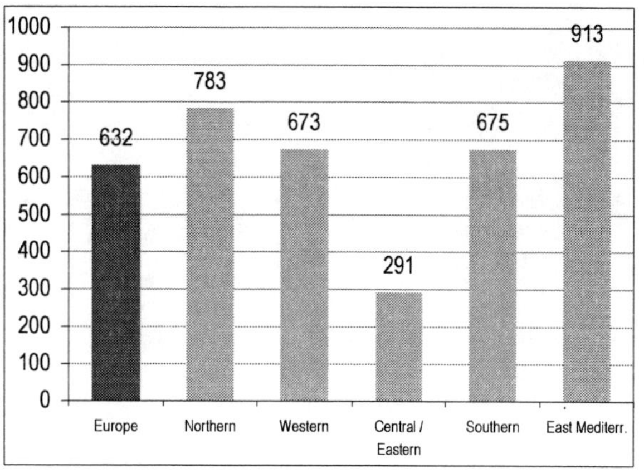


Source: World Tourism Organization (WTO) ©

On average, European destinations earned 632 euro per international tourist arrival in 2003. The highest value was achieved by East Mediterranean Europe collecting 913 euro per arrival. In the second position was Northern Europe with 783 euro per arrival, while Central and Eastern Europe holds the last position with 291 euro per arrival, still very far from all the other subregions where receipts per arrival were superior to 660 euro.

**International Tourism Receipts, Europe**

| | International Tourism Receipts (billion) | | | | | | Change current prices (%) | | | Change constant prices (%) | | |
|---|---|---|---|---|---|---|---|---|---|---|---|---|
| | 1990 | 1995 | 2000 | 2001 | 2002 | 2003* | 01/00 | 02/01 | 03*/02 | 01/00 | 02/01 | 03*/02 |
| **Local currencies** | | | | | | | 5.3 | 2.8 | 0.7 | -0.5 | -1.8 | -2.7 |
| **US$** | 145.7 | 212.2 | 232.5 | 228.3 | 243.2 | 285.1 | -1.8 | 6.6 | 17.2 | -4.5 | 4.9 | 14.6 |
| **Euro** | 114.4 | 162.2 | 251.8 | 254.9 | 257.2 | 252.0 | 1.2 | 0.9 | -2.0 | -1.1 | -1.3 | -4.0 |

Source: World Tourism Organization (WTO) © (Data as collected by WTO December 2004)

**International Tourism Receipts by (Sub)region**

| | Change Local currencies, constant prices (%) | | | | US$ (billion) | | Receipts per arrival | euro (billion) | | Receipts per arrival | Market share (%) |
|---|---|---|---|---|---|---|---|---|---|---|---|
| | 00/99 | 01/00 | 02/01 | 03*/02 | 2002 | 2003* | 2003* | 2002 | 2003* | 2003* | 2003* |
| **World** | **9.2** | **-0.4** | **0.3** | **-1.9** | **482.3** | **524.2** | **759** | **510.0** | **463.4** | **671** | **100** |
| ***Europe*** | ***9.4*** | ***-0.5*** | ***-1.8*** | ***-2.7*** | ***243.2*** | ***285.1*** | ***715*** | ***257.2*** | ***252.0*** | ***632*** | ***54.4*** |
| Northern Europe | 3.7 | -3.1 | 3.3 | -2.1 | 37.1 | 42.0 | 886 | 39.3 | 37.1 | 783 | 8.0 |
| Western Europe | 11.7 | -1.0 | -0.1 | -2.5 | 87.6 | 103.6 | 761 | 92.7 | 91.6 | 673 | 19.8 |
| Central/Eastern Europe | -2.4 | -8.2 | -5.7 | -4.1 | 20.2 | 22.3 | 329 | 21.4 | 19.7 | 291 | 4.3 |
| Southern Europe | 10.7 | 1.8 | -4.4 | -1.2 | 82.4 | 100.0 | 763 | 87.2 | 88.4 | 675 | 19.1 |
| East Mediterranean Eu. | 21.3 | 5.5 | -3.6 | -11.1 | 15.8 | 17.3 | 1,033 | 16.7 | 15.3 | 913 | 3.3 |

Source: World Tourism Organization (WTO) © (Data as collected by WTO December 2004)

World and regions: Inbound tourism
Receipts per Arrival, 2003* (euro)

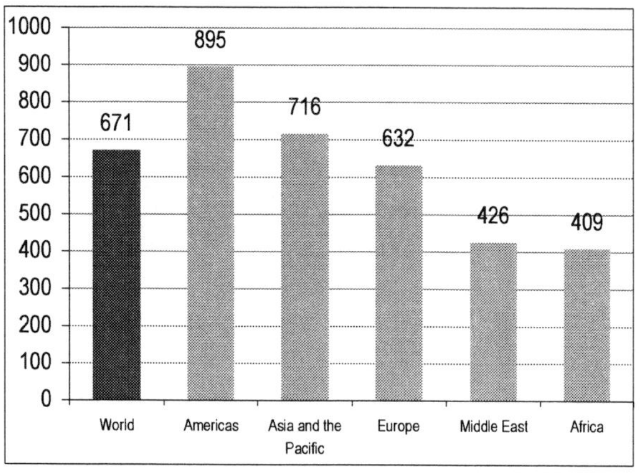


Source: World Tourism Organization (WTO) ©

World and regions: Inbound tourism (% change 03*/02,
International Tourism Receipts local currencies, constant prices)

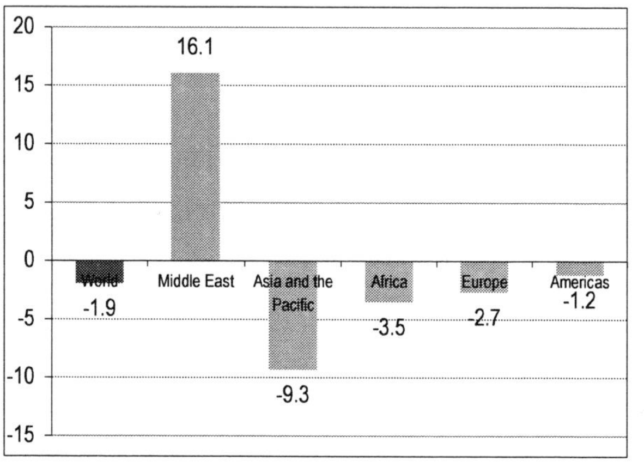


Source: World Tourism Organization (WTO) ©

## *Inbound tourism by region of origin*

In 2003, nearly 90 per cent of international tourist arrivals in Europe corresponded to tourists from the same region and only 10 per cent to interregional tourism, while for the remaining 0.7 per cent the origin was not specified. The reinforcement of intraregional traffic in Europe has been clear in recent years with the share of tourists from Europe increasing from 86 per cent in 2000 to nearly 90 per cent in 2003. Although in the last decade intra and interregional traffic in Europe grew almost at the same pace (3.9% and 3.4% respectively), since 2001 there has been a reversed trend. Interregional inbound has been decreasing for the last three years, having thus accumulated a loss of almost 18 percent as compared to 2000. The decline was particularly strong in the traffic from the Americas (-23% in 2003 when compared to 2000 figures), which has been decreasing for three consecutive years. In 2003, under the impact of the war in Iraq and of the weakness of the US dollar against the euro, the fall of traffic from the Americas reached almost 7 per cent to a total of 21.6 million, therefore far from the 27.9 million mark attained in 2000. In 2003 interregional traffic to Europe decreased from all regions, except from the Middle East, which grew by 1.3 per cent as compared to 2002.

Notwithstanding the recent decrease in flows from the Americas, interregional tourist arrivals to Europe are still dominated by this region, which accounted for 55 per cent of all inbound from outside the region in 2003, followed by Asia and the Pacific with a 35 per cent market share in terms of interregional traffic (13.6 million tourist arrivals). Tourists from the other two regions –Africa and the Middle East– represented a market share of 6 and 4 per cent each concerning total arrivals from outside Europe.

Europe: Inbound tourism by region of origin
International Tourist Arrivals, 2003* (share, %)

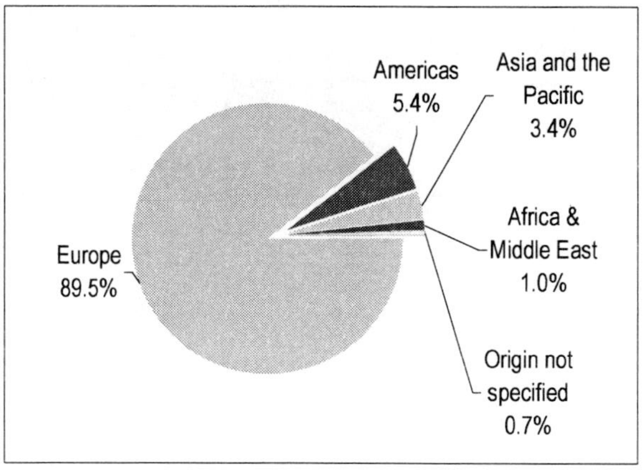


Source: World Tourism Organization (WTO) ©

Europe: Inbound tourism by region of origin
International Tourist Arrivals (share, %)

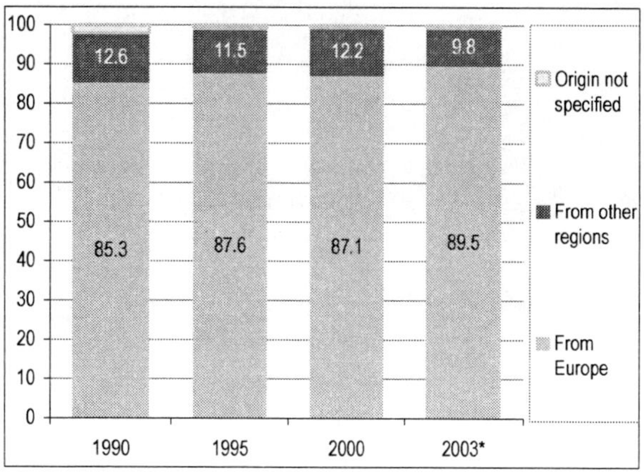


Source: World Tourism Organization (WTO) ©

**Europe**
**Inbound Tourism by Region of Origin (including estimations for countries with missing data)**

| | International Tourist Arrivals (1000) | | | | | Market share (%) | | | Growth rate (%) | | Average annual growth (%) | |
|---|---|---|---|---|---|---|---|---|---|---|---|---|
| | 1990 | 1995 | 2000 | 2002 | 2003* | 1990 | 1995 | 2003* | 02/01 | 03*/02 | 90-00 | 95-00 |
| **Europe** | **270,364** | **316,410** | **389,591** | **397,305** | **398,952** | **100** | **100** | **100** | **2.4** | **0.4** | **3.7** | **4.2** |
| From: | | | | | | | | | | | | |
| *Europe* | *230,547* | *277,148* | *339,419* | *353,091* | *357,133* | *85.3* | *87.6* | *89.5* | *3.2* | *1.1* | *3.9* | *4.1* |
| *Other regions* | *34,100* | *36,435* | *47,639* | *41,902* | *39,083* | *12.6* | *11.5* | *9.8* | *-3.1* | *-6.7* | *3.4* | *5.5* |
| Africa | 2,914 | 2,340 | 2,693 | 2,583 | 2,340 | 1.1 | 0.7 | 0.6 | 1.0 | -9.4 | -0.8 | 2.9 |
| Americas | 21,199 | 20,197 | 27,947 | 23,130 | 21,568 | 7.8 | 6.4 | 5.4 | -7.6 | -6.8 | 2.8 | 6.7 |
| Asia and the Pacific | 8,403 | 11,860 | 15,203 | 14,644 | 13,611 | 3.1 | 3.7 | 3.4 | 4.5 | -7.1 | 6.1 | 5.1 |
| Middle East | 1,583 | 2,039 | 1,796 | 1,545 | 1,564 | 0.6 | 0.6 | 0.4 | -5.5 | 1.3 | 1.3 | -2.5 |
| *Origin not specified* | *5,718* | *2,827* | *2,533* | *2,312* | *2,737* | *2.1* | *0.9* | *0.7* | *-5.8* | *18.3* | | |

Source: World Tourism Organization (WTO) © (Data as collected by WTO December 2004)

World and regions: Inbound tourism by region of origin
International Tourist Arrivals, 2003* (share, %)

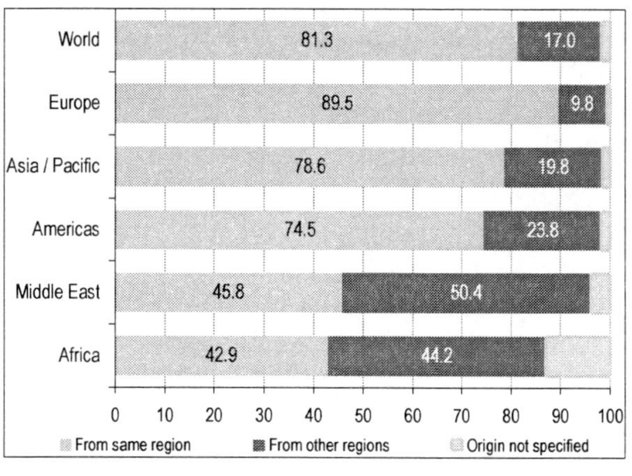


Source: World Tourism Organization (WTO) ©

World regions: Inbound tourism by region of origin
International Tourist Arrivals, 2003* (million)

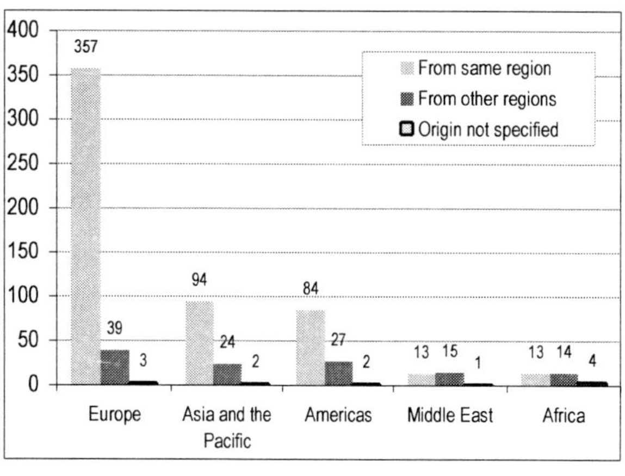


Source: World Tourism Organization (WTO) ©

Europe: Inbound tourism by region of origin
International Tourist Arrivals, 2003* (million)

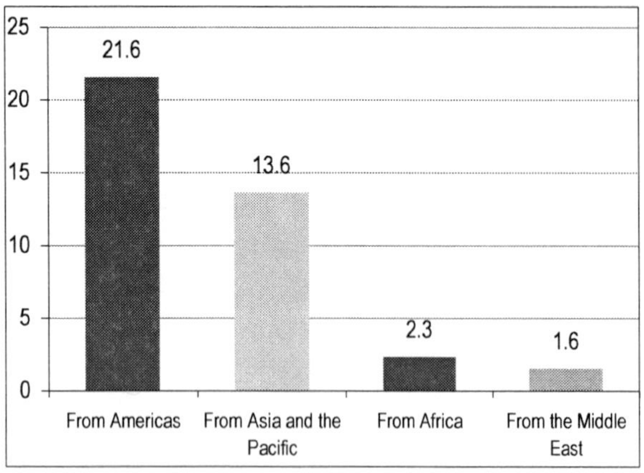


Source: World Tourism Organization (WTO) ©

Europe: Inbound tourism by region of origin
International Tourist Arrivals (change 03*/02, %)

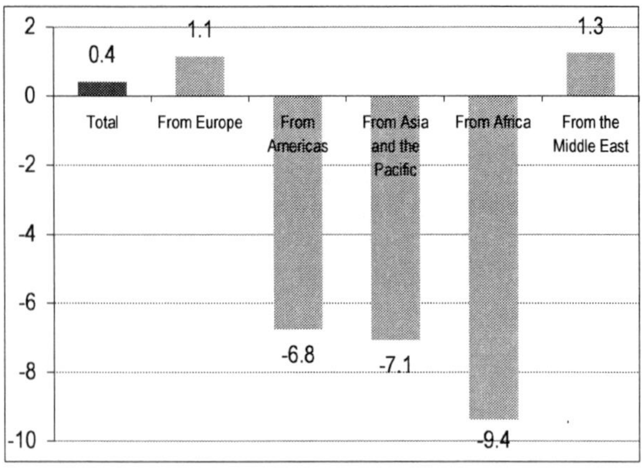


Source: World Tourism Organization (WTO) ©

Within European subregions, intra-regional traffic continues to be particularly strong in Central and Eastern Europe (94%), driven by strong flows between neighbouring countries, and in Southern Europe (94%), where holiday traffic from the Northern and Western European countries is predominantly important, with Germany and the United Kingdom as the major generating markets for almost all destinations in the subregion. On the other hand, Northern Europe is the subregion with comparatively the lowest percentage of intraregional arrivals but still with a high share (78%). The Americas is the most important interregional source market for all European subregions, except for Central and Eastern Europe and for East Mediterranean Europe, where the geographical proximity with Asia and the Pacific reinforces the importance of this region. Traffic from the Americas is particularly relevant for Northern Europe (13 per cent of the total arrivals and 61 per cent of interregional arrivals) due to the strong flows from the United States of America to the United Kingdom and Ireland. Asia and the Pacific, on the other hand, dominates interregional arrivals to Central and Eastern Europe (3 per cent share of overall arrivals and almost 55 per cent of interregional arrivals) and to East Mediterranean Europe (5 per cent of the total and 42 per cent of the interregional volume). Arrivals from Africa and the Middle East represent shares of less than 2 per cent in every subregion, except in Eastern Mediterranean Europe, where arrivals from the Middle East represent 2.6 per cent of the total arrivals and 22 per cent of arrivals from outside Europe.

Europe and subregions: Inbound tourism by region of origin
International Tourist Arrivals, 2003* (share, %)

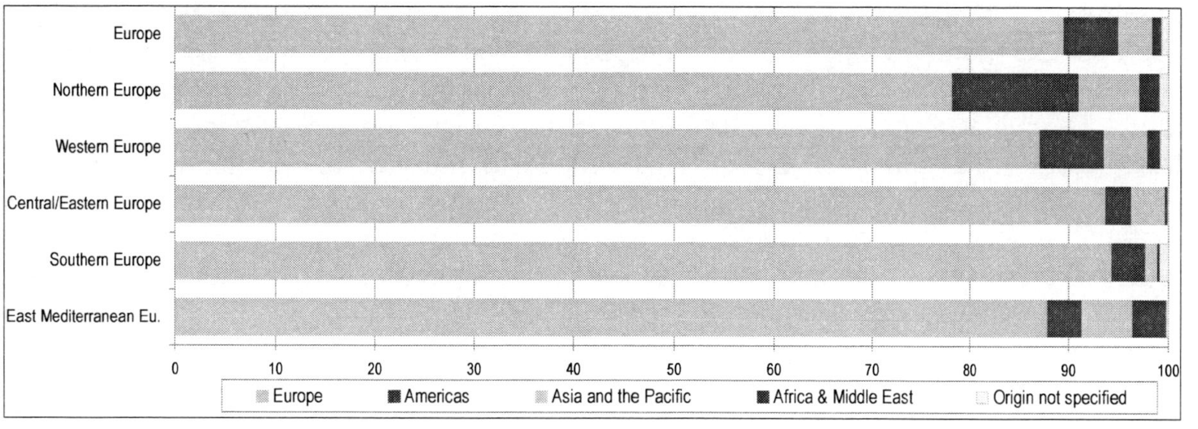


Source: World Tourism Organization (WTO) ©

**Europe**

**Inbound Tourism by Region of Origin (including estimations for countries with missing data), 2003***

| | | Europe | | | | | |
|---|---|---|---|---|---|---|---|
| | | **Total** | **Northern** | **Western** | **Central/Eastern** | **Southern** | **East Mediterr.** |
| | | **International Tourist Arrivals (000)** | | | | | |
| **Total** | | **398,952** | **47,368** | **136,070** | **67,763** | **131,043** | **16,707** |
| from: | Europe | 357,133 | 36,988 | 118,461 | 63,488 | 123,520 | 14,677 |
| | Other regions | 39,083 | 9,951 | 16,501 | 4,247 | 6,381 | 2,003 |
| | Americas | 21,568 | 6,114 | 8,778 | 1,692 | 4,399 | 584 |
| | Asia and the Pacific | 13,611 | 2,868 | 5,916 | 2,326 | 1,669 | 832 |
| | Africa | 2,340 | 623 | 1,328 | 85 | 149 | 156 |
| | Middle East | 1,564 | 346 | 479 | 144 | 164 | 431 |
| | Origin not specified | 2,737 | 430 | 1,108 | 28 | 1,142 | 27 |
| | | **% destination broken down by origin** | | | | | |
| **Total** | | **100** | **100** | **100** | **100** | **100** | **100** |
| from: | Europe | 89.5 | 78.1 | 87.1 | 93.7 | 94.3 | 87.8 |
| | Other regions | 9.8 | 21.0 | 12.1 | 6.3 | 4.9 | 12.0 |
| | Americas | 5.4 | 12.9 | 6.5 | 2.5 | 3.4 | 3.5 |
| | Asia and the Pacific | 3.4 | 6.1 | 4.3 | 3.4 | 1.3 | 5.0 |
| | Africa | 0.6 | 1.3 | 1.0 | 0.1 | 0.1 | 0.9 |
| | Middle East | 0.4 | 0.7 | 0.4 | 0.2 | 0.1 | 2.6 |
| | Origin not specified | 0.7 | 0.9 | 0.8 | 0.0 | 0.9 | 0.2 |
| | | **% origin broken down by destination** | | | | | |
| **Total** | | **100** | **11.9** | **34.1** | **17.0** | **32.8** | **4.2** |
| from: | Europe | 100 | 10.4 | 33.2 | 17.8 | 34.6 | 4.1 |
| | Other regions | 100 | 25.5 | 42.2 | 10.9 | 16.3 | 5.1 |
| | Americas | 100 | 28.3 | 40.7 | 7.8 | 20.4 | 2.7 |
| | Asia and the Pacific | 100 | 21.1 | 43.5 | 17.1 | 12.3 | 6.1 |
| | Africa | 100 | 26.6 | 56.7 | 3.6 | 6.4 | 6.7 |
| | Middle East | 100 | 22.1 | 30.6 | 9.2 | 10.5 | 27.6 |
| | Origin not specified | 100 | 15.7 | 40.5 | 1.0 | 41.7 | 1.0 |

Source: World Tourism Organization (WTO) © (Data as collected by WTO December 2004)

*Inbound tourism by mode of transport*

Land transport is by far still the most common means of transport for tourists travelling in or to Europe. Compared to other regions Europe is the region along with the Middle East which enjoys the highest share of arrivals by land (56%). This fact is easy to understand given the importance of intraregional tourism for Europe, together with the well-developed road and rail infrastructures, the comparatively short distances to most of the destinations, the easy accessibility in many cases in terms of border formalities and the increasing economic integration among European countries. However, land transport has lost some percentage points in market share over the last decade, decreasing from 61 per cent in 1990 to 56 per cent in 2003, in favour of air transport. The latter has become more and more affordable and the regional network has developed considerably with more routes and higher frequencies. In recent years air traffic has also been boosted by the strong advance of low-cost airlines. Arrivals to Europe by air have increased its weight in total arrivals from 31 per cent in 1990 to 36 per cent in 2003, notwithstanding the flat results of 2001, as arrivals by air grew at an average yearly rate of 4 per cent between 1990 and 2003, when compared to the 3 per cent rate of road traffic. Transport by water accounted for more than 7 per cent of the total international tourist arrivals in 2003.

Europe: Inbound tourism by mode of transport

International Tourist Arrivals (share, %)

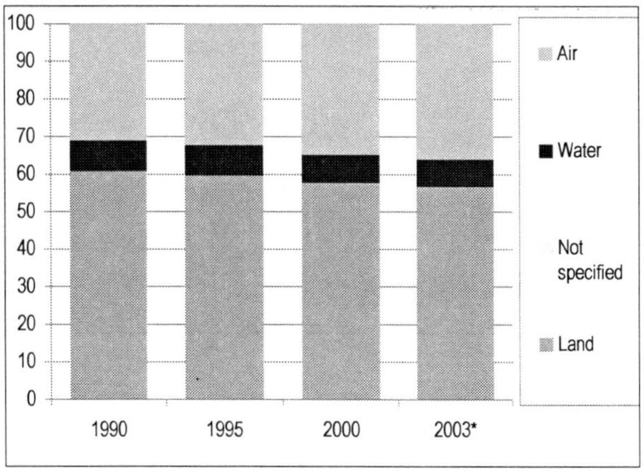


Source: World Tourism Organization (WTO) ©

Europe and subregions: Inbound tourism by mode of transport

International Tourist Arrivals, 2003* (share, %)

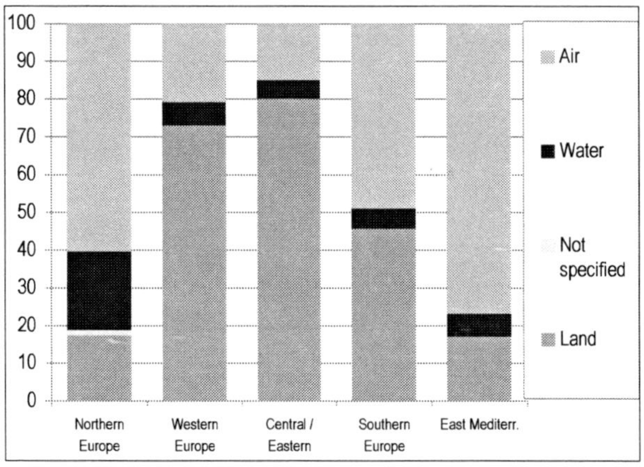


Source: World Tourism Organization (WTO) ©

**Europe**

**Arrivals by mode of transport (including estimations for countries with missing data)**

| | International Tourist Arrivals | | | | | Share | | | | Change | | Average annual |
|---|---|---|---|---|---|---|---|---|---|---|---|---|
| | | | | | (million) | | | | (%) | | (%) | growth (%) |
| | 1990 | 1995 | 2000 | 2002 | 2003* | 1990 | 1995 | 2000 | 2003* | 02/01 | 03*/02 | 1990-2000 |
| **Total** | 270.4 | 316.4 | 389.6 | 397.3 | 399.0 | 100 | 100 | 100 | 100 | 2.4 | 0.4 | 3.7 |
| Air | 84.1 | 101.9 | 135.6 | 140.0 | 143.8 | 31.1 | 32.2 | 34.8 | 36.0 | 2.7 | 2.7 | 4.9 |
| Land | 164.7 | 189.0 | 224.1 | 227.0 | 224.8 | 60.9 | 59.7 | 57.5 | 56.3 | 2.1 | -1.0 | 3.1 |
| Road | 138.0 | 165.2 | 196.3 | 199.5 | 197.5 | 51.0 | 52.2 | 50.4 | 49.5 | 2.6 | -1.0 | 3.6 |
| Rail | 26.7 | 23.8 | 27.8 | 27.5 | 27.3 | 9.9 | 7.5 | 7.1 | 6.8 | -1.8 | -0.7 | 0.4 |
| Water | 21.5 | 25.5 | 29.5 | 29.8 | 29.7 | 8.0 | 8.1 | 7.6 | 7.4 | 4.0 | -0.4 | 3.2 |
| Not specified | 0.0 | 0.0 | 0.4 | 0.5 | 0.6 | 0.0 | 0.0 | 0.1 | 0.2 | | | |

Source: World Tourism Organization (WTO) © (Data as collected by WTO December 2004)

Air traffic accounts for a major percentage of arrivals in Northern (60%) and in East Mediterranean Europe (77%). This last subregion is particularly dependant on this mode of transport as access to countries in the area is limited by other means and by the fact that many generating markets are located at a considerable long distance for the use of land transport. On the contrary, the highly developed road infrastructure and the proximity among countries in Western and Central and Eastern Europe determine that most arrivals to both subregions occur by land. In the case of Western Europe such rate reaches 73 per cent of all arrivals, while in Central and Eastern Europe it represents 80 per cent. On the other hand, arrivals by water, that account for 7 per cent in all Europe, achieve a particularly significant market share in Northern Europe, where they account for 21 per cent of all arrivals.

**Arrivals by mode of transport (including estimations for countries with missing data), 2003***

| | Total | Air | Land | Water | Not specified |
|---|---|---|---|---|---|
| | International Tourist Arrivals (million) | | | | |
| Europe | 399.0 | 143.8 | 224.8 | 29.7 | 0.6 |
| Northern Europe | 47.4 | 28.5 | 8.3 | 10.0 | 0.6 |
| Western Europe | 136.1 | 28.2 | 99.4 | 8.4 | 0.0 |
| Central/Eastern Europe | 67.8 | 10.1 | 54.3 | 3.4 | 0.0 |
| Southern Europe | 131.0 | 64.1 | 60.0 | 6.9 | 0.0 |
| East Mediterranean Eu. | 16.7 | 12.8 | 2.8 | 1.0 | 0.0 |
| | % | | | | |
| Europe | 100 | 36.0 | 56.3 | 7.4 | 0.2 |
| Northern Europe | 100 | 60.2 | 17.5 | 21.0 | 1.3 |
| Western Europe | 100 | 20.7 | 73.1 | 6.2 | 0.0 |
| Central/Eastern Europe | 100 | 14.9 | 80.1 | 5.0 | 0.0 |
| Southern Europe | 100 | 48.9 | 45.8 | 5.3 | 0.0 |
| East Mediterranean Eu. | 100 | 76.7 | 17.0 | 6.2 | 0.0 |

Source: World Tourism Organization (WTO) © (Data as collected by WTO December 2004)

*Inbound tourism by purpose of visit*

In 2003, more than half of total international tourist arrivals to Europe were for the purpose of leisure, recreation and holidays (55%), representing 3 percentage points more than the world average. However, this category has decreased significantly in weight during recent years: from 61 per cent in 1990 to 55 per cent in 2003. In contrast, there was an increased share of tourists who visited European destinations for business and professional purposes, which in 2003 totalled 22 per cent of all arrivals. The category "business and professional", which experienced an average annual growth rate of nearly 5 per cent during the period 1990-2000, decreased by 4 per cent in 2001 under the impact of the economic situation and the 11th September events. Although in 2002 and 2003 arrivals to Europe for business purposes recovered, they are still slightly below the 2000 levels (88 million). Compared to other regions, Europe is the region with the largest share of arrivals in the category "business and professional". The remaining quarter of international tourist arrivals are grouped together in the category "VFR –visiting friends and relatives–, health, religion and other" with a total volume of almost 92 million. This category, which grew on average 5 per cent a year between 1990 and 2000, was particularly reinforced in recent years, having incremented by nearly 8 per cent when compared to 2000 figures.

"Leisure, recreation and holidays" are the main purpose of visit in most of the European subregions, but are particularly important in East Mediterranean and in Southern Europe (75% and 69% respectively), the traditional holiday destinations in Europe. On the other hand, "business and professional" travel reaches the highest market share in Northern and Western Europe (30% and 25% respectively), while the category of "VFR, health, religion and other" is the main purpose of visit for arrivals in Central and Eastern Europe (47%).

Europe: Inbound tourism by purpose of visit

International Tourist Arrivals (share, %)

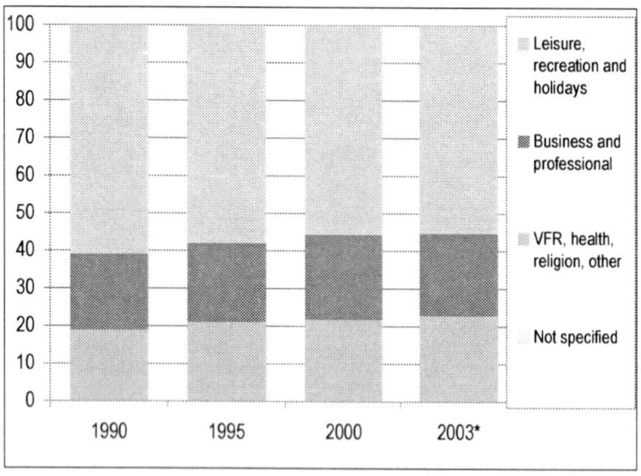


Source: World Tourism Organization (WTO) ©

Europe and subregions: Inbound tourism by purpose of visit

International Tourist Arrivals, 2003* (share, %)

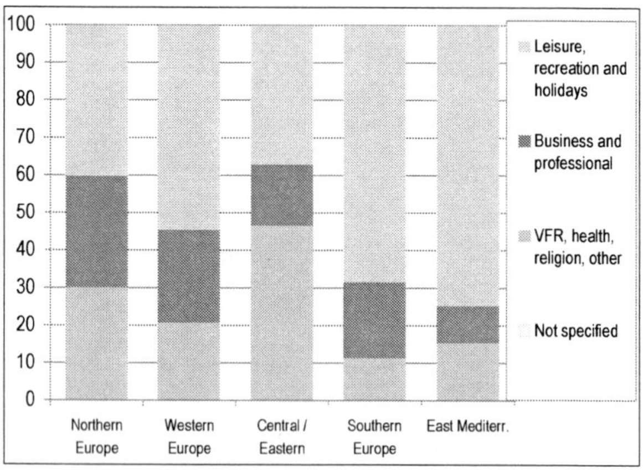


Source: World Tourism Organization (WTO) ©

**Europe**

**Arrivals by purpose of visit (including estimations for countries with missing data)**

| | International Tourist Arrivals (million) | | | | | Share (%) | | | | Change (%) | | Average annual growth (%) |
|---|---|---|---|---|---|---|---|---|---|---|---|---|
| | 1990 | 1995 | 2000 | 2002 | 2003* | 1990 | 1995 | 2000 | 2003* | 02/01 | 03*/02 | 1990-2000 |
| **Total** | 270.4 | 316.4 | 389.6 | 397.3 | 399.0 | 100 | 100 | 100 | 100 | 2.4 | 0.4 | 3.7 |
| Leisure, recreation and holidays | 164.5 | 183.5 | 216.5 | 219.9 | 220.6 | 60.8 | 58.0 | 55.6 | 55.3 | 2.1 | 0.3 | 2.8 |
| Business and professional | 54.7 | 65.9 | 88.1 | 85.9 | 86.7 | 20.2 | 20.8 | 22.6 | 21.7 | 1.5 | 0.8 | 4.9 |
| VFR, health, religion, other | 51.1 | 66.9 | 85.0 | 91.4 | 91.5 | 18.9 | 21.2 | 21.8 | 22.9 | 4.3 | 0.1 | 5.2 |

Source: World Tourism Organization (WTO) © (Data as collected by WTO December 2004)

**Arrivals by purpose of visit (including estimations for countries with missing data), 2003***

| | Total | Leisure, recreation and holidays | Business and professional | VFR, health, religion, other | Not specified |
|---|---|---|---|---|---|
| | International Tourist Arrivals (million) | | | | |
| Europe | 399.0 | 220.6 | 86.7 | 91.5 | 0.2 |
| Northern Europe | 47.4 | 19.1 | 14.0 | 14.1 | 0.1 |
| Western Europe | 136.1 | 74.2 | 33.5 | 28.3 | 0.0 |
| Central/Eastern Europe | 67.8 | 25.1 | 11.0 | 31.6 | 0.0 |
| Southern Europe | 131.0 | 89.7 | 26.4 | 14.9 | 0.0 |
| East Mediterranean Eu. | 16.7 | 12.5 | 1.6 | 2.6 | 0.0 |
| | % | | | | |
| Europe | 100 | 55.3 | 21.7 | 22.9 | 0.0 |
| Northern Europe | 100 | 40.3 | 29.7 | 29.8 | 0.3 |
| Western Europe | 100 | 54.6 | 24.7 | 20.8 | 0.0 |
| Central/Eastern Europe | 100 | 37.1 | 16.3 | 46.7 | 0.0 |
| Southern Europe | 100 | 68.5 | 20.2 | 11.3 | 0.0 |
| East Mediterranean Eu. | 100 | 74.8 | 9.7 | 15.5 | 0.0 |

Source: World Tourism Organization (WTO) © (Data as collected by WTO December 2004)

## II.1.2 Outbound Tourism

*Outbound tourism by (sub)region of destination*

In 2003 Europe generated almost 409 million international tourist arrivals corresponding to nearly 60 per cent of the world total. In the period 1995-2000 European outbound tourism grew at an average rate of 4.5 per cent a year, only slightly below the world average of 4.7 per cent a year.

World and regions: Outbound tourism by region of destination
International Tourist Arrivals, 2003* (share, %)

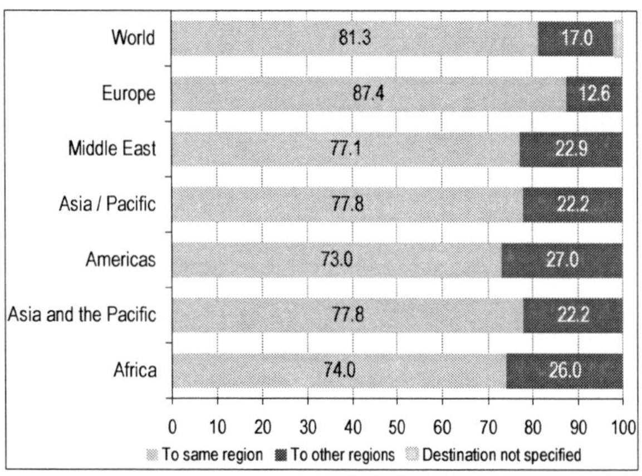


Source: World Tourism Organization (WTO) ©

World regions: Outbound tourism by region of destination
International Tourist Arrivals, 2003* (million)

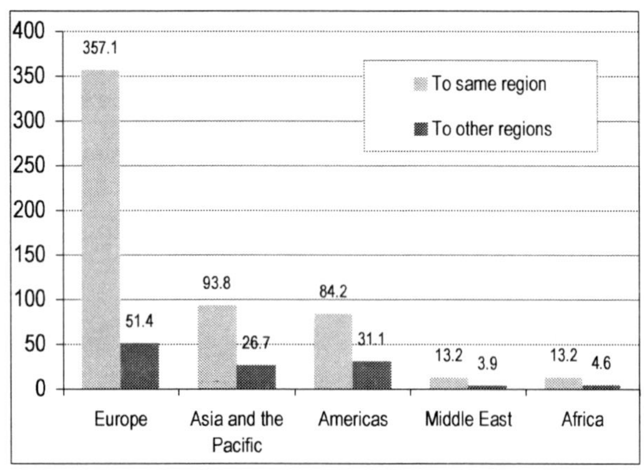


Source: World Tourism Organization (WTO) ©

Europe: Outbound tourism by region of destination
International Tourist Arrivals, 2003* (share, %)

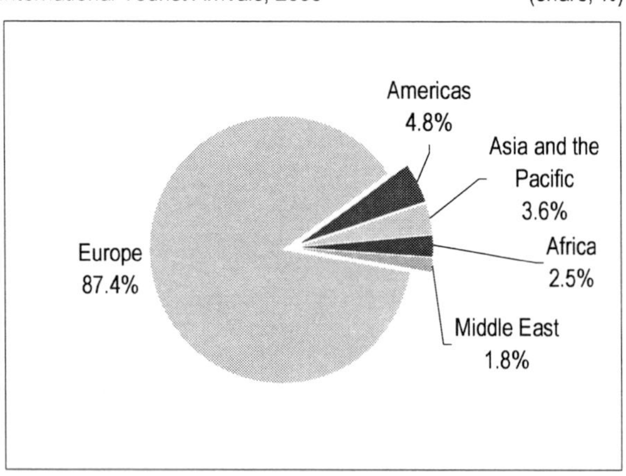


Source: World Tourism Organization (WTO) ©

Europe: Outbound tourism by region of destination
International Tourist Arrivals (share, %)

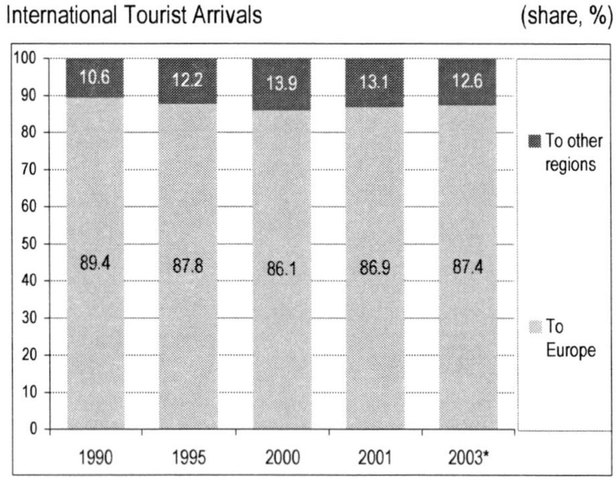


Source: World Tourism Organization (WTO) ©

Maintaining the previous trend, European countries lead the way as the main destinations of European outbound with an 87 per cent share. In 2003, tourism from Europe to destinations in the same region amounted to more than 357 million, the majority of which to Southern (124 million) and Western Europe (118 million), being that both subregions received almost 60 per cent of all outbound traffic generated by Europe. In the period between 1995 and 2000 outbound tourism to the same region grew at an annual average rate of 4 per cent and was particularly strong to Southern Europe and to Eastern Mediterranean Europe, with a 7 and 6 per cent growth rate a year on average respectively. After a positive performance in

2002 (+3%), in 2003 intraregional outbound grew by a mere 1 per cent, due in particular to the slow down of outbound to the major two sub-regions (-0.2% to Western Europe and +0.2% to Southern Europe).

Europe: Outbound tourism by region of destination
International Tourist Arrivals, 2003* (million)

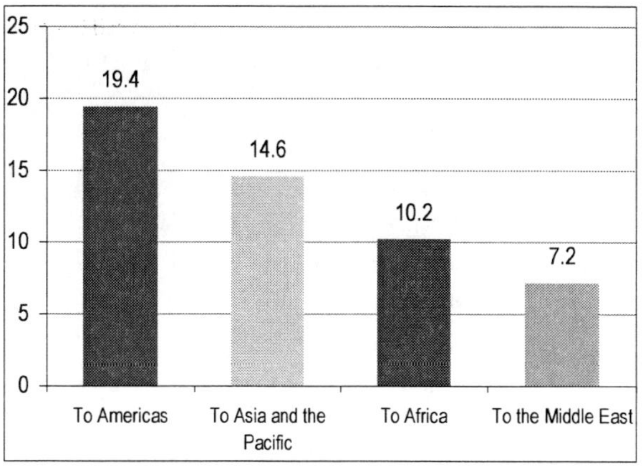


Source: World Tourism Organization (WTO) ©

Europe: Outbound tourism by region of destination
International Tourist Arrivals (change 03*/02, %)

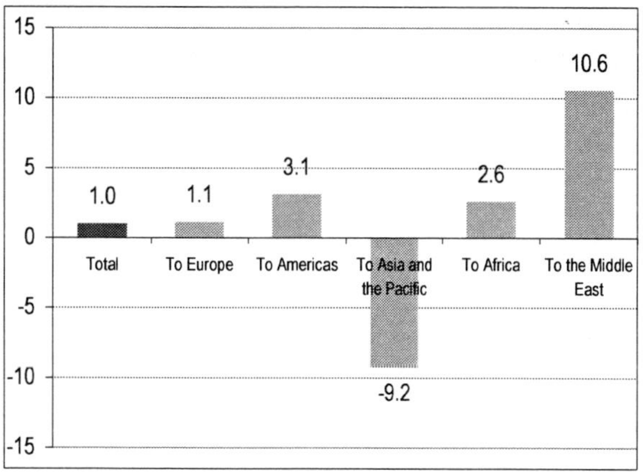


Source: World Tourism Organization (WTO) ©

**Europe**
**Outbound Tourism by (sub)region of destination (including estimations for countries with missing data)**

| | International Tourist Arrivals | | | | (1000) | Market share | | (%) | Growth rate | (%) | Average annual | growth (%) |
|---|---|---|---|---|---|---|---|---|---|---|---|---|
| | 1990 | 1995 | 2000 | 2002 | 2003* | 1990 | 1995 | 2003* | 02/01 | 03*/02 | 90-00 | 95-00 |
| **Total** | **257,944** | **315,727** | **394,306** | **404,408** | **408,501** | **100** | **100** | **100** | **2.7** | **1.0** | **4.3** | **4.5** |
| To: | | | | | | | | | | | | |
| ***Europe*** | ***230,547*** | ***277,148*** | ***339,419*** | ***353,091*** | ***357,133*** | ***89.4*** | ***87.8*** | ***87.4*** | ***3.2*** | ***1.1*** | ***3.9*** | ***4.1*** |
| Northern Europe | 23,412 | 31,383 | 34,678 | 35,736 | 36,988 | 9.1 | 9.9 | 9.1 | 5.2 | 3.5 | 4.0 | 2.0 |
| Western Europe | 89,415 | 95,127 | 117,075 | 118,693 | 118,461 | 34.7 | 30.1 | 29.0 | 2.8 | -0.2 | 2.7 | 4.2 |
| Central/Eastern Europe | 34,087 | 57,322 | 58,389 | 61,241 | 63,488 | 13.2 | 18.2 | 15.5 | 3.0 | 3.7 | 5.5 | 0.4 |
| Southern Europe | 77,654 | 84,207 | 117,047 | 123,254 | 123,520 | 30.1 | 26.7 | 30.2 | 2.3 | 0.2 | 4.2 | 6.8 |
| East Mediterranean Eu. | 5,979 | 9,109 | 12,230 | 14,167 | 14,677 | 2.3 | 2.9 | 3.6 | 10.9 | 3.6 | 7.4 | 6.1 |
| ***Interregional*** | ***27,398*** | ***38,579*** | ***54,887*** | ***51,317*** | ***51,368*** | ***10.6*** | ***12.2*** | ***12.6*** | ***-0.7*** | ***0.1*** | ***7.2*** | ***7.3*** |
| **Americas** | **12,217** | **16,744** | **22,848** | **18,837** | **19,426** | **4.7** | **5.3** | **4.8** | **-7.3** | **3.1** | **6.5** | **6.4** |
| North America | 8,720 | 11,590 | 14,952 | 11,538 | 11,298 | 3.4 | 3.7 | 2.8 | -8.4 | -2.1 | 5.5 | 5.2 |
| Caribbean | 1,944 | 2,877 | 4,484 | 3,819 | 4,209 | 0.8 | 0.9 | 1.0 | -7.2 | 10.2 | 8.7 | 9.3 |
| Central America | 228 | 388 | 459 | 514 | 568 | 0.1 | 0.1 | 0.1 | 7.3 | 10.6 | 7.2 | 3.4 |
| South America | 1,323 | 1,889 | 2,954 | 2,966 | 3,352 | 0.5 | 0.6 | 0.8 | -5.4 | 13.0 | 8.4 | 9.4 |
| **Asia and the Pacific** | **7,812** | **11,425** | **15,088** | **16,064** | **14,584** | **3.0** | **3.6** | **3.6** | **4.8** | **-9.2** | **6.8** | **5.7** |
| North-East Asia | 2,348 | 4,055 | 5,134 | 5,759 | 4,901 | 0.9 | 1.3 | 1.2 | 9.8 | -14.9 | 8.1 | 4.8 |
| South-East Asia | 3,321 | 4,268 | 5,418 | 5,948 | 5,016 | 1.3 | 1.4 | 1.2 | 3.5 | -15.7 | 5.0 | 4.9 |
| Oceania | 868 | 1,226 | 1,729 | 1,736 | 1,815 | 0.3 | 0.4 | 0.4 | 2.4 | 4.6 | 7.1 | 7.1 |
| South Asia | 1,275 | 1,876 | 2,807 | 2,621 | 2,852 | 0.5 | 0.6 | 0.7 | -0.9 | 8.8 | 8.2 | 8.4 |
| **Africa** | **5,481** | **6,906** | **10,550** | **9,937** | **10,195** | **2.1** | **2.2** | **2.5** | **-5.2** | **2.6** | **6.8** | **8.8** |
| North Africa | 3,133 | 3,648 | 5,643 | 4,940 | 4,889 | 1.2 | 1.2 | 1.2 | -11.7 | -1.0 | 6.1 | 9.1 |
| West Africa | 560 | 678 | 973 | 1,127 | 1,068 | 0.2 | 0.2 | 0.3 | 10.7 | -5.3 | 5.7 | 7.5 |
| Central Africa | 147 | 193 | 336 | 195 | 202 | 0.1 | 0.1 | 0.0 | -39.2 | 3.8 | 8.6 | 11.8 |
| East Africa | 1,131 | 1,486 | 2,262 | 2,141 | 2,313 | 0.4 | 0.5 | 0.6 | -4.7 | 8.0 | 7.2 | 8.8 |
| Southern Africa | 510 | 901 | 1,336 | 1,534 | 1,723 | 0.2 | 0.3 | 0.4 | 16.9 | 12.4 | 10.1 | 8.2 |
| **Middle East** | **1,889** | **3,504** | **6,401** | **6,479** | **7,163** | **0.7** | **1.1** | **1.8** | **17.0** | **10.6** | **13.0** | **12.8** |

Source: World Tourism Organization (WTO) © (Data as collected by WTO December 2004)

As for interregional outbound tourism, Europe generated a total of more than 51 million arrivals in other regions in 2003, or almost the same volume as in 2002 (+0.1%), among which 19 million in the Americas (4.8%), 15 million in Asia and the Pacific (3.6%), 10 million in Africa (2.5%) and more than 7 million in the Middle East (1.8%). All regions, except for Asia and the Pacific (-9%) registered increased arrivals from Europe, with the most significant growth occurring in the Middle East (+11%). While long-haul traffic to the Americas start to recover from the setbacks of the two previous years (-11% and -7% respectively) growing in 2003 by 3 per cent, outbound to Asia and the Pacific plunged under the effect of SARS. The most affected subregions were as expected North and South-East Asia (-15% and -16% respectively), whereas traffic to South Asia and Oceania performed rather positively (+9% and +5%). As for the Americas the growth trend was particularly driven by the Caribbean (+10%) and by South America (+13%), while outbound to North America, though recovering comparatively to 2001 and 2002 rates, was still on the negative side (-2%).

*International tourism expenditure*

The international tourism expenditure relating to overnight as well as same-day trips abroad taken by Europeans reached an estimated 248 billion euro (US$ 281 billion) in 2003 corresponding to a decrease of 1 per cent over 2002. Europe concentrates 54 per cent of the world's tourism expenditure, including seven of the ten world tourism top spenders - Germany (57 billion euro), the United Kingdom (43 billion), France (21 billion), Italy (18 billion), the Netherlands (13 billion), the Russian Federation (11 billion), Belgium (11 billion) and Austria (10 billion). Outside the "major spenders league" there is also a large group of countries with expenditure on international tourism of over 5 billion euro (Sweden, Denmark, Spain, Switzerland and Norway).

In 2003 Europe registered expenditure per capita (travellers and non-travellers) on international tourism of 283 euro, significantly above the world average (74 euro). The highest figures are recorded by Northern and Western Europe with 774 and 652 euro respectively. Residents from countries in Southern Europe (216 euro), East Mediterranean Europe (62 euro) and Central Eastern Europe (58 euro) spend on average a more modest amount on international tourism.

World and regions: Outbound tourism
International Tourism Expenditure, 2003* (share, %)

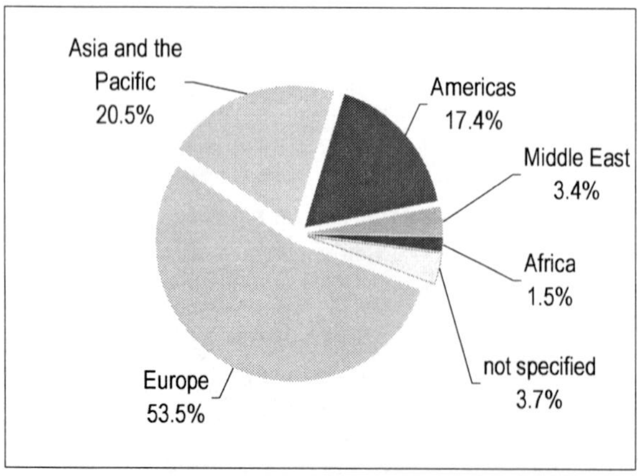


Source: World Tourism Organization (WTO) ©

World and regions: Outbound tourism
International Tourism Expenditure, 2003* (euro per capita)

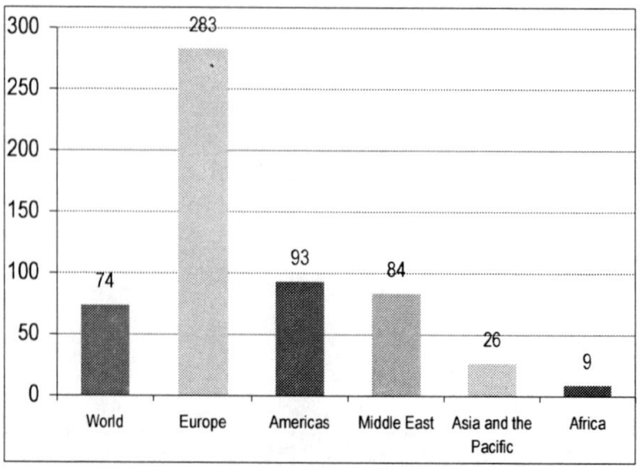


Source: World Tourism Organization (WTO) ©

Europe: Outbound tourism
International Tourism Expenditure, 2003* (euro billion)

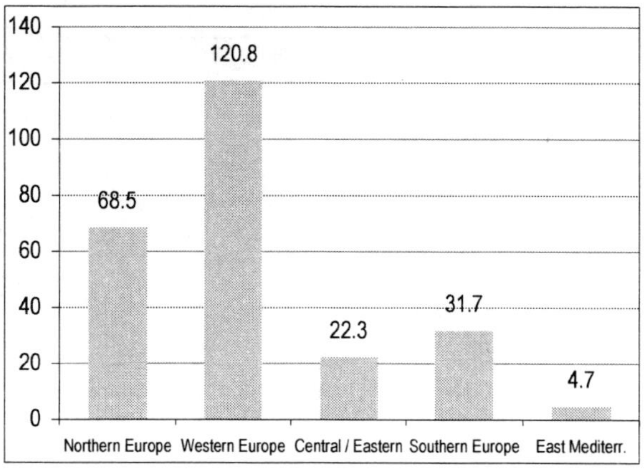


Source: World Tourism Organization (WTO) ©

Europe: Outbound tourism
International Tourism Expenditure, 2003* (euro per capita)

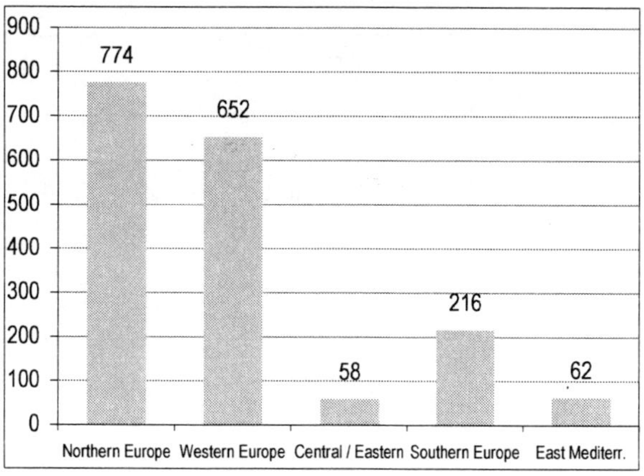


Source: World Tourism Organization (WTO) ©

In terms of source markets, by far the highest figure of the region regarding expenditure per capita is registered by Luxembourg (4,624 euro). It is likely that a significant part of this expenditure relates to same-day trips to neighbouring Belgium, France or Germany for shopping, services, leisure, etc. In general it are the smaller European countries that show the highest expenditure per capita: Iceland (1,582 euro), Austria (1,274 euro), Norway (1,244 euro), Denmark (1,091 euro), Ireland (1,061 euro) and Belgium (1,037 euro), all with over 1,000 euro per capita.

**Outbound Tourism, International Tourism Expenditure**

| | | | | | | (euro million) | Share (%) | per capita[1] (euro) | Change (%) 02/01 | Change (%) 03*/02 | Average (%) 1995-2000 |
|---|---|---|---|---|---|---|---|---|---|---|---|
| | 1990 | 1995 | 2000 | 2001 | 2002 | 2003* | | | | | |
| ***Europe*** | ***107,620*** | ***160,159*** | ***240,758*** | ***247,173*** | ***250,861*** | ***248,064*** | ***100.0*** | ***283*** | ***1.5*** | ***-1.1*** | ***8.5*** |
| **Northern Europe** | **28,459** | **33,360** | **65,462** | **66,078** | **69,857** | **68,490** | **27.6** | **774** | **5.7** | **-2.0** | **14.4** |
| Denmark | 3,048 | 3,337 | 5,068 | 5,433 | 6,164 | 5,886 | 2.4 | 1,091 | 13.4 | -4.5 | 8.7 |
| Finland | 2,192 | 1,742 | 2,005 | 2,068 | 2,121 | 2,128 | 0.9 | 409 | 2.6 | 0.3 | 2.9 |
| Iceland | 225 | 216 | 510 | 415 | 391 | 461 | 0.2 | 1,582 | -5.8 | 17.7 | 18.8 |
| Ireland | 913 | 1,609 | 2,804 | 3,211 | 3,956 | 4,163 | 1.7 | 1,061 | 23.2 | 5.2 | 11.7 |
| Norway | 2,889 | 3,235 | 4,935 | 4,871 | 5,357 | 5,665 | 2.3 | 1,244 | 10.0 | 5.8 | 8.8 |
| Sweden | 4,936 | 4,165 | 8,714 | 7,728 | 7,721 | 7,334 | 3.0 | 818 | -0.1 | -5.0 | 15.9 |
| United Kingdom | 14,256 | 19,056 | 41,426 | 42,351 | 44,147 | 42,854 | 17.3 | 713 | 4.2 | -2.9 | 16.8 |
| **Western Europe** | **61,120** | **88,201** | **117,756** | **121,212** | **119,969** | **120,817** | **48.7** | **652** | **-1.0** | **0.7** | **6.0** |
| Austria | 6,084 | 7,958 | 9,216 | 10,032 | 9,923 | 10,397 | 4.2 | 1,274 | -1.1 | 4.8 | 3.0 |
| Belgium | .. | 6,204 | 10,209 | 10,922 | 10,759 | 10,718 | 4.3 | 1,037 | -1.5 | -0.4 | 10.5 |
| Belgium/Luxembourg | 4,281 | .. | .. | .. | .. | .. | | | .. | .. | |
| France | 9,756 | 12,506 | 19,387 | 20,219 | 20,842 | 20,842 | 8.4 | 346 | 3.1 | 0.0 | 9.2 |
| Germany | 30,574 | 45,994 | 57,427 | 57,985 | 55,504 | 57,187 | 23.1 | 694 | -4.3 | 3.0 | 4.5 |
| Liechtenstein | .. | .. | .. | .. | .. | .. | | | .. | .. | |
| Luxembourg | .. | 911 | 1,417 | 1,635 | 2,018 | 2,112 | 0.9 | 4,624 | 23.4 | 4.7 | 9.2 |
| Monaco | .. | .. | .. | .. | .. | .. | | | .. | .. | |
| Netherlands | 5,792 | 8,925 | 13,199 | 13,392 | 13,888 | 12,915 | 5.2 | 796 | 3.7 | -7.0 | 8.1 |
| Switzerland | 4,612 | 5,673 | 6,859 | 6,985 | 6,993 | 6,605 | 2.7 | 892 | 0.1 | -5.6 | 3.9 |

Continued on the next page.

**Outbound Tourism, International Tourism Expenditure**

| | 1990 | 1995 | 2000 | 2001 | 2002 | 2003* | Share (%) | per capita[1] (euro) | Change (%) 02/01 | Change (%) 03*/02 | Average (%) 1995-2000 |
|---|---|---|---|---|---|---|---|---|---|---|---|
| | | | | | (euro million) | | | | | | |
| **Central/Eastern Europe** | **2,526** | **17,587** | **20,292** | **22,244** | **24,007** | **22,341** | **9.0** | **58** | **7.9** | **-6.9** | **2.9** |
| Armenia | .. | 2 | 43 | 45 | 57 | 59 | 0.0 | 20 | 27.9 | 3.7 | 80.0 |
| Azerbaijan | .. | 112 | 143 | 122 | 111 | 98 | 0.0 | 13 | -8.8 | -11.6 | 5.1 |
| Belarus | .. | 67 | 263 | 559 | 591 | 436 | 0.2 | 42 | 5.7 | -26.3 | 31.7 |
| Bulgaria | 148 | 149 | 582 | 509 | 564 | 663 | 0.3 | 87 | 10.7 | 17.6 | 31.3 |
| Czech Rep | 357 | 1,250 | 1,382 | 1,548 | 1,689 | 1,710 | 0.7 | 167 | 9.1 | 1.2 | 2.0 |
| Estonia | .. | 70 | 221 | 214 | 244 | 284 | 0.1 | 210 | 14.0 | 16.2 | 26.0 |
| Former U.S.S.R. | .. | .. | .. | .. | .. | .. | | | .. | .. | |
| Georgia | .. | .. | 119 | 119 | 158 | 117 | 0.0 | 25 | 31.9 | -25.9 | |
| Hungary | 375 | 1,144 | 1,502 | 1,626 | 1,821 | 1,788 | 0.7 | 178 | 12.0 | -1.8 | 5.6 |
| Kazakhstan | .. | 216 | 442 | 751 | 801 | 591 | 0.2 | 39 | 6.5 | -26.1 | 15.3 |
| Kyrgyzstan | .. | 5 | 17 | 13 | 11 | 15 | 0.0 | 3 | -21.1 | 42.1 | 26.5 |
| Latvia | .. | 18 | 267 | 249 | 243 | 290 | 0.1 | 125 | -2.3 | 19.2 | 70.9 |
| Lithuania | .. | 81 | 274 | 245 | 345 | 416 | 0.2 | 115 | 41.0 | 20.8 | 27.6 |
| Poland | 332 | 4,205 | 3,587 | 3,902 | 3,386 | 2,476 | 1.0 | 64 | -13.2 | -26.9 | -3.1 |
| Rep Moldova | .. | 43 | 78 | 78 | 90 | 86 | 0.0 | 19 | 15.0 | -4.6 | 12.7 |
| Romania | 81 | 533 | 466 | 503 | 416 | 423 | 0.2 | 19 | -17.3 | 1.7 | -2.6 |
| Russian Federation | .. | 8,868 | 9,580 | 10,367 | 11,933 | 11,386 | 4.6 | 79 | 15.1 | -4.6 | 1.6 |
| Slovakia | 111 | 245 | 320 | 323 | 467 | 507 | 0.2 | 94 | 44.9 | 8.4 | 5.5 |
| Tajikistan | .. | .. | .. | .. | 2 | 2 | 0.0 | 0 | .. | -16.4 | |
| Turkmenistan | .. | .. | .. | .. | .. | .. | | | .. | .. | |
| Ukraine | .. | 161 | 509 | 632 | 695 | 697 | 0.3 | 15 | 9.9 | 0.4 | 26.0 |
| Uzbekistan | .. | .. | .. | .. | .. | .. | | | .. | .. | |
| **Southern Europe** | **13,887** | **18,442** | **31,911** | **31,933** | **31,809** | **31,736** | **12.8** | **216** | **-0.4** | **-0.2** | **11.6** |
| Albania | .. | 5 | 294 | 287 | 387 | 432 | 0.2 | 123 | 34.9 | 11.7 | 122.9 |
| Andorra | .. | .. | .. | .. | .. | .. | | | .. | .. | |
| Bosnia & Herzg | 13 | .. | 38 | 44 | 52 | 52 | 0.0 | 13 | 19.0 | 0.6 | |
| Croatia | 572 | 323 | 615 | 677 | 826 | 594 | 0.2 | 132 | 22.1 | -28.1 | 13.8 |
| F.Yug.Rp.Macedonia | 14 | 21 | 37 | 44 | 48 | 42 | 0.0 | 21 | 9.3 | -10.8 | 12.3 |
| Greece | 856 | 1,011 | 4,935 | 4,651 | 2,549 | 2,109 | 0.9 | 198 | -45.2 | -17.3 | 37.3 |
| Italy | 8,092 | 11,337 | 16,982 | 16,519 | 17,898 | 18,147 | 7.3 | 313 | 8.3 | 1.4 | 8.4 |
| Malta | 108 | 164 | 217 | 201 | 162 | 190 | 0.1 | 480 | -19.5 | 17.2 | 5.8 |
| Portugal | 681 | 1,605 | 2,412 | 2,347 | 2,385 | 2,389 | 1.0 | 228 | 1.6 | 0.2 | 8.5 |
| San Marino | .. | .. | .. | .. | .. | .. | | | .. | .. | |
| Serbia & Montenegro | 48 | .. | .. | .. | 111 | 127 | 0.1 | 12 | .. | 14.6 | |
| Slovenia | 139 | 440 | 554 | 596 | 642 | 668 | 0.3 | 332 | 7.8 | 4.0 | 4.7 |
| Spain | 3,341 | 3,424 | 5,929 | 6,655 | 7,045 | 7,324 | 3.0 | 182 | 5.9 | 4.0 | 11.6 |
| **East Mediterranean Eu.** | **1,628** | **2,569** | **5,338** | **5,707** | **5,218** | **4,680** | **1.9** | **62** | **-8.6** | **-10.3** | **15.8** |
| Cyprus | 87 | 252 | 447 | 478 | 539 | 558 | 0.2 | 723 | 12.9 | 3.4 | 12.2 |
| Israel | 1,132 | 1,621 | 3,036 | 3,288 | 2,689 | 2,255 | 0.9 | 369 | -18.2 | -16.2 | 13.4 |
| Turkey | 408 | 696 | 1,855 | 1,941 | 1,989 | 1,868 | 0.8 | 27 | 2.5 | -6.1 | 21.6 |

Source: World Tourism Organization (WTO) © (Data as collected by WTO December 2004)

[1] values correspond to most recent year with data available

*Trips Abroad*

When evaluating the data on the number of trips abroad from countries in the region, it should be taken into account that statistics on outbound trips are still lacking for many countries and that it is not always clear whether the reported figures refer to visitors in general or only to tourists (visitors who stay overnight). This situation is confirmed by the high volume of trips abroad reported by countries such as Poland (39 million) or the Czech Republic (36 million), as compared to the figures of other generating markets such as the Germany (75 million), the United Kingdom (61 million) or Italy (27 million). In the first case it is likely that a large share of same-day visitors (excursionists) is included crossing the country borders regularly for leisure, business or other purposes but not spending the night abroad.

**Outbound Tourism, Trips abroad (trips can either refer to overnight visits only, or also include same-day visits)**

| | | | | | | (1000) | per 100 popu- | | | Change (%) | Average (%) |
|---|---|---|---|---|---|---|---|---|---|---|---|
| | 1990 | 1995 | 2000 | 2001 | 2002 | 2003* | lation[1] | 01/00 | 02/01 | 03*/02 | 1995-2000 |
| ***Europe*** | | | | | | | | | | | |
| **Northern Europe** | | | | | | | | | | | |
| Denmark | 2,530 | .. | 5,011 | 4,946 | 4,935 | 5,564 | 240 | -1.3 | -0.2 | 12.7 | |
| Finland | 1,169 | 5,147 | 5,914 | 5,824 | 5,857 | 5,585 | 111 | -1.5 | 0.6 | -4.6 | 2.8 |
| Iceland | 142 | 166 | 283 | .. | .. | .. | | | | | 11.3 |
| Ireland | 1,798 | 2,547 | 3,783 | 4,216 | 4,634 | .. | 5 | 11.4 | 9.9 | | 8.2 |
| Norway | 508 | 590 | .. | .. | .. | .. | | | | | |
| Sweden | 8,691 | 10,127 | 10,400 | 10,500 | 12,927 | 12,579 | 125 | 1.0 | 23.1 | -2.7 | 0.5 |
| United Kingdom | 31,150 | 41,345 | 56,837 | 58,281 | 59,377 | 61,424 | 809 | 2.5 | 1.9 | 3.4 | 6.6 |
| **Western Europe** | | | | | | | | | | | |
| Austria | 2,572 | .. | 4,660 | 4,207 | 3,907 | 5,060 | 140 | -9.7 | -7.1 | 29.5 | |
| Belgium | .. | .. | 7,932 | 6,570 | 6,773 | 7,268 | 48 | -17.2 | 3.1 | 7.3 | |
| France | 19,430 | 18,686 | 19,886 | 19,265 | 17,404 | 17,426 | | -3.1 | -9.7 | 0.1 | 1.3 |
| Germany | .. | .. | 74,400 | 76,400 | 73,300 | 74,600 | 723 | 2.7 | -4.1 | 1.8 | |
| Luxembourg | .. | .. | 263 | 261 | .. | .. | 5 | -0.8 | | | |
| Netherlands | 9,000 | 12,320 | 13,896 | 14,220 | 16,760 | .. | 5,819 | 2.3 | 17.9 | | 2.4 |
| Switzerland | 9,627 | 11,148 | 12,240 | 11,554 | 11,427 | .. | 295 | -5.6 | -1.1 | | 1.9 |

Continued on the next page.

**Outbound Tourism, Trips abroad (trips can either refer to overnight visits only, or also include same-day visits)**

| | | | | | | (1000) | per 100 popu- | | | Change (%) | Average (%) |
|---|---|---|---|---|---|---|---|---|---|---|---|
| | 1990 | 1995 | 2000 | 2001 | 2002 | 2003* | lation[1] | 01/00 | 02/01 | 03*/02 | 1995-2000 |
| **Central/Eastern Europe** | | | | | | | | | | | |
| Armenia | .. | .. | 111 | 110 | 131 | 169 | 0 | -0.9 | 19.1 | 29.0 | |
| Azerbaijan | .. | .. | 1,326 | 1,130 | 1,141 | .. | 25 | -14.8 | 1.0 | | |
| Belarus | .. | 626 | 1,289 | 1,386 | .. | .. | 16 | 7.5 | | | 15.5 |
| Bulgaria | 2,395 | 3,524 | 2,337 | 2,730 | 3,188 | 3,403 | 77 | 16.8 | 16.8 | 6.7 | -7.9 |
| Czech Rep | 13,380 | 44,873 | 38,177 | 36,224 | 34,303 | 36,074 | 2,671 | -5.1 | -5.3 | 5.2 | -3.2 |
| Estonia | .. | 1,764 | 1,800 | 1,658 | 1,849 | 2,075 | 38 | -7.9 | 11.5 | 12.2 | 0.4 |
| Former U.S.S.R. | 9,086 | .. | .. | .. | .. | .. | | | | | |
| Georgia | .. | 228 | 315 | 306 | 317 | .. | 0 | -2.9 | 3.6 | | 6.7 |
| Hungary | 13,596 | 13,083 | 11,065 | 11,167 | 12,966 | 14,283 | 303 | 0.9 | 16.1 | 10.2 | -3.3 |
| Kazakhstan | .. | .. | 1,247 | 2,294 | 2,274 | 2,374 | 11 | 84.0 | -0.9 | 4.4 | |
| Kyrgyzstan | .. | 42 | 47 | 46 | 45 | .. | 1 | -2.1 | -2.2 | | 2.3 |
| Latvia | .. | 1,812 | 2,596 | 2,697 | 2,306 | 2,286 | 2 | 3.9 | -14.5 | -0.9 | 7.5 |
| Lithuania | .. | 1,925 | 3,632 | 3,390 | 3,584 | 3,502 | 9 | -6.7 | 5.7 | -2.3 | 13.5 |
| Poland | 22,131 | 36,387 | 56,677 | 53,122 | 45,043 | 38,730 | 378 | -6.3 | -15.2 | -14.0 | 9.3 |
| Rep Moldova | 129 | 71 | 32 | 30 | 52 | 67 | 0 | -6.3 | 73.3 | 28.8 | -14.7 |
| Romania | 11,247 | 5,737 | 6,388 | 6,408 | 5,757 | .. | 56 | 0.3 | -10.2 | | 2.2 |
| Russian Federation | .. | 21,329 | 18,371 | 17,939 | 20,343 | .. | 34 | -2.4 | 13.4 | | -2.9 |
| Slovakia | .. | 218 | 388 | 373 | 437 | 408 | 6 | -3.9 | 17.2 | -6.6 | 12.2 |
| Tajikistan | .. | .. | 6 | 3 | .. | .. | 0 | -57.8 | | | |
| Turkmenistan | .. | 21 | .. | .. | .. | .. | | | | | |
| Ukraine | .. | 6,552 | 8,654 | 9,412 | 9,270 | .. | 57 | 8.8 | -1.5 | | 5.7 |
| Uzbekistan | .. | .. | 217 | 183 | 264 | 400 | 8 | -15.7 | 44.3 | 51.5 | |
| **Southern Europe** | | | | | | | | | | | |
| Albania | .. | 12 | .. | .. | .. | .. | | | | | |
| Italy | .. | .. | 21,993 | 22,421 | 25,126 | 26,817 | 46 | 1.9 | 12.1 | 6.7 | |
| Malta | 122 | 163 | 200 | 179 | .. | .. | 46 | -10.5 | | | 4.2 |
| Portugal | 192 | .. | .. | .. | .. | .. | | | | | |
| Slovenia | .. | .. | 1,965 | 2,055 | 2,127 | 2,114 | 105 | 4.6 | 3.5 | -0.6 | |
| Spain | 21,878 | 3,648 | 4,100 | 4,139 | 3,871 | 4,094 | 10 | 1.0 | -6.5 | 5.8 | 2.4 |
| **East Mediterranean Eu.** | | | | | | | | | | | |
| Cyprus | 228 | 360 | 503 | 589 | 645 | 629 | 82 | 17.1 | 9.5 | -2.5 | 6.9 |
| Israel | 883 | 2,259 | 3,530 | 3,561 | 3,273 | 3,299 | 54 | 0.9 | -8.1 | 0.8 | 9.3 |
| Turkey | 2,917 | 3,981 | 5,284 | 4,856 | 5,131 | 5,928 | 9 | -8.1 | 5.7 | 15.5 | 5.8 |

Source: World Tourism Organization (WTO) © (Data as collected by WTO December 2004)

[1] values correspond to most recent year with data available

# II.2 Tourism Trends by Subregion

## II.2.1 Northern Europe

*International tourist arrivals*

During 2003 Northern Europe, which holds a 12 per cent share of all European tourist arrivals, received more than 47 million arrivals, resulting in a 2.1 per cent increase over a positive 2002 (+3.5%).

All countries in the subregion show positive results in 2003, with the exception of Finland, recording a considerable drop (-10%) induced in particular by the fall of tourist arrivals from Russia (-10%) under the unfavourable exchange rate of the US dollar. Best performances were recorded in Iceland (+10%), Norway (+5%) and Ireland (+5%). Growth was more moderate in the United Kingdom and Sweden (both +2%). Denmark posted a slight increase (+0.3%), maintaining thus the stagnating trend of 2002.

The United Kingdom continues to hold the first position as main destination in the subregion, with a 52 per cent market share, followed by Sweden, which accounts for 16 per cent of the subregional arrivals. Ireland ranks third with a 13 per cent market share.

Northern Europe: Inbound tourism
International Tourist Arrivals (million)

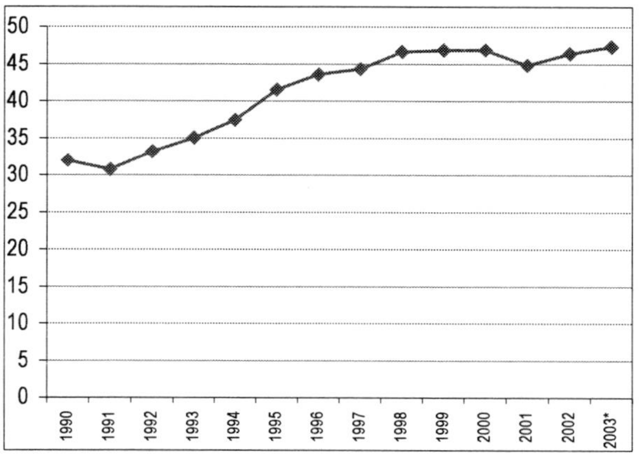


Source: World Tourism Organization (WTO) ©

Northern Europe: Inbound tourism
International Tourist Arrivals (change over previous year, %)

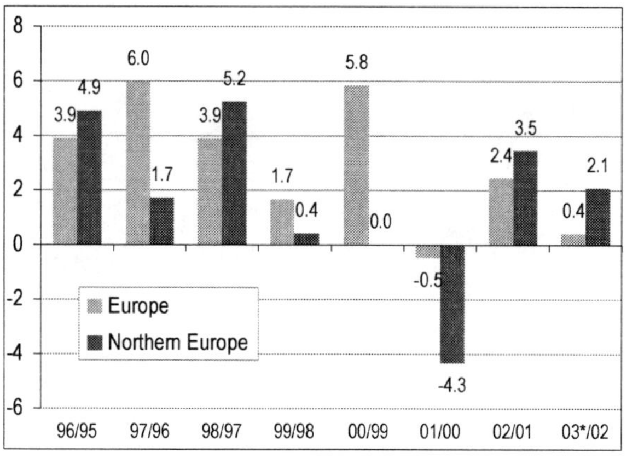


Source: World Tourism Organization (WTO) ©

*International tourism receipts*

International tourism receipts in Northern Europe amounted to 37 billion euro in 2003, or over 2 million euro less as compared to 2002. Computed in local currencies, constant prices, Northern Europe showed a 2 per cent decreased over 2002, slightly lower than the region's decline of 2.7 per cent. The United Kingdom, which generates the highest volume of revenues (20 billion euro), represents more than 54 per cent of all tourism receipts earned by the subregion. Following are Sweden and Denmark, both with volumes of nearly 4.7 billion euro (13% share each). International tourism receipts as computed in euro, suffered major decreases in Denmark (-8%), the United Kingdom (-7%) and in Sweden (-6%). On the other hand, good results were achieved by Ireland (+5%) and Iceland (+4%), whereas Finland just maintained its 2002 results (+0.3%). It is important to note, however, that, except in the case of countries within the euro zone, these variations are much influenced by exchange rates fluctuations as the euro appreciated during 2003 strongly against currencies such as the Pound.

Receipts per arrival in Northern Europe reached an average of 783 euro in 2003, positioning the subregion as second regarding this indicator. In terms of destinations, the highest value belongs to Denmark (2,309 euro), followed at a significant distance by the United Kingdom (814 euro) and Norway (687 euro). The lowest value of receipt per arrival occurred in Iceland (366 euro).

Northern Europe: Inbound tourism
International Tourism Receipts (euro billion, current prices)

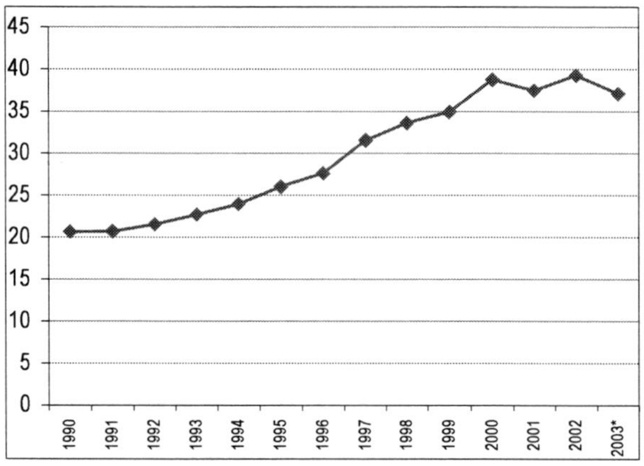


Source: World Tourism Organization (WTO) ©

Northern Europe: Inbound tourism (share in regional total, %)
International arrivals & receipts

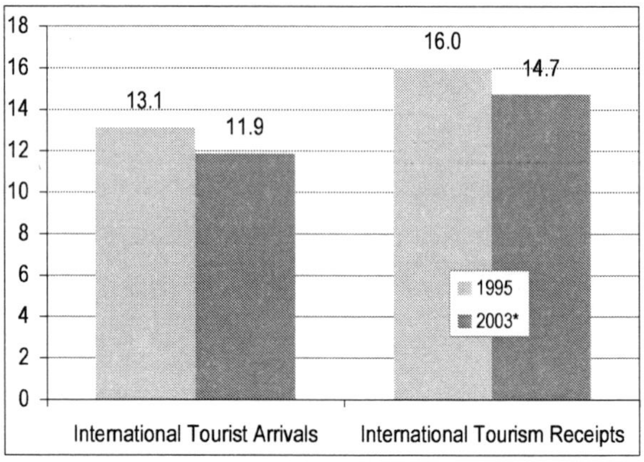


Source: World Tourism Organization (WTO) ©

**Northern Europe**

**International Tourist Arrivals and Tourism Receipts by Country of Destination**

| | | | | | | | Market share | | | Growth rate | | | Average annual growth | |
|---|---|---|---|---|---|---|---|---|---|---|---|---|---|---|
| | | 1990 | 1995 | 2000 | 2002 | 2003* | 1995 | 2000 | 2003* | 01/00 | 02/01 | 03*/02 | '90-'95 | '95-'00 |
| | Series | International Tourist Arrivals (1000) | | | | | | | % | | | % | | % |
| **Northern Europe** | | **31,955** | **41,554** | **46,880** | **46,405** | **47,368** | **100** | **100** | **100** | **-4.3** | **3.5** | **2.1** | **5.4** | **2.4** |
| Denmark | TCE | .. | .. | 2,088 | 2,010 | 2,016 | | 4.5 | 4.3 | -2.9 | -0.9 | 0.3 | | |
| Finland | TF | .. | 1,779 | 2,714 | 2,875 | 2,601 | 4.3 | 5.8 | 5.5 | 4.1 | 1.7 | -9.5 | | 8.8 |
| Iceland | TCE | 142 | 190 | 634 | 705 | 771 | 0.5 | 1.4 | 1.6 | 6.0 | 4.8 | 9.5 | 6.0 | 27.3 |
| Ireland | TF | 3,666 | 4,818 | 6,313 | 6,065 | 6,369 | 11.6 | 13.5 | 13.4 | -5.1 | 1.2 | 5.0 | 5.6 | 5.6 |
| Norway | TCE | 1,955 | 2,880 | 3,104 | 3,111 | 3,269 | 6.9 | 6.6 | 6.9 | -1.0 | 1.2 | 5.1 | 8.1 | 1.5 |
| Sweden | TCE/TF | .. | 2,310 | 2,746\| | 7,459 | 7,627 | 5.6 | 5.9 | 16.1 | | 0.4 | 2.3 | | 3.5 |
| United Kingdom | VF | 18,013 | 23,537 | 25,209 | 24,180 | 24,715 | 56.6 | 53.8 | 52.2 | -9.4 | 5.9 | 2.2 | 5.5 | 1.4 |
| | | International Tourism Receipts (euro million) | | | | | | | % | | | % | | % |
| **Northern Europe** | | **20,622** | **25,979** | **38,780** | **39,258** | **37,085** | **100** | **100** | **100** | **-3.4** | **4.8** | **-5.5** | **4.7** | **8.3** |
| Denmark | | 2,862 | 2,808 | 3,999 | 5,035 | 4,655 | 10.8 | 10.3 | 12.6 | 12.1 | 12.4 | -7.6 | -0.4 | 7.3 |
| Finland | | 916 | 1,254 | 1,522 | 1,669 | 1,674 | 4.8 | 3.9 | 4.5 | 5.4 | 4.0 | 0.3 | 6.5 | 4.0 |
| Iceland | | 109 | 142 | 246 | 271 | 282 | 0.5 | 0.6 | 0.8 | 5.4 | 4.5 | 4.2 | 5.4 | 11.6 |
| Ireland | | 1,146 | 1,748 | 2,824 | 3,266 | 3,426 | 6.7 | 7.3 | 9.2 | 10.3 | 4.8 | 4.9 | 8.8 | 10.1 |
| Norway | | 1,233 | 1,711 | 2,220 | 2,304 | 2,246 | 6.6 | 5.7 | 6.1 | -1.5 | 5.4 | -2.5 | 6.8 | 5.3 |
| Sweden | | 2,282 | 2,654 | 4,400 | 4,981 | 4,689 | 10.2 | 11.3 | 12.6 | 7.9 | 4.9 | -5.9 | 3.1 | 10.6 |
| United Kingdom | | 12,074 | 15,663 | 23,569 | 21,732 | 20,113 | 60.3 | 60.8 | 54.2 | -10.6 | 3.2 | -7.4 | 5.3 | 8.5 |
| | | Receipts per Arrival (euro) | | | | | | | | | | % | | % |
| **Northern Europe** | | **645** | **625** | **827** | **846** | **783** | | | | **0.9** | **1.3** | **-7.5** | **-0.6** | **5.8** |
| Denmark | | | | 1,915 | 2,505 | 2,309 | | | | 15.4 | 13.4 | -7.8 | | |
| Finland | | | 705 | 561 | 580 | 644 | | | | 1.2 | 2.2 | 10.9 | | -4.5 |
| Iceland | | 769 | 748 | 388 | 384 | 366 | | | | -0.6 | -0.3 | -4.8 | -0.5 | -12.3 |
| Ireland | | 313 | 363 | 447 | 539 | 538 | | | | 16.3 | 3.6 | -0.1 | 3.0 | 4.3 |
| Norway | | 631 | 594 | 715 | 741 | 687 | | | | -0.5 | 4.1 | -7.2 | -1.2 | 3.8 |
| Sweden | | | 1,149 | 1,602\| | 668 | 615 | | | | | 4.5 | -7.9 | | 6.9 |
| United Kingdom | | 670 | 665 | 935 | 899 | 814 | | | | -1.3 | -2.6 | -9.5 | -0.1 | 7.0 |

Source: World Tourism Organization (WTO) ©

(Data as collected by WTO December 2004)

## II.2.2 Western Europe

*International tourist arrivals*

Western Europe continues to be the lead subregion in terms of tourist arrivals - not only in Europe, but also worldwide – with a share of 34 per cent of the regional total and 20 per cent of the world total respectively. In 2003 it received over 136 million arrivals, which represents a slight 1.4 per cent decrease over the previous year. However, being a subregion composed by a highly developed and mature tourism sector, its market share tends to decline in favour of faster growing emerging destinations in Asia and the Pacific, the Middle East and Africa. Within Europe, Western Europe is also losing out to other subregions, such as Southern and East Mediterranean Europe. Since 1990 its market share of all tourist arrivals in Europe decreased by 6 percentage points, from 40 per cent to 34 per cent in 2003.

Results were negative in the majority of destinations of Western Europe in 2003. Only Austria (+2.5%) and Germany (+2.4%) managed to record growth, while the top destination - France - faced a 2.6 per cent decrease, due in particular to the general fall of arrivals from its top source markets and to the significant decline in arrivals from the United States of America (-18%). France's results determined thus significantly the overall performance of the subregion where it holds a 55 per cent share. In spite of the decrease, France, with 75 million tourist arrivals, still holds the first position as the world's top destination. Negative results were also recorded in major destinations such as The Netherlands (7% share), where arrival dropped by more than 4 per cent, and Switzerland (5% share) with a 5 per cent decrease over the previous year.

Western Europe: Inbound tourism
International Tourist Arrivals (million)

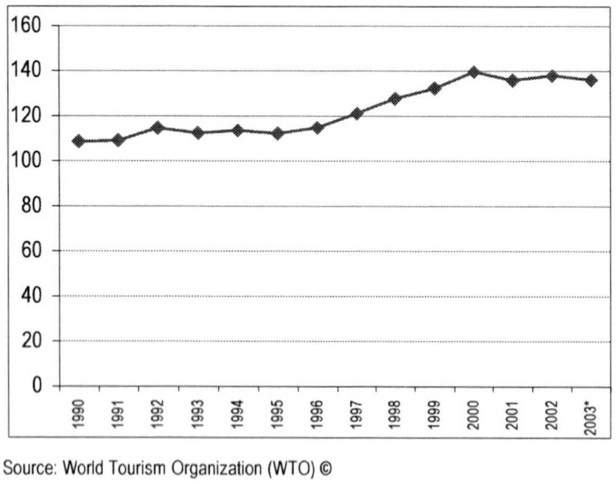


Source: World Tourism Organization (WTO) ©

Western Europe: Inbound tourism
International Tourist Arrivals (change over previous year, %)

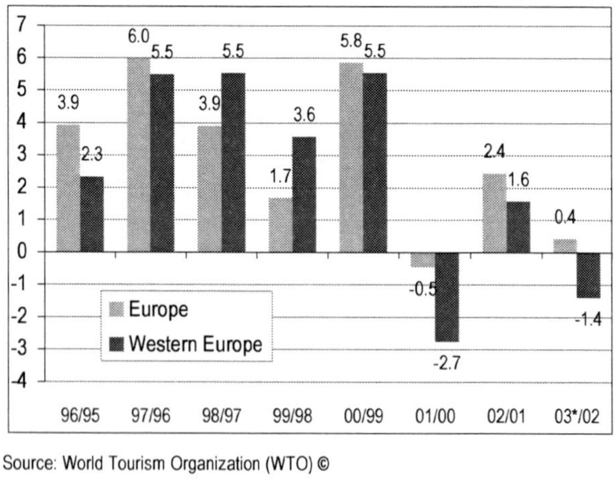


Source: World Tourism Organization (WTO) ©

*International tourism receipts*

International tourism receipts in Western Europe reached 91.6 billion euro in 2003, or 1 billion euro less than in 2002, and represented 36 per cent of the region's total receipts for international tourism and 20 per cent of the world's volume. Among the main earners in the subregion, France and Germany (with a combined market share of almost 60%), results are mixed. While Germany grew by 1.3 per cent, recovering from the slowdown of the two previous years, France posted a drop of 5.4 per cent under the impact of diminished overseas traffic. Particularly good results were obtained by Luxembourg (+7%) and by Austria (+5%), whereas the remaining destinations performed negatively (Belgium, -1.4% and Switzerland, -1.2%) or just maintained the previous years results (the Netherlands, +0.3%).

Receipts per arrivals in Western Europe amount to 673 euro. Highest values were achieved by Luxembourg (2,848 euro) and Switzerland (1,262 euro), while the lowest occurred in France (436 euro).

Western Europe: Inbound tourism
International Tourism Receipts (euro billion, current prices)

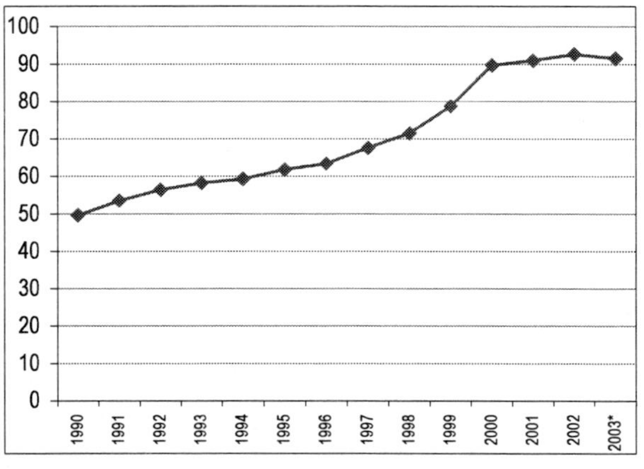


Source: World Tourism Organization (WTO) ©

Western Europe: Inbound tourism (share in regional total, %)
International arrivals & receipts

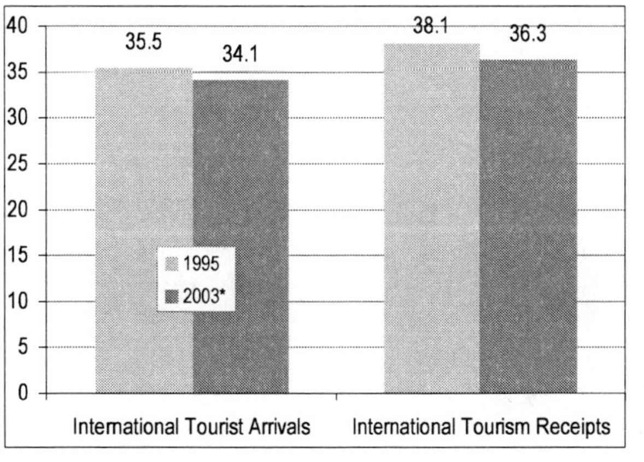


Source: World Tourism Organization (WTO) ©

**Western Europe**

**International Tourist Arrivals and Tourism Receipts by Country of Destination**

| | | | | | | | Market share | | | Growth rate | | | Average annual growth | |
|---|---|---|---|---|---|---|---|---|---|---|---|---|---|---|
| | | **1990** | **1995** | **2000** | **2002** | **2003*** | **1995** | **2000** | **2003*** | **01/00** | **02/01** | **03*/02** | **'90-'95** | **'95-'00** |
| | **Series** | **International Tourist Arrivals (1000)** | | | | | | | **%** | | | **%** | | **%** |
| **Western Europe** | | **108,627** | **112,184** | **139,659** | **137,961** | **136,070** | **100** | **100** | **100** | **-2.7** | **1.6** | **-1.4** | **0.6** | **4.5** |
| Austria | TCE | 19,011 | 17,173 | 17,982 | 18,611 | 19,078 | 15.3 | 12.9 | 14.0 | 1.1 | 2.4 | 2.5 | -2.0 | 0.9 |
| Belgium | TCE | .. | 5,560 | 6,457 | 6,720 | 6,690 | 5.0 | 4.6 | 4.9 | -0.1 | 4.2 | -0.4 | | 3.0 |
| France | TF | 52,497 | 60,033 | 77,190 | 77,012 | 75,048 | 53.5 | 55.3 | 55.2 | -2.6 | 2.4 | -2.6 | 2.7 | 5.2 |
| Germany | TCE | 17,045 | 14,838 | 18,992 | 17,959 | 18,392 | 13.2 | 13.6 | 13.5 | -6.0 | 0.6 | 2.4 | -2.7 | 5.1 |
| Liechtenstein | THS | 78 | 59 | 62 | 49 | 49 | 0.1 | 0.0 | 0.0 | -8.9 | -13.7 | 0.6 | -5.4 | 1.0 |
| Luxembourg | TCE | 820 | 768 | 852 | 885 | 867 | 0.7 | 0.6 | 0.6 | -1.1 | 5.0 | -2.0 | -1.3 | 2.1 |
| Monaco | THS | 245 | 233 | 300 | 263 | 235 | 0.2 | 0.2 | 0.2 | -10.0 | -2.7 | -10.5 | -1.0 | 5.2 |
| Netherlands | TCE | 5,795 | 6,574 | 10,003 | 9,595 | 9,181 | 5.9 | 7.2 | 6.7 | -5.0 | 1.0 | -4.3 | 2.6 | 8.8 |
| Switzerland | TC | 7,963 | 6,946 | 7,821 | 6,868 | 6,530 | 6.2 | 5.6 | 4.8 | -4.7 | -7.9 | -4.9 | -2.7 | 2.4 |
| | | **International Tourism Receipts (euro million)** | | | | | | | **%** | | | **%** | | **%** |
| **Western Europe** | | **49,562** | **61,769** | **89,664** | **92,660** | **91,572** | **100** | **100** | **100** | **1.4** | **1.9** | **-1.2** | **4.5** | **7.7** |
| Austria | | 10,536 | 9,883 | 10,752 | 11,886 | 12,436 | 16.0 | 12.0 | 13.6 | 6.5 | 3.8 | 4.6 | -1.3 | 1.7 |
| Belgium | | .. | 3,477 | 7,137 | 7,287 | 7,187 | 5.6 | 8.0 | 7.8 | 8.0 | -5.5 | -1.4 | | 15.5 |
| France | | 15,850 | 21,091 | 33,543 | 34,622 | 32,742 | 34.1 | 37.4 | 35.8 | 1.1 | 2.1 | -5.4 | 5.9 | 9.7 |
| Germany | | 11,187 | 13,762 | 20,179 | 20,060 | 20,318 | 22.3 | 22.5 | 22.2 | -0.7 | 0.1 | 1.3 | 4.2 | 8.0 |
| Luxembourg | | .. | 1,296 | 1,825 | 2,310 | 2,469 | 2.1 | 2.0 | 2.7 | 8.9 | 16.2 | 6.9 | | 7.1 |
| Netherlands | | 3,263 | 5,029 | 7,792 | 8,154 | 8,176 | 8.1 | 8.7 | 8.9 | -3.9 | 8.9 | 0.3 | 9.0 | 9.2 |
| Switzerland | | 5,820 | 7,232 | 8,435 | 8,342 | 8,243 | 11.7 | 9.4 | 9.0 | -0.7 | -0.4 | -1.2 | 4.4 | 3.1 |
| | | **Receipts per Arrival (euro)** | | | | | | | | | | **%** | | **%** |
| **Western Europe** | | **456** | **551** | **642** | **672** | **673** | | | | **4.3** | **0.3** | **0.2** | **3.8** | **3.1** |
| Austria | | 554 | 575 | 598 | 639 | 652 | | | | 5.4 | 1.4 | 2.1 | 0.8 | 0.8 |
| Belgium | | | 625 | 1,105 | 1,084 | 1,074 | | | | 8.1 | -9.2 | -0.9 | | 12.1 |
| France | | 302 | 351 | 435 | 450 | 436 | | | | 3.7 | -0.3 | -3.0 | 3.1 | 4.3 |
| Germany | | 656 | 927 | 1,062 | 1,117 | 1,105 | | | | 5.6 | -0.4 | -1.1 | 7.2 | 2.8 |
| Luxembourg | | | 1,687 | 2,143 | 2,610 | 2,848 | | | | 10.0 | 10.7 | 9.1 | | 4.9 |
| Netherlands | | 563 | 765 | 779 | 850 | 891 | | | | 1.2 | 7.8 | 4.8 | 6.3 | 0.4 |
| Switzerland | | 731 | 1,041 | 1,079 | 1,215 | 1,262 | | | | 4.2 | 8.1 | 3.9 | 7.3 | 0.7 |

Source: World Tourism Organization (WTO) © (Data as collected by WTO December 2004)

# II.2.3 Central and Eastern Europe

*International tourist arrivals*

In 2003 Central and Eastern Europe recorded nearly 68 million international tourist arrivals, corresponding to an increase of 3.7 per cent over an already positive 2002 (+3%), and in spite of the slight declines felt by the two main destinations, Hungary (-1%) and Poland (-2%) and of the rather flat results of the Russian Federation (+0.9%). In the past years the region has been steadily consolidating the recovery initiated after the 1998 and 1999 setbacks under the influence of the nearby Kosovo conflict and the impact of the Russian financial crisis, and is now on the growing path for the fourth consecutive years.

Tourist arrivals in subregion are still dominated by Hungary (16 million), Poland (14 million) and the Russian Federation (8 million), which represent on the overall more than 55 per cent of all arrivals. In the past years, Hungary and Poland have been gradually loosing market share in favour of other destinations such as Bulgaria. In a second line, with over 4 million arrivals are Ukraine (6 million in 2002), the Czech Republic (5 million) and Bulgaria (4 milllion), which passed the 4 million record for the first time in 2003. The Czech Republic, which had seen its tourist arrivals decreasing by nearly 12 per cent in 2002 under the effects of severe floods, recovered in 2003 with an 11 per cent increase, but is still slightly below its 2001 record (5.2 million).

Central/Eastern Europe: Inbound tourism
International Tourist Arrivals (million)

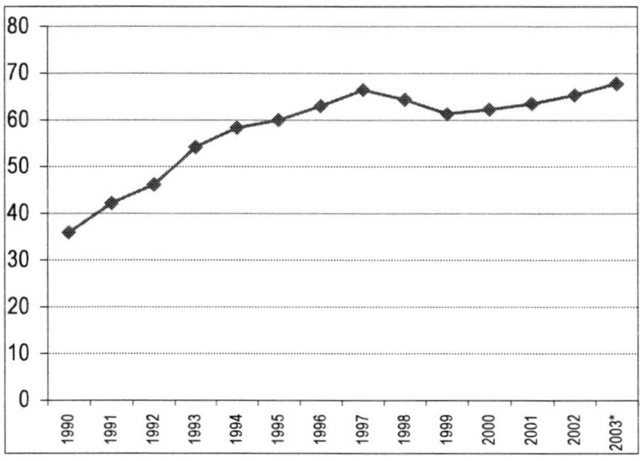


Source: World Tourism Organization (WTO) ©

Central/Eastern Europe: Inbound tourism
International Tourist Arrivals (change over previous year, %)

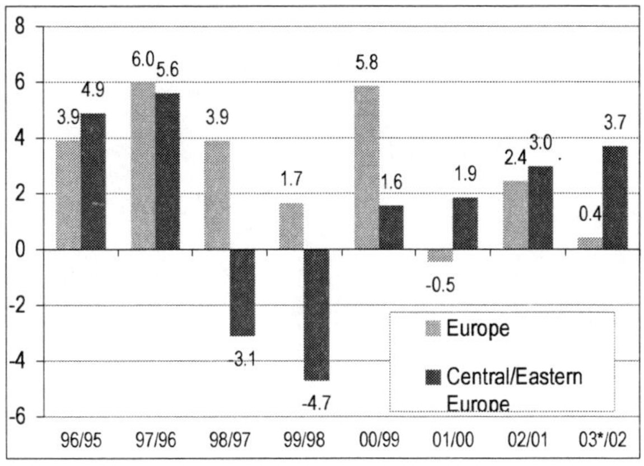


Source: World Tourism Organization (WTO) ©

*International tourism receipts*

In 2003 international tourism receipts in Central and Eastern Europe reached nearly 20 billion euro, or some 1.7 million less than in 2002 (-4% as computed in local currencies, constant prices) as all the major destinations suffered setbacks.

Notwithstanding the decline of almost 10 per cent, the Russian Federation was still the top earner of the subregion with receipts of nearly 4 billion euro and a market share of 20 per cent. The country in 2002 took the leading position occupied previously by Poland (3.6

billion). The Czech Republic and Hungary both reported receipts slightly over 3 billion. Except for Bulgaria, with 1.5 billion euro receipts, all other destinations account for values of less than one billion euro.

Performances of the destinations in the subregion in 2003 ranged from significant decreases, occurring, as already happened in 2002, in some of the major key players – Hungary (-12%) and Poland (-21%) – to good results in "emerging destinations" such as Latvia (+15%) and Lithuania (+6%). It is however important to stress again that such percentage changes are influenced by the exchange rate factor.

Central and Eastern Europe recorded receipts per arrival of 291 euro in 2003, the lowest figure of Europe and well below the average of the region (632 euro). Significantly higher than the subregional average values were registered by Belarus (3,671 euro), the Republic of Moldova (2,442 euro), Czech Republic (619 euro) and Slovakia (551 euro), while the lowest values were reported by Uzbekistan (184 euro) and Romania (106 euro).

Central/Eastern Europe: Inbound tourism
International Tourism Receipts (euro billion, current prices)

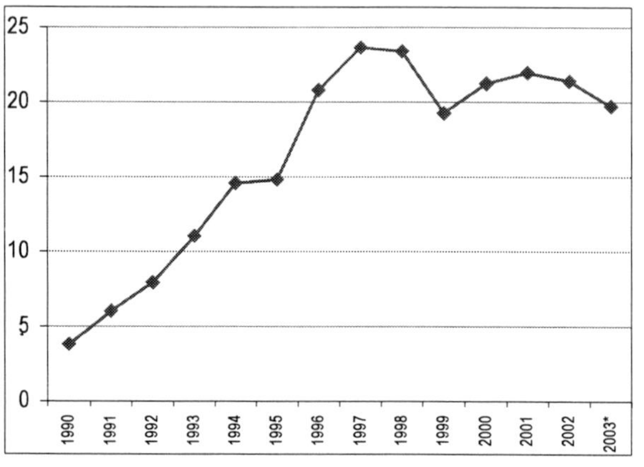


Source: World Tourism Organization (WTO) ©

Central/Eastern Europe: Inbound tourism (share in regional total,
International arrivals & receipts %)

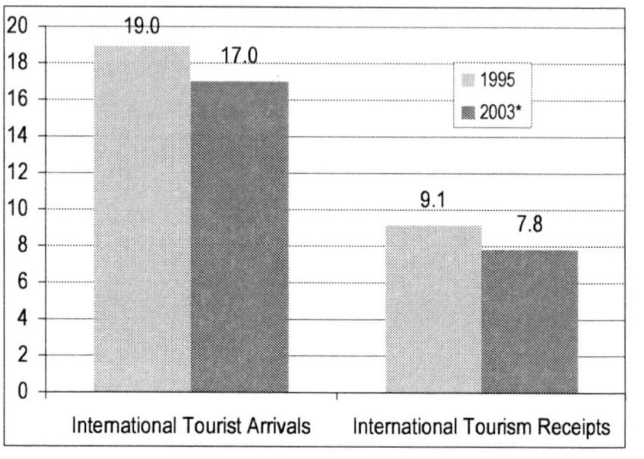


Source: World Tourism Organization (WTO) ©

**Central and Eastern Europe**
**International Tourist Arrivals and Tourism Receipts by Country of Destination**

| | | | | | | | Market share | | | Growth rate | | | Average annual growth | |
|---|---|---|---|---|---|---|---|---|---|---|---|---|---|---|
| | | 1990 | 1995 | 2000 | 2002 | 2003* | 1995 | 2000 | 2003* | 01/00 | 02/01 | 03*/02 | '90-'95 | '95-'00 |
| | Series | International Tourist Arrivals (1000) | | | | | | | % | | | % | | % |
| **Central and Eastern Europe** | | **35,876** | **59,993** | **62,297** | **65,341** | **67,763** | **100** | **100** | **100** | **1.9** | **3.0** | **3.7** | **10.8** | **0.8** |
| Armenia | TCE | .. | 12 | 45 | 162 | 206 | 0.0 | 0.1 | 0.3 | 173.9 | 31.5 | 27.1 | | 30.3 |
| Azerbaijan | TF | .. | 93 | 681 | 834 | .. | 0.2 | 1.1 | | 12.6 | 8.8 | | | 48.9 |
| Belarus | TF | .. | 161 | 60 | .. | 64 | 0.3 | 0.1 | 0.1 | 1.7 | | | | -17.9 |
| Bulgaria | TF | .. | 3,466 | 2,785 | 3,433 | 4,048 | 5.8 | 4.5 | 6.0 | 14.4 | 7.8 | 17.9 | | -4.3 |
| Czech Rep | TCE | .. | 3,381 | 4,666 | 4,579 | 5,076 | 5.6 | 7.5 | 7.5 | 11.3 | -11.8 | 10.8 | | 6.7 |
| Estonia | TF | .. | 530 | 1,220 | 1,362 | 1,462 | 0.9 | 2.0 | 2.2 | 8.2 | 3.2 | 7.3 | | 18.1 |
| Former U.S.S.R. | TF | 2,286 | .. | .. | .. | .. | | | | | | | | |
| Georgia | TF | .. | 85 | 387 | 298 | .. | 0.1 | 0.6 | | -21.9 | -1.2 | | | 35.4 |
| Hungary | VF/2 | 20,510 | 20,690 | 15,571 | 15,870 | 15,706 | 34.5 | 25.0 | 23.2 | -1.5 | 3.5 | -1.0 | 0.2 | -5.5 |
| Kazakhstan | TF | .. | .. | 1,471 | 2,832 | 2,410 | | 2.4 | 3.6 | 25.4 | 53.5 | -14.9 | | |
| Kyrgyzstan | TF | .. | 36 | 59 | 140 | .. | 0.1 | 0.1 | | 67.0 | 41.6 | | | 10.4 |
| Latvia | TF | .. | 539 | 509 | 848 | 971 | 0.9 | 0.8 | 1.4 | 16.1 | 43.5 | 14.5 | | -1.1 |
| Lithuania | TF | .. | 650 | 1,083 | 1,428 | 1,491 | 1.1 | 1.7 | 2.2 | 17.4 | 12.4 | 4.4 | | 10.7 |
| Poland | TF | .. | 19,215 | 17,400 | 13,980 | 13,720 | 32.0 | 27.9 | 20.2 | -13.8 | -6.8 | -1.9 | | -2.0 |
| Rep Moldova | TF | .. | 32 | 18 | 18 | 21 | 0.1 | 0.0 | 0.0 | -11.1 | 12.5 | 16.7 | | -10.9 |
| Romania | TF | 3,099 | 2,757 | 3,274 | 3,204 | 3,739 | 4.6 | 5.3 | 5.5 | 0.8 | -2.9 | 16.7 | -2.3 | 3.5 |
| Russian Federation | TF | .. | .. | 7,030 | 7,943 | 8,015 | | 11.3 | 11.8 | 5.3 | 7.3 | 0.9 | | |
| Slovakia | TCE | 822 | 903 | 1,053 | 1,399 | 1,387 | 1.5 | 1.7 | 2.0 | 15.8 | 14.7 | -0.9 | 1.9 | 3.1 |
| Tajikistan | TF | .. | .. | 4 | .. | .. | | 0.0 | | -7.9 | | | | |
| Turkmenistan | TF | .. | 218 | .. | .. | .. | 0.4 | | | | | | | |
| Ukraine | TF | .. | 3,716 | 4,406 | 6,326 | .. | 6.2 | 7.1 | | 31.4 | 9.2 | | | 3.5 |
| Uzbekistan | TF | .. | 92 | 302 | 332 | 231 | 0.2 | 0.5 | 0.3 | 14.2 | -3.9 | -30.3 | | 26.8 |
| | | International Tourism Receipts (euro million) | | | | | | | % | | | % | | % |
| **Central and Eastern Europe** | | **3,808** | **14,811** | **21,225** | **21,400** | **19,719** | **100** | **100** | **100** | **3.4** | **-2.5** | **-7.9** | **31.2** | **7.5** |
| Armenia | | .. | 1 | 41 | 67 | 65 | 0.0 | 0.2 | 0.3 | 76.4 | -8.2 | -3.1 | | 121.9 |
| Azerbaijan | | 179 | 54 | 68 | 54 | 51 | 0.4 | 0.3 | 0.3 | -29.6 | 12.3 | -4.9 | -21.5 | 5.0 |
| Belarus | | .. | 18 | 101 | 247 | 236 | 0.1 | 0.5 | 1.2 | 89.6 | 29.6 | -4.6 | | 41.8 |
| Bulgaria | | 251 | 362 | 1,163 | 1,220 | 1,466 | 2.4 | 5.5 | 7.4 | -7.5 | 13.5 | 20.1 | 7.6 | 26.3 |
| Czech Rep | | 329 | 2,202 | 3,219 | 3,135 | 3,144 | 14.9 | 15.2 | 15.9 | 7.7 | -9.6 | 0.3 | 46.3 | 7.9 |
| Estonia | | .. | 273 | 546 | 587 | 596 | 1.8 | 2.6 | 3.0 | 3.7 | 3.7 | 1.5 | | 14.9 |
| Georgia | | .. | .. | 105 | 133 | 130 | | 0.5 | 0.7 | 24.4 | 2.0 | -2.5 | | |
| Hungary | | 647 | 2,239 | 3,729 | 3,462 | 3,041 | 15.1 | 17.6 | 15.4 | 12.9 | -17.7 | -12.2 | 28.2 | 10.7 |
| Kazakhstan | | .. | 93 | 385 | 658 | 499 | 0.6 | 1.8 | 2.5 | 30.9 | 30.3 | -24.2 | | 32.8 |
| Kyrgyzstan | | .. | 4 | 16 | 38 | 42 | 0.0 | 0.1 | 0.2 | 65.0 | 42.1 | 11.5 | | 33.6 |
| Latvia | | .. | 15 | 142 | 170 | 196 | 0.1 | 0.7 | 1.0 | -5.5 | 27.1 | 15.3 | | 56.1 |
| Lithuania | | .. | 59 | 423 | 534 | 564 | 0.4 | 2.0 | 2.9 | 1.0 | 24.9 | 5.6 | | 48.4 |
| Poland | | 281 | 5,057 | 6,147 | 4,562 | 3,597 | 34.1 | 29.0 | 18.2 | -15.6 | -12.1 | -21.2 | 78.2 | 4.0 |
| Rep Moldova | | .. | 44 | 42 | 53 | 51 | 0.3 | 0.2 | 0.3 | 3.1 | 21.4 | -3.0 | | -0.6 |
| Romania | | 83 | 451 | 389 | 354 | 397 | 3.0 | 1.8 | 2.0 | 4.0 | -12.3 | 12.0 | 40.2 | -2.9 |
| Russian Federation | | .. | 3,297 | 3,714 | 4,407 | 3,980 | 22.3 | 17.5 | 20.2 | 7.4 | 10.5 | -9.7 | | 2.4 |
| Slovakia | | 55 | 476 | 469 | 778 | 765 | 3.2 | 2.2 | 3.9 | 52.7 | 8.8 | -1.8 | 54.0 | -0.3 |
| Tajikistan | | .. | .. | .. | 2 | 2 | | | 0.0 | | | -16.4 | | |
| Ukraine | | .. | 146 | 427 | 833 | 827 | 1.0 | 2.0 | 4.2 | 50.0 | 30.3 | -0.8 | | 23.9 |
| Uzbekistan | | .. | .. | 68 | 72 | 42 | | 0.3 | 0.2 | 17.9 | -10.5 | -41.0 | | |

Continued on the next page.

**Central and Eastern Europe**
**International Tourist Arrivals and Tourism Receipts by Country of Destination**

| | 1990 | 1995 | 2000 | 2002 | 2003* | Market share 1995 | Market share 2000 | Market share 2003* | Growth rate 01/00 | Growth rate 02/01 | Growth rate 03*/02 | Average annual growth '90-'95 | Average annual growth '95-'00 |
|---|---|---|---|---|---|---|---|---|---|---|---|---|---|
| | Receipts per Arrival (euro) | | | | | | | | | | % | | % |
| **Central and Eastern Europe** | **106** | **247** | **341** | **328** | **291** | | | | **1.5** | **-5.3** | **-11.2** | **18.4** | **6.7** |
| Armenia | | 64 | 914 | 411 | 313 | | | | -35.6 | -30.2 | -23.8 | | 70.4 |
| Azerbaijan | | 575 | 100 | 65 | | | | | -37.5 | 3.3 | | | -29.5 |
| Belarus | | 109 | 1,678 | | 3,671 | | | | 86.5 | | | | 72.7 |
| Bulgaria | | 104 | 418 | 355 | 362 | | | | -19.2 | 5.3 | 1.9 | | 32.0 |
| Czech Rep | | 651 | 690 | 685 | 619 | | | | -3.3 | 2.6 | -9.5 | | 1.2 |
| Estonia | | 515 | 447 | 431 | 408 | | | | -4.1 | 0.5 | -5.4 | | -2.8 |
| Georgia | | | 271 | 446 | | | | | 59.3 | 3.3 | | | |
| Hungary | 32 | 108 | 239 | 218 | 194 | | | | 14.6 | -20.5 | -11.3 | 28.0 | 17.2 |
| Kazakhstan | | | 262 | 232 | 207 | | | | 4.4 | -15.1 | -10.9 | | |
| Kyrgyzstan | | 106 | 275 | 273 | | | | | -1.2 | 0.3 | | | 21.0 |
| Latvia | | 28 | 279 | 201 | 202 | | | | -18.6 | -11.4 | 0.7 | | 57.9 |
| Lithuania | | 91 | 391 | 374 | 378 | | | | -13.9 | 11.2 | 1.1 | | 34.0 |
| Poland | | 263 | 353 | 326 | 262 | | | | -2.1 | -5.6 | -19.7 | | 6.1 |
| Rep Moldova | | 1,362 | 2,346 | 2,938 | 2,442 | | | | 16.0 | 7.9 | -16.9 | | 11.5 |
| Romania | 27 | 164 | 119 | 111 | 106 | | | | 3.2 | -9.7 | -4.0 | 43.5 | -6.2 |
| Russian Federation | | | 528 | 555 | 497 | | | | 2.0 | 2.9 | -10.5 | | |
| Slovakia | 67 | 527 | 445 | 556 | 551 | | | | 31.9 | -5.2 | -0.9 | 51.1 | -3.3 |
| Tajikistan | | | | | | | | | | | | | |
| Ukraine | | 39 | 97 | 132 | | | | | 14.1 | 19.2 | | | 19.8 |
| Uzbekistan | | | 226 | 217 | 184 | | | | 3.2 | -6.9 | -15.3 | | |

Source: World Tourism Organization (WTO) © (Data as collected by WTO December 2004)

## II.2.4 Southern Europe

*International tourist arrivals*

Southern Europe is the second most important subregion in the world and in Europe regarding international tourist arrivals, with a 19 per cent of world share and 33 per cent of the overall regional volume. In 2003 it received over 131 million arrivals, which represents a stagnation over 2002 results (-0.4%).

In spite of being a subregion constituted by mature destinations, Southern Europe experienced a substantial development in recent years with an impressive average annual growth rate of almost 7 per cent between 1995 and 2000. Almost all destinations of the region shared this growth, and particularly the more developed destinations, such as Spain and Italy, which recorded average annual growth rates of 6.5 and 5.8 per cent respectively in this same period. Simultaneously, some of the new countries that emerged after the disintegration of the former Socialist Republic of Yugoslavia are firm on their way to build or rebuild their tourism industry, in particular Croatia and Slovenia. However, growth to Southern Europe has slowed down in the last three years. In 2001 and 2002, and in spite of the overall unfavourable climate, arrivals grew by 2 per cent as the destinations in the area were seen by many as "safe havens". In 2003 the strength of the euro and the increased competition from other subregions, lead to declines or to modest results in the main subregional destinations. While international tourist arrivals to Portugal went no further than 0.5 per cent increase, Spain (-1%), Italy (-0.5%) and Greece (-1.5%) reported negative results. On the other hand, significant gains were still obtained by southern non-euro zone destinations, such as Croatia (+7%) and Slovenia (+6%).

Southern Europe: Inbound tourism
International Tourist Arrivals (million)

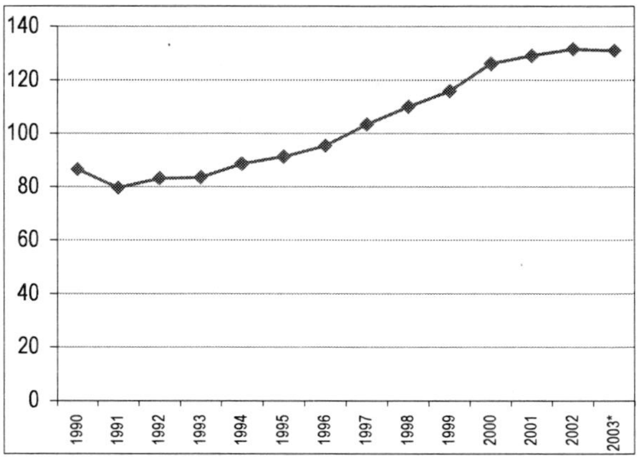


Source: World Tourism Organization (WTO) ©

Southern Europe: Inbound tourism
International Tourist Arrivals (change over previous year, %)

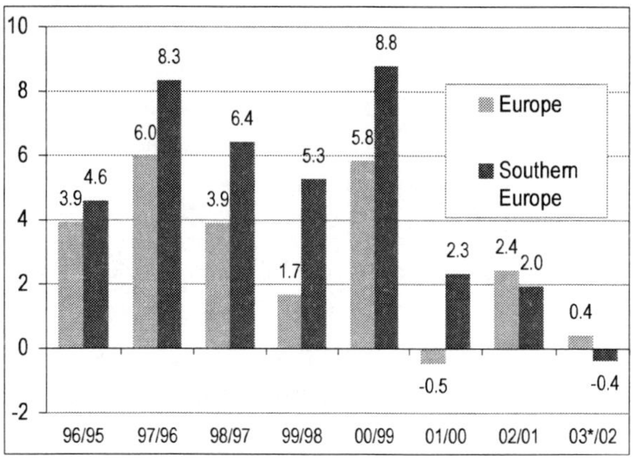


Source: World Tourism Organization (WTO) ©

In 2003, Spain holds the leading position by a distance, with a 40 per cent market share of all arrivals to Southern Europe and an overall volume of almost 52 million arrivals, followed by Italy with almost 40 arrivals and a 30 per cent market share. The third and the fourth positions belong to Greece (11% share) and to Portugal (9% share), both with over 11 million arrivals. Furthermore, it is worth noting the position of Croatia, currently with 7.4 million tourist arrivals. The country recovered strongly in recent years from the strong setback of the first half of the 90's and was able to post an average growth rate of 22 per cent between 1995 and 2003.

*International tourism receipts*

Receipts for international tourism in Southern Europe increased by a bit more than 1 billion euro and totalled 88 billion euro in 2003. In local currencies and constant prices (taking inflation into account), however, this result represented a slight decrease as compared to 2002 (-1.2%). The subregion holds a share of receipts that amounts to 35 per cent, which means that it is, together with Western Europe, responsible for more than 70 per cent of tourism receipts generated in Europe.

More than 85 per cent of tourism receipts in Southern Europe are generated in three countries: Spain accounting for 42 per cent (36.9 billion euro), Italy for 31 per cent (27.6 billion euro) and Greece for 11 per cent (9.5 billion euro). In 2003 Italy saw its tourism receipts decrease for the third year in a row, probably influenced by the continuing decrease in long-haul travel, in particular from the United States of America, and continues to lose market share (from 43% in 1995 to 31% in 2003). Other important earners are Portugal with a 7 per cent market share (6 billion euro) and Croatia representing a 6 per cent share (5.6 billion euro). Except for Slovenia (1.2 billion euro) and Malta (615 million euro), all other destinations reported results below the 500 million euro mark.

Southern Europe: Inbound tourism
International Tourism Receipts (euro billion, current prices)

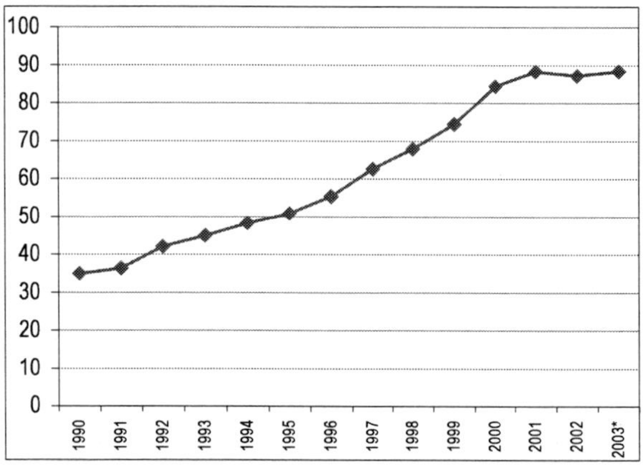


Source: World Tourism Organization (WTO) ©

Southern Europe: Inbound tourism (share in regional total, %)
International arrivals & receipts

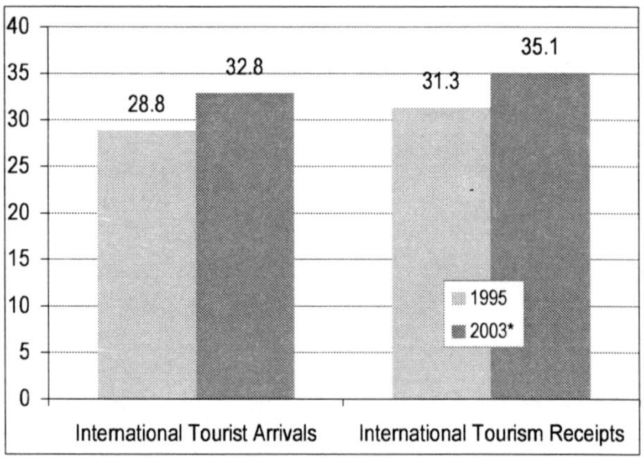


Source: World Tourism Organization (WTO) ©

In 2003, as it had already happen the previous year, some of the main destinations have suffered the impact of the decrease of high-yield long-haul traffic, the trading down by consumers, the general trend of pressure on prices and the drop of demand from Germany. International tourism receipts decreased in Greece (-8%) and in Italy (-3%), while they stagnated in Portugal (+0.7%). Spain was the only euro zone destination that managed to grow (+3.4%), recovering thus from the previous year's negative results (-2.1%). By contrast, Croatia did particularly well (+40% values computed in euro), and so did the smaller earners such as Serbia and Montenegro (+29%) and the Former Yugoslav Republic of Macedonia (+22%). In the case of "non-euro" countries these variations must nonetheless be taken with care as they might be to a higher or lesser extent be impacted by the appreciation of the euro in 2003.

Southern European destinations earned on average 675 euro per tourist arrival, positioning third on this indicator after East Mediterranean Europe (913 euro) and Northern Europe (783 euro). Highest receipts per arrivals were recorded in Albania (11,255 euro), Bosnia and Herzegovina (1,256 euro), Slovenia (864 euro) and Croatia (761 euro).

**Southern Europe**
**International Tourist Arrivals and Tourism Receipts by Country of Destination**

| | | | | | | | Market share | | | Growth rate | | | Average annual growth | |
|---|---|---|---|---|---|---|---|---|---|---|---|---|---|---|
| | | 1990 | 1995 | 2000 | 2002 | 2003* | 1995 | 2000 | 2003* | 01/00 | 02/01 | 03*/02 | '90-'95 | '95-'00 |
| | Series | International Tourist Arrivals (1000) | | | | | | | % | | | % | | % |
| **Southern Europe** | | **86,484** | **91,280** | **126,067** | **131,529** | **131,043** | **100** | **100** | **100** | **2.3** | **2.0** | **-0.4** | **1.1** | **6.7** |
| Albania | THS | 30 | 40 | 32 | 36 | 41 | 0.0 | 0.0 | 0.0 | 6.3 | 5.9 | 13.9 | 5.9 | -4.4 |
| Andorra | TF | .. | .. | 2,949 | 3,387 | 3,138 | | 2.3 | 2.4 | 19.2 | -3.7 | -7.4 | | |
| Bosnia & Herzg | TCE | .. | .. | 171 | 160 | 165 | | 0.1 | 0.1 | -19.0 | 15.3 | 3.6 | | |
| Croatia | TCE | .. | 1,485 | 5,831 | 6,944 | 7,409 | 1.6 | 4.6 | 5.7 | 12.2 | 6.1 | 6.7 | | 31.5 |
| F.Yug.Rp.Macedonia | TCE | .. | 147 | 224 | 123 | 158 | 0.2 | 0.2 | 0.1 | -55.8 | 24.2 | 28.3 | | 8.8 |
| Greece | TF | 8,873 | 10,130 | 13,096 | 14,180 | 13,969 | 11.1 | 10.4 | 10.7 | 7.3 | 0.9 | -1.5 | 2.7 | 5.3 |
| Italy | TF | 26,679 | 31,052 | 41,181 | 39,799 | 39,604 | 34.0 | 32.7 | 30.2 | -3.9 | 0.6 | -0.5 | 3.1 | 5.8 |
| Malta | TF | 872 | 1,116 | 1,216 | 1,134 | 1,127 | 1.2 | 1.0 | 0.9 | -3.0 | -3.9 | -0.6 | 5.1 | 1.7 |
| Portugal | TF | 8,020 | 9,511 | 12,097 | 11,644 | 11,707 | 10.4 | 9.6 | 8.9 | 0.6 | -4.3 | 0.5 | 3.5 | 4.9 |
| San Marino | THS | 45 | 28 | 43 | 45 | 41 | 0.0 | 0.0 | 0.0 | 14.0 | -8.2 | -8.9 | -9.1 | 9.0 |
| Serbia & Montenegro | TCE | .. | 228 | 239 | 448 | 481 | 0.2 | 0.2 | 0.4 | 46.9 | 27.6 | 7.4 | | 0.9 |
| Slovenia | TC | .. | 732 | 1,090 | 1,302 | 1,373 | 0.8 | 0.9 | 1.0 | 11.8 | 6.8 | 5.5 | | 8.3 |
| Spain | TF | 34,085 | 34,920 | 47,898 | 52,327 | 51,830 | 38.3 | 38.0 | 39.6 | 4.6 | 4.5 | -1.0 | 0.5 | 6.5 |
| | | International Tourism Receipts (euro million) | | | | | | | % | | | % | | % |
| **Southern Europe** | | **34,919** | **50,834** | **84,326** | **87,169** | **88,409** | **100** | **100** | **100** | **4.7** | **-1.3** | **1.4** | **7.8** | **10.7** |
| Albania | | 3 | 50 | 421 | 515 | 461 | 0.1 | 0.5 | 0.5 | 18.2 | 3.4 | -10.4 | 73.7 | 53.3 |
| Bosnia & Herzg | | .. | .. | 179 | 203 | 208 | | 0.2 | 0.2 | 9.4 | 3.9 | 2.3 | | |
| Croatia | | | 1,031 | 2,986 | 4,030 | 5,636 | 2.0 | 3.5 | 6.4 | 24.7 | 8.2 | 39.9 | | 23.7 |
| F.Yug.Rp.Macedonia | | | 15 | 41 | 41 | 50 | 0.0 | 0.0 | 0.1 | -29.4 | 42.1 | 22.2 | | 23.1 |
| Greece | | 2,032 | 3,161 | 9,981 | 10,285 | 9,460 | 6.2 | 11.8 | 10.7 | 6.0 | -2.8 | -8.0 | 9.2 | 25.9 |
| Italy | | 12,924 | 21,965 | 29,767 | 28,420 | 27,601 | 43.2 | 35.3 | 31.2 | -3.1 | -1.4 | -2.9 | 11.2 | 6.3 |
| Malta | | 389 | 505 | 660 | 604 | 615 | 1.0 | 0.8 | 0.7 | -2.3 | -6.4 | 1.9 | 5.3 | 5.5 |
| Portugal | | 2,792 | 3,693 | 5,677 | 6,093 | 6,132 | 7.3 | 6.7 | 6.9 | 7.6 | -0.2 | 0.7 | 5.8 | 9.0 |
| Serbia & Montenegro | | .. | 32 | 32 | 103 | 133 | 0.1 | 0.0 | 0.1 | 85.6 | 70.1 | 29.3 | | 0.2 |
| Slovenia | | .. | 829 | 1,040 | 1,148 | 1,186 | 1.6 | 1.2 | 1.3 | 5.9 | 4.2 | 3.3 | | 4.7 |
| Spain | | 14,601 | 19,503 | 33,541 | 35,728 | 36,925 | 38.4 | 39.8 | 41.8 | 8.8 | -2.1 | 3.4 | 6.0 | 11.5 |
| | | Receipts per Arrival (euro) | | | | | | | | | | % | | % |
| **Southern Europe** | | **404** | **557** | **669** | **663** | **675** | | | | **2.3** | **-3.1** | **1.8** | **6.6** | **3.7** |
| Albania | | 105 | 1,242 | 13,162 | 14,306 | 11,255 | | | | 11.3 | -2.3 | -21.3 | 64.0 | 60.3 |
| Bosnia & Herzg | | | | 1,045 | 1,271 | 1,256 | | | | 35.0 | -9.9 | -1.2 | | |
| Croatia | | | 695 | 512 | 580 | 761 | | | | 11.1 | 2.0 | 31.1 | | -5.9 |
| F.Yug.Rp.Macedonia | | | 99 | 184 | 336 | 320 | | | | 59.7 | 14.4 | -4.8 | | 13.2 |
| Greece | | 229 | 312 | 762 | 725 | 677 | | | | -1.3 | -3.6 | -6.6 | 6.4 | 19.6 |
| Italy | | 484 | 707 | 723 | 714 | 697 | | | | 0.8 | -2.0 | -2.4 | 7.9 | 0.4 |
| Malta | | 447 | 453 | 543 | 533 | 546 | | | | 0.7 | -2.6 | 2.5 | 0.3 | 3.7 |
| Portugal | | 348 | 388 | 469 | 523 | 524 | | | | 7.0 | 4.2 | 0.1 | 2.2 | 3.9 |
| Serbia & Montenegro | | | 141 | 136 | 229 | 276 | | | | 26.4 | 33.3 | 20.4 | | -0.7 |
| Slovenia | | | 1,132 | 954 | 882 | 864 | | | | -5.3 | -2.4 | -2.0 | | -3.4 |
| Spain | | 428 | 559 | 700 | 683 | 712 | | | | 4.1 | -6.3 | 4.3 | 5.4 | 4.6 |

Source: World Tourism Organization (WTO) © (Data as collected by WTO December 2004)

## II.2.5 East Mediterranean Europe

*International tourist arrivals*

In 2003 East Mediterranean Europe continued the growth path gained back in 2002 and achieved the best performance in Europe, significantly above the region's average 0.4 per cent increase. International tourist arrivals reached nearly 17 million, which represents a 4 per cent increase over 2002.

East Mediterranean Europe: Inbound tourism
International Tourist Arrivals (million)

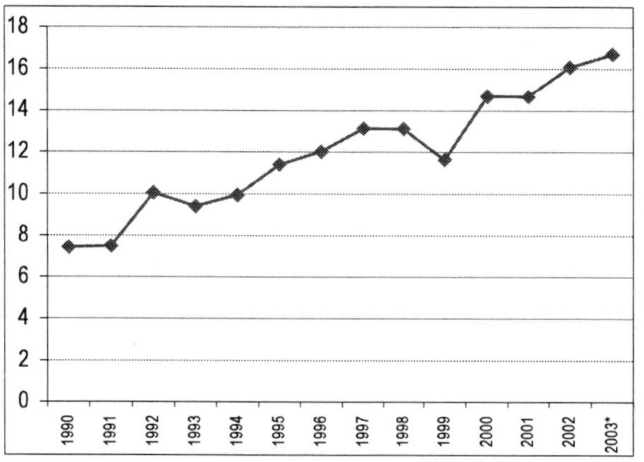


Source: World Tourism Organization (WTO) ©

East Mediterranean Europe: Inbound tourism
International Tourist Arrivals (change over previous year, %)

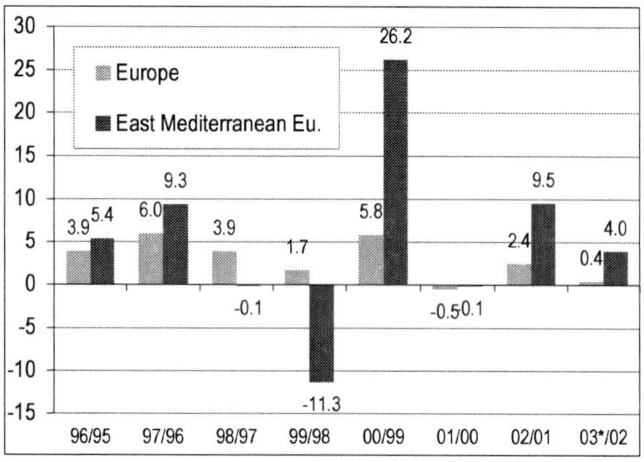


Source: World Tourism Organization (WTO) ©

This result is mainly attributable to Turkey's 4 per cent growth due to its relative importance in the subregion (80% market share). Between 1995 and 2000 tourist arrivals to Turkey grew at an average rate of 6 per cent a year, and in 2001, in spite of the events of 11th September, the country still recorded a significant 13 per cent increase. In 2003, though Turkey still posted particularly positive results, growth slowed down as compared to the double digit rate of 2001 and 2002. Further growth in the subregion has been offset in recent years by the sharp decrease of arrivals to Israel due to the Israeli-Palestinian conflict. Nevertheless, after losing almost two-thirds of its international tourist arrivals in 2001 and 2002, Israel reported a 23 per cent increase in 2003. International tourist arrivals were negative for the second consecutive year in Cyprus, which in 2003 lost almost 5 per cent.

*International tourism receipts*

East Mediterranean Europe earned 15.3 billion euro in international tourism receipts in 2003, corresponding to a significant 11 per cent drop over 2002, as computed in local currencies, constant prices. All the destinations in the subregion saw their receipts, computed in euro, decline: -16 per cent in Israel, -11 per cent in Cyprus and -7 per cent in Turkey.

Expressed in receipts per arrival, East Mediterranean Europe earned 913 euro, with Israel reporting the highest value (1,695 euro) and Cyprus the lowest (773 euro).

East Mediterranean Europe: Inbound tourism
International Tourism Receipts (euro billion, current prices)

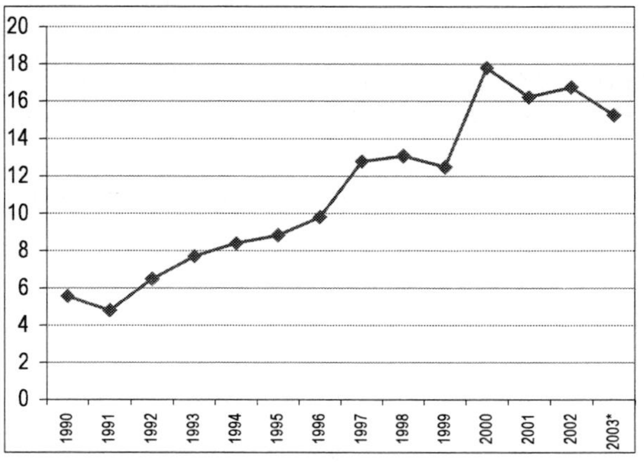


Source: World Tourism Organization (WTO) ©

East Mediterranean Europe (share in regional total, %)
International arrivals & receipts

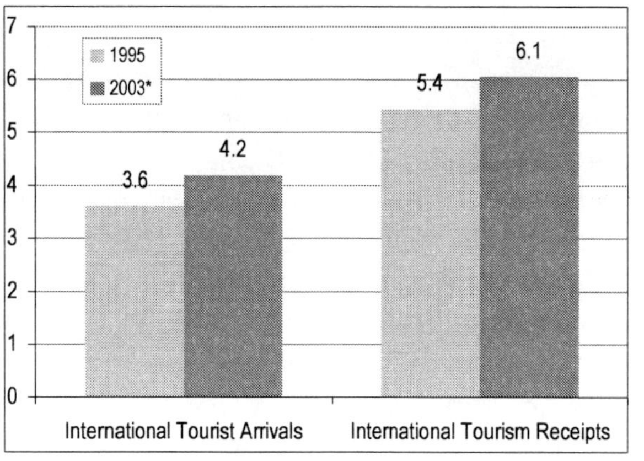


Source: World Tourism Organization (WTO) ©

**East Mediterranean Europe**
**International Tourist Arrivals and Tourism Receipts by Country of Destination**

| | | | | | | | Market share | | | Growth rate | | | Average annual growth | |
|---|---|---|---|---|---|---|---|---|---|---|---|---|---|---|
| | | 1990 | 1995 | 2000 | 2002 | 2003* | 1995 | 2000 | 2003* | 01/00 | 02/01 | 03*/02 | '90-'95 | '95-'00 |
| | Series | International Tourist Arrivals (1000) | | | | | | | % | | | % | | % |
| **East Mediterranean Europe** | | **7,423** | **11,398** | **14,689** | **16,070** | **16,707** | **100** | **100** | **100** | **-0.1** | **9.5** | **4.0** | **9.0** | **5.2** |
| Cyprus | TF | 1,561 | 2,100 | 2,686 | 2,418 | 2,303 | 18.4 | 18.3 | 13.8 | 0.4 | -10.3 | -4.8 | 6.1 | 5.0 |
| Israel | TF | 1,063 | 2,215 | 2,417 | 862 | 1,063 | 19.4 | 16.5 | 6.4 | -50.5 | -27.9 | 23.4 | 15.8 | 1.8 |
| Turkey | TF | 4,799 | 7,083 | 9,586 | 12,790 | 13,341 | 62.1 | 65.3 | 79.9 | 12.5 | 18.6 | 4.3 | 8.1 | 6.2 |
| | | International Tourism Receipts (euro million) | | | | | | | % | | | % | | % |
| **East Mediterranean Europe** | | **5,536** | **8,827** | **17,778** | **16,749** | **15,255** | **100** | **100** | **100** | **-8.7** | **3.2** | **-8.9** | **9.8** | **15.0** |
| Cyprus | | 988 | 1,374 | 2,098 | 2,006 | 1,781 | 15.6 | 11.8 | 11.7 | 6.7 | -10.4 | -11.2 | 6.8 | 8.8 |
| Israel | | 1,096 | 2,288 | 4,411 | 2,156 | 1,803 | 25.9 | 24.8 | 11.8 | -37.7 | -21.6 | -16.4 | 15.9 | 14.0 |
| Turkey | | 2,533 | 3,790 | 8,268 \| | 12,586 | 11,672 | 42.9 | 46.5 | 76.5 | | 12.0 | -7.3 | 8.4 | 16.9 |
| | | Receipts per Arrival (euro) | | | | | | | | | | % | | % |
| **East Mediterranean Europe** | | **746** | **774** | **1,210** | **1,042** | **913** | | | | **-8.6** | **-5.8** | **-12.4** | **0.8** | **9.3** |
| Cyprus | | 633 | 654 | 781 | 830 | 773 | | | | 6.3 | -0.1 | -6.8 | 0.7 | 3.6 |
| Israel | | 1,031 | 1,033 | 1,825 | 2,502 | 1,695 | | | | 26.0 | 8.8 | -32.2 | 0.0 | 12.1 |
| Turkey | | 528 | 535 | 862 | 984 | 875 | | | | 20.9 | -5.6 | -11.1 | 0.3 | 10.0 |

Source: World Tourism Organization (WTO) © (Data as collected by WTO December 2004)

# II.3 Tourism Trends in Mediterranean Destinations

In 2002, the Mediterranean still posted a 3 per cent growth in spite of a difficult beginning in the first months of the year, when the majority of destinations saw their tourist arrivals plunge under the effects of 11th September. In fact, and regardless of the geopolitical climate and economic slowdown in some of its important markets such as Germany, results were overall positive partly just because the Mediterranean benefited from the fact that major source markets are near and that there is a long tradition and loyal clientele that is very familiar with the various destination countries. In 2003, however, tourism in the Mediterranean, which includes a group of twenty-four countries engaged under the diverse influences of Europe, Africa and the Middle East, was marked by the sign of stagnation. This important tourism area, which holds 35 per cent of the world's international tourist arrivals (242 million), reports a slight 0.2 per cent decline over the previous year, as most of the major destinations obtained negative or rather feeble results.

International tourism earnings showed an even more unfavourable evolution. The strength of the euro, along with an overall trend for increased pressure on prices which is particularly strong in the area as destinations are facing growing competition –among them and from other world key destinations such as the Caribbean– and are strongly influenced by major tour operators, lead international tourism receipts in the region to decrease, as expressed in euro at current prices, by 2 per cent to a total of 147 billion euro.

**Mediterranean: tourism results 2003**

International Tourist Arrivals:
242 million

International Tourism Receipts:
US$ 167 billion / 147 billion euro

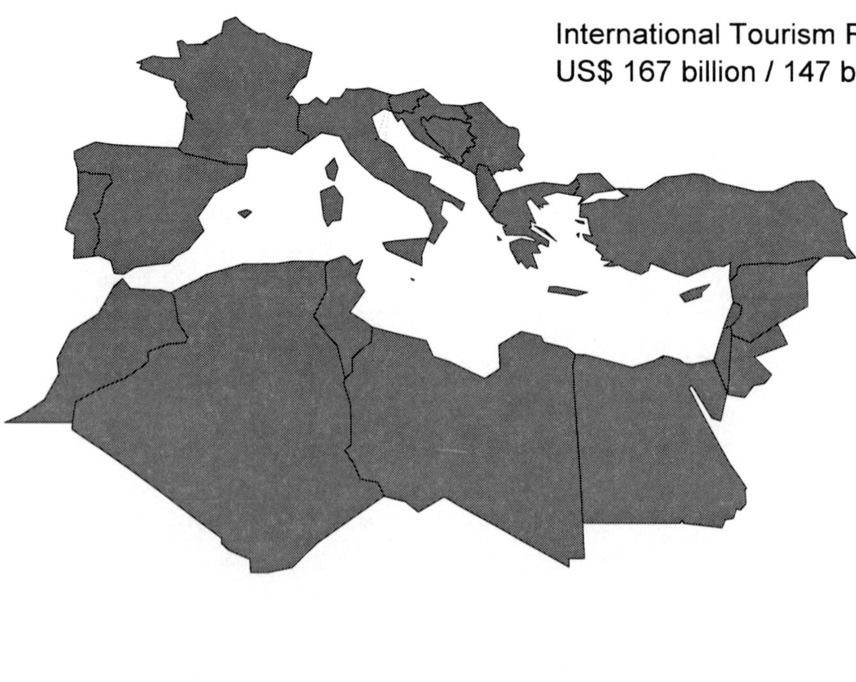

*International Tourist Arrivals*

In 2003 tourist arrivals to the Mediterranean maintained almost the same level of 2002 (-0.2%), attaining a total volume of 242 million, as most of the major destinations posted negative results or just equalled the ones of the previous year.

Mediterranean: Inbound tourism
International Tourist Arrivals (million)

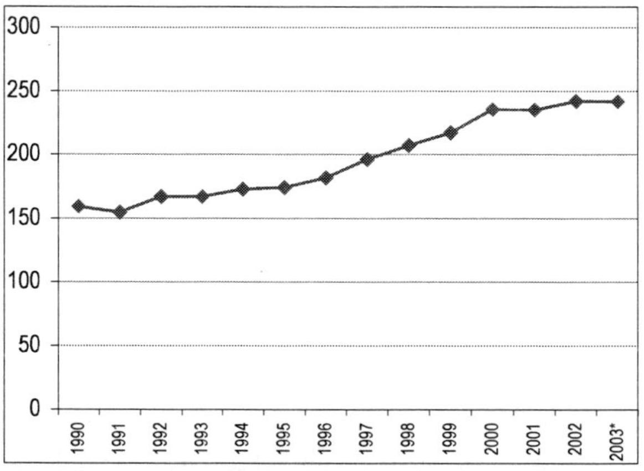


Source: World Tourism Organization (WTO) ©

Mediterranean: Inbound tourism
International Tourist Arrivals (change over previous year, %)

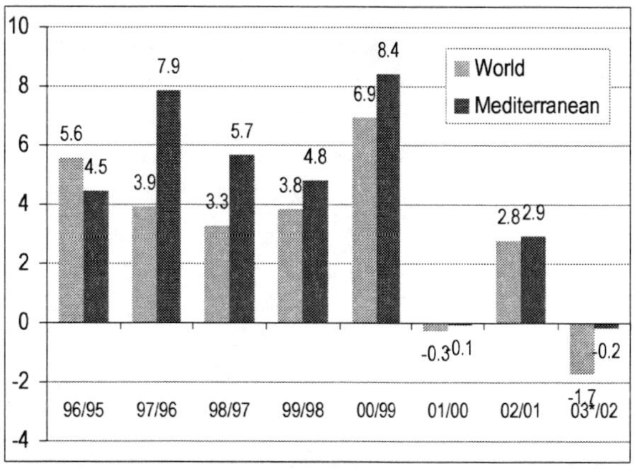


Source: World Tourism Organization (WTO) ©

While the decline in long-haul traffic from the Americas and from Asia and the Pacific, under the spectre of the war in Iraq and of SARS, affected in particular the major destinations such as France (-2.6%) and Italy (-0.5%), the strength of the euro determined some changes in the traditional summer traffic from Northern to Southern Europe. The 'sun and sea' destinations in the euro area (Portugal, Greece, Spain, and as mentioned, France and Italy) posted negative or modest results. Tourist arrivals decreased in Greece (-1.5%) and in Spain (-1%), while in Portugal growth was almost nil (+0.5%). On the other hand, the "so called" emerging European destinations outside the euro area, and the destinations of the Middle East and of North Africa, benefited from a favourable exchange rate situation. Arrivals grew at an exceptional 17 per cent rate in Egypt, 7 per cent in Croatia, and 6 per cent in Slovenia and in Morocco.

The Mediterranean has exceeded worldwide results since 1997, even in the difficult past three years. Although the Mediterranean incorporates a number of significantly mature destinations, its annual growth rate in the period 1995-2000 reached more than 6 per cent, driven not only by the exceptional performances of the 'emerging destinations' (32% a year in Croatia and 8% in Slovenia) but also by the relatively good results of destinations such as Spain (7% a year on average), Italy (6%) or France (5%).

In spite of the emergency of new destinations, the main share of arrivals in the region continues to belong to France, Spain and Italy, which together accounted for nearly 70 per cent of all tourist arrivals.

In 2003, best growth rates occurred in Israel (+23%), which is finally recovering from the exceptional declines of the two previous years (-50% and -28% in 2001 and 2002 respectively), in Algeria (+18%) and in Egypt (+17%).

**Mediterranean**

**International Tourist Arrivals and Tourism Receipts by Country of Destination**

| | | | | | | | Market share | | | Growth rate | | | Average annual growth | |
|---|---|---|---|---|---|---|---|---|---|---|---|---|---|---|
| | | 1990 | 1995 | 2000 | 2002 | 2003* | 1995 | 2000 | 2003* | 01/00 | 02/01 | 03*/02 | '90-'95 | '95-'00 |
| | Series | International Tourist Arrivals (1000) | | | | | | | % | | | % | | % |
| **Mediterranean** | | **159,021** | **174,024** | **235,434** | **242,203** | **241,833** | **100** | **100** | **100** | **-0.1** | **2.9** | **-0.2** | **1.8** | **6.2** |
| Portugal | TF | 8,020 | 9,511 | 12,097 | 11,644 | 11,707 | 5.5 | 5.1 | 4.8 | 0.6 | -4.3 | 0.5 | 3.5 | 4.9 |
| Spain | TF | 34,085\| | 34,920 | 47,898 | 52,327 | 51,830 | 20.1 | 20.3 | 21.4 | 4.6 | 4.5 | -1.0 | | 6.5 |
| France | TF | 52,497 | 60,033 | 77,190 | 77,012 | 75,048 | 34.5 | 32.8 | 31.0 | -2.6 | 2.4 | -2.6 | 2.7 | 5.2 |
| Monaco | THS | 245 | 233 | 300 | 263 | 235 | 0.1 | 0.1 | 0.1 | -10.0 | -2.7 | -10.5 | -1.0 | 5.2 |
| Italy | TF | 26,679 | 31,052 | 41,181 | 39,799 | 39,604 | 17.8 | 17.5 | 16.4 | -3.9 | 0.6 | -0.5 | 3.1 | 5.8 |
| Malta | TF | 872 | 1,116 | 1,216 | 1,134 | 1,127 | 0.6 | 0.5 | 0.5 | -3.0 | -3.9 | -0.6 | 5.1 | 1.7 |
| Yugoslav SFR | | 7,880 | | | | | | | | | | | | |
| Slovenia | TCE | | 732 | 1,090 | 1,302 | 1,373 | 0.4 | 0.5 | 0.6 | 11.8 | 6.8 | 5.5 | | 8.3 |
| Croatia | TCE | | 1,485 | 5,831 | 6,944 | 7,409 | 0.9 | 2.5 | 3.1 | 12.2 | 6.1 | 6.7 | | 31.5 |
| Bosnia & Herzg | TCE | | .. | 171 | 160 | 165 | | 0.1 | 0.1 | -19.0 | 15.3 | 3.6 | | |
| Serbia & Montenegro | TCE | | 228 | 239 | 448 | 481 | 0.1 | 0.1 | 0.2 | 46.9 | 27.6 | 7.4 | | 0.9 |
| Albania | THS | 30 | 40 | 32 | 36 | 41 | 0.0 | 0.0 | 0.0 | 6.3 | 5.9 | 13.9 | 5.9 | -4.4 |
| Greece | TF | 8,873 | 10,130 | 13,096 | 14,180 | 13,969 | 5.8 | 5.6 | 5.8 | 7.3 | 0.9 | -1.5 | 2.7 | 5.3 |
| Turkey | TF | 4,799 | 7,083 | 9,586 | 12,790 | 13,341 | 4.1 | 4.1 | 5.5 | 12.5 | 18.6 | 4.3 | 8.1 | 6.2 |
| Cyprus | TF | 1,561 | 2,100 | 2,686 | 2,418 | 2,303 | 1.2 | 1.1 | 1.0 | 0.4 | -10.3 | -4.8 | 6.1 | 5.0 |
| Syrian Arab Republic | TCE | 562 | 815 | 1,416\| | 2,870 | 2,788 | 0.5 | 0.6 | 1.2 | -6.9 | | -2.9 | 7.7 | 11.7 |
| Lebanon | TF | .. | 450 | 742 | 956 | 1,015 | 0.3 | 0.3 | 0.4 | 12.8 | 14.3 | 6.1 | | 10.5 |
| Israel | TF | 1,063 | 2,215 | 2,417 | 862 | 1,063 | 1.3 | 1.0 | 0.4 | -50.5 | -27.9 | 23.4 | 15.8 | 1.8 |
| Palestine | TF | .. | .. | 330 | 40 | 40 | | 0.1 | 0.0 | -85.2 | -18.4 | 0.0 | | |
| Jordan | TF | 572 | 1,074 | 1,427 | 1,622 | 1,573 | 0.6 | 0.6 | 0.7 | 3.6 | 9.8 | -3.0 | 13.4 | 5.8 |
| Egypt | TF | 2,411 | 2,871 | 5,116 | 4,906 | 5,746 | 1.6 | 2.2 | 2.4 | -14.8 | 12.6 | 17.1 | 3.6 | 12.2 |
| Libyan Arab Jamahiriya | TF | 96 | 56 | 174 | 135 | 142 | 0.0 | 0.1 | 0.1 | -2.9 | -20.1 | 5.2 | -10.2 | 25.5 |
| Tunisia | TF | 3,204 | 4,120 | 5,058 | 5,064 | 5,114 | 2.4 | 2.1 | 2.1 | 6.5 | -6.0 | 1.0 | 5.2 | 4.2 |
| Algeria | VF | 1,137 | 520 | 866 | 988 | 1,166 | 0.3 | 0.4 | 0.5 | 4.1 | 9.6 | 18.0 | -14.5 | 10.7 |
| Morocco | TF | 4,024 | 2,602 | 4,240 | 4,303 | 4,552 | 1.5 | 1.8 | 1.9 | 2.4 | -0.9 | 5.8 | -8.4 | 10.3 |

Continued on the next page.

## *International tourism receipts*

The Mediterranean received more than 147 billion euro in tourism receipts in 2003, representing a drop of almost 2 per cent over the previous year, when tourism receipts, had already declined by 0.6 per cent. Results are expressed here in euro, as it is the currency of reference for most destinations as well as source markets. The euro is the official currency of five of the major earners -Spain (37 billion euro), France (33 billion euro), Italy (28 billion euro), Greece (9 billion euro) and Portugal (6 billion euro)-, together accounting for 80 per cent of international tourism receipts generated in the Mediterranean. As the US dollar depreciated strongly against the euro in the past years, changes expressed in US dollar make not much sense. Results obtained by countries in the euro area, show an overall trend of decrease. Tourism receipts dropped by 8 per cent in Greece, by 5 per cent in France, and by almost 3 per cent in Italy under the impact of the decreased long-haul traffic. On the other hand, tourism receipts grew in Spain (+3%) and in Portugal (+0.7%), as these destinations are less dependent on interregional arrivals.

Unlike with tourist arrivals, the first destination in terms of tourism receipts was Spain with a share of 25 per cent, followed by France and Italy, with shares of 22 per cent and 19 per cent respectively. It is important to note the decrease in the market share of Italy. As compared to 1995, the country lost more than 6 percentage points, dropping from a market share of just over a quarter to a share just below 19 per cent in 2003. On the other hand, destinations such as Spain and Turkey gained around 3 percentage points each as compared to 1995.

Receipts per arrival in the Mediterranean region reached 610 euro. The destinations with major receipts per arrival in 2003, were Albania (11,255 euro), Israel (1,695 euro) and Bosnia and Herzegovina (1,256 euro), followed by Lebanon (885 euro), Turkey (875 euro) and Slovenia (864 euro), while the destinations that show the lowest receipts per arrival were Palestine (88 euro) and Algeria (122 euro).

**Mediterranean**

**International Tourist Arrivals and Tourism Receipts by Country of Destination**

| | | | | | | Market share | | | Growth rate | | | Average annual growth | |
|---|---|---|---|---|---|---|---|---|---|---|---|---|---|
| | 1990 | 1995 | 2000 | 2002 | 2003* | 1995 | 2000 | 2003* | 01/00 | 02/01 | 03*/02 | '90-'95 | '95-'00 |
| | International Tourism Receipts (euro million) | | | | | | | % | | | % | | % |
| **Mediterranean** | **60,025** | **87,614** | **148,228** | **150,457** | **147,412** | **100** | **98** | **100** | **2.2** | **-0.6** | **-2.0** | **7.9** | **11.1** |
| Portugal | 2,792 | 3,693 | 5,677 | 6,093 | 6,132 | 4.2 | 3.8 | 4.2 | 7.6 | -0.2 | 0.7 | 5.8 | 9.0 |
| Spain | 14,601 | 19,503 | 33,541 | 35,728 | 36,925 | 22.3 | 22.6 | 25.0 | 8.8 | -2.1 | 3.4 | 6.0 | 11.5 |
| France | 15,850 | 21,091 | 33,543 | 34,622 | 32,742 | 24.1 | 22.6 | 22.2 | 1.1 | 2.1 | -5.4 | 5.9 | 9.7 |
| Italy | 12,924 | 21,965 | 29,767 | 28,420 | 27,601 | 25.1 | 20.1 | 18.7 | -3.1 | -1.4 | -2.9 | 11.2 | 6.3 |
| Malta | 389 | 505 | 660 | 604 | 615 | 0.6 | 0.4 | 0.4 | -2.3 | -6.4 | 1.9 | 5.3 | 5.5 |
| Yugoslav SFR | 2,178 | | | | | | | | | | | | |
| Slovenia | | 829 | 1,040 | 1,148 | 1,186 | 0.9 | 0.7 | 0.8 | 5.9 | 4.2 | 3.3 | | 4.7 |
| Croatia | | 1,031 | 2,986 | 4,030 | 5,636 | 1.2 | 2.0 | 3.8 | 24.7 | 8.2 | 39.9 | | 23.7 |
| Bosnia & Herzg | | .. | 179 | 203 | 208 | | 0.1 | 0.1 | 9.4 | 3.9 | 2.3 | | |
| Serbia & Montenegro | | 32 | 32 | 103 | 133 | 0.0 | 0.0 | 0.1 | 85.6 | 70.1 | 29.3 | | 0.2 |
| Albania | 3 | 50 | 421 | 515 | 461 | 0.1 | 0.3 | 0.3 | 18.2 | 3.4 | -10.4 | 73.7 | 53.3 |
| Greece | 2,032 | 3,161 | 9,981 | 10,285 | 9,460 | 3.6 | 6.7 | 6.4 | 6.0 | -2.8 | -8.0 | 9.2 | 25.9 |
| Turkey | 2,533 | 3,790 | 8,268 | 12,586 | 11,672 | 4.3 | 5.6 | 7.9 | 36.0 | 12.0 | -7.3 | 8.4 | 16.9 |
| Cyprus | 988 | 1,374 | 2,098 | 2,006 | 1,781 | 1.6 | 1.4 | 1.2 | 6.7 | -10.4 | -11.2 | 6.8 | 8.8 |
| Syrian Arab Republic | 251 | 962 | 1,171 | 1,506 | 1,245 | 1.1 | 0.8 | 0.8 | 9.6 | 17.3 | -17.3 | 30.8 | 4.0 |
| Lebanon | .. | 543 | 803 | 1,011 | 898 | 0.6 | 0.5 | 0.6 | 16.3 | 8.2 | -11.2 | | 8.2 |
| Israel | 1,096 | 2,288 | 4,411 | 2,156 | 1,803 | 2.6 | 3.0 | 1.2 | -37.7 | -21.6 | -16.4 | 15.9 | 14.0 |
| Palestine | .. | .. | 245 | 1 | 4 | | 0.2 | 0.0 | -96.8 | -86.5 | 234.4 | | |
| Jordan | 402 | 505 | 783 | 831 | 720 | 0.6 | 0.5 | 0.5 | -0.2 | 6.4 | -13.3 | 4.6 | 9.2 |
| Egypt | 864 | 2,052 | 4,704 | 3,981 | 4,052 | 2.3 | 3.2 | 2.7 | -9.8 | -6.2 | 1.8 | 18.9 | 18.0 |
| Libyan Arab Jamahiriya | 5 | 2 | 105 | 79 | 70 | 0.0 | 0.1 | 0.0 | -0.1 | -24.4 | -12.0 | -20.2 | 133.0 |
| Tunisia | 744 | 1,170 | 1,821 | 1,611 | 1,399 | 1.3 | 1.2 | 0.9 | 7.4 | -17.6 | -13.1 | 9.5 | 9.3 |
| Algeria | 82 | 25 | 104 | 141 | 142 | 0.0 | 0.1 | 0.1 | 7.2 | 26.6 | 1.2 | -21.2 | 32.9 |
| Morocco | 989 | 991 | 2,208 | 2,798 | 2,525 | 1.1 | 1.5 | 1.7 | 30.6 | -3.0 | -9.8 | 0.0 | 17.4 |

Continued on the next page.

**Mediterranean**

**International Tourist Arrivals and Tourism Receipts by Country of Destination**

| | 1990 | 1995 | 2000 | 2002 | 2003* | Market share 1995 | Market share 2000 | Market share 2003* | Growth rate 01/00 | Growth rate 02/01 | Growth rate 03*/02 | Average annual growth '90-'95 | Average annual growth '95-'00 |
|---|---|---|---|---|---|---|---|---|---|---|---|---|---|
| | Receipts per Arrival (euro) | | | | | | | | | | % | | % |
| **Mediterranean** | **377** | **503** | **630** | **621** | **610** | | | | **2.2** | **-3.5** | **-1.9** | **5.9** | **4.6** |
| Portugal | 348 | 388 | 469 | 523 | 524 | | | | 7.0 | 4.2 | 0.1 | 2.2 | 3.9 |
| Spain | 428 | 559 | 700 | 683 | 712 | | | | 4.1 | -6.3 | 4.3 | 5.4 | 4.6 |
| France | 302 | 351 | 435 | 450 | 436 | | | | 3.7 | -0.3 | -3.0 | 3.1 | 4.3 |
| Italy | 484 | 707 | 723 | 714 | 697 | | | | 0.8 | -2.0 | -2.4 | 7.9 | 0.4 |
| Malta | 447 | 453 | 543 | 533 | 546 | | | | 0.7 | -2.6 | 2.5 | 0.3 | 3.7 |
| Yugoslav SFR | 276 | | | | | | | | | | | | |
| Slovenia | | 1,132 | 954 | 882 | 864 | | | | -5.3 | -2.4 | -2.0 | | -3.4 |
| Croatia | | 695 | 512 | 580 | 761 | | | | 11.1 | 2.0 | 31.1 | | -5.9 |
| Bosnia & Herzg | | | 1,045 | 1,271 | 1,256 | | | | 35.0 | -9.9 | -1.2 | | |
| Serbia & Montenegro | | 141 | 136 | 229 | 276 | | | | 26.4 | 33.3 | 20.4 | | -0.7 |
| Albania | 105 | 1,242 | 13,162 | 14,306 | 11,255 | | | | 11.3 | -2.3 | -21.3 | 64.0 | 60.3 |
| Greece | 229 | 312 | 762 | 725 | 677 | | | | -1.3 | -3.6 | -6.6 | 6.4 | 19.6 |
| Turkey | 528 | 535 | 862 | 984 | 875 | | | | 20.9 | -5.6 | -11.1 | 0.3 | 10.0 |
| Cyprus | 633 | 654 | 781 | 830 | 773 | | | | 6.3 | -0.1 | -6.8 | 0.7 | 3.6 |
| Syrian Arab Republic | 447 | 1,180 | 827\| | 525 | 446 | | | | 17.8 | | -14.9 | 21.4 | -6.9 |
| Lebanon | | 1,206 | 1,083 | 1,057 | 885 | | | | 3.1 | -5.3 | -16.3 | | -2.1 |
| Israel | 1,031 | 1,033 | 1,825 | 2,502 | 1,695 | | | | 26.0 | 8.8 | -32.2 | 0.0 | 12.1 |
| Palestine | | | 741 | 26 | 88 | | | | -78.5 | -83.4 | 234.4 | | |
| Jordan | 703 | 470 | 549 | 513 | 458 | | | | -3.6 | -3.1 | -10.6 | -7.7 | 3.1 |
| Egypt | 358 | 715 | 920 | 811 | 705 | | | | 5.9 | -16.7 | -13.1 | 14.8 | 5.2 |
| Libyan Arab Jamahiriya | 49 | 27 | 604 | 588 | 492 | | | | 2.9 | -5.4 | -16.3 | -11.1 | 85.7 |
| Tunisia | 232 | 284 | 360 | 318 | 274 | | | | 0.8 | -12.4 | -14.0 | 4.1 | 4.9 |
| Algeria | 73 | 48 | 120 | 142 | 122 | | | | 3.0 | 15.5 | -14.3 | -7.9 | 20.0 |
| Morocco | 246 | 381 | 521 | 650 | 555 | | | | 27.6 | -2.1 | -14.7 | 9.2 | 6.5 |

Source: World Tourism Organization (WTO) © (Data as collected by WTO December 2004)

Mediterranean: Inbound tourism
International Tourism Receipts (euro billion, current prices)

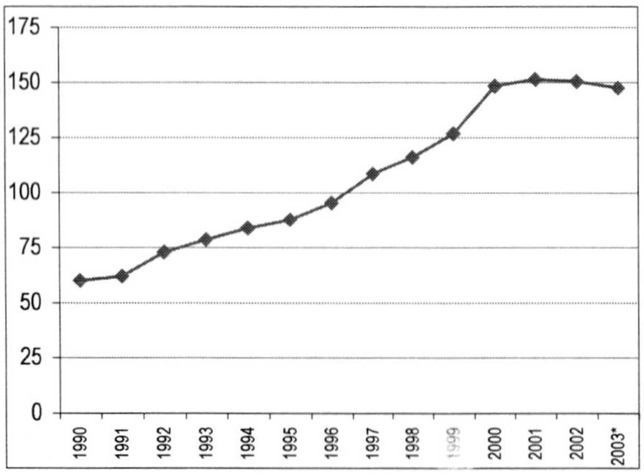


Source: World Tourism Organization (WTO) ©

Mediterranean: Inbound tourism
Receipts per Arrival, 2003* (euro)

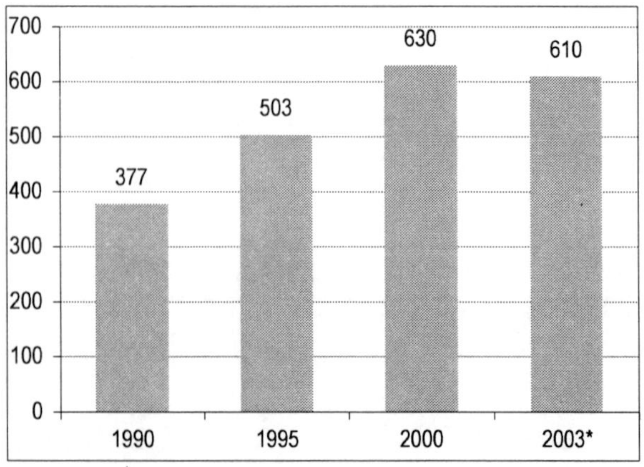


Source: World Tourism Organization (WTO) ©

Mediterranean: Inbound tourism

International Tourist Arrivals (share in world total, %)

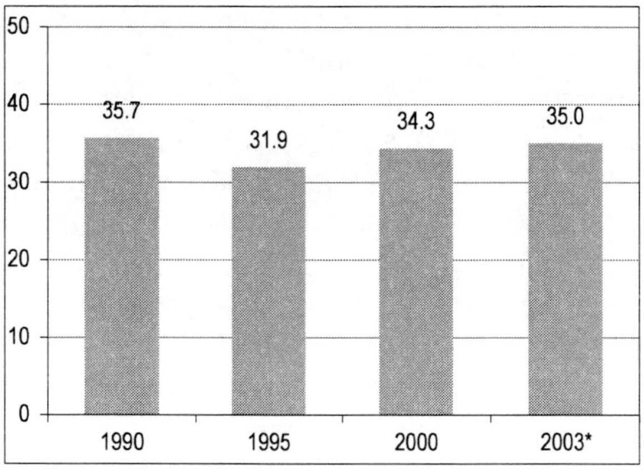


Source: World Tourism Organization (WTO) ©

Mediterranean: Inbound tourism

International Tourism Receipts (share in world total, %)

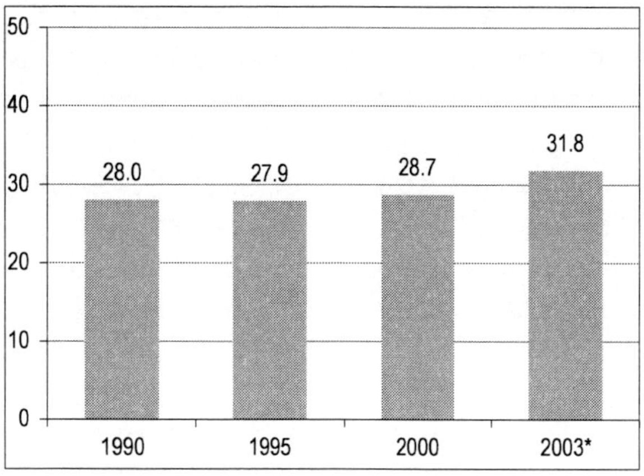


Source: World Tourism Organization (WTO) ©

*Cruises in the Mediterranean*

In spite of a particular difficult international travel climate, the world cruise industry has continued its strong performance in the last two years, growing around 10 per cent in the two main generating markets, North America and Europe, in 2002. According to Passenger Shipping Association (PSA) - IRN CruiseStat data (Annual Cruise Review 2003), 2003 was another positive year for the industry. A total of 12.2 million cruise passengers were booked in the world. The North American market (USA and Canada) grew by more than 7 per cent to a total of more than 8 million in spite of the uncertain atmosphere created by the war in Iraq. Although the volume of cruise passengers from the North American market taking a cruise out of Europe declined, the market resisted due to the development of cruising out of North American ports. In Europe, growth was even stronger (+27%) as all main markets posted very positive results. It is noteworthy to mention the exceptional 24 per cent increase in Germany and the growth of Spain (135%), which is becoming an increasingly important generating market.

**Cruise demand in Europe and America**

| | Passengers by region (1000) | | | | Growth rate (%) | | | Average annual growth (%) |
|---|---|---|---|---|---|---|---|---|
| Market | 2000 | 2001 | 2002 | 2003* | 01/00 | 02/01 | 03*/02 | 2000/2003 |
| United Kingdom | 754 | 776 | 820 | 962 | 2.9 | 5.7 | 17.3 | 8.5 |
| Germany | 379 | 392 | 425 | 529 | 3.4 | 8.4 | 24.4 | 11.7 |
| Italy | 220 | 255 | 300 | 346 | 15.9 | 17.6 | 15.2 | 16.2 |
| Spain | 68 | 118 | 135 | 317 | 74.0 | 14.1 | 135.1 | 67.1 |
| France | 266 | 200 | 215 | 212 | -24.9 | 7.5 | -1.2 | -7.2 |
| Other | 164 | 165 | 201 | 305 | 0.5 | 22.0 | 51.5 | 22.9 |
| **Total Europe** | 1,852 | 1,906 | 2,097 | 2,671 | 2.9 | 10.0 | 27.4 | 13.0 |
| **North America** | 6,882 | 6,906 | 7,640 | 8,195 | 0.3 | 10.6 | 7.3 | 6.0 |
| **Total Europe & America** | 8,734 | 8,812 | 9,737 | 10,866 | 0.9 | 10.5 | 11.6 | 7.6 |

Source: Compiled by WTO from Passengers Shipping Association (PSA), Cruise Lines International Association (CLIA) and European Cruise Council (IRN Research)

In the Mediterranean, among the major ports, except for Naples in Italy and Limassol in Cyprus, all ports with cruise passenger data available for 2003 show positive results. Barcelona, the top port of the Mediterranean, with more than 1 million passengers for the first time in 2003, maintained its steady double-digit growth (+25%). The four other major ports with more than half a million passengers also posted strong results: Palma de Mallorca (+13%) also in Spain, Venice (+36%) and Genoa (+8%) in Italy and Piraeus (+54%) in Greece. Ports that were somewhat affected by the geopolitical instability in 2001 and 2002, such as Piraeus (+54%) in Greece or Kusadasi (+47%) in Turkey, recovered significantly in 2003, though in the case of Kusadasi still far from the volume of passengers received before. Finally, Dubrovnik in Croatia, which grew on average 35 per cent between 1998 and 2003, has rapidly incorporated itself as an important port in the Mediterranean. In 2003, passenger figures to Dubrovnik reached almost 400 thousand, corresponding to an increase of 49 per cent.

**Cruise passenger movement at the main Mediterranean ports (thousands)**

| Country | Port | 1998 | 1999 | 2000 | 2001 | 2002 | 2003* | Growth rate (%) 02/01 | Growth rate (%) 03*/02 | Average annual growth (%) 98/2003 |
|---|---|---|---|---|---|---|---|---|---|---|
| Cyprus | Limassol | 604 | 690 | 885 | 551 | 378 | 369 | -31.3 | -2.4 | -9.4 |
| Croatia | Dubrovnick | 89 | 14 | 127 | 205 | 265 | 395 | 29.2 | 49.2 | 34.9 |
| | Split | 8 | 1 | 0 | 7 | 23 | 46 | 245.4 | 97.3 | 42.8 |
| Egypt | Alexandria | 42 | 51 | 125 | 93 | - | - | - | - | - |
| | Port Said | 433 | 535 | 600 | 438 | - | - | - | - | - |
| France | Ajaccio | 87 | 77 | 117 | - | - | - | - | - | - |
| | Cannes | 56 | 61 | 106 | 99 | 103 | 114 | 3.8 | 10.7 | 15.2 |
| | Marseille | 153 | 149 | 165 | 239 | 258 | 357 | 8.1 | 38.2 | 18.5 |
| | Nice- Villefranche | 156 | 194 | 195 | 251 | 299 | 347 | 19.3 | 15.7 | 17.3 |
| | Toulon - Saint Tropez | | | | | | 60 | - | - | |
| Greece | Piraeus | 437 | 335 | 508 | 525 | 388 | 595 | -26.2 | 53.5 | 6.4 |
| Israel | Haifa | 234 | 255 | 339 | 99 | - | 131 | - | - | - |
| | Eliat | 2 | 2 | 1 | 0 | - | - | - | - | - |
| | Ashdod | 107 | 87 | 77 | 74 | - | - | - | - | - |
| Italy | Bari | 121 | 2 | 61 | 146 | 203 | 214 | 39.5 | 5.2 | 12.2 |
| | Cagliari | 13 | 25 | 39 | 17 | 20 | 47 | 21.8 | 134.4 | 29.8 |
| | Catania | 51 | 41 | 43 | - | - | - | - | - | - |
| | Civitavecchia | 256 | 296 | 392 | 170 | - | 433 | - | - | 11.1 |
| | Genoa | 365 | 569 | 408 | 471 | 568 | 615 | 20.4 | 8.4 | 11.0 |
| | La Spezia | | | | | 15 | 26 | | 68.7 | |
| | Livrono | 196 | 251 | 229 | 264 | 298 | 364 | 13.0 | 22.1 | 13.2 |
| | Messina | 121 | 112 | 126 | - | - | 242 | - | - | 14.9 |
| | Naples | 334 | 503 | 406 | 470 | 485 | 413 | 3.3 | -14.9 | 4.3 |
| | Palermo | 83 | 135 | 157 | 181 | 197 | 207 | 9.0 | 4.7 | 20.0 |
| | Portoferraio | 37 | 24 | 28 | 26 | 28 | 23 | 6.3 | -17.1 | -8.7 |
| | Ravenna | 2 | 2 | 1 | 3 | 3 | 48 | 14.1 | - | - |
| | Savona | 103 | 89 | 120 | 110 | 105 | 195 | -3.8 | 85.2 | 13.7 |
| | Venice | 335 | 97 | 337 | 526 | 508 | 690 | -3.6 | 35.9 | 15.5 |
| Malta | Valetta | 147 | 193 | 174 | 274 | 357 | 389 | 30.4 | 9.2 | 21.4 |
| Monaco | Monaco | 56 | 60 | 76 | 72 | 56 | 80 | - | - | - |
| Morocco | Casablanca | 154 | 183 | 116 | 111 | 115 | - | 3.6 | - | - |
| | Tanger | 34 | 84 | 117 | 116 | 128 | - | 10.6 | - | - |
| Portugal | Lisbon | 140 | 161 | 189 | 149 | 164 | 209 | 10.3 | 27.4 | 8.4 |
| Spain | Alicante | 14 | 18 | 20 | 34 | 26 | 45 | -24.3 | 71.6 | 26.6 |
| | Barcelona | 466 | 546 | 574 | 655 | 844 | 1,054 | 28.8 | 25.0 | 17.7 |
| | Ibiza | 36 | 47 | 38 | 23 | 37 | 80 | 60.2 | 116.3 | 17.3 |
| | Malaga | 106 | 167 | 134 | 128 | 163 | 200 | 27.5 | 23.0 | 13.6 |
| | Mahón | 71 | 93 | 77 | 83 | 77 | 83 | -6.7 | 7.4 | 3.3 |
| | Palma Mallorca | 393 | 582 | 507 | 531 | 658 | 743 | 23.9 | 12.8 | 13.6 |
| | Valencia | 1 | 3 | 10 | 11 | 48 | 58 | 348.7 | 20.1 | 145.3 |
| Tunisia | Tunis | 101 | 156 | 186 | 234 | - | 330 | - | - | 26.8 |
| Turkey | Kusadasi | | | 442 | 481 | 212 | 313 | -55.8 | 47.4 | -10.9 |
| | Alanya | | | | | 37 | 31 | - | -16.7 | - |
| UK | Gibraltar | 90 | 122 | 133 | 119 | 117 | 215 | -1.4 | 84.2 | 19.0 |

Source: Compiled by WTO from Medcruise and National Port Authorities

Includes Embarking, Disembarking and Transit passengers

# III

# Tourism Trends by Country

# III.1 Northern Europe

## III.1.1 Denmark Northern Europe

### Profile

# Denmark

Europe
Northern Europe

| | |
|---|---|
| Capital | Copenhagen |
| Area (1000 km²) | 43 |
| Population (2003, million) | 5.4 |
| Gross Domestic Product (GDP) (2003, euro million) | 224,483 |
| GDP per capita (2003, euro) | 41,720 |
| GDP growth (real, %) | |
| '-> 2002: 1.0; 2003: 0.5; 2004*: 2.1; 2005*: 2.5 | |

| | 2001 | 2002 | 2003* | 2002/2001 | 2003*/2002 |
|---|---|---|---|---|---|
| **International Arrivals** | | | | | |
| Tourists (overnight visitors) (1000) | 2,028 | 2,010 | 2,016 | -0.9 | 0.3 |
| - per 100 of inhabitants | 38 | 37 | 37 | | |
| **Tourism accommodation** | | | | | |
| Number of rooms | 40,181 | 41,194 | 41,729 | 2.5 | 1.3 |
| *Nights spent in collective establishments (1000)* | 25,197 | 25,685 | 26,372 | 1.9 | 2.7 |
| by non-residents (inbound tourism) | 9,748 | 9,582 | 9,883 | -1.7 | 3.1 |
| by residents (domestic tourism) | 15,449 | 16,103 | 16,489 | 4.2 | 2.4 |
| *Nights spent in hotels and similar establishments (1000)* | 9,140 | 9,226 | 9,138 | 0.9 | -1.0 |
| by non-residents (inbound tourism) | 4,551 | 4,483 | 4,507 | -1.5 | 0.5 |
| by residents (domestic tourism) | 4,589 | 4,743 | 4,631 | 3.4 | -2.4 |
| **Outbound Tourism** | | | | | |
| Trips abroad (1000) | 4,946 | 4,935 | 5,564 | -0.2 | 12.7 |
| - per 100 of inhabitants | 92 | 92 | 103 | | |
| **Receipts and Expenditure for International Tourism** | | | | | |
| International Tourism Receipts (euro million) | 4,345 | 5,316 | 5,568 | 22.3 | 4.8 |
| - per Tourist Arrival (euro) | 2,143 | 2,645 | 2,762 | 23.4 | 4.4 |
| - per capita (euro) | 811 | 989 | 1,032 | | |
| International Tourism Expenditure (euro million) | 5,269 | 6,508 | 7,041 | 23.5 | 8.2 |
| - per trip (euro) | 1,065 | 1,319 | 1,266 | 23.8 | -4.0 |
| - per capita (euro) | 984 | 1,211 | 1,305 | | |
| △ International Tourism Balance (euro million) | -923 | -1,192 | -1,473 | | |

Source: World Tourism Organization (WTO) (Data as collected by WTO December 2004)

See annex for methodological notes and reference of external sources used.

# Survey

Contributed by *The Danish Tourist Board*
www.visitdenmark.com (promotional)
www.danskturisme.dk (institutional/corporate)
www.danskturisme.dk (Danish Tourist Board) ; www.visitdenmark.com (Danish Tourist Board) ; www.dst.dk (Statistics Denmark) (research and data)

## Tourism development and outlook

**Overall evaluation of results**

Danish tourism performed well in 2003 with an overall 2.6 per cent increase in bednights, the highest growth for more than a decade. There was a positive development in both domestic (3.2%) and international (2.1%) tourism. Growth in international tourism was mainly generated by neighbouring/near markets, particularly Germany, Norway and the Netherlands. Tourism related to camping and holiday houses performed particularly well, whereas tourism related to hotels, holiday centres and hostels declined.

Preliminary estimates of tourism spending indicate a moderate growth of approximately one per cent in commercial tourism (i.e. excluding same-day visitors and tourists in private accommodation). A structural shift has moderated growth. Nationality and accommodation mix in 2003 has shifted towards less consuming types of tourism.

The coastal tourism segment saw the highest growth rate, but also the city break segment recorded progress. The MICE segment appears to have declined slightly.

**Supply**

The structure of the tourism industry is characterised by a very large number of small enterprises, typically single proprietorships.

Especially in sub-industries such as hotels and travel agencies, small enterprises constitute the substantial part. In fact the structure is characterised by many very small enterprises, since 90 per cent of enterprises have less than 10 employees, and travel agencies and restaurants, in particular, that operate with very few employees.

The Danish tourism industry has adapted to the growing international competition by increasing its focus on product development, efficient and cost-saving production systems and by forming voluntary partnerships and alliances in marketing and distribution.

A number of initiatives have been undertaken to develop and improve the variety and quality of the tourism product.

**External factors**

A turbulent international environment (crisis and war in Iraq, the outbreak of the Severe Acute Respiratory Syndrome (SARS) and fear of terrorists) may have stimulated Danish tourism which is heavily dependent on tourists from neighbouring/near markets. Tourism from overseas markets constitutes a relatively small part of bednights and tourism spending in Denmark. Overseas tourism declined in 2003. However, tourism from the major overseas market, the United States of America, was a positive exception (1.2% increase).

A 16 per cent increase in the Danish kroner towards the United States dollar contributed negatively to the competitiveness of Danish tourism vis á vis a range of non-euro countries.

1st October: Denmark lowered its excises on alcohol and other items sensitive to border trade. This reduction has increased border shopping from Norway and Sweden, but may also have stimulated tourism (particularly same-day tourism).

**Tourism policy**

In 2003, the Danish tourism policy has focused on implementing the Government's Action Plan on Tourism which was launched by the present government in May 2002. Some of the initiatives in the action plan which have been implemented are:
- A quality labelling scheme for Danish attractions and museums;
- A new concept for meeting planning;
- A quality labelling scheme for physical accessibility;
- A new common concept for developing and marketing city breaks in Denmark;
- Five quality labels concerning golf, wellness, fishing, gastronomy and cycling related to active holiday facilities, places providing overnight accommodation, etc.;
- A stronger marketing co-operation on branding of Denmark in specific foreign markets;
- A coordinated effort in order to professionalize cultural events.

Furthermore, the Danish Tourist Board launched a general debate with the industry, organisations, politicians etc. on a new vision of Danish tourism 2010. The debate was launched on the board's annual Tourism Conference in November 2003 where different scenarios for Danish tourism in the future was discussed.
The debate continues in 2004 on national, regional and local levels and will lead to a common vision for Danish tourism 2010. The vision will be launched in May 2004.

**Outlook 2004**

The outlook for 2004 is positive. Development in bednights has been very promising and expectations for the important summer season are high.
Regarding special events, more focus will be put on developing international event tourism in the years to come. Based on a government initiative, the Danish Tourist Board on 1st January 2004, established "Event Denmark", a unit with the objective of developing more cultural events with appeal to an international audience. The prime target group is the city break segment.
In 2004, the royal wedding between H.R.H Crown Prince Frederik and the Australian Ms. Mary Donaldson is expected to create an extraordinary awareness of Denmark, but no direct tourism effects in itself, other than domestic and international press.
In 2005, the celebration of Hans Christian Andersen's 200th anniversary will be followed by hundreds of cultural events, new attractions, etc., that are expected to give an increase in tourism demand, mainly from Europe, Japan and from the new Chinese market.
Long-term expectations are generally positive depending on a continuation of growth on the important established markets, but also a considerable growth potential from emerging tourism markets in East Europe and Asia. In February 2004, an agreement between Denmark and China was signed giving Denmark an Approved Destination Status. This agreement is expected to stimulate overseas tourism in the medium/long term.
Long-term expectations are linked to a successful implementation of the new vision for Danish tourism 2010.

## International Meetings Industry (MI)

**Characteristics of supply**

Denmark has a large variety of meeting and conference facilities ranging from graceful castles and manor houses to modern hotels. Copenhagen has a particularly wide selection of centrally-located hotels. International, state-of-the-art congress centres are located in Copenhagen, Aalborg, Århus, Herning and Odense.
Hotels and conference facility rating system ranging from 1-5 stars.
Representation of international hotel chains.
A wide range of teambuilding possibilities are available: treasure hunts, speedboat navigation zorbing, archery, radio communication, rappelling, fishing and golf as well as cultural/historical incentive programmes.

**Organisation of promotion**

The international promotion of MICE tourism is organized through the Danish Tourist Board and our market offices <www.visitdenmark.com>.

We have specialized MICE staff at our offices in Sweden, Norway, the United Kingdom/Ireland, Germany, the United States of America, Belgium and at the head office in Copenhagen.

There are regional convention bureau in Copenhagen, Aalborg, Århus, South East Jutland and Funen.

**Importance / size**

Preliminary estimates of the MICE segment indicate an estimated turn over of approximately 5.7 billion Danish Kroner in 2003 (approximately 0.75 billion euro). This is approximately one-fifth of commercial tourism (i.e. excluding same-day visitors and tourists in private accommodation).

## International Tourism by Origin

**Denmark**

**International Tourist Arrivals in All Accommodation Establishments**

Region of Origin, 2003* — Change over previous year (%)

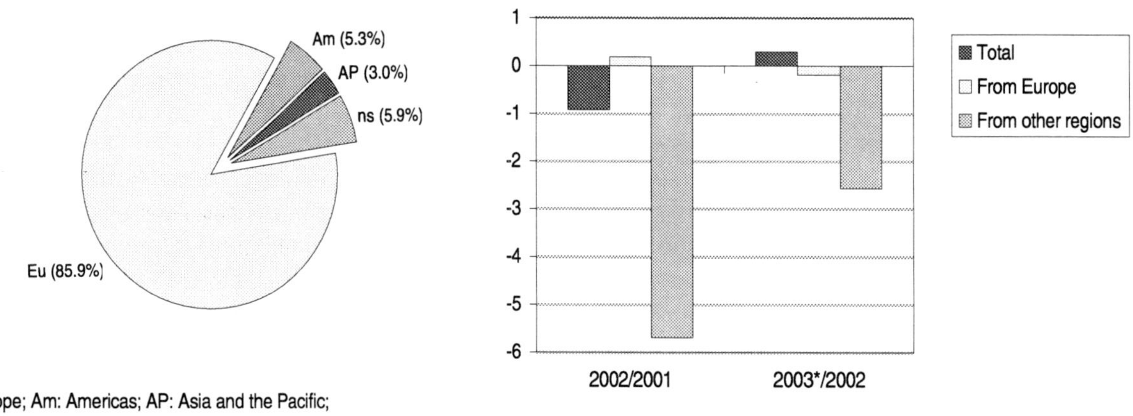


Eu: Europe; Am: Americas; AP: Asia and the Pacific;
ns: Not specified; Ot: Other;

Source: World Tourism Organization (WTO) ©

**Denmark**

**Nights of International Tourists in All Accommodation Establishments**

Region of Origin, 2003* — Change over previous year (%)

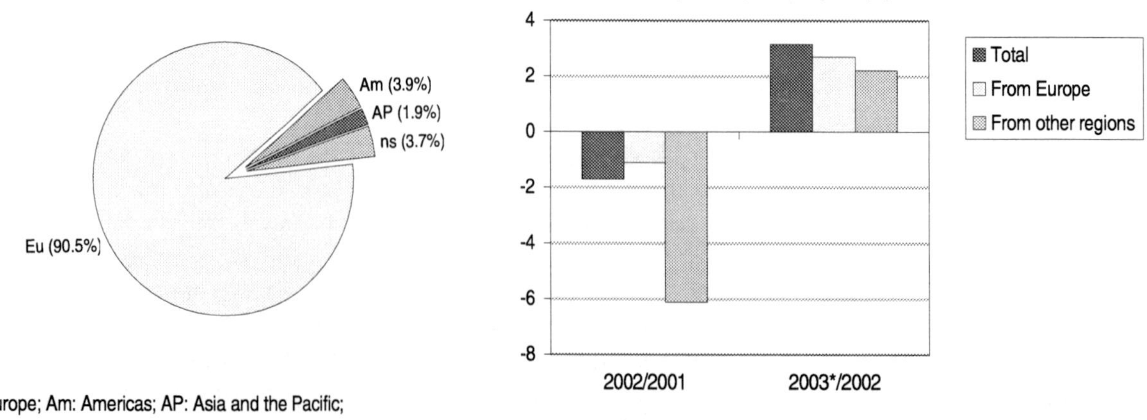


Eu: Europe; Am: Americas; AP: Asia and the Pacific;
ns: Not specified;

Source: World Tourism Organization (WTO) ©

**Denmark**

**International Tourist Arrivals in All Accommodation Establishments (by residence)**

| | | | | (thousand) | Market share (%) | | Growth rate (%) | | Average per year (%) |
|---|---|---|---|---|---|---|---|---|---|
| | 1995 | 2001 | 2002 | 2003* | 1995 | 2003* | 2002/01 | 2003*/02 | 1995-2003* |
| **Total** | .. | **2,028** | **2,010** | **2,016** | | **100** | **-0.9** | **0.3** | |
| *From Europe* | .. | *1,731* | *1,734* | *1,731* | | *85.9* | *0.2* | *-0.2* | |
| Sweden | .. | 565 | 546 | 542 | | 26.9 | -3.4 | -0.6 | |
| Germany | .. | 363 | 359 | 355 | | 17.6 | -1.1 | -1.1 | |
| Norway | .. | 301 | 335 | 347 | | 17.2 | 11.1 | 3.7 | |
| United Kingdom | .. | 118 | 111 | 104 | | 5.1 | -6.1 | -6.2 | |
| Netherlands | .. | 82 | 81 | 88 | | 4.3 | -1.4 | 8.5 | |
| Italy | .. | 46 | 45 | 46 | | 2.3 | -2.1 | 2.9 | |
| Finland | .. | 40 | 38 | 38 | | 1.9 | -5.0 | -0.1 | |
| France | .. | 26 | 28 | 28 | | 1.4 | 7.0 | -1.7 | |
| Switzerland | .. | 28 | 29 | 27 | | 1.3 | 3.5 | -7.1 | |
| Spain | .. | 19 | 23 | 22 | | 1.1 | 18.3 | -2.9 | |
| Poland | .. | 20 | 24 | 19 | | 0.9 | 20.2 | -20.3 | |
| Belgium/Luxembourg | .. | 16 | 17 | 15 | | 0.8 | 7.9 | -11.8 | |
| Austria | .. | 11 | 9 | 9 | | 0.4 | -13.4 | -3.9 | |
| Other Europe | .. | 95 | 90 | 91 | | 4.5 | -6.1 | 1.3 | |
| *From other regions* | .. | *182* | *171* | *167* | | *8.3* | *-5.7* | *-2.6* | |
| United States | .. | 97 | 86 | 87 | | 4.3 | -11.7 | 1.0 | |
| Japan | .. | 33 | 33 | 32 | | 1.6 | -0.5 | -3.6 | |
| All South-East Asia | .. | 28 | 30 | 29 | | 1.4 | 5.9 | -4.9 | |
| Canada | .. | 12 | 12 | 11 | | 0.6 | 2.4 | -9.0 | |
| Other interregional | .. | 11 | 10 | 8 | | 0.4 | -6.7 | -15.3 | |
| *Other World/Not specified* | .. | *116* | *105* | *118* | | *5.9* | *-10.0* | *13.0* | |

Source: World Tourism Organization (WTO) © (Data as collected by WTO December 2004)

**Denmark**

**Nights of International Tourists in All Accommodation Establishments (by residence)**

| | | | | (thousand) | Market share (%) | | Growth rate (%) | | Average per year (%) |
|---|---|---|---|---|---|---|---|---|---|
| | **1995** | **2001** | **2002** | **2003*** | **1995** | **2003*** | **2002/01** | **2003*/02** | **1995-2003*** |
| **Total** | **10,790** | **9,748** | **9,582** | **9,883** | **100** | **100** | **-1.7** | **3.1** | **-1.1** |
| *From Europe* | *9,872* | *8,804* | *8,707* | *8,942* | *91.5* | *90.5* | *-1.1* | *2.7* | *-1.2* |
| Germany | 4,789 | 3,220 | 3,086 | 3,237 | 44.4 | 32.8 | -4.1 | 4.9 | -4.8 |
| Sweden | 1,735 | 1,817 | 1,765 | 1,753 | 16.1 | 17.7 | -2.9 | -0.7 | 0.1 |
| Norway | 1,097 | 1,418 | 1,563 | 1,614 | 10.2 | 16.3 | 10.2 | 3.3 | 4.9 |
| Netherlands | 856 | 664 | 630 | 732 | 7.9 | 7.4 | -5.1 | 16.2 | -1.9 |
| United Kingdom | 402 | 557 | 525 | 492 | 3.7 | 5.0 | -5.7 | -6.3 | 2.6 |
| Italy | 177 | 193 | 188 | 196 | 1.6 | 2.0 | -2.6 | 4.2 | 1.3 |
| Finland | 132 | 146 | 138 | 139 | 1.2 | 1.4 | -5.7 | 0.6 | 0.6 |
| France | 133 | 115 | 123 | 125 | 1.2 | 1.3 | 6.4 | 1.9 | -0.7 |
| Switzerland | 34 | 96 | 100 | 91 | 0.3 | 0.9 | 4.5 | -8.8 | 13.0 |
| Spain | .. | 67 | 79 | 78 | | 0.8 | 18.4 | -1.9 | |
| Belgium/Luxembourg | .. | 69 | 75 | 70 | | 0.7 | 8.3 | -6.4 | |
| Poland | .. | 66 | 80 | 63 | | 0.6 | 20.1 | -20.5 | |
| Austria | .. | 36 | 31 | 29 | | 0.3 | -13.5 | -4.5 | |
| Belgium | 11 | .. | .. | .. | 0.1 | | | | |
| Other Europe | 506 | 340 | 325 | 322 | 4.7 | 3.3 | -4.6 | -0.9 | -5.5 |
| *From other regions* | *399* | *600* | *564* | *576* | *3.7* | *5.8* | *-6.1* | *2.2* | *4.7* |
| United States | 300 | 348 | 308 | 323 | 2.8 | 3.3 | -11.4 | 4.9 | 0.9 |
| Japan | 99 | 101 | 100 | 100 | 0.9 | 1.0 | -0.4 | 0.0 | 0.2 |
| All South-East Asia | .. | 85 | 90 | 88 | | 0.9 | 5.7 | -2.4 | |
| Canada | .. | 36 | 37 | 38 | | 0.4 | 1.7 | 4.7 | |
| Other Americas | .. | 31 | 29 | 27 | | 0.3 | -6.5 | -8.1 | |
| *Other World/Not specified* | *519* | *343* | *311* | *365* | *4.8* | *3.7* | *-9.4* | *17.3* | *-4.3* |

Source: World Tourism Organization (WTO) © (Data as collected by WTO December 2004)

# III.1.2 Finland Northern Europe

## Profile

# Finland

Europe
Northern Europe

| | |
|---|---|
| Capital | Helsinki |
| Area (1000 km²) | 338 |
| Population (2003, million) | 5.2 |
| Gross Domestic Product (GDP) (2003, euro million) | 170,417 |
| GDP per capita (2003, euro) | 32,702 |
| GDP growth (real, %) | |
| '-> 2002: 2.3; 2003: 2.0; 2004*: 2.8; 2005*: 2.6 | |

| | 2001 | 2002 | 2003* | 2002/2001 | 2003*/2002 |
|---|---|---|---|---|---|
| **International Arrivals** | | | | | |
| Visitors (1000) | 4,252 | 4,687 | 4,527 | 10.2 | -3.4 |
| Tourists (overnight visitors) (1000) | 2,826 | 2,875 | 2,601 | 1.7 | -9.5 |
| - per 100 of inhabitants | 55 | 55 | 50 | | |
| Same-day visitors (1000) | 1,426 | 1,812 | 1,926 | 27.1 | 6.3 |
| **Tourism accommodation** | | | | | |
| Number of rooms | 55,268 | 54,916 | 55,767 | -0.6 | 1.5 |
| *Nights spent in collective establishments (1000)* | 16,212 | 15,993 | 16,082 | -1.4 | 0.6 |
| by non-residents (inbound tourism) | 4,183 | 4,290 | 4,331 | 2.6 | 1.0 |
| by residents (domestic tourism) | 12,029 | 11,703 | 11,751 | -2.7 | 0.4 |
| *Nights spent in hotels and similar establishments (1000)* | 13,557 | 13,273 | 13,429 | -2.1 | 1.2 |
| by non-residents (inbound tourism) | 3,675 | 3,721 | 3,758 | 1.3 | 1.0 |
| by residents (domestic tourism) | 9,882 | 9,552 | 9,671 | -3.3 | 1.2 |
| **Outbound Tourism** | | | | | |
| Trips abroad (1000) | 5,824 | 5,857 | 5,585 | 0.6 | -4.6 |
| - per 100 of inhabitants | 112 | 113 | 107 | | |
| **Receipts and Expenditure for International Tourism** | | | | | |
| International Tourism Receipts (euro million) | 1,556 | 1,762 | 2,003 | 13.2 | 13.7 |
| - per Tourist Arrival (euro) | 551 | 613 | 770 | 11.3 | 25.7 |
| - per Visitor Arrival (euro) | 366 | 376 | 442 | 2.7 | 17.7 |
| - per capita (euro) | 300 | 339 | 385 | | |
| International Fare Receipts (euro million) | 680 | 741 | 804 | 9.0 | 8.4 |
| International Tourism Expenditure (euro million) | 2,005 | 2,240 | 2,546 | 11.7 | 13.7 |
| - per trip (euro) | 344 | 382 | 456 | 11.1 | 19.2 |
| - per capita (euro) | 387 | 431 | 489 | | |
| International Fare Expenditure (euro million) | 639 | 481 | 523 | -24.7 | 8.8 |
| △ International Tourism Balance (euro million) | -449 | -478 | -543 | | |
| △ International Fare Balance (euro million) | 41 | 260 | 280 | | |

Source: World Tourism Organization (WTO) (Data as collected by WTO December 2004)

See annex for methodological notes and reference of external sources used.

# Survey

Contributed by *Finnish Tourist Board*
www.visitfinland.com (promotional)
www.mek.fi (institutional/corporate)
www.mek.fi (research and data)

## Tourism development and outlook

**Overall evaluation of results**

The figures for 2003 show an overall decrease of one per cent. Domestic overnights decreased by 1.3 per cent and foreign by 0.3 per cent. The weak result concerning incoming tourism was mainly caused by a sharp drop of 122 per cent in Russian overnights and quite big decreases in Norwegian and American overnights too. On the other hand very good growth figures were achieved in overnights from the United Kingdom, the Netherlands, France, Italy, Switzerland and Spain.

**External factors**

The high exchange rate of the euro against the United States dollar was unfavourable for tourism from Russia to Finland.

**Marketing & promotion**

A big summer tourism marketing campaign was launched with the aim of increasing summer tourism to Finland from the main markets. The growth of summer tourism to Finland has stagnated and by concentrating funds on a big consumer campaign with wide media coverage, e.g. TV-spots, the Finnish Tourist Board (FTB) aims to achieve better results than before. Product development is an essential part of this project.

**Outlook 2004**

A growth of 3-4 per cent in incoming tourism is estimated for the years 2004 and 2005. The growth markets are likely to be Central and South Europe and the United States of America and Japan.

## International Meetings Industry (MI)

**Characteristics of supply**

Finland has very good facilities for congresses, not only in the big cities like Helsinki and Tampere, but also in most provincial capitals. Among the world's leading congress countries, Finland is the 15$^{th}$ biggest.
Incentive travel to Finland is estimated to include visits of altogether 80 thousand guests annually.

**Organisation of promotion**

The main organisation in charge of promoting congresses and conferences to Finland is the Finland Convention Bureau.
The Helsinki City Tourist Office also has a congress department to promote Helsinki as a conference venue.
The Finnish Tourist Board is in charge of the promotion of incentive travel and event tourism.
Websites: www.finlandconventionbureau.fi/eng/index ; www.hel.fi/convention/EN/

**Collection of statistics on the Meetings Industry?:** yes.

**Description**

The Finland Convention Bureau (FCB) regularly carries out surveys and collects data on international congresses in Finland. The surveys include interviews with congress participants and congress organizers. At present the FCB is carrrying out an extensive study of the entire Finnish meeting market. The objective is to determine the number of domestic and international meetings held in Finland and their impact on the economy and employment.

Data on the number of foreign visitors taking part in congresses or seminars in Finland can also be found in the Border Survey of the Finnish Tourist Board/Statistics Finland.

**Importance / size**

Some 300 international congresses with a total of 60 thousand delegates are held in Finland every year. Compared to the total number of overnight visitors in Finland (2.6 million in 2003) the share of congress tourists is about 2.3 per cent.

In 2001, the expenditure of foreign congress participants totalled 42 million euro, which was approximately 2.6 per cent of the total expenditure of foreign tourists.

**Evolution MI**

The development of congress tourism has been stable and the future outlook is also very good.

In 2006, Finland will once again be assuming the Presidency of the European Union and 2006 and 2007 also look like being extremely good congress years.

# International Tourism by Origin

**Finland**

**International Tourist Arrivals in All Accommodation Establishments**

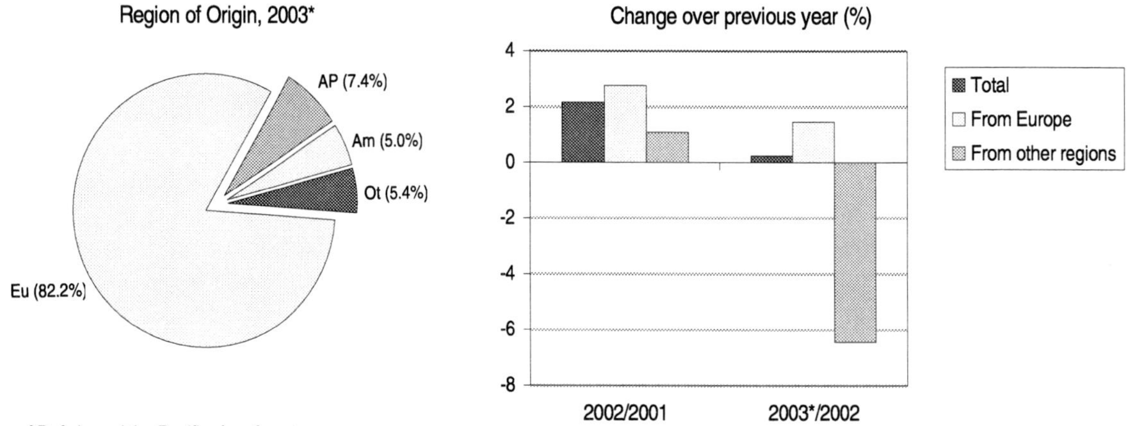


Eu: Europe; AP: Asia and the Pacific; Am: Americas;
Ot: Other;

Source: World Tourism Organization (WTO) ©

**Finland**

**Nights of International Tourists in All Accommodation Establishments**

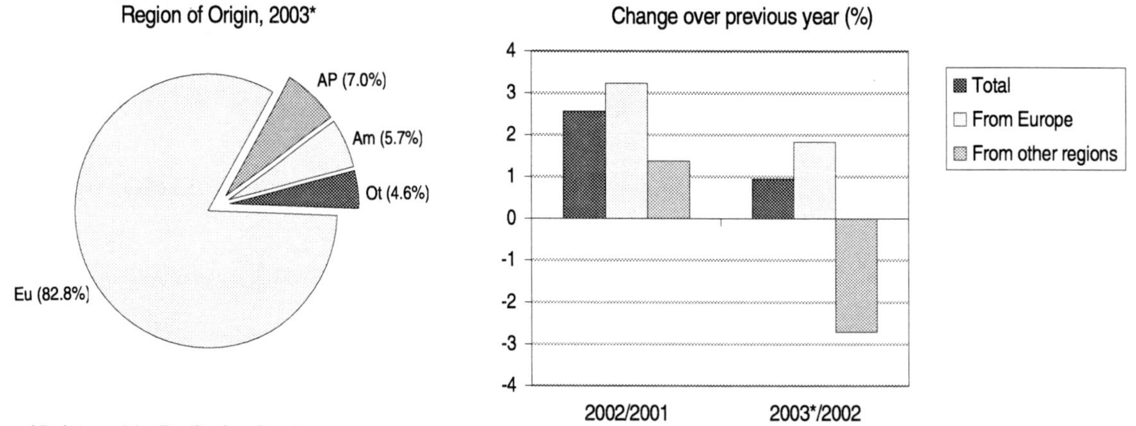


Eu: Europe; AP: Asia and the Pacific; Am: Americas;
Ot: Other;

Source: World Tourism Organization (WTO) ©

**Finland**

**International Tourist Arrivals in All Accommodation Establishments (by residence)**

| | | | | (thousand) | Market share (%) | | Growth rate (%) | | Average per year (%) |
|---|---|---|---|---|---|---|---|---|---|
| | 1995 | 2001 | 2002 | 2003* | 1995 | 2003* | 2002/01 | 2003*/02 | 1995-2003* |
| **Total** | .. | **1,999** | **2,043** | **2,047** | | **100** | **2.2** | **0.2** | |
| *From Europe* | .. | *1,615* | *1,660* | *1,684* | | *82.2* | *2.8* | *1.5* | |
| Sweden | .. | 353 | 344 | 341 | | 16.7 | -2.5 | -0.9 | |
| Germany | .. | 233 | 247 | 256 | | 12.5 | 5.9 | 3.6 | |
| Russian Federation | .. | 204 | 215 | 194 | | 9.5 | 5.2 | -9.7 | |
| United Kingdom | .. | 161 | 152 | 168 | | 8.2 | -5.8 | 10.4 | |
| Netherlands | .. | 82 | 104 | 111 | | 5.4 | 27.0 | 6.3 | |
| Norway | .. | 110 | 110 | 101 | | 5.0 | 0.1 | -8.0 | |
| France | .. | 67 | 74 | 81 | | 4.0 | 9.2 | 10.2 | |
| Italy | .. | 65 | 68 | 73 | | 3.5 | 3.3 | 7.1 | |
| Estonia | .. | 55 | 52 | 55 | | 2.7 | -5.0 | 5.4 | |
| Denmark | .. | 54 | 55 | 54 | | 2.7 | 2.7 | -1.4 | |
| Switzerland | .. | 49 | 47 | 54 | | 2.6 | -4.4 | 15.3 | |
| Spain | .. | 41 | 49 | 51 | | 2.5 | 19.1 | 2.5 | |
| Belgium | .. | 19 | 21 | 23 | | 1.1 | 9.9 | 10.2 | |
| Austria | .. | 19 | 19 | 19 | | 0.9 | 0.1 | 0.3 | |
| Poland | .. | 16 | 17 | 16 | | 0.8 | 6.0 | -3.6 | |
| Latvia | .. | 13 | 13 | 13 | | 0.6 | -4.9 | 3.5 | |
| Czech Rep | .. | 8 | 8 | 9 | | 0.5 | 1.3 | 12.9 | |
| Ireland | .. | 9 | 10 | 9 | | 0.5 | 7.7 | -3.9 | |
| Greece | .. | 7 | 9 | 7 | | 0.4 | 20.4 | -17.0 | |
| Hungary | .. | 8 | 8 | 7 | | 0.4 | -1.2 | -1.5 | |
| Lithuania | .. | 6 | 6 | 7 | | 0.3 | 6.1 | 4.4 | |
| Portugal | .. | 6 | 5 | 6 | | 0.3 | -14.8 | 13.9 | |
| Israel | .. | 6 | 4 | 4 | | 0.2 | -30.9 | -14.9 | |
| Iceland | .. | 3 | 3 | 4 | | 0.2 | -7.7 | 26.8 | |
| Turkey | .. | 3 | 3 | 3 | | 0.1 | 6.1 | -0.7 | |
| Other intraregional | .. | 15 | 16 | 17 | | 0.8 | 9.2 | 3.0 | |
| *From other regions* | .. | *276* | *279* | *261* | | *12.7* | *1.1* | *-6.5* | |
| United States | .. | 101 | 90 | 83 | | 4.0 | -10.7 | -8.3 | |
| Japan | .. | 82 | 74 | 69 | | 3.4 | -9.9 | -6.9 | |
| China | .. | 25 | 45 | 41 | | 2.0 | 78.4 | -8.6 | |
| Canada | .. | 11 | 10 | 12 | | 0.6 | -0.3 | 16.3 | |
| Australia | .. | 12 | 13 | 12 | | 0.6 | 7.2 | -5.8 | |
| Korea, Republic of | .. | 7 | 9 | 10 | | 0.5 | 26.6 | 15.5 | |
| India | .. | 4 | 3 | 4 | | 0.2 | -9.6 | 8.1 | |
| Taiwan (pr. of China) | .. | 7 | 5 | 3 | | 0.2 | -25.5 | -34.3 | |
| Thailand | .. | 2 | 4 | 3 | | 0.1 | 60.8 | -30.4 | |
| Hong Kong (China) | .. | 1 | 2 | 2 | | 0.1 | 88.8 | 14.2 | |
| Brazil | .. | 2 | 3 | 2 | | 0.1 | 21.5 | -26.4 | |
| Singapore | .. | 2 | 2 | 2 | | 0.1 | -13.6 | 18.1 | |
| New Zealand | .. | 2 | 2 | 2 | | 0.1 | -2.6 | -4.3 | |
| South Africa | .. | 2 | 2 | 2 | | 0.1 | -8.2 | -2.6 | |
| Mexico | .. | 2 | 1 | 1 | | 0.1 | -39.5 | 2.1 | |
| Saudi Arabia | .. | 1 | 1 | 1 | | 0.1 | 16.9 | 4.1 | |
| Other interregional | .. | 13 | 13 | 11 | | 0.6 | 0.0 | -8.7 | |
| *Other World/Not specified* | .. | *108* | *104* | *103* | | *5.0* | *-3.9* | *-1.1* | |

Source: World Tourism Organization (WTO) ©

(Data as collected by WTO December 2004)

**Finland**

**Nights of International Tourists in All Accommodation Establishments (by residence)**

| | | | | (thousand) | Market share (%) | | Growth rate (%) | | Average per year (%) |
|---|---|---|---|---|---|---|---|---|---|
| | 1995 | 2001 | 2002 | 2003* | 1995 | 2003* | 2002/01 | 2003*/02 | 1995-2003* |
| **Total** | **3,292** | **4,183** | **4,290** | **4,331** | **100** | **100** | **2.6** | **0.9** | **3.5** |
| *From Europe* | *2,713* | *3,411* | *3,521* | *3,585* | *82.4* | *82.8* | *3.2* | *1.8* | *3.5* |
| Sweden | 485 | 628 | 613 | 613 | 14.7 | 14.1 | -2.4 | -0.1 | 3.0 |
| Germany | 628 | 489 | 515 | 533 | 19.1 | 12.3 | 5.3 | 3.5 | -2.0 |
| Russian Federation | 392 | 521 | 532 | 478 | 11.9 | 11.0 | 2.1 | -10.0 | 2.5 |
| United Kingdom | 205 | 369 | 379 | 414 | 6.2 | 9.6 | 2.6 | 9.3 | 9.2 |
| Netherlands | 109 | 159 | 197 | 219 | 3.3 | 5.1 | 24.0 | 11.5 | 9.1 |
| Norway | 141 | 231 | 236 | 215 | 4.3 | 5.0 | 2.2 | -8.8 | 5.4 |
| France | 115 | 152 | 165 | 192 | 3.5 | 4.4 | 8.2 | 16.8 | 6.6 |
| Italy | 100 | 135 | 139 | 151 | 3.0 | 3.5 | 2.8 | 8.5 | 5.3 |
| Switzerland | 98 | 102 | 95 | 116 | 3.0 | 2.7 | -6.5 | 21.6 | 2.1 |
| Estonia | 71 | 107 | 105 | 106 | 2.2 | 2.4 | -1.7 | 1.1 | 5.0 |
| Spain | 55 | 84 | 97 | 102 | 1.7 | 2.3 | 15.4 | 4.4 | 8.0 |
| Denmark | 85 | 100 | 103 | 98 | 2.6 | 2.3 | 2.7 | -4.5 | 1.8 |
| Belgium | 31 | 40 | 42 | 47 | 0.9 | 1.1 | 6.8 | 10.8 | 5.5 |
| Austria | 33 | 47 | 48 | 46 | 1.0 | 1.1 | 0.8 | -4.3 | 4.2 |
| Poland | 33 | 40 | 45 | 40 | 1.0 | 0.9 | 11.4 | -11.2 | 2.5 |
| Latvia | 13 | 26 | 25 | 28 | 0.4 | 0.6 | -1.8 | 9.6 | 10.0 |
| Ireland | 5 | 22 | 22 | 27 | 0.2 | 0.6 | 1.2 | 19.7 | 22.2 |
| Czech Rep | 17 | 22 | 23 | 24 | 0.5 | 0.5 | 4.9 | 3.2 | 4.0 |
| Greece | 16 | 18 | 24 | 20 | 0.5 | 0.5 | 28.2 | -13.3 | 3.2 |
| Hungary | 17 | 21 | 22 | 20 | 0.5 | 0.5 | 4.2 | -11.4 | 1.8 |
| Portugal | 7 | 15 | 12 | 15 | 0.2 | 0.3 | -16.3 | 21.8 | 10.2 |
| Lithuania | 9 | 12 | 14 | 14 | 0.3 | 0.3 | 14.7 | -1.9 | 5.5 |
| Iceland | 7 | 7 | 7 | 9 | 0.2 | 0.2 | -9.6 | 32.7 | 3.9 |
| Israel | 9 | 13 | 10 | 8 | 0.3 | 0.2 | -25.0 | -17.3 | -1.0 |
| Turkey | 6 | 7 | 7 | 6 | 0.2 | 0.1 | 6.6 | -14.4 | 0.6 |
| Other intraregional | 25 | 42 | 44 | 44 | 0.8 | 1.0 | 4.2 | 2.2 | 7.3 |
| *From other regions* | *469* | *578* | *585* | *570* | *14.3* | *13.2* | *1.4* | *-2.7* | *2.4* |
| United States | 191 | 221 | 206 | 192 | 5.8 | 4.4 | -6.9 | -6.4 | 0.1 |
| Japan | 116 | 144 | 136 | 131 | 3.5 | 3.0 | -5.1 | -3.8 | 1.6 |
| China | 23 | 53 | 81 | 77 | 0.7 | 1.8 | 52.9 | -4.4 | 16.5 |
| Canada | 25 | 28 | 27 | 33 | 0.7 | 0.8 | -2.2 | 22.2 | 3.9 |
| Australia | 23 | 25 | 26 | 25 | 0.7 | 0.6 | 2.1 | -1.9 | 1.0 |
| Korea, Republic of | 12 | 13 | 14 | 18 | 0.4 | 0.4 | 12.7 | 28.0 | 5.4 |
| India | 8 | 19 | 14 | 14 | 0.2 | 0.3 | -27.6 | 0.8 | 7.7 |
| Saudi Arabia | 1 | 4 | 6 | 6 | 0.0 | 0.1 | 59.3 | 3.0 | 22.6 |
| Brazil | 9 | 6 | 7 | 6 | 0.3 | 0.1 | 18.1 | -19.0 | -5.2 |
| Singapore | 3 | 5 | 5 | 6 | 0.1 | 0.1 | -3.0 | 18.5 | 7.7 |
| Taiwan (pr. of China) | 10 | 9 | 7 | 5 | 0.3 | 0.1 | -18.6 | -26.1 | -7.4 |
| Thailand | 6 | 4 | 7 | 5 | 0.2 | 0.1 | 59.2 | -25.9 | -3.4 |
| South Africa | 3 | 6 | 5 | 5 | 0.1 | 0.1 | -18.3 | 3.5 | 5.9 |
| Greenland | 0 | 0 | 0 | 4 | 0.0 | 0.1 | -83.2 | 13866.7 | 102.2 |
| New Zealand | 4 | 4 | 4 | 4 | 0.1 | 0.1 | 1.8 | 0.5 | 0.9 |
| Hong Kong (China) | 3 | 2 | 3 | 4 | 0.1 | 0.1 | 61.4 | 12.4 | 2.7 |
| Other interregional | 33 | 36 | 38 | 33 | 1.0 | 0.8 | 6.6 | -12.0 | 0.0 |
| *Other World/Not specified* | *110* | *195* | *184* | *176* | *3.3* | *4.1* | *-5.6* | *-4.3* | *6.0* |

Source: World Tourism Organization (WTO) © (Data as collected by WTO December 2004)

# III.1.3 Iceland Northern Europe

## Profile

# Iceland

**Europe**
**Northern Europe**

| | |
|---|---|
| Capital | Reykjavik |
| Area (1000 km²) | 103 |
| Population (2003, 1000) | 291 |
| Gross Domestic Product (GDP) (2003, euro million) | 11,118 |
| GDP per capita (2003, euro) | 38,274 |
| GDP growth (real, %) | |
| -> 2002: -0.5; 2003: 4.0; 2004*: 4.4; 2005*: 5.3 | |

| | 2001 | 2002 | 2003* | 2002/2001 | 2003*/2002 |
|---|---|---|---|---|---|
| **International Arrivals** | | | | | |
| Tourists (overnight visitors) (1000) | 672 | 705 | 771 | 4.8 | 9.5 |
| - per 100 of inhabitants | 236 | 245 | 265 | | |
| Cruise passengers (1000) | 28 | 30 | 31 | 7.1 | 3.3 |
| **Tourism accommodation** | | | | | |
| Number of rooms | 6,174 | 6,807 | 7,330 | 10.3 | 7.7 |
| *Nights spent in collective establishments (1000)* | 1,744 | 1,861 | 1,985 | 6.7 | 6.7 |
| by non-residents (inbound tourism) | 1,184 | 1,257 | 1,377 | 6.2 | 9.5 |
| by residents (domestic tourism) | 560 | 604 | 608 | 7.9 | 0.7 |
| *Nights spent in hotels and similar establishments (1000)* | 1,183 | 1,260 | 1,369 | 6.5 | 8.7 |
| by non-residents (inbound tourism) | 908 | 970 | 1,070 | 6.8 | 10.3 |
| by residents (domestic tourism) | 275 | 290 | 299 | 5.5 | 3.1 |
| **Receipts and Expenditure for International Tourism** | | | | | |
| International Tourism Receipts (euro million) | 251 | 286 | 337 | 13.8 | 18.0 |
| - per Tourist Arrival (euro) | 374 | 406 | 437 | 8.5 | 7.8 |
| - per capita (euro) | 882 | 992 | 1,159 | | |
| International Fare Receipts (euro million) | 163 | 178 | 177 | 8.6 | -0.5 |
| International Tourism Expenditure (euro million) | 403 | 413 | 551 | 2.6 | 33.4 |
| - per capita (euro) | 1,414 | 1,434 | 1,893 | | |
| △ International Tourism Balance (euro million) | -152 | -127 | -214 | | |

Source: World Tourism Organization (WTO) (Data as collected by WTO December 2004)

See annex for methodological notes and reference of external sources used.

# International Tourism by Origin

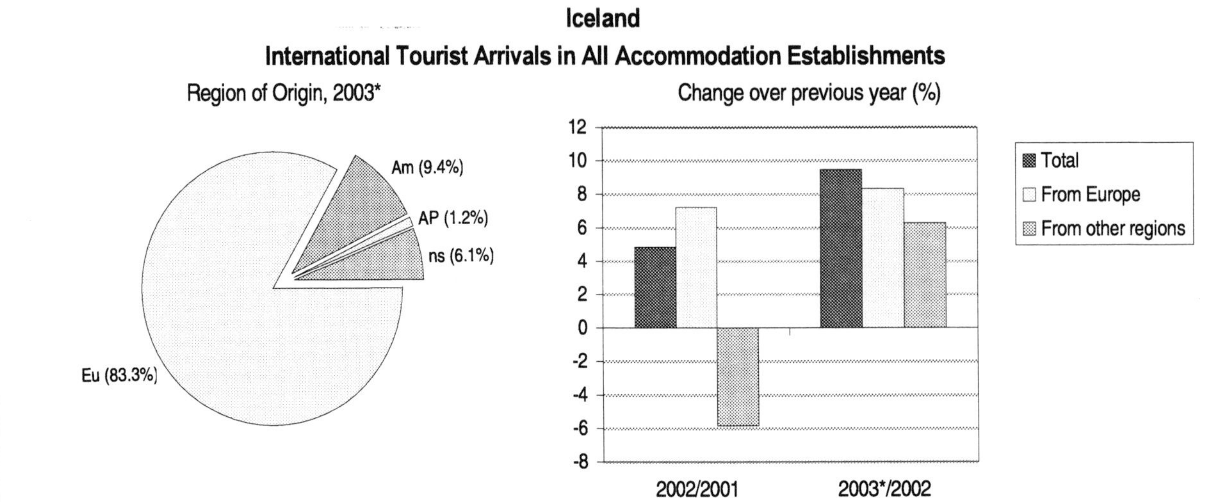


Eu: Europe; Am: Americas; AP: Asia and the Pacific;
ns: Not specified;

Source: World Tourism Organization (WTO) ©

**Iceland**
**International Tourist Arrivals in All Accommodation Establishments (by nationality)**

| | (thousand) | | | | Market share (%) | | Growth rate (%) | | Average per year (%) |
|---|---|---|---|---|---|---|---|---|---|
| | 1995 | 2001 | 2002 | 2003* | 1995 | 2003* | 2002/01 | 2003*/02 | 1995-2003* |
| **Total** | .. | **672** | **705** | **771** | | **100** | **4.8** | **9.5** | |
| *From Europe* | .. | *553* | *593* | *643* | | *83.3* | *7.2* | *8.3* | |
| Germany | .. | 159 | 149 | 160 | | 20.7 | -6.0 | 7.0 | |
| France | .. | 66 | 88 | 91 | | 11.7 | 34.5 | 2.6 | |
| United Kingdom | .. | 77 | 80 | 90 | | 11.6 | 4.1 | 12.5 | |
| Italy | .. | 39 | 41 | 48 | | 6.3 | 7.0 | 16.8 | |
| Netherlands | .. | 36 | 39 | 42 | | 5.4 | 7.9 | 7.5 | |
| Denmark | .. | 32 | 40 | 42 | | 5.4 | 25.3 | 3.6 | |
| Sweden | .. | 33 | 32 | 34 | | 4.5 | -0.8 | 6.4 | |
| Norway | .. | 26 | 29 | 33 | | 4.2 | 9.4 | 13.5 | |
| Switzerland | .. | 21 | 26 | 29 | | 3.7 | 23.0 | 9.3 | |
| Spain | .. | 15 | 17 | 22 | | 2.9 | 9.4 | 31.3 | |
| Austria | .. | 11 | 12 | 13 | | 1.7 | 5.2 | 9.9 | |
| Belgium | .. | 11 | 9 | 9 | | 1.2 | -16.4 | -0.8 | |
| Finland | .. | 8 | 9 | 8 | | 1.0 | 1.6 | -12.5 | |
| Ireland | .. | 4 | 3 | 3 | | 0.4 | -30.8 | 12.5 | |
| Other Europe | .. | 15 | 19 | 21 | | 2.7 | 24.6 | 6.9 | |
| *From other regions* | .. | *81* | *76* | *81* | | *10.5* | *-5.8* | *6.3* | |
| United States | .. | 68 | 64 | 65 | | 8.4 | -6.6 | 2.5 | |
| Japan | .. | 7 | 7 | 9 | | 1.2 | 4.7 | 27.9 | |
| Canada | .. | 6 | 6 | 7 | | 0.9 | -9.3 | 21.9 | |
| *Other World/Not specified* | .. | *38* | *35* | *47* | | *6.1* | *-7.4* | *35.6* | |

Source: World Tourism Organization (WTO) ©

(Data as collected by WTO December 2004)

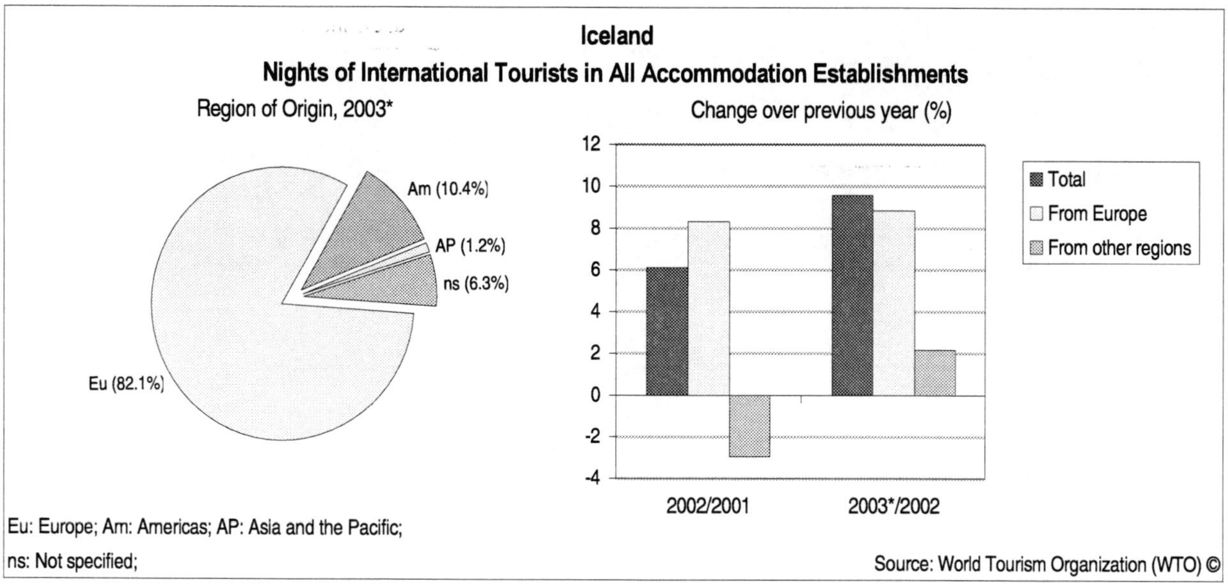


**Iceland**
**Nights of International Tourists in All Accommodation Establishments (by nationality)**

| | (thousand) | | | | Market share (%) | | Growth rate (%) | | Average per year (%) |
|---|---|---|---|---|---|---|---|---|---|
| | 1995 | 2001 | 2002 | 2003* | 1995 | 2003* | 2002/01 | 2003*/02 | 1995-2003* |
| **Total** | **815** | **1,184** | **1,257** | **1,377** | **100** | **100** | **6.1** | **9.6** | **6.8** |
| *From Europe* | *729* | *959* | *1,039* | *1,130* | *89.4* | *82.1* | *8.3* | *8.8* | *5.6* |
| Germany | 253 | 248 | 243 | 262 | 31.0 | 19.0 | -1.8 | 7.7 | 0.5 |
| United Kingdom | 66 | 172 | 175 | 195 | 8.1 | 14.2 | 2.2 | 11.2 | 14.4 |
| France | 67 | 90 | 122 | 128 | 8.3 | 9.3 | 34.9 | 4.7 | 8.3 |
| Denmark | 52 | 62 | 77 | 81 | 6.3 | 5.9 | 23.5 | 5.1 | 5.8 |
| Sweden | 62 | 73 | 76 | 79 | 7.6 | 5.7 | 4.3 | 3.5 | 3.0 |
| Norway | 45 | 62 | 67 | 74 | 5.5 | 5.3 | 7.2 | 10.0 | 6.4 |
| Netherlands | 32 | 58 | 63 | 71 | 3.9 | 5.1 | 8.5 | 11.6 | 10.6 |
| Italy | 23 | 50 | 54 | 63 | 2.8 | 4.6 | 7.5 | 16.2 | 13.4 |
| Switzerland | 42 | 33 | 40 | 46 | 5.2 | 3.3 | 22.6 | 15.2 | 1.1 |
| Spain | 9 | 21 | 24 | 32 | 1.1 | 2.3 | 14.7 | 30.7 | 17.3 |
| Finland | 13 | 20 | 22 | 21 | 1.6 | 1.5 | 11.6 | -4.9 | 6.0 |
| Austria | 21 | 15 | 18 | 19 | 2.6 | 1.4 | 19.0 | 6.8 | -0.8 |
| Belgium | 6 | 16 | 15 | 14 | 0.7 | 1.0 | -10.0 | -4.1 | 11.7 |
| Ireland | 2 | 7 | 5 | 7 | 0.3 | 0.5 | -22.2 | 30.9 | 16.2 |
| Other Europe | 36 | 30 | 36 | 39 | 4.4 | 2.8 | 17.0 | 9.2 | 0.9 |
| *From other regions* | *57* | *162* | *157* | *160* | *7.0* | *11.6* | *-3.0* | *2.2* | *13.7* |
| United States | 47 | 137 | 131 | 128 | 5.8 | 9.3 | -4.4 | -2.6 | 13.2 |
| Japan | 7 | 12 | 13 | 17 | 0.9 | 1.2 | 11.0 | 28.1 | 11.4 |
| Canada | 3 | 13 | 13 | 16 | 0.3 | 1.1 | -0.1 | 24.7 | 25.0 |
| *Other World/Not specified* | *29* | *64* | *61* | *86* | *3.6* | *6.3* | *-4.1* | *41.1* | *14.5* |

Source: World Tourism Organization (WTO) © (Data as collected by WTO December 2004)

# III.1.4 Ireland Northern Europe

## Profile

# Ireland

**Europe**
**Northern Europe**

| | |
|---|---|
| Capital | Dublin |
| Area (1000 km²) | 70 |
| Population (2003, million) | 3.9 |
| Gross Domestic Product (GDP) (2003, euro million) | 161,172 |
| GDP per capita (2003, euro) | 40,507 |
| GDP growth (real, %) | |
| '-> 2002: 6.1; 2003: 3.7; 2004*: 4.7; 2005*: 5.0 | |

| | 2001 | 2002 | 2003* | 2002/2001 | 2003*/2002 |
|---|---|---|---|---|---|
| **International Arrivals** | | | | | |
| Tourists (overnight visitors) (1000) | 5,990 | 6,065 | 6,369 | 1.2 | 5.0 |
| - per 100 of inhabitants | 156 | 156 | 162 | | |
| Same-day visitors (1000) | 344 | 305 | .. | -11.3 | |
| **Tourism accommodation** | | | | | |
| Number of rooms | 61,230 | 62,807 | .. | 2.6 | |
| *Nights spent in collective establishments (1000)* | 29,340 | 25,970 | | -11.5 | |
| by non-residents (inbound tourism) | 18,332 | 17,677 | .. | -3.6 | |
| by residents (domestic tourism) | 11,008 | 8,293 | .. | -24.7 | |
| *Nights spent in hotels and similar establishments (1000)* | 23,107 | 20,996 | | -9.1 | |
| by non-residents (inbound tourism) | 15,315 | 14,562 | .. | -4.9 | |
| by residents (domestic tourism) | 7,792 | 6,434 | .. | -17.4 | |
| **Outbound Tourism** | | | | | |
| Trips abroad (1000) | 4,216 | 4,634 | .. | 9.9 | |
| - per 100 of inhabitants | 110 | 119 | .. | | |
| **Receipts and Expenditure for International Tourism** | | | | | |
| International Tourism Receipts (euro million) | 3,021 | 3,448 | 4,099 | 14.2 | 18.9 |
| - per Tourist Arrival (euro) | 504 | 569 | 644 | 12.7 | 13.2 |
| - per capita (euro) | 788 | 889 | 1,044 | | |
| International Fare Receipts (euro million) | 795 | 763 | 811 | -4.0 | 6.3 |
| International Tourism Expenditure (euro million) | 3,114 | 4,177 | 4,980 | 34.1 | 19.2 |
| - per trip (euro) | 739 | 901 | .. | 22.0 | |
| - per capita (euro) | 812 | 1,077 | 1,269 | | |
| International Fare Expenditure (euro million) | 495 | 500 | 644 | 1.2 | 28.6 |
| △ International Tourism Balance (euro million) | -93 | -728 | -882 | | |
| △ International Fare Balance (euro million) | 301 | 263 | 167 | | |

Source: World Tourism Organization (WTO) (Data as collected by WTO December 2004)

See annex for methodological notes and reference of external sources used.

Data on Tourist Arrrivals 2002 and 2003 updated. Correspondingly data by country of residence are not available.

# Survey

Contributed by *Failte Ireland*
www.tourismireland.com (promotional)
www.bordfailte.ie (institutional/corporate)
www.bordfailte.ie (research and data)

## Tourism development and outlook

**Overall evaluation of results**

Foreign tourist arrivals increased by 5 per cent to 6.8 million in 2003, and while Britain remains the largest market at 3.6 million, the strongest growth was recorded from mainland Europe and as a result of the continuing recovery from North America. North America remains down on the record levels achieved in 2000. Foreign earnings from tourism increased by 3 per cent to 4.1 billion euro. Holiday tourism grew by 2 per cent to 3.3 million visits.

**Supply**

The number of beds and rooms available in registered hotels increased by almost 3 per cent, however, beds and rooms in less formal accommodation declined, resulting in an overall increase of less than one per cent in paid, serviced accommodation capacity.
Weekly capacity on scheduled air services between the United States of America and Ireland increased by 22 per cent. New air route development continued on mainland European routes with non-stop scheduled service capacity up by 5 per cent. Capacity on Britain-Ireland air routes increased by 4 per cent.

**External factors**

The Iraq war slowed down the recovery in the United States of America and other long-haul markets and has impacted on the type of holiday visitor from the United States of America e.g. less coach tours.
There is a continuing trend towards shorter holidays from Britain with knock-on effects on spatial spread and participation in active pursuits.
Increases in costs, particularly insurance costs, continue to put pressure on business margins.
Attracting and retaining skilled staff continues to be a key challenge for the industry.
The continuing decline in the value of the United States dollar and the drop in the value of the Sterling versus the euro both impacted on performance from the United States of America and Britain, respectively, particularly in terms of perceived value for money.

**Tourism policy**

The Government produced a major report of the Tourism Policy Review Group, a group drawn from the state tourism agencies and the private sector, entitled "New Horizons for Irish Tourism – An Agenda for Action" providing a framework for the development of Irish Tourism to 2012.
Failte Ireland, the new development authority for Irish tourism, was established by the Government through the merger of two state agencies, Bord Failte and CERT. The new agency provides strategic and practical support to develop and sustain a high quality and competitive tourist destination in partnership with the tourism industry. Tourism Ireland is responsible for marketing the island of Ireland overseas.

**Marketing & promotion**

Tourism Ireland has developed a marketing strategy for the island of Ireland for the period 2004 to 2006 and has published an Operating Plan for 2004. The bulk of resources will be focused on Great Britain, the United States of America, France and Germany. Almost two-thirds of allocated funds will be spent on advertising with the

balance spent on below-the-line activities such as promotions, direct marketing, print, distribution and trade activities.
Failte Ireland has published Operational Plans for 2004 in respect of niche tourism products such as walking, cycling, golf, equestrian pursuits, heritage and gardens, angling, language learning and business tourism, and for home holidays and regional development.

**Outlook 2004** Target is to increase foreign visitors to Ireland by almost 6 per cent per annum to 2006, while increasing "promotable" visitors (holiday, conference, incentive, language learning) by almost 7 per cent per annum. The Government has set a target of doubling foreign visitor spending by 2012.
The target for 2004 is for an increase of 4 per cent in foreign tourist arrivals.

## International Meetings Industry (MI)

**Characteristics of supply** There has been a 5 billion euro investment in hotel and venue facilities over the last few years, which means Ireland has meeting rooms and conference rooms of top quality. Ireland has also a team of professional conference organisers to assist Associations and Corporations with their meetings. Our range of four and five-star properties, creative Destination Management Companies and variety of activities make Ireland an ideal Incentive Travel destination.

**Organisation of promotion** Primarily by the Business Tourism Section of the National Tourism Authority and through overseas Market Offices. Significant promotion is carried out by individual trade partners and city convention bureaux.
<www.conference-ireland.ie> and <www.incentive-ireland.ie>.

**Collection of statistics on the Meetings Industry?:** yes.

**Description** We collect data through our international visitor survey conducted at points of departure from the country. Business trips are identified as Association conference or convention, Corporate event or seminar, Trade fair or exhibition, or other business.

**Importance / size** The number of international conference and corporate meeting visitors in 2002 was estimated at 122 thousand; worth an estimated 146 million euro in visitor spend.

**Evolution MI** The international Conference/Corporate Meetings sector to Ireland has grown by 11 per cent per annum over the past 10 years, despite a slowdown in growth in recent years as a result of unprecedented international events. Based on continuing strong economies and a stable international environment, the sector should continue to perform well in the future.

# International Tourism by Origin

**Ireland**
**International Tourist Arrivals at Frontiers**

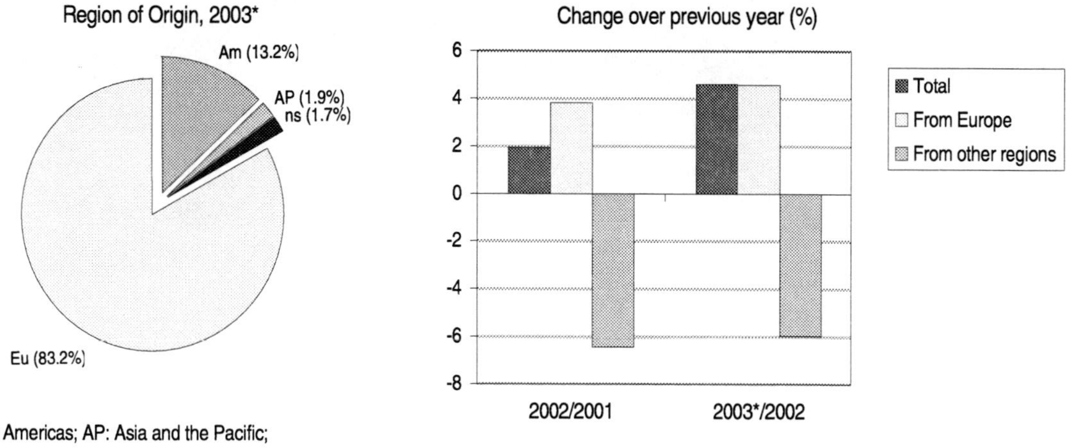


Eu: Europe; Am: Americas; AP: Asia and the Pacific;
ns: Not specified;

Source: World Tourism Organization (WTO) ©

**Ireland**
**International Tourist Arrivals at Frontiers (by residence)**

| | | | | (thousand) | Market share (%) | | Growth rate (%) | | Average per year (%) |
|---|---|---|---|---|---|---|---|---|---|
| | 1995 | 2001 | 2002 | 2003* | 1995 | 2003* | 2002/01 | 2003*/02 | 1995-2003* |
| **Total** | **4,818** | **6,353** | **6,476** | **6,774** | **100** | **100** | **1.9** | **4.6** | **4.4** |
| *From Europe* | *3,977* | *5,189* | *5,387* | *5,633* | *82.5* | *83.2* | *3.8* | *4.6* | *4.4* |
| United Kingdom | 2,875 | 3,853 | 4,009 | 4,149 | 59.7 | 61.2 | 4.0 | 3.5 | 4.7 |
| France | 234 | 280 | 298 | 321 | 4.9 | 4.7 | 6.4 | 7.7 | 4.0 |
| Germany | 319 | 285 | 288 | 302 | 6.6 | 4.5 | 1.1 | 4.9 | -0.7 |
| Italy | 112 | 157 | 157 | 176 | 2.3 | 2.6 | 0.0 | 12.1 | 5.8 |
| Netherlands | 94 | 182 | 162 | 146 | 2.0 | 2.2 | -11.0 | -9.9 | 5.7 |
| Spain | 67 | 100 | 113 | 133 | 1.4 | 2.0 | 13.0 | 17.7 | 8.9 |
| Belgium/Luxembourg | 53 | 81 | 104 | 96 | 1.1 | 1.4 | 28.4 | -7.7 | 7.7 |
| Scandinavia | 46 | 104 | 84 | .. | 1.0 | | -19.2 | | |
| Switzerland | 62 | 38 | 42 | 51 | 1.3 | 0.8 | 10.5 | 21.4 | -2.4 |
| Denmark | 22 | 25 | 24 | 27 | 0.5 | 0.4 | -4.0 | 12.5 | 2.6 |
| Austria | .. | 25 | 26 | .. | | | 4.0 | | |
| Greece | .. | 6 | 8 | .. | | | 33.3 | | |
| Portugal | .. | 10 | 8 | .. | | | -20.0 | | |
| Other Europe | 93 | 43 | 64 | 232 | 1.9 | 3.4 | 48.8 | 262.5 | 12.1 |
| *From other regions* | *760* | *1,164* | *1,089* | *1,024* | *15.8* | *15.1* | *-6.4* | *-6.0* | *3.8* |
| United States | 587 | 829 | 759 | 809 | 12.2 | 11.9 | -8.4 | 6.6 | 4.1 |
| Australia, New Zealand | 89 | 132 | 113 | 109 | 1.8 | 1.6 | -14.4 | -3.5 | 2.6 |
| Canada | 54 | 74 | 85 | 84 | 1.1 | 1.2 | 14.9 | -1.2 | 5.7 |
| All Africa | .. | 32 | 29 | .. | | | -9.4 | | |
| Japan | 30 | 22 | 22 | 22 | 0.6 | 0.3 | 0.0 | 0.0 | -3.8 |
| Other Americas | .. | 12 | 16 | .. | | | 33.3 | | |
| Other East Asia/Pacific | .. | 63 | 65 | .. | | | 3.2 | | |
| *Other World/Not specified* | *81* | .. | .. | *117* | *1.7* | *1.7* | | | *4.7* |

Source: World Tourism Organization (WTO) ©

(Data as collected by WTO December 2004)

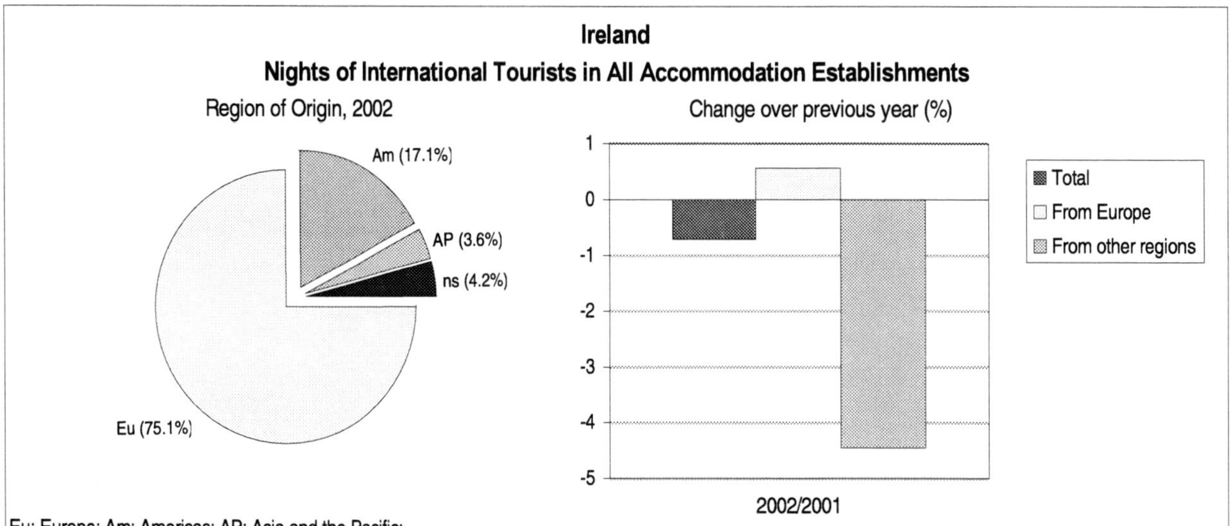


**Ireland**

**Nights of International Tourists in All Accommodation Establishments (by residence)**

| | (thousand) 1995 | 2000 | 2001 | 2002 | Market share (%) 1995 | 2002 | Growth rate (%) 2001/00 | 2002/01 | Average per year (%) 1995-2002 |
|---|---|---|---|---|---|---|---|---|---|
| **Total** | **40,592** | **..** | **47,315** | **46,979** | **100** | **100** | | **-0.7** | **2.1** |
| *From Europe* | *31,562* | .. | *35,085* | *35,282* | *77.8* | *75.1* | | *0.6* | *1.6* |
| United Kingdom | 18,941 | .. | 20,294 | 19,924 | 46.7 | 42.4 | | -1.8 | 0.7 |
| France | 2,720 | .. | 3,451 | 3,354 | 6.7 | 7.1 | | -2.8 | 3.0 |
| Germany | 3,254 | .. | 3,242 | 3,025 | 8.0 | 6.4 | | -6.7 | -1.0 |
| Italy | 1,238 | .. | 1,806 | 2,058 | 3.0 | 4.4 | | 14.0 | 7.5 |
| Spain | 1,800 | .. | .. | .. | 4.4 | | | | |
| Netherlands | 645 | .. | 1,230 | 1,185 | 1.6 | 2.5 | | -3.7 | 9.1 |
| Scandinavia | 563 | .. | 1,143 | 1,087 | 1.4 | 2.3 | | -4.9 | 9.9 |
| Belgium/Luxembourg | 499 | .. | 496 | 662 | 1.2 | 1.4 | | 33.5 | 4.1 |
| Switzerland | 614 | .. | 416 | 451 | 1.5 | 1.0 | | 8.4 | -4.3 |
| Other Europe | 1,288 | .. | 3,007 | 3,536 | 3.2 | 7.5 | | 17.6 | 15.5 |
| *From other regions* | *7,459* | .. | *10,200* | *9,746* | *18.4* | *20.7* | | *-4.5* | *3.9* |
| United States | 6,002 | .. | 7,902 | 7,149 | 14.8 | 15.2 | | -9.5 | 2.5 |
| Australia, New Zealand | 937 | .. | 1,499 | 1,693 | 2.3 | 3.6 | | 12.9 | 8.8 |
| Canada | 520 | .. | 799 | 904 | 1.3 | 1.9 | | 13.1 | 8.2 |
| *Other World/Not specified* | *1,571* | .. | *2,030* | *1,951* | *3.9* | *4.2* | | *-3.9* | *3.1* |

Source: World Tourism Organization (WTO) © (Data as collected by WTO December 2004)

Note: Including private accommodation

# III.1.5 Norway Northern Europe

## Profile

# Norway

Europe
Northern Europe

| | |
|---|---|
| Capital | Oslo |
| Area (1000 km²) | 324 |
| Population (2003, million) | 4.6 |
| Gross Domestic Product (GDP) (2003, euro million) | 233,565 |
| GDP per capita (2003, euro) | 51,120 |
| GDP growth (real, %) | |
| '-> 2002: 1.4; 2003: 0.4; 2004*: 2.7; 2005*: 2.7 | |

| | 2001 | 2002 | 2003* | 2002/2001 | 2003*/2002 |
|---|---|---|---|---|---|
| **International Arrivals** | | | | | |
| Visitors (1000) | 5,115 | 5,247 | 5,288 | 2.6 | 0.8 |
| Tourists (overnight visitors) (1000) | 3,073 | 3,111 | 3,269 | 1.2 | 5.1 |
| - per 100 of inhabitants | 68 | 69 | 72 | | |
| Same-day visitors (1000) | 1,238 | 1,222 | 1,142 | -1.3 | -6.5 |
| Cruise passengers (1000) | 804 | 914 | 1,000 | 13.7 | 9.4 |
| **Tourism accommodation** | | | | | |
| Number of rooms | 66,428 | 66,727 | 67,114 | 0.5 | 0.6 |
| *Nights spent in collective establishments (1000)* | 24,332 | 24,384 | 23,809 | 0.2 | -2.4 |
| by non-residents (inbound tourism) | 7,322 | 7,275 | 6,956 | -0.6 | -4.4 |
| by residents (domestic tourism) | 17,010 | 17,109 | 16,853 | 0.6 | -1.5 |
| *Nights spent in hotels and similar establishments (1000)* | 16,416 | 16,188 | 15,637 | -1.4 | -3.4 |
| by non-residents (inbound tourism) | 4,817 | 4,706 | 4,375 | -2.3 | -7.0 |
| by residents (domestic tourism) | 11,599 | 11,482 | 11,262 | -1.0 | -1.9 |
| **Receipts and Expenditure for International Tourism** | | | | | |
| International Tourism Receipts (euro million) | 2,120 | 2,433 | 2,687 | 14.8 | 10.5 |
| - per Tourist Arrival (euro) | 690 | 782 | 822 | 13.4 | 5.1 |
| - per Visitor Arrival (euro) | 414 | 464 | 508 | 11.9 | 9.6 |
| - per capita (euro) | 470 | 536 | 590 | | |
| International Fare Receipts (euro million) | 457 | 540 | 572 | 18.3 | 5.9 |
| International Tourism Expenditure (euro million) | 4,724 | 5,655 | 6,777 | 19.7 | 19.8 |
| - per capita (euro) | 1,046 | 1,247 | 1,488 | | |
| International Fare Expenditure (euro million) | 333 | 470 | 357 | 41.0 | -24.0 |
| △ International Tourism Balance (euro million) | -2,604 | -3,222 | -4,090 | | |
| △ International Fare Balance (euro million) | 123 | 70 | 215 | | |

Source: World Tourism Organization (WTO) (Data as collected by WTO December 2004)

See annex for methodological notes and reference of external sources used.

# Survey

Contributed by *Innovation Norway*
www.visitnorway.com (promotional)
www.invanor.no (institutional/corporate)
www.invanor.no (research and data)

## Tourism development and outlook

| | |
|---|---|
| **Overall evaluation of results** | There was an increase of 3 per cent in overall holiday arrivals.<br>A general increase was experienced in all major markets.<br>There was a significant increase from Southern Europe, Spain, France and Italy.<br>A decrease was noted in domestic overnights (-2%). |
| **Supply** | A shift in supply from hotel to self-catering accommodation (e.g. an increase in sale-lease back).<br>There was an increase in direct flights to Norway.<br>There was also an increase in the supply of wellness products. |
| **External factors** | The exchange rate was positive.<br>Extra funding was available for campaigns.<br>The winter season started early. |
| **Tourism policy** | The Norwegian Trade Council (NTC), the Governmental Consultative Office for Inventors (SVO), the Norwegian Tourist Board (NTB) and the Norwegian Industrial and Regional Development Fund (SND) merged into a new company on 1st January 2004: "Innovation Norway".<br>The travel market is one of the main focus areas for Innovation Norway. |
| **Marketing & promotion** | A branding program started in 2001 and we are still following the same strategy.<br>The new strategic markets will be Russia and China. |
| **Outlook 2004** | Based on our Tourist Barometer, we expect a slight increase from most markets this summer.<br>The strongest uncertainty concerns the Danish and German markets. |

## International Meetings Industry (MI)

| | |
|---|---|
| **Characteristics of supply** | The largest hotel chains, the flight company and the largest cities are cooperating in offering MICE products. |
| **Organisation of promotion** | The Norwegian Convention Bureau (NCB) is responsible for promoting the MICE industry. The Bureau has been newly organised with a privately funded secretariat. In addition to the NCB there are several events and travel bureaux with MICE products.<br>In 2004 Innovation Norway has a MICE project for the domestic market. |

**Collection of statistics on the Meetings Industry?:** yes.

| | |
|---|---|
| **Importance / size** | Fifteen per cent of the guest nights in hotels are related to meetings. |
| **Evolution MI** | The share has been relatively stable in the recent past. |

# International Tourism by Origin

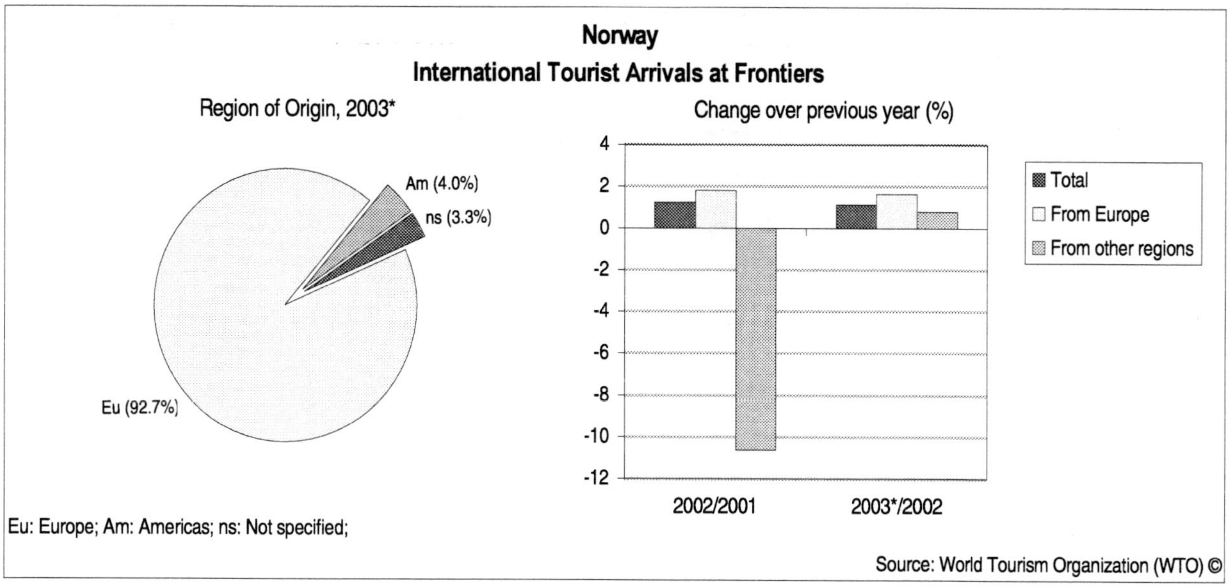


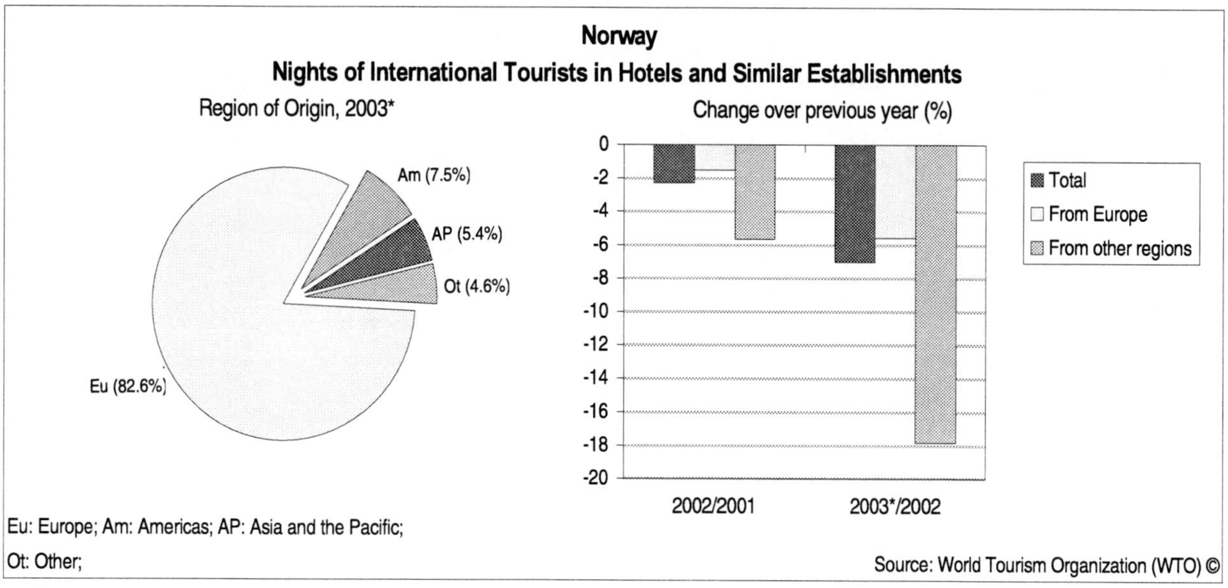

**Norway**

**International Tourist Arrivals at Frontiers (by nationality)**

| | | | | (thousand) | Market share (%) | | Growth rate (%) | | Average per year (%) |
|---|---|---|---|---|---|---|---|---|---|
| | 1995 | 2001 | 2002 | 2003* | 1995 | 2003* | 2002/01 | 2003*/02 | 1995-2003* |
| **Total** | .. | **3,073** | **3,111** | **3,146** | | **100** | **1.2** | **1.1** | |
| *From Europe* | .. | *2,817* | *2,868* | *2,915* | | *92.7* | *1.8* | *1.6* | |
| Sweden | .. | 884 | 860 | 844 | | 26.8 | -2.7 | -1.9 | |
| Denmark | .. | 545 | 554 | 556 | | 17.7 | 1.7 | 0.4 | |
| Germany | .. | 492 | 507 | 543 | | 17.3 | 3.0 | 7.1 | |
| United Kingdom | .. | 231 | 249 | 243 | | 7.7 | 7.8 | -2.4 | |
| Finland | .. | 190 | 215 | 185 | | 5.9 | 13.2 | -14.0 | |
| Netherlands | .. | 121 | 120 | 126 | | 4.0 | -0.8 | 5.0 | |
| France | .. | 79 | 83 | 90 | | 2.9 | 5.1 | 8.4 | |
| Italy | .. | 41 | 44 | 53 | | 1.7 | 7.3 | 20.5 | |
| Switzerland | .. | 39 | 38 | 38 | | 1.2 | -2.6 | 0.0 | |
| Spain | .. | 29 | 32 | 36 | | 1.1 | 10.3 | 12.5 | |
| Belgium | .. | 25 | 28 | 33 | | 1.0 | 12.0 | 17.9 | |
| Austria | .. | 22 | 22 | 22 | | 0.7 | 0.0 | 0.0 | |
| Other Europe | .. | 119 | 116 | 146 | | 4.6 | -2.5 | 25.9 | |
| *From other regions* | .. | *141* | *126* | *127* | | *4.0* | *-10.6* | *0.8* | |
| United States | .. | 141 | 126 | 127 | | 4.0 | -10.6 | 0.8 | |
| *Other World/Not specified* | .. | *115* | *117* | *104* | | *3.3* | *1.7* | *-11.1* | |

Source: World Tourism Organization (WTO) © (Data as collected by WTO December 2004)

**Norway**

**Nights of International Tourists in Hotels and Similar Establishments (by nationality)**

| | | | | (thousand) | Market share (%) | | Growth rate (%) | | Average per year (%) |
|---|---|---|---|---|---|---|---|---|---|
| | 1995 | 2001 | 2002 | 2003* | 1995 | 2003* | 2002/01 | 2003*/02 | 1995-2003* |
| **Total** | **4,985** | **4,815** | **4,706** | **4,375** | **100** | **100** | **-2.3** | **-7.0** | **-1.6** |
| *From Europe* | *4,164* | *3,887* | *3,828* | *3,614* | *83.5* | *82.6* | *-1.5* | *-5.6* | *-1.8* |
| Germany | 1,065 | 814 | 768 | 774 | 21.4 | 17.7 | -5.7 | 0.8 | -3.9 |
| Denmark | 951 | 777 | 736 | 617 | 19.1 | 14.1 | -5.2 | -16.2 | -5.3 |
| United Kingdom | 422 | 517 | 545 | 516 | 8.5 | 11.8 | 5.4 | -5.2 | 2.6 |
| Sweden | 643 | 585 | 550 | 475 | 12.9 | 10.9 | -6.1 | -13.6 | -3.7 |
| Netherlands | 248 | 270 | 280 | 283 | 5.0 | 6.5 | 3.6 | 1.2 | 1.7 |
| France | 272 | 230 | 230 | 220 | 5.5 | 5.0 | -0.2 | -4.2 | -2.6 |
| Spain | 59 | 172 | 176 | 180 | 1.2 | 4.1 | 2.4 | 2.7 | 14.9 |
| Italy | 110 | 122 | 130 | 142 | 2.2 | 3.3 | 6.8 | 9.1 | 3.2 |
| Finland | 90 | 69 | 70 | 60 | 1.8 | 1.4 | 0.9 | -13.7 | -4.9 |
| Switzerland | 71 | 61 | 65 | 60 | 1.4 | 1.4 | 6.2 | -7.8 | -2.1 |
| Belgium | 29 | 26 | 27 | 32 | 0.6 | 0.7 | 2.8 | 19.2 | 1.3 |
| Austria | 30 | 28 | 24 | 25 | 0.6 | 0.6 | -11.8 | 3.3 | -2.3 |
| Poland | 9 | 19 | 21 | 22 | 0.2 | 0.5 | 9.5 | 6.8 | 11.1 |
| Greece | 7 | 12 | 13 | 14 | 0.1 | 0.3 | 12.0 | 10.7 | 8.5 |
| Portugal | 6 | 13 | 14 | 14 | 0.1 | 0.3 | 5.0 | -1.4 | 10.9 |
| Czech Rep | 12 | 12 | 11 | 12 | 0.2 | 0.3 | -10.7 | 5.5 | -0.4 |
| Iceland | 11 | 12 | 12 | 12 | 0.2 | 0.3 | -4.1 | -1.3 | 1.1 |
| Hungary | 3 | 5 | 6 | 8 | 0.1 | 0.2 | 14.4 | 27.0 | 14.7 |
| Ireland | 2 | 7 | 8 | 7 | 0.0 | 0.2 | 8.2 | -6.3 | 16.8 |
| Turkey | 2 | 3 | 4 | 3 | 0.0 | 0.1 | 46.1 | -13.8 | 7.6 |
| Slovakia | 3 | 4 | 3 | 3 | 0.1 | 0.1 | -18.2 | 6.3 | 2.1 |
| Luxembourg | 1 | 2 | 2 | 3 | 0.0 | 0.1 | 23.5 | 7.2 | 7.6 |
| Other Europe | 117 | 126 | 133 | 130 | 2.3 | 3.0 | 5.9 | -2.2 | 1.3 |
| *From other regions* | *619* | *740* | *698* | *574* | *12.4* | *13.1* | *-5.7* | *-17.8* | *-0.9* |
| United States | 347 | 382 | 356 | 298 | 7.0 | 6.8 | -6.7 | -16.3 | -1.9 |
| Japan | 150 | 167 | 147 | 113 | 3.0 | 2.6 | -12.2 | -23.5 | -3.6 |
| Canada | 13 | 14 | 15 | 15 | 0.3 | 0.3 | 6.8 | -1.0 | 1.5 |
| Australia | 15 | 15 | 18 | 15 | 0.3 | 0.3 | 24.0 | -19.5 | -0.8 |
| All Africa | 8 | 10 | 14 | 13 | 0.2 | 0.3 | 39.0 | -4.9 | 7.1 |
| Mexico | 1 | 2 | 3 | 3 | 0.0 | 0.1 | 43.1 | 4.2 | 13.6 |
| New Zealand | 2 | 2 | 2 | 2 | 0.0 | 0.1 | -5.7 | 29.5 | 3.3 |
| Other Americas | 14 | 16 | 13 | 11 | 0.3 | 0.3 | -18.2 | -15.7 | -2.5 |
| Other Asia | 70 | 132 | 131 | 104 | 1.4 | 2.4 | -1.5 | -20.0 | 5.2 |
| *Other World/Not specified* | *202* | *189* | *180* | *187* | *4.1* | *4.3* | *-4.7* | *4.1* | *-1.0* |

Source: World Tourism Organization (WTO) ©

(Data as collected by WTO December 2004)

# III.1.6 Sweden Northern Europe

## Profile

| Sweden | | |
|---|---|---|
| | Capital | Stockholm |
| | Area (1000 km²) | 450 |
| | Population (2003, million) | 9.0 |
| | Gross Domestic Product (GDP) (2003, euro million) | 318,966 |
| | GDP per capita (2003, euro) | 35,539 |
| **Europe** | GDP growth (real, %) | |
| **Northern Europe** | '-> 2002: 2.1; 2003: 1.6; 2004*: 3.0; 2005*: 2.5 | |

| | 2001 | 2002 | 2003* | 2002/2001 | 2003*/2002 |
|---|---|---|---|---|---|
| **International Arrivals** | | | | | |
| Visitors (1000) | 14,721 | 14,271 | .. | -3.1 | |
| Tourists (overnight visitors) (1000) | 7,431 \| | 7,459 | 7,627 | 0.4 | 2.3 |
| - per 100 of inhabitants | 83 | 83 | 85 | | |
| Same-day visitors (1000) | 7,290 | 6,813 | .. | -6.5 | |
| **Tourism accommodation** | | | | | |
| Number of rooms | 99,267 | 95,125 | 96,372 | -4.2 | 1.3 |
| *Nights spent in collective establishments (1000)* | 41,194 | 42,896 | 44,054 | 4.1 | 2.7 |
| by non-residents (inbound tourism) | 9,133 | 9,768 | 9,715 | 7.0 | -0.5 |
| by residents (domestic tourism) | 32,061 | 33,128 | 34,339 | 3.3 | 3.7 |
| *Nights spent in hotels and similar establishments (1000)* | 21,664 | 21,011 | 21,068 | -3.0 | 0.3 |
| by non-residents (inbound tourism) | 4,927 | 4,868 | 4,833 | -1.2 | -0.7 |
| by residents (domestic tourism) | 16,737 | 16,143 | 16,235 | -3.5 | 0.6 |
| **Outbound Tourism** | | | | | |
| Trips abroad (1000) | 10,500 | 12,927 | 12,579 | 23.1 | -2.7 |
| - per 100 of inhabitants | 117 | 144 | 140 | | |
| **Receipts and Expenditure for International Tourism** | | | | | |
| International Tourism Receipts (euro million) | 4,605 | 5,259 | 5,609 | 14.2 | 6.7 |
| - per Tourist Arrival (euro) | 620 | 705 | 735 | 13.8 | 4.3 |
| - per Visitor Arrival (euro) | 313 | 369 | .. | 17.8 | |
| - per capita (euro) | 515 | 587 | 625 | | |
| International Fare Receipts (euro million) | 1,025 | 1,073 | 1,316 | 4.6 | 22.6 |
| International Tourism Expenditure (euro million) | 7,493 | 8,152 | 8,774 | 8.8 | 7.6 |
| - per trip (euro) | 714 | 631 | 697 | -11.6 | 10.6 |
| - per capita (euro) | 838 | 910 | 978 | | |
| International Fare Expenditure (euro million) | 1,077 | 1,027 | 1,141 | -4.6 | 11.1 |
| △ International Tourism Balance (euro million) | -2,889 | -2,893 | -3,164 | | |
| △ International Fare Balance (euro million) | -52 | 46 | 174 | | |

Source: World Tourism Organization (WTO) (Data as collected by WTO December 2004)

See annex for methodological notes and reference of external sources used.

# Survey

Contributed by *Swedish Tourist Authority*
www.visit-sweden.com (The Swedish Travel & Tourism Council). (promotional)
www.tourist.se (Swedish Tourist Authority) ;www.swetourism.se (The Swedish Travel & Tourism Council). (institutional/corporate)
www.tourist.se (Swedish Tourist Authority) ; www.scb.se (Statistics Sweden). (research and data)

## Tourism development and outlook

**Overall evaluation of results**

An increase in volume (nights spent) was recorded during 2003 (+3,1%). Inbound tourism decreased by 0,5 per cent and domestic nights increased by 4,2 per cent. But the economic development (revenues for all types of commercial accommodations) did not follow the same development, and decreased by 2,2 per cent. The most significant factor for this development is a shift of demand, with a reduction of the MICE market and an increase of the leisure/private market.

An unstable domestic and international economic situation contributed to a reduction of inbound tourism to Sweden. According to the official TSA calculations for Sweden, the total tourist consumption decreased by 0,5 per cent to 167 billion SEK (2,5% of total GDP) in 2003. Domestic private consumption increased by 2,9 per cent to 82 billion SEK and the export value of inbound tourism decreased by 6,2 per cent to 47 billion SEK.

Employment in the travel and tourism industry increased by 1,4 per cent to 127 thousand employed (years worked). During the period 1995 to 2003 employment in the travel and tourism industry has increased by 35 per cent.

**Supply**

*Accommodation:*

Classification of hotels (1 to 5 stars) in Sweden started during 2003, total capacity increased by 1,6 per cent. The occupancy rate in percent of available beds stayed at the same level (33%). Employment also stayed at the same level as 2002.

*Travel agencies / tour operators:*

According to TSA calculations the consumption decreased by 7,7 per cent and employment dropped by 2,2 per cent.

*Transport capacity:*

According to TSA calculations the production value for rail, bus, sea and air transport decreased by 1,9 per cent. But employment in the sector increased by 5,2 per cent.

*Attractions / entertainment:*

The total number of visitors to attractions in Sweden increased by approximately 1,2 per cent and employment in the tourist sectors of culture, recreation and sports increased by 9,7 per cent.

**External factors**

The general political situation in Sweden is characterised by stability. 2003 was a year of slow business development and this lead to an increase in domestic tourism and a decrease in outgoing tourism.

Entry formalities are few and Sweden is well connected to the international air, train, road and ferry networks.

**Tourism policy**

The ongoing implementation of a strategic programme for tourism, produced in 2001, involving several hundred organizations, companies and government authorities with connection to tourism. The programme consists of more than one hundred separate projects.

**Marketing & promotion**

A continued focus on major and new markets in Europe as well as development of some highly interesting markets in Asia.

**Outlook 2004**

Slow and steady growth during the coming years, highly dependent on the general development in the economy.

## International Meetings Industry (MI)

**Characteristics of supply**

The MICE industry has a great potential in Sweden.
A lot of cities of Sweden boasts with all characteristics for successful meetings, conventions, exotic incentives & events, exhibitions, namely:

- Professionalism and excellent organisational skills;
- Easily accessible with direct daily flights from major European hubs (main cities);
- A wide range of centrally located congress centres;
- Everything is within walking distance (small cities);
- A friendly, welcoming environment in a country where English is widely spoken;
- Unknown and exotic meeting/incentive products;
- Value for money: good price/standard relation in hotels and restaurants.

Main destinations for big events, conventions and meetings would be Stockholm, Göteborg and Malmö.
For small and medium sized events, Meetings and Incentives Sweden offers a wide range of different and unique regions with professional products such as, the Northern Sweden (Ice Hotel, Motorcoach safaris, virgin nature etc), the Stockholm area with the Archipelago, etc,.

**Organisation of promotion**

The international promotion on a national level is done by the Swedish Travel & Tourism Council (www.visit-sweden.com).
Sweden has a number of regional Convention Bureaux (Stockholm: <www.meetstockholm.se> ; Göteborg: <www.goteborg.com> ; Malmö: <www.malmo.se/congress>, etc.).
Professional Congress Organizers are also doing their own International promotion (as an example see Congress Stockholm: <www.stockholmtown.com/congress> and Stockholm Convention Bureau: <www.stocon.se>).

**Collection of statistics on the Meetings Industry?:** no.

**Description**

We have results which permit to measure meeting capacity on a national level and the regional distribution.

**Importance / size**

No statistics available.
An estimate for 2002 shows a turnover of SEK 32 billion for the Meetings Industry.

**Evolution MI**

The evolution in recent years is difficult to measure. Based on the TSA there has been a noticeable decrease in domestic business consumption since 2002 and it is reasonable to assume that the decrease also comprises the Meeting Industry.
On the other hand, there has been a notable focus on the Meeting Industry from regions, cities, and the travel industry it self.
It is believed that this part of the Tourism Industry has a great growth potential in the future development of the tourism industry. The economic importance is prevalent, i.e. it is a fact that the spending of a meeting/convention attendee is much higher than that of the leisure traveller.

# International Tourism by Origin

**Sweden**

**International Tourist Arrivals at Frontiers**

Region of Origin, 2003* | Change over previous year (%)

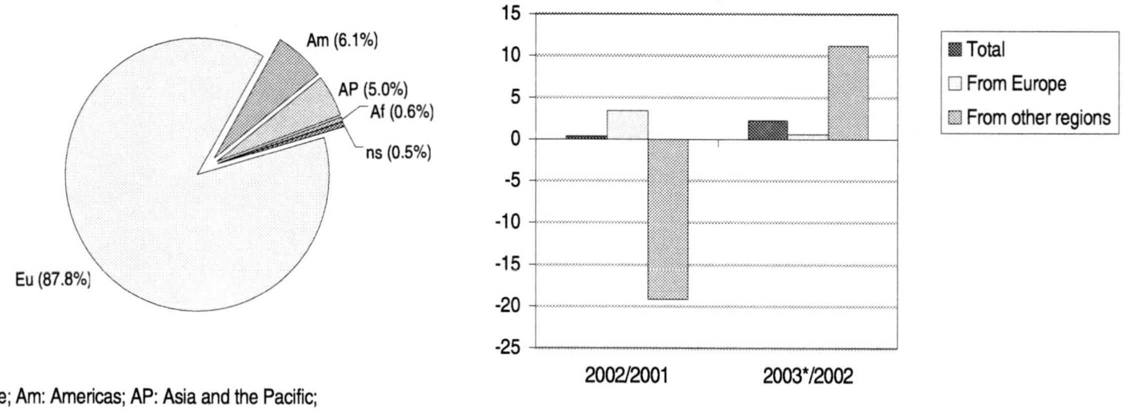


Eu: Europe; Am: Americas; AP: Asia and the Pacific;

Af: Africa; ns: Not specified;

Source: World Tourism Organization (WTO) ©

**Sweden**

**Nights of International Tourists in All Accommodation Establishments**

Region of Origin, 2003* | Change over previous year (%)

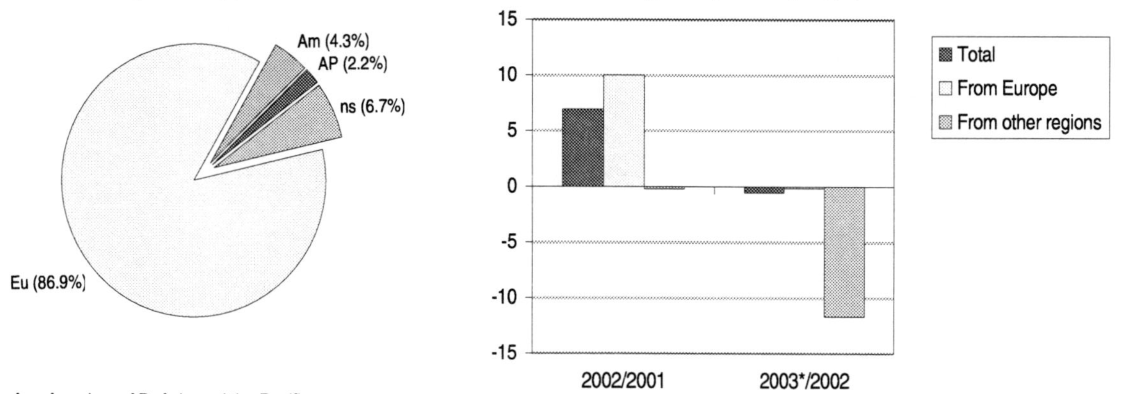


Eu: Europe; Am: Americas; AP: Asia and the Pacific;

ns: Not specified;

Source: World Tourism Organization (WTO) ©

**Sweden**

**International Tourist Arrivals at Frontiers (by residence)**

| | | | | (thousand) | Market share (%) | | Growth rate (%) | | Average per year (%) |
|---|---|---|---|---|---|---|---|---|---|
| | 1995 | 2001 | 2002 | 2003* | 1995 | 2003* | 2002/01 | 2003*/02 | 1995-2003* |
| **Total** | .. | **7,431** | **7,459** | **7,627** | | **100** | **0.4** | **2.3** | |
| *From Europe* | .. | *6,437* | *6,656* | *6,696* | | *87.8* | *3.4* | *0.6* | |
| Germany | .. | 1,493 | 1,696 | 1,736 | | 22.8 | 13.6 | 2.4 | |
| Denmark | .. | 1,351 | 1,361 | 1,556 | | 20.4 | 0.7 | 14.3 | |
| Finland | .. | 817 | 795 | 639 | | 8.4 | -2.7 | -19.6 | |
| United Kingdom | .. | 577 | 499 | 527 | | 6.9 | -13.5 | 5.6 | |
| Norway | .. | 477 | 587 | 519 | | 6.8 | 23.1 | -11.6 | |
| All Central/Eastern Europe | .. | 304 | 326 | 375 | | 4.9 | 7.2 | 15.0 | |
| Netherlands | .. | 322 | 309 | 318 | | 4.2 | -4.0 | 2.9 | |
| France | .. | 284 | 279 | 239 | | 3.1 | -1.8 | -14.3 | |
| Other Europe | .. | 812 | 804 | 787 | | 10.3 | -1.0 | -2.1 | |
| *From other regions* | .. | *994* | *803* | *893* | | *11.7* | *-19.2* | *11.2* | |
| United States | .. | 402 | 328 | 349 | | 4.6 | -18.4 | 6.4 | |
| All Asia | .. | 357 | 282 | 309 | | 4.1 | -21.0 | 9.6 | |
| All Oceania | .. | 54 | 66 | 71 | | 0.9 | 22.2 | 7.6 | |
| Canada | .. | 73 | 41 | 50 | | 0.7 | -43.8 | 22.0 | |
| All Africa | .. | 37 | 42 | 46 | | 0.6 | 13.5 | 9.5 | |
| Other Americas | .. | 71 | 44 | 68 | | 0.9 | -38.0 | 54.5 | |
| *Other World/Not specified* | .. | .. | .. | *38* | | *0.5* | | | |

Source: World Tourism Organization (WTO) © (Data as collected by WTO December 2004)

**Sweden**

**Nights of International Tourists in All Accommodation Establishments (by residence)**

| | | | | (thousand) | Market share (%) | | Growth rate (%) | | Average per year (%) |
|---|---|---|---|---|---|---|---|---|---|
| | 1995 | 2001 | 2002 | 2003* | 1995 | 2003* | 2002/01 | 2003*/02 | 1995-2003* |
| **Total** | **7,861** | **9,133** | **9,768** | **9,715** | **100** | **100** | **6.9** | **-0.5** | **2.7** |
| *From Europe* | *6,863* | *7,684* | *8,452* | *8,440* | *87.3* | *86.9* | *10.0* | *-0.2* | *2.6* |
| Norway | 1,602 | 2,053 | 2,541 | 2,466 | 20.4 | 25.4 | 23.8 | -3.0 | 5.5 |
| Germany | 2,079 | 1,832 | 1,914 | 2,013 | 26.5 | 20.7 | 4.5 | 5.2 | -0.4 |
| Denmark | 956 | 910 | 1,000 | 1,024 | 12.2 | 10.5 | 9.9 | 2.4 | 0.9 |
| United Kingdom | 358 | 612 | 617 | 593 | 4.6 | 6.1 | 0.9 | -4.0 | 6.5 |
| Netherlands | 455 | 491 | 541 | 577 | 5.8 | 5.9 | 10.2 | 6.5 | 3.0 |
| Finland | 420 | 407 | 449 | 418 | 5.3 | 4.3 | 10.3 | -6.9 | -0.1 |
| France | 177 | 212 | 216 | 201 | 2.2 | 2.1 | 1.7 | -6.9 | 1.6 |
| Italy | 166 | 190 | 193 | 179 | 2.1 | 1.8 | 1.2 | -7.0 | 0.9 |
| Switzerland | 122 | 142 | 167 | 139 | 1.6 | 1.4 | 18.1 | -16.9 | 1.6 |
| Russian Federation | 53 | 84 | 114 | 113 | 0.7 | 1.2 | 35.1 | -0.8 | 10.0 |
| Spain | 35 | 105 | 101 | 95 | 0.4 | 1.0 | -3.9 | -6.0 | 13.1 |
| Poland | 37 | 110 | 106 | 88 | 0.5 | 0.9 | -4.2 | -16.8 | 11.6 |
| Belgium | 35 | 67 | 56 | 61 | 0.4 | 0.6 | -16.1 | 9.3 | 7.4 |
| Austria | 32 | 37 | 40 | 41 | 0.4 | 0.4 | 5.9 | 2.4 | 3.2 |
| Estonia | 13 | 24 | 30 | 23 | 0.2 | 0.2 | 26.2 | -22.7 | 7.2 |
| Ireland | .. | 12 | 13 | 19 | | 0.2 | 11.3 | 41.8 | |
| Czech Rep | .. | 13 | 14 | 18 | | 0.2 | 9.9 | 27.5 | |
| Latvia | 12 | 13 | 16 | 15 | 0.1 | 0.1 | 20.6 | -9.1 | 3.0 |
| Lithuania | 11 | 13 | 10 | 13 | 0.1 | 0.1 | -23.3 | 27.9 | 1.3 |
| Iceland | .. | 4 | 5 | 9 | | 0.1 | 19.9 | 73.0 | |
| Portugal | .. | 6 | 7 | 8 | | 0.1 | 5.2 | 26.8 | |
| Turkey | .. | 3 | 3 | 7 | | 0.1 | 20.5 | 116.3 | |
| Hungary | .. | 7 | 5 | 7 | | 0.1 | -28.5 | 43.8 | |
| Greece | .. | 6 | 5 | 7 | | 0.1 | -13.2 | 42.5 | |
| Luxembourg | .. | 2 | 2 | 4 | | 0.0 | -12.0 | 144.7 | |
| Other intraregional | 300 | 330 | 288 | 303 | 3.8 | 3.1 | -12.5 | 5.1 | 0.1 |
| *From other regions* | *496* | *713* | *711* | *628* | *6.3* | *6.5* | *-0.2* | *-11.7* | *3.0* |
| United States | 327 | 424 | 392 | 365 | 4.2 | 3.8 | -7.5 | -6.9 | 1.4 |
| Japan | 109 | 130 | 138 | 110 | 1.4 | 1.1 | 5.6 | -20.4 | 0.0 |
| Canada | 23 | 56 | 62 | 34 | 0.3 | 0.3 | 11.7 | -45.7 | 5.0 |
| Australia | 26 | 26 | 31 | 29 | 0.3 | 0.3 | 22.9 | -8.0 | 1.5 |
| Korea, Republic of | 11 | 11 | 17 | 13 | 0.1 | 0.1 | 52.7 | -21.4 | 2.1 |
| New Zealand | .. | 2 | 2 | 3 | | 0.0 | 10.6 | 25.4 | |
| Other Americas | .. | 13 | 13 | 20 | | 0.2 | -1.6 | 50.6 | |
| Other Asia | .. | 51 | 56 | 55 | | 0.6 | 10.0 | -1.0 | |
| *Other World/Not specified* | *501* | *736* | *604* | *647* | *6.4* | *6.7* | *-18.0* | *7.1* | *3.2* |

Source: World Tourism Organization (WTO) © (Data as collected by WTO December 2004)

# III.1.7 the United Kingdom Northern Europe

## Profile

# United Kingdom

Europe
Northern Europe

| | |
|---|---|
| Capital | London |
| Area (1000 km²) | 243 |
| Population (2003, million) | 60.1 |
| Gross Domestic Product (GDP) (2003, euro million) | 1,901,111 |
| GDP per capita (2003, euro) | 31,875 |
| GDP growth (real, %) | |
| '-> 2002: 1.8; 2003: 2.2; 2004*: 3.4; 2005*: 2.5 | |

| | 2001 | 2002 | 2003* | 2002/2001 | 2003*/2002 |
|---|---|---|---|---|---|
| **International Arrivals** | | | | | |
| Visitors (1000) | 22,835 | 24,180 | 24,715 | 5.9 | 2.2 |
| - per 100 of inhabitants | 38 | 40 | 41 | | |
| Same-day visitors (1000) | 1,853 | 1,873 | 1,928 | 1.1 | 2.9 |
| **Tourism accommodation** | | | | | |
| *Nights spent in collective establishments (1000)* | 719,116 | 731,225 | 693,972 | 1.7 | -5.1 |
| by non-residents (inbound tourism) | 189,516 | 199,285 | 203,432 | 5.2 | 2.1 |
| by residents (domestic tourism) | 529,600 | 531,940 | 490,540 | 0.4 | -7.8 |
| **Outbound Tourism** | | | | | |
| Trips abroad (1000) | 58,281 | 59,377 | 61,424 | 1.9 | 3.4 |
| - per 100 of inhabitants | 98 | 99 | 102 | | |
| **Receipts and Expenditure for International Tourism** | | | | | |
| International Tourism Receipts (euro million) | 20,424 | 22,944 | 24,062 | 12.3 | 4.9 |
| - per Visitor Arrival (euro) | 894 | 949 | 974 | 6.1 | 2.6 |
| - per capita (euro) | 342 | 383 | 400 | | |
| International Fare Receipts (euro million) | 7,733 | 8,225 | 8,359 | 6.4 | 1.6 |
| International Tourism Expenditure (euro million) | 41,068 | 46,609 | 51,267 | 13.5 | 10.0 |
| - per trip (euro) | 705 | 785 | 835 | 11.4 | 6.3 |
| - per capita (euro) | 688 | 778 | 853 | | |
| International Fare Expenditure (euro million) | 8,840 | 9,895 | 10,708 | 11.9 | 8.2 |
| △ International Tourism Balance (euro million) | -20,644 | -23,665 | -27,206 | | |
| △ International Fare Balance (euro million) | -1,108 | -1,669 | -2,349 | | |

Source: World Tourism Organization (WTO) (Data as collected by WTO December 2004)

See annex for methodological notes and reference of external sources used.

# Survey

Contributed by *VisitBritain*
www.visitbritain.com (promotional)
www.visitbritain.org/ukindustry/ (institutional/corporate)
www.staruk.org.uk/ (research and data)

## Tourism development and outlook

**Overall evaluation of results**

Inbound arrivals grew 3 per cent, a good performance in the context of reduced travel from the United States of America (because of the Iraq situation) and from the Far East (Severe Acute Respiratory Syndrome outbreak). The last quarter showed good recovery with arrivals up 8 per cent.
Arrivals from Europe were stronger through most of the year, particularly Eastern Europe. There was a small reduction in length of stay of europeans.
Arrivals on Business trips saw a small decline, while holiday and especially Visits to Friends and Relatives trips increased.
Official statistics for domestic tourism show volume decline with small value growth, but this conflicts with most anecdotal evidence that suggests a good year.

**Supply**

The main impact in supply is from the growth of low-cost flight operators and budget hotels.
There is some evidence of contraction of supply for bed and breakfast and guesthouse accommodation as owners convert to residential use and sell up, taking advantage of high and (still) rising house prices in the United Kingdom.

**External factors**

The situation in Iraq and the outbreak of Severe Acute Respiratory Syndrome (SARS) had a major impact, particularly in the second quarter.
The strength of the euro and the weakening of the dollar will also have had an impact.
The United Kingdom enjoyed some exceptionally hot weather in August.
In the last quarter the electrification of the railway line in South East England reduced journey times on Eurostar.

**Tourism policy**

*The National Tourism Office (NTO) merger:*
The main development last year was the changed role of the NTO. On 1st April 2003, a new NTO structure came into effect to allow a greater focus on marketing activity. The British Tourist Authority merged with the English Tourism Council to form VisitBritain. The role of the new organisation is to promote England within Britain and Britain to the rest of the world.
*Legislation:*
A new Licensing Act was passed on 10th July 2003 controlling the sale of alcohol. The Act brings together in one statute the regulation of the use of premises for licensed activities. The 2003 Act is in the process of being implemented. Key measures contained in the Act include:

- More flexible opening hours for premises, potentially up to 24 hours, seven days a week;
- A single premises licence which permit premises to be used to supply alcohol, to provide regulated entertainment and to provide refreshment late at night. This will bring together the six existing licensing regimes (alcohol, public entertainment, cinemas, theatres, late-night refreshment houses and night cafes) thereby cutting down on red tape;
- A new system of personal licences relating to the supply of alcohol which will enable holders to move more freely between premises where a premise licence is in force; subject to police scrutiny.

A draft Gambling Bill was published. The proposed changes are aimed at achieving a managed relaxation of outdated restrictions and greater choice for adult gamblers, balanced by greater emphasis on social responsibility and protection of the vulnerable, particularly children. The Bill will allow for the establishment of a new regulator, the Gambling Commission, transforming the existing Gaming Board for Great Britain into a new body with wider functions, greater flexibility to act and stronger enforcement powers.
*Consultation:*
There have also been government consultations on the future development of air transport in the United Kingdom to further the development of a sustainable airport policy for the next 30 years.

**Marketing & promotion**

The International Marketing Strategy "Leading the World to Britain" provided a strategic framework for VisitBritain's international marketing. It aims to boost inbound tourism to every part of England, Scotland and Wales in the longer term by working with all parts of the tourism industry. The highlights of the strategy include:
- Sharpening the brand position of Britain in relation to the nations and regions of the United Kingdom;
- Honing our marketing skills and exploiting the potential of new media;
- Engaging our public and private stakeholders in the marketing of Britain;
- Aligning our organisation and culture to deliver these objectives.

The restructuring of our international operations into regional 'hubs' or centres of excellence to monitor and respond to opportunities throughout its region, not just in our core markets. Plans were also laid for four 'new' markets that held the most potential. It also set clear priorities in areas such as Customer Relationship Management (CRM), business tourism, Internet marketing and 'new' market development as well as development of a strong brand for Britain. Continued fundamental shift in distribution, with the Internet and direct marketing replacing walk-in centres and telephone calls as the main point of customer contact.
2003 also saw:
- A very successful European short-break campaign in response to the impact of the Severe Acute Respiratory Syndrome (SARS) virus and the war in Iraq on tourism from longer-haul destinations;
- The first co-ordinated domestic marketing strategy for England in 10 years
- Enjoy England;
- The first Royal Tourism Day in June.

**Outlook 2004**

We are forecasting a 3 per cent growth in 2004 for inbound visitors, assuming that there will be no further major disasters.
Similar growth rates are anticipated for domestic tourism.

## International Meetings Industry (MI)

**Characteristics of supply**

Meetings, congress, conference and convention product supply is the United Kingdom wide, key international conference destinations with purpose built venues include: Aberdeen, Belfast, Birmingham, Bournemouth, Brighton, Cardiff, Edinburgh, Glasgow, Harrogate, Liverpool, London, Manchester, Newcastle and Gateshead.
Incentive product supply is the United Kingdom wide with a strong emphasis on luxury products particularly in London and Scotland, outdoor activities and increasingly spa products.
Exhibitions and Fairs product supply is the United Kingdom wide, key international exhibition venues with purpose built facilities (single venue 10,000$m^2$) include: Birmingham, Belfast, Manchester, Glasgow and London.

**Organisation of promotion**

International MICE industry destination promotion in the United Kingdom is organised on national, regional and city levels. With regard to international marketing, the key players are:

- VisitBritain Business Tourism Department, responsible for marketing the United Kingdom wide MICE product internationally <www.visitbritain.com/businesstourism>;
- Visit Scotland Business Tourism Unit, responsible for marketing Scottish MICE product internationally <ww.conventionscotland.com>;
- Wales Tourist Board, responsible for marketing Welsh MICE product internationally <www.meetings.visitwales.com>;
- Visit London Business and Conventions, responsible for marketing London MICE product internationally <www.visitlondon.com/business>;
- Regional and City Convention Bureau, normally divisions within regional and city tourist boards. Budgets and levels of activity vary greatly and these organisations are variously funded by regional development agencies, local authorities, membership fees and conference sales lead commissions. Links to most key organisations can be seen via the British Association of Conference Destinations <www.bacd.org.uk>.

**Collection of statistics on the Meetings Industry?:** yes.

**Description**

International Passenger Survey: Outbound international visitor survey on reason for visit, duration of visit, expenditure, etc. Ongoing with quarterly reports and yearly publication <www.tourismtrade.org.uk/uktrade/MarketIntelligence>.

The United Kingdom Conference Market Survey: the United Kingdom conference buyer survey <www.meetings.org>.

British Conference Venues Survey: the United Kingdom conference supplier survey <www.bacd.org.uk>.

The United Kingdom Exhibition Facts: statistical profile of the United Kingdom exhibition industry <www.exhibitionvenues.com>.

Various levels of business conversion analysis amongst destination marketing organisations for their stakeholder interest.

ICCA members feedback on confirmed international association conferences held.

**Importance / size**

According to International Passenger Survey figures for 2002:

- International visits to Britain where purpose of visit was to attend a conference in 2002 accounted for a total of 682 thousand visits, 2.8 million nights and £441 million in direct expenditure;
- International visits to Britain where purpose of visit was to attend an exhibition in 2002 accounted for a total of 254 thousand visits, one million nights and £173 million in direct expenditure;
- International visits to Britain where purpose of visit was for other business in 2002 accounted for a total of 6.2 million visits, 25 million nights and £2,959 million in direct expenditure;
- Information on the above may be obtained on: <www.tourismtrade.org.uk/uktrade/MarketIntelligence>.

According to the International Congress and Convention Association (ICCA) statistics on the international meetings market, the United Kingdom held the third highest number of international meetings in the world during 2002 (149 international meetings according to ICCA criteria <www.iccaworld.com>).

According to Union of International Associations (UIA/UAI) statistics on the top international meetings countries in 2002 the United Kingdom held the third highest number of international meetings in 2002 (5.5% of all international meetings by UIA measurement criteria <www.uia.org>).

**Evolution MI** International Passenger Survey data demonstrates year-on-year figures and is the basis for future growth projections: <www.tourismtrade.org.uk/uktrade/MarketIntelligence>.

# International Tourism by Origin

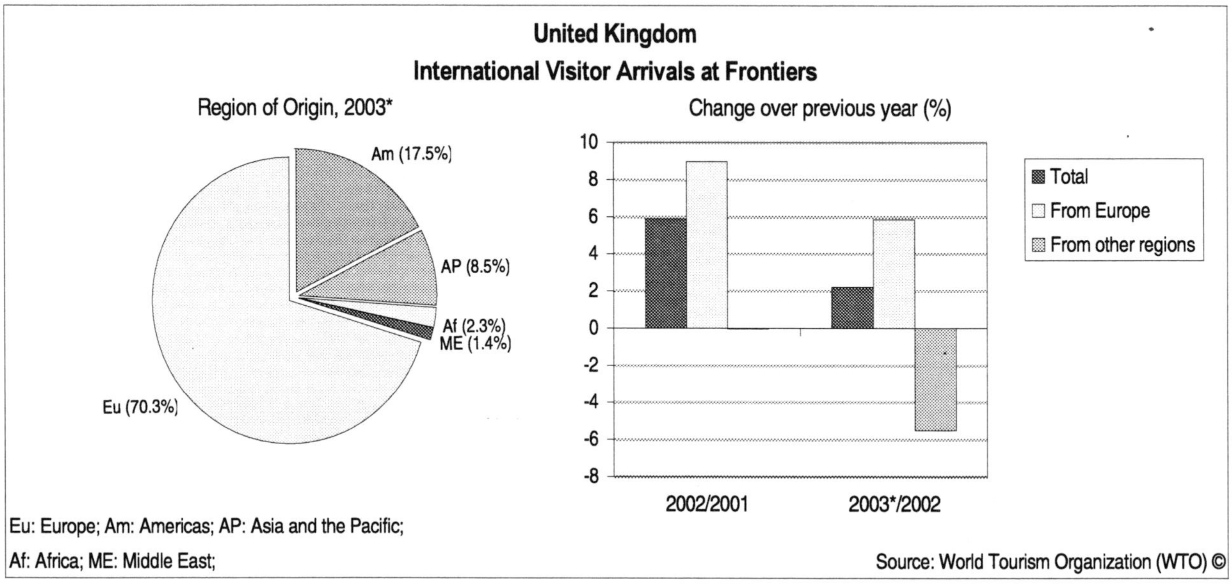


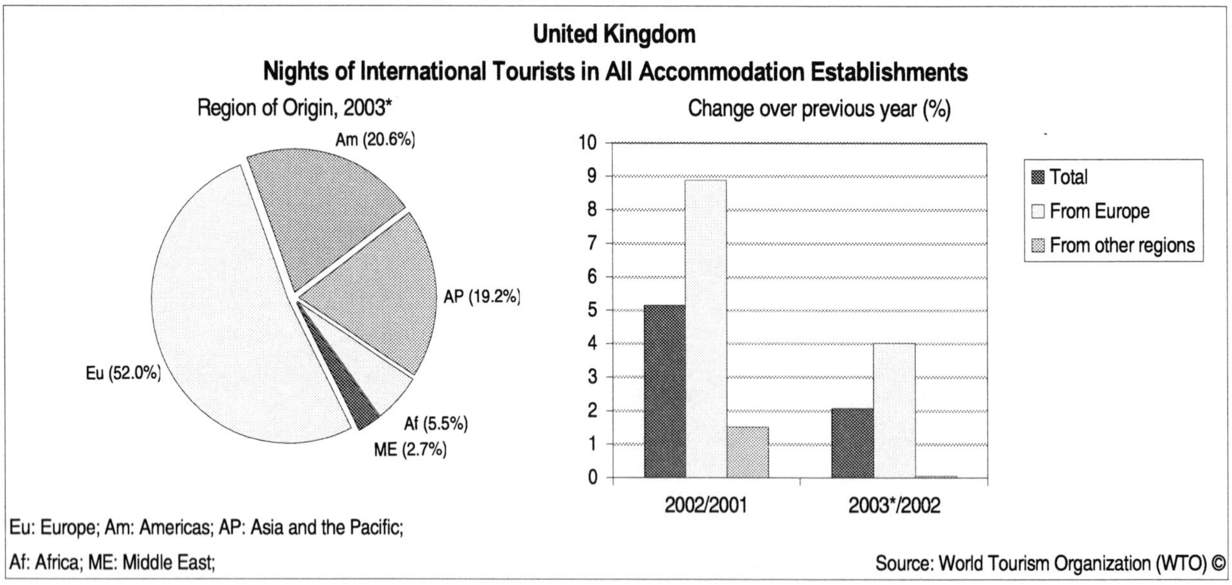

**United Kingdom**
**International Visitor Arrivals at Frontiers (by residence)**

| | | | | (thousand) | Market share (%) | | Growth rate (%) | | Average per year (%) |
|---|---|---|---|---|---|---|---|---|---|
| | 1995 | 2001 | 2002 | 2003* | 1995 | 2003* | 2002/01 | 2003*/02 | 1995-2003* |
| **Total** | **23,537** | **22,835** | **24,181** | **24,715** | **100** | **100** | **5.9** | **2.2** | **0.6** |
| *From Europe* | *15,790* | *15,060* | *16,409* | *17,371* | *67.1* | *70.3* | *9.0* | *5.9* | *1.2* |
| France | 3,184 | 2,852 | 3,077 | 3,073 | 13.5 | 12.4 | 7.9 | -0.1 | -0.4 |
| Germany | 2,654 | 2,309 | 2,556 | 2,611 | 11.3 | 10.6 | 10.7 | 2.2 | -0.2 |
| Ireland | 1,988 | 2,039 | 2,439 | 2,488 | 8.4 | 10.1 | 19.6 | 2.0 | 2.8 |
| Netherlands | 1,408 | 1,411 | 1,419 | 1,549 | 6.0 | 6.3 | 0.6 | 9.2 | 1.2 |
| Spain | 772 | 856 | 1,010 | 1,206 | 3.3 | 4.9 | 18.0 | 19.4 | 5.7 |
| Italy | 924 | 857 | 977 | 1,168 | 3.9 | 4.7 | 14.0 | 19.5 | 3.0 |
| Belgium | 1,296 | 916 | 966 | 936 | 5.5 | 3.8 | 5.5 | -3.1 | -4.0 |
| Switzerland | 541 | 514 | 593 | 564 | 2.3 | 2.3 | 15.4 | -4.9 | 0.5 |
| Sweden | 552 | 527 | 530 | 533 | 2.3 | 2.2 | 0.6 | 0.6 | -0.4 |
| Norway | 427 | 403 | 397 | 433 | 1.8 | 1.8 | -1.5 | 9.1 | 0.2 |
| Denmark | 327 | 394 | 431 | 425 | 1.4 | 1.7 | 9.4 | -1.4 | 3.3 |
| Poland | 183 | 225 | 188 | 325 | 0.8 | 1.3 | -16.4 | 72.9 | 7.4 |
| Austria | 255 | 191 | 219 | 263 | 1.1 | 1.1 | 14.7 | 20.1 | 0.4 |
| Czech Rep | 149 | 115 | 122 | 202 | 0.6 | 0.8 | 6.1 | 65.6 | 3.9 |
| Portugal | 157 | 172 | 170 | 193 | 0.7 | 0.8 | -1.2 | 13.5 | 2.6 |
| Greece | 166 | 185 | 169 | 185 | 0.7 | 0.7 | -8.6 | 9.5 | 1.4 |
| Israel | .. | 205 | 191 | 162 | | 0.7 | -6.8 | -15.2 | |
| Russian Federation | 141 | 108 | 117 | 138 | 0.6 | 0.6 | 8.3 | 17.9 | -0.3 |
| Finland | 123 | 100 | 121 | 122 | 0.5 | 0.5 | 21.0 | 0.8 | -0.1 |
| Hungary | 57 | 104 | 132 | 111 | 0.2 | 0.4 | 26.9 | -15.9 | 8.7 |
| Cyprus | .. | 76 | 80 | 104 | | 0.4 | 5.3 | 30.0 | |
| Turkey | 75 | 69 | 65 | 92 | 0.3 | 0.4 | -5.8 | 41.5 | 2.6 |
| Malta | .. | 46 | 36 | 50 | | 0.2 | -21.7 | 38.9 | |
| Other intraregional | 411 | 386 | 404 | 438 | 1.7 | 1.8 | 4.7 | 8.4 | 0.8 |
| *From other regions* | *7,747* | *7,775* | *7,772* | *7,344* | *32.9* | *29.7* | *0.0* | *-5.5* | *-0.7* |
| United States | 3,146 | 3,580 | 3,611 | 3,346 | 13.4 | 13.5 | 0.9 | -7.3 | 0.8 |
| Australia | 607 | 694 | 702 | 723 | 2.6 | 2.9 | 1.2 | 3.0 | 2.2 |
| Canada | 609 | 647 | 660 | 652 | 2.6 | 2.6 | 2.0 | -1.2 | 0.9 |
| Japan | 619 | 366 | 368 | 314 | 2.6 | 1.3 | 0.5 | -14.7 | -8.1 |
| South Africa | 243 | 319 | 276 | 266 | 1.0 | 1.1 | -13.5 | -3.6 | 1.1 |
| India | 163 | 189 | 205 | 199 | 0.7 | 0.8 | 8.5 | -2.9 | 2.5 |
| New Zealand | 131 | 151 | 137 | 144 | 0.6 | 0.6 | -9.3 | 5.1 | 1.2 |
| Hong Kong (China) | 169 | 146 | 158 | 131 | 0.7 | 0.5 | 8.2 | -17.1 | -3.1 |
| Untd Arab Emirates | .. | 112 | 109 | 113 | | 0.5 | -2.7 | 3.7 | |
| Korea, Republic of | 119 | 81 | 92 | 109 | 0.5 | 0.4 | 13.6 | 18.5 | -1.1 |
| Nigeria | 68 | 92 | 111 | 102 | 0.3 | 0.4 | 20.7 | -8.1 | 5.2 |
| All the Caribbean | 62 | 98 | 109 | 90 | 0.3 | 0.4 | 11.2 | -17.4 | 4.8 |
| Singapore | 97 | 86 | 84 | 79 | 0.4 | 0.3 | -2.3 | -6.0 | -2.5 |
| Mexico | 31 | 63 | 71 | 76 | 0.1 | 0.3 | 12.7 | 7.0 | 11.9 |
| Malaysia | 120 | 78 | 80 | 74 | 0.5 | 0.3 | 2.6 | -7.5 | -5.9 |
| Brazil | 105 | 69 | 83 | 70 | 0.4 | 0.3 | 20.3 | -15.7 | -4.9 |
| China | 31 | 58 | 64 | 68 | 0.1 | 0.3 | 10.3 | 6.3 | 10.3 |
| Saudi Arabia | 120 | 90 | 78 | 63 | 0.5 | 0.3 | -13.3 | -19.2 | -7.7 |
| Pakistan | 73 | 96 | 62 | 57 | 0.3 | 0.2 | -35.4 | -8.1 | -3.0 |
| Other interregional | 1,234 | 760 | 712 | 668 | 5.2 | 2.7 | -6.3 | -6.2 | -7.4 |

Source: World Tourism Organization (WTO) © (Data as collected by WTO December 2004)

**United Kingdom**

**Nights of International Tourists in All Accommodation Establishments (by residence)**

| | | | | (thousand) | Market share (%) | | Growth rate (%) | | Average per year (%) |
|---|---|---|---|---|---|---|---|---|---|
| | 1995 | 2001 | 2002 | 2003* | 1995 | 2003* | 2002/01 | 2003*/02 | 1995-2003* |
| **Total** | **220,300** | **189,513** | **199,283** | **203,431** | **100** | **100** | **5.2** | **2.1** | **-1.0** |
| *From Europe* | *122,800* | *93,437* | *101,739* | *105,831* | *55.7* | *52.0* | *8.9* | *4.0* | *-1.8* |
| Germany | 22,000 | 14,182 | 15,392 | 15,435 | 10.0 | 7.6 | 8.5 | 0.3 | -4.3 |
| France | 17,900 | 16,274 | 17,735 | 13,765 | 8.1 | 6.8 | 9.0 | -22.4 | -3.2 |
| Spain | 10,900 | 8,562 | 9,348 | 10,957 | 4.9 | 5.4 | 9.2 | 17.2 | 0.1 |
| Ireland | 15,400 | 8,077 | 9,927 | 9,675 | 7.0 | 4.8 | 22.9 | -2.5 | -5.6 |
| Italy | 10,700 | 7,186 | 7,749 | 8,048 | 4.9 | 4.0 | 7.8 | 3.9 | -3.5 |
| Poland | 3,400 | 2,865 | 3,870 | 7,993 | 1.5 | 3.9 | 35.1 | 106.5 | 11.3 |
| Netherlands | 6,500 | 5,859 | 6,276 | 7,032 | 3.0 | 3.5 | 7.1 | 12.0 | 1.0 |
| Switzerland | 3,800 | 3,599 | 4,118 | 3,514 | 1.7 | 1.7 | 14.4 | -14.7 | -1.0 |
| Sweden | 3,900 | 3,199 | 2,716 | 3,106 | 1.8 | 1.5 | -15.1 | 14.4 | -2.8 |
| Belgium | 3,600 | 2,721 | 2,999 | 2,667 | 1.6 | 1.3 | 10.2 | -11.1 | -3.7 |
| Norway | 2,700 | 2,107 | 1,829 | 1,948 | 1.2 | 1.0 | -13.2 | 6.5 | -4.0 |
| Denmark | 2,400 | 2,097 | 2,558 | 1,944 | 1.1 | 1.0 | 22.0 | -24.0 | -2.6 |
| Czech Rep | 2,600 | 987 | 770 | 1,940 | 1.2 | 1.0 | -22.0 | 151.9 | -3.6 |
| Austria | 2,000 | 1,268 | 1,761 | 1,813 | 0.9 | 0.9 | 38.9 | 3.0 | -1.2 |
| Greece | 2,000 | 1,618 | 2,015 | 1,715 | 0.9 | 0.8 | 24.5 | -14.9 | -1.9 |
| Hungary | 1,000 | 881 | 985 | 1,709 | 0.5 | 0.8 | 11.8 | 73.5 | 6.9 |
| Russian Federation | 1,900 | 1,688 | 1,395 | 1,548 | 0.9 | 0.8 | -17.4 | 11.0 | -2.5 |
| Portugal | 1,300 | 1,381 | 1,439 | 1,206 | 0.6 | 0.6 | 4.2 | -16.2 | -0.9 |
| Israel | .. | 1,622 | 1,452 | 1,166 | | 0.6 | -10.5 | -19.7 | |
| Turkey | 1,300 | 1,260 | 846 | 1,002 | 0.6 | 0.5 | -32.9 | 18.4 | -3.2 |
| Finland | 1,200 | 912 | 958 | 795 | 0.5 | 0.4 | 5.0 | -17.0 | -5.0 |
| Yugoslav SFR | 700 | 773 | 540 | 656 | 0.3 | 0.3 | -30.1 | 21.5 | -0.8 |
| Other Central/Eastern Europe | 3,100 | 2,218 | 2,563 | 3,809 | 1.4 | 1.9 | 15.6 | 48.6 | 2.6 |
| Other intraregional | 2,500 | 2,101 | 2,498 | 2,388 | 1.1 | 1.2 | 18.9 | -4.4 | -0.6 |
| *From other regions* | *97,500* | *96,076* | *97,544* | *97,600* | *44.3* | *48.0* | *1.5* | *0.1* | *0.0* |
| United States | 28,500 | 28,463 | 29,737 | 28,136 | 12.9 | 13.8 | 4.5 | -5.4 | -0.2 |
| Australia | 11,600 | 12,914 | 11,678 | 13,125 | 5.3 | 6.5 | -9.6 | 12.4 | 1.6 |
| Canada | 8,100 | 7,395 | 7,810 | 7,351 | 3.7 | 3.6 | 5.6 | -5.9 | -1.2 |
| India | 2,500 | 3,924 | 4,753 | 5,054 | 1.1 | 2.5 | 21.1 | 6.3 | 9.2 |
| South Africa | 3,700 | 5,482 | 5,100 | 4,668 | 1.7 | 2.3 | -7.0 | -8.5 | 2.9 |
| Japan | 6,600 | 3,502 | 3,931 | 3,406 | 3.0 | 1.7 | 12.3 | -13.4 | -7.9 |
| All the Caribbean | 1,500 | 2,012 | 2,458 | 2,583 | 0.7 | 1.3 | 22.2 | 5.1 | 7.0 |
| New Zealand | 3,300 | 2,775 | 2,758 | 2,409 | 1.5 | 1.2 | -0.6 | -12.7 | -3.9 |
| Taiwan (pr. of China) | 700 | 453 | 1,029 | 1,955 | 0.3 | 1.0 | 127.2 | 90.0 | 13.7 |
| Nigeria | 1,400 | 1,274 | 1,746 | 1,776 | 0.6 | 0.9 | 37.0 | 1.7 | 3.0 |
| China | 700 | 1,730 | 1,216 | 1,770 | 0.3 | 0.9 | -29.7 | 45.6 | 12.3 |
| Brazil | 1,200 | 1,358 | 1,159 | 1,744 | 0.5 | 0.9 | -14.7 | 50.5 | 4.8 |
| Pakistan | 1,800 | 1,896 | 1,582 | 1,741 | 0.8 | 0.9 | -16.6 | 10.1 | -0.4 |
| Malaysia | 1,200 | 939 | 1,683 | 1,694 | 0.5 | 0.8 | 79.2 | 0.7 | 4.4 |
| Untd Arab Emirates | .. | .. | 1,831 | 1,626 | | 0.8 | | -11.2 | |
| Hong Kong (China) | 2,400 | 2,298 | 1,804 | 1,466 | 1.1 | 0.7 | -21.5 | -18.7 | -6.0 |
| Korea, Republic of | 1,100 | 1,573 | 970 | 1,389 | 0.5 | 0.7 | -38.3 | 43.2 | 3.0 |
| Saudi Arabia | 2,100 | 1,400 | 1,325 | 1,209 | 1.0 | 0.6 | -5.4 | -8.8 | -6.7 |
| Singapore | 1,100 | 877 | 906 | 981 | 0.5 | 0.5 | 3.3 | 8.3 | -1.4 |
| Other interregional | 18,000 | 15,811 | 14,068 | 13,517 | 8.2 | 6.6 | -11.0 | -3.9 | -3.5 |

Source: World Tourism Organization (WTO) © (Data as collected by WTO December 2004)

# III.2 Western Europe

## III.2.1 Austria Western Europe

### Profile

| **Austria** | | |
|---|---|---|
| | Capital | Vienna |
| | Year of entry in WTO | 1975 |
| | Area (1000 km²) | 84 |
| | Population (2003, million) | 8.2 |
| | Gross Domestic Product (GDP) (2003, euro million) | 268,173 |
| | GDP per capita (2003, euro) | 32,872 |
| **Europe** | GDP growth (real, %) | |
| **Western Europe** | '-> 2002: 1.4; 2003: 0.7; 2004*: 1.6; 2005*: 2.4 | |

| | 2001 | 2002 | 2003* | 2002/2001 | 2003*/2002 |
|---|---|---|---|---|---|
| **International Arrivals** | | | | | |
| Tourists (overnight visitors) (1000) | 18,180 | 18,611 | 19,078 | 2.4 | 2.5 |
| - per 100 of inhabitants | 224 | 228 | 234 | | |
| **Tourism accommodation** | | | | | |
| Number of rooms | 288,346 | 282,735 | 282,614 | -1.9 | 0.0 |
| *Nights spent in collective establishments (1000)* | 92,138 | 93,770 | 95,240 | 1.8 | 1.6 |
| by non-residents (inbound tourism) | 65,523 | 67,346 | 68,217 | 2.8 | 1.3 |
| by residents (domestic tourism) | 26,615 | 26,424 | 27,023 | -0.7 | 2.3 |
| *Nights spent in hotels and similar establishments (1000)* | 78,066 | 79,551 | 80,256 | 1.9 | 0.9 |
| by non-residents (inbound tourism) | 58,737 | 60,249 | 60,622 | 2.6 | 0.6 |
| by residents (domestic tourism) | 19,329 | 19,302 | 19,634 | -0.1 | 1.7 |
| **Outbound Tourism** | | | | | |
| Trips abroad (1000) | 4,207 | 3,907 | 5,060 | -7.1 | 29.5 |
| - per 100 of inhabitants | 52 | 48 | 62 | | |
| **Receipts and Expenditure for International Tourism** | | | | | |
| International Tourism Receipts (euro million) | 11,108 | 12,549 | 14,877 | 13.0 | 18.6 |
| - per Tourist Arrival (euro) | 611 | 674 | 780 | 10.4 | 15.7 |
| - per capita (euro) | 1,366 | 1,540 | 1,823 | | |
| International Fare Receipts (euro million) | 1,886 | 2,133 | 2,646 | 13.1 | 24.1 |
| International Tourism Expenditure (euro million) | 9,728 | 10,476 | 12,438 | 7.7 | 18.7 |
| - per trip (euro) | 2,312 | 2,681 | 2,458 | 16.0 | -8.3 |
| - per capita (euro) | 1,196 | 1,286 | 1,524 | | |
| International Fare Expenditure (euro million) | 901 | 938 | 1,200 | 4.1 | 28.0 |
| △ International Tourism Balance (euro million) | 1,380 | 2,072 | 2,439 | | |
| △ International Fare Balance (euro million) | 985 | 1,195 | 1,446 | | |

Source: World Tourism Organization (WTO) (Data as collected by WTO December 2004)

See annex for methodological notes and reference of external sources used.

# Survey

Contributed by *Federal Ministry for Economic Affairs and Labour*
www.austria.info (promotional)
www.bmwa.gv.at/tourismus (institutional/corporate)
www.statistik.gv.at (research and data)

## Tourism development and outlook

**Overall evaluation of results**

2003 brought an increase in arrivals and overnights in Austria. Particularly large was the increase from the adhesion countries, especially Hungary, the Czech Republic, Slovenia and Slovakia.
Due to the Severe Acute Respiratory Syndrome (SARS) the arrivals and overnights from Asia decreased, and also the United States of America again recorded a decline.
A number of economic, sports and marketing cooperations have boosted the Austrian image.
To stress the increasing importance of congress and incentive tourism, a new strategic business segment the "Austrian Business and Convention Network" (ABCN) has been founded.
For Austrian visitors an international information and service center for the markets Austria, Germany, Switzerland and France has been installed. A new competence center to achieve more customer orientation and market closeness was opened in Berlin.

**Supply**

Accommodation: 70 thousand establishments; 4-5 star hotels increased by 3.5 per cent.
Travel agencies/Tour operators: 2,200.
Attractions: innumerable (e.g. Vienna, Salzburg, Innsbruck etc).
Focus:

- Further development of both strategic programmes on "Destination Management Monitoring" and "Well being-tourism" leading to more quality and competitiveness of Austrian tourism products in general;
- Sport tourism (skiing, hiking, etc.,);
- Wellness;
- City tourism (Graz European Culture Capital 2003);
- Culture tourism (e.g. Mozart year 2006);
- Congress tourism (meetings, incentives, conventions and events).

**External factors**

Impact by Severe Acute Respiratory Syndrome (SARS) outbreak but relatively insignificant effect and the overall economic situation.
Low-cost carriers.
Good weather conditions in all seasons.

**Tourism policy**

Launching of the "e-Gästeblatt": an instrument recording tourist data in accommodations for easier handling and better analysis.
The development of T-Mona (Tourism Monitor Austria): an instrument collecting regular data for tourism analysis based on survey results.

**Marketing & promotion**

Development of a new advertising campaign.
The implementation of the three values: intensive, civilized, straight.
Affinity group marketing ( e.g. lover of classical music).
Major markets: Austria, Germany, Italy, the Netherlands and the United Kingdom.
New modern information service center.

**Outlook 2004**

The commencement of the new advertising campaign.
The overnight stays in the Winter season (November 2003 - March 2004) grew by 1.7 per cent (domestic visitors +3%, foreign visitors +1.3%).
The turnover for November 2003 - March 2004 brought an increase of 3.6 per cent; for the whole Winter season an increase of about 4 per cent is expected.
For the coming Summer season, the Austrian Institute for Economic Research (WIFO) expects an increase of about 4.5 per cent.

## International Meetings Industry (MI)

**Organisation of promotion**

The Austrian Business and Convention Network (ABCN) is the new dedicated department of the Austrian National Tourist Office with the sole aim to pro-actively promote Austria and to work more closely with conference, incentive and event planners. ABCN, with it's world-wide network of offices provides a quick and efficient service to the industry, <www.austria-tourism.biz>.
Austria's provinces/regions/cities:

- Vienna Convention Bureau, <www.vienna.convention.at>.
- Lower Austrian Tourist Board, <www.mice-noe.at>.
- Burgenland Tourist Board, <www.burgenland.info>.
- Styrian Tourist Board/ARGE MICE Styria, <www.mice-Steiermark.com>.
- Graz Convention Bureau, <www.graztourismus.at/congress>.
- Upper Austrian Tourist Board, <www.oberoesterreich.at/mice>.
- Romantikstadt Steyr, <www.tourism-steyr.at/mice>.
- Salzburg Convention Bureau, <www.salzburgcb.com>.
- Kur- und Tourismusverband Bad Hofgastein, <www.badhofgastein.com>.
- Conventionland Carinthia, <www.convention.kaernten.at>.
- Carinthian Convention, <www.carinthianconvention.at>.
- Klagenfurt Tourismus, <www.info.klagenfurt.at>.
- Guest Service Tirol Ltd -Congress Incentive Seminar Alpine, <www.kisa.tirol.at>.
- Convention Bureau Vorarlberg, <www.kongressland.at>.
- Tourism alliances/organisations:
- Austrian Convention Bureau, <www.acb.at>.
- RTK Round Table Konferenzhotels, <www.rtk.at>.

**Collection of statistics on the Meetings Industry?:** yes.

**Description**

Vienna Meeting Statistics:
International meetings with a minimum of 50 per cent of the delegates from a foreign country.
Methodology: real data comes directly from the organiser, is checked with meeting suppliers (i.e. convention centre, meeting hotel, PCO, etc.) and published on a yearly basis <www.venue.at/images/files/wks_2003.pdf>, <www.vienna.convention.at>.
Austrian Meeting Statistics are planned for the future.

**Importance / size**

According to the ranking of the Union of International Associations (UIA) for 2002, Austria is listed at an excellent 12$^{th}$ place of the most popular convention destinations world-wide; according to the city ranking of the International Congress and Convention Association (ICCA), Vienna is even listed at fourth place.

**Evolution MI**

Overnights produced in the meeting and conference segment in total has nearly tripled in the past 15 years and now even presents approximately 4 per cent (4 million overnights) of total overnight stays. Summing up, it can be said that the congress industry in Austria leads to an Austrian employment rate of 21,700 to 26,800 employees.

The strategic goals of the Austrian National Tourist Office for the future are to combine and co-ordinate Austrian efforts in regional focus markets for sales and marketing in order to increase the above-mentioned figures, the volume of overnights and revenue and therefore support year-round tourism.

# International Tourism by Origin

**Austria**

**International Tourist Arrivals in All Accommodation Establishments**

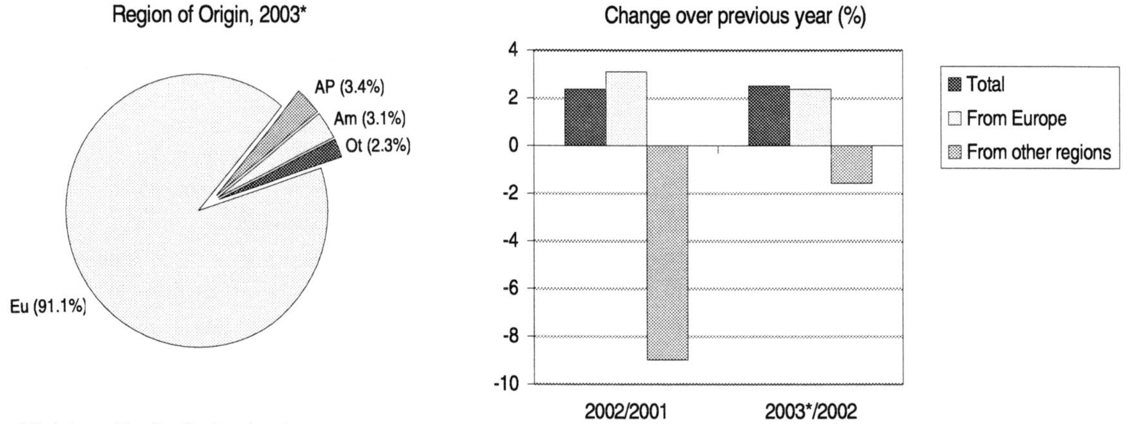


Eu: Europe; AP: Asia and the Pacific; Am: Americas;
Ot: Other;

Source: World Tourism Organization (WTO) ©

**Austria**

**Nights of International Tourists in All Accommodation Establishments**

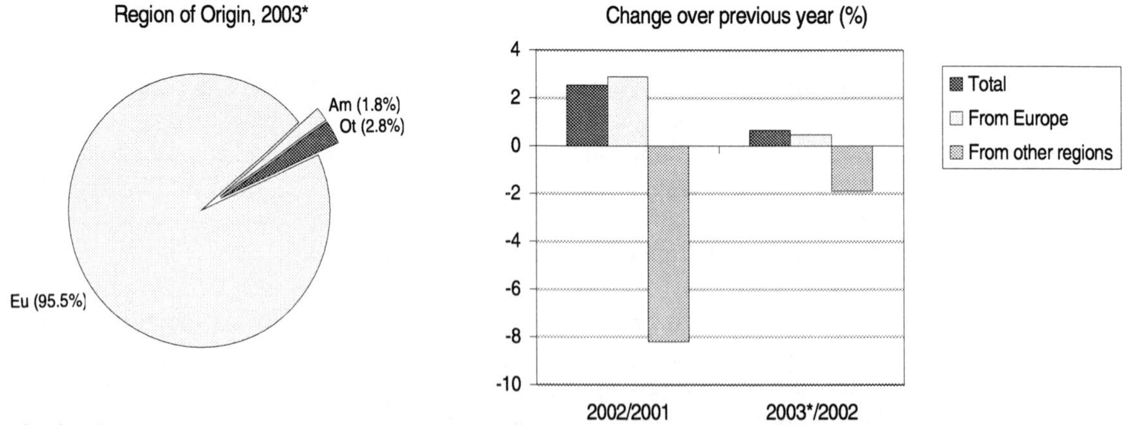


Eu: Europe; Am: Americas;
Ot: Other;

Source: World Tourism Organization (WTO) ©

**Austria**

**International Tourist Arrivals in All Accommodation Establishments (by residence)**

| | | | | (thousand) | Market share (%) | | Growth rate (%) | | Average per year (%) |
|---|---|---|---|---|---|---|---|---|---|
| | 1995 | 2001 | 2002 | 2003* | 1995 | 2003* | 2002/01 | 2003*/02 | 1995-2003* |
| **Total** | **17,173** | **18,180** | **18,611** | **19,078** | **100** | **100** | **2.4** | **2.5** | **1.3** |
| *From Europe* | *15,722* | *16,474* | *16,984* | *17,387* | *91.6* | *91.1* | *3.1* | *2.4* | *1.3* |
| Germany | 10,014 | 10,145 | 10,349 | 10,468 | 58.3 | 54.9 | 2.0 | 1.1 | 0.6 |
| Netherlands | 1,128 | 1,238 | 1,350 | 1,418 | 6.6 | 7.4 | 9.0 | 5.1 | 2.9 |
| Italy | 821 | 964 | 995 | 1,090 | 4.8 | 5.7 | 3.2 | 9.5 | 3.6 |
| Switzerland | 726 | 779 | 817 | 888 | 4.2 | 4.7 | 5.0 | 8.7 | 2.6 |
| United Kingdom | 538 | 646 | 685 | 663 | 3.1 | 3.5 | 6.1 | -3.2 | 2.6 |
| France | 564 | 385 | 406 | 436 | 3.3 | 2.3 | 5.4 | 7.3 | -3.2 |
| Belgium/Luxembourg | 427 | .. | .. | .. | 2.5 | | | | |
| Belgium | .. | 360 | 374 | 391 | | 2.1 | 3.9 | 4.6 | |
| Hungary | 196 | 235 | 248 | 287 | 1.1 | 1.5 | 5.6 | 15.7 | 4.8 |
| Czech Rep | 141 | 223 | 226 | 265 | 0.8 | 1.4 | 1.3 | 17.2 | 8.2 |
| Denmark | 164 | 202 | 207 | 214 | 1.0 | 1.1 | 2.8 | 3.2 | 3.4 |
| Spain | 174 | 195 | 183 | 193 | 1.0 | 1.0 | -6.1 | 5.5 | 1.3 |
| Poland | 115 | 187 | 193 | 185 | 0.7 | 1.0 | 3.7 | -4.6 | 6.1 |
| Sweden | 167 | 163 | 161 | 157 | 1.0 | 0.8 | -1.6 | -2.2 | -0.7 |
| Commonwealth Indep. States | 67 | 123 | 142 | 149 | 0.4 | 0.8 | 16.1 | 4.8 | 10.5 |
| Croatia | 51 | 71 | 70 | 74 | 0.3 | 0.4 | -1.2 | 5.6 | 4.9 |
| Slovenia | 55 | 58 | 63 | 68 | 0.3 | 0.4 | 7.7 | 8.4 | 2.6 |
| Greece | 43 | 60 | 62 | 67 | 0.2 | 0.3 | 2.6 | 8.0 | 5.7 |
| Romania | 27 | 39 | 56 | .. | 0.2 | | 41.9 | | |
| Slovakia | 29 | 50 | 49 | 55 | 0.2 | 0.3 | -1.3 | 11.2 | 8.4 |
| Israel | 57 | 64 | 52 | 53 | 0.3 | 0.3 | -18.7 | 1.9 | -0.9 |
| Finland | 30 | 55 | 53 | 53 | 0.2 | 0.3 | -4.3 | 0.4 | 7.2 |
| Norway | 39 | 48 | 53 | 51 | 0.2 | 0.3 | 10.9 | -3.7 | 3.7 |
| Luxembourg | .. | 32 | 35 | 40 | | 0.2 | 6.7 | 15.4 | |
| Ireland | 12 | 33 | 36 | 40 | 0.1 | 0.2 | 9.9 | 10.0 | 16.0 |
| Other intraregional | 137 | 118 | 116 | 81 | 0.8 | 0.4 | -1.6 | -30.4 | -6.4 |
| *From other regions* | *1,218* | *1,465* | *1,334* | *1,313* | *7.1* | *6.9* | *-9.0* | *-1.6* | *0.9* |
| United States | 539 | 639 | 512 | 485 | 3.1 | 2.5 | -19.8 | -5.4 | -1.3 |
| Japan | 240 | 255 | 240 | 222 | 1.4 | 1.2 | -5.9 | -7.4 | -0.9 |
| Australia | .. | 100 | 88 | 91 | | 0.5 | -11.9 | 3.7 | |
| Australia, New Zealand | 78 | .. | .. | .. | 0.5 | | | | |
| All South-East Asia | .. | 91 | 96 | 73 | | 0.4 | 4.8 | -23.3 | |
| Canada | 55 | 66 | 65 | 66 | 0.3 | 0.3 | -1.3 | 1.9 | 2.3 |
| Korea, Republic of | .. | 24 | 28 | 41 | | 0.2 | 17.2 | 48.3 | |
| All Middle East | .. | 33 | 29 | 38 | | 0.2 | -14.4 | 32.1 | |
| All South Asia | 24 | 32 | 39 | 30 | 0.1 | 0.2 | 21.3 | -24.1 | 2.7 |
| Taiwan (pr. of China) | .. | 28 | 25 | 24 | | 0.1 | -11.5 | -4.7 | |
| Other Africa | 7 | 16 | 11 | 14 | 0.0 | 0.1 | -31.9 | 21.9 | 9.5 |
| Other Americas | 21 | 24 | 29 | 49 | 0.1 | 0.3 | 21.7 | 66.4 | 11.4 |
| Other Middle East | 18 | .. | .. | .. | 0.1 | | | | |
| Other Asia | .. | 67 | 105 | 71 | | 0.4 | 57.9 | -32.8 | |
| Other East Asia/Pacific | 159 | .. | .. | 83 | 0.9 | 0.4 | | | -7.8 |
| Other Oceania | .. | 3 | 2 | .. | | | -24.5 | | |
| Other interregional | 77 | 86 | 64 | 26 | 0.4 | 0.1 | -25.7 | -59.0 | -12.6 |
| *Other World/Not specified* | *233* | *241* | *293* | *378* | *1.4* | *2.0* | *21.9* | *28.9* | *6.2* |

Source: World Tourism Organization (WTO) © (Data as collected by WTO December 2004)

**Austria**

**Nights of International Tourists in All Accommodation Establishments (by residence)**

| | | | | (thousand) | Market share (%) | | Growth rate (%) | | Average per year (%) |
|---|---|---|---|---|---|---|---|---|---|
| | **1995** | **2001** | **2002** | **2003*** | **1995** | **2003*** | **2002/01** | **2003*/02** | **1995-2003*** |
| **Total** | **86,991** | **83,669** | **85,792** | **86,348** | **100** | **100** | **2.5** | **0.6** | **-0.1** |
| *From Europe* | *83,611* | *79,738* | *82,041* | *82,423* | *96.1* | *95.5* | *2.9* | *0.5* | *-0.2* |
| Germany | 58,430 | 52,786 | 53,521 | 52,805 | 67.2 | 61.2 | 1.4 | -1.3 | -1.3 |
| Netherlands | 7,516 | 7,682 | 8,226 | 8,518 | 8.6 | 9.9 | 7.1 | 3.5 | 1.6 |
| Switzerland | 2,903 | 3,092 | 3,285 | 3,540 | 3.3 | 4.1 | 6.3 | 7.7 | 2.5 |
| United Kingdom | 2,716 | 3,037 | 3,241 | 3,200 | 3.1 | 3.7 | 6.7 | -1.3 | 2.1 |
| Italy | 2,211 | 2,684 | 2,812 | 3,004 | 2.5 | 3.5 | 4.8 | 6.8 | 3.9 |
| Belgium/Luxembourg | 2,615 | .. | .. | .. | 3.0 | | | | |
| Belgium | .. | 2,077 | 2,185 | 2,250 | | 2.6 | 5.2 | 2.9 | |
| France | 2,134 | 1,443 | 1,562 | 1,612 | 2.5 | 1.9 | 8.2 | 3.2 | -3.4 |
| Hungary | 623 | 788 | 860 | 1,009 | 0.7 | 1.2 | 9.1 | 17.4 | 6.2 |
| Denmark | 803 | 953 | 980 | 988 | 0.9 | 1.1 | 2.9 | 0.8 | 2.6 |
| Czech Rep | 405 | 760 | 788 | 922 | 0.5 | 1.1 | 3.7 | 17.0 | 10.8 |
| Poland | 391 | 791 | 841 | 830 | 0.4 | 1.0 | 6.3 | -1.2 | 9.9 |
| Sweden | 710 | 650 | 649 | 627 | 0.8 | 0.7 | -0.3 | -3.4 | -1.5 |
| Commonwealth Indep. States | 267 | 466 | 526 | 605 | 0.3 | 0.7 | 12.9 | 15.0 | 10.8 |
| Spain | 392 | 469 | 438 | 469 | 0.5 | 0.5 | -6.7 | 7.1 | 2.3 |
| Croatia | 162 | 254 | 257 | 278 | 0.2 | 0.3 | 1.3 | 8.1 | 7.0 |
| Luxembourg | .. | 189 | 204 | 232 | | 0.3 | 7.9 | 13.8 | |
| Slovenia | 177 | 189 | 197 | 216 | 0.2 | 0.3 | 3.9 | 9.7 | 2.5 |
| Greece | 135 | 171 | 179 | 196 | 0.2 | 0.2 | 4.3 | 9.6 | 4.7 |
| Ireland | 57 | 153 | 170 | 185 | 0.1 | 0.2 | 11.1 | 8.5 | 15.9 |
| Slovakia | 83 | 160 | 165 | 185 | 0.1 | 0.2 | 2.8 | 12.2 | 10.5 |
| Finland | 112 | 187 | 180 | 183 | 0.1 | 0.2 | -3.6 | 1.5 | 6.3 |
| Israel | 191 | 194 | 177 | 181 | 0.2 | 0.2 | -8.4 | 2.0 | -0.6 |
| Norway | 127 | 159 | 171 | 165 | 0.1 | 0.2 | 7.5 | -3.5 | 3.4 |
| Romania | 72 | 95 | 116 | .. | 0.1 | | 22.0 | | |
| Other intraregional | 379 | 308 | 311 | 224 | 0.4 | 0.3 | 0.9 | -27.8 | -6.4 |
| *From other regions* | *2,792* | *3,330* | *3,057* | *2,999* | *3.2* | *3.5* | *-8.2* | *-1.9* | *0.9* |
| United States | 1,328 | 1,580 | 1,341 | 1,249 | 1.5 | 1.4 | -15.1 | -6.9 | -0.8 |
| Japan | 498 | 528 | 482 | 457 | 0.6 | 0.5 | -8.6 | -5.2 | -1.1 |
| Australia | .. | 223 | 218 | 209 | | 0.2 | -2.6 | -4.2 | |
| Australia, New Zealand | 180 | .. | .. | .. | 0.2 | | | | |
| Canada | 152 | 176 | 172 | 174 | 0.2 | 0.2 | -2.1 | 1.0 | 1.7 |
| All Middle East | .. | 129 | 115 | 138 | | 0.2 | -10.7 | 20.3 | |
| All South-East Asia | .. | 135 | 135 | 108 | | 0.1 | -0.3 | -19.8 | |
| South Africa | 63 | 81 | 67 | 63 | 0.1 | 0.1 | -18.0 | -6.3 | 0.0 |
| Korea, Republic of | .. | 34 | 42 | 62 | | 0.1 | 26.2 | 47.1 | |
| All South Asia | 45 | 48 | 58 | 49 | 0.1 | 0.1 | 21.0 | -16.1 | 1.1 |
| Other Africa | 23 | 44 | 36 | 46 | 0.0 | 0.1 | -17.0 | 27.3 | 9.2 |
| Other Americas | 42 | 53 | 65 | 111 | 0.0 | 0.1 | 22.0 | 70.5 | 13.0 |
| Other Middle East | 66 | .. | .. | .. | 0.1 | | | | |
| Other Asia | .. | 110 | 170 | 141 | | 0.2 | 53.8 | -16.7 | |
| Other East Asia/Pacific | 265 | .. | .. | 120 | 0.3 | 0.1 | | | -9.4 |
| Other interregional | 132 | 189 | 156 | 72 | 0.2 | 0.1 | -17.4 | -53.8 | -7.3 |
| *Other World/Not specified* | *589* | *601* | *694* | *926* | *0.7* | *1.1* | *15.4* | *33.5* | *5.8* |

Source: World Tourism Organization (WTO) © (Data as collected by WTO December 2004)

Note: Including private accommodation

# III.2.2 Belgium Western Europe

## Profile

**Belgium**

**Europe**
**Western Europe**

| | |
|---|---|
| Capital | Brussels |
| Area (1000 km²) | 31 |
| Population (2003, million) | 10.3 |
| Gross Domestic Product (GDP) (2003, euro million) | 319,690 |
| GDP per capita (2003, euro) | 31,100 |
| GDP growth (real, %) | |
| '-> 2002: 0.7; 2003: 1.1; 2004*: 2.5; 2005*: 2.3 | |

| | 2001 | 2002 | 2003* | 2002/2001 | 2003*/2002 |
|---|---|---|---|---|---|
| **International Arrivals** | | | | | |
| Tourists (overnight visitors) (1000) | 6,452 | 6,720 | 6,690 | 4.2 | -0.4 |
| - per 100 of inhabitants | 63 | 65 | 65 | | |
| **Tourism accommodation** | | | | | |
| Number of rooms | 61,769 | 62,686 | 63,220 | 1.5 | 0.9 |
| *Nights spent in collective establishments (1000)* | 28,694 | 29,072 | 29,018 | 1.3 | -0.2 |
| by non-residents (inbound tourism) | 15,373 | 15,895 | 15,929 | 3.4 | 0.2 |
| by residents (domestic tourism) | 13,321 | 13,177 | 13,089 | -1.1 | -0.7 |
| *Nights spent in hotels and similar establishments (1000)* | 14,068 | 14,501 | 14,341 | 3.1 | -1.1 |
| by non-residents (inbound tourism) | 10,011 | 10,410 | 10,280 | 4.0 | -1.2 |
| by residents (domestic tourism) | 4,057 | 4,091 | 4,061 | 0.8 | -0.7 |
| **Outbound Tourism** | | | | | |
| Trips abroad (1000) | 6,570 | 6,773 | 7,268 | 3.1 | 7.3 |
| - per 100 of inhabitants | 64 | 66 | 70 | | |
| **Receipts and Expenditure for International Tourism** | | | | | |
| International Tourism Receipts (euro million) | 7,474 | 7,693 | 8,598 | 2.9 | 11.8 |
| - per Tourist Arrival (euro) | 1,158 | 1,145 | 1,285 | -1.2 | 12.3 |
| - per capita (euro) | 726 | 746 | 832 | | |
| International Fare Receipts (euro million) | .. | 737 | 664 | | -9.9 |
| International Tourism Expenditure (euro million) | 10,591 | 11,358 | 12,822 | 7.2 | 12.9 |
| - per trip (euro) | 1,612 | 1,677 | 1,764 | 4.0 | 5.2 |
| - per capita (euro) | 1,029 | 1,101 | 1,241 | | |
| International Fare Expenditure (euro million) | .. | 1,134 | 1,134 | | -0.1 |
| △ International Tourism Balance (euro million) | -3,117 | -3,666 | -4,224 | | |
| △ International Fare Balance (euro million) | .. | -397 | -470 | | |

Source: World Tourism Organization (WTO) (Data as collected by WTO December 2004)

See annex for methodological notes and reference of external sources used.

# International Tourism by Origin

**Belgium**

**International Tourist Arrivals in All Accommodation Establishments**

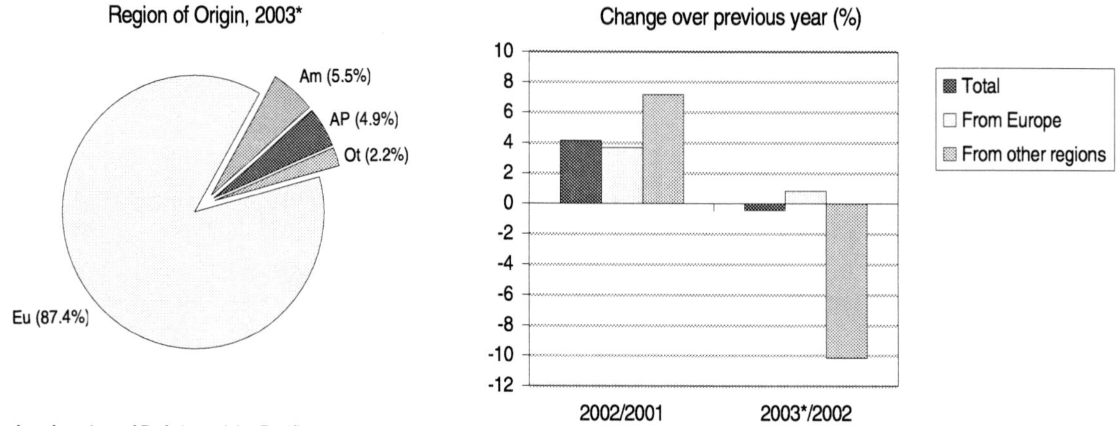


Eu: Europe; Am: Americas; AP: Asia and the Pacific;
Ot: Other;

Source: World Tourism Organization (WTO) ©

**Belgium**

**Nights of International Tourists in All Accommodation Establishments**

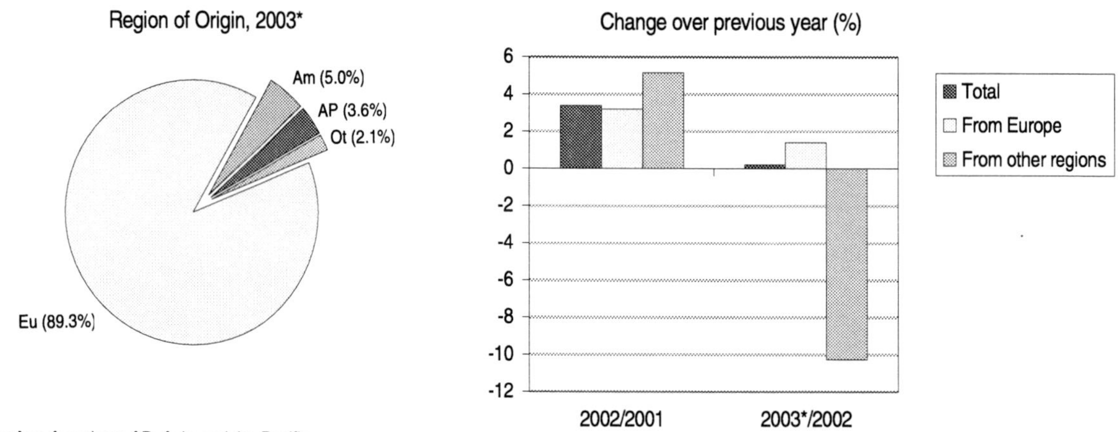


Eu: Europe; Am: Americas; AP: Asia and the Pacific;
Ot: Other;

Source: World Tourism Organization (WTO) ©

**Belgium**

**International Tourist Arrivals in All Accommodation Establishments (by residence)**

| | | | | (thousand) | Market share (%) | | Growth rate (%) | | Average per year (%) |
|---|---|---|---|---|---|---|---|---|---|
| | 1995 | 2001 | 2002 | 2003* | 1995 | 2003* | 2002/01 | 2003*/02 | 1995-2003* |
| **Total** | **5,560** | **6,452** | **6,720** | **6,690** | **100** | **100** | **4.2** | **-0.4** | **2.3** |
| *From Europe* | *4,827* | *5,592* | *5,798* | *5,847* | *86.8* | *87.4* | *3.7* | *0.8* | *2.4* |
| Netherlands | 1,373 | 1,657 | 1,677 | 1,746 | 24.7 | 26.1 | 1.2 | 4.1 | 3.0 |
| United Kingdom | 731 | 1,254 | 1,250 | 1,195 | 13.1 | 17.9 | -0.3 | -4.4 | 6.3 |
| France | 732 | 835 | 909 | 941 | 13.2 | 14.1 | 8.8 | 3.5 | 3.2 |
| Germany | 924 | 783 | 815 | 781 | 16.6 | 11.7 | 4.2 | -4.2 | -2.1 |
| Italy | 187 | 206 | 223 | 231 | 3.4 | 3.5 | 8.6 | 3.5 | 2.7 |
| Spain | 148 | 180 | 215 | 215 | 2.7 | 3.2 | 19.7 | -0.1 | 4.8 |
| Sweden | 89 | 76 | 75 | 79 | 1.6 | 1.2 | -2.2 | 6.4 | -1.5 |
| Luxembourg | 65 | 64 | 66 | 68 | 1.2 | 1.0 | 3.3 | 2.9 | 0.5 |
| Denmark | 69 | 59 | 63 | 59 | 1.2 | 0.9 | 7.0 | -6.0 | -1.9 |
| Switzerland | 60 | 46 | 59 | 58 | 1.1 | 0.9 | 28.0 | -0.4 | -0.4 |
| Ireland | 30 | 38 | 48 | 53 | 0.5 | 0.8 | 26.2 | 11.2 | 7.1 |
| Poland | 42 | 46 | 49 | 44 | 0.8 | 0.7 | 6.0 | -9.1 | 0.6 |
| Greece | 45 | 27 | 31 | 36 | 0.8 | 0.5 | 14.1 | 16.2 | -2.6 |
| Norway | 31 | 32 | 35 | 35 | 0.6 | 0.5 | 7.6 | 2.0 | 1.8 |
| Portugal | 59 | 31 | 33 | 34 | 1.1 | 0.5 | 8.2 | 2.8 | -6.6 |
| Russian Federation | 26 | 34 | 33 | 34 | 0.5 | 0.5 | -1.5 | 3.1 | 3.5 |
| Finland | 40 | 29 | 32 | 33 | 0.7 | 0.5 | 10.8 | 3.2 | -2.4 |
| Austria | 48 | 29 | 30 | 31 | 0.9 | 0.5 | 5.1 | 2.4 | -5.4 |
| Israel | 24 | 34 | 30 | 29 | 0.4 | 0.4 | -11.8 | -2.8 | 2.3 |
| Hungary | 12 | 17 | 15 | 20 | 0.2 | 0.3 | -10.6 | 33.8 | 7.2 |
| Turkey | 13 | 14 | 16 | 18 | 0.2 | 0.3 | 12.5 | 14.9 | 4.5 |
| Czech Rep | 26 | 16 | 17 | 18 | 0.5 | 0.3 | 1.9 | 8.8 | -4.5 |
| Romania | 9 | 6 | 9 | 10 | 0.2 | 0.1 | 52.2 | 4.1 | 1.4 |
| Albania | 5 | 5 | 6 | 8 | 0.1 | 0.1 | 8.6 | 47.2 | 7.1 |
| Lithuania | 2 | 4 | 6 | 7 | 0.0 | 0.1 | 27.3 | 31.4 | 15.1 |
| Other intraregional | 37 | 72 | 57 | 61 | 0.7 | 0.9 | -20.4 | 7.5 | 6.5 |
| *From other regions* | *697* | *806* | *864* | *776* | *12.5* | *11.6* | *7.2* | *-10.2* | *1.4* |
| United States | 284 | 326 | 301 | 275 | 5.1 | 4.1 | -7.6 | -8.8 | -0.4 |
| Japan | 149 | 140 | 154 | 114 | 2.7 | 1.7 | 10.1 | -25.7 | -3.3 |
| China | 17 | 62 | 113 | 107 | 0.3 | 1.6 | 81.6 | -5.0 | 25.5 |
| Canada | 34 | 44 | 40 | 41 | 0.6 | 0.6 | -8.0 | 2.1 | 2.6 |
| Australia | 23 | 24 | 27 | 27 | 0.4 | 0.4 | 10.5 | 2.7 | 2.5 |
| India | 9 | 15 | 25 | 20 | 0.2 | 0.3 | 69.2 | -22.2 | 11.1 |
| Mexico | 6 | 18 | 21 | 18 | 0.1 | 0.3 | 18.0 | -14.7 | 14.1 |
| Morocco | 12 | 13 | 14 | 14 | 0.2 | 0.2 | 8.3 | 4.5 | 2.0 |
| Korea, Republic of | 11 | 7 | 10 | 13 | 0.2 | 0.2 | 42.3 | 30.4 | 2.0 |
| Brazil | 24 | 13 | 12 | 13 | 0.4 | 0.2 | -7.6 | 7.8 | -7.8 |
| South Africa | 8 | 8 | 8 | 7 | 0.1 | 0.1 | -6.0 | -5.9 | -0.7 |
| New Zealand | 4 | 6 | 7 | 6 | 0.1 | 0.1 | 13.6 | -3.6 | 7.4 |
| Bangladesh | 8 | 5 | 4 | 4 | 0.1 | 0.1 | -9.6 | -1.2 | -7.5 |
| Argentina | 8 | 8 | 5 | 4 | 0.1 | 0.1 | -35.3 | -16.5 | -7.8 |
| Saudi Arabia | 2 | 4 | 4 | 4 | 0.0 | 0.1 | 5.9 | 9.0 | 7.4 |
| Dem.R.Congo | 10 | 4 | 4 | 4 | 0.2 | 0.1 | 5.4 | -0.4 | -9.6 |
| Other interregional | 88 | 110 | 115 | 103 | 1.6 | 1.5 | 4.4 | -10.6 | 1.9 |
| *Other World/Not specified* | *37* | *54* | *58* | *67* | *0.7* | *1.0* | *7.6* | *16.4* | *7.9* |

Source: World Tourism Organization (WTO) © (Data as collected by WTO December 2004)

**Belgium**
**Nights of International Tourists in All Accommodation Establishments (by residence)**

| | | | | (thousand) | Market share (%) | | Growth rate (%) | | Average per year (%) |
|---|---|---|---|---|---|---|---|---|---|
| | 1995 | 2001 | 2002 | 2003* | 1995 | 2003* | 2002/01 | 2003*/02 | 1995-2003* |
| **Total** | **13,878** | **15,373** | **15,895** | **15,929** | **100** | **100** | **3.4** | **0.2** | **1.7** |
| *From Europe* | *12,367* | *13,599* | *14,031* | *14,230* | *89.1* | *89.3* | *3.2* | *1.4* | *1.8* |
| Netherlands | 4,429 | 4,911 | 5,023 | 5,246 | 31.9 | 32.9 | 2.3 | 4.5 | 2.1 |
| United Kingdom | 1,513 | 2,647 | 2,645 | 2,509 | 10.9 | 15.8 | -0.1 | -5.1 | 6.5 |
| Germany | 2,890 | 2,193 | 2,228 | 2,119 | 20.8 | 13.3 | 1.6 | -4.9 | -3.8 |
| France | 1,383 | 1,574 | 1,703 | 1,786 | 10.0 | 11.2 | 8.2 | 4.9 | 3.3 |
| Italy | 378 | 409 | 444 | 489 | 2.7 | 3.1 | 8.5 | 10.2 | 3.3 |
| Spain | 265 | 333 | 407 | 417 | 1.9 | 2.6 | 22.3 | 2.3 | 5.8 |
| Luxembourg | 193 | 190 | 177 | 185 | 1.4 | 1.2 | -7.1 | 4.9 | -0.5 |
| Sweden | 164 | 142 | 141 | 156 | 1.2 | 1.0 | -0.3 | 10.8 | -0.6 |
| Denmark | 137 | 125 | 131 | 129 | 1.0 | 0.8 | 5.1 | -1.5 | -0.7 |
| Switzerland | 122 | 93 | 118 | 118 | 0.9 | 0.7 | 27.3 | -0.3 | -0.4 |
| Ireland | 57 | 76 | 96 | 106 | 0.4 | 0.7 | 26.2 | 9.9 | 8.1 |
| Poland | .. | 99 | 106 | 96 | | 0.6 | 6.9 | -9.4 | |
| Greece | 96 | 67 | 73 | 96 | 0.7 | 0.6 | 8.3 | 31.5 | 0.0 |
| Portugal | 118 | 71 | 70 | 79 | 0.9 | 0.5 | -0.9 | 12.0 | -5.0 |
| Finland | 79 | 58 | 69 | 73 | 0.6 | 0.5 | 18.6 | 7.1 | -0.8 |
| Norway | .. | 60 | 69 | 72 | | 0.4 | 15.3 | 2.9 | |
| Russian Federation | 72 | 85 | 82 | 70 | 0.5 | 0.4 | -3.5 | -14.9 | -0.4 |
| Israel | .. | 73 | 68 | 69 | | 0.4 | -6.7 | 1.0 | |
| Austria | 100 | 59 | 64 | 64 | 0.7 | 0.4 | 8.5 | 0.4 | -5.3 |
| Turkey | 29 | 37 | 44 | 49 | 0.2 | 0.3 | 19.2 | 12.7 | 6.9 |
| Czech Rep | .. | 47 | 41 | 46 | | 0.3 | -12.3 | 11.7 | |
| Hungary | .. | 38 | 36 | 44 | | 0.3 | -4.8 | 22.9 | |
| Romania | .. | 19 | 27 | 28 | | 0.2 | 40.4 | 3.2 | |
| Lithuania | .. | 11 | 13 | 19 | | 0.1 | 18.0 | 49.6 | |
| Bulgaria | .. | 14 | 17 | 17 | | 0.1 | 21.4 | -1.2 | |
| Other intraregional | 344 | 170 | 140 | 148 | 2.5 | 0.9 | -17.3 | 5.6 | -10.0 |
| *From other regions* | *1,437* | *1,662* | *1,747* | *1,568* | *10.4* | *9.8* | *5.1* | *-10.3* | *1.1* |
| United States | 581 | 692 | 665 | 606 | 4.2 | 3.8 | -4.0 | -8.8 | 0.5 |
| Japan | 249 | 250 | 293 | 221 | 1.8 | 1.4 | 17.2 | -24.8 | -1.5 |
| China | .. | 94 | 141 | 135 | | 0.8 | 50.3 | -4.9 | |
| Canada | 67 | 94 | 90 | 90 | 0.5 | 0.6 | -4.5 | 0.3 | 3.7 |
| All South America | 84 | .. | .. | .. | 0.6 | | | | |
| Australia | .. | 43 | 48 | 48 | | 0.3 | 12.4 | -1.5 | |
| All Oceania | 47 | .. | .. | .. | 0.3 | | | | |
| India | .. | 39 | 60 | 45 | | 0.3 | 54.2 | -23.7 | |
| Mexico | .. | 29 | 33 | 31 | | 0.2 | 13.0 | -6.0 | |
| Morocco | .. | 21 | 22 | 26 | | 0.2 | 3.5 | 22.0 | |
| Brazil | .. | 27 | 23 | 25 | | 0.2 | -14.6 | 5.7 | |
| All Central America | 21 | .. | .. | .. | 0.2 | | | | |
| Korea, Republic of | .. | 11 | 15 | 18 | | 0.1 | 37.2 | 17.8 | |
| Untd Arab Emirates | .. | 24 | 19 | 16 | | 0.1 | -22.1 | -14.5 | |
| New Zealand | .. | 10 | 13 | 13 | | 0.1 | 24.5 | 0.2 | |
| Bangladesh | .. | 13 | 13 | 13 | | 0.1 | 4.4 | -4.3 | |
| Other interregional | 389 | 313 | 311 | 281 | 2.8 | 1.8 | -0.5 | -9.6 | -4.0 |
| *Other World/Not specified* | *73* | *113* | *117* | *132* | *0.5* | *0.8* | *3.5* | *12.7* | *7.6* |

Source: World Tourism Organization (WTO) © (Data as collected by WTO December 2004)

# Survey (Flanders region)

Contributed by *Tourist Office for Flanders*
www.visitflanders.com (promotional)
www.visitflanders.com/figures (research and data)

## Tourism development and outlook

**Overall evaluation of results**

Global trends:
- All overnights: -0.2 per cent;
- Inbound: +0.2 per cent;
- Domestic: -0.7 per cent.

Like many other countries in 2003, we felt the effects of the world-wide threats of terrorism, the influence of the Severe Acute Respiratory Syndrome (SARS) outbreaks and the conflict in Iraq. The global economic situation in 2003 was not very good and tourism is a sector that is very dependent on the economic situation.
Despite these problems, tourism to Belgium remained relatively stable. Incoming overnights to Brussels increased by 2.3 per cent in 2003 and many strong markets for Belgium are strengthening. Some examples are: the Netherlands +4.5 per cent, France +4.9 per cent, Italy +10.2 per cent and Spain +2.3 per cent. Overnights from the United Kingdom, the United States of America and Japan are decreasing (–5.1%, –8.8% and –24.8%), probably due to overall feelings of uncertainty with respect to the war in Iraq and the SARS contagion in the Far East.

**External factors**

Global world-wide factors like the remaining influences of 11th September 2001, the threat of war and economic instability are presumed to be the most important determining factors affecting tourism to Belgium in 2003.

**Tourism policy**

In the year 2003, preparations were made to reorganise the structure of the Ministries in the Flanders Region. The Tourist Office for Flanders is one of the first parts to become an 'Internal autonomous agency' within the administrational structure. The consequences of these changes are that the Board of Directors has been omitted, and the Head of the Agency gets more autonomous decision-taking power.

**Marketing & promotion**

The main marketing activities are focussed on press, trade and the (potential) consumer. Besides the headquarters in Brussels, we conduct promotional activities in 11 major generating foreign markets. These markets are divided into three major areas: the domestic market, neighbouring and long-haul countries. Also our event marketing has proven to be very successful (Beaufort 2003, Khnopff etc.) .

**Outlook 2004**

We expect the following trends:
- Improvement of economic stability in 2004;
- An increase of Chinese travellers to Europe and Belgium;
- An increase of activities by SN-Brussels Airlines will induce more passenger traffic.

## International Meetings Industry (MI)

**Characteristics of supply**

In 2004, we commissioned a market research project concerning MICE tourism in the Flanders and Brussels region (supply analysis, demand, trends, etc.). Data from the project will be available mid-2004 and the final report is expected for the beginning of 2005.

| | |
|---|---|
| **Organisation of promotion** | The Tourist Office for Flanders is responsible for the MICE promotion of the Flanders and the Brussels region. These activities are managed by the "Flanders-Brussels Convention Bureau", a service within the Tourist Office for Flanders, in collaboration with our 11 foreign offices. Several important major cities in Flanders-Brussels have their own congress bureau. Also recently some subregional authorities have become active in the field of MICE tourism promotion. |

**Collection of statistics on the Meetings Industry?:** yes.

| | |
|---|---|
| **Description** | The National Institute for Statistics (NIS) collects monthly data on arrivals and overnights in all commercial establishments. These data (only residential tourism) are differentiated by motive of stay e.g. leisure, MICE and other business purposes. It is possible to extract the specific data of MICE tourists (period of stay, length of stay, region of origin, region of stay, type of accommodation) out of the global database. |
| **Importance / size** | Inbound MICE tourism accounts for 15 per cent of the overnight stays in Belgium and domestic MICE tourism is estimated at 5 per cent of the overnight stays. |
| **Evolution MI** | In Brussels, the major MICE destination in Belgium, the closure of the "Congress Palace" could lead to a decrease in the volume of the MICE sector. On the other hand, the activities from new member state-employees will contribute to the MICE sector in Brussels too. |

# Survey (Walloon region and Brussels)

Contributed by *Office de Promotion du Tourisme Wallonie-Bruxelles (OPT)*
www.belgique-tourisme.net ; au Japon www.belgium-travel.jp ; aux Etats-Unis www.visitbelgium.com (promotional)
http://pro.opt.be ; http://mrw.wallonie.be/dgee/cgt (institutional/corporate)
www.observatoiretourisme.irisnet.be ; www.observatoriumtoerisme.irisnet.be (site de l'Observatoire du Tourisme à Bruxelles) ; http://mrw.wallonie.be/dgee/cgt/otw (site de l'Observatoire du Tourisme Wallon). (research and data)

## Tourism development and outlook

**Supply**

*Accommodation:* Increased rural tourism offerings, quality control in all accommodation establishments.
*Attractions:* Opening of new attractions, elaboration with the tourism attractions sector of legislation for their recognition and classification according to quality of service (Wallonia region).
*Events:*
- Major events - Brel in Brussels and Simenon in Liège;
- Annual promotional theme - architecture and the development of local cultural and tourism events.

*Transport:*
- Development of TGV links to Germany and increased speed of the Eurostar train from London;
- Expansion of regional airports in Charleroi (passengers, low-cost airlines) and Liège (freight + passengers).

**External factors**

Brussels National Airport:
following the shock represented by the disappearance of Sabena, the opening of new airlines led to a resurgence of activity at the airport, with more hubs.
United States, Japan: lower frequency and disappearance of direct air links, security issues and unfavourable exchange rate.
Preparations for the accession into the European Union of ten new member countries, increased business travel from these countries to Brussels.
Weather conditions: rainy pre-season and hot summer, which discouraged travel, with people who travel frequently taking short stays and day-trips using last-minute bookings according to how sunny it is. Increase in facilities and competition from the French market, with campaigns urging Britons to stay in Great Britain.

**Tourism policy**

Investment incentives (European and regional co-financing within the framework of various European programmes and regional structural funds). Higher level of professionalism in inbound tourism services through the creation of tourism bureaus grouping together several communes.

**Marketing & promotion**

Marketing plans targeted by market (market-product pairs).
Annual promotional theme; in 2003, architecture.
Image campaign in the Wallonia region.
Development and use of Internet sites: general public, leisure tourism professionals, business tourism professionals.

**Outlook 2004**

Belgium: departure rates are on the decline for long vacations, short holidays and day trips; promotional and price policies to re-launch the market and increase its share; principal market for Wallonia.
The Netherlands: growth needs to be sustained.
Germany, Great Britain, and France: increasing their market share by working on three aspects: quality of lifestyle, quality of service and price.

## International Meetings Industry (MI)

**Characteristics of supply**

Brussels, as the capital of Europe and the headquarters of multinational firms and international organizations, is strongly positioned in the meetings segment; services, facilities and accommodation are accordingly developed, although two major problems remain: the closure of the Palais des Congrès convention centre and the lack of a permanent large convention centre for meeting of at least 5 thousand people. Brussels is beginning to position itself in the area of incentive travel. Its development should focus on mid-category hotels. Wallonia positions itself in the meetings and incentives segment with three components: small hotels or chain-operated hotels, the quality of the gastronomy and the development of real incentive services. Its development should focus on large chain hotels.

**Organisation of promotion**

We select markets where promotion is necessary, useful and visible. The priority markets are Belgium, the Netherlands, Germany, Great Britain and northern France. The techniques used are information via the Internet, complemented by a service in the Tourism Promotion Office or in major cities. Also notable are incentives in Brussels and Wallonia (teambuilding).

**Website(s)**

<www.meetingpointbelgium.be>.

**Collection of statistics on the Meetings Industry?:** yes.

**Description**

Sources:
- Institut National de Statistique;
- Observatoire du Tourisme à Bruxelles;
- Measurement of the impact of our MICE service among providers;
- Market studies;
- Trend chart of strategic indicators.

For more information: <www.observatoiretourisme.irisnet.be> (Béatrice Walgraeve, 00 322 5040236) and <www.optpro.be> (François Verdin).

**Importance / size**

Brussels: 60 per cent of overnights for business purposes.
Wallonia: 12 per cent of overnights for business purposes.

# III.2.3 France Western Europe

## Profile

# France

| | |
|---|---|
| Capital | Paris |
| Year of entry in WTO | 1975 |
| Area (1000 km²) | 552 |
| Population (2003, million) | 60.2 |
| Gross Domestic Product (GDP) (2003, euro million) | 1,863,624 |
| GDP per capita (2003, euro) | 30,283 |
| GDP growth (real, %) | |
| '-> 2002: 1.1; 2003: 0.5; 2004*: 2.6; 2005*: 2.3 | |

**Europe**
**Western Europe**

| | 2001 | 2002 | 2003* | 2002/2001 | 2003*/2002 |
|---|---|---|---|---|---|
| **International Arrivals** | | | | | |
| Tourists (overnight visitors) (1000) | 75,202 | 77,012 | 75,048 | 2.4 | -2.6 |
| - per 100 of inhabitants | 126 | 129 | 125 | | |
| **Tourism accommodation** | | | | | |
| Number of rooms | 600,492 | 603,619 | 603,279 | 0.5 | -0.1 |
| *Nights spent in collective establishments (1000)* | 1,550,781 | 1,593,423 | 1,569,003 | 2.7 | -1.5 |
| by non-residents (inbound tourism) | 581,037 | 588,430 | 567,006 | 1.3 | -3.6 |
| by residents (domestic tourism) | 969,744 | 1,004,993 | 1,001,997 | 3.6 | -0.3 |
| *Nights spent in hotels and similar establishments (1000)* | 191,228 | 192,056 | 184,859 | 0.4 | -3.7 |
| by non-residents (inbound tourism) | 75,652 | 77,602 | 69,323 | 2.6 | -10.7 |
| by residents (domestic tourism) | 115,576 | 114,454 | 115,536 | -1.0 | 0.9 |
| **Outbound Tourism** | | | | | |
| Trips abroad (1000) | 19,265 | 17,404 | 17,426 | -9.7 | 0.1 |
| - per 100 of inhabitants | 32 | 29 | 29 | | |
| **Receipts and Expenditure for International Tourism** | | | | | |
| International Tourism Receipts (euro million) | 32,874 | 36,553 | 39,170 | 11.2 | 7.2 |
| - per Tourist Arrival (euro) | 437 | 475 | 522 | 8.6 | 10.0 |
| - per capita (euro) | 551 | 610 | 651 | | |
| International Tourism Expenditure (euro million) | 19,607 | 22,005 | 24,933 | 12.2 | 13.3 |
| - per trip (euro) | 1,018 | 1,264 | 1,431 | 24.2 | 13.2 |
| - per capita (euro) | 329 | 367 | 414 | | |
| △ International Tourism Balance (euro million) | 13,267 | 14,548 | 14,237 | | |

Source: World Tourism Organization (WTO) (Data as collected by WTO December 2004)

See annex for methodological notes and reference of external sources used.

# Survey

Contributed by *Maison de la France*
www.franceguide.com (promotional)
www.tourisme.gouv.fr ; www.franceguide.com (institutional/corporate)
www.franceguide.com ; www.tourisme.gouv.fr (research and data)

## Tourism development and outlook

**Overall evaluation of results**

France's tourism results in 2003 were affected by various national and international factors, and suffered a decline of around 2.6 per cent in foreign visitor arrivals, due mainly to fewer long-haul visitors, from the United States and Japan in particular.
In terms of receipts, the decline was sharper: -5.4 per cent according to initial estimates available, due in particular to the decline in long-haul visitor arrivals, whose average expenditure is markedly higher than average.
The unfavourable international context: the wait-and-see attitude prior to the war in Iraq, the war in Iraq, the SARS epidemic, the economic downturn in many generating markets, the sharp decline of the dollar against the euro, and also by the sterling relative to the euro, combined to create a situation that was unfavourable for the development of international tourism.
Other factors specific to France could have also had an impact on the perception of the country's image and attractiveness: the difficult situation of United States-France relations following France's stance prior to the Iraq war, forest fires in the Var region, which were given heavy media coverage in some markets, cancellation of festivals, the heat wave, pollution of the Aquitaine coast following the sinking of the Prestige.
The confluence of these different events had a negative impact in terms of image, especially with regard to the attractiveness of our destination.

**Supply**

The development of low-cost airlines constitutes a positive factor for our destination, enhancing the attractiveness of certain cities or regions. The strengthening of certain air links (from Moscow, for example) and the opening of new air routes such as connections to Canton, also constitute a positive factor for the development of generating markets for France.

**External factors**

Also to be noted: the fact that the "Schengen" countries have been authorised by China as a tourist destination, which should lead to strong growth of the Chinese market over the coming months and years.
The heat wave during the summer may have dissuaded certain tourists from visiting the country during this period. This is possibly the case of tourists from northern Europe, who opted to stay in their respective countries, where the weather was just as good.

**Marketing & promotion**

Maison de la France conducted in late 2003 a survey on France's tourism image and its positioning relative to the competition in the main generating markets, and undertook a reflection process with a view to the publication of its new Marketing Strategy in late 2004.
208 advertising campaigns were carried out in all of the foreign markets, representing a 17 per cent increase relative to 2002. Communication via the Internet increased substantially (32 online campaigns).
Maison de la France participated in 119 trade shows, both for professionals and for the general public. A plan to promote the destination was launched during the third quarter in numerous European and long haul markets, including advertising campaigns and "events". Examples include the ski campaign in the Belgian market in

partnership with Liberty Television, the billboard campaign in Times Square (New York), the France 2007 event in Australia aimed at promoting the cities hosting the matches of the Rugby World Cup 2007 in France.
As for thematic promotion, a new promotional club (Club Outremer) was created to promote the tourism offerings of overseas territories in the French mainland market and certain foreign markets. One of the elements in this effort was an advertising campaign using theme "France of the Three Oceans". Moreover, thematization of the website <www.franceguide.com> has been reinforced. Following the pollution caused by the sinking of the Prestige, a campaign to promote tourism in the Aquitaine region was carried out in the form of television ads, while specific actions were undertaken in certain nearby markets.
A rural tourism promotion campaign was also carried out, aimed at the general public in the French market, with the support of various ministerial departments.
The promotion of the coast in the off-season (spring) was carried out through billboard campaigns in France and other campaigns in the foreign markets concerned. In order to increase traffic to the franceguide.com website, measures were taken to enhance its results in search engines. Club France, which is aimed at enhancing the loyalty of foreign clientele visiting France, was launched in several test markets.
The Club France membership card is sold exclusively over the Internet and provides access to offers that provide specific benefits.

**Outlook 2004**

After a highly satisfactory 2003-2004 winter sports season, the trends for spring-summer 2004 are variable according to market, with increasing last-minute purchases and more direct bookings (especially via Internet) make it difficult to forecast medium-term development.
In 2004 we expect a recovery of certain markets, especially long-haul ones (United States, Japan) and continued growth in markets such as Russia or China.
As for the major European markets, the outlook is variable depending on the market, considering the specific economic situation of each country.
The principal generating markets for France (Germany and Great Britain) are expected to perform better in terms of arrivals, relative to 2003.

## International Meetings Industry (MI)

**Characteristics of supply**

France's offerings are highly diverse, with some 2000 establishments having the capacity to host professional events of at least 200 people. The supply environment is also highly competitive due to the diversity and high number of players in the market. Moreover, three large French regions alone account for 40 per cent of the supply in the business tourism segment in France: Paris- Île-de-France, Rhône-Alpes and Provence-Alpes-Côte d'Azur.
Some 1,500 hotels in France have developed "business" services in their establishments. They offer services tailored to the needs of business clients, as well as large-capacity conference halls with specialized equipment. There are currently 120 convention centres of different sizes in France. This makes France the top European country in terms of convention facilities, with 36 per cent of convention capacity, which can be broken down as follows:

- around 15 centres with a capacity of over 4 thousand people in major cities serving the regional, national and international markets;
- around 30 centres with capacities between 2 thousand and 4 thousand people in large cities, also catering to the same markets;
- the rest of the convention centres are either in regional capitals or resort towns.

In terms of exhibition centres, France has exhibit areas totalling over 1,586,878 m² ; offerings are very diverse, with only two exhibition centres of over 100,000 m², Paris Expo and Paris Nord Villepinte.

**Organisation of promotion**

Maison de la France handles the promotion of business tourism in foreign markets, in particular, through the Tourisme d'Affaires club, which groups together the main inbound operators in this sector. With 160 members (convention centres, convention bureaus, hotels and hotel chains, market planners) the Club establishes an annual plan of action according to the targets and priority markets it establishes.
Other bodies take part in the international promotion of business tourism: this is the case of convention bureaus in the major cities (in conjunction with Tourism Offices) and the Association France Congrès, which is the association of mayors of convention cities.

**Collection of statistics on the Meetings Industry?:** yes.

**Importance / size**

According to available estimates, business tourism accounted for around 30 per cent of France's tourism receipts.

**Evolution MI**

The segment experienced some difficulties and a considerable slowdown following the events of 11th September 2001, and the war in Iraq. Even so, service providers are increasing their professionalism and place a great deal of stock in this segment, which remains very lucrative.

# International Tourism by Origin

**France**

**International Tourist Arrivals at Frontiers**

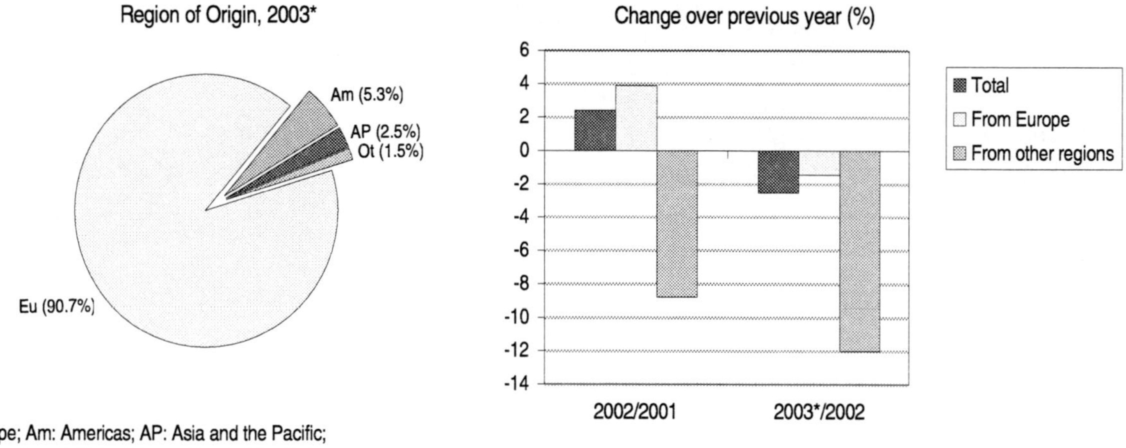


Eu: Europe; Am: Americas; AP: Asia and the Pacific;
Ot: Other;

Source: World Tourism Organization (WTO) ©

**France**

**Nights of International Tourists in All Accommodation Establishments**

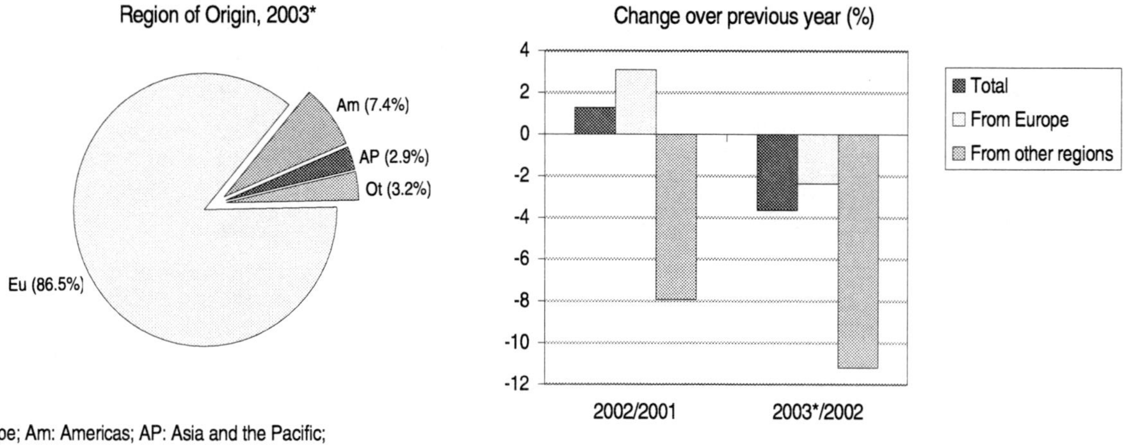


Eu: Europe; Am: Americas; AP: Asia and the Pacific;
Ot: Other;

Source: World Tourism Organization (WTO) ©

**France**

**International Tourist Arrivals at Frontiers (by residence)**

| | | | | (thousand) | Market share (%) | | Growth rate (%) | | Average per year (%) |
|---|---|---|---|---|---|---|---|---|---|
| | 1995 | 2001 | 2002 | 2003* | 1995 | 2003* | 2002/01 | 2003*/02 | 1995-2003* |
| **Total** | **60,033** | **75,202** | **77,012** | **75,048** | **100** | **100** | **2.4** | **-2.6** | **2.8** |
| *From Europe* | *46,438* | *66,491* | *69,078* | *68,072* | *77.4* | *90.7* | *3.9* | *-1.5* | *4.9* |
| United Kingdom/Ireland | 11,159 | 14,885 | 14,958 | 14,845 | 18.6 | 19.8 | 0.5 | -0.8 | 3.6 |
| Germany | 10,588 | 13,880 | 14,346 | 14,047 | 17.6 | 18.7 | 3.4 | -2.1 | 3.6 |
| Netherlands | 5,380 | 11,776 | 12,631 | 12,486 | 9.0 | 16.6 | 7.3 | -1.1 | 11.1 |
| Belgium/Luxembourg | 7,298 | 8,238 | 8,472 | 8,614 | 12.2 | 11.5 | 2.8 | 1.7 | 2.1 |
| Italy | 5,041 | 7,058 | 7,874 | 7,511 | 8.4 | 10.0 | 11.6 | -4.6 | 5.1 |
| Switzerland | 3,107 | 3,296 | 3,074 | 3,002 | 5.2 | 4.0 | -6.7 | -2.3 | -0.4 |
| Spain | 3,865 | 2,858 | 2,965 | 2,861 | 6.4 | 3.8 | 3.7 | -3.5 | -3.7 |
| Scandinavia | .. | .. | .. | 1,518 | | 2.0 | | | |
| Denmark | .. | 709 | 776 | .. | | | 9.4 | | |
| Poland | .. | 594 | 593 | .. | | | -0.2 | | |
| Portugal | .. | 585 | 607 | 586 | | 0.8 | 3.8 | -3.5 | |
| Greece | .. | 379 | 503 | 496 | | 0.7 | 32.7 | -1.4 | |
| Sweden | .. | 493 | 469 | .. | | | -4.9 | | |
| Austria | .. | 418 | 452 | 461 | | 0.6 | 8.1 | 2.0 | |
| Former Czechoslovakia | .. | 396 | 389 | .. | | | -1.8 | | |
| Norway | .. | 153 | 168 | .. | | | 9.8 | | |
| Finland | .. | 110 | 113 | .. | | | 2.7 | | |
| Turkey | .. | 79 | 81 | .. | | | 2.5 | | |
| Other Central/Eastern Europe | .. | 584 | 607 | .. | | | 3.9 | | |
| Other Europe | .. | .. | .. | 1,645 | | 2.2 | | | |
| *From other regions* | *3,149* | *8,651* | *7,892* | *6,943* | *5.2* | *9.3* | *-8.8* | *-12.0* | *10.4* |
| United States | 2,184 | 3,539 | 2,996 | 2,447 | 3.6 | 3.3 | -15.3 | -18.3 | 1.4 |
| All Oceania | .. | .. | .. | 1,289 | | 1.7 | | | |
| All Africa | .. | .. | .. | 889 | | 1.2 | | | |
| Japan | 965 | 728 | 723 | 601 | 1.6 | 0.8 | -0.7 | -16.9 | -5.7 |
| Canada | .. | 710 | 636 | 562 | | 0.7 | -10.4 | -11.6 | |
| Australia, New Zealand | .. | 479 | 493 | .. | | | 2.9 | | |
| All North Africa | .. | 433 | 442 | .. | | | 2.1 | | |
| All Middle East | .. | 325 | 249 | 210 | | 0.3 | -23.4 | -15.7 | |
| Mexico | .. | 104 | 101 | .. | | | -2.9 | | |
| Other Africa | .. | 488 | 482 | .. | | | -1.2 | | |
| Other Americas | .. | 938 | 906 | 945 | | 1.3 | -3.4 | 4.3 | |
| Other East Asia/Pacific | .. | 907 | 864 | .. | | | -4.7 | | |
| *Other World/Not specified* | *10,446* | *60* | *42* | *33* | *17.4* | *0.0* | *-30.0* | *-21.4* | *-51.3* |

Source: World Tourism Organization (WTO) © (Data as collected by WTO December 2004)

**France**

**Nights of International Tourists in All Accommodation Establishments (by residence)**

| | | | | (thousand) | Market share (%) | | Growth rate (%) | | Average per year (%) |
|---|---|---|---|---|---|---|---|---|---|
| | 1995 | 2001 | 2002 | 2003* | 1995 | 2003* | 2002/01 | 2003*/02 | 1995-2003* |
| **Total** | **490,877** | **581,037** | **588,430** | **567,006** | **100** | **100** | **1.3** | **-3.6** | **1.8** |
| *From Europe* | *350,631* | *487,113* | *502,210* | *490,294* | *71.4* | *86.5* | *3.1* | *-2.4* | *4.3* |
| United Kingdom/Ireland | 78,452 | 108,006 | 109,269 | 108,957 | 16.0 | 19.2 | 1.2 | -0.3 | 4.2 |
| Germany | 90,862 | 107,787 | 109,634 | 105,848 | 18.5 | 18.7 | 1.7 | -3.5 | 1.9 |
| Netherlands | 45,903 | 77,279 | 82,018 | 79,053 | 9.4 | 13.9 | 6.1 | -3.6 | 7.0 |
| Belgium/Luxembourg | 50,914 | 63,089 | 64,315 | 63,958 | 10.4 | 11.3 | 1.9 | -0.6 | 2.9 |
| Italy | 36,467 | 48,350 | 53,416 | 50,186 | 7.4 | 8.9 | 10.5 | -6.0 | 4.1 |
| Switzerland | 25,589 | 21,872 | 20,302 | 19,784 | 5.2 | 3.5 | -7.2 | -2.6 | -3.2 |
| Spain | 22,444 | 18,925 | 20,158 | 19,119 | 4.6 | 3.4 | 6.5 | -5.2 | -2.0 |
| Scandinavia | .. | .. | .. | 15,052 | | 2.7 | | | |
| Denmark | .. | 7,764 | 7,880 | .. | | | 1.5 | | |
| Greece | .. | 4,607 | 5,477 | 5,268 | | 0.9 | 18.9 | -3.8 | |
| Sweden | .. | 4,806 | 4,459 | .. | | | -7.2 | | |
| Austria | .. | 4,042 | 4,167 | 4,429 | | 0.8 | 3.1 | 6.3 | |
| Portugal | .. | 3,498 | 3,726 | 3,534 | | 0.6 | 6.5 | -5.2 | |
| Former Czechoslovakia | .. | 3,320 | 3,372 | .. | | | 1.6 | | |
| Poland | .. | 3,209 | 3,230 | .. | | | 0.7 | | |
| Norway | .. | 1,038 | 1,169 | .. | | | 12.6 | | |
| Finland | .. | 1,038 | 1,028 | .. | | | -1.0 | | |
| Turkey | .. | 848 | 852 | .. | | | 0.5 | | |
| Other Central/Eastern Europe | .. | 7,635 | 7,738 | .. | | | 1.3 | | |
| Other Europe | .. | .. | .. | 15,106 | | 2.7 | | | |
| *From other regions* | *29,364* | *92,391* | *85,063* | *75,551* | *6.0* | *13.3* | *-7.9* | *-11.2* | *12.5* |
| United States | 25,536 | 35,995 | 30,832 | 24,979 | 5.2 | 4.4 | -14.3 | -19.0 | -0.3 |
| All Africa | .. | .. | .. | 14,638 | | 2.6 | | | |
| All Oceania | .. | .. | .. | 12,729 | | 2.2 | | | |
| Canada | .. | 9,592 | 9,307 | 7,936 | | 1.4 | -3.0 | -14.7 | |
| All North Africa | .. | 7,322 | 7,392 | .. | | | 1.0 | | |
| Australia, New Zealand | .. | 6,610 | 6,723 | .. | | | 1.7 | | |
| Japan | 3,828 | 4,512 | 4,414 | 3,813 | 0.8 | 0.7 | -2.2 | -13.6 | 0.0 |
| All Middle East | .. | 3,475 | 2,531 | 2,246 | | 0.4 | -27.2 | -11.3 | |
| Mexico | .. | 1,009 | 961 | .. | | | -4.8 | | |
| Other Africa | .. | 7,932 | 7,693 | .. | | | -3.0 | | |
| Other Americas | .. | 9,080 | 8,646 | 9,210 | | 1.6 | -4.8 | 6.5 | |
| Other East Asia/Pacific | .. | 6,864 | 6,564 | .. | | | -4.4 | | |
| *Other World/Not specified* | *110,882* | *1,533* | *1,157* | *1,161* | *22.6* | *0.2* | *-24.5* | *0.3* | *-43.4* |

Source: World Tourism Organization (WTO) © (Data as collected by WTO December 2004)

# III.2.4 Germany Western Europe

## Profile

# Germany

| | |
|---|---|
| Capital | Berlin |
| Year of entry in WTO | 1976 |
| Area (1000 km²) | 357 |
| Population (2003, million) | 82.4 |
| Gross Domestic Product (GDP) (2003, euro million) | 2,544,819 |
| GDP per capita (2003, euro) | 30,853 |
| GDP growth (real, %) | |
| -> 2002: 0.1; 2003: -0.1; 2004*: 2.0; 2005*: 1.8 | |

**Europe**
**Western Europe**

| | 2001 | 2002 | 2003* | 2002/2001 | 2003*/2002 |
|---|---|---|---|---|---|
| **International Arrivals** | | | | | |
| Tourists (overnight visitors) (1000) | 17,860 | 17,959 | 18,392 | 0.6 | 2.4 |
| - per 100 of inhabitants | 22 | 22 | 22 | | |
| **Tourism accommodation** | | | | | |
| Number of rooms | 884,534 | 891,879 | 892,302 | 0.8 | 0.0 |
| *Nights spent in collective establishments (1000)* | 347,941 | 338,696 | 338,588 | -2.7 | 0.0 |
| by non-residents (inbound tourism) | 40,798 | 40,655 | 41,746 | -0.4 | 2.7 |
| by residents (domestic tourism) | 307,143 | 298,041 | 296,842 | -3.0 | -0.4 |
| *Nights spent in hotels and similar establishments (1000)* | 206,334 | 198,936 | 198,726 | -3.6 | -0.1 |
| by non-residents (inbound tourism) | 34,660 | 34,553 | 35,172 | -0.3 | 1.8 |
| by residents (domestic tourism) | 171,674 | 164,383 | 163,554 | -4.2 | -0.5 |
| **Outbound Tourism** | | | | | |
| Trips abroad (1000) | 76,400 | 73,300 | 74,600 | -4.1 | 1.8 |
| - per 100 of inhabitants | 93 | 89 | 91 | | |
| **Receipts and Expenditure for International Tourism** | | | | | |
| International Tourism Receipts (euro million) | 19,423 | 21,178 | 24,307 | 9.0 | 14.8 |
| - per Tourist Arrival (euro) | 1,088 | 1,179 | 1,322 | 8.4 | 12.1 |
| - per capita (euro) | 236 | 257 | 295 | | |
| International Fare Receipts (euro million) | 6,652 | 10,606 | 9,136 | 59.4 | -13.9 |
| International Tourism Expenditure (euro million) | 56,229 | 58,600 | 68,413 | 4.2 | 16.7 |
| - per trip (euro) | 736 | 799 | 917 | 8.6 | 14.7 |
| - per capita (euro) | 683 | 712 | 830 | | |
| International Fare Expenditure (euro million) | 5,304 | 9,961 | 9,543 | 87.8 | -4.2 |
| △ International Tourism Balance (euro million) | -36,805 | -37,421 | -44,106 | | |
| △ International Fare Balance (euro million) | 1,348 | 645 | -407 | | |

Source: World Tourism Organization (WTO) (Data as collected by WTO December 2004)

See annex for methodological notes and reference of external sources used.

# Survey

Contributed by *German National Tourist Board (GNTB)*
www.germany-tourism.de (promotional)
www.bmwi.de ; www.germany-extranet.net (institutional/corporate)
www.drv.de ; www.fur.de ; www.destatis.de (research and data)

## Tourism development and outlook

**Overall evaluation of results**

Tourism is one of the most important economic factors for Germany:

- With 339 million overnight stays (incl. camp. sites) and 8 per cent of GDP;
- Capacity utilization of 500 thousand available rooms is 60 per cent;
- 18.4 million international arrivals in 2003 (WTO 2004);
- 76 per cent of all overnight stays by visitors from Europe, 11 per cent from America, 8.8 per cent from Asia;
- 11.4 billion euro revenue from all travel in 2003 from Western Europe alone.

There is a positive trend for Germany as a travel destination.

The number of overnight stays (excl. Camp sites) by visitors from abroad (2003) increased by an encouraging 2.1 per cent.

Europe, which is responsible for around three quarters of the overnight stays by visitors from abroad, increased its market share by 2 percentage points in 2003. This increase came mainly from the Netherlands, Germany's most important source market, with a 2.5 per cent increase. Other important source countries are: Switzerland (+9.3%), Belgium (+8%), Italy (+6.3%), France (+5.3%) and Denmark (+5.1%).

For 2003 as a whole, there was a 1.6 per cent overall increase in the number of overnights stays in Germany by visitors from eastern Europe. The Baltic States recorded a 6.5 per cent increase, while the number of overnight stays from Hungary and the Czech Republic rose by 3.9 per cent and 3 per cent respectively. Based on the German National Tourist Board's (GNTB) own market research, a core potential of 5.6 million trips could be generated from the east European European Union accession countries alone by 2005.

The most important overseas market for Germany, the United States pf America, recorded a 5.6 per cent decrease in 2003. China, on the other hand, fared very well with a slight increase of 0.9 per cent to a total of around 580 thousand overnight stays. The number of overnight stays by visitors from China will reach the one million mark by 2009. The number of overnight stays by visitors from Japan fell by 9.8 per cent. The GNTB is expecting four million overnight stays per annum by visitors from the Far East. The Arab Gulf States recorded a significant increase with 11 per cent more overnight stays (2003).

*Domestic tourism:*

In 2003, there was a 0.6 per cent increase in the number of domestic arrivals. Although the number of overnight stays by German visitors fell by 1.1 per cent. In 2003, Germany increased its market share of all holidays taken by Germans by 2 percentage points to 60 per cent.

The survey "Reasons for booking a holiday in Germany" showed that, for 64 per cent of the Germans surveyed, Germany still holds a number of unexplored regions. One of the main reasons for taking a holiday in Germany is that it is close to home. The German holiday regions are easily accessible by car (51%), by rail (23%) and by coach (17%). Sixty per cent of Germans were satisfied with their holiday in Germany and 41 per cent were regular visitors. For 40 per cent of Germans, good value for money and the ease of organising the holiday were behind their decision to take a holiday in Germany.

**Supply**

Accommodation capacity in Germany (July 2003):
- Hotels 13,098 (share 24%);
- Bed and breakfast hotels 8,972 (17%);
- Inns 10,150 (19%);
- Guesthouses 5,329 (9.9%);
- Total traditional accommodation providers 37,549 (70%).
- Leisure, recreational and training centres 2,674 (5%);
- Holiday centres 86 (0.2%);
- Holiday homes or apartments 10,794 (20%);
- Holiday cottages, youth hostels 1,606 (3%);
- Preventative medical clinics and rehabilitation clinics 1,062 (2%);
- All accommodation types 53,771 (100%).

Number of rooms (hotels and similar): 892,302.
Number of beds (hotels and similar): 1.6 million.

**External factors**

The following success factors will have a positive impact on Germany's future as a travel destination:
- Travel to Germany by visitors from western Europe continues to grow: intracontinental travel (overnights) to Germany increased in 2003 by 2.1 per cent. There was an increase of 3.9 per cent in the number of visitors from Western Europe. The number of overnight stays in Germany by visitors from across Europe increased by 2 percentage points to 74 per cent in 2003.
- Germany secures its position as a destination for visitors from Eastern Europe: according to the European Travel Monitor, the eastern European states recorded a total volume of 39.7 million trips abroad in 2000, including 6.1 million tours (15%) to Germany. This generated total revenue of 2.7 billion euro for the German incoming sector.
- Japan is still the most important Asian source market for Germany with around 1.2 million overnight stays in 2003. The GNTB is highlighting this with the "Germany in Japan" campaign for 2005/2006 (initiated by the German government) and by increasing its marketing activities in both markets.
- Germany increased its share of the domestic travel market by two percentage points in 2003, with an annual market share of 60 per cent (German Travel Monitor). For 2003 as a whole, there was a slight increase (+1%) in the number of trips. The holiday sector as a whole recorded an increase of one per cent, whereby mini-breaks (1-3 nights) showed strong growth (+31%), while longer holidays decreased by 19 per cent. The business travel sector also saw a 2 per cent increase, while the number of visits to friends and family remained unchanged.
- Germany is well positioned for City Tours/Events, General Tours and Health and Fitness Holidays product lines, based on the health and culture mega-trends. The over 55 age group offers great potential for Germany as a holiday destination with 31.1 million additional trips abroad alone up to the year 2020. With 63 per cent more trips, this segment has the highest growth rate, compared to 28 per cent for the 35-54 age group and 11 per cent for the 15-34 age group.
- In 2003, according to FUR, the low-cost carriers were used by 4.2 million germans alone.
- According to Miniwatts, Germany took the lead over the United Kingdom and France in February 2004 with 44.8 million internet users. Sweden, with 76.9 per cent coverage is one of the leading nations within Europe for internet use. The number of online reservations made by people travelling to Germany from the rest of Europe increased from 1.2 million in 2000 to 2.1 million in 2002, (83%). In Germany the comparative figure for online reservations in 2002 was 15.2 million.
- The 2006 FIFA Football World Cup Germany™ represents an important opportunity for promoting Germany as a travel destination around the world. For 2006 as a whole, the GNTB is expecting an additional increase in the number of

overnight stays of around 1.7 per cent as a result of this sporting event.
- A recent survey of the GNTB revealed that 90 per cent of travel agency managers in Germany anticipate growth in travel within Germany in 2004. The areas of health/wellness (86%) and city breaks/event-related travel (85%) were identified as having the greatest potential for growth. Thirty-seven per cent of travel agency managers forecast growth in demand for domestic holidays in 2004 and 33 per cent already registered this effect in 2003.
- According to the head of the GNTB, the tenth factor in the success of the tourism in Germany is the work of the organisation itself. In 2004, the GNTB is expecting an increase of one per cent in the number of overnight stays by german nationals, and an increase of more than 2 per cent in overnight stays by visitors from abroad.

**Tourism policy**

In Germany, tourism represents 8 per cent of Gross Domestic Product and 2.8 million employees. The german tourism industry is characterised mainly by medium-sized enterprises except for the number of big tour operators and airline companies.

The German Government is supporting the GNTB via the Federal Ministry of Economics and Labour (BMWA). The GNTB budget has been continuously increased during past years by the German government and places special emphasis on the medium-sized tourism enterprises in Germany thus giving them the possibility to offer their tourism products in international markets.

It also supports general domestic tourism promotion.

The main goals of the BMWA tourism policy are:
- Improving the quality of tourism products;
- Increasing the number of employees in the german tourism industry;
- Researching and evaluating economic potentials in specific segments of demand for the tourism industry/enterprises;
- Increasing sustainability in tourism.

**Marketing & promotion**

Market analysis is the basis of the GNTB's activities. The GNTB will have to continue to focus on city breaks and health and fitness holidays. Spain, Italy and Sweden, in particular, offer hidden potential for growth. The GNTB also wishes to take advantage of opportunities created by the eastward expansion of the European Union and to develop new target groups for business travel and holidays. China, South Korea and the Arab Emirates are also markets in which the GNTB aims to secure and develop a competitive advantage. Previous growth in traditional overseas markets, in particular the United States of America and Japan, will have to be consolidated and continued.

For the first time, the GNTB is publishing a collection of important market data on incoming tourism to Germany in time for the ITB.

**Outlook 2004**

The mega-trends culture and health are the two themes on which the GNTB consistently focuses its global activities, and on which both the "City Tours/Events" and "Health and Fitness Holidays" product lines are based.

From 2006, the GNTB will concentrate on one central theme per year. In addition to the main annual theme, it will also focus each year on anniversaries and major events with market-specific campaigns. In 2005, for example, there will be a variety of events in Germany associated with the 200$^{th}$ anniversary of the death of Friedrich Schiller, as well as the re-consecration of the Church of Our Lady in Dresden. In 2006, the year Germany hosts the Football World Cup, theme "250 Years of Mozart" will offer a cultural counterpoint. Global marketing of tourism in Germany via the travel industry is one of the cornerstones of the GNTB's strategy.

For 2005, other additional campaigns are: "Vibrant Towns and Cities" and "Family Holidays".

The festival atmosphere of the World Youth Day and Federal Garden Show, Cologne is expecting up to 800 thousand visitors in August 2005 for the XX World Youth Day.

In 2005, there will be a number of events commemorating Friedrich Schiller, primarily

in Baden-Württemberg and Thuringia, but also in other regions of Germany.
Dresden will be commemorating the 250th anniversary of the birth of the famous composer, Wolfgang Amadeus Mozart. The anniversary year will also be celebrated in Chemnitz with the all-year-round Mozart festival, Augsburg, and along the cross-border Mozart cycle route, which runs from Chiemgau through the Berchtesgadener Land to the Salzburg region.
With new web areas, an e-book in 30 languages and additional online services, the German National Tourist Board (GNTB) is continuing to expand and improve its central marketing platform, the Germany website.
From March 2004, young travellers visiting the GNTB's German or English portals at <www.deutschland-tourismus.de/junges-reisen> and <www.germany-tourism.de/young-travel> have been able to find a comprehensive range of information about events and sport.
A new, dedicated section of the GNTB website for the 2006 FIFA World Cup Germany™ also came online in March 2004. Further information is available via the link to the official FIFA World Cup Germany 2006™ website at <www.FIFAworldcup.com>.
E-book provides internet users around the world with up-to-the-minute information on Germany, even in countries where the GNTB has no local representation.
In the future, the GNTB wishes to place greater emphasis in its websites on the highlights Germany has to offer as a travel destination.
*Domestic Tourism Promotion:*
The GNTB is aiming to consolidate and strengthen domestic tourism in Germany based on three main approaches: cooperation projects with traditional nationwide media, information management on the Germany portal at <www.deutschland-tourismus.de>, and sales and promotional campaigns for the travel industry.
Basic training for the GNTB's new e-learning programme has been successfully concluded; advanced training to be started in Autumn 2004. 2,500 travel agents have already taken part in the course entitled "Expedition Germany – The Seminar for Explorers". The objective is to effectively increase the quality of travel advice and to increase the number of holiday bookings for Germany. In 2002, the number of holidays in Germany booked through travel agencies has already increased by 15 per cent.

## International Meetings Industry (MI)

**Characteristics of supply**

According to the Association of the German Trade Fair Industry (AUMA), the 6 largest trade fair and exhibition centres in Germany in 2003 were: Hannover, Frankfurt/Main, Cologne, Düsseldorf, Munich and Berlin. The importance of these six locations alone is shown by the fact that four of them are among the top five locations within Europe and all six are among the TOP 12 cities.

**Organisation of promotion**

The GNTB has a long-established cooperation with the German Convention Bureau (GCB). The goal is to consolidate and develop Germany's position as a destination for conferences and seminars in conjunction with the GCB to achieve the following:
- Integration of unusual conference venues;
- Presentation at trade fairs, workshops and site inspections;
- Mailshots and specific business development activities.

Combination of outstanding infrastructure and added tourism value:
- Presentation of the variety of attractions that Germany offers as a travel destination;
- Encouraging visitors to add a few days to their stay in Germany or to return for a holiday at a later date.

Germany offers a wealth of advantages as a destination in the run-up to major events such as the Olympics, the World Championships or the 2006 Football World Cup in Germany.

**Website(s)** <www.gcb.de>.

**Collection of statistics on the Meetings Industry?:** yes.

**Importance / size** According to the European Travel Monitor, of the 7.7 million business trips from Europe to Germany taken in 2003, 56 per cent were non-promotable or traditional business trips, 22 per cent were trips to trade fairs and exhibitions, 19 per cent were trips to conferences and congresses, and 3 per cent were incentive trips.

**Evolution MI** With a total of 70 billion euro gross added value from Germany and abroad, the trade fair and conference travel sectors are clearly of economic importance for Germany as a tourist destination. Overall, it is also clear that the sector is dominated by domestic travel. However, there is potential for future growth from abroad and this is certainly set to become more dynamic as the result of the eastward expansion of the European Union. That is why, in addition to promoting holiday travel, the German National Tourist Board (GNTB) in Frankfurt is focusing its international activities on the trade fair, congress and conference sector.

# International Tourism by Origin

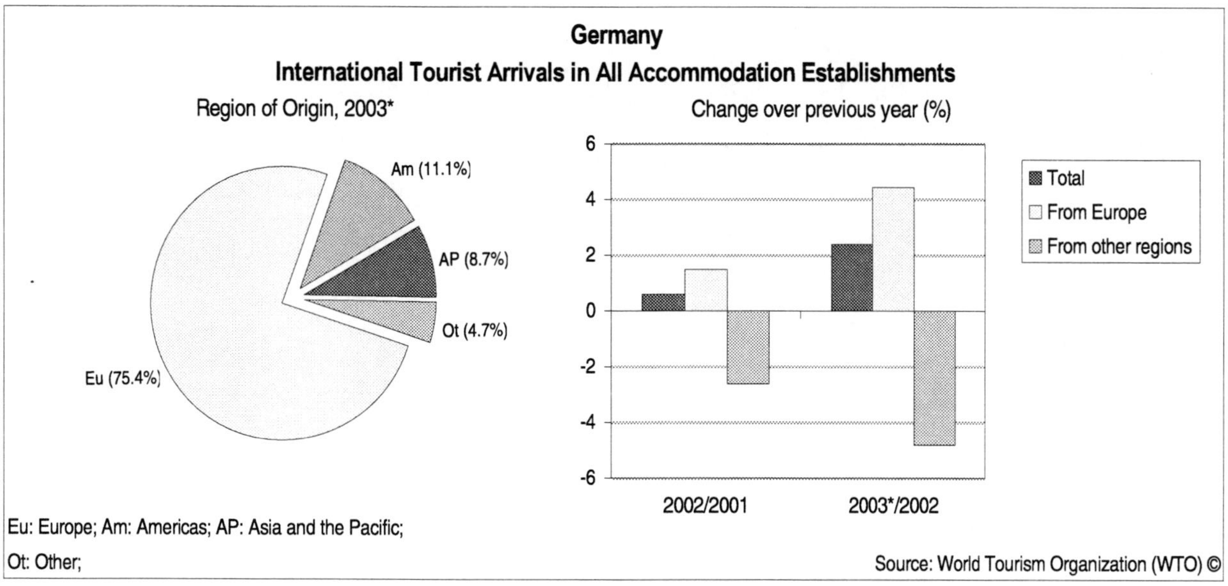


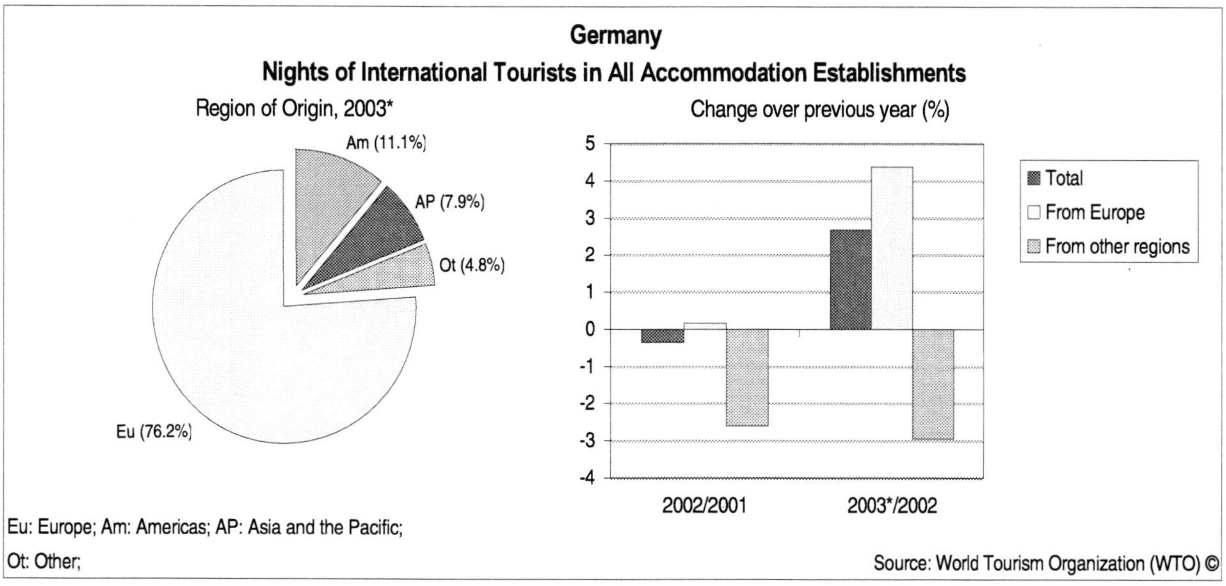

**Germany**

**International Tourist Arrivals in All Accommodation Establishments (by residence)**

| | | | | (thousand) | Market share (%) | | Growth rate (%) | | Average per year (%) |
|---|---|---|---|---|---|---|---|---|---|
| | 1995 | 2001 | 2002 | 2003* | 1995 | 2003* | 2002/01 | 2003*/02 | 1995-2003* |
| **Total** | **14,847** | **17,861** | **17,969** | **18,399** | **100** | **100** | **0.6** | **2.4** | **2.7** |
| *From Europe* | *10,820* | *13,093* | *13,289* | *13,878* | *72.9* | *75.4* | *1.5* | *4.4* | *3.2* |
| Netherlands | 2,297 | 2,590 | 2,657 | 2,765 | 15.5 | 15.0 | 2.6 | 4.1 | 2.3 |
| United Kingdom | 1,362 | 1,713 | 1,645 | 1,635 | 9.2 | 8.9 | -4.0 | -0.6 | 2.3 |
| Switzerland | 833 | 1,092 | 1,162 | 1,271 | 5.6 | 6.9 | 6.4 | 9.4 | 5.4 |
| Italy | 762 | 1,030 | 1,052 | 1,123 | 5.1 | 6.1 | 2.1 | 6.7 | 5.0 |
| France | 802 | 845 | 851 | 900 | 5.4 | 4.9 | 0.6 | 5.7 | 1.4 |
| Austria | 616 | 809 | 821 | 866 | 4.2 | 4.7 | 1.5 | 5.5 | 4.3 |
| Sweden | 588 | 748 | 761 | 778 | 4.0 | 4.2 | 1.7 | 2.3 | 3.6 |
| Denmark | 641 | 733 | 734 | 759 | 4.3 | 4.1 | 0.2 | 3.4 | 2.1 |
| Belgium | .. | 673 | 688 | 731 | | 4.0 | 2.3 | 6.3 | |
| Belgium/Luxembourg | 654 | .. | .. | .. | 4.4 | | | | |
| Spain | 307 | 423 | 448 | 468 | 2.1 | 2.5 | 6.0 | 4.4 | 5.4 |
| Poland | 280 | 342 | 322 | 331 | 1.9 | 1.8 | -5.9 | 2.7 | 2.1 |
| Russian Federation | 279 | 253 | 270 | 277 | 1.9 | 1.5 | 6.9 | 2.5 | -0.1 |
| Norway | 222 | 256 | 273 | 260 | 1.5 | 1.4 | 6.6 | -4.7 | 2.0 |
| Czech Rep | 185 | 203 | 201 | 216 | 1.2 | 1.2 | -1.1 | 7.7 | 2.0 |
| Finland | 145 | 177 | 180 | 193 | 1.0 | 1.0 | 1.8 | 7.2 | 3.6 |
| Hungary | 141 | 158 | 154 | 159 | 0.9 | 0.9 | -2.7 | 3.7 | 1.5 |
| Turkey | 109 | 113 | 118 | 135 | 0.7 | 0.7 | 4.1 | 14.7 | 2.8 |
| Luxembourg | .. | 104 | 114 | 126 | | 0.7 | 9.3 | 10.7 | |
| Baltic Countries | .. | 102 | 110 | 122 | | 0.7 | 8.0 | 11.7 | |
| Greece | 97 | 107 | 106 | 116 | 0.7 | 0.6 | -1.1 | 9.6 | 2.3 |
| Israel | 100 | 128 | 114 | 116 | 0.7 | 0.6 | -10.8 | 1.5 | 1.9 |
| Portugal | 73 | 76 | 74 | 80 | 0.5 | 0.4 | -2.7 | 7.5 | 1.2 |
| Ireland | 50 | 68 | 69 | 69 | 0.3 | 0.4 | 1.5 | 0.4 | 4.3 |
| Iceland | 21 | 21 | 21 | 22 | 0.1 | 0.1 | -3.1 | 7.7 | 0.6 |
| Other intraregional | 257 | 330 | 346 | 360 | 1.7 | 2.0 | 4.8 | 4.3 | 4.3 |
| *From other regions* | *3,621* | *4,250* | *4,139* | *3,940* | *24.4* | *21.4* | *-2.6* | *-4.8* | *1.1* |
| United States | 1,549 | 1,924 | 1,768 | 1,678 | 10.4 | 9.1 | -8.1 | -5.1 | 1.0 |
| Japan | 813 | 779 | 762 | 647 | 5.5 | 3.5 | -2.1 | -15.2 | -2.8 |
| China | 117 | 237 | 270 | 268 | 0.8 | 1.5 | 14.0 | -0.9 | 10.9 |
| Canada | 130 | 176 | 172 | 169 | 0.9 | 0.9 | -2.2 | -1.7 | 3.4 |
| Australia, New Zealand | 167 | 165 | 166 | 168 | 1.1 | 0.9 | 0.8 | 1.3 | 0.1 |
| All Middle East | 62 | 117 | 128 | 143 | 0.4 | 0.8 | 9.7 | 11.5 | 11.0 |
| Korea, Republic of | 87 | 86 | 111 | 114 | 0.6 | 0.6 | 29.6 | 2.6 | 3.5 |
| Brazil | 93 | 87 | 72 | 70 | 0.6 | 0.4 | -16.6 | -2.3 | -3.4 |
| Taiwan (pr. of China) | 51 | 62 | 56 | 69 | 0.3 | 0.4 | -9.4 | 23.2 | 3.8 |
| Mexico | 30 | 48 | 48 | 46 | 0.2 | 0.2 | -0.2 | -4.8 | 5.5 |
| South Africa | 51 | 47 | 43 | 39 | 0.3 | 0.2 | -10.0 | -9.3 | -3.3 |
| Other Africa | 73 | 100 | 101 | 105 | 0.5 | 0.6 | 1.1 | 3.3 | 4.5 |
| Other Americas | 88 | 100 | 90 | 85 | 0.6 | 0.5 | -9.3 | -5.7 | -0.4 |
| Other East Asia/Pacific | 312 | 323 | 350 | 339 | 2.1 | 1.8 | 8.4 | -3.1 | 1.1 |
| *Other World/Not specified* | *406* | *518* | *542* | *581* | *2.7* | *3.2* | *4.5* | *7.3* | *4.6* |

Source: World Tourism Organization (WTO) © (Data as collected by WTO December 2004)

**Germany**

**Nights of International Tourists in All Accommodation Establishments (by residence)**

| | | | | (thousand) | Market share (%) | | Growth rate (%) | | Average per year (%) |
|---|---|---|---|---|---|---|---|---|---|
| | 1995 | 2001 | 2002 | 2003* | 1995 | 2003* | 2002/01 | 2003*/02 | 1995-2003* |
| **Total** | **35,481** | **40,798** | **40,655** | **41,746** | **100** | **100** | **-0.4** | **2.7** | **2.1** |
| *From Europe* | *27,042* | *30,429* | *30,478* | *31,812* | *76.2* | *76.2* | *0.2* | *4.4* | *2.1* |
| Netherlands | 7,121 | 7,399 | 7,535 | 7,859 | 20.1 | 18.8 | 1.8 | 4.3 | 1.2 |
| United Kingdom | 3,238 | 3,662 | 3,521 | 3,477 | 9.1 | 8.3 | -3.8 | -1.2 | 0.9 |
| Switzerland | 1,745 | 2,247 | 2,374 | 2,623 | 4.9 | 6.3 | 5.7 | 10.5 | 5.2 |
| Italy | 1,720 | 2,177 | 2,183 | 2,327 | 4.8 | 5.6 | 0.2 | 6.6 | 3.8 |
| Belgium | .. | 1,641 | 1,682 | 1,834 | | 4.4 | 2.5 | 9.0 | |
| France | 1,671 | 1,713 | 1,690 | 1,788 | 4.7 | 4.3 | -1.3 | 5.8 | 0.8 |
| Austria | 1,340 | 1,718 | 1,711 | 1,779 | 3.8 | 4.3 | -0.4 | 4.0 | 3.6 |
| Belgium/Luxembourg | 1,682 | .. | .. | .. | 4.7 | | | | |
| Denmark | 1,317 | 1,423 | 1,434 | 1,520 | 3.7 | 3.6 | 0.8 | 6.0 | 1.8 |
| Sweden | 1,020 | 1,254 | 1,267 | 1,308 | 2.9 | 3.1 | 1.1 | 3.2 | 3.2 |
| Spain | 669 | 929 | 983 | 1,025 | 1.9 | 2.5 | 5.8 | 4.3 | 5.5 |
| Poland | 977 | 959 | 840 | 838 | 2.8 | 2.0 | -12.4 | -0.2 | -1.9 |
| Russian Federation | 954 | 739 | 777 | 779 | 2.7 | 1.9 | 5.1 | 0.3 | -2.5 |
| Czech Rep | 486 | 552 | 513 | 530 | 1.4 | 1.3 | -7.1 | 3.4 | 1.1 |
| Norway | 433 | 443 | 473 | 452 | 1.2 | 1.1 | 6.7 | -4.4 | 0.5 |
| Hungary | 381 | 412 | 371 | 385 | 1.1 | 0.9 | -10.0 | 3.8 | 0.1 |
| Finland | 300 | 364 | 356 | 374 | 0.8 | 0.9 | -2.3 | 5.1 | 2.8 |
| Luxembourg | .. | 283 | 311 | 343 | | 0.8 | 10.1 | 10.1 | |
| Turkey | 292 | 289 | 293 | 336 | 0.8 | 0.8 | 1.4 | 14.7 | 1.8 |
| Baltic Countries | .. | 292 | 301 | 321 | | 0.8 | 3.4 | 6.6 | |
| Greece | 259 | 295 | 292 | 302 | 0.7 | 0.7 | -1.3 | 3.5 | 1.9 |
| Israel | 279 | 343 | 290 | 297 | 0.8 | 0.7 | -15.6 | 2.4 | 0.8 |
| Portugal | 231 | 203 | 190 | 196 | 0.7 | 0.5 | -6.6 | 3.3 | -2.0 |
| Ireland | 136 | 175 | 171 | 163 | 0.4 | 0.4 | -2.1 | -4.7 | 2.2 |
| Iceland | 52 | 49 | 45 | 48 | 0.1 | 0.1 | -7.8 | 7.8 | -1.0 |
| Other intraregional | 738 | 870 | 878 | 911 | 2.1 | 2.2 | 0.9 | 3.7 | 2.7 |
| *From other regions* | *7,591* | *9,299* | *9,057* | *8,790* | *21.4* | *21.1* | *-2.6* | *-2.9* | *1.9* |
| United States | 3,209 | 4,213 | 3,976 | 3,752 | 9.0 | 9.0 | -5.6 | -5.7 | 2.0 |
| Japan | 1,308 | 1,342 | 1,299 | 1,172 | 3.7 | 2.8 | -3.2 | -9.8 | -1.4 |
| China | 336 | 514 | 573 | 578 | 0.9 | 1.4 | 11.5 | 0.9 | 7.0 |
| All Middle East | 205 | 372 | 399 | 442 | 0.6 | 1.1 | 7.3 | 10.6 | 10.1 |
| Canada | 274 | 384 | 375 | 373 | 0.8 | 0.9 | -2.4 | -0.3 | 3.9 |
| Australia, New Zealand | 348 | 348 | 349 | 349 | 1.0 | 0.8 | 0.1 | 0.2 | 0.1 |
| Korea, Republic of | 166 | 179 | 222 | 226 | 0.5 | 0.5 | 24.1 | 1.9 | 3.9 |
| Brazil | 222 | 243 | 196 | 184 | 0.6 | 0.4 | -19.3 | -6.0 | -2.3 |
| Taiwan (pr. of China) | 102 | 134 | 129 | 139 | 0.3 | 0.3 | -3.7 | 8.1 | 4.0 |
| Mexico | 76 | 122 | 120 | 114 | 0.2 | 0.3 | -1.9 | -4.5 | 5.2 |
| South Africa | 126 | 126 | 108 | 111 | 0.4 | 0.3 | -14.4 | 2.5 | -1.6 |
| Other Africa | 232 | 298 | 283 | 304 | 0.7 | 0.7 | -5.1 | 7.6 | 3.4 |
| Other Americas | 212 | 247 | 224 | 212 | 0.6 | 0.5 | -9.2 | -5.4 | 0.0 |
| Other East Asia/Pacific | 775 | 777 | 806 | 834 | 2.2 | 2.0 | 3.7 | 3.5 | 0.9 |
| *Other World/Not specified* | *848* | *1,069* | *1,119* | *1,143* | *2.4* | *2.7* | *4.6* | *2.1* | *3.8* |

Source: World Tourism Organization (WTO) © (Data as collected by WTO December 2004)

# III.2.5 Liechtenstein Western Europe

## Profile

# Liechtenstein

**Europe**
**Western Europe**

| | |
|---|---|
| Capital | Vaduz |
| Area (10 km²) | 16 |
| Population (2003, 1000) | 33 |

| | 2001 | 2002 | 2003* | 2002/2001 | 2003*/2002 |
|---|---|---|---|---|---|
| **International Arrivals** | | | | | |
| Tourists (overnight visitors) (1000) | 56 | 49 | 49 | -13.7 | 0.6 |
| - per 100 of inhabitants | 174 | 148 | 148 | | |
| **Tourism accommodation** | | | | | |
| Number of rooms | 609 | 581 | 591 | -4.6 | 1.7 |
| *Nights spent in hotels and similar establishments (1000)* | 123 | 108 | 108 | -12.2 | |
| by non-residents (inbound tourism) | 120 | 106 | 105 | -11.7 | -0.9 |
| by residents (domestic tourism) | 3 | 2 | 3 | -33.3 | 50.0 |

Source: World Tourism Organization (WTO) (Data as collected by WTO December 2004)

See annex for methodological notes and reference of external sources used.

## Survey

Contributed by *Liechtenstein Tourism*
www.tourismus.li (promotional)
www.liechtenstein.li (institutional/corporate)
www.avw.llv.li (research and data)

## Tourism development and outlook

**Overall evaluation of results**

Overall tourism is equal to last year.
The main factor was the influence of the international economic situation.

**Supply**

Accommodation: equal capacity.
Travel agencies/tour operators: equal.
Transport capacity (routes and frequency): equal.
Attractions/entertainment: new Landesmuseum Liechtenstein.
Specific products such as MICE, cultural tourism, wellness, sports tourism; etc., a new travel market "inside", diverse new flyers and packages.

**External factors**

Main factor: influence of the international economic situation.
Good weather conditions during the summer.

| | |
|---|---|
| **Tourism policy** | Various cooperation agreements were made.<br>A number of workshops were organised. |
| **Marketing & promotion** | New travel market "inside".<br>Live-Cam for Malbun and Vaduz.<br>Internet development.<br>Route "Gastronomie & Wine".<br>Diverse new roadshows.<br>Public Relations campaigns undertaken.<br>Promotion on the website <www.sommeraktion.ch>. |
| **Outlook 2004** | A new theme has been developed "Mit Goethe durch Vaduz".<br>A 3D-map of Vaduz will be distributed.<br>Hotel classification to be undertaken.<br>Summer campaign will be initiated in Germany. |

## International Meetings Industry (MI)

| | |
|---|---|
| **Characteristics of supply** | Good infrastructure.<br>Central location in Europe. |
| **Organisation of promotion** | Flyers.<br>Internet.<br>Private companies. |

**Collection of statistics on the Meetings Industry?:** yes.

| | |
|---|---|
| **Description** | Numbers of meetings co-organised by Liechtenstein Tourism. |
| **Evolution MI** | The Meetings Industry has been an important factor of overall tourism in the past and will also be an important factor in the future. |

# International Tourism by Origin

**Liechtenstein**

**International Tourist Arrivals in Hotels and Similar Establishments**

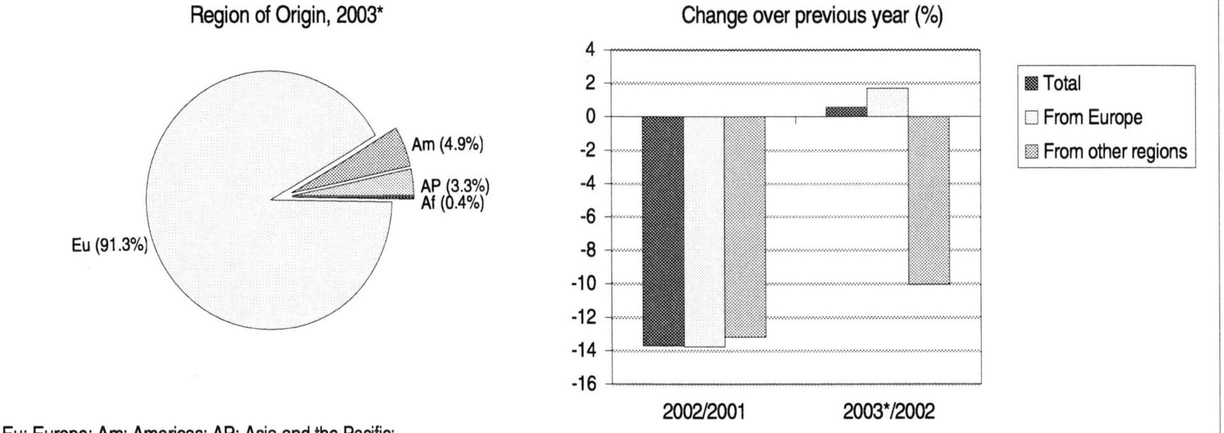


Eu: Europe; Am: Americas; AP: Asia and the Pacific;
Af: Africa;

Source: World Tourism Organization (WTO) ©

**Liechtenstein**

**Nights of International Tourists in Hotels and Similar Establishments**

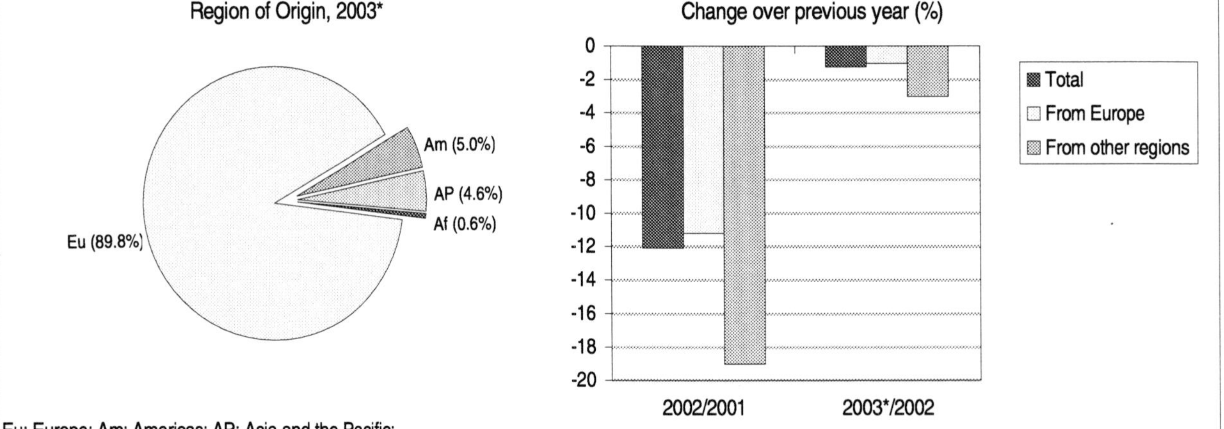


Eu: Europe; Am: Americas; AP: Asia and the Pacific;
Af: Africa;

Source: World Tourism Organization (WTO) ©

**Liechtenstein**

**International Tourist Arrivals in Hotels and Similar Establishments (by residence)**

| | | | | (thousand) | Market share (%) | | Growth rate (%) | | Average per year (%) |
|---|---|---|---|---|---|---|---|---|---|
| | 1995 | 2001 | 2002 | 2003* | 1995 | 2003* | 2002/01 | 2003*/02 | 1995-2003* |
| **Total** | **59** | **56** | **49** | **49** | **100** | **100** | **-13.7** | **0.6** | **-2.4** |
| *From Europe* | *52* | *51* | *44* | *45* | *87.8* | *91.3* | *-13.8* | *1.7* | *-1.9* |
| Germany | 21 | 21 | 17 | 16 | 34.6 | 31.9 | -18.6 | -8.8 | -3.4 |
| Switzerland | 14 | 14 | 13 | 14 | 24.2 | 28.6 | -3.7 | 7.7 | -0.3 |
| United Kingdom | 2 | 2 | 2 | 2 | 3.0 | 4.9 | -23.2 | 31.8 | 3.7 |
| Austria | 3 | 3 | 2 | 2 | 4.5 | 4.6 | -11.7 | -1.3 | -2.0 |
| Former U.S.S.R. | 2 | .. | .. | .. | 3.7 | | | | |
| Italy | 2 | 2 | 2 | 2 | 3.6 | 4.3 | -12.8 | 11.7 | -0.3 |
| France | 2 | 2 | 1 | 1 | 2.9 | 2.8 | -23.8 | 2.5 | -2.7 |
| Netherlands | 1 | 1 | 1 | 1 | 2.1 | 2.4 | -14.4 | 1.3 | -0.8 |
| Belgium | 1 | 1 | 1 | 1 | 1.4 | 1.4 | 7.7 | 3.4 | -2.5 |
| Spain | 1 | 1 | 1 | 1 | 1.3 | 1.2 | -7.9 | 0.4 | -3.7 |
| Czech Rep | .. | 0 | 0 | 0 | | 1.0 | -24.7 | 29.6 | |
| Luxembourg | .. | 0 | 0 | 0 | | 0.8 | 1.2 | 15.1 | |
| Sweden | 1 | 0 | 0 | 0 | 1.4 | 0.7 | -25.4 | -1.6 | -10.2 |
| Norway | 0 | 0 | 0 | 0 | 0.4 | 0.7 | -10.3 | 10.5 | 3.0 |
| Yugoslav SFR | 1 | 0 | 0 | 0 | 1.1 | 0.5 | -9.2 | 10.6 | -11.5 |
| Greece | 0 | 0 | 0 | 0 | 0.5 | 0.5 | -7.2 | 27.6 | -2.7 |
| Hungary | .. | 0 | 0 | 0 | | 0.5 | -13.9 | 13.4 | |
| Poland | .. | 0 | 0 | 0 | | 0.5 | -17.1 | -12.2 | |
| Portugal | 0 | 0 | 0 | 0 | 0.4 | 0.5 | -14.6 | 25.6 | -1.8 |
| Denmark | 0 | 0 | 0 | 0 | 0.5 | 0.4 | -30.0 | -23.2 | -4.8 |
| Finland | 0 | 0 | 0 | 0 | 0.3 | 0.4 | -4.8 | 30.2 | 2.3 |
| Romania | 0 | .. | .. | .. | 0.3 | | | | |
| Israel | 0 | 0 | 0 | 0 | 0.3 | 0.3 | -31.1 | 17.6 | -0.2 |
| Slovakia | .. | 0 | 0 | 0 | | 0.3 | 5.2 | -20.3 | |
| Ireland | .. | 0 | 0 | 0 | | 0.2 | 42.6 | -17.4 | |
| Other intraregional | 1 | 1 | 1 | 1 | 1.2 | 1.9 | -27.4 | 22.6 | 3.8 |
| *From other regions* | *7* | *5* | *5* | *4* | *11.7* | *8.7* | *-13.2* | *-10.0* | *-5.9* |
| United States | 4 | 3 | 2 | 2 | 6.5 | 3.8 | -21.3 | -17.5 | -8.7 |
| Japan | 1 | 1 | 1 | 1 | 2.3 | 1.3 | 4.8 | -9.8 | -9.2 |
| Canada | 0 | 0 | 0 | 0 | 0.6 | 0.5 | -34.3 | 13.0 | -3.6 |
| Korea, Republic of | .. | 0 | 0 | 0 | | 0.2 | 1.0 | 6.7 | |
| South Africa | 0 | 0 | 0 | 0 | 0.1 | 0.2 | -25.6 | 13.8 | 1.5 |
| New Zealand | .. | 0 | 0 | 0 | | 0.1 | -32.1 | 147.4 | |
| Other Africa | 0 | 0 | 0 | 0 | 0.1 | 0.2 | 78.9 | -15.4 | 5.8 |
| Other Americas | 0 | 0 | 0 | 0 | 0.8 | 0.6 | -18.5 | -20.1 | -6.3 |
| Other Asia | 0 | 1 | 1 | 1 | 0.8 | 1.4 | 4.2 | 0.4 | 4.6 |
| Other Oceania | 0 | 0 | 0 | 0 | 0.4 | 0.4 | 9.0 | 1.2 | -4.4 |
| *Other World/Not specified* | *0* | .. | .. | .. | *0.6* | | | | |

Source: World Tourism Organization (WTO) © (Data as collected by WTO December 2004)

**Liechtenstein**

**Nights of International Tourists in Hotels and Similar Establishments (by residence)**

| | | | | (thousand) | Market share (%) | | Growth rate (%) | | Average per year (%) |
|---|---|---|---|---|---|---|---|---|---|
| | 1995 | 2001 | 2002 | 2003* | 1995 | 2003* | 2002/01 | 2003*/02 | 1995-2003* |
| **Total** | **127** | **120** | **106** | **105** | **100** | **100** | **-12.1** | **-1.2** | **-2.4** |
| *From Europe* | *113* | *107* | *95* | *94* | *89.1* | *89.8* | *-11.2* | *-1.0* | *-2.3* |
| Germany | 48 | 46 | 39 | 34 | 37.8 | 32.1 | -14.7 | -14.7 | -4.3 |
| Switzerland | 31 | 27 | 28 | 29 | 24.2 | 27.3 | 3.0 | 1.0 | -0.9 |
| United Kingdom | 4 | 5 | 4 | 5 | 2.9 | 4.8 | -24.4 | 35.0 | 3.7 |
| Austria | 7 | 5 | 4 | 4 | 5.2 | 4.0 | -24.7 | 7.3 | -5.5 |
| Former U.S.S.R. | 4 | .. | .. | .. | 3.3 | | | | |
| Italy | 3 | 4 | 3 | 4 | 2.4 | 3.4 | -20.8 | 28.2 | 2.2 |
| France | 3 | 3 | 2 | 3 | 2.0 | 2.8 | -27.1 | 18.4 | 1.9 |
| Netherlands | 4 | 3 | 3 | 3 | 3.0 | 2.5 | -6.8 | -6.1 | -4.5 |
| Luxembourg | .. | 1 | 1 | 2 | | 1.7 | 2.4 | 39.8 | |
| Belgium | 2 | 1 | 1 | 2 | 1.9 | 1.5 | 16.3 | 7.2 | -4.8 |
| Czech Rep | .. | 1 | 1 | 1 | | 0.9 | -8.6 | 30.0 | |
| Spain | 1 | 1 | 1 | 1 | 0.9 | 0.9 | -21.0 | 9.4 | -2.3 |
| Greece | 1 | 1 | 1 | 1 | 0.7 | 0.7 | 0.9 | 20.2 | -1.9 |
| Portugal | 0 | 0 | 0 | 1 | 0.3 | 0.6 | -12.9 | 58.0 | 5.6 |
| Norway | 0 | 1 | 0 | 1 | 0.3 | 0.6 | -17.3 | 43.1 | 6.4 |
| Sweden | 1 | 1 | 1 | 1 | 0.9 | 0.6 | -19.1 | -9.1 | -7.9 |
| Yugoslav SFR | 1 | 1 | 1 | 1 | 0.8 | 0.5 | -10.5 | -13.8 | -7.2 |
| Poland | .. | 1 | 0 | 0 | | 0.5 | -20.9 | 7.2 | |
| Romania | 0 | .. | .. | .. | 0.4 | | | | |
| Finland | 0 | 0 | 0 | 0 | 0.2 | 0.4 | 26.7 | 7.5 | 4.8 |
| Hungary | .. | 0 | 0 | 0 | | 0.4 | -20.0 | 7.2 | |
| Denmark | 1 | 1 | 1 | 0 | 0.4 | 0.3 | -30.6 | -33.7 | -5.4 |
| Israel | 0 | 0 | 0 | 0 | 0.2 | 0.3 | -23.9 | -14.3 | -0.6 |
| Ireland | .. | 0 | 0 | 0 | | 0.3 | 10.0 | -18.2 | |
| Turkey | .. | 0 | 0 | 0 | | 0.2 | -35.8 | 189.9 | |
| Other intraregional | 1 | 3 | 2 | 3 | 1.2 | 2.5 | -28.2 | 28.4 | 7.4 |
| *From other regions* | *12* | *14* | *11* | *11* | *9.2* | *10.2* | *-19.0* | *-3.0* | *-1.0* |
| United States | 6 | 7 | 4 | 4 | 4.8 | 3.8 | -32.6 | -10.6 | -5.1 |
| Japan | 2 | 2 | 2 | 1 | 1.4 | 1.3 | 8.5 | -16.4 | -3.0 |
| Korea, Republic of | .. | 0 | 0 | 1 | | 0.5 | -3.8 | 81.3 | |
| Canada | 1 | 1 | 0 | 0 | 0.5 | 0.4 | -45.4 | 24.6 | -4.6 |
| South Africa | 0 | 0 | 0 | 0 | 0.1 | 0.2 | -24.8 | 13.0 | 3.5 |
| New Zealand | .. | 0 | 0 | 0 | | 0.1 | -29.3 | 224.1 | |
| Other Africa | 0 | 0 | 0 | 0 | 0.1 | 0.3 | 81.8 | -18.4 | 10.1 |
| Other Americas | 1 | 1 | 1 | 1 | 0.8 | 0.8 | -22.1 | -8.6 | -3.2 |
| Other Asia | 1 | 3 | 2 | 3 | 1.0 | 2.5 | -4.9 | 9.1 | 9.0 |
| Other Oceania | 0 | 0 | 0 | 0 | 0.3 | 0.2 | 4.4 | -16.7 | -5.1 |
| *Other World/Not specified* | *2* | .. | .. | .. | *1.7* | | | | |

Source: World Tourism Organization (WTO) © (Data as collected by WTO December 2004)

# III.2.6 Luxembourg Western Europe

## Profile

# Luxembourg

Europe
Western Europe

| | |
|---|---|
| Capital | Luxembourg |
| Area (100 km²) | 26 |
| Population (2003, 1000) | 457 |
| Gross Domestic Product (GDP) (2003, euro million) | 28,071 |
| GDP per capita (2003, euro) | 62,380 |
| GDP growth (real, %) | |
| '-> 2002: 1.7; 2003: 2.1; 2004*: 2.8; 2005*: 3.4 | |

| | 2001 | 2002 | 2003* | 2002/2001 | 2003*/2002 |
|---|---|---|---|---|---|
| **International Arrivals** | | | | | |
| Tourists (overnight visitors) (1000) | 843 | 885 | 867 | 5.0 | -2.0 |
| - per 100 of inhabitants | 190 | 196 | 190 | | |
| **Tourism accommodation** | | | | | |
| Number of rooms | 7,536 | 7,719 | 7,626 | 2.4 | -1.2 |
| *Nights spent in collective establishments (1000)* | 2,696 | 2,750 | 2,810 | 2.0 | 2.2 |
| by non-residents (inbound tourism) | 2,422 | 2,469 | 2,541 | 1.9 | 2.9 |
| by residents (domestic tourism) | 274 | 281 | 269 | 2.6 | -4.3 |
| *Nights spent in hotels and similar establishments (1000)* | 1,246 | 1,245 | 1,224 | -0.1 | -1.7 |
| by non-residents (inbound tourism) | 1,174 | 1,167 | 1,144 | -0.6 | -2.0 |
| by residents (domestic tourism) | 72 | 78 | 80 | 8.3 | 2.6 |
| **Outbound Tourism** | | | | | |
| Trips abroad (1000) | 261 | .. | .. | | |
| - per 100 of inhabitants | 59 | .. | .. | | |
| **Receipts and Expenditure for International Tourism** | | | | | |
| International Tourism Receipts (euro million) | 1,927 | 2,439 | 2,954 | 26.5 | 21.1 |
| - per Tourist Arrival (euro) | 2,286 | 2,755 | 3,407 | 20.5 | 23.6 |
| - per capita (euro) | 4,333 | 5,409 | 6,467 | | |
| International Fare Receipts (euro million) | .. | 153 | 179 | | 16.8 |
| International Tourism Expenditure (euro million) | 1,585 | 2,130 | 2,527 | 34.4 | 18.6 |
| - per trip (euro) | 6,073 | .. | .. | | |
| - per capita (euro) | 3,564 | 4,726 | 5,531 | | |
| International Fare Expenditure (euro million) | .. | 10 | 14 | | 36.8 |
| △ International Tourism Balance (euro million) | 342 | 308 | 427 | | |
| △ International Fare Balance (euro million) | .. | 143 | 165 | | |

Source: World Tourism Organization (WTO) (Data as collected by WTO December 2004)

See annex for methodological notes and reference of external sources used.

# Survey

Contributed by *Office National du Tourisme du Grand-Duché de Luxembourg*
www.ont.lu (promotional)
www.mdt.public.lu (institutional/corporate)
www.ont.lu (research and data)

## Tourism development and outlook

| | |
|---|---|
| **Overall evaluation of results** | Hotels: slight decrease in arrivals and overnights; stronger decrease in the city of Luxembourg.<br>Camping: significant rise in arrivals and overnights.<br>Rise in incoming tourism from the Netherlands and Denmark.<br>Decrease in incoming tourism from Britain, the United States of America and Asia.<br>Weakness of business and congress tourism (compared to previous years). |
| **Supply** | The Luxembourg-Saarbrücken motorway was opened. |
| **External factors** | Weak economy: a decrease in the hotel sector, especially in the capital.<br>Severe Acute Respiratory Syndrome (SARS) outbreak affected tourism flows.<br>Hot weather: good for camping sector, less for hotel sector depending on the regions, and leading to a decrease in restauration.<br>Strong competition of low-priced Mediterranean and Eastern Europe destinations.<br>Competition of low-cost airlines.<br>Belgium: new federal tax policy will probably lead to an absence of some Belgian clients. |
| **Tourism policy** | A new Five-Year Plan has been introduced by the Tourism Ministry for subsidies to tourism infrastructures.<br>Discussions have taken place on the introduction of a visitors' tax.<br>The possibility of a Quality Management Study is under discussion. |
| **Marketing & promotion** | A new publication for family tourism ("Luxembourg for Kids") has been released.<br>Focus is being put on cultural tourism, with respect to the Cultural Year 2007.<br>Increased joint promotion with the hotel and holiday apartment sector is being encouraged to promote special thematic offers.<br>Poster advertisements are promoting the tourist pass (Luxembourg Card) and agenda.<br>A tram in Brussels has been decorated for 2 months in order to promote cycling tourism in Luxembourg. |
| **Outlook 2004** | Campaigns: extension to Eastern Europe, stronger emphasis on Belgium, the United Kingdom, Scandinavia and Asia.<br>Increased promotion in professional press.<br>Events: Landesgartenschau (Garden show), 60th Anniversary of Battle of the Bulge, 2005: European Union presidency.<br>Increased cooperation with the national airline Luxair (especially in the United Kingdom and Hungary).<br>Expectations: Belgium, the United States of America and China will hopefully regain strength and that Denmark and the Netherlands maintain levels.<br>New publications: Garden and Parks and Cycling in Luxembourg. |

## International Meetings Industry (MI)

| | |
|---|---|
| **Characteristics of supply** | Meetings, Congresses, Conferences, Conventions: Luxembourg Convention Bureau, Luxembourg Congrès (conference center in European quarter "Kirchberg"), Meetings, W.I.T.S and Médiation.<br>Incentives: New Spirit and Destination Luxembourg.<br>Exhibitions and Fairs: Lux Expo. |
| **Organisation of promotion** | The industry is organised in specialized structures under the aegis of the National Convention Bureau (for contacts see above).<br>Internet:<br>Luxembourg Convention Bureau: <www.lcto.lu>, then click Meetings and Events.<br>Luxembourg Congrès: <www.luxcongress.lu>. |

**Collection of statistics on the Meetings Industry?:** yes.

| | |
|---|---|
| **Statistics included** | The statistics are collected by the Luxembourg Convention Bureau and Luxembourg Congrès. |
| **Importance / size** | Luxembourg Convention Bureau and Luxembourg Congrès total an average of about 15 thousand overnights per year.<br>For all the other organizations in the congress, conference and incentives field, no collective statistics are available. |
| **Evolution MI** | There was a significant rise until 2003, when there was a sudden decrease.<br>There is a need for new infrastructure (also in luxury hotels), as congresses get larger (but decrease in numbers).<br>A new congress center will open in 2005. |

# International Tourism by Origin

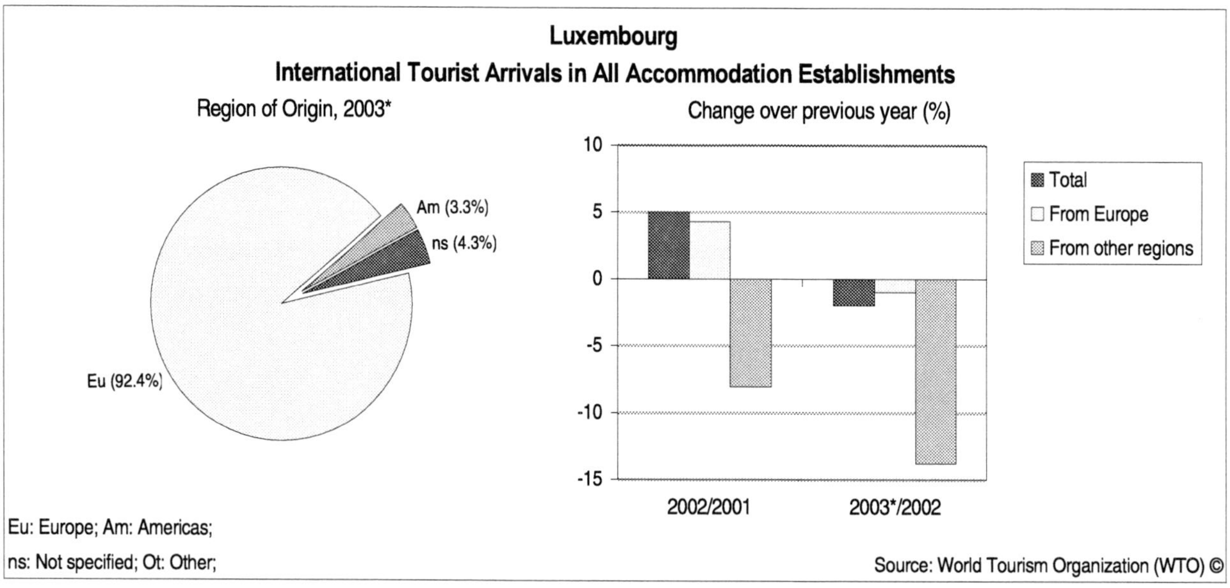


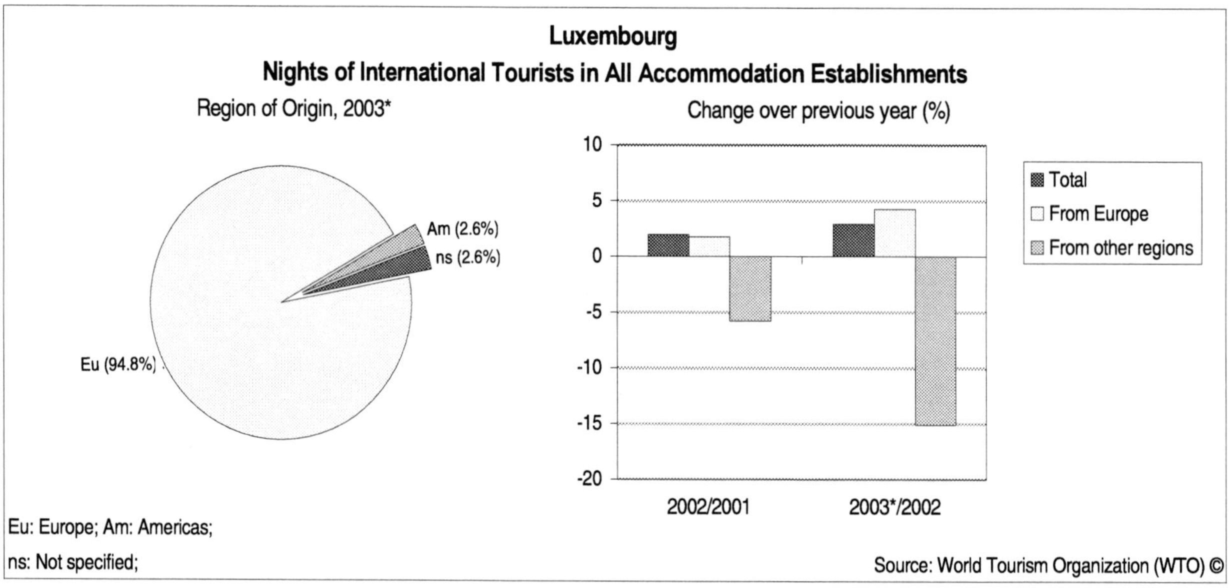

**Luxembourg**

**International Tourist Arrivals in All Accommodation Establishments (by residence)**

| | | | | (thousand) | Market share (%) | | Growth rate (%) | | Average per year (%) |
|---|---|---|---|---|---|---|---|---|---|
| | 1995 | 2001 | 2002 | 2003* | 1995 | 2003* | 2002/01 | 2003*/02 | 1995-2003* |
| **Total** | **768** | **843** | **885** | **867** | **100** | **100** | **5.0** | **-2.0** | **1.5** |
| *From Europe* | *713* | *776* | *809* | *801* | *92.9* | *92.4* | *4.3* | *-1.0* | *1.5* |
| Netherlands | 235 | 229 | 254 | 255 | 30.6 | 29.4 | 10.6 | 0.6 | 1.1 |
| Belgium | 179 | 203 | 188 | 186 | 23.3 | 21.4 | -7.6 | -1.0 | 0.5 |
| Germany | 111 | 103 | 113 | 117 | 14.5 | 13.5 | 9.5 | 4.0 | 0.6 |
| France | 53 | 70 | 75 | 77 | 6.9 | 8.9 | 7.1 | 2.3 | 4.8 |
| United Kingdom | 38 | 60 | 59 | 50 | 5.0 | 5.7 | -0.9 | -15.8 | 3.3 |
| Italy | 16 | 19 | 23 | 20 | 2.1 | 2.4 | 22.0 | -11.6 | 3.2 |
| Switzerland | 14 | 16 | 16 | 15 | 1.8 | 1.8 | 1.8 | -7.9 | 1.4 |
| Spain | 10 | 13 | 17 | 14 | 1.3 | 1.7 | 27.0 | -12.4 | 4.8 |
| Denmark | 10 | 10 | 8 | 9 | 1.3 | 1.0 | -13.2 | 1.6 | -1.4 |
| Sweden | 7 | 8 | 8 | 7 | 0.9 | 0.9 | -7.9 | -2.2 | 1.1 |
| Portugal | 6 | 5 | 6 | 6 | 0.8 | 0.7 | 27.5 | 2.3 | 0.9 |
| Austria | 5 | 5 | 5 | 5 | 0.6 | 0.6 | 8.5 | 5.9 | 1.2 |
| Finland | 4 | 3 | 3 | 4 | 0.5 | 0.4 | 1.3 | 5.5 | 0.4 |
| Ireland | 3 | 4 | 3 | 3 | 0.4 | 0.4 | -6.9 | 2.2 | 2.9 |
| Poland | .. | 3 | 4 | 3 | | 0.4 | 40.9 | -25.0 | |
| Iceland | 3 | .. | .. | .. | 0.4 | | | | |
| Greece | 2 | 3 | 3 | 3 | 0.3 | 0.3 | 5.1 | 7.2 | 3.6 |
| Czech Rep | .. | 2 | 2 | 2 | | 0.3 | 1.6 | 20.1 | |
| Hungary | .. | 1 | 2 | 2 | | 0.2 | 35.2 | 14.4 | |
| Slovenia | .. | 1 | 1 | 1 | | 0.1 | 5.3 | 18.9 | |
| Slovakia | .. | 0 | 0 | 1 | | 0.1 | 1.3 | 59.4 | |
| Lithuania | .. | 0 | 1 | 1 | | 0.1 | 27.8 | 1.5 | |
| Estonia | .. | 0 | 0 | 0 | | 0.0 | -5.8 | 39.2 | |
| Malta | .. | 0 | 0 | 0 | | 0.0 | 46.5 | 2.4 | |
| Cyprus | .. | 0 | 0 | 0 | | 0.0 | 51.2 | -18.3 | |
| Other intraregional | 19 | 17 | 17 | 18 | 2.5 | 2.0 | 3.1 | 3.1 | -1.0 |
| *From other regions* | *33* | *36* | *33* | *29* | *4.3* | *3.3* | *-8.1* | *-13.8* | *-1.9* |
| United States | 25 | 26 | 24 | 21 | 3.2 | 2.4 | -6.8 | -15.5 | -2.2 |
| Other Americas | 9 | 10 | 9 | 8 | 1.1 | 0.9 | -11.4 | -9.2 | -0.9 |
| *Other World/Not specified* | *21* | *31* | *42* | *37* | *2.7* | *4.3* | *37.4* | *-11.4* | *7.5* |

Source: World Tourism Organization (WTO) ©  (Data as collected by WTO December 2004)

**Luxembourg**

**Nights of International Tourists in All Accommodation Establishments (by residence)**

| | | | | (thousand) | Market share (%) | | Growth rate (%) | | Average per year (%) |
|---|---|---|---|---|---|---|---|---|---|
| | 1995 | 2001 | 2002 | 2003* | 1995 | 2003* | 2002/01 | 2003*/02 | 1995-2003* |
| **Total** | **2,378** | **2,422** | **2,469** | **2,541** | **100** | **100** | **2.0** | **2.9** | **0.8** |
| *From Europe* | *2,266* | *2,271* | *2,311* | *2,409* | *95.3* | *94.8* | *1.8* | *4.2* | *0.8* |
| Netherlands | 1,039 | 970 | 1,035 | 1,125 | 43.7 | 44.3 | 6.7 | 8.7 | 1.0 |
| Belgium | 537 | 527 | 511 | 513 | 22.6 | 20.2 | -3.2 | 0.4 | -0.6 |
| Germany | 237 | 222 | 229 | 248 | 9.9 | 9.8 | 3.1 | 8.6 | 0.6 |
| France | 112 | 151 | 148 | 164 | 4.7 | 6.5 | -1.6 | 10.8 | 4.9 |
| United Kingdom | 94 | 146 | 137 | 109 | 3.9 | 4.3 | -5.9 | -20.5 | 1.9 |
| Italy | 44 | 45 | 44 | 40 | 1.9 | 1.6 | -1.8 | -8.4 | -1.3 |
| Spain | 19 | 25 | 28 | 27 | 0.8 | 1.0 | 12.3 | -6.1 | 4.6 |
| Switzerland | 26 | 28 | 29 | 26 | 1.1 | 1.0 | 3.9 | -10.5 | 0.2 |
| Denmark | 25 | 22 | 19 | 19 | 1.1 | 0.7 | -15.1 | 1.0 | -3.5 |
| Portugal | 21 | 16 | 15 | 17 | 0.9 | 0.7 | -3.4 | 14.1 | -2.3 |
| Sweden | 14 | 16 | 14 | 14 | 0.6 | 0.6 | -11.0 | 1.2 | -0.3 |
| Austria | 11 | 11 | 11 | 11 | 0.5 | 0.4 | 3.8 | -2.1 | -0.2 |
| Poland | .. | 8 | 10 | 9 | | 0.4 | 26.5 | -10.1 | |
| Ireland | 8 | 12 | 9 | 8 | 0.3 | 0.3 | -23.2 | -10.5 | 0.7 |
| Finland | 9 | 7 | 6 | 7 | 0.4 | 0.3 | -5.5 | 10.3 | -3.2 |
| Greece | 7 | 6 | 6 | 7 | 0.3 | 0.3 | 4.2 | 11.0 | -0.1 |
| Czech Rep | .. | 6 | 5 | 6 | | 0.3 | -13.8 | 22.9 | |
| Hungary | .. | 4 | 5 | 6 | | 0.2 | 22.3 | 18.4 | |
| Iceland | 6 | .. | .. | .. | 0.2 | | | | |
| Slovakia | .. | 1 | 2 | 2 | | 0.1 | 31.1 | 33.3 | |
| Slovenia | .. | 2 | 2 | 2 | | 0.1 | 11.3 | 0.0 | |
| Estonia | .. | 1 | 1 | 1 | | 0.1 | -13.0 | 83.1 | |
| Lithuania | .. | 2 | 2 | 1 | | 0.1 | -2.3 | -9.7 | |
| Malta | .. | 1 | 1 | 1 | | 0.0 | 49.5 | -19.5 | |
| Cyprus | .. | 1 | 1 | 1 | | 0.0 | 91.3 | -31.2 | |
| Other intraregional | 58 | 43 | 40 | 43 | 2.4 | 1.7 | -7.2 | 6.5 | -3.7 |
| *From other regions* | *72* | *83* | *78* | *67* | *3.0* | *2.6* | *-5.8* | *-15.1* | *-1.0* |
| United States | 54 | 62 | 58 | 49 | 2.3 | 1.9 | -6.4 | -15.7 | -1.2 |
| Other Americas | 18 | 21 | 20 | 18 | 0.8 | 0.7 | -3.8 | -13.3 | -0.5 |
| *Other World/Not specified* | *40* | *68* | *80* | *65* | *1.7* | *2.6* | *17.3* | *-18.0* | *6.3* |

Source: World Tourism Organization (WTO) © (Data as collected by WTO December 2004)

# III.2.7 Monaco Western Europe

## Profile

# Monaco

| | |
|---|---|
| Capital | Monaco |
| Year of entry in WTO | 2001 |
| Population (2003, 1000) | 32 |

**Europe**
**Western Europe**

| | 2001 | 2002 | 2003* | 2002/2001 | 2003*/2002 |
|---|---|---|---|---|---|
| **International Arrivals** | | | | | |
| Tourists (overnight visitors) (1000) | 270 | 263 | 235 | -2.7 | -10.5 |
| - per 100 of inhabitants | 848 | 821 | 731 | | |
| Cruise passengers (1000) | 72 | 56 | 80 | -22.2 | 42.9 |
| **Tourism accommodation** | | | | | |
| Number of rooms | 2,206 | 2,191 | 2,212 | -0.7 | 1.0 |
| *Nights spent in hotels and similar establishments (1000)* | | | | | |
| by non-residents (inbound tourism) | 798 | 765 | 674 | -4.1 | -11.9 |

Source: World Tourism Organization (WTO) (Data as collected by WTO December 2004)
See annex for methodological notes and reference of external sources used.

## Survey

Contributed by *Direction du Tourisme et des Congrès*
www.monaco-tourisme.com (promotional)
www.gouv.mc (institutional/corporate)
www.gouv.mc (research and data)

## Tourism development and outlook

**Overall evaluation of results**

Tourism in the Principality of Monaco suffered a decline in 2003 in every visitor category and nationality.
Business tourism was particularly affected with a drop of 31 per cent (in overnight stays) with respect to 2002.
Leisure tourism was also down by 4 per cent. This negative figure however gives less cause for concern than that of business tourism in that it is in line with a tourism trend common to all countries.

**Supply**

*Accommodation:*
Most 4 and 5 stars luxury hotels undertook major renovation, extension and modernization work in 2003. A new hotel was also opened. By 2007 hotel capacity should increase by 30 per cent, bringing the number of rooms to some 2,900.
*Specific products:*
The Spa segment is thriving in most hotel establishments and given prominence in campaigns promoting leisure tourism.

A large-scale promotional effort is under way to develop business tourism in the low season.
The cruise business is expanding with the building of a new jetty to enlarge Monaco's harbour.

**External factors**

Tourism in 2003 was severely affected by the war in Iraq, health risks, the increase in terrorism, the depreciation of the dollar against the euro, ever-more aggressive competition and unusual weather patterns.
These factors gave rise to a general feeling of uncertainty about travel and a shift in demand.

**Tourism policy**

The global economic climate and changes in tourism consumption in 2003 led to some restructuring within the Directorate for Tourism and Congresses. New departments (Communications, the Monaco Convention Bureau) have been set up, and others have merged or increased their staff.

**Marketing & promotion**

Preparation of a five-year strategic plan (to 2008), which will be periodically updated as part of an exercise in which all businessmen and other professionals with direct or indirect links to tourism in the Principality will take part.

**Outlook 2004**

The outlook for 2004 is encouraging, and hotel occupancy has increased in the first five months of the year. There is however still a clear downturn in tourism from the United States of America, and customers from elsewhere are paying close attention to the political and economic situation. The tourism market is still shaky in the wake of the events marking 2003.

## International Meetings Industry (MI)

**Characteristics of supply**

The Principality of Monaco has been a business tourism destination since 1972, and all its hotels and conference centres have the necessary facilities to cater for the segment as a whole: conferences, conventions, seminars, product launches, fairs, exhibitions, etc.

**Organisation of promotion**

The Principality's promotion is carried out through six tourism offices abroad:
- Düsseldorf office: <monaco-duesseldorf@t-online.de> ; <www.monaco-congres.de>;
- London office: <dtc.london@monaco-tourisme.com>;
- Milan office: <principato.monaco@monaco.inet.it>;
- New York office: <www.visitmonaco.com; info@visitmonaco.com>;
- Paris office: <dtcparis@monaco-tourisme.com>;
- Tokyo office: <www.monaco.or.jp> ; <kikio@cf.mbn.or.jp>;

Participation in tourism fairsInternational advertising media and direct marketing Partnerships with specialized bodies (e.g. Maison de la France).

**Collection of statistics on the Meetings Industry?:** yes.

**Description**

Monaco has been collecting fairly comprehensive statistics on this kind of tourism since 2000. There is a full list of related events that have taken place in Monaco with details of the number of participants, overnight stays, customer type, the sector connected with the event, the nature of the event, the nationality of the organizer, etc. Moreover, a database common to the various departments of the Directorate for Tourism and Congresses is being set up and updated so as to allow for real-time communications and the sharing of information on all the files opened by the offices (we would note that in one year alone there were 600 applications to stage events in the Principality).

| | |
|---|---|
| **Importance / size** | Business tourism today accounts for 30 per cent of the Principality's arrivals (as opposed to 10 per cent in 1972). |
| **Evolution MI** | So far as business tourism is concerned, the Principality of Monaco has no peak or low seasons. The strategy is to promote business tourism still further, in particular with the launch, in the autumn of 2004, of the Monaco Convention Bureau. In this way, business tourism may eventually account for 50 per cent of Monaco's visitors. |

# International Tourism by Origin

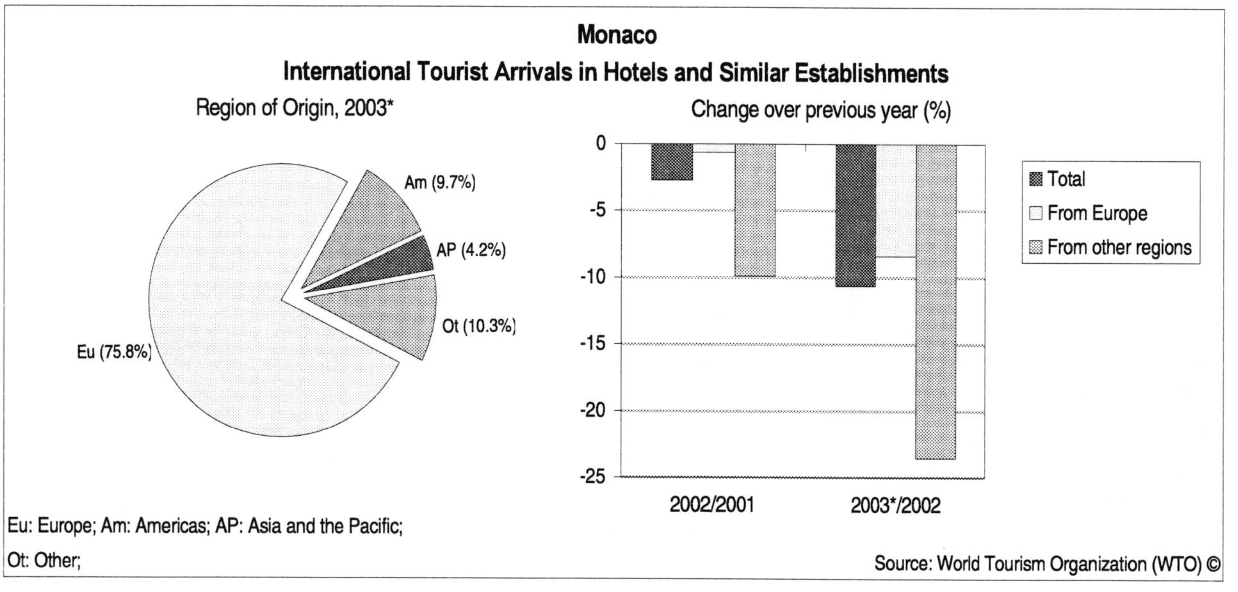


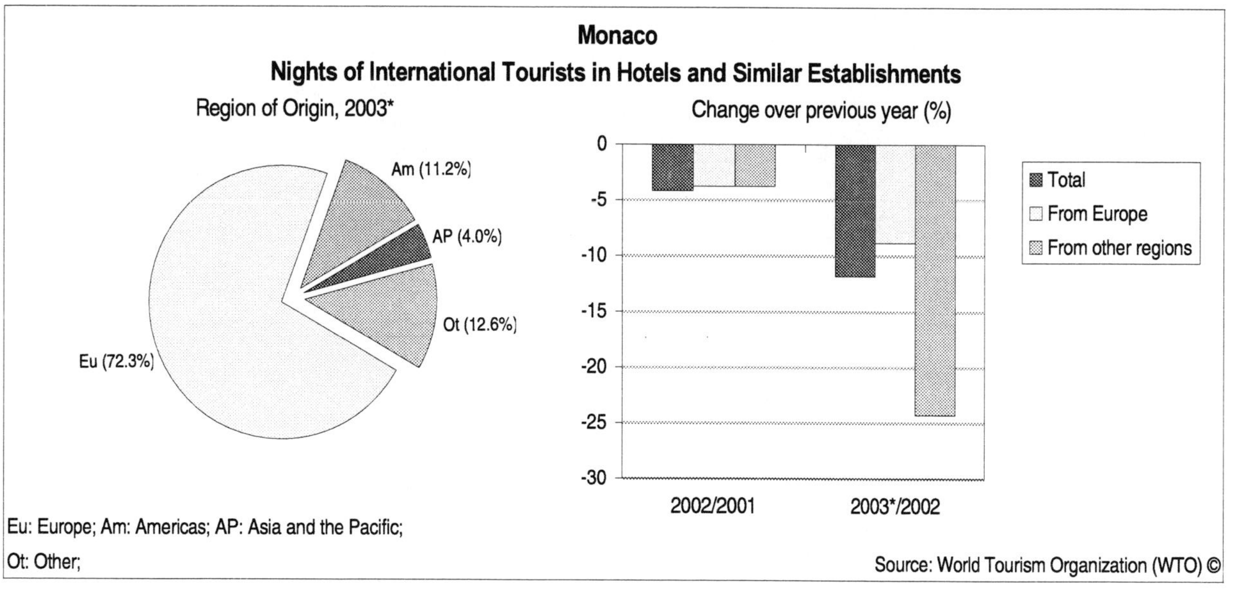

**Monaco**

**International Tourist Arrivals in Hotels and Similar Establishments (by nationality)**

| | | | | (thousand) | Market share (%) | | Growth rate (%) | | Average per year (%) |
|---|---|---|---|---|---|---|---|---|---|
| | 1995 | 2001 | 2002 | 2003* | 1995 | 2003* | 2002/01 | 2003*/02 | 1995-2003* |
| **Total** | **233** | **270** | **263** | **235** | **100** | **100** | **-2.7** | **-10.6** | **0.1** |
| *From Europe* | *167* | *196* | *194* | *178* | *71.8* | *75.8* | *-0.7* | *-8.4* | *0.8* |
| Italy | 58 | 64 | 61 | 59 | 24.8 | 25.1 | -4.4 | -3.3 | 0.2 |
| France | 49 | 44 | 41 | 41 | 21.1 | 17.3 | -6.9 | -1.8 | -2.3 |
| United Kingdom | 19 | 34 | 38 | 33 | 8.2 | 13.9 | 10.6 | -14.4 | 6.9 |
| Germany | 14 | 14 | 15 | 12 | 5.8 | 5.3 | 7.1 | -16.9 | -1.1 |
| Switzerland | 7 | 9 | 8 | 7 | 3.1 | 2.8 | -4.4 | -20.5 | -1.3 |
| Spain | 6 | 6 | 6 | 6 | 2.4 | 2.6 | 2.8 | -5.2 | 0.9 |
| Netherlands | 4 | 5 | 5 | 4 | 1.7 | 1.9 | 14.7 | -15.7 | 1.9 |
| Belgium | 4 | 5 | 5 | 4 | 1.6 | 1.7 | -2.6 | -13.7 | 0.7 |
| Russian Federation | .. | 3 | 4 | 3 | | 1.3 | 8.2 | -18.7 | |
| Austria | 2 | 2 | 2 | 3 | 0.9 | 1.1 | -10.8 | 22.2 | 2.8 |
| Denmark | 1 | 2 | 2 | 2 | 0.5 | 0.8 | -2.7 | 18.9 | 6.4 |
| Sweden | 2 | 3 | 3 | 2 | 0.9 | 0.8 | -10.3 | -33.3 | -2.6 |
| Israel | .. | 2 | 1 | 1 | | 0.5 | -10.1 | -23.3 | |
| Norway | 1 | 2 | 2 | 1 | 0.6 | 0.5 | 6.3 | -33.2 | -4.1 |
| Portugal | .. | 1 | 1 | 1 | | 0.4 | 2.3 | -30.2 | |
| *From other regions* | *49* | *55* | *50* | *38* | *20.9* | *16.2* | *-9.9* | *-23.6* | *-3.0* |
| United States | 27 | 30 | 25 | 18 | 11.7 | 7.6 | -15.2 | -30.1 | -5.2 |
| Japan | 11 | 10 | 8 | 6 | 4.8 | 2.7 | -17.5 | -22.7 | -6.7 |
| All Middle East | 3 | 3 | 4 | 3 | 1.2 | 1.4 | 21.0 | -17.5 | 2.2 |
| Canada | 3 | 3 | 3 | 2 | 1.2 | 1.0 | 2.8 | -21.3 | -1.7 |
| All Africa | .. | 2 | 2 | 2 | | 0.9 | 2.9 | -8.7 | |
| Australia | 1 | 2 | 2 | 2 | 0.6 | 0.9 | 1.1 | -4.2 | 4.4 |
| China | .. | 1 | 2 | 1 | | 0.6 | 30.2 | -23.1 | |
| Brazil | 1 | 1 | 1 | 1 | 0.6 | 0.4 | -4.0 | -9.0 | -3.4 |
| Mexico | 1 | 1 | 1 | 1 | 0.3 | 0.3 | -4.2 | -23.8 | 3.5 |
| Argentina | 1 | 1 | 0 | 1 | 0.3 | 0.3 | -44.1 | 52.6 | -1.1 |
| South Africa | 0 | .. | .. | .. | 0.2 | | | | |
| Venezuela | 0 | .. | .. | .. | 0.1 | | | | |
| *Other World/Not specified* | *17* | *19* | *19* | *19* | *7.3* | *8.0* | *-3.4* | *0.8* | *1.2* |

Source: World Tourism Organization (WTO) © (Data as collected by WTO December 2004)

**Monaco**

**Nights of International Tourists in Hotels and Similar Establishments (by nationality)**

| | | | | (thousand) | Market share (%) | | Growth rate (%) | | Average per year (%) |
|---|---|---|---|---|---|---|---|---|---|
| | 1995 | 2001 | 2002 | 2003* | 1995 | 2003* | 2002/01 | 2003*/02 | 1995-2003* |
| **Total** | **626** | **798** | **765** | **674** | **100** | **100** | **-4.2** | **-11.8** | **0.9** |
| *From Europe* | *427* | *555* | *535* | *487* | *68.3* | *72.3* | *-3.8* | *-8.9* | *1.7* |
| Italy | 140 | 163 | 149 | 142 | 22.4 | 21.1 | -8.3 | -4.8 | 0.2 |
| France | 113 | 109 | 98 | 95 | 18.0 | 14.1 | -10.7 | -2.9 | -2.1 |
| United Kingdom | 59 | 104 | 110 | 93 | 9.5 | 13.8 | 5.2 | -15.4 | 5.8 |
| Germany | 37 | 45 | 39 | 34 | 5.9 | 5.1 | -13.2 | -11.2 | -0.9 |
| Switzerland | 21 | 27 | 28 | 25 | 3.4 | 3.7 | 3.4 | -9.6 | 2.3 |
| Spain | 14 | 19 | 19 | 19 | 2.2 | 2.8 | 3.6 | -3.8 | 4.1 |
| Russian Federation | .. | 15 | 18 | 16 | | 2.3 | 15.7 | -10.8 | |
| Netherlands | 12 | 15 | 18 | 14 | 1.9 | 2.1 | 15.1 | -18.6 | 2.3 |
| Belgium | 11 | 17 | 14 | 13 | 1.8 | 2.0 | -18.5 | -7.5 | 1.7 |
| Austria | 7 | 11 | 9 | 11 | 1.0 | 1.7 | -16.3 | 21.4 | 6.9 |
| Denmark | 4 | 5 | 6 | 6 | 0.6 | 0.9 | 22.1 | 5.7 | 6.7 |
| Sweden | 7 | 9 | 9 | 6 | 1.0 | 0.9 | -0.1 | -36.9 | -1.4 |
| Portugal | .. | 4 | 6 | 5 | | 0.7 | 48.9 | -17.5 | |
| Israel | .. | 6 | 6 | 5 | | 0.7 | 3.9 | -27.1 | |
| Norway | 4 | 5 | 6 | 3 | 0.6 | 0.5 | 8.2 | -45.1 | -1.4 |
| *From other regions* | *147* | *174* | *167* | *126* | *23.5* | *18.8* | *-3.8* | *-24.3* | *-1.9* |
| United States | 89 | 95 | 84 | 56 | 14.3 | 8.3 | -11.6 | -34.0 | -5.7 |
| Japan | 25 | 25 | 22 | 17 | 3.9 | 2.6 | -11.4 | -20.8 | -4.3 |
| All Middle East | 10 | 17 | 21 | 15 | 1.6 | 2.2 | 24.1 | -29.9 | 5.4 |
| Canada | 10 | 11 | 12 | 10 | 1.6 | 1.4 | 6.2 | -19.1 | 0.0 |
| All Africa | .. | 8 | 9 | 9 | | 1.4 | 15.2 | 4.8 | |
| Australia | 4 | 6 | 7 | 6 | 0.7 | 1.0 | 3.5 | -1.8 | 5.2 |
| Brazil | 4 | 4 | 4 | 4 | 0.7 | 0.6 | 2.1 | 17.4 | 0.9 |
| China | .. | 3 | 4 | 3 | | 0.5 | 27.6 | -27.9 | |
| Argentina | 2 | 2 | 1 | 3 | 0.3 | 0.4 | -29.9 | 132.4 | 7.0 |
| Mexico | 2 | 2 | 3 | 3 | 0.3 | 0.4 | 31.9 | -3.9 | 6.2 |
| South Africa | 1 | .. | .. | .. | 0.2 | | | | |
| Venezuela | 1 | .. | .. | .. | 0.1 | | | | |
| *Other World/Not specified* | *51* | *69* | *63* | *61* | *8.2* | *9.0* | *-8.4* | *-4.1* | *2.1* |

Source: World Tourism Organization (WTO) © (Data as collected by WTO December 2004)

# III.2.8 Netherlands Western Europe

## Profile

### Netherlands

Europe
Western Europe

| | |
|---|---|
| Capital | Amsterdam |
| Year of entry in WTO | 1976 |
| Area (1000 km²) | 42 |
| Population (2003, million) | 16.2 |
| Gross Domestic Product (GDP) (2003, euro million) | 543,206 |
| GDP per capita (2003, euro) | 33,547 |
| GDP growth (real, %) | |
| -> 2002: 0.6; 2003: -0.9; 2004*: 1.1; 2005*: 1.8 | |

| | 2001 | 2002 | 2003* | 2002/2001 | 2003*/2002 |
|---|---|---|---|---|---|
| **International Arrivals** | | | | | |
| Tourists (overnight visitors) (1000) | 9,500 | 9,595 | 9,181 | 1.0 | -4.3 |
| - per 100 of inhabitants | 59 | 60 | 57 | | |
| **Tourism accommodation** | | | | | |
| Number of rooms | .. | 86,247 | 88,146 | | 2.2 |
| *Nights spent in collective establishments (1000)* | 80,475 | 82,372 | 81,205 | 2.4 | -1.4 |
| by non-residents (inbound tourism) | 25,502 | 26,368 | 25,341 | 3.4 | -3.9 |
| by residents (domestic tourism) | 54,973 | 56,004 | 55,864 | 1.9 | -0.2 |
| *Nights spent in hotels and similar establishments (1000)* | 28,563 | 28,515 | 27,182 | -0.2 | -4.7 |
| by non-residents (inbound tourism) | 14,955 | 14,922 | 13,798 | -0.2 | -7.5 |
| by residents (domestic tourism) | 13,608 | 13,593 | 13,384 | -0.1 | -1.5 |
| **Outbound Tourism** | | | | | |
| Trips abroad (1000) | 14,220 | 16,760 | .. | 17.9 | |
| - per 100 of inhabitants | 89 | 104 | .. | | |
| **Receipts and Expenditure for International Tourism** | | | | | |
| International Tourism Receipts (euro million) | 7,263 | 8,608 | 9,781 | 18.5 | 13.6 |
| - per Tourist Arrival (euro) | 765 | 897 | 1,065 | 17.4 | 18.7 |
| - per capita (euro) | 453 | 534 | 603 | | |
| International Fare Receipts (euro million) | 4,806 | 4,505 | .. | -6.3 | |
| International Tourism Expenditure (euro million) | 12,986 | 14,662 | 15,450 | 12.9 | 5.4 |
| - per trip (euro) | 913 | 875 | .. | -4.2 | |
| - per capita (euro) | 811 | 909 | 952 | | |
| International Fare Expenditure (euro million) | 1,155 | 1,368 | .. | 18.4 | |
| △ International Tourism Balance (euro million) | -5,723 | -6,054 | -5,669 | | |
| △ International Fare Balance (euro million) | 3,651 | 3,137 | .. | | |

Source: World Tourism Organization (WTO) (Data as collected by WTO December 2004)

See annex for methodological notes and reference of external sources used.

# Survey

Contributed by *Netherlands Board of Tourism and Conventions*
www.holland.com (promotional)
www.holland2.com/corporate/tm.html (institutional/corporate)

## Tourism development and outlook

**Overall evaluation of results**

The year 2003 has been a difficult year for inbound tourism to the Netherlands. Due to the Severe Acute Respiratory Syndrome (SARS), the war in Iraq and the economic slowdown, the number of international arrivals declined by 4 per cent to 9.2 million. The long-haul markets especially showed negative figures. The number of visitors from Asia and America declined by 15 per cent and 9 per cent respectively. The picture for the European countries was more diverse. The number of tourists from the neighbouring countries Germany and Belgium increased by 2 per cent and 11 per cent respectively. However, the number of British tourists declined by 11 per cent, mainly due to the more expensive euro.

**Supply**

No significant changes took place on the supply side.

**External factors**

International uncertainty, SARS and worsening economic circumstances influenced the development of incoming tourism negatively.

**Tourism policy**

In October 2003, the Ministry of Economic Affairs presented a new Tourism Policy Plan (in Dutch called the Vernieuwde Toeristische Agenda). In the plan, the Ministry describes its policy for the next coming years. The Ministry sees as its main objective for the national tourism policy, the stimulation of incoming tourism. Besides more general policy making, the Ministry will focus especially on the development of four important tourism segments, namely the coast, cities/culture, events and the MICE segment.

**Marketing & promotion**

The new tourism policy and a serious budget cut from the Ministry of Economic Affairs had significant consequences for the national tourism organization.
In June 2004, the Ministry and the Netherlands Board of Tourism and Conventions (NBTC) settled a new contract for the period 2004-2006. The main objective for the NBTC will be to gain market share from its competitors in North-West Europe. In 2003, the market share amounts to 14 per cent; in 2006, the target is set at 14.3 per cent.
In order to reach the objective, the NBTC has developed a new marketing strategy. In that strategy choices are made on product-market combinations. In the coming years, the NBTC will concentrate on the following products: Holland classics, city trips, the coast and the rest of Holland. On the promotion side, NBTC will develop some big promotional campaigns directed mainly to the neighbouring countries. In promotion, theme years and international events will play an important role.

**Outlook 2004**

A growth of 2.5 per cent is expected for incoming tourism.

## International Meetings Industry (MI)

**Characteristics of supply**

The Netherlands is a congress destination that offers a lot of qualities. Creativity, co-operative thinking and flexibility is characteristic of the Netherlands. The wide range of places of interest are located in easy reach from each other, which offers a lot of possibilities for organising a social program.

Besides the excellent infrastructure, the Netherlands has a balanced price/quality relation, a wide offer of hotels and many multifunctional congress centres which guarantees the Netherlands as an attractive congress destination. The main congress destinations in the Netherlands are: Amsterdam, The Hague, Rotterdam, Noordwijk, Maastricht, Utrecht, Groningen and Eindhoven.

**Organisation of promotion**

The Netherlands Board of Tourism and Conventions (NBTC) has been given the exclusive task, by the government, to promote the country as an international congress destination. Regional Convention Bureaux (RCB) are partners of the NBTC and take part in the activities organised by the NBTC.
The NBTC supports and stimulates the Dutch congress sector to secure the current position of the Netherlands as an important international congress destination and, where possible, to improve it.

**Website(s)**

<www.holland.com/ncb>

**Collection of statistics on the Meetings Industry?:** yes.

**Description**

An important instrument in reaching the above mentioned goal is good and reliable market information. The number of international congresses in the Netherlands is registered on a yearly basis by the NBTC. Also, this year the NBTC has undertaken research on the expenditures of the international non-corporate congress participants to gain insights into the economical importance of this market segment, national as well as regional.
Every year all RCB gather information from their region on the international congresses that were held in the year before. In their turn: the RCB hand over this information to NBTC.
The NBTC applies the following criteria for international conventions and business meetings:

- The event may be an associative or corporate meeting;
- The convention or business conference must last at least two days, with at least one overnight stay;
- The number of participants on the first day must be at least 40;
- At least one third of all participants must reside outside the Netherlands;
- The meeting must take place at external accommodation, including universities and academic medical centres;
- The purpose of the external meeting must be to transfer knowledge.

The NBTC receives data on the title of the congress, the dates, the accommodation used, the number of participants and area of interest and uses this information to analyse trends on number of international congresses annually, number of participant/days, average number of participants per congress and average duration.
The information is spread among the RCB for internal comparison and as a country figure published in the press.

**Importance / size**

The average duration of international conventions in the Netherlands in 2002 was 4 days, with an average number of visitors of 222 per convention. There were 998 international conventions and business meetings in the Netherlands in 2002. This figure is based on data collected from the Regional Congress Bureaux (RCB), organisers and accommodation providers in the Netherlands.
The Netherlands as a convention destination in 2002:

- Total number of international conventions: 998;
- Total number of convention participant/days: 881 thousand;
- Average number of participants: 222;
- Average duration in days: 4.

Source: NBTC 2003 (figures for 2002).

The NBTC also uses information from the International Congress and Convention Association (ICCA) and the Union of International Associations (UIA) to view the position of the Netherlands in the world wide list of Congress Destinations.The most important outcome of the research on the expenditure of the international non-corporate congress participants is that in 2002, 360 international non-corporate congresses were held in the Netherlands. The international non-corporate congress market is approximately one-third of the total international congress market. The foreign non-corporate congress participant spends on average 344 euro per day in the Netherlands. More than two-thirds of this benefits the "local economy of the congress accommodation". The research shows that total expenditure by foreign participants in non-corporate congresses in 2002 was 116 million euro.

**Evolution MI**

More destinations are becoming more competitive when compared to the more traditional congress destinations. Especially with the enlargement of the European Union, competition has strengthened. The NBTC is specifically focussing on promoting the Nethewrlands abroad, and has put more internal focus on promoting the country as a congress destination with specific Product-Market-Partner-Combinations.

# International Tourism by Origin

**Netherlands**

**International Tourist Arrivals in All Accommodation Establishments**

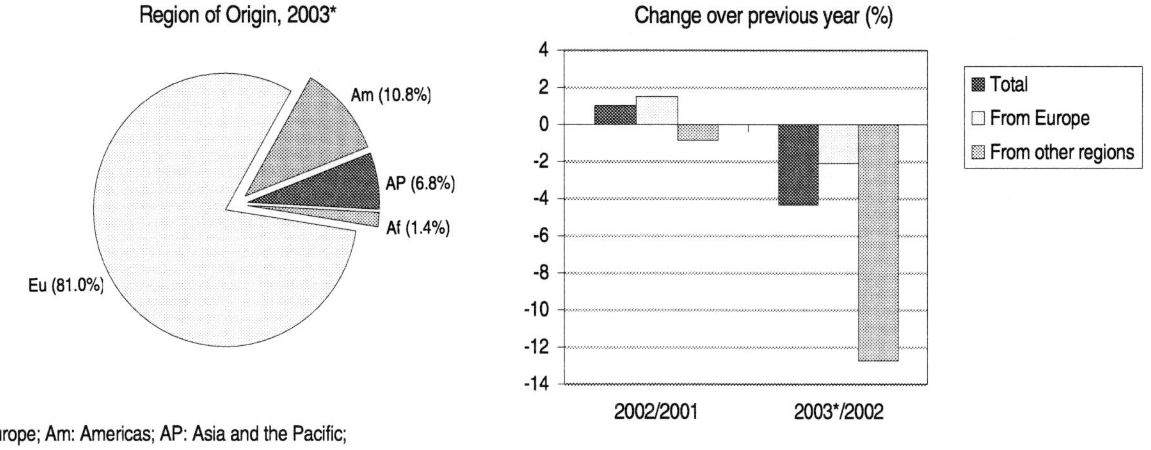


Eu: Europe; Am: Americas; AP: Asia and the Pacific;
Af: Africa; Ot: Other;

Source: World Tourism Organization (WTO) ©

**Netherlands**

**International Tourist Arrivals in All Accommodation Establishments (by residence)**

| | | | | (thousand) | Market share (%) | | Growth rate (%) | | Average per year (%) |
|---|---|---|---|---|---|---|---|---|---|
| | 1995 | 2001 | 2002 | 2003* | 1995 | 2003* | 2002/01 | 2003*/02 | 1995-2003* |
| **Total** | **6,574** | **9,500** | **9,595** | **9,181** | **100** | **100** | **1.0** | **-4.3** | **4.3** |
| *From Europe* | *5,307* | *7,479* | *7,592* | *7,432* | *80.7* | *81.0* | *1.5* | *-2.1* | *4.3* |
| Germany | 2,461 | 2,657 | 2,755 | 2,803 | 37.4 | 30.5 | 3.7 | 1.8 | 1.6 |
| United Kingdom | 871 | 1,939 | 1,851 | 1,646 | 13.2 | 17.9 | -4.5 | -11.1 | 8.3 |
| Belgium | 436 | 629 | 705 | 779 | 6.6 | 8.5 | 12.1 | 10.6 | 7.5 |
| France | 387 | 455 | 511 | 465 | 5.9 | 5.1 | 12.3 | -9.0 | 2.3 |
| Italy | 214 | 343 | 346 | 339 | 3.3 | 3.7 | 0.9 | -2.0 | 5.9 |
| Spain | .. | 259 | 276 | 275 | | 3.0 | 6.7 | -0.4 | |
| Spain, Portugal | 165 | .. | .. | .. | 2.5 | | | | |
| Denmark | 87 | 105 | 103 | 116 | 1.3 | 1.3 | -1.8 | 13.1 | 3.7 |
| Switzerland | 111 | 122 | 127 | 115 | 1.7 | 1.2 | 4.9 | -10.0 | 0.4 |
| Sweden | 107 | .. | 112 | 106 | 1.6 | 1.2 | | -5.2 | -0.2 |
| Norway | 53 | .. | .. | .. | 0.8 | | | | |
| Ireland | 34 | .. | .. | .. | 0.5 | | | | |
| Finland | 29 | .. | .. | .. | 0.4 | | | | |
| Luxembourg | 24 | .. | .. | .. | 0.4 | | | | |
| Other Europe | 329 | 972 | 807 | 788 | 5.0 | 8.6 | -17.0 | -2.3 | 11.5 |
| *From other regions* | *1,267* | *2,021* | *2,004* | *1,749* | *19.3* | *19.0* | *-0.9* | *-12.7* | *4.1* |
| All Americas | .. | 1,203 | 1,100 | 996 | | 10.8 | -8.6 | -9.4 | |
| United States | 531 | .. | .. | .. | 8.1 | | | | |
| All Asia | .. | 564 | 624 | 531 | | 5.8 | 10.8 | -15.0 | |
| All Africa | 50 | 141 | 173 | 131 | 0.8 | 1.4 | 23.0 | -24.4 | 12.8 |
| Japan | 119 | .. | .. | .. | 1.8 | | | | |
| All Oceania | .. | 114 | 107 | 92 | | 1.0 | -6.4 | -14.3 | |
| Canada | 86 | .. | .. | .. | 1.3 | | | | |
| Other Americas | 104 | .. | .. | .. | 1.6 | | | | |
| Other Asia | 287 | .. | .. | .. | 4.4 | | | | |
| Other Oceania | 91 | .. | .. | .. | 1.4 | | | | |

Source: World Tourism Organization (WTO) © (Data as collected by WTO December 2004)

**Netherlands**
**Nights of International Tourists in All Accommodation Establishments**

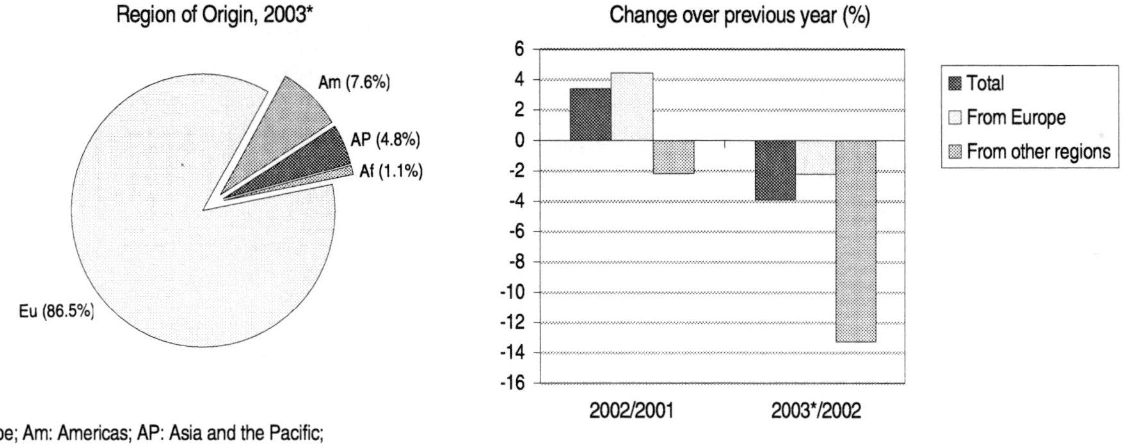


Eu: Europe; Am: Americas; AP: Asia and the Pacific;
Af: Africa;

Source: World Tourism Organization (WTO) ©

**Netherlands**
**Nights of International Tourists in All Accommodation Establishments (by residence)**

| | | | | (thousand) | Market share (%) | | Growth rate (%) | | Average per year (%) |
|---|---|---|---|---|---|---|---|---|---|
| | 1995 | 2001 | 2002 | 2003* | 1995 | 2003* | 2002/01 | 2003*/02 | 1995-2003* |
| **Total** | **19,736** | **25,502** | **26,368** | **25,341** | **100** | **100** | **3.4** | **-3.9** | **3.2** |
| *From Europe* | *17,057* | *21,473* | *22,427* | *21,924* | *86.4* | *86.5* | *4.4* | *-2.2* | *3.2* |
| Germany | 10,412 | 10,707 | 11,482 | 11,350 | 52.8 | 44.8 | 7.2 | -1.1 | 1.1 |
| United Kingdom | 1,940 | 4,168 | 4,016 | 3,484 | 9.8 | 13.7 | -3.7 | -13.2 | 7.6 |
| Belgium | 1,300 | 1,684 | 1,941 | 2,137 | 6.6 | 8.4 | 15.3 | 10.1 | 6.4 |
| France | 748 | 893 | 998 | 955 | 3.8 | 3.8 | 11.8 | -4.3 | 3.1 |
| Italy | 480 | 768 | 775 | 786 | 2.4 | 3.1 | 1.0 | 1.4 | 6.4 |
| Spain | .. | 582 | 607 | 630 | | 2.5 | 4.3 | 3.8 | |
| Spain, Portugal | 373 | .. | .. | .. | 1.9 | | | | |
| Denmark | 205 | 235 | 226 | 266 | 1.0 | 1.0 | -3.8 | 17.4 | 3.3 |
| Switzerland | 276 | 258 | 288 | 265 | 1.4 | 1.0 | 11.7 | -8.1 | -0.5 |
| Sweden | 219 | .. | 223 | 225 | 1.1 | 0.9 | | 0.9 | 0.3 |
| Norway | 108 | .. | .. | .. | 0.5 | | | | |
| Ireland | 85 | .. | .. | .. | 0.4 | | | | |
| Finland | 62 | .. | .. | .. | 0.3 | | | | |
| Luxembourg | 49 | .. | .. | .. | 0.2 | | | | |
| Other Europe | 800 | 2,179 | 1,871 | 1,826 | 4.1 | 7.2 | -14.1 | -2.4 | 10.9 |
| *From other regions* | *2,679* | *4,029* | *3,941* | *3,418* | *13.6* | *13.5* | *-2.2* | *-13.3* | *3.1* |
| All Americas | .. | 2,418 | 2,168 | 1,937 | | 7.6 | -10.4 | -10.6 | |
| United States | 1,120 | .. | .. | .. | 5.7 | | | | |
| All Asia | .. | 1,088 | 1,197 | 1,017 | | 4.0 | 10.0 | -15.0 | |
| All Africa | 144 | 297 | 368 | 274 | 0.7 | 1.1 | 24.0 | -25.6 | 8.3 |
| Japan | 242 | .. | .. | .. | 1.2 | | | | |
| All Oceania | 194 | 226 | 209 | 190 | 1.0 | 0.7 | -7.8 | -9.2 | -0.3 |
| Canada | 177 | .. | .. | .. | 0.9 | | | | |
| Other Americas | 212 | .. | .. | .. | 1.1 | | | | |
| Other Asia | 590 | .. | .. | .. | 3.0 | | | | |

Source: World Tourism Organization (WTO) © (Data as collected by WTO December 2004)

# III.2.9 Switzerland Western Europe

## Profile

# Switzerland

Europe
Western Europe

| | |
|---|---|
| Capital | Bern |
| Year of entry in WTO | 1976 |
| Area (1000 km²) | 41 |
| Population (2003, million) | 7.4 |
| Gross Domestic Product (GDP) (2003, euro million) | 338,052 |
| GDP per capita (2003, euro) | 45,888 |
| GDP growth (real, %) | |
| -> 2002: 0.2; 2003: -0.5; 2004*: 1.8; 2005*: 2.2 | |

| | 2001 | 2002 | 2003* | 2002/2001 | 2003*/2002 |
|---|---|---|---|---|---|
| **International Arrivals** | | | | | |
| Tourists (overnight visitors) (1000) | 7,455 | 6,868 | 6,530 | -7.9 | -4.9 |
| - per 100 of inhabitants | 102 | 93 | 88 | | |
| **Tourism accommodation** | | | | | |
| Number of rooms | 140,644 | 139,943 | 139,969 | -0.5 | 0.0 |
| *Nights spent in collective establishments (1000)* | 68,330 | 65,895 | 64,961 | -3.6 | -1.4 |
| by non-residents (inbound tourism) | 32,111 | 29,641 | 28,569 | -7.7 | -3.6 |
| by residents (domestic tourism) | 36,219 | 36,254 | 36,392 | 0.1 | 0.4 |
| *Nights spent in hotels and similar establishments (1000)* | 33,586 | 31,964 | 31,200 | -4.8 | -2.4 |
| by non-residents (inbound tourism) | 19,273 | 17,768 | 16,964 | -7.8 | -4.5 |
| by residents (domestic tourism) | 14,313 | 14,196 | 14,236 | -0.8 | 0.3 |
| **Outbound Tourism** | | | | | |
| Trips abroad (1000) | 11,554 | 11,427 | .. | -1.1 | |
| - per 100 of inhabitants | 158 | 155 | .. | | |
| **Receipts and Expenditure for International Tourism** | | | | | |
| International Tourism Receipts (euro million) | 8,126 | 8,807 | 9,862 | 8.4 | 12.0 |
| - per Tourist Arrival (euro) | 1,090 | 1,282 | 1,510 | 17.7 | 17.8 |
| - per capita (euro) | 1,111 | 1,196 | 1,331 | | |
| International Fare Receipts (euro million) | 2,715 | 2,073 | 2,135 | -23.6 | 3.0 |
| International Tourism Expenditure (euro million) | 6,773 | 7,383 | 7,901 | 9.0 | 7.0 |
| - per trip (euro) | 586 | 646 | .. | 10.2 | |
| - per capita (euro) | 926 | 1,003 | 1,067 | | |
| International Fare Expenditure (euro million) | 2,105 | 1,868 | 2,101 | -11.3 | 12.5 |
| △ International Tourism Balance (euro million) | 1,353 | 1,424 | 1,961 | | |
| △ International Fare Balance (euro million) | 611 | 205 | 34 | | |

Source: World Tourism Organization (WTO) (Data as collected by WTO December 2004)

See annex for methodological notes and reference of external sources used.

## Survey

Contributed by *Swiss Federal Statistical Office*
http://myswitzerland.com (promotional)
www.swisstourfed.ch ; www.presence.ch/prs_dir/e/start ; www.seco-admin.ch ; www.idt.unisg.ch (institutional/corporate)
www.statistik.admin.ch (Swiss Federal Statistical Office) ; www.bakbasel.ch (Prognosis) ; www.stnet.ch (site for ST Partners) (research and data)

## Tourism development and outlook

**Overall evaluation of results**

Overnights in Swiss hotels: Overall: -2.7 per cent.
Negative world economic situation in main source markets, but day-trippers to Switzerland due to the great summer weather. It was a year with extremes.
Mountain and wellness resorts registered slight positive figures (+0.4% / +0.5%).

**Supply**

A Mystery Park opened in May 2003 in the Berner Oberland.
Transport capacities: the new SWISS Airline has cancelled some direct flights (e.g. from and to Beijing, Delhi, St. Petersburg, Buenos Aires, etc.).

**External factors**

China: Switzerland registered 106 thousand overnights from Chinese guests in Swiss hotels. The Approved Destination Status for Switzerland was formalised in 2004. The forecast for 2006 is estimated at 300 thousand overnights.
The high price level in Switzerland.
Reduced capacity of our national carrier SWISS Airline.
Strong euro against the Swiss Franc.

**Tourism policy**

Renewal of tourism programmes focusing on the improvement of tourism supply:
- Swiss hotel credit association: 60 million swiss francs for the period 2003-2007;
- Inno Tour programme: 35 million swiss francs for 2003-2007 to improve innovation and cooperation.

**Marketing & promotion**

Customer Relation Management (CRM) project in 2 modules for "Enjoy Switzerland" from 1st June 2006 to 31th December 2010:
- Module 1: e-marketing;
- Module 2: Electronic communication and Customercard. The basic aim is to create one-to-one communication with the customer via the web.

**Outlook 2004**

Switzerland Tourism believes there will be a turnaround this year with a deviation in the figures for former years:
- 2004: total +0.4 per cent; foreigners +0.6 per cent; home market -0.7 per cent;
- 2005: total +1.4 per cent; foreigners +0.8 per cent; home market: +1.8 per cent;
- Summer season 2004: total +1 per cent; foreign countries +2.3 per cent; home market -0.5 per cent.

## International Meetings Industry (MI)

**Characteristics of supply**

A selection from among the fourteen tourism fairs in Switzerland are:
- Ferienmesse in Basel;
- Salon Vacances, Sports et Loisirs in Geneva;
- FESPO in Zürich;
- Ferien-und Gesundheitsmesse in Bern;
- Ferienmesse + Touristiertag in St-Gall.

The main destinations are Basel, Bern, Crans-Montana, Davos, Flims, Fribourg, Geneva, Interlaken, Lausanne, Lugano, Luzern, Montreux, Pontresina, St. Gallen, St. Moritz and Zürich.

**Organisation of promotion**

City level: Regional convention bureaux and within the structure of the regional tourism organizations.
National level: National convention bureau within the structure of the national tourist office <www.MySwitzerland.com/mice>.
Some references of independent organizations acting at regional level are: <www.wigra.com>, <www.olma-messen.ch>, <www.viva50plus.org>.

**Collection of statistics on the Meetings Industry?:** no.

**Importance / size**

Average stay in Switzerland: 3 nights.
Of all foreign outbound trips from Europe, approximately 6 per cent market share (20 million journeys).
Overnight share of all tourism nights in Switzerland: 5 per cent.
Estimation: Basel 30 thousand visitors; Geneva 26 thousand visitors; Zürich 69 thousand visitors; Bern 43 thousand visitors; and St-Gall 27 thousand visitors.

**Evolution MI**

Recent years: stable.
Coming years: slight increase.

# International Tourism by Origin

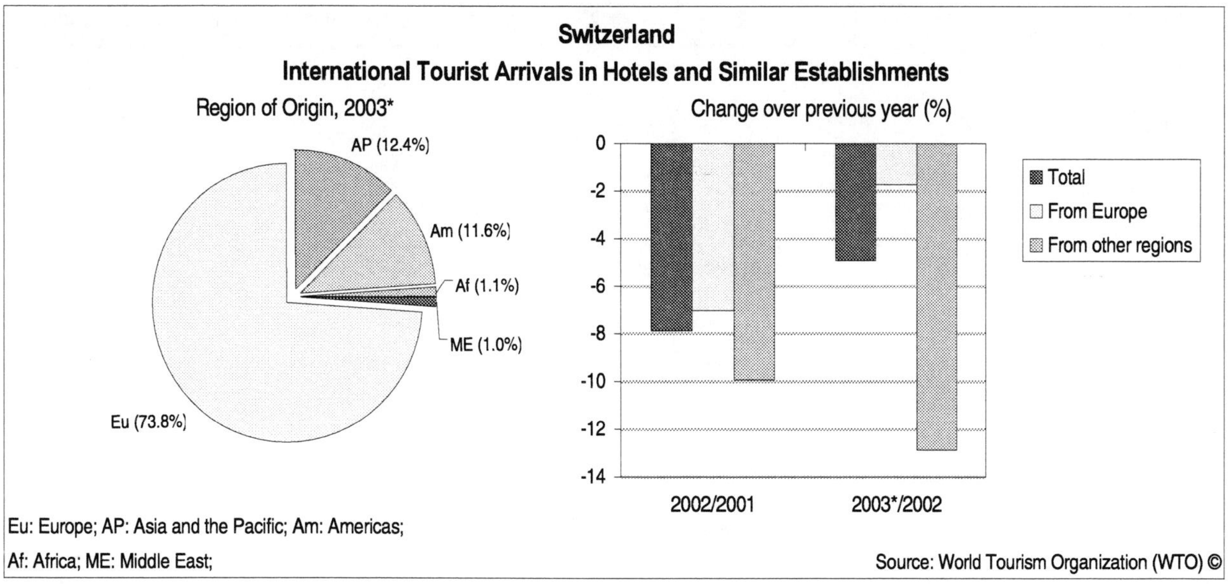


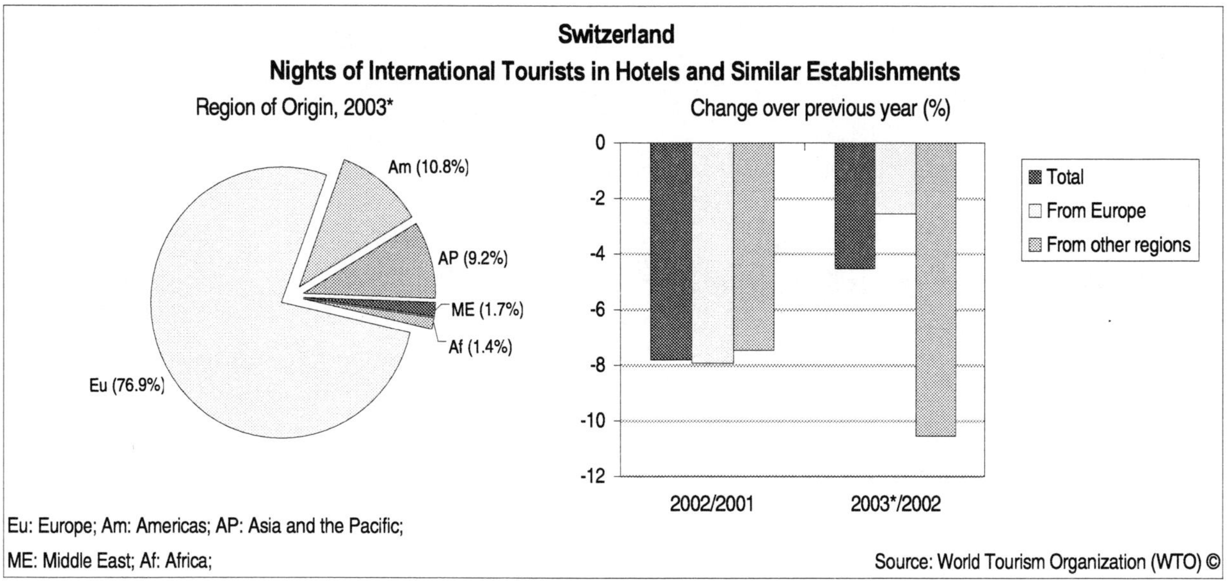

**Switzerland**

**International Tourist Arrivals in Hotels and Similar Establishments (by residence)**

| | | | | (thousand) | Market share (%) | | Growth rate (%) | | Average per year (%) |
|---|---|---|---|---|---|---|---|---|---|
| | 1995 | 2001 | 2002 | 2003* | 1995 | 2003* | 2002/01 | 2003*/02 | 1995-2003* |
| **Total** | **6,946** | **7,455** | **6,868** | **6,530** | **100** | **100** | **-7.9** | **-4.9** | **-0.8** |
| *From Europe* | *4,785* | *5,277* | *4,906* | *4,821* | *68.9* | *73.8* | *-7.0* | *-1.7* | *0.1* |
| Germany | 2,111 | 2,179 | 1,952 | 1,882 | 30.4 | 28.8 | -10.4 | -3.6 | -1.4 |
| United Kingdom | 448 | 661 | 619 | 612 | 6.4 | 9.4 | -6.4 | -1.1 | 4.0 |
| France | 461 | 503 | 489 | 488 | 6.6 | 7.5 | -2.8 | -0.1 | 0.7 |
| Italy | 372 | 439 | 429 | 435 | 5.4 | 6.7 | -2.1 | 1.2 | 2.0 |
| Netherlands | 254 | 312 | 289 | 285 | 3.7 | 4.4 | -7.4 | -1.4 | 1.4 |
| Belgium | 223 | 209 | 198 | 191 | 3.2 | 2.9 | -5.1 | -3.3 | -1.9 |
| Austria | 143 | 147 | 145 | 144 | 2.1 | 2.2 | -1.1 | -0.5 | 0.1 |
| Spain | 154 | 156 | 145 | 138 | 2.2 | 2.1 | -7.0 | -5.0 | -1.4 |
| Russian Federation | .. | 61 | 64 | 69 | | 1.1 | 4.7 | 7.2 | |
| Sweden | 75 | 73 | 65 | 65 | 1.1 | 1.0 | -11.1 | -0.2 | -1.7 |
| Israel | 96 | 79 | 66 | 61 | 1.4 | 0.9 | -16.3 | -8.3 | -5.6 |
| Denmark | 37 | 41 | 41 | 40 | 0.5 | 0.6 | -0.7 | -2.8 | 1.0 |
| Greece | 38 | 34 | 38 | 36 | 0.5 | 0.6 | 12.6 | -5.0 | -0.5 |
| Luxembourg | 32 | 36 | 35 | 32 | 0.5 | 0.5 | -3.3 | -8.3 | 0.1 |
| Norway | 26 | 31 | 28 | 31 | 0.4 | 0.5 | -10.6 | 11.2 | 1.9 |
| Poland | 21 | 31 | 27 | 26 | 0.3 | 0.4 | -10.3 | -3.4 | 3.2 |
| Portugal | 32 | 29 | 27 | 25 | 0.5 | 0.4 | -5.0 | -6.9 | -2.7 |
| Turkey | 26 | 24 | 23 | 25 | 0.4 | 0.4 | -2.7 | 5.2 | -0.8 |
| Finland | 22 | 27 | 24 | 24 | 0.3 | 0.4 | -10.9 | -0.9 | 0.9 |
| Ireland | 14 | 18 | 19 | 23 | 0.2 | 0.4 | 1.4 | 24.2 | 6.2 |
| Hungary | 19 | 21 | 22 | 21 | 0.3 | 0.3 | 6.0 | -5.1 | 1.4 |
| Czech Rep | .. | 22 | 20 | 20 | | 0.3 | -9.6 | 1.2 | |
| Serbia & Montenegro | .. | 16 | 15 | 14 | | 0.2 | -8.9 | -8.8 | |
| Other intraregional | 181 | 128 | 124 | 133 | 2.6 | 2.0 | -2.7 | 7.4 | -3.7 |
| *From other regions* | *2,161* | *2,178* | *1,961* | *1,709* | *31.1* | *26.2* | *-9.9* | *-12.9* | *-2.9* |
| United States | 783 | 827 | 689 | 598 | 11.3 | 9.2 | -16.7 | -13.2 | -3.3 |
| Japan | 561 | 523 | 416 | 321 | 8.1 | 4.9 | -20.4 | -23.0 | -6.8 |
| India | 37 | 72 | 80 | 85 | 0.5 | 1.3 | 11.3 | 5.3 | 11.1 |
| Korea, Republic of | .. | 57 | 69 | 71 | | 1.1 | 21.7 | 3.3 | |
| All Oceania | 74 | 86 | 80 | 68 | 1.1 | 1.0 | -7.2 | -14.4 | -0.9 |
| Canada | 63 | 76 | 70 | 66 | 0.9 | 1.0 | -8.5 | -5.5 | 0.6 |
| China | .. | 49 | 69 | 63 | | 1.0 | 40.3 | -9.7 | |
| All Middle East | 53 | .. | .. | .. | 0.8 | | | | |
| Taiwan (pr. of China) | .. | 39 | 42 | 34 | | 0.5 | 5.9 | -17.2 | |
| Thailand | .. | 30 | 33 | 30 | | 0.5 | 8.5 | -7.9 | |
| Hong Kong (China) | .. | 39 | 36 | 28 | | 0.4 | -6.6 | -21.8 | |
| Brazil | 58 | 36 | 34 | 28 | 0.8 | 0.4 | -3.2 | -18.8 | -8.7 |
| South Africa | 22 | 26 | 22 | 22 | 0.3 | 0.3 | -15.6 | -1.5 | -0.3 |
| Singapore | .. | 21 | 20 | 19 | | 0.3 | -3.9 | -6.6 | |
| All Central America | 17 | .. | .. | .. | 0.2 | | | | |
| All North Africa | 30 | 20 | 19 | 17 | 0.4 | 0.3 | -6.2 | -9.7 | -7.0 |
| Malaysia | .. | 15 | 18 | 16 | | 0.2 | 19.0 | -13.5 | |
| Egypt | .. | 11 | 11 | 12 | | 0.2 | 4.4 | 2.6 | |
| Indonesia | .. | 10 | 11 | 10 | | 0.2 | 17.2 | -11.7 | |
| Other interregional | 463 | 241 | 241 | 222 | 6.7 | 3.4 | 0.2 | -8.0 | -8.8 |

Source: World Tourism Organization (WTO) © (Data as collected by WTO December 2004)

**Switzerland**

**Nights of International Tourists in Hotels and Similar Establishments (by residence)**

| | | | | (thousand) | Market share (%) | | Growth rate (%) | | Average per year (%) |
|---|---|---|---|---|---|---|---|---|---|
| | 1995 | 2001 | 2002 | 2003* | 1995 | 2003* | 2002/01 | 2003*/02 | 1995-2003* |
| **Total** | **18,386** | **19,273** | **17,768** | **16,964** | **100** | **100** | **-7.8** | **-4.5** | **-1.0** |
| *From Europe* | *13,845* | *14,543* | *13,391* | *13,048* | *75.3* | *76.9* | *-7.9* | *-2.6* | *-0.7* |
| Germany | 6,585 | 6,278 | 5,544 | 5,302 | 35.8 | 31.3 | -11.7 | -4.4 | -2.7 |
| United Kingdom | 1,336 | 1,983 | 1,866 | 1,813 | 7.3 | 10.7 | -5.9 | -2.9 | 3.9 |
| France | 1,230 | 1,244 | 1,166 | 1,149 | 6.7 | 6.8 | -6.3 | -1.4 | -0.8 |
| Italy | 759 | 948 | 933 | 958 | 4.1 | 5.7 | -1.6 | 2.8 | 3.0 |
| Netherlands | 804 | 904 | 818 | 787 | 4.4 | 4.6 | -9.5 | -3.7 | -0.3 |
| Belgium | 910 | 749 | 715 | 699 | 4.9 | 4.1 | -4.6 | -2.1 | -3.2 |
| Austria | 331 | 332 | 327 | 326 | 1.8 | 1.9 | -1.5 | -0.1 | -0.2 |
| Spain | 292 | 313 | 304 | 292 | 1.6 | 1.7 | -2.8 | -3.9 | 0.0 |
| Russian Federation | .. | 209 | 232 | 240 | | 1.4 | 10.8 | 3.3 | |
| Israel | 236 | 203 | 176 | 164 | 1.3 | 1.0 | -13.4 | -6.9 | -4.5 |
| Sweden | 169 | 176 | 150 | 151 | 0.9 | 0.9 | -14.8 | 0.6 | -1.4 |
| Luxembourg | 124 | 124 | 116 | 109 | 0.7 | 0.6 | -6.5 | -5.4 | -1.6 |
| Greece | 96 | 87 | 96 | 93 | 0.5 | 0.5 | 10.2 | -2.5 | -0.4 |
| Denmark | 88 | 95 | 91 | 90 | 0.5 | 0.5 | -3.4 | -2.1 | 0.2 |
| Norway | 59 | 70 | 62 | 72 | 0.3 | 0.4 | -12.1 | 17.0 | 2.6 |
| Poland | 50 | 76 | 70 | 66 | 0.3 | 0.4 | -7.8 | -5.6 | 3.5 |
| Turkey | 71 | 69 | 64 | 64 | 0.4 | 0.4 | -6.6 | 0.0 | -1.2 |
| Portugal | 68 | 74 | 69 | 64 | 0.4 | 0.4 | -5.7 | -7.8 | -0.8 |
| Ireland | 36 | 49 | 48 | 59 | 0.2 | 0.4 | -1.5 | 23.1 | 6.6 |
| Hungary | 50 | 61 | 63 | 59 | 0.3 | 0.3 | 2.5 | -6.2 | 2.1 |
| Finland | 54 | 64 | 57 | 58 | 0.3 | 0.3 | -10.0 | 1.5 | 1.1 |
| Czech Rep | .. | 56 | 53 | 53 | | 0.3 | -5.4 | 0.7 | |
| Other intraregional | 496 | 381 | 370 | 377 | 2.7 | 2.2 | -2.9 | 1.9 | -3.4 |
| *From other regions* | *4,541* | *4,730* | *4,377* | *3,916* | *24.7* | *23.1* | *-7.5* | *-10.5* | *-1.8* |
| United States | 1,720 | 1,877 | 1,587 | 1,398 | 9.4 | 8.2 | -15.5 | -11.9 | -2.6 |
| Japan | 929 | 829 | 690 | 558 | 5.1 | 3.3 | -16.7 | -19.2 | -6.2 |
| India | 89 | 184 | 200 | 197 | 0.5 | 1.2 | 9.0 | -1.6 | 10.4 |
| All Middle East | 185 | .. | .. | .. | 1.0 | | | | |
| Canada | 150 | 187 | 165 | 164 | 0.8 | 1.0 | -11.6 | -1.1 | 1.1 |
| All Oceania | 158 | 191 | 178 | 162 | 0.9 | 1.0 | -6.7 | -9.0 | 0.3 |
| China | .. | 95 | 119 | 106 | | 0.6 | 25.2 | -11.1 | |
| Korea, Republic of | .. | 81 | 99 | 105 | | 0.6 | 21.1 | 6.9 | |
| Brazil | 126 | 107 | 106 | 94 | 0.7 | 0.6 | -1.0 | -11.1 | -3.6 |
| All North Africa | 108 | 72 | 75 | 72 | 0.6 | 0.4 | 4.8 | -4.4 | -5.0 |
| South Africa | 57 | 70 | 57 | 58 | 0.3 | 0.3 | -19.0 | 2.7 | 0.4 |
| Thailand | .. | 57 | 57 | 57 | | 0.3 | 0.8 | 0.0 | |
| Taiwan (pr. of China) | .. | 60 | 63 | 52 | | 0.3 | 5.3 | -18.6 | |
| Hong Kong (China) | .. | 68 | 59 | 49 | | 0.3 | -12.4 | -17.1 | |
| All Central America | 46 | .. | .. | .. | 0.3 | | | | |
| Singapore | .. | 49 | 46 | 44 | | 0.3 | -7.5 | -4.2 | |
| Malaysia | .. | 41 | 42 | 40 | | 0.2 | 2.2 | -5.4 | |
| Other Africa | 97 | 108 | 110 | 112 | 0.5 | 0.7 | 2.5 | 1.4 | 1.9 |
| Other South America | 127 | 62 | 61 | 50 | 0.7 | 0.3 | -2.2 | -18.9 | -11.1 |
| Other Americas | .. | 92 | 96 | 86 | | 0.5 | 4.6 | -10.6 | |
| Other interregional | 749 | 500 | 565 | 513 | 4.1 | 3.0 | 13.2 | -9.3 | -4.6 |

Source: World Tourism Organization (WTO) © (Data as collected by WTO December 2004)

# III.3 Central and Eastern Europe

## III.3.1 Armenia Central and Eastern Europe

### Profile

# Armenia

Europe
Central and Eastern Europe

| | |
|---|---|
| Capital | Yerevan |
| Year of entry in WTO | 1997 |
| Area (1000 km²) | 30 |
| Population (2003, million) | 3.0 |
| Gross Domestic Product (GDP) (2003, euro million) | 2,919 |
| GDP per capita (2003, euro) | 767 |
| GDP growth (real, %) | |

'-> 2002: 12.9; 2003: 13.9; 2004*: 7.0; 2005*: 6.0

| | 2001 | 2002 | 2003* | 2002/2001 | 2003*/2002 |
|---|---|---|---|---|---|
| **International Arrivals** | | | | | |
| Tourists (overnight visitors) (1000) | 123 | 162 | 206 | 31.5 | 27.1 |
| - per 100 of inhabitants | 4 | 5 | 7 | | |
| **Tourism accommodation** | | | | | |
| Number of bed-places | 12,132 | 12,578 | 14,115 | 3.7 | 12.2 |
| *Nights spent in collective establishments (1000)* | 668 | 928 | 1,318 | 38.9 | 42.0 |
| by non-residents (inbound tourism) | 200 | 202 | 343 | 1.0 | 69.8 |
| by residents (domestic tourism) | 468 | 726 | 975 | 55.1 | 34.3 |
| **Outbound Tourism** | | | | | |
| Trips abroad (1000) | 110 | 131 | 169 | 19.1 | 29.0 |
| - per 100 of inhabitants | 4 | 4 | 6 | | |
| **Receipts and Expenditure for International Tourism** | | | | | |
| International Tourism Receipts (euro million) | 70 | 70 | 77 | 0.0 | 9.8 |
| - per Tourist Arrival (euro) | 571 | 434 | 375 | -24.0 | -13.7 |
| - per capita (euro) | 23 | 23 | 26 | | |
| International Fare Receipts (euro million) | 17 | 20 | 18 | 16.0 | -10.5 |
| International Tourism Expenditure (euro million) | 43 | 60 | 71 | 39.2 | 17.5 |
| - per trip (euro) | 394 | 460 | 419 | 16.9 | -8.9 |
| - per capita (euro) | 14 | 20 | 24 | | |
| International Fare Expenditure (euro million) | 21 | 35 | 32 | 68.3 | -8.3 |
| △ International Tourism Balance (euro million) | 27 | 10 | 6 | | |
| △ International Fare Balance (euro million) | -3 | -15 | -14 | | |

Source: World Tourism Organization (WTO) (Data as collected by WTO December 2004)

See annex for methodological notes and reference of external sources used.

# Survey

Contributed by *Ministry of Trade and Economic Development*
www.armeniainfo.am (promotional)
www.minted.am (institutional/corporate)
www.armstat.am (research and data)

## Tourism development and outlook

**Overall evaluation of results**

Tourism has been one of the fastest expanding economic sectors in recent years. Despite Armenia's geo-political position which tends to restrict arrivals, tourism increased in 2003.

The road network generally is in normal condition. An extensive programme was commenced in 2001 for the reconstruction of highways, roads signs and streets of Yerevan in conjunction with a Museum renovation programme. These projects have now been completed. Both public transport buses, private tour buses and car hire services are currently operating and the number of private buses operating in the tourism sphere doubled last year.

A negative factor is the underdeveloped tourism infrastructure in regions and the absence of hotels etc.

**Supply**

During 2001 and the first half of 2002, the number of hotels in Yerevan and the regions of Armenia increased. Sixteen new high-quality hotels were opened.

In 2003, two high-quality hotels were opened: the hotel Europe in Yerevan and the Tsapatagh in Gegharkunik. The law on investments and grants was designed to encourage investment in tourism, and the policy of encouraging the establishment of new hotels in the Armenian regions will continue. Economic reforms have had a positive impact and this has been reflected in an increase in the number of arrivals.

The rail routes to Turkey and Azerbaijan are presently closed but the route from Yerevan to Tbilisi (Georgia) was opened. There exist various means of transportation in large towns such as buses, streetcars, taxis and taxi-vans with fixed functioning routes.

A negative factor is the underdeveloped tourism infrastructure in regional areas.

**External factors**

The stable political and economic situation in Armenia is the major determinant.

The great majority of visitors arrive through a single airport, Zvartnots. It is an international airport situated 20 minutes driving distance from Yerevan. The airport itself has undergone an expansion and reconstruction program. However, proposals for change in the visa procedures are currently being examined by the Ministry of Foreign Affairs.

At the present time, some of the operating air companies are Armenian Airlines, British Airways, Czech Airlines, Russian Airlines (Aeroflot), etc., and Armenia can be reached from all major airports.

Armenia has sunny weather the whole year with mild winters.

There is an absence of wide spread diseases, a low level of organized crime etc., which has made the Armenian tourism product more interesting for foreign tourists.

**Tourism policy**

The Tourism Master Plan for Armenia is being developed at the present time.

The Government of the Republic of Armenia has adopted the following:

- A law on tourism and tourism activity of the Republic of Armenia was passed on 17th December 2003;
- A State program for health resort and summer house development in Armenia was passed on 10th October 2003.

The House of National Assembly of the Republic of Armenia accepted a tax parcel and as a result value-added tax has been lifted from tourism. At the same time some programs for the development of human resources, kindly provided by our partners (Egypt, Japan, Germany, Greece, Cyprus etc.) have been undertaken.

**Marketing & promotion**

The Armenian Tourism Development Agency specialising in the marketing and promotion of the Armenian tourism product all over the world has been created.

The Tourism Development in the Provinces Programme has been evaluated and is now being implemented.

Armenia participated as an umbrella stand under the Armenian Tourism Development Agency (ATDA) at international exhibitions such as ITB 2003 Berlin, WTM 2003 London and the Silk Route of Tbilisi and Kiev 2003.

Participation in the seminar on "Sustainable Tourism in the Caucasian Region" in Georgia 2nd-10th August 2003.

The Ministry of Trade and Economic Development in cooperation with the International Executive Service Corps (IESC) and the United States Agency for International Development (USAID) organized a Pilot Project, in Dilijan and Ijevan under the scope of the "Tourism Development Project in communities of the Republic of Armenia".

Current project plans to arrange intensive courses on the “How tourism works” theme and practical activities on the preparation of advertising materials and information bulletins presenting the city.

The Kenats Festival was organised under the umbrella of ATDA in September 2003. It is now planned to hold the festival annually, featuring Armenian culture and historical background destinations, churches and cultural monuments.

The publication of new advertising materials (booklets, brochures, etc.).

A new Marketing Plan for the next three years has been developed as follows:

- Target markets now include Russia and the Middle East;
- New distribution channels have been identified, in particular country advertising on CNN and the BBC;
- Armenia has joined the American Society of Travel Agents (ASTA) and participated in its convention.

**Outlook 2004**

The major generating markets for Armenian tourism are the United States of America and Western Europe. New emerging markets are visitors from South America, Japan and South-Eastern Asian Countries. Our niche market is based on regional tourism (Silk Road); many visitors travel to Armenia from neighbouring Georgia and Iran. The major target group are visitors for cultural, historical and rural tourism, ecotourism and religious tourism.

The annual Kenats festival is to be expanded to the regions.

A Wine and Cheese Festival will take place in the regions of Armenia.

## International Meetings Industry (MI)

**Characteristics of supply**

The first Armenia-Diaspora Economic Forum was held in Armenia in 2003.

The Ministry of Trade and Economic Development of the Republic of Armenia organized an International Seminar on "Tendencies and Methods of World Tourism Development" in Yerevan on 13rd-14th November 2003.

Within the framework of Armenian-Greek cooperation, preparative work was undertaken in Armenia to found a tourism school.

**Organisation of promotion**

International promotion is organised by the Armenian Tourism Development Agency (ATDA).

| | |
|---|---|
| **Website(s)** | <www. armeniainfo.am>. |
| **Importance / size** | It is estimated at around 5 per cent. |

## International Tourism by Origin

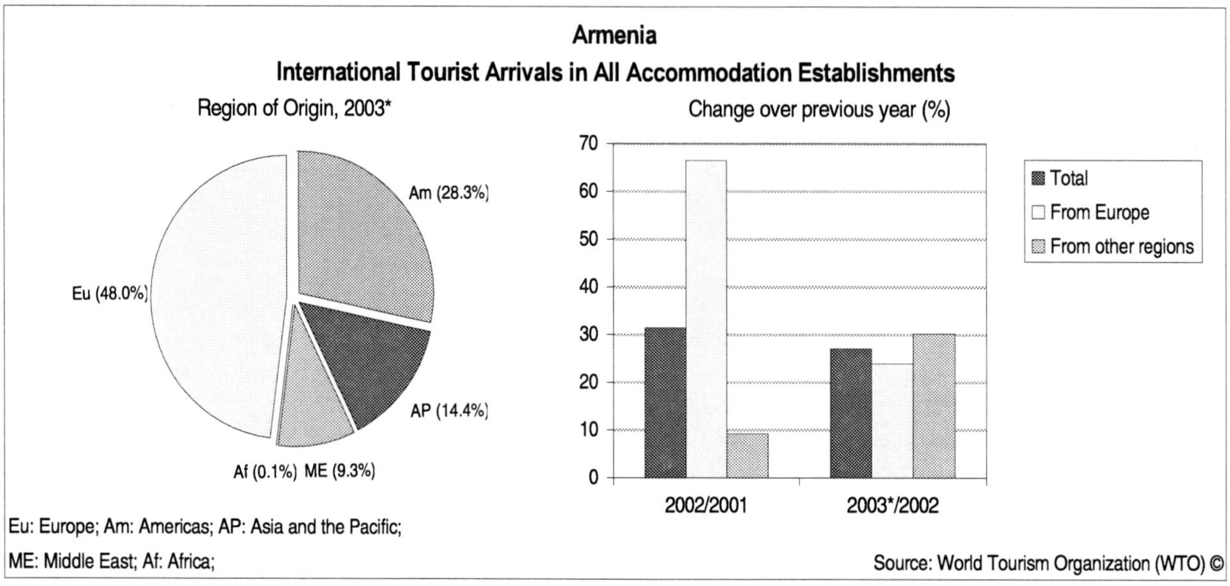

**Armenia**

**International Tourist Arrivals in All Accommodation Establishments (by residence)**

| | | | | (thousand) | Market share (%) | | Growth rate (%) | | Average per year (%) |
|---|---|---|---|---|---|---|---|---|---|
| | 1995 | 2001 | 2002 | 2003* | 1995 | 2003* | 2002/01 | 2003*/02 | 1995-2003* |
| **Total** | **12** | **123** | **162** | **206** | **100** | **100** | **31.5** | **27.1** | **42.6** |
| *From Europe* | *8* | *48* | *80* | *99* | *69.6* | *48.0* | *66.5* | *24.0* | *36.1* |
| Commonwealth Indep. States | 5 | 24 | 53 | 59 | 37.6 | 28.5 | 116.5 | 11.5 | 37.8 |
| France | 1 | 7 | 8 | 10 | 6.9 | 4.7 | 14.9 | 23.1 | 36.2 |
| Germany | 1 | 4 | 5 | 8 | 4.3 | 3.8 | 42.7 | 50.3 | 40.4 |
| United Kingdom | 1 | 2 | 2 | 5 | 5.4 | 2.4 | 11.0 | 183.7 | 28.7 |
| Italy | 0 | 1 | 2 | 3 | 0.9 | 1.4 | 37.3 | 62.3 | 50.7 |
| Greece | 0 | 2 | 2 | 3 | 1.9 | 1.4 | 4.1 | 54.4 | 36.6 |
| Belgium | 0 | 1 | 1 | 1 | 1.1 | 0.5 | 31.6 | 24.8 | 31.2 |
| Austria | 0 | 1 | 1 | 1 | 0.4 | 0.5 | 35.0 | 25.8 | 45.1 |
| Turkey | 0 | 1 | 1 | 1 | 1.4 | 0.5 | 4.2 | 32.4 | 24.6 |
| Switzerland | 0 | 1 | 1 | 1 | 1.1 | 0.4 | 25.0 | 12.6 | 26.9 |
| Netherlands | 0 | 1 | 1 | 1 | 2.1 | 0.4 | 4.4 | 2.5 | 17.1 |
| Israel | 0 | 0 | 1 | 1 | 0.8 | 0.4 | 22.2 | 41.1 | 30.2 |
| Bulgaria | 0 | 0 | 0 | 1 | 0.6 | 0.4 | 3.0 | 142.3 | 34.5 |
| Poland | 0 | 1 | 0 | 1 | 0.1 | 0.3 | -68.9 | 133.9 | 56.5 |
| Bosnia & Herzg | .. | 0 | 0 | 1 | | 0.3 | 10.8 | 33.0 | |
| Norway | 0 | 0 | 0 | 1 | 0.1 | 0.2 | 20.3 | 40.3 | 59.7 |
| Cyprus | 0 | 0 | 0 | 1 | 0.1 | 0.2 | 2.1 | 29.5 | 63.3 |
| Denmark | 0 | 0 | 0 | 0 | 0.4 | 0.2 | 8.8 | 57.1 | 32.6 |
| Portugal | 0 | 0 | 0 | 0 | 0.1 | 0.2 | 16.5 | 17.2 | 57.5 |
| Romania | 0 | 0 | 0 | 0 | 0.2 | 0.1 | -7.9 | 17.6 | 36.4 |
| Estonia | .. | 0 | 0 | 0 | | 0.1 | 6.8 | 119.2 | |
| Czech Rep | 0 | 0 | 0 | 0 | 0.2 | 0.1 | 10.2 | 106.2 | 35.2 |
| Latvia | 0 | 0 | 0 | 0 | 0.0 | 0.1 | 19.0 | 66.0 | 99.3 |
| Hungary | 0 | 0 | 0 | 0 | 0.7 | 0.1 | -43.3 | 51.9 | 13.5 |
| Spain | 0 | 0 | 0 | 0 | 1.2 | 0.1 | 13.7 | 23.0 | 6.7 |
| Other intraregional | 0 | 1 | 1 | 1 | 2.0 | 0.5 | -3.6 | 58.7 | 19.6 |
| *From other regions* | *4* | *75* | *82* | *107* | *30.4* | *52.0* | *9.2* | *30.2* | *52.5* |
| United States | 2 | 21 | 25 | 31 | 15.4 | 15.0 | 17.4 | 23.2 | 42.1 |
| Iran | 1 | 18 | 18 | 23 | 9.1 | 11.0 | 2.7 | 24.6 | 46.1 |
| Canada | 0 | 9 | 9 | 12 | 0.8 | 5.8 | 5.7 | 26.9 | 83.6 |
| Lebanon | 0 | 7 | 7 | 10 | 1.0 | 4.8 | 6.3 | 32.0 | 72.8 |
| Argentina | 0 | 6 | 7 | 10 | 0.5 | 4.8 | 5.0 | 47.7 | 91.3 |
| Syrian Arab Republic | 0 | 5 | 6 | 9 | 0.8 | 4.3 | 7.7 | 51.8 | 76.3 |
| Brazil | 0 | 4 | 4 | 5 | 0.1 | 2.2 | 2.3 | 9.4 | 104.6 |
| Japan | 0 | 1 | 2 | 4 | 0.5 | 1.9 | 34.2 | 115.1 | 69.7 |
| Australia | 0 | 1 | 1 | 1 | 0.1 | 0.5 | 1.3 | 7.8 | 78.0 |
| India | 0 | 0 | 0 | 1 | 0.6 | 0.4 | 33.9 | 66.0 | 35.7 |
| Mexico | 0 | 0 | 0 | 0 | 0.0 | 0.2 | 7.3 | 44.6 | 94.2 |
| Uruguay | 0 | 0 | 0 | 0 | 0.3 | 0.2 | 4.8 | 19.9 | 32.4 |
| China | 0 | 0 | 0 | 0 | 0.0 | 0.2 | 35.6 | 13.1 | 65.9 |
| Afghanistan | .. | 0 | 0 | 0 | | 0.2 | 61.8 | 52.3 | |
| Other interregional | 0 | 1 | 1 | 2 | 1.3 | 0.7 | 20.6 | 24.4 | 33.0 |

Source: World Tourism Organization (WTO) © (Data as collected by WTO December 2004)

# III.3.2 Azerbaijan Central and Eastern Europe

## Profile

# Azerbaijan

Europe
Central and Eastern Europe

| | |
|---|---|
| Capital | Baku |
| Year of entry in WTO | 2001 |
| Area (1000 km²) | 87 |
| Population (2003, million) | 7.8 |
| Gross Domestic Product (GDP) (2003, euro million) | 7,764 |
| GDP per capita (2003, euro) | 938 |
| GDP growth (real, %) | |

2002: 10.6; 2003: 11.2; 2004*: 9.1; 2005*: 11.4

| | 2001 | 2002 | 2003* | 2002/2001 | 2003*/2002 |
|---|---|---|---|---|---|
| **International Arrivals** | | | | | |
| Tourists (overnight visitors) (1000) | 767 | 834 | .. | 8.8 | |
| - per 100 of inhabitants | 10 | 11 | .. | | |
| **Tourism accommodation** | | | | | |
| Number of rooms | 5,259 | .. | .. | | |
| *Nights spent in hotels and similar establishments (1000)* | | | | | |
| by non-residents (inbound tourism) | 184 | .. | .. | | |
| **Outbound Tourism** | | | | | |
| Trips abroad (1000) | 1,130 | 1,141 | .. | 1.0 | |
| - per 100 of inhabitants | 15 | 15 | .. | | |
| **Receipts and Expenditure for International Tourism** | | | | | |
| International Tourism Receipts (euro million) | 47 | 57 | 61 | 22.3 | 7.7 |
| - per Tourist Arrival (euro) | 61 | 68 | .. | 12.4 | |
| - per capita (euro) | 6 | 7 | 8 | | |
| International Fare Receipts (euro million) | 15 | 13 | 13 | -11.6 | -5.3 |
| International Tourism Expenditure (euro million) | 118 | 117 | 117 | -0.7 | 0.1 |
| - per trip (euro) | 104 | 103 | .. | -1.6 | |
| - per capita (euro) | 15 | 15 | 15 | | |
| International Fare Expenditure (euro million) | 11 | 6 | 10 | -48.4 | 70.5 |
| △ International Tourism Balance (euro million) | -71 | -60 | -56 | | |
| △ International Fare Balance (euro million) | 4 | 8 | 3 | | |

Source: World Tourism Organization (WTO) (Data as collected by WTO December 2004)

See annex for methodological notes and reference of external sources used.

# Survey

Contributed by *Ministry of Youth, Sport and Tourism*
www.tourism.az (promotional)
www.myst.gov.az (institutional/corporate)

## Tourism development and outlook

**Overall evaluation of results**
There has been a positive development in the economy of our country.
The government is supporting the tourism sector.
The creation of new tourism infrastructure is being carried out.

**Supply**
The quantity and quality of accommodation has been improved.
Travel agencies and tour operators are introducing new types of tourism as well as creating new tourism routes within the country.

**External factors**
The economic situation of the country is stable.
The cost of a tourist visa for Azerbaijan has been reduced from US$ 40 to US$ 20.
The highways and roads are being reconstructed. A new airport meeting world standards has recently been built.

**Tourism policy**
The United States Trade and Development Association (USTDA) has approved funding for a grant to the Ministry of Youth, Sport and Tourism for technical assistance to develop a tourism strategy for Azerbaijan.

**Marketing & promotion**
Printing of promotion materials (magazines, guides, books, etc.).
Participation in local and international fairs.
New websites have been created.

## International Meetings Industry (MI)

**Characteristics of supply**
Taking into consideration Azerbaijan as an oil producing country, its geographical situation and the membership of Azerbaijan in many international organisations, it must be mentioned that many meetings, congresses, conferences, exhibitions and fairs take place in Azerbaijan.

**Collection of statistics on the Meetings Industry?:** no.

# International Tourism by Origin

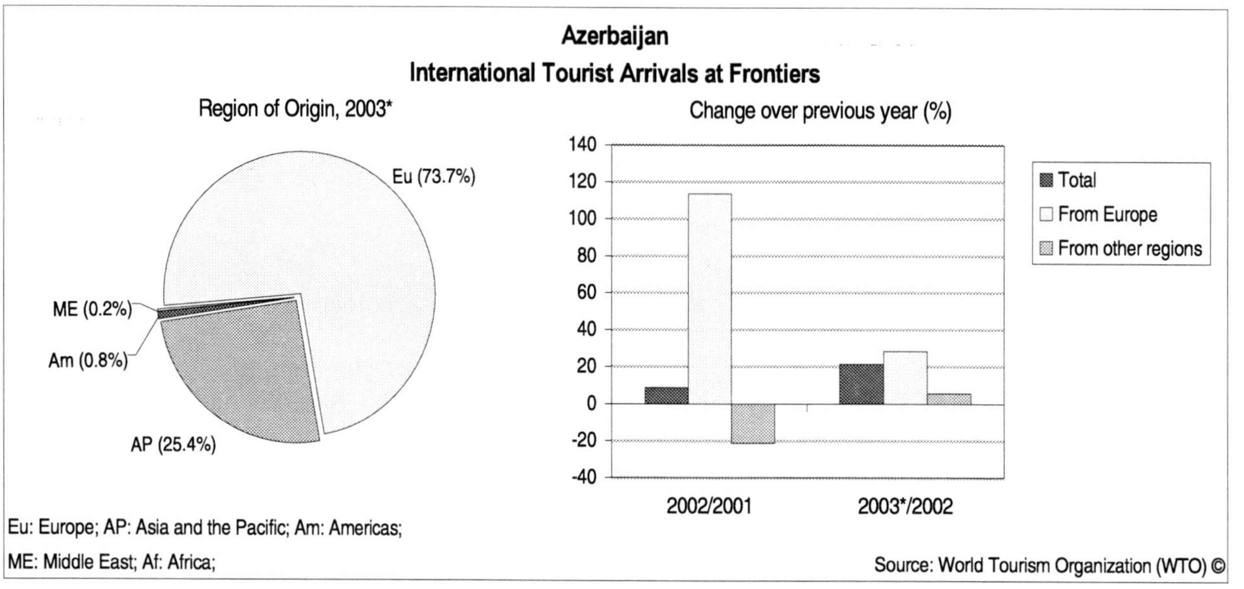

**Azerbaijan**

**International Tourist Arrivals at Frontiers (by residence)**

| | | | | (thousand) | Market share (%) | | Growth rate (%) | | Average per year (%) |
|---|---|---|---|---|---|---|---|---|---|
| | 1995 | 2001 | 2002 | 2003* | 1995 | 2003* | 2002/01 | 2003*/02 | 1995-2003* |
| **Total** | .. | **767** | **834** | **1,014** | | **100** | **8.8** | **21.5** | |
| *From Europe* | .. | *272* | *582* | *747* | | *73.7* | *113.6* | *28.4* | |
| Russian Federation | .. | .. | 217 | 402 | | 39.6 | | 85.1 | |
| Commonwealth Indep. States | .. | 264 | .. | .. | | | | | |
| Georgia | .. | .. | 252 | 210 | | 20.7 | | -16.9 | |
| Turkey | .. | 8 | 54 | 69 | | 6.8 | 535.5 | 28.0 | |
| Ukraine | .. | .. | 21 | 26 | | 2.6 | | 23.4 | |
| United Kingdom | .. | .. | 11 | 11 | | 1.1 | | 7.1 | |
| Kazakhstan | .. | .. | 5 | 6 | | 0.6 | | 9.5 | |
| Germany | .. | .. | 3 | 3 | | 0.3 | | 12.9 | |
| Uzbekistan | .. | .. | 3 | 3 | | 0.3 | | -6.4 | |
| Israel | .. | .. | 2 | 2 | | 0.2 | | 10.7 | |
| Turkmenistan | .. | .. | 3 | 2 | | 0.2 | | -23.5 | |
| Belarus | .. | .. | 2 | 2 | | 0.2 | | 4.0 | |
| Norway | .. | .. | 1 | 1 | | 0.1 | | 41.6 | |
| Italy | .. | .. | 1 | 1 | | 0.1 | | -17.6 | |
| Netherlands | .. | .. | 1 | 1 | | 0.1 | | -6.9 | |
| Kyrgyzstan | .. | .. | 0 | 1 | | 0.1 | | 62.4 | |
| Greece | .. | .. | 0 | 1 | | 0.1 | | 271.2 | |
| Rep Moldova | .. | .. | 0 | 1 | | 0.1 | | 41.7 | |
| Poland | .. | .. | 0 | 1 | | 0.1 | | 20.8 | |
| Austria | .. | .. | 0 | 1 | | 0.0 | | 22.0 | |
| Denmark | .. | .. | 0 | 0 | | 0.0 | | 50.0 | |
| Sweden | .. | .. | 0 | 0 | | 0.0 | | 23.2 | |
| Switzerland | .. | .. | 0 | 0 | | 0.0 | | 115.5 | |
| Finland | .. | .. | 0 | 0 | | 0.0 | | 138.3 | |
| Bulgaria | .. | .. | 0 | 0 | | 0.0 | | 0.3 | |
| Other intraregional | .. | .. | 3 | 3 | | 0.3 | | 11.2 | |
| *From other regions* | .. | *322* | *253* | *267* | | *26.3* | *-21.5* | *5.6* | |
| Iran | .. | 322 | 240 | 250 | | 24.6 | -25.5 | 4.2 | |
| United States | .. | .. | 6 | 6 | | 0.6 | | 16.0 | |
| India | .. | .. | 1 | 2 | | 0.2 | | 53.3 | |
| China | .. | .. | 1 | 1 | | 0.1 | | 116.6 | |
| Canada | .. | .. | 1 | 1 | | 0.1 | | 29.1 | |
| Pakistan | .. | .. | 1 | 1 | | 0.1 | | 70.9 | |
| Japan | .. | .. | 1 | 1 | | 0.1 | | -28.3 | |
| Australia | .. | .. | 0 | 0 | | 0.0 | | 4.8 | |
| Lebanon | .. | .. | 0 | 0 | | 0.0 | | 367.1 | |
| Syrian Arab Republic | .. | .. | 0 | 0 | | 0.0 | | 63.1 | |
| Other interregional | .. | .. | 3 | 4 | | 0.4 | | 47.4 | |
| *Other World/Not specified* | .. | *173* | .. | .. | | | | | |

Source: World Tourism Organization (WTO) © (Data as collected by WTO December 2004)

# III.3.3 Belarus Central and Eastern Europe

## Profile

# Belarus

Europe
Central and Eastern Europe

| | |
|---|---|
| Capital | Minsk |
| Area (1000 km²) | 208 |
| Population (2003, million) | 10.3 |
| Gross Domestic Product (GDP) (2003, euro million) | 18,518 |
| GDP per capita (2003, euro) | 2,085 |
| GDP growth (real, %) | |

'-> 2002: 5.0; 2003: 6.8; 2004*: 6.4; 2005*: 5.5

| | 2001 | 2002 | 2003* | 2002/2001 | 2003*/2002 |
|---|---|---|---|---|---|
| **International Arrivals** | | | | | |
| Tourists (overnight visitors) (1000) | 61 | .. | 64 | | |
| - per 100 of inhabitants | 1 | .. | 1 | | |
| **Outbound Tourism** | | | | | |
| Trips abroad (1000) | 1,386 | .. | .. | | |
| - per 100 of inhabitants | 13 | .. | .. | | |
| **Receipts and Expenditure for International Tourism** | | | | | |
| International Tourism Receipts (euro million) | 185 | 261 | 282 | 41.1 | 8.1 |
| - per Tourist Arrival (euro) | 3,035 | .. | 4,392 | | |
| - pèr capita (euro) | 18 | 25 | 27 | | |
| International Fare Receipts (euro million) | 66 | 68 | 76 | 3.1 | 11.8 |
| International Tourism Expenditure (euro million) | 542 | 624 | 521 | 15.1 | -16.5 |
| - per trip (euro) | 391 | .. | .. | | |
| - per capita (euro) | 52 | 60 | 51 | | |
| International Fare Expenditure (euro million) | 35 | 38 | 39 | 9.6 | 3.1 |
| △ International Tourism Balance (euro million) | -357 | -363 | -239 | | |
| △ International Fare Balance (euro million) | 31 | 30 | 37 | | |

Source: World Tourism Organization (WTO) (Data as collected by WTO December 2004)

See annex for methodological notes and reference of external sources used.

# Survey

Contributed by *Ministry of Sports and Tourism*
www.mst.solo.by ; www.touragency.by (promotional)
www.mst.by ; www.touragency.by (institutional/corporate)
www.mst.by ; www.touragency.by (research and data)

## Tourism development and outlook

**Overall evaluation of results**

64 thousand foreign tourists visited the Republic of Belarus in 2003. In the same year, 1.1 million belarussian tourists visited others countries.
Overall amount of tourist receipts is evaluated at US$ 11 million in 2003.

**Supply**

In 2003, Belarusian tourist services were provided by 400 tourist organizations licensed to perform such services:
- accommodation capacity: 285 (accomodation units);
- organizations offering sanatorium and health resort services: 318.

The following is a list of other relevant items that would be of interest to all potential visitors:
- 189 state museums; 302 cinemas; 60 theatres; 37 art galleries; 103 concert halls; 80 disco-bars and night clubs; 41 public swimming-pools and diving-clubs; 196 beauty parlors; 47 public parks; 33 casinos/gamers; 240 restaurants; 81 bars; 166, cafés; 21 religious organizations; 2 stationary circuses;
- communication services such as: 645 post offices and telegraph offices, internet-clubs/cafés and public telephone booths (available in most of the cities), mobile phone services with worldwide roaming;
- other related services: 535 banks, ATM machines, 47 insurance companies, 29 foreign embassies to Belarus; 7 consulates, around 100 foreign embassies to Belarus on the concurrent basis with residence in Moscow, 41 embassies of the Republic of Belarus abroad.

Belarus has a well-developed international and domestic infrastructures:
- National airline: "Belavia";
- Belorussian railroad network;
- River transport and a well-developed network of international and domestic auto transportation.

**External factors**

Belarus sustains a stable, safe and balanced political and economic situation. At the present time the Republic of Belarus maintains well-developed heavy, light and food-processing industries as well as a large-scale agricultural industry. The climate throughout the whole country is temperate, continental. The duration of the warm period (spring-summer, beginning of fall season) is about 250-260 days. Temperature in July rises up to 35ºC-37ºC and falls down in January to -35ºC.

**Tourism policy**

State policy in the field of tourism is being realized through the Ministry of Sports and Tourism according to the conception of the "National Programme". Investment planning in the sphere of tourism is being made possible on the basis of cooperation and joint international projects with the Russian Federation, Poland, and Lithuania in the framework of international agreements between the mentioned countries.
Tax exemptions and privileges in the sphere of tourism are being planned in the framework of tourist zones that are being created in Belarus.
*Human resources issues:*
- 14 institutions of higher education are offering training of specialists for the tourism industry;

- In 2003 tour guides and tourist group leaders were attested (the Ministry of Sports and Tourism requirement);
- The number of specialists involved in the sphere of tourism services reaches more than two thousand people.

**Marketing & promotion**

Marketing and promotion of tourism product is realized on the basis of "National Programme of Tourism Development in the Republic of Belarus".

The following socially significant literature and promotion materials covering tourism potential of the Republic of Belarus have been prepared by the Ministry of Sports and Tourism within the framework of the "National Programme":
- "Minsk": guide-book (in Russian, English and German languages);
- "Polotsk", "Gomel", "Braslav","Nesvizh": guide-books;
- Photo album about Pinsk (in Belorussian, Russian and English languages):
- Historic architectural itinerary on Belarus (in Belorussian, Russian and English languages);
- Photo album on Grodno (in Belorussian, Russian and English languages).

In order to promote the image of Belarus as of country favourable for tourism the following is being targeted:
- Organization (by the Belorussian side), holding and hosting of international tourist exhibitions;
- Yearly participation by means of single or collective national stand in international tourism exhibitions, like WTM (London), ITB (Berlin), MITT (Moscow);
- Organization of a single or collective national stand of the Republic of Belarus at the major international tourism exhibitions abroad;
- A lasting advertisement campaign in the foreign mass-media sources, organization of introductory (promotion) tours around Belarus for representatives of foreign mass-media and tourism agencies;
- Promotion of Belorussian tourism possibilities through Internet sites;
- Preparation for founding regional tourism information centres.

**Outlook 2004**

According to activities based on "National Programme", prospects for the year 2004 are:
- the adoption of the Law of the Republic of Belarus on "World Tourism Organization statute ratification";
- joining the World Tourism Organization (WTO);
- revisions and amendments of the Law of the Republic of Belarus "On Tourism";
- up-coming certification of tourism services;
- active participation in the work of international tourism organizations, such as WTO and the Community of Independant States (CEI);
- production of a thematic calendar on tourism events in Belarus;
- promotion campaigns in various foreign mass-media;
- creation of the Republican Tourism Development foundation;
- conducting marketing research based on projection and evaluation of tourism services market conditions. The "Programme" also stipulates an increase in exports of tourism services in 2005 by 18 per cent as compared to 2000.

## International Meetings Industry (MI)

**Characteristics of supply**

Information on exhibitions taking place in Minsk is available on the website: <www.belexpo.by>

**Organisation of promotion**

National tourist agency is responsible for the promotion of Meetings Industry in Belarus: <www.touragency.by>

**Collection of statistics on the Meetings Industry?:** no.

# International Tourism by Origin

**Belarus**

**International Tourist Arrivals at Frontiers**

Region of Origin, 2003*

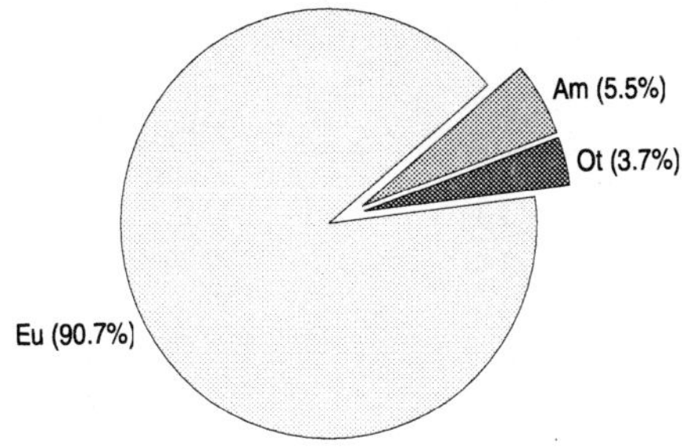


Eu: Europe; Am: Americas;
Ot: Other;

Source: World Tourism Organization (WTO) ©

**Belarus**

**International Tourist Arrivals at Frontiers (by nationality)**

| | | | | (thousand) | Market share (%) | | Growth rate (%) | | Average per year (%) |
|---|---|---|---|---|---|---|---|---|---|
| | 1995 | 2001 | 2002 | 2003* | 1995 | 2003* | 2002/01 | 2003*/02 | 1995-2003* |
| **Total** | **161** | **61** | **..** | **64** | **100** | **100** | | | **-11.0** |
| *From Europe* | *154* | *55* | *..* | *58* | *95.2* | *90.7* | | | *-11.5* |
| Poland | 32 | 12 | .. | 10 | 20.0 | 16.1 | | | -13.3 |
| Latvia | 3 | 8 | .. | 8 | 1.9 | 12.0 | | | 11.8 |
| Lithuania | 5 | 3 | .. | 7 | 2.8 | 11.7 | | | 6.4 |
| Germany | 10 | 5 | .. | 7 | 6.0 | 11.1 | | | -3.8 |
| Russian Federation | 58 | 10 | .. | 7 | 35.8 | 10.7 | | | -23.5 |
| Italy | 5 | 2 | .. | 4 | 3.4 | 6.6 | | | -3.2 |
| United Kingdom | 6 | 9 | .. | 3 | 3.7 | 5.1 | | | -7.3 |
| Cyprus | 1 | 1 | .. | 3 | 0.3 | 4.1 | | | 22.3 |
| Former U.S.S.R. | 3 | .. | .. | .. | 1.6 | | | | |
| Netherlands | 1 | 1 | .. | 1 | 0.7 | 2.1 | | | 1.4 |
| Israel | 1 | 1 | .. | 1 | 0.4 | 1.2 | | | 0.9 |
| Estonia | 1 | 1 | .. | 1 | 0.4 | 1.1 | | | 0.3 |
| Ukraine | 15 | 1 | .. | 1 | 9.3 | 1.0 | | | -32.5 |
| Austria | 1 | 1 | .. | 1 | 0.6 | 0.9 | | | -5.7 |
| Denmark | 0 | 0 | .. | 1 | 0.3 | 0.8 | | | 2.7 |
| France | 1 | 1 | .. | 0 | 0.7 | 0.8 | | | -10.6 |
| Sweden | 1 | 0 | .. | 0 | 0.3 | 0.7 | | | -2.8 |
| Turkey | 0 | 0 | .. | 0 | 0.1 | 0.6 | | | 7.1 |
| Spain | 0 | 0 | .. | 0 | 0.2 | 0.6 | | | 5.2 |
| Czech Rep | 1 | 0 | .. | 0 | 0.6 | 0.6 | | | -10.2 |
| Switzerland | 0 | 0 | .. | 0 | 0.2 | 0.6 | | | -0.9 |
| Belgium | 1 | 0 | .. | 0 | 0.4 | 0.5 | | | -7.6 |
| Norway | 0 | 0 | .. | 0 | 0.2 | 0.2 | | | -6.6 |
| Finland | 1 | 0 | .. | 0 | 0.3 | 0.2 | | | -16.4 |
| Croatia | 0 | 0 | .. | 0 | 0.1 | 0.2 | | | -7.5 |
| Other intraregional | 7 | 0 | .. | 1 | 4.6 | 1.1 | | | -25.7 |
| *From other regions* | *8* | *6* | *..* | *6* | *4.8* | *9.3* | | | *-3.3* |
| United States | 5 | 5 | .. | 3 | 3.1 | 5.3 | | | -4.7 |
| New Zealand | 0 | 0 | .. | 1 | 0.0 | 0.9 | | | 59.3 |
| Japan | 1 | 0 | .. | 0 | 0.3 | 0.6 | | | -4.4 |
| Australia | 0 | 0 | .. | 0 | 0.1 | 0.5 | | | 13.4 |
| India | 0 | 0 | .. | 0 | 0.1 | 0.4 | | | 4.9 |
| Korea, Republic of | 0 | .. | .. | .. | 0.1 | | | | |
| Iran | 0 | 0 | .. | 0 | 0.0 | 0.2 | | | 8.2 |
| Lebanon | 0 | .. | .. | 0 | 0.1 | 0.2 | | | 1.0 |
| China | 0 | 0 | .. | .. | 0.1 | | | | |
| Taiwan (pr. of China) | 0 | 0 | .. | 0 | 0.0 | 0.2 | | | 48.8 |
| Vietnam | 0 | 0 | .. | 0 | 0.0 | 0.1 | | | 4.6 |
| Syrian Arab Republic | 0 | 0 | .. | 0 | 0.0 | 0.1 | | | 0.7 |
| Untd Arab Emirates | 0 | 0 | .. | 0 | 0.0 | 0.1 | | | 21.4 |
| Canada | 0 | 0 | .. | 0 | 0.2 | 0.1 | | | -16.3 |
| Argentina | 0 | 0 | .. | 0 | 0.0 | 0.1 | | | 1.2 |
| South Africa | 0 | 0 | .. | 0 | 0.1 | 0.1 | | | -16.5 |
| Bangladesh | 0 | 0 | .. | 0 | 0.0 | 0.1 | | | 25.1 |
| Other interregional | 1 | 0 | .. | 0 | 0.4 | 0.3 | | | -13.0 |

Source: World Tourism Organization (WTO) © (Data as collected by WTO December 2004)

# III.3.4 Bulgaria Central and Eastern Europe

## Profile

# Bulgaria

**Europe**
**Central and Eastern Europe**

| | |
|---|---|
| Capital | Sofia |
| Year of entry in WTO | 1976 |
| Area (1000 km²) | 111 |
| Population (2003, million) | 7.6 |
| Gross Domestic Product (GDP) (2003, euro million) | 21,038 |
| GDP per capita (2003, euro) | 2,697 |
| GDP growth (real, %) | |
| '-> 2002: 4.9; 2003: 4.3; 2004*: 5.2; 2005*: 5.2 | |

| | 2001 | 2002 | 2003* | 2002/2001 | 2003*/2002 |
|---|---|---|---|---|---|
| **International Arrivals** | | | | | |
| Visitors (1000) | 5,104 | 5,563 | 6,241 | 9.0 | 12.2 |
| Tourists (overnight visitors) (1000) | 3,186 | 3,433 | 4,048 | 7.8 | 17.9 |
| - per 100 of inhabitants | 41 | 45 | 53 | | |
| Same-day visitors (1000) | 1,918 | 2,130 | 2,193 | 11.1 | 3.0 |
| **Tourism accommodation** | | | | | |
| Number of bed-places | 116,044 | 132,024 | 143,960 | 13.8 | 9.0 |
| *Nights spent in collective establishments (1000)* | 9,384 | 10,286 | 12,521 | 9.6 | 21.7 |
| by non-residents (inbound tourism) | 6,190 | 7,055 | 9,142 | 14.0 | 29.6 |
| by residents (domestic tourism) | 3,194 | 3,231 | 3,379 | 1.2 | 4.6 |
| *Nights spent in hotels and similar establishments (1000)* | 8,960 | 9,967 | 12,045 | 11.2 | 20.8 |
| by non-residents (inbound tourism) | 6,118 | 6,985 | 8,987 | 14.2 | 28.7 |
| by residents (domestic tourism) | 2,842 | 2,982 | 3,058 | 4.9 | 2.5 |
| **Outbound Tourism** | | | | | |
| Trips abroad (1000) | 2,730 | 3,188 | 3,403 | 16.8 | 6.7 |
| - per 100 of inhabitants | 35 | 42 | 45 | | |
| **Receipts and Expenditure for International Tourism** | | | | | |
| International Tourism Receipts (euro million) | 1,043 | 1,288 | 1,753 | 23.6 | 36.1 |
| - per Tourist Arrival (euro) | 327 | 375 | 433 | 14.7 | 15.4 |
| - per Visitor Arrival (euro) | 204 | 232 | 281 | 13.4 | 21.3 |
| - per capita (euro) | 135 | 168 | 231 | | |
| International Fare Receipts (euro million) | 282 | 347 | 474 | 23.4 | 36.4 |
| International Tourism Expenditure (euro million) | 494 | 595 | 793 | 20.5 | 33.3 |
| - per trip (euro) | 181 | 187 | 233 | 3.2 | 24.9 |
| - per capita (euro) | 64 | 78 | 105 | | |
| International Fare Expenditure (euro million) | 207 | 250 | 333 | 20.9 | 33.2 |
| △ International Tourism Balance (euro million) | 549 | 693 | 960 | | |
| △ International Fare Balance (euro million) | 75 | 97 | 141 | | |

Source: World Tourism Organization (WTO) (Data as collected by WTO December 2004)

See annex for methodological notes and reference of external sources used.

# International Tourism by Origin

**Bulgaria**

**International Visitor Arrivals at Frontiers**

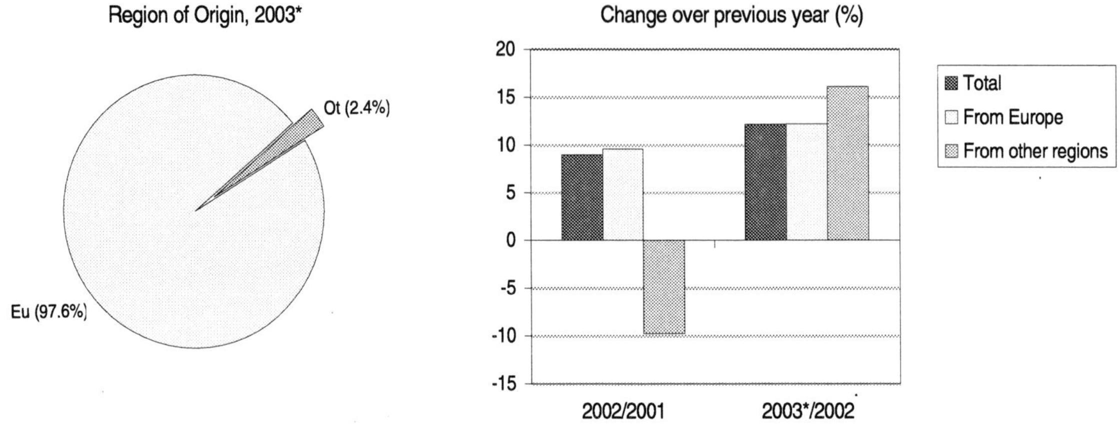


Eu: Europe;

Ot: Other;

Source: World Tourism Organization (WTO) ©

**Bulgaria**

**Nights of International Tourists in All Accommodation Establishments**

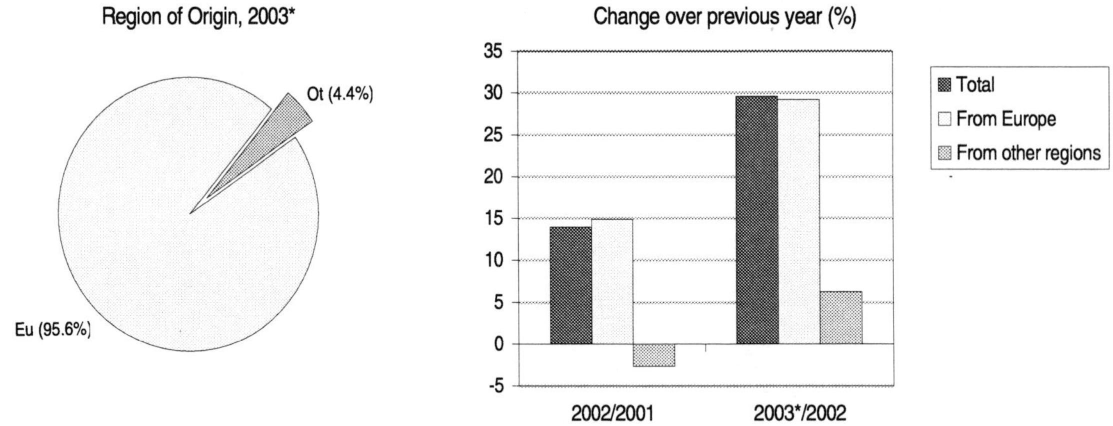


Eu: Europe;

Ot: Other;

Source: World Tourism Organization (WTO) ©

**Bulgaria**

**International Visitor Arrivals at Frontiers (by residence)**

| | | | | (thousand) | Market share (%) | | Growth rate (%) | | Average per year (%) |
|---|---|---|---|---|---|---|---|---|---|
| | 1995 | 2001 | 2002 | 2003* | 1995 | 2003* | 2002/01 | 2003*/02 | 1995-2003* |
| **Total** | **8,005** | **5,104** | **5,563** | **6,241** | **100** | **100** | **9.0** | **12.2** | **-3.1** |
| *From Europe* | *7,687* | *4,951* | *5,426* | *6,088* | *96.0* | *97.6* | *9.6* | *12.2* | *-2.9* |
| Yugoslav SFR | 2,346 | .. | .. | .. | 29.3 | | | | |
| Former U.S.S.R. | 1,216 | .. | .. | .. | 15.2 | | | | |
| Serbia & Montenegro | .. | 617 | 841 | 887 | | 14.2 | 36.3 | 5.5 | |
| F.Yug.Rp.Macedonia | .. | 859 | 849 | 887 | | 14.2 | -1.2 | 4.5 | |
| Greece | 231 | 451 | 487 | 645 | 2.9 | 10.3 | 8.0 | 32.4 | 13.7 |
| Germany | 202 | 435 | 562 | 631 | 2.5 | 10.1 | 29.1 | 12.3 | 15.3 |
| Turkey | 1,825 | 560 | 581 | 608 | 22.8 | 9.7 | 3.7 | 4.6 | -12.8 |
| Romania | 1,510 | 674 | 572 | 607 | 18.9 | 9.7 | -15.2 | 6.1 | -10.8 |
| Hungary | 32 | 57 | 203 | 205 | 0.4 | 3.3 | 255.9 | 0.8 | 26.0 |
| Poland | 37 | 104 | 102 | 194 | 0.5 | 3.1 | -1.4 | 90.0 | 22.9 |
| United Kingdom | 51 | 82 | 124 | 174 | 0.6 | 2.8 | 51.9 | 39.7 | 16.5 |
| Russian Federation | .. | 177 | 130 | 154 | | 2.5 | -26.6 | 18.8 | |
| Slovakia | .. | 119 | 145 | 144 | | 2.3 | 21.5 | -0.4 | |
| Czech Rep | .. | 112 | 130 | 142 | | 2.3 | 16.4 | 9.4 | |
| Ukraine | .. | 190 | 96 | 104 | | 1.7 | -49.4 | 8.9 | |
| Netherlands | 19 | 55 | 67 | 80 | 0.2 | 1.3 | 22.2 | 19.5 | 19.7 |
| Sweden | 17 | 53 | 61 | 79 | 0.2 | 1.3 | 15.6 | 28.8 | 21.0 |
| Former Czechoslovakia | 75 | .. | .. | .. | 0.9 | | | | |
| Israel | 5 | 54 | 68 | 73 | 0.1 | 1.2 | 25.5 | 7.2 | 38.8 |
| Austria | 10 | 55 | 59 | 67 | 0.1 | 1.1 | 6.5 | 14.7 | 26.3 |
| Belgium | 5 | 33 | 45 | 53 | 0.1 | 0.8 | 37.2 | 16.5 | 34.9 |
| Finland | 5 | 31 | 39 | 50 | 0.1 | 0.8 | 28.4 | 27.6 | 32.3 |
| France | 20 | 39 | 43 | 50 | 0.2 | 0.8 | 10.7 | 15.2 | 12.3 |
| Denmark | 11 | 23 | 36 | 47 | 0.1 | 0.8 | 56.9 | 32.5 | 19.7 |
| Italy | 24 | 37 | 41 | 46 | 0.3 | 0.7 | 11.6 | 13.5 | 8.8 |
| Other intraregional | 44 | 135 | 145 | 160 | 0.6 | 2.6 | 6.8 | 10.5 | 17.3 |
| *From other regions* | *73* | *107* | *96* | *112* | *0.9* | *1.8* | *-9.7* | *16.1* | *5.4* |
| United States | 17 | 43 | 39 | 46 | 0.2 | 0.7 | -8.1 | 17.2 | 12.9 |
| Iran | 6 | 9 | 7 | 8 | 0.1 | 0.1 | -28.4 | 25.8 | 4.9 |
| Japan | 3 | 7 | 7 | 8 | 0.0 | 0.1 | 4.2 | 5.4 | 10.5 |
| Canada | 2 | 6 | 6 | 7 | 0.0 | 0.1 | -6.0 | 21.0 | 15.5 |
| Australia | 2 | 5 | 5 | 5 | 0.0 | 0.1 | 8.7 | 7.3 | 10.4 |
| Syrian Arab Republic | 11 | 5 | 5 | 5 | 0.1 | 0.1 | 5.7 | -3.2 | -9.7 |
| Korea, Republic of | 2 | 3 | 0 | 4 | 0.0 | 0.1 | -86.1 | 999.7 | 12.2 |
| Lebanon | 4 | 4 | 4 | 4 | 0.1 | 0.1 | -6.3 | 4.4 | -1.4 |
| China | 3 | 3 | 4 | 3 | 0.0 | 0.1 | 15.9 | -4.5 | 0.5 |
| Vietnam | 0 | 3 | 4 | 3 | 0.0 | 0.0 | 9.3 | -12.4 | 30.0 |
| India | 2 | 3 | 2 | 2 | 0.0 | 0.0 | -20.7 | 12.5 | 0.4 |
| Algeria | 1 | 1 | 2 | 2 | 0.0 | 0.0 | 87.0 | 0.1 | 11.6 |
| Jordan | 2 | 1 | 1 | 2 | 0.0 | 0.0 | -3.1 | 74.8 | -1.8 |
| Egypt | 2 | 1 | 1 | 2 | 0.0 | 0.0 | -0.7 | 22.3 | -3.7 |
| New Zealand | 1 | 1 | 1 | 1 | 0.0 | 0.0 | 3.1 | 8.8 | 1.8 |
| Kuwait | 1 | 1 | 1 | 1 | 0.0 | 0.0 | -31.3 | 7.6 | 4.6 |
| Other interregional | 12 | 11 | 8 | 8 | 0.2 | 0.1 | -27.4 | 4.1 | -4.8 |
| *Other World/Not specified* | *244* | *46* | *40* | *41* | *3.0* | *0.7* | *-12.3* | *1.6* | *-20.0* |

Source: World Tourism Organization (WTO) © (Data as collected by WTO December 2004)

**Bulgaria**

**Nights of International Tourists in All Accommodation Establishments (by residence)**

| | | | | (thousand) | Market share (%) | | Growth rate (%) | | Average per year (%) |
|---|---|---|---|---|---|---|---|---|---|
| | 1995 | 2001 | 2002 | 2003* | 1995 | 2003* | 2002/01 | 2003*/02 | 1995-2003* |
| **Total** | **5,438** | **6,190** | **7,055** | **9,142** | **100** | **100** | **14.0** | **29.6** | **6.7** |
| *From Europe* | *5,244* | *5,890* | *6,766* | *8,742* | *96.4* | *95.6* | *14.9* | *29.2* | *6.6* |
| Germany | 2,148 | 2,764 | 3,415 | 4,173 | 39.5 | 45.6 | 23.6 | 22.2 | 8.7 |
| Former U.S.S.R. | 1,324 | .. | .. | .. | 24.3 | | | | |
| United Kingdom | 518 | 389 | 666 | 1,053 | 9.5 | 11.5 | 71.3 | 58.2 | 9.3 |
| Russian Federation | .. | 743 | 484 | 714 | | 7.8 | -34.9 | 47.7 | |
| Sweden | 173 | 295 | 241 | 404 | 3.2 | 4.4 | -18.1 | 67.4 | 11.2 |
| Finland | 45 | 185 | 192 | 247 | 0.8 | 2.7 | 4.1 | 28.6 | 23.8 |
| Israel | 26 | 157 | 209 | 237 | 0.5 | 2.6 | 33.0 | 13.7 | 32.1 |
| Belgium | 27 | 214 | 228 | 237 | 0.5 | 2.6 | 6.6 | 4.1 | 31.4 |
| Denmark | 72 | 93 | 115 | 210 | 1.3 | 2.3 | 23.8 | 82.5 | 14.2 |
| France | 146 | 155 | 166 | 167 | 2.7 | 1.8 | 7.4 | 0.9 | 1.7 |
| Serbia & Montenegro | .. | 44 | 78 | 133 | | 1.5 | 76.7 | 71.5 | |
| Greece | 126 | 67 | 89 | 116 | 2.3 | 1.3 | 32.7 | 30.4 | -1.1 |
| Czech Rep | .. | 49 | 70 | 104 | | 1.1 | 43.4 | 47.3 | |
| F.Yug.Rp.Macedonia | .. | 47 | 88 | 103 | | 1.1 | 89.7 | 17.0 | |
| Yugoslav SFR | 102 | .. | .. | .. | 1.9 | | | | |
| Austria | 35 | 168 | 115 | 99 | 0.6 | 1.1 | -31.9 | -13.4 | 14.1 |
| Poland | 21 | 27 | 84 | 99 | 0.4 | 1.1 | 206.9 | 18.0 | 21.2 |
| Norway | 113 | 82 | 74 | 91 | 2.1 | 1.0 | -9.7 | 23.2 | -2.6 |
| Switzerland | 25 | 25 | 57 | 83 | 0.5 | 0.9 | 124.6 | 45.9 | 16.4 |
| Former Czechoslovakia | 83 | .. | .. | .. | 1.5 | | | | |
| Netherlands | 125 | 66 | 64 | 80 | 2.3 | 0.9 | -2.5 | 23.4 | -5.4 |
| Ukraine | .. | 101 | 67 | 79 | | 0.9 | -33.0 | 17.3 | |
| Turkey | 40 | 46 | 57 | 70 | 0.7 | 0.8 | 25.6 | 22.4 | 7.2 |
| Italy | 49 | 45 | 60 | 68 | 0.9 | 0.7 | 31.1 | 14.1 | 4.3 |
| Slovakia | .. | 34 | 44 | 64 | | 0.7 | 30.4 | 45.4 | |
| Other intraregional | 47 | 96 | 103 | 110 | 0.9 | 1.2 | 7.2 | 6.3 | 11.1 |
| *From other regions* | *64* | *106* | *103* | *109* | *1.2* | *1.2* | *-2.7* | *6.2* | *7.0* |
| United States | 41 | 87 | 81 | 86 | 0.8 | 0.9 | -6.8 | 5.8 | 9.7 |
| Japan | 15 | 14 | 17 | 16 | 0.3 | 0.2 | 15.5 | -4.8 | 1.0 |
| Canada | 7 | 4 | 5 | 8 | 0.1 | 0.1 | 20.1 | 50.1 | 1.8 |
| Iraq | 2 | .. | .. | .. | 0.0 | | | | |
| *Other World/Not specified* | *131* | *195* | *187* | *291* | *2.4* | *3.2* | *-4.1* | *55.9* | *10.5* |

Source: World Tourism Organization (WTO) © (Data as collected by WTO December 2004)

# III.3.5 Czech Republic Central and Eastern Europe

## Profile

### Czech Republic

| | |
|---|---|
| Capital | Prague |
| Year of entry in WTO | 1976 |
| Area (1000 km²) | 79 |
| Population (2003, million) | 10.3 |
| Gross Domestic Product (GDP) (2003, euro million) | 94,939 |
| GDP per capita (2003, euro) | 9,298 |
| GDP growth (real, %) | |
| '-> 2002: 1.5; 2003: 3.1; 2004*: 3.3; 2005*: 3.4 | |

**Europe**
**Central and Eastern Europe**

| | 2001 | 2002 | 2003* | 2002/2001 | 2003*/2002 |
|---|---|---|---|---|---|
| **International Arrivals** | | | | | |
| Visitors (1000) | 103,070 | 97,606 | 94,984 | -5.3 | -2.7 |
| Tourists (overnight visitors) (1000) | 5,194 | 4,579 | 5,076 | -11.8 | 10.8 |
| - per 100 of inhabitants | 51 | 45 | 50 | | |
| **Tourism accommodation** | | | | | |
| Number of rooms | 91,490 | 104,491 | 97,282 | 14.2 | -6.9 |
| *Nights spent in collective establishments (1000)* | 37,720 | 33,295 | 39,344 | -11.7 | 18.2 |
| by non-residents (inbound tourism) | 16,564 | 14,589 | 16,511 | -11.9 | 13.2 |
| by residents (domestic tourism) | 21,156 | 18,706 | 22,833 | -11.6 | 22.1 |
| *Nights spent in hotels and similar establishments (1000)* | 22,162 | 21,228 | 23,467 | -4.2 | 10.5 |
| by non-residents (inbound tourism) | 13,647 | 12,520 | 13,688 | -8.3 | 9.3 |
| by residents (domestic tourism) | 8,515 | 8,708 | 9,779 | 2.3 | 12.3 |
| **Outbound Tourism** | | | | | |
| Trips abroad (1000) | 36,224 | 34,303 | 36,074 | -5.3 | 5.2 |
| - per 100 of inhabitants | 353 | 334 | 352 | | |
| **Receipts and Expenditure for International Tourism** | | | | | |
| International Tourism Receipts (euro million) | 3,361 | 3,309 | 3,761 | -1.5 | 13.6 |
| - per Tourist Arrival (euro) | 647 | 723 | 741 | 11.7 | 2.5 |
| - per Visitor Arrival (euro) | 33 | 34 | 40 | 4.0 | 16.8 |
| - per capita (euro) | 327 | 323 | 367 | | |
| International Fare Receipts (euro million) | .. | 460 | 532 | | 15.6 |
| International Tourism Expenditure (euro million) | 1,501 | 1,783 | 2,045 | 18.8 | 14.7 |
| - per trip (euro) | 41 | 52 | 57 | 25.5 | 9.1 |
| - per capita (euro) | 146 | 174 | 200 | | |
| International Fare Expenditure (euro million) | .. | 223 | 257 | | 15.1 |
| △ International Tourism Balance (euro million) | 1,860 | 1,526 | 1,715 | | |
| △ International Fare Balance (euro million) | .. | 237 | 275 | | |

Source: World Tourism Organization (WTO) (Data as collected by WTO December 2004)

See annex for methodological notes and reference of external sources used.

# Survey

Contributed by *Ministry for Regional Development*
www.visitczechia.cz ; www.mmr.cz (promotional)
www.mmr.cz ; www.czechtourservice.cz (institutional/corporate)
www.mmr.cz ; www.czso.cz (research and data)

## Tourism development and outlook

**Overall evaluation of results**

Compared with 2002, there were 2.7 per cent less foreign visitors arrivals in 2003. Nevertheless, the inbound tourism income reached an increase of 21 per cent in US dollar in comparaison with 2002. In 2003, 8.9 per cent more tourists used the accommodation facilities in the Czech Republic. 7 per cent of them were foreign tourists, 11 per cent domestic tourists (16.5 million overnights).

**Supply**

As far as the foreign hotel chains are concerned, almost all the most important ones are already represented in the Czech market. On the contrary, new Czech hotel chains are emerging.
There are about 900 travel agencies and this number more or less constant over the last three years. All of them are insured against bankruptcy and in case of any troubles of a travel agency the homecoming of the clients is guaranteed.
The transport capacity is being enlarged. There are new tunnels, a new bypass around big cities (Pilsen), new motorway from Olomouc to the border with Poland.
*Attractions:*
A new multifunctional Sazka arena was completed in Prague, a new large aquacentrum in Pruhonice is under construction.
*Specific products:*
Many folklore music festivals all around the republic, film (Karlovy Vary, TOURFILM), theatre (Summer Shakespeare Celebration), music (Prague Spring, Mezi Ploty) festivals. Among the priorities of the tourism state policy belong the spa tourism, agro tourism or cyclo tourism.

**External factors**

The political and the economic situation regarding the external tourism are stable in the long term.
With the entrance to the European Union the entry formalities with the most important European countries has become simpler. The Czech Republic is considered to be a safe destination (in January 2003 there was a conference "Czech Republic – The Safe Tourist Destination" held in Prague).
Infrastructures: new airport terminals are in construction at the Prague airport, new roads.
Health: a good health care, foreign centres providing high quality medical services primarily for foreign residents and visitors (Canadian Medical Care).
The Czech Republic is situated in the temperate zone with the favourable and stable climate.

**Tourism policy**

The most important feature of the present State Tourism Policy is the accent on the promotion of the Czech Republic abroad as a peaceful destination. Various programmes for training and education of the human resources with the support of the financial grants from the European Union are being prepared (The Joint Regional Operational Programme prepared by the Ministry for Regional Development in cooperation with the regional authorities).
At the level of regions or towns the limited liability companies are founded with the

purpose of bringing more tourists to the regions. Partners of such companies are representatives both from the public and the private sectors. Every region has its own long-term study on the tourism development. All these conceptional materials are elaborated in accordance with the claim to the environment protection.

**Marketing & promotion**

The area of marketing and Promotion is fully administered by the Czech Tourist Authority –CzechTourism <www.czechtourism.com>, which organizes familiarization trips for incoming travel agencies and press trips for foreign journalists, presents the Czech Republic at trade fairs both at home and abroad, and issues and distributes an enormous amount of prospectuses and other publicity materials. Its other important task is the support of the country's tourist regions (the holding of seminars, regional presentations, rural tourism, etc.). The Czech Center is also involved in analyzing the market, conducting statistical surveys on incoming tourism, investigating the motivations of arriving tourists and above all determining why tourists have not visited the Czech Republic.

The Authority administers 23 branches abroad. In present, the Czech Republic is presented abroad by way of five principal tourist-related themes:

- The beauty of the country´s castles, chateaus and historic towns and cities;
- A healthy and active vacation;
- Golden Prague (three aspects: a city of history, a city of culture, a city for the young);
- Health spas as places of relaxation and enjoyment;
- Ecclesiastical monuments and places of pilgrimage.

There is also the first standard presentation of the Czech Republic targeted to the European Union members called "Visit New Neighbour". This TV spot is running at four prestigious foreign TV channels (BBC World Europe, CNN, Discovery Europe and Eurosport). In a longer-term prospect the promotion strategy defines the basic features of a holiday in the Czech Republic as comfortable, peaceful, unchallenging, calm, pleasant and get-at-able.

**Outlook 2004**

In 2004 the growing tendency of tourism is expected. We suppose that the number of the foreign tourists coming to the Czech Republic could grow over 10 per cent compared to 2003, which means 7.1 million foreign tourists in 2004. From $18^{th}$ to $20^{th}$ October 2004 there will be held a Regional Seminar on Sustainability Certification in Tourism in Mariánské lázne. Apart from that, Czech Republic is preparing for the ASTA Conference which will be held in Prague in 2006. From $5^{th}$ to $9^{th}$ October the $37^{th}$ International Festival TOURFILM and $11^{th}$ Festival TOUR REGION FILM will be held in Karlovy Vary. As far as the tourism fairs are concerned, Czech republic was or is planning to be represented at 53 fairs all around the world. Two of them (GO+Regiontour and Holiday World) are held in the Czech Republic. Apart from that the CzechTourism is organizing "Czech Days" in various countries.

## International Meetings Industry (MI)

**Characteristics of supply**

Attractiveness of the destination.
Traffic availability.
Safeness.
Prague Convention Center.
In the centre of Prague, high capacity, high level of technical services.
Possibility to arrange conferences in historical buildings.
High professionalism of PCO´s in congress and incentive tourism.
Two large areas for Exhibitions and Fairs in Prague and Brno.

| | |
|---|---|
| **Organisation of promotion** | By now the promotion is done at region or directly at city level. International promotion of the Czech Republic is done by the CzechTourism. In present the White Paper (strategic document for congress tourism) is finished and an establishment of the Prague Convention Bureau is planned. The Ministry for Regional Development and the City of Prague cooperate on this document. |

**Collection of statistics on the Meetings Industry?:** no.

| | |
|---|---|
| **Description** | The Prague Convention Center has its own statistics as well as the PCO´s. CzechTourism has started with the research this year. |
| **Importance / size** | Estimations according to the White Paper (based on the statistics of the ICCA) for the year 2003: 180 thousand conference guests and 630 thousand delegate days. |
| **Evolution MI** | The number of conferences is growing from the year 2003 (when the Czech Republic hosted IMF). The vision to the future is to be regularly among the 5 top european meetings destinations for the association meetings by 2008 and by 2010 to be the leading European destination for the small and medium size associations. |

# International Tourism by Origin

**Czech Republic**

**International Tourist Arrivals in All Accommodation Establishments**

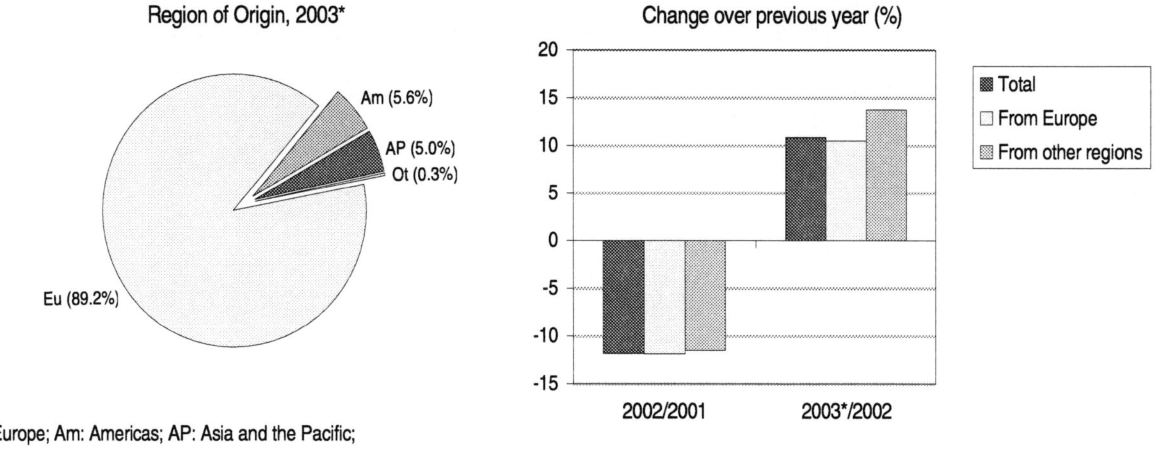


Eu: Europe; Am: Americas; AP: Asia and the Pacific;
Ot: Other;

Source: World Tourism Organization (WTO) ©

**Czech Republic**

**Nights of International Tourists in All Accommodation Establishments**

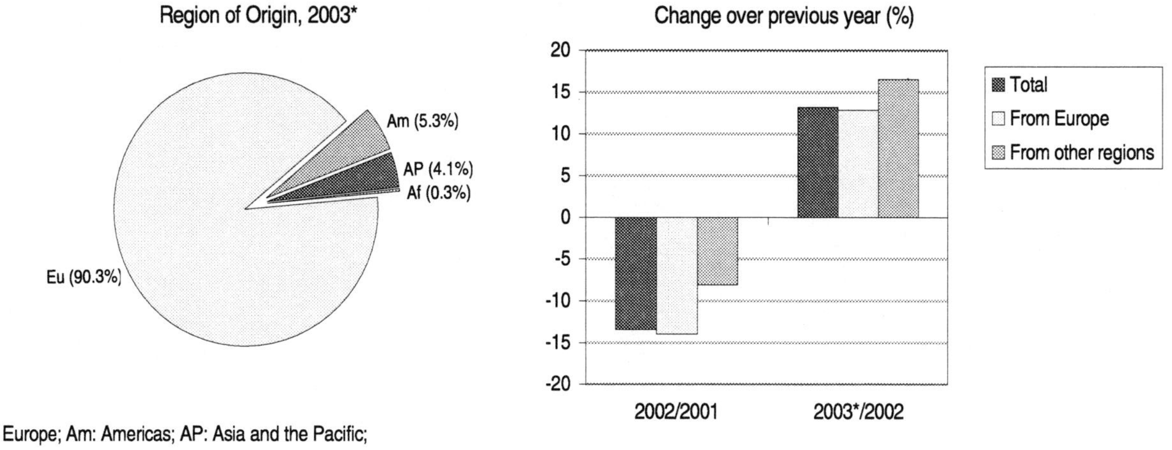


Eu: Europe; Am: Americas; AP: Asia and the Pacific;
Af: Africa;

Source: World Tourism Organization (WTO) ©

**Czech Republic**

**International Tourist Arrivals in All Accommodation Establishments (by nationality)**

| | | | | (thousand) | Market share (%) | | Growth rate (%) | | Average per year (%) |
|---|---|---|---|---|---|---|---|---|---|
| | 1995 | 2001 | 2002 | 2003* | 1995 | 2003* | 2002/01 | 2003*/02 | 1995-2003* |
| **Total** | **3,381** | **5,194** | **4,579** | **5,076** | **100** | **100** | **-11.8** | **10.8** | **5.2** |
| *From Europe* | *3,107* | *4,650* | *4,098* | *4,528* | *91.9* | *89.2* | *-11.9* | *10.5* | *4.8* |
| Germany | 1,243 | 1,551 | 1,395 | 1,439 | 36.8 | 28.4 | -10.1 | 3.2 | 1.8 |
| United Kingdom | 129 | 279 | 287 | 412 | 3.8 | 8.1 | 2.8 | 43.8 | 15.7 |
| Poland | 130 | 370 | 318 | 291 | 3.8 | 5.7 | -14.0 | -8.5 | 10.6 |
| Italy | 207 | 310 | 254 | 281 | 6.1 | 5.5 | -17.9 | 10.8 | 3.9 |
| Slovakia | 157 | 209 | 211 | 253 | 4.6 | 5.0 | 0.9 | 19.6 | 6.1 |
| Netherlands | 229 | 271 | 191 | 239 | 6.8 | 4.7 | -29.5 | 25.0 | 0.5 |
| France | 123 | 187 | 185 | 193 | 3.6 | 3.8 | -1.0 | 4.3 | 5.8 |
| Austria | 183 | 164 | 181 | 165 | 5.4 | 3.3 | 10.3 | -8.5 | -1.3 |
| Spain | 129 | 157 | 140 | 153 | 3.8 | 3.0 | -10.6 | 9.5 | 2.1 |
| Russian Federation | 78 | 120 | 106 | 125 | 2.3 | 2.5 | -12.1 | 18.1 | 6.1 |
| Denmark | 76 | 138 | 97 | 105 | 2.2 | 2.1 | -30.0 | 9.1 | 4.2 |
| Sweden | 49 | 97 | 72 | 80 | 1.4 | 1.6 | -25.9 | 12.5 | 6.4 |
| Hungary | 20 | 63 | 56 | 72 | 0.6 | 1.4 | -12.4 | 30.2 | 17.2 |
| Israel | 28 | 183 | 105 | 72 | 0.8 | 1.4 | -42.6 | -32.0 | 12.5 |
| Belgium | 70 | 70 | 57 | 66 | 2.1 | 1.3 | -17.5 | 15.1 | -0.6 |
| Switzerland | 50 | 58 | 55 | 58 | 1.5 | 1.1 | -5.3 | 5.0 | 1.8 |
| Norway | 15 | 44 | 38 | 53 | 0.4 | 1.0 | -14.8 | 39.6 | 17.1 |
| Greece | 16 | 29 | 41 | 45 | 0.5 | 0.9 | 42.8 | 8.7 | 13.9 |
| Finland | 18 | 47 | 33 | 40 | 0.5 | 0.8 | -30.9 | 21.9 | 10.2 |
| Ireland | .. | 17 | 13 | 33 | | 0.6 | -24.8 | 151.4 | |
| Croatia | .. | 31 | 25 | 31 | | 0.6 | -18.1 | 22.4 | |
| Turkey | .. | 16 | 16 | 24 | | 0.5 | 0.0 | 55.1 | |
| Lithuania | .. | 24 | 21 | 24 | | 0.5 | -11.9 | 14.7 | |
| Bulgaria | 10 | 13 | 12 | 19 | 0.3 | 0.4 | -1.4 | 57.2 | 8.7 |
| Slovenia | .. | 16 | 14 | 15 | | 0.3 | -12.3 | 4.6 | |
| Other intraregional | 147 | 186 | 176 | 239 | 4.4 | 4.7 | -5.7 | 35.8 | 6.2 |
| *From other regions* | *274* | *544* | *481* | *548* | *8.1* | *10.8* | *-11.5* | *13.8* | *9.0* |
| United States | 120 | 218 | 188 | 221 | 3.6 | 4.4 | -13.9 | 17.8 | 7.9 |
| Japan | 50 | 99 | 101 | 93 | 1.5 | 1.8 | 2.3 | -7.8 | 8.0 |
| Australia | 15 | 36 | 22 | 25 | 0.5 | 0.5 | -39.4 | 14.2 | 6.4 |
| Canada | 14 | 23 | 17 | 25 | 0.4 | 0.5 | -23.1 | 42.3 | 7.6 |
| All Africa | 12 | 15 | 12 | 14 | 0.4 | 0.3 | -22.4 | 17.3 | 1.8 |
| Mexico | .. | 10 | 10 | 11 | | 0.2 | -0.1 | 7.5 | |
| New Zealand | .. | 5 | 2 | 5 | | 0.1 | -53.8 | 133.9 | |
| Other Americas | 15 | 28 | 20 | 25 | 0.4 | 0.5 | -30.1 | 26.7 | 6.6 |
| Other Asia | 47 | 110 | 109 | 128 | 1.4 | 2.5 | -0.5 | 17.3 | 13.4 |

Source: World Tourism Organization (WTO) © (Data as collected by WTO December 2004)

**Czech Republic**

**Nights of International Tourists in All Accommodation Establishments (by nationality)**

| | | | | (thousand) | Market share (%) | | Growth rate (%) | | Average per year (%) |
|---|---|---|---|---|---|---|---|---|---|
| | **1995** | **2001** | **2002** | **2003*** | **1995** | **2003*** | **2002/01** | **2003*/02** | **1995-2003*** |
| **Total** | **10,327** | **16,854** | **14,589** | **16,511** | **100** | **100** | **-13.4** | **13.2** | **6.0** |
| *From Europe* | *9,577* | *15,355* | *13,211* | *14,905* | *92.7* | *90.3* | *-14.0* | *12.8* | *5.7* |
| Germany | 3,902 | 5,990 | 5,462 | 5,662 | 37.8 | 34.3 | -8.8 | 3.7 | 4.8 |
| United Kingdom | 373 | 756 | 783 | 1,167 | 3.6 | 7.1 | 3.5 | 49.2 | 15.3 |
| Netherlands | 812 | 966 | 641 | 866 | 7.9 | 5.2 | -33.6 | 35.0 | 0.8 |
| Italy | 620 | 922 | 736 | 816 | 6.0 | 4.9 | -20.2 | 10.8 | 3.5 |
| Slovakia | 513 | 610 | 591 | 766 | 5.0 | 4.6 | -3.1 | 29.5 | 5.1 |
| Russian Federation | 431 | 693 | 607 | 721 | 4.2 | 4.4 | -12.4 | 18.8 | 6.6 |
| Poland | 341 | 949 | 730 | 655 | 3.3 | 4.0 | -23.1 | -10.2 | 8.5 |
| France | 336 | 521 | 471 | 520 | 3.3 | 3.1 | -9.5 | 10.4 | 5.6 |
| Spain | 379 | 491 | 430 | 489 | 3.7 | 3.0 | -12.4 | 13.6 | 3.2 |
| Austria | 390 | 350 | 369 | 352 | 3.8 | 2.1 | 5.4 | -4.7 | -1.3 |
| Denmark | 247 | 424 | 311 | 334 | 2.4 | 2.0 | -26.6 | 7.3 | 3.9 |
| Israel | 85 | 592 | 338 | 279 | 0.8 | 1.7 | -42.8 | -17.6 | 16.0 |
| Sweden | 138 | 266 | 197 | 230 | 1.3 | 1.4 | -25.8 | 16.9 | 6.6 |
| Belgium | 210 | 182 | 160 | 191 | 2.0 | 1.2 | -12.2 | 19.5 | -1.2 |
| Hungary | 49 | 158 | 138 | 182 | 0.5 | 1.1 | -12.6 | 31.8 | 17.8 |
| Switzerland | 137 | 160 | 144 | 156 | 1.3 | 0.9 | -9.8 | 8.0 | 1.6 |
| Norway | 41 | 127 | 102 | 150 | 0.4 | 0.9 | -19.4 | 46.6 | 17.6 |
| Finland | 63 | 162 | 105 | 135 | 0.6 | 0.8 | -34.9 | 27.6 | 10.0 |
| Greece | 48 | 86 | 111 | 131 | 0.5 | 0.8 | 30.2 | 17.5 | 13.2 |
| Croatia | .. | 97 | 81 | 98 | | 0.6 | -16.1 | 21.2 | |
| Ireland | .. | 49 | 34 | 92 | | 0.6 | -30.8 | 171.3 | |
| Turkey | .. | 47 | 43 | 66 | | 0.4 | -8.4 | 53.5 | |
| Bulgaria | 31 | 27 | 30 | 49 | 0.3 | 0.3 | 12.8 | 59.3 | 6.0 |
| Lithuania | .. | 50 | 40 | 44 | | 0.3 | -20.1 | 11.8 | |
| Portugal | .. | 33 | 32 | 37 | | 0.2 | -2.5 | 15.4 | |
| Other intraregional | 432 | 648 | 523 | 719 | 4.2 | 4.4 | -19.4 | 37.5 | 6.6 |
| *From other regions* | *750* | *1,499* | *1,378* | *1,606* | *7.3* | *9.7* | *-8.1* | *16.5* | *10.0* |
| United States | 350 | 642 | 566 | 691 | 3.4 | 4.2 | -11.8 | 22.1 | 8.9 |
| Japan | 119 | 199 | 209 | 216 | 1.2 | 1.3 | 5.0 | 2.9 | 7.7 |
| Canada | 39 | 67 | 62 | 75 | 0.4 | 0.5 | -6.7 | 20.8 | 8.5 |
| Australia | 41 | 73 | 46 | 61 | 0.4 | 0.4 | -37.8 | 33.9 | 5.2 |
| All Africa | 40 | 72 | 53 | 57 | 0.4 | 0.3 | -26.4 | 7.9 | 4.5 |
| Mexico | .. | 29 | 32 | 30 | | 0.2 | 8.4 | -5.1 | |
| New Zealand | .. | 12 | 5 | 13 | | 0.1 | -57.7 | 151.7 | |
| Other Americas | 40 | 88 | 60 | 73 | 0.4 | 0.4 | -31.9 | 21.0 | 7.6 |
| Other Asia | 120 | 315 | 344 | 389 | 1.2 | 2.4 | 9.1 | 13.2 | 15.8 |

Source: World Tourism Organization (WTO) © (Data as collected by WTO December 2004)

Note: 2002 and 2003 change of series

## III.3.6 Estonia — Central and Eastern Europe

# Profile

## Estonia

| | |
|---|---|
| Capital | Tallinn |
| Area (1000 km²) | 45 |
| Population (2003, million) | 1.4 |
| Gross Domestic Product (GDP) (2003, euro million) | 9,599 |
| GDP per capita (2003, euro) | 6,844 |
| GDP growth (real, %) | '-> 2002: 7.2; 2003: 5.1; 2004*: 5.8; 2005*: 5.4 |

**Europe**
**Central and Eastern Europe**

| | 2001 | 2002 | 2003* | 2002/2001 | 2003*/2002 |
|---|---|---|---|---|---|
| **International Arrivals** | | | | | |
| Visitors (1000) | 3,230 | 3,253 | 3,378 | 0.7 | 3.8 |
| Tourists (overnight visitors) (1000) | 1,320 | 1,362 | 1,462 | 3.2 | 7.3 |
| - per 100 of inhabitants | 96 | 100 | 108 | | |
| Same-day visitors (1000) | 1,778 | 1,773 | 1,741 | -0.3 | -1.8 |
| Cruise passengers (1000) | 132 | 118 | 175 | -10.6 | 48.3 |
| **Tourism accommodation** | | | | | |
| Number of rooms | 8,452 | 10,845 | 12,445 | 28.3 | 14.8 |
| *Nights spent in collective establishments (1000)* | 2,537 | 2,696 | 3,085 | 6.3 | 14.4 |
| by non-residents (inbound tourism) | 1,911 | 1,998 | 2,268 | 4.6 | 13.5 |
| by residents (domestic tourism) | 626 | 698 | 817 | 11.5 | 17.0 |
| *Nights spent in hotels and similar establishments (1000)* | | 2,337 | 2,644 | | 13.1 |
| by non-residents (inbound tourism) | 1,341 | 1,887 | 2,086 | 40.7 | 10.5 |
| by residents (domestic tourism) | .. | 450 | 558 | | 24.0 |
| **Outbound Tourism** | | | | | |
| Trips abroad (1000) | 1,658 | 1,849 | 2,075 | 11.5 | 12.2 |
| - per 100 of inhabitants | 121 | 136 | 154 | | |
| **Receipts and Expenditure for International Tourism** | | | | | |
| International Tourism Receipts (euro million) | 549 | 620 | 713 | 12.9 | 15.0 |
| - per Tourist Arrival (euro) | 416 | 455 | 488 | 9.4 | 7.2 |
| - per Visitor Arrival (euro) | 170 | 190 | 211 | 12.1 | 10.8 |
| - per capita (euro) | 401 | 456 | 528 | | |
| International Fare Receipts (euro million) | 167 | 203 | 224 | 21.9 | 10.3 |
| International Tourism Expenditure (euro million) | 208 | 258 | 339 | 24.1 | 31.6 |
| - per trip (euro) | 125 | 139 | 164 | 11.3 | 17.3 |
| - per capita (euro) | 152 | 190 | 251 | | |
| International Fare Expenditure (euro million) | 66 | 83 | 96 | 25.1 | 16.5 |
| △ International Tourism Balance (euro million) | 341 | 362 | 373 | | |
| △ International Fare Balance (euro million) | 101 | 121 | 128 | | |

Source: World Tourism Organization (WTO) (Data as collected by WTO December 2004)

See annex for methodological notes and reference of external sources used.

# Survey

Contributed by *Estonian Tourist Board (Enterprise Estonia)*
www.visitestonia.com (promotional)
www.visitestonia.com (institutional/corporate)
www.visitestonia.com (research and data)

## Tourism development and outlook

**Overall evaluation of results**

In 2003, the number of foreign visitors to Estonia reached 3.4 million, the highest level ever. Compared with 2002, tourism flows to Estonia grew 4 per cent. Among them, 1.4 million or 42 per cent were overnight visitors (increased by 5% compared to 2002). For a few consecutive years now, arrival flows from neighbouring Finland, Latvia and Russia have increased modestly or even decreased while arrivals from more distant countries, especially Germany, Norway and Poland, but also the United Kingdom, Italy and France have shown continuous substantial increases.
The main contributing factors were: new direct air routes, substantially lowered rates by the national carrier Estonian Air, an 11 per cent increase in the hotel capacity of Tallinn, added capacity and facilities at health spas and a significant increase in the number of cruise ships calling at the port of Tallinn.

**Supply**

Transport:
- A major positive factor was the opening of five new direct air routes to Tallinn (from Prague, Paris, Berlin, Amsterdam and Oslo) during 2003 as well as the new pricing policy and the substantially lower rates offered by the national carrier Estonian Air. Visitor arrivals by plane increased 15 per cent (by almost 24 thousand people). These changes contributed positively especially to the number of air passengers from Germany, Norway, the United Kingdom and the Netherlands;
- The number of cruise ships calling at the port of Tallinn increased from 165 in 2002 to 236 in 2003 (an increase of 43%). Consequently, the number of cruise passenger arrivals increased by more than 50 per cent. The number of cruise passengers from the United States of America, Germany, the United Kingdom, Italy, Spain and France showed a significant increase;
- One new catamaran and one new ferry started to sail between Tallinn and Helsinki.

Accommodation:
- In October 2003, Sokos Hotel Viru in Tallinn opened its new conference and banquet centre. Together, the new multifunctional seminar rooms can seat up to 900 delegates, the largest can seat up to 400 delegates;
- The hotels of Tallinn continue to join international hotel chains. To date, 2003 has added the Choice Hotels Scandinavia, Design Hotels, and Sokos Hotels to the Estonian hotel market;
- Bed capacity at health spas increased by 15 per cent.

**External factors**

Weather:
The severe ice conditions in the Gulf of Finland in early 2003 hindered ferry traffic and, compared with 2002, postponed the start of the sea jet navigation between Helsinki and Tallinn by one and a half months.
This negatively affected visitor arrivals from Estonia's biggest market, Finland, but also slightly affected transit traffic from the Baltic countries to Nordic countries. The

decrease in the arrival flows from Finland continued in June and July as well, partly due to the late start of summer, but recovered and started to increase in August. Therefore, visitor arrivals by regular ships for the whole year decreased only slightly (–1%).

**Tourism policy**

For the first time, the Statistical Office of Estonia compiled an analysis on the contribution of tourism to the Estonian Gross Domestic Product (GDP) and employment in 1997-2000 according to the Tourism Satellite Account (TSA) methodology. According to the analysis completed in 2003, tourism contributed 8.2 per cent of Estonia's GDP, and engaged 8.2 per cent of the total employed workforce in the year 2000 (together with indirect effects).

**Marketing & promotion**

International workshop and familiarisation trip to Estonia, which was very informative for foreign tour operators in Autumn 2003 (targeting especially directed at tour operators who do not yet sell trips to Estonia).
Advertising campaign organised for the first time in Latvia in the Summer of 2003.
Advertising campaign organised for the first time in Estonia to promote domestic tourism in the Summer of 2003.

**Outlook 2004**

*Major developments in the tourism services and facilities of Estonia in 2004*
Shipping:

- A brand new ship Victoria I (for 2,500 passengers and 550 cars) started sailing between Tallinn and Stockholm from March 2004, replacing a smaller ferry. Ships sailing on the Tallinn-Stockholm route have started making stopovers on Aland island (Finland) to continue onboard duty-free sales after Estonia joins the European Union on 1st May 2004;
- The opening of the Tallinn-St. Petersburg shipping route: from April 2004, the biggest Estonian shipping company Tallink started regular ship traffic on Helsinki-Tallinn-St. Petersburg route. In June 2004, the Silja Line is expected to start regular ship traffic on the same route, in combination with the Tallinn-Rostock route;
- Two new catamarans will start sailing between Tallinn and Helsinki in May 2004;
- After 1st May when duty-free trade will be abolished on the ships sailing between Tallinn and Helsinki, catamarans are gradually expected to gain and ferries to lose market share on the Tallinn-Helsinki shipping route. In the case that the number of passengers will not increase as forecasted after Estonia joins the European Union, the prices of ship tickets on the Tallinn-Helsinki route may increase somewhat due to lost revenues from onboard duty-free sales.

Air traffic:

- Some new air routes have been opened in 2004; Tallinn-Tampere (from March), Tallinn-Munich (from May);
- Lufthansa resumed its daily flights between Tallinn and Frankfurt (previously only operated by Estonian Air);
- Estonian Air has added frequencies on several existing routes (Tallinn-Copenhagen, Tallinn-Hamburg, Tallinn-London, Tallinn-Oslo) to commence in Spring 2004;
- The first low-cost airline to enter Estonia is Italian Volare which plans to start direct flights between Tallinn and Milan in May (twice a week).

Accommodation establishments:

- Tallinn is expected to get about 830 new hotel rooms during 2004 (most of them will be opened in Spring 2004 and will be on the level of 2 or 3 stars). Consequently, the hotel capacity in Tallinn will increase by more than 20 per cent;
- A new spa hotel with 91 rooms will be opened on Saaremaa island in May 2004;
- A big water park with various water attractions and a hotel with 250 beds were opened in Pärnu in March 2004.

Joining the European Union on 1st May 2004:

- Additional promotion that the new European Union members receive in the foreign press and also improved image of the new European Union members (e.g. regarding safety, improved confidence of foreign investors, etc.);
- Easier border crossing formalities for citizens of European Union countries. European Union citizens will not be registered any more so the time spent on checking their passports will decrease. This will also lead to shorter border crossing times when travelling through the Baltic countries. This is important as Estonia and the Baltic countries are increasingly popular among car and bus tourists from Central Europe, especially from Germany. In the near future, the European Union citizens will be able to travel to Estonia showing only their ID cards, not passports;
- Additional European Union funds for the development of tourism infrastructure and tourism products will become available in Estonia and facilitate further investments from the private sector as well.

Promotion:

In 2004, the total budget of the Estonian Tourist Board for promoting Estonia abroad increased by 2.6 times compared to 2003. The Marketing Action Plan for 2004-2006 was completed at the beginning of 2004.

Forecasts:

Foreign overnights at accommodation establishments of Estonia are expected to increase by 10 per cent in 2004. The most important growth markets are expected to be the European source markets that have shown good growth rates during the past few years to date: Germany, the United Kingdom, Norway, Italy, to a smaller extent also Poland, France and Spain.

## International Meetings Industry (MI)

**Characteristics of supply**

The main destination for international conferences and seminars is the capital Tallinn (78% of foreign conference tourists staying at accommodation establishments of Estonia), followed by the university town Tartu (8%) and the resort town Pärnu (5%). Most of the conferences and seminars have up to 300 participants (most of the providers of meeting rooms offer facilities of this capacity). There are a few bigger conference halls (suitable for up to one thousand delegates) and one arena which can seat up to 6 thousand delegates.

**Organisation of promotion**

Promotion is organised at the national (Estonian Tourist Board) and city level (town governments of Tallinn, Tartu and Pärnu) in cooperation with private enterprises. Tallinn and Pärnu also promote themselves via membership in the European Federation of Conference Towns. Tallinn City Tourist Office and Convention Bureau employs one convention project manager (promotional website: <www.tourism.tallinn.ee>).

**Collection of statistics on the Meetings Industry?:** yes.

**Description**

As from 2002, the Statistical Office of Estonia has collected monthly data on domestic and foreign tourists staying at accommodation establishments with the aim of participating in conferences or seminars of any size.

**Importance / size**

In 2003, there were almost 39 thousand domestic tourists staying at accommodation establishments of Estonia with the aim of participating in conferences or seminars (9% of all domestic tourists at accommodation establishments) and 49 thousand foreign tourists (5% of all foreign tourists at accommodation establishments).

**Evolution MI** Conference tourism in Estonia has been increasing due to increased supply of facilities and increased promotion (e.g. participating in specialised travel trade fairs, EIBTM, IMEX, etc.,) but due to the lack of statistics or surveys it is hard to assess the development over the years in detail.

# International Tourism by Origin

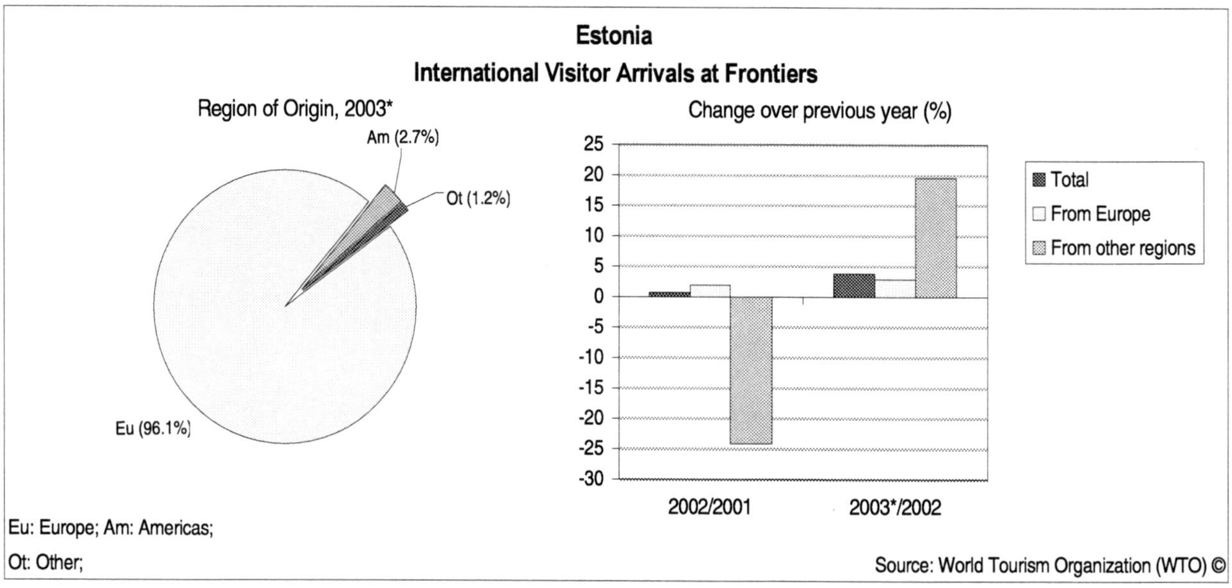


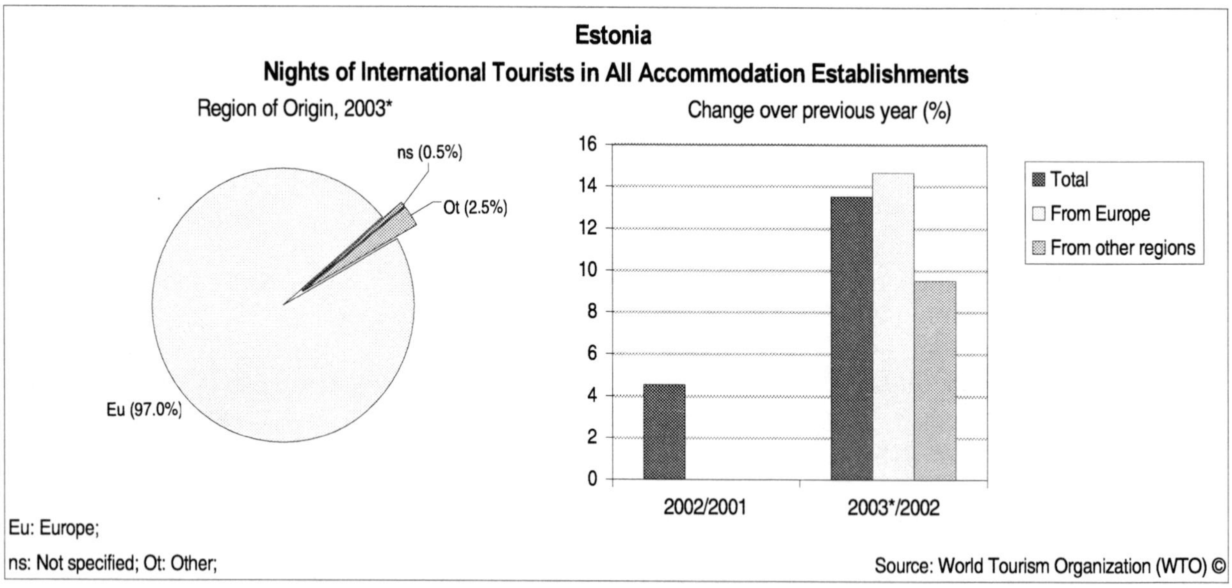

**Estonia**

**International Visitor Arrivals at Frontiers (by residence)**

| | | | | (thousand) | Market share (%) | | Growth rate (%) | | Average per year (%) |
|---|---|---|---|---|---|---|---|---|---|
| | 1995 | 2001 | 2002 | 2003* | 1995 | 2003* | 2002/01 | 2003*/02 | 1995-2003* |
| **Total** | **2,111** | **3,230** | **3,253** | **3,378** | **100** | **100** | **0.7** | **3.8** | **6.1** |
| *From Europe* | *2,072* | *3,093* | *3,154* | *3,244* | *98.2* | *96.1* | *2.0* | *2.9* | *5.8* |
| Finland | 1,523 | 1,810 | 1,825 | 1,788 | 72.1 | 52.9 | 0.8 | -2.0 | 2.0 |
| Latvia | 200 | 452 | 402 | 414 | 9.5 | 12.3 | -11.1 | 3.2 | 9.5 |
| Russian Federation | 107 | 281 | 281 | 296 | 5.1 | 8.8 | 0.1 | 5.2 | 13.5 |
| Sweden | 55 | 110 | 134 | 150 | 2.6 | 4.4 | 22.3 | 11.6 | 13.3 |
| Lithuania | 46 | 113 | 129 | 127 | 2.2 | 3.8 | 14.6 | -1.7 | 13.4 |
| Germany | 30 | 70 | 86 | 105 | 1.4 | 3.1 | 21.8 | 22.3 | 16.7 |
| United Kingdom | 10 | 57 | 59 | 71 | 0.5 | 2.1 | 4.0 | 19.8 | 27.1 |
| Norway | .. | 28 | 36 | 43 | | 1.3 | 28.9 | 20.6 | |
| Poland | .. | 22 | 29 | 38 | | 1.1 | 30.6 | 30.1 | |
| Italy | .. | 19 | 21 | 33 | | 1.0 | 13.8 | 56.6 | |
| Spain | .. | 13 | 17 | 22 | | 0.7 | 34.5 | 28.3 | |
| France | .. | 12 | 15 | 20 | | 0.6 | 22.2 | 36.6 | |
| Denmark | .. | 16 | 17 | 18 | | 0.5 | 3.1 | 6.6 | |
| Ukraine | .. | 15 | 16 | 17 | | 0.5 | 3.2 | 6.3 | |
| Netherlands | .. | 11 | 12 | 16 | | 0.5 | 13.1 | 37.8 | |
| Czech Rep | .. | 9 | 11 | 12 | | 0.4 | 18.7 | 13.6 | |
| Austria | .. | 7 | 8 | 10 | | 0.3 | 18.0 | 13.4 | |
| Hungary | .. | 8 | 8 | 9 | | 0.3 | -3.9 | 14.6 | |
| Switzerland | .. | 7 | 6 | 8 | | 0.2 | -2.8 | 24.1 | |
| Belarus | .. | 7 | 7 | 7 | | 0.2 | 8.4 | -12.0 | |
| Belgium | .. | 4 | 5 | 6 | | 0.2 | 32.0 | 26.6 | |
| Ireland | .. | 6 | 4 | 5 | | 0.1 | -24.7 | 14.7 | |
| Iceland | .. | 1 | 1 | 1 | | 0.0 | 33.7 | 3.9 | |
| Other Central/Eastern Europe | .. | 7 | 9 | 10 | | 0.3 | 21.3 | 19.3 | |
| Other Southern Europe | .. | 7 | 9 | 11 | | 0.3 | 44.7 | 16.5 | |
| Other intraregional | 100 | 3 | 5 | 6 | 4.7 | 0.2 | 58.4 | 18.4 | -30.0 |
| *From other regions* | *37* | *122* | *92* | *110* | *1.8* | *3.3* | *-24.1* | *19.6* | *14.6* |
| United States | .. | 99 | 71 | 83 | | 2.5 | -28.1 | 17.2 | |
| All Americas | 30 | .. | .. | .. | 1.4 | | | | |
| Japan | .. | 10 | 9 | 9 | | 0.3 | -8.7 | 8.2 | |
| Canada | .. | 8 | 7 | 9 | | 0.3 | -13.9 | 34.2 | |
| Australia | .. | 5 | 5 | 6 | | 0.2 | 7.1 | 26.8 | |
| Philippines | .. | 1 | 1 | 2 | | 0.1 | -5.8 | 228.7 | |
| All East Asia/Pacific | 7 | .. | .. | .. | 0.3 | | | | |
| *Other World/Not specified* | 2 | *15* | *7* | *23* | *0.1* | *0.7* | *-54.0* | *224.2* | *40.7* |

Source: World Tourism Organization (WTO) ©

(Data as collected by WTO December 2004)

**Estonia**

**Nights of International Tourists in All Accommodation Establishments (by residence)**

| | | | | (thousand) | Market share (%) | | Growth rate (%) | | Average per year (%) |
|---|---|---|---|---|---|---|---|---|---|
| | 1995 | 2001 | 2002 | 2003* | 1995 | 2003* | 2002/01 | 2003*/02 | 1995-2003* |
| **Total** | .. | **1,911** | **1,998** | **2,268** | | **100** | **4.5** | **13.5** | |
| *From Europe* | .. | *1,718* | *1,918* | *2,200* | | *97.0* | *11.6* | *14.7* | |
| Finland | .. | 1,211 | 1,242 | 1,412 | | 62.2 | 2.5 | 13.7 | |
| Sweden | .. | 97 | 124 | 134 | | 5.9 | 27.6 | 8.4 | |
| Germany | .. | 82 | 110 | 122 | | 5.4 | 34.4 | 11.0 | |
| Russian Federation | .. | 56 | 73 | 81 | | 3.6 | 29.2 | 11.4 | |
| Poland | .. | 11 | 15 | 77 | | 3.4 | 35.5 | 409.5 | |
| United Kingdom | .. | .. | .. | 73 | | 3.2 | | | |
| United Kingdom/Ireland | .. | 56 | 70 | .. | | | 23.8 | | |
| Norway | .. | 34 | 47 | 61 | | 2.7 | 39.3 | 29.3 | |
| Latvia | .. | 38 | 58 | 43 | | 1.9 | 53.1 | -26.2 | |
| Italy | .. | 16 | 21 | 28 | | 1.2 | 32.8 | 35.1 | |
| Denmark | .. | 22 | 31 | 26 | | 1.1 | 39.7 | -15.0 | |
| Lithuania | .. | 21 | 30 | 23 | | 1.0 | 44.2 | -23.0 | |
| Benelux | .. | 15 | 20 | .. | | | 31.6 | | |
| Netherlands | .. | .. | .. | 16 | | 0.7 | | | |
| France | .. | 10 | 13 | 15 | | 0.7 | 34.5 | 15.4 | |
| Spain | .. | .. | .. | 14 | | 0.6 | | | |
| Spain, Portugal | .. | 8 | 13 | .. | | | 53.9 | | |
| Switzerland | .. | 6 | 6 | 7 | | 0.3 | 6.6 | 13.0 | |
| Austria | .. | 5 | 7 | 6 | | 0.3 | 47.7 | -7.0 | |
| Belgium | .. | .. | .. | 6 | | 0.3 | | | |
| Ireland | .. | .. | .. | 5 | | 0.2 | | | |
| Czech Rep | .. | .. | .. | 4 | | 0.2 | | | |
| Hungary | .. | 3 | 4 | 4 | | 0.2 | 26.9 | 9.4 | |
| Former Czechoslovakia | .. | 3 | 4 | .. | | | 24.0 | | |
| Greece | .. | 1 | 2 | 3 | | 0.1 | 108.6 | 49.8 | |
| Other intraregional | .. | 23 | 29 | 38 | | 1.7 | 27.3 | 29.4 | |
| *From other regions* | .. | *51* | *52* | *57* | | *2.5* | *1.5* | *9.5* | |
| United States | .. | 35 | 35 | 30 | | 1.3 | -0.8 | -12.8 | |
| Japan | .. | 11 | 12 | 13 | | 0.6 | 5.6 | 5.3 | |
| Canada | .. | 5 | 6 | 4 | | 0.2 | 8.3 | -22.9 | |
| Australia | .. | .. | .. | 3 | | 0.1 | | | |
| All Africa | .. | .. | .. | 1 | | 0.0 | | | |
| New Zealand | .. | .. | .. | 0 | | 0.0 | | | |
| Other Americas | .. | .. | .. | 1 | | 0.0 | | | |
| Other Asia | .. | .. | .. | 4 | | 0.2 | | | |
| Other Oceania | .. | .. | .. | 0 | | 0.0 | | | |
| *Other World/Not specified* | .. | *141* | *27* | *11* | | *0.5* | *-80.7* | *-59.1* | |

Source: World Tourism Organization (WTO) ©

(Data as collected by WTO December 2004)

# III.3.7 Georgia Central and Eastern Europe

## Profile

# Georgia

| | |
|---|---|
| Capital | T'bilisi |
| Year of entry in WTO | 1993 |
| Area (1000 km²) | 70 |
| Population (2003, million) | 4.7 |
| Gross Domestic Product (GDP) (2003, euro million) | 4,213 |
| GDP per capita (2003, euro) | 814 |
| GDP growth (real, %) | |
| -> 2002: 5.5; 2003: 11.1; 2004*: 8.5; 2005*: 6.0 | |

**Europe**
**Central and Eastern Europe**

| | 2001 | 2002 | 2003* | 2002/2001 | 2003*/2002 |
|---|---|---|---|---|---|
| **International Arrivals** | | | | | |
| Tourists (overnight visitors) (1000) | 302 | 298 | .. | -1.2 | |
| - per 100 of inhabitants | 6 | 6 | .. | | |
| **Tourism accommodation** | | | | | |
| Number of rooms | 2,015 | 3,712 | .. | 84.2 | |
| *Nights spent in collective establishments (1000)* | | | | | |
| by non-residents (inbound tourism) | 2,417 | 2,387 | .. | -1.2 | |
| *Nights spent in hotels and similar establishments (1000)* | 4,262 | | | | |
| by non-residents (inbound tourism) | 2,083 | .. | .. | | |
| by residents (domestic tourism) | 2,179 | .. | .. | | |
| **Outbound Tourism** | | | | | |
| Trips abroad (1000) | 306 | 317 | .. | 3.6 | |
| - per 100 of inhabitants | 6 | 7 | .. | | |
| **Receipts and Expenditure for International Tourism** | | | | | |
| International Tourism Receipts (euro million) | 127 | 141 | 155 | 11.1 | 10.5 |
| - per Tourist Arrival (euro) | 419 | 471 | .. | 12.5 | |
| - per capita (euro) | 27 | 30 | 33 | | |
| International Fare Receipts (euro million) | 21 | 20 | 26 | -2.3 | 31.6 |
| International Tourism Expenditure (euro million) | 116 | 166 | 140 | 43.6 | -16.1 |
| - per trip (euro) | 379 | 525 | .. | 38.6 | |
| - per capita (euro) | 24 | 35 | 30 | | |
| International Fare Expenditure (euro million) | 31 | 45 | 42 | 42.2 | -5.3 |
| △ International Tourism Balance (euro million) | 11 | -26 | 16 | | |
| △ International Fare Balance (euro million) | -11 | -25 | -16 | | |

Source: World Tourism Organization (WTO) (Data as collected by WTO December 2004)

See annex for methodological notes and reference of external sources used.

# International Tourism by Origin

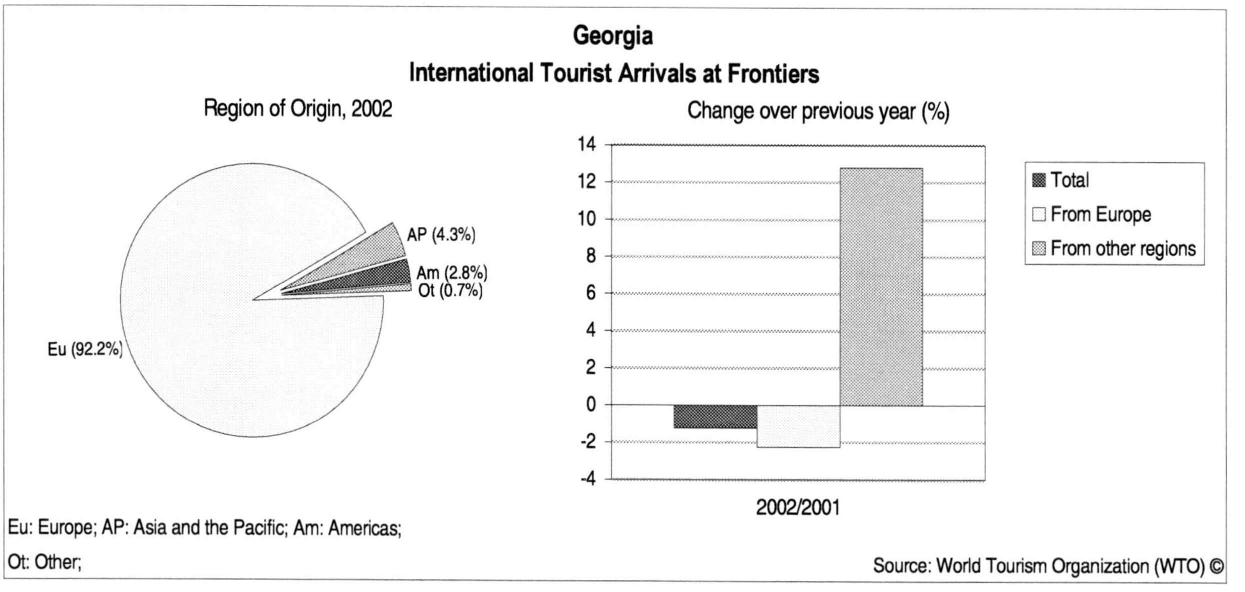


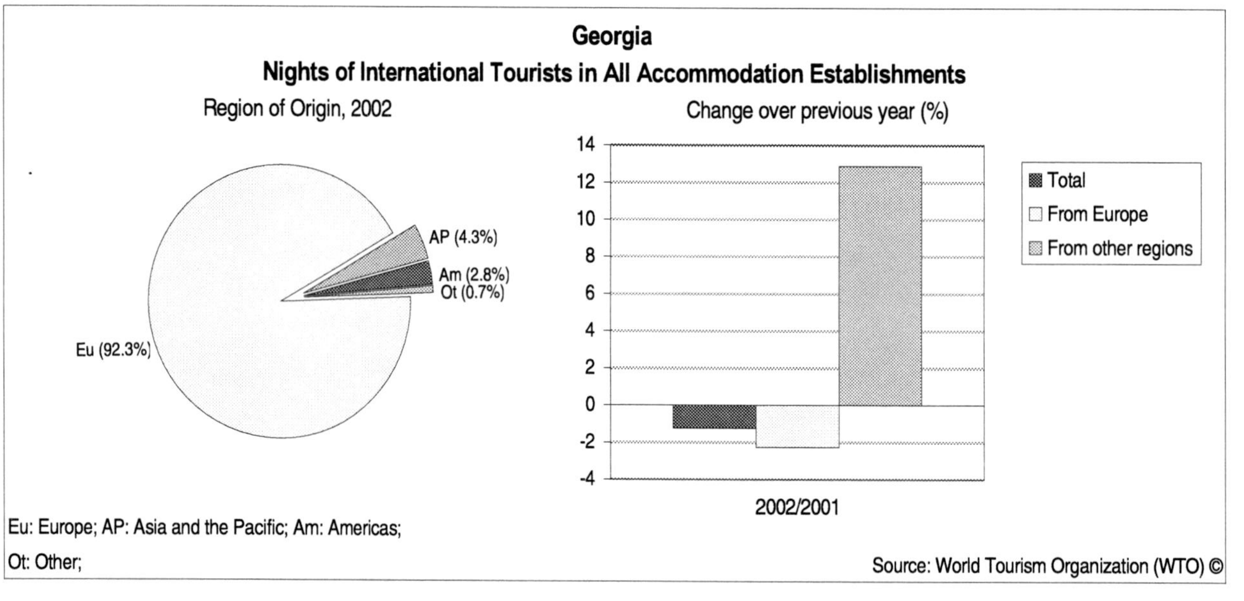

**Georgia**

**International Tourist Arrivals at Frontiers (by residence)**

| | | | | (thousand) | Market share (%) | | Growth rate (%) | | Average per year (%) |
|---|---|---|---|---|---|---|---|---|---|
| | 1995 | 2000 | 2001 | 2002 | 1995 | 2002 | 2001/00 | 2002/01 | 1995-2002 |
| **Total** | **85** | **..** | **302** | **298** | **100** | **100** | | **-1.2** | **19.6** |
| *From Europe* | *78* | *..* | *282* | *275* | *91.7* | *92.2* | | *-2.3* | *19.7* |
| Commonwealth Indep. States | 51 | .. | 184 | 176 | 59.5 | 59.1 | | -4.1 | 19.4 |
| Turkey | 25 | .. | 57 | 56 | 28.8 | 18.9 | | -1.0 | 12.6 |
| Germany | .. | .. | 6 | 6 | | 2.2 | | 16.6 | |
| United Kingdom | .. | .. | 4 | 4 | | 1.5 | | 3.9 | |
| Greece | 0 | .. | 5 | 4 | 0.4 | 1.4 | | -10.0 | 41.4 |
| Israel | 1 | .. | 3 | 3 | 0.9 | 1.1 | | 3.4 | 23.0 |
| Romania | .. | .. | 2 | 2 | | 0.8 | | 32.6 | |
| France | .. | .. | 2 | 2 | | 0.8 | | 5.0 | |
| Italy | 0 | .. | 2 | 2 | 0.2 | 0.6 | | -12.5 | 41.5 |
| Netherlands | 0 | .. | 1 | 2 | 0.2 | 0.5 | | 12.2 | 34.9 |
| Poland | .. | .. | 1 | 1 | | 0.4 | | 18.1 | |
| Switzerland | 0 | .. | 1 | 1 | 0.3 | 0.3 | | 7.0 | 20.4 |
| Austria | 0 | .. | 1 | 1 | 0.2 | 0.3 | | -16.6 | 24.8 |
| Czech Rep | .. | .. | 1 | 1 | | 0.3 | | 44.6 | |
| Denmark | 0 | .. | 1 | 1 | 0.0 | 0.2 | | -1.8 | 56.3 |
| Latvia | .. | .. | 0 | 1 | | 0.2 | | 31.5 | |
| Lithuania | .. | .. | 0 | 1 | | 0.2 | | 30.0 | |
| Sweden | 0 | .. | 0 | 1 | 0.3 | 0.2 | | 5.8 | 10.7 |
| Ireland | 0 | .. | 0 | 0 | 0.0 | 0.2 | | -2.0 | 42.3 |
| Spain | 0 | .. | 0 | 0 | 0.1 | 0.1 | | -25.4 | 20.7 |
| Croatia | .. | .. | 0 | 0 | | 0.1 | | 52.8 | |
| Hungary | .. | .. | 0 | 0 | | 0.1 | | -10.8 | |
| Norway | 0 | .. | 0 | 0 | 0.0 | 0.1 | | 26.4 | 70.0 |
| Estonia | .. | .. | 0 | 0 | | 0.1 | | 30.8 | |
| Finland | 0 | .. | 0 | 0 | 0.0 | 0.1 | | -15.6 | 48.3 |
| Other intraregional | 1 | .. | 8 | 8 | 0.7 | 2.7 | | -1.8 | 46.8 |
| *From other regions* | *4* | *..* | *20* | *23* | *5.0* | *7.7* | | *12.8* | *27.2* |
| United States | 3 | .. | 7 | 7 | 3.3 | 2.4 | | 9.1 | 14.3 |
| Philippines | .. | .. | 3 | 4 | | 1.5 | | 34.7 | |
| Iran | 1 | .. | 3 | 3 | 1.5 | 1.2 | | 6.5 | 15.7 |
| India | 0 | .. | 2 | 2 | 0.1 | 0.6 | | 17.0 | 65.8 |
| Syrian Arab Republic | .. | .. | 1 | 1 | | 0.3 | | 4.2 | |
| China | 0 | .. | 1 | 1 | 0.0 | 0.3 | | 37.6 | 159.4 |
| Japan | 0 | .. | 1 | 1 | 0.0 | 0.2 | | 11.3 | 116.9 |
| Canada | 0 | .. | 0 | 1 | 0.1 | 0.2 | | 22.1 | 40.2 |
| Australia | 0 | .. | 0 | 0 | 0.0 | 0.1 | | 9.7 | 50.8 |
| Pakistan | .. | .. | 0 | 0 | | 0.1 | | 20.5 | |
| South Africa | .. | .. | 0 | 0 | | 0.1 | | 57.0 | |
| Indonesia | .. | .. | 0 | 0 | | 0.1 | | 134.3 | |
| Egypt | .. | .. | 0 | 0 | | 0.1 | | 12.4 | |
| Korea, D P Rp | 0 | .. | 0 | 0 | 0.0 | 0.1 | | 40.0 | 53.5 |
| New Zealand | 0 | .. | 0 | 0 | 0.0 | 0.0 | | 2.8 | 96.0 |
| Sri Lanka | .. | .. | 0 | 0 | | 0.0 | | -5.4 | |
| Other interregional | 0 | .. | 2 | 1 | 0.1 | 0.5 | | -21.5 | 61.0 |
| *Other World/Not specified* | *3* | *..* | *0* | *0* | *3.4* | *0.1* | | *7.7* | *-28.3* |

Source: World Tourism Organization (WTO) © (Data as collected by WTO December 2004)

**Georgia**

**Nights of International Tourists in All Accommodation Establishments (by residence)**

| | | | | (thousand) | Market share (%) | | Growth rate (%) | | Average per year (%) |
|---|---|---|---|---|---|---|---|---|---|
| | 1995 | 2000 | 2001 | 2002 | 1995 | 2002 | 2001/00 | 2002/01 | 1995-2002 |
| **Total** | | .. | **2,417** | **2,387** | | **100** | | **-1.2** | |
| *From Europe* | .. | .. | *2,254* | *2,203* | | *92.3* | | *-2.3* | |
| Commonwealth Indep. States | .. | .. | 1,472 | 1,411 | | 59.1 | | -4.1 | |
| Turkey | .. | .. | 456 | 452 | | 18.9 | | -1.0 | |
| Germany | .. | .. | 44 | 51 | | 2.2 | | 16.6 | |
| United Kingdom | .. | .. | 34 | 35 | | 1.5 | | 3.9 | |
| Greece | .. | .. | 37 | 33 | | 1.4 | | -10.0 | |
| Israel | .. | .. | 25 | 26 | | 1.1 | | 3.4 | |
| Romania | .. | .. | 14 | 19 | | 0.8 | | 32.6 | |
| France | .. | .. | 17 | 18 | | 0.8 | | 5.0 | |
| Italy | .. | .. | 15 | 13 | | 0.6 | | -12.5 | |
| Netherlands | .. | .. | 11 | 12 | | 0.5 | | 12.2 | |
| Poland | .. | .. | 8 | 9 | | 0.4 | | 18.1 | |
| Switzerland | .. | .. | 7 | 7 | | 0.3 | | 7.0 | |
| Austria | .. | .. | 8 | 6 | | 0.3 | | -16.6 | |
| Czech Rep | .. | .. | 4 | 6 | | 0.3 | | 44.7 | |
| Denmark | .. | .. | 6 | 6 | | 0.2 | | -1.8 | |
| Latvia | .. | .. | 4 | 5 | | 0.2 | | 31.5 | |
| Lithuania | .. | .. | 3 | 5 | | 0.2 | | 30.0 | |
| Sweden | .. | .. | 4 | 4 | | 0.2 | | 5.8 | |
| Ireland | .. | .. | 4 | 4 | | 0.2 | | -2.0 | |
| Spain | .. | .. | 4 | 3 | | 0.1 | | -25.4 | |
| Croatia | .. | .. | 2 | 3 | | 0.1 | | 52.8 | |
| Hungary | .. | .. | 3 | 3 | | 0.1 | | -10.8 | |
| Norway | .. | .. | 2 | 2 | | 0.1 | | 26.4 | |
| Estonia | .. | .. | 1 | 2 | | 0.1 | | 30.8 | |
| Finland | .. | .. | 2 | 2 | | 0.1 | | -15.6 | |
| Other intraregional | .. | .. | 67 | 66 | | 2.7 | | -1.8 | |
| *From other regions* | | .. | *161* | *182* | | *7.6* | | *12.9* | |
| United States | .. | .. | 52 | 57 | | 2.4 | | 9.1 | |
| Philippines | .. | .. | 27 | 36 | | 1.5 | | 34.7 | |
| Iran | .. | .. | 26 | 28 | | 1.2 | | 6.5 | |
| India | .. | .. | 13 | 15 | | 0.6 | | 17.0 | |
| Syrian Arab Republic | .. | .. | 7 | 7 | | 0.3 | | 4.2 | |
| China | .. | .. | 5 | 6 | | 0.3 | | 37.6 | |
| Japan | .. | .. | 5 | 5 | | 0.2 | | 11.3 | |
| Canada | .. | .. | 4 | 5 | | 0.2 | | 22.1 | |
| Australia | .. | .. | 3 | 3 | | 0.1 | | 9.7 | |
| Pakistan | .. | .. | 2 | 2 | | 0.1 | | 20.5 | |
| Korea, Republic of | .. | .. | 2 | 2 | | 0.1 | | 5.9 | |
| South Africa | .. | .. | 1 | 2 | | 0.1 | | 57.0 | |
| Indonesia | .. | .. | 1 | 1 | | 0.1 | | 134.3 | |
| Egypt | .. | .. | 1 | 1 | | 0.1 | | 12.4 | |
| New Zealand | .. | .. | 1 | 1 | | 0.0 | | 2.8 | |
| Sri Lanka | .. | .. | 1 | 1 | | 0.0 | | -5.4 | |
| Other interregional | | .. | 13 | 10 | | 0.4 | | -20.5 | |
| *Other World/Not specified* | .. | .. | *2* | *2* | | *0.1* | | *7.7* | |

Source: World Tourism Organization (WTO) © (Data as collected by WTO December 2004)

# III.3.8 Hungary — Central and Eastern Europe

## Profile

# Hungary

Europe
Central and Eastern Europe

| | |
|---|---|
| Capital | Budapest |
| Year of entry in WTO | 1975 |
| Area (1000 km²) | 93 |
| Population (2003, million) | 10.1 |
| Gross Domestic Product (GDP) (2003, euro million) | 87,572 |
| GDP per capita (2003, euro) | 8,884 |
| GDP growth (real, %) | |
| '-> 2002: 3.5; 2003: 2.9; 2004*: 3.5; 2005*: 3.7 | |

| | 2001 | 2002 | 2003* | 2002/2001 | 2003*/2002 |
|---|---|---|---|---|---|
| **International Arrivals** | | | | | |
| Visitors (1000) | 30,679 | 31,739 | 31,412 | 3.5 | -1.0 |
| Tourists (overnight visitors) (1000) | 3,070 | 3,013 | 2,948 | -1.9 | -2.2 |
| - per 100 of inhabitants | 30 | 30 | 29 | | |
| **Tourism accommodation** | | | | | |
| Number of rooms | 59,897 | 62,415 | 64,091 | 4.2 | 2.7 |
| *Nights spent in collective establishments (1000)* | 18,648 | 18,450 | 18,611 | -1.1 | 0.9 |
| by non-residents (inbound tourism) | 10,894 | 10,361 | 10,040 | -4.9 | -3.1 |
| by residents (domestic tourism) | 7,754 | 8,089 | 8,571 | 4.3 | 6.0 |
| *Nights spent in hotels and similar establishments (1000)* | 13,726 | 13,834 | 13,452 | 0.8 | -2.8 |
| by non-residents (inbound tourism) | 8,405 | 8,260 | 7,870 | -1.7 | -4.7 |
| by residents (domestic tourism) | 5,321 | 5,574 | 5,582 | 4.8 | 0.1 |
| **Outbound Tourism** | | | | | |
| Trips abroad (1000) | 11,167 | 12,966 | 14,283 | 16.1 | 10.2 |
| - per 100 of inhabitants | 110 | 129 | 142 | | |
| **Receipts and Expenditure for International Tourism** | | | | | |
| International Tourism Receipts (euro million) | 4,082 | 3,656 | 3,638 | -10.4 | -0.5 |
| - per Tourist Arrival (euro) | 1,330 | 1,213 | 1,234 | -8.7 | 1.7 |
| - per Visitor Arrival (euro) | 133 | 115 | 116 | -13.4 | 0.6 |
| - per capita (euro) | 404 | 363 | 362 | | |
| International Fare Receipts (euro million) | 40 | 51 | 61 | 28.2 | 19.4 |
| International Tourism Expenditure (euro million) | 1,576 | 1,923 | 2,139 | 22.0 | 11.3 |
| - per trip (euro) | 141 | 148 | 150 | 5.0 | 1.0 |
| - per capita (euro) | 156 | 191 | 213 | | |
| International Fare Expenditure (euro million) | 86 | 87 | 112 | 1.8 | 28.7 |
| △ International Tourism Balance (euro million) | 2,505 | 1,733 | 1,499 | | |
| △ International Fare Balance (euro million) | -45 | -36 | -51 | | |

Source: World Tourism Organization (WTO) (Data as collected by WTO December 2004)

See annex for methodological notes and reference of external sources used.

# Survey

Contributed by *Hungarian National Tourist Office*
www.hungary.com (public pages) (promotional)
www.hungary.com (Travel Trade pages) (institutional/corporate)
www.hungary.com (Travel Trade Pages) ; www.ksh.hu ; www.mnb.hu ;
www.tourmis.info (research and data)

## Tourism development and outlook

**Overall evaluation of results**

Tourism data 2003:
The top five inbound markets (visitor arrivals at frontiers) were Romania (+5.6%), Austria (+2.9%), Slovakia (+9.2%), Serbia and Montenegro (-14%) and Germany (+5%). Other important markets for Hungary are Italy (+12%), France (+6.9%) and Switzerland (+24%).

**Supply**

The most positive factor has been the improvement in access.
Hotel capacity increased during 2003, mainly in the 4-5 star category.
A growing number of tour operators are programming Hungary.
Traditional events stay successful and some new events and programmes proved to be successful as well.
Increasing interest in health tourism (spa and wellness). Hungary has very good local conditions for health tourism and due to last years intensive and deliberate development programmes, the quality of services has improved as well.
Budapest: new hotels and improvment of accessibility.
Lake Balaton: new products to spread the demand over the year, a bicycle road around the lake was established, new higher-category hotels and congress centres were constructed.
Conference and incentive tourism: new venues outside Budapest.

**External factors**

The most positive factor was the European Union enlargement.
The most negative factor was the world economy recession.
In Hungary there were no strikes, or other kinds of social movements/disturbances, which affected inbound tourism. The security situation in Hungary is more favourable than in Western Europe, but the general fear of the Iraq war and terrorism had a negative affect on Hungarian inbound tourism.
The Hungarian economy is stable, but certainly the global problems had some negative effects. The growth rate of Gross Domestic Product (GDP) declined to 2.9 per cent from 3.3 per cent, but CPI decreased to 4.7 per cent from 5.3 per cent and the unemployment rate decreased to 5.5 per cent (from 5.9%).
The exchange rate of the national currency (the Hungarian Forint - HUF) changed in a favourable way (fast and significant decrease) from the point of view of inbound tourism.
The economic problems within the largest European tourism generating markets kept many potential tourists at home in 2003. There were some other factors connected with this issue e.g. shorter paid holidays in Germany, a new type of contribution to employee's holidays in Poland, which can be spent only on domestic holidays. Some of our large tourism generating countries, e.g. the Ukraine and Russia suffered from the visa requirements and the more complicated entry processes.
The country's access has improved due to: development of regional airports, appearance of budget airlines and decreasing prices in the Hungarian flag carrier as well.

In Hungary there were no health risks.
The weather is less extreme than in the neighbouring countries. The low water lever of Europe's rivers (e.g. in Hungary: the Danube and Tisza) and lakes (e.g. in Hungary: Lake Balaton) had a negative impact.
The last phase of the European Union enlargement process gave a large opportunity to Hungary to improve its image, which together with the increasing interest in the new member states had positive effects. Positive publicity caused an increase in knowledge about Hungary in Europe.

**Tourism policy**

In 2003 the budgetary provision for tourism was 19 billion HUF (79.1 million euro, monthly average exchange rate, January 2003), but this can be increased up to 32.3 billion HUF (134.5 million euro) by provisional decisions over the next two years' budget.
There are other resources for tourism which are not allocated directly to the Secretariat in charge of tourism:
- A budget for 'holiday vouchers' (incentive for domestic tourism): 6 billion HUF (25 million euro);
- A budget (registered at the Ministry of Health, Social and Family Affairs) for holiday vouchers for inactive people: 400 million HUF (1.7 million euro);
- A budget for spa treatments assisted by social insurance: 5.5 billion HUF (22.9 million euro).

The successful mid-term development plan has continued with new incentives and with a more clear evaluation process. Two main focus points of the National Development Plan are the development of Hungary's image as a tourism destination and the development of the supply side and tourist attractions <www.nfh.hu>.
*The National Development Plan:*
Hungary will join the European Union on 1st May 2004 and subsequently will become eligible for support from the European Union Structural Funds and Cohesion Fund.
The National Development Plan will constitute the basis for the discussions with the Commission, as a result of which the Community Support Framework (CSF), representing the legal framework of support, is completed.
The Hungarian Central Statistical Office (HCSO) is currently changing its methodology of data collection due to its the European Union duties. The regular survey of domestic and foreign tourists was started in 2003 and on the basis of this HCSO will develop Hungary's Tourism Satellite Account (TSA). The state secretariat in charge of tourism and Hungarian National Tourist Office closely works together with HCSO on the tourist surveys and the TSA project.

**Marketing & promotion**

HNTO's total budget was increased by nearly 21 per cent in 2003, of which its marketing budget was increased by 25 per cent.
*Marketing activity in Hungary:*
- Successful participation in large domestic travel trade fairs and events: Utazás (Travel) 2003, Conference of Event Organizers, 12th Welcome to Hungary inbound workshop, Wellness Expo, II Sport and Activity Conference and Fair, Spa Hungary and the Business Travel Show.

*Marketing activity abroad:*
- An update of successful brochures, new brochures for MICE market, CD-ROM for MICE market and for a general introduction of Hungary;
- Co-operation with four Visegrád countries (Czech Republic, Hungary, Poland and Slovakia): homepage <www.european-quartet.com>;
- The year of Hungarian Culture in the United Kingdom: "Magyar Magic - Hungary in Focus" events;
- Large billboard campaigns in Rome and Milan (in the underground), bus advertisements in London and Tokyo, billboard campaign in the London Underground;

- Joint campaign with Budapest Tourism Office in Germany, France, Italy and the Scandinavian countries in May-June;
- Television advertisement campaign on international channels in June;
- International television advertisement campaign during Autumn (spa centres);
- Promotion of Island Festival (Sziget Fesztivál);
- Study tours;
- European Site Networking and Educational Conference (ESNEP) in March and the Association Française des Agences de Voyages (AFAT) voyage in November;
- Travel fairs and exhibitions (136 in 2003);
- The establishment of a new representative office in Dublin and a new information office in Copenhagen;
- Improving co-operation in the field of tourism marketing with the Hungarian Investment and Trade Development Public Benefit Company (ITD) Hungary.

*HNTO's improving partnership with service providers:*

- Free registration in Tourinform (www.tourinform.hu) Network's database (OTIR);
- Free registration in the new on-line database/tourism portal (ONTIR; www.hungary.com) offering the possibility of expression of opinions on HNTO's marketing plan via the professional associations and organizations.

*Cooperation with:*

- MALEV (Hungarian Airlines) and the Hungarian Association of Tour Operators and Travel Agencies and the Hungarian Hotel Association in case of special promotion campaigns, study tours, etc.;
- Professional organisations, associations and clubs;
- The main transport companies;
- Other professional and cultural associations and organizations;
- ITDH, AMC, BTH;
- The Ministry of National Cultural Heritage;
- The Hungaricum Club (Hungarian specialities);
- Educational institutions (lectures and trainees);
- Hungarian Central Statistical Office (they provide HNTO with statistical data);
- Hungarian and local partners in the United States of America and Austria;
- The HNTO has a very good relationship with the World Tourism Organization and the European Travel Commission.

**Outlook 2004**

The official forecast of the HNTO for 2004 is as follows:

- Domestic bed-nights at public accommodation establishments: +4 per cent (year-on-year);
- Foreign bed-nights at public accommodation establishments: +3 per cent (year-on-year);

The reasons for this optimism are:

- The higher marketing budget in 2003 and more intensive marketing activity of HNTO;
- The population of our main inbound markets have started to travel more;
- The European Union enlargement;
- Domestic tourism is getting stronger;
- Hungary is becoming more and more accessible;
- The exchange rate is expected to be more favourable for inbound tourism.

In 2004 HNTO plans to put great emphasis on the following products and markets:

- Budapest;
- Lake Balaton (in Germany, Austria, Switzerland, the Netherlands, Denmark and Central Eastern Europe);
- Health tourism/spa tourism;
- Conference and Incentive tourism mainly in Western Europe;
- Activity tourism, mainly sports;
- Cultural tourism;

- Youth and senior tourism;
- Domestic tourism.

All the traditional, successful events, which took place in 2003 and the previous years, will be organized in 2004 as well.
The European Union accession and the 15th anniversary of the opening-up of borders between Austria and Hungary, the year of Hungarian Culture in the United Kingdom (Magyar Magic), Hungary's ADS and intensive marketing activity and presence.

## International Meetings Industry (MI)

**Characteristics of supply** In the last year, about 30 per cent of visitors came with some kind of business purpose, both business in general and conference tourism.
In Hungary, scientific congresses have the highest participation rate. About 25 per cent of these are organised in the field of the medical sciences. If we consider the whole Hungarian conference market, we notice a rapid growth of corporate meetings, and an increased demand for trade shows as well.
Organisers like unusual meeting places and new hotels. Sometimes direct business from abroad e.g. without a local Professional Congress Organizer (PCO) might cause problems of organisation.

**Organisation of promotion** Since 1st January 2000, the Hungarian Convention Bureau (HCB) has been working as a division of the Hungarian National Tourist Office. Its aim is to provide free and neutral information on Hungary as a MICE destination. The Bureau is operating on public funds and has membership in several international organizations such as UIA, ICCA.

**Website(s)** <www.hcb.hu>

**Collection of statistics on the Meetings Industry?:** yes.

**Description** Besides the Hungarian Central Statistical Office, the Hungarian Convention Bureau collects statistical information.
Methodology: 220 questionnaires are sent quarterly to venues, organisers and associations.

**Statistics included** For more information please visit the website of the Hungarian Convention Bureau <www.hcb.hu> under the link "Statistics".

**Importance / size** In Hungary, in 2003, 351 international conferences were held with altogether 83 thousand participants from 73 countries of the world. The average length of stay is 3.2 days. March seemed to be the most busy period, and what is more the number of meetings doubled compared to last year. Most of the delegates came from Germany, Great Britain, Austria and France.

**Evolution MI** The most important factor this year for Hungary was the European Union accession. After the last entries (Austria, Sweden and Finland, 1995) the MICE industry growth was 20-50 per cent in these countries. We hope we will reach this growth too.

# International Tourism by Origin

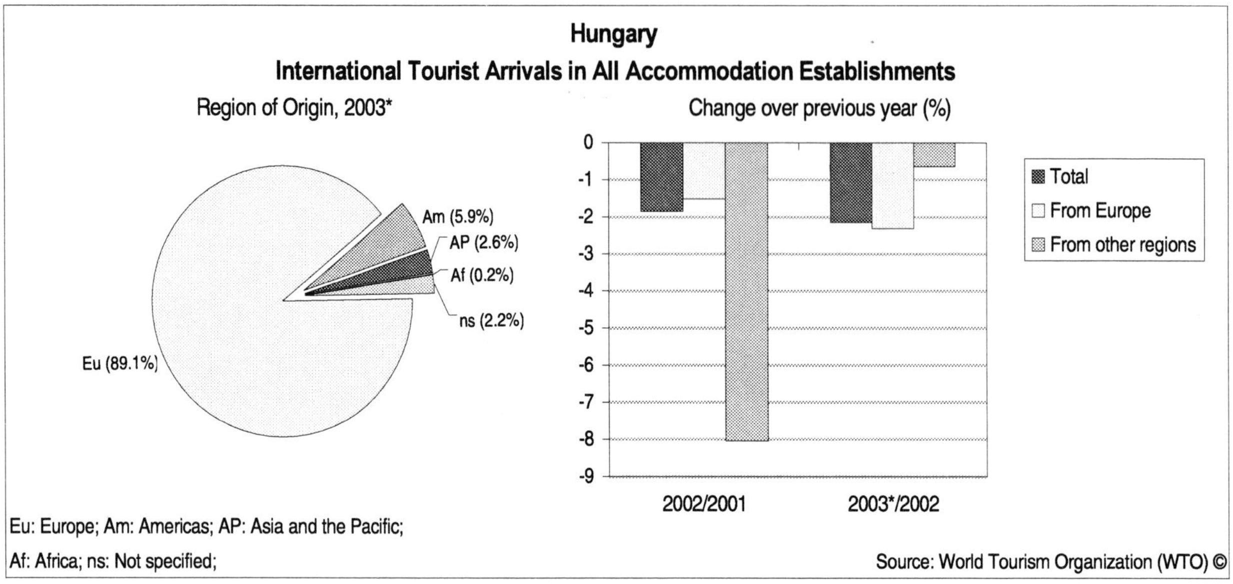


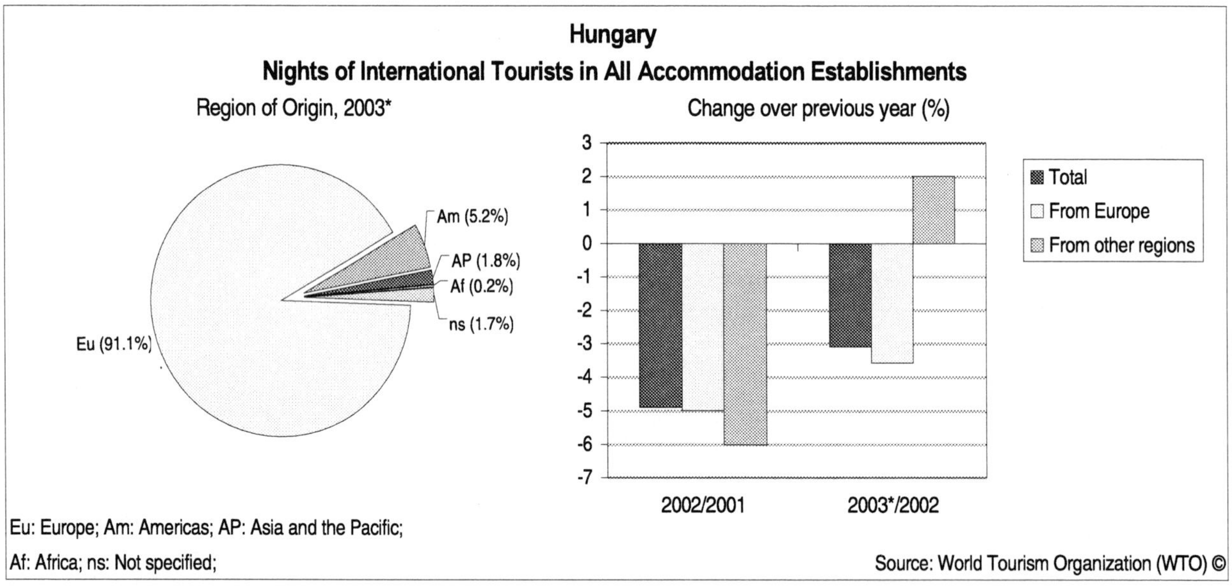

**Hungary**

**International Tourist Arrivals in All Accommodation Establishments (by nationality)**

| | | | | (thousand) | Market share (%) | | Growth rate (%) | | Average per year (%) |
|---|---|---|---|---|---|---|---|---|---|
| | 1995 | 2001 | 2002 | 2003* | 1995 | 2003* | 2002/01 | 2003*/02 | 1995-2003* |
| **Total** | **2,878** | **3,070** | **3,013** | **2,948** | **100** | **100** | **-1.9** | **-2.2** | **0.3** |
| *From Europe* | *2,562* | *2,730* | *2,689* | *2,627* | *89.0* | *89.1* | *-1.5* | *-2.3* | *0.3* |
| Germany | 866 | 860 | 810 | 748 | 30.1 | 25.4 | -5.8 | -7.6 | -1.8 |
| Austria | 247 | 232 | 247 | 245 | 8.6 | 8.3 | 6.3 | -0.6 | -0.1 |
| Italy | 157 | 184 | 174 | 185 | 5.4 | 6.3 | -5.4 | 6.7 | 2.1 |
| United Kingdom | 93 | 130 | 143 | 142 | 3.2 | 4.8 | 10.1 | -0.7 | 5.4 |
| France | 88 | 102 | 113 | 120 | 3.1 | 4.1 | 10.5 | 6.0 | 4.0 |
| Netherlands | 124 | 115 | 107 | 103 | 4.3 | 3.5 | -7.2 | -3.7 | -2.3 |
| Spain | 61 | 95 | 90 | 94 | 2.1 | 3.2 | -5.1 | 4.4 | 5.5 |
| Romania | 93 | 80 | 90 | 89 | 3.2 | 3.0 | 12.3 | -0.7 | -0.6 |
| Poland | 82 | 113 | 112 | 87 | 2.9 | 2.9 | -0.8 | -22.7 | 0.7 |
| Serbia & Montenegro | 96 | 77 | 80 | 65 | 3.3 | 2.2 | 4.5 | -18.5 | -4.7 |
| Israel | 30 | 95 | 67 | 62 | 1.1 | 2.1 | -29.8 | -7.3 | 9.4 |
| Czech Rep | 25 | 43 | 51 | 56 | 0.9 | 1.9 | 19.8 | 9.1 | 10.6 |
| Sweden | 34 | 52 | 50 | 56 | 1.2 | 1.9 | -3.2 | 10.6 | 6.5 |
| Switzerland | 67 | 52 | 55 | 55 | 2.3 | 1.9 | 5.8 | 1.0 | -2.3 |
| Russian Federation | 126 | 50 | 48 | 54 | 4.4 | 1.8 | -4.1 | 11.6 | -10.1 |
| Ukraine | 72 | 41 | 52 | 54 | 2.5 | 1.8 | 27.9 | 2.7 | -3.5 |
| Denmark | 35 | 45 | 48 | 51 | 1.2 | 1.7 | 6.4 | 7.6 | 4.7 |
| Belgium | 45 | 43 | 40 | 41 | 1.6 | 1.4 | -8.2 | 4.2 | -0.9 |
| Finland | 28 | 45 | 42 | 40 | 1.0 | 1.4 | -6.8 | -3.0 | 4.8 |
| Slovakia | 19 | 34 | 34 | 36 | 0.6 | 1.2 | -0.9 | 3.9 | 8.4 |
| Croatia | 31 | 35 | 30 | 33 | 1.1 | 1.1 | -12.8 | 9.8 | 0.8 |
| Greece | 22 | 25 | 27 | 30 | 0.8 | 1.0 | 7.2 | 11.2 | 4.1 |
| Norway | 16 | 21 | 20 | 22 | 0.6 | 0.7 | -4.5 | 7.1 | 4.0 |
| Slovenia | 22 | 18 | 19 | 21 | 0.7 | 0.7 | 3.2 | 8.4 | -0.6 |
| Turkey | 18 | 12 | 14 | 19 | 0.6 | 0.6 | 12.3 | 39.1 | 0.4 |
| Other intraregional | 67 | 131 | 127 | 119 | 2.3 | 4.0 | -3.5 | -5.9 | 7.4 |
| *From other regions* | *237* | *281* | *258* | *257* | *8.2* | *8.7* | *-8.0* | *-0.6* | *1.0* |
| United States | 111 | 146 | 134 | 138 | 3.8 | 4.7 | -8.2 | 3.2 | 2.8 |
| Japan | 49 | 83 | 71 | 66 | 1.7 | 2.2 | -13.9 | -8.1 | 3.7 |
| Canada | 13 | 15 | 15 | 14 | 0.5 | 0.5 | -5.5 | -5.2 | 0.6 |
| Australia | 11 | 10 | 11 | 12 | 0.4 | 0.4 | 14.7 | 1.4 | 0.2 |
| All Africa | 7 | 7 | 6 | 6 | 0.2 | 0.2 | -19.4 | 0.3 | -1.5 |
| Other Americas | 46 | 20 | 22 | 22 | 1.6 | 0.7 | 8.3 | 1.5 | -9.0 |
| *Other World/Not specified* | *79* | *59* | *66* | *65* | *2.7* | *2.2* | *11.8* | *-1.4* | *-2.4* |

Source: World Tourism Organization (WTO) © (Data as collected by WTO December 2004)

**Hungary**
**Nights of International Tourists in All Accommodation Establishments (by nationality)**

| | | | | (thousand) | Market share (%) | | Growth rate (%) | | Average per year (%) |
|---|---|---|---|---|---|---|---|---|---|
| | 1995 | 2001 | 2002 | 2003* | 1995 | 2003* | 2002/01 | 2003*/02 | 1995-2003* |
| **Total** | **9,998** | **10,894** | **10,361** | **10,040** | **100** | **100** | **-4.9** | **-3.1** | **0.1** |
| *From Europe* | *9,130* | *9,984* | *9,485* | *9,146* | *91.3* | *91.1* | *-5.0* | *-3.6* | *0.0* |
| Germany | 4,262 | 4,391 | 4,020 | 3,648 | 42.6 | 36.3 | -8.4 | -9.2 | -1.9 |
| Austria | 793 | 717 | 743 | 719 | 7.9 | 7.2 | 3.7 | -3.3 | -1.2 |
| Italy | 399 | 495 | 450 | 480 | 4.0 | 4.8 | -9.0 | 6.7 | 2.4 |
| Netherlands | 552 | 527 | 441 | 434 | 5.5 | 4.3 | -16.4 | -1.4 | -3.0 |
| United Kingdom | 262 | 348 | 391 | 386 | 2.6 | 3.8 | 12.5 | -1.4 | 5.0 |
| Denmark | 173 | 237 | 257 | 293 | 1.7 | 2.9 | 8.1 | 14.0 | 6.8 |
| France | 202 | 242 | 267 | 290 | 2.0 | 2.9 | 10.2 | 8.7 | 4.6 |
| Spain | 162 | 245 | 240 | 250 | 1.6 | 2.5 | -2.0 | 4.3 | 5.6 |
| Poland | 323 | 416 | 371 | 246 | 3.2 | 2.5 | -10.8 | -33.5 | -3.3 |
| Israel | 98 | 284 | 211 | 212 | 1.0 | 2.1 | -25.9 | 0.7 | 10.1 |
| Romania | 189 | 158 | 179 | 210 | 1.9 | 2.1 | 13.4 | 17.2 | 1.4 |
| Switzerland | 226 | 194 | 199 | 205 | 2.3 | 2.0 | 2.7 | 2.9 | -1.2 |
| Russian Federation | 315 | 194 | 178 | 199 | 3.1 | 2.0 | -8.3 | 11.5 | -5.6 |
| Sweden | 103 | 158 | 149 | 167 | 1.0 | 1.7 | -6.0 | 12.3 | 6.3 |
| Czech Rep | 63 | 118 | 144 | 155 | 0.6 | 1.5 | 21.5 | 8.1 | 11.8 |
| Serbia & Montenegro | 182 | 168 | 170 | 146 | 1.8 | 1.5 | 1.3 | -14.2 | -2.8 |
| Belgium | 169 | 141 | 130 | 139 | 1.7 | 1.4 | -8.0 | 6.7 | -2.5 |
| Ukraine | 148 | 84 | 118 | 128 | 1.5 | 1.3 | 40.5 | 8.6 | -1.8 |
| Finland | 98 | 145 | 132 | 126 | 1.0 | 1.3 | -9.0 | -4.0 | 3.2 |
| Slovakia | 50 | 105 | 90 | 87 | 0.5 | 0.9 | -14.4 | -2.9 | 7.1 |
| Greece | 57 | 67 | 70 | 79 | 0.6 | 0.8 | 4.2 | 12.6 | 4.1 |
| Norway | 49 | 67 | 64 | 67 | 0.5 | 0.7 | -4.5 | 5.0 | 4.2 |
| Croatia | 59 | 73 | 61 | 66 | 0.6 | 0.7 | -17.3 | 8.3 | 1.3 |
| Turkey | 38 | 34 | 37 | 52 | 0.4 | 0.5 | 9.4 | 38.4 | 3.9 |
| Slovenia | 44 | 35 | 39 | 41 | 0.4 | 0.4 | 10.6 | 4.1 | -0.9 |
| Other intraregional | 114 | 341 | 336 | 321 | 1.1 | 3.2 | -1.3 | -4.5 | 13.8 |
| *From other regions* | *658* | *754* | *709* | *723* | *6.6* | *7.2* | *-6.0* | *2.0* | *1.2* |
| United States | 327 | 426 | 399 | 416 | 3.3 | 4.1 | -6.2 | 4.1 | 3.0 |
| Japan | 104 | 170 | 153 | 148 | 1.0 | 1.5 | -10.1 | -3.4 | 4.5 |
| Canada | 48 | 52 | 48 | 45 | 0.5 | 0.5 | -7.1 | -5.2 | -0.6 |
| Australia | 29 | 28 | 30 | 32 | 0.3 | 0.3 | 9.5 | 5.7 | 1.2 |
| All Africa | 22 | 25 | 19 | 21 | 0.2 | 0.2 | -21.5 | 6.3 | -0.5 |
| Other Americas | 129 | 54 | 59 | 61 | 1.3 | 0.6 | 8.9 | 4.4 | -8.8 |
| *Other World/Not specified* | *210* | *156* | *167* | *171* | *2.1* | *1.7* | *6.7* | *2.6* | *-2.5* |

Source: World Tourism Organization (WTO) © (Data as collected by WTO December 2004)

# III.3.9 Kazakhstan Central and Eastern Europe

## Profile

# Kazakhstan

| | |
|---|---|
| Capital | Astana |
| Year of entry in WTO | 1993 |
| Area (1000 km²) | 2,725 |
| Population (2003, million) | 15.1 |
| Gross Domestic Product (GDP) (2003, euro million) | 31,445 |
| GDP per capita (2003, euro) | 2,116 |
| GDP growth (real, %) | |
| '-> 2002: 9.8; 2003: 9.2; 2004*: 9.0; 2005*: 8.5 | |

**Europe**
**Central and Eastern Europe**

| | 2001 | 2002 | 2003* | 2002/2001 | 2003*/2002 |
|---|---|---|---|---|---|
| **International Arrivals** | | | | | |
| Visitors (1000) | 2,693 | 3,678 | 3,237 | 36.6 | -12.0 |
| Tourists (overnight visitors) (1000) | 1,845 | 2,832 | 2,410 | 53.5 | -14.9 |
| - per 100 of inhabitants | 12 | 19 | 16 | | |
| Same-day visitors (1000) | 848 | 846 | 827 | -0.2 | -2.2 |
| **Tourism accommodation** | | | | | |
| Number of rooms | 8,821 | 9,838 | 11,104 | 11.5 | 12.9 |
| *Nights spent in hotels and similar establishments (1000)* | 1,360 | 1,218 | 1,441 | -10.4 | 18.3 |
| by non-residents (inbound tourism) | 304 | 445 | 554 | 46.4 | 24.5 |
| by residents (domestic tourism) | 1,056 | 773 | 887 | -26.8 | 14.7 |
| **Outbound Tourism** | | | | | |
| Trips abroad (1000) | 2,294 | 2,274 | 2,374 | -0.9 | 4.4 |
| - per 100 of inhabitants | 15 | 15 | 16 | | |
| **Receipts and Expenditure for International Tourism** | | | | | |
| International Tourism Receipts (euro million) | 489 | 694 | 596 | 41.9 | -14.1 |
| - per Tourist Arrival (euro) | 265 | 245 | 247 | -7.5 | 0.9 |
| - per Visitor Arrival (euro) | 182 | 189 | 184 | 3.9 | -2.4 |
| - per capita (euro) | 33 | 46 | 39 | | |
| International Fare Receipts (euro million) | 54 | 65 | 78 | 19.6 | 20.8 |
| International Tourism Expenditure (euro million) | 729 | 845 | 708 | 16.0 | -16.3 |
| - per trip (euro) | 318 | 372 | 298 | 17.0 | -19.8 |
| - per capita (euro) | 48 | 56 | 47 | | |
| International Fare Expenditure (euro million) | 95 | 119 | 121 | 25.4 | 0.9 |
| △ International Tourism Balance (euro million) | -239 | -151 | -111 | | |
| △ International Fare Balance (euro million) | -41 | -55 | -42 | | |

Source: World Tourism Organization (WTO) (Data as collected by WTO December 2004)

See annex for methodological notes and reference of external sources used.

# Survey

Contributed by *Agency of the Republic of Kazakhstan for Tourism and Sport*
www.kaztour.kz (promotional)
www.kaztour.kz (institutional/corporate)

## Tourism development and outlook

**Overall evaluation of results**

Stable political and economic situation in Kazakhstan is the major determinant.
In comparison with 2002, the number of tourists visiting Kazakhstan in 2003 has increased by 79 per cent. The number of tourists traveling within Kazakhstan has increaded by 75 per cent.

**Supply**

New scheduled flight of "Air Astana" to London from Almaty among others within Kazakhstan and abroad.

**External factors**

Facilitation of visa formalities for tourists form main generating markets.
Improvement and maintenance of inter-urban, urban and rural roads.
Rebuilding and improvement of airport infrastructure in Almaty.

**Tourism policy**

In 2003 adopted:
The Tourism Industry Development Programme for 2003-2005.
The Law of the Republic of Kazakhstan "About obligatory insurance of the civil-law responsibility of a travel agent and tour operator" Close co-operation with the World Tourism Organisation (organising of the WTO seminars, participation in WTO events).
Better co-operation with the Ministry of Foreign Affairs (facilitation of visa formalities for tourists form main generating markets)

**Marketing & promotion**

Constant participation in the main international travel fairs: FITUR, ITB, WTM, MITT.
Development of Kazakhstan travel fairs: Otdukh Leisure (in Astana), KITF (in Almaty).
Enlarged number of Kazakhstan regional tourism administrations participating in the main travel fairs.

**Outlook 2004**

International and domestic tourism growth.
Creation of a tourism research institute in 2006 with a view of constant monitoring of tourism development.

## International Meetings Industry (MI)

**Characteristics of supply**

Taking into account the geopolitic location and economic boom, Kazakhstan became a place of many international meetings, conferences, etc., including in areas of politics and economy.
The most known annual events are "The Eurasian media-forum", "Congress of world and traditional-national religions", "Oil and gas" exhibition, "Kazakhstan international tourism fair".

**Organisation of promotion**

It is not given sufficient attention to international promotion of the Meetings Industry in Kazakhstan.
We hope, that in process of popularisation of Kazakhstan as a tourist destination, Kazakhstan becomes recognised as the centre of business tourism too.

**Collection of statistics on the Meetings Industry?:** no.

**Importance / size** The share of the Meetings Industry in tourism makes approximately 20 per cent.

**Evolution MI** We assume that the Meetings Industry in our country will develop fast according to rates of development of a national economy.

# International Tourism by Origin

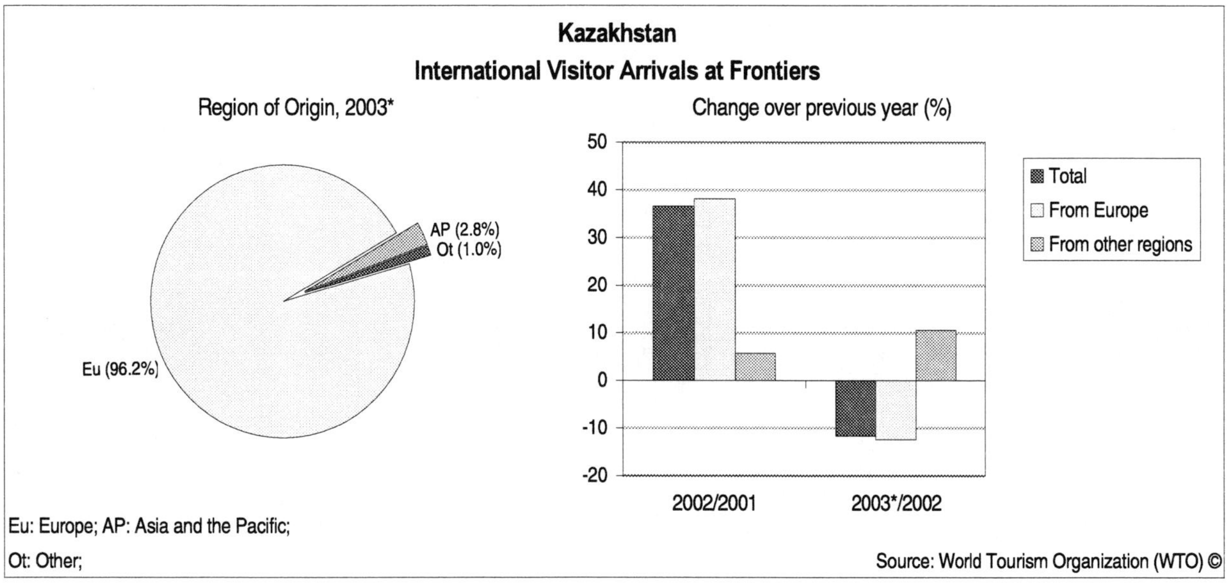

**Kazakhstan**

**International Visitor Arrivals at Frontiers (by residence)**

| | | | | (thousand) | Market share (%) | | Growth rate (%) | | Average per year (%) |
|---|---|---|---|---|---|---|---|---|---|
| | 1995 | 2001 | 2002 | 2003* | 1995 | 2003* | 2002/01 | 2003*/02 | 1995-2003* |
| **Total** | .. | **2,693** | **3,678** | **3,249** | | **100** | **36.6** | **-11.7** | |
| *From Europe* | .. | *2,585* | *3,569* | *3,125* | | *96.2* | *38.1* | *-12.4* | |
| Kyrgyzstan | .. | 1,367 | 1,962 | 1,383 | | 42.6 | 43.5 | -29.5 | |
| Uzbekistan | .. | 878 | 1,181 | 696 | | 21.4 | 34.6 | -41.0 | |
| Russian Federation | .. | 146 | 164 | 606 | | 18.6 | 12.4 | 269.9 | |
| Tajikistan | .. | 50 | 95 | 203 | | 6.2 | 91.2 | 113.3 | |
| Germany | .. | 44 | 48 | 56 | | 1.7 | 9.0 | 17.5 | |
| Turkey | .. | 16 | 25 | 31 | | 1.0 | 57.7 | 27.0 | |
| Ukraine | .. | 6 | 7 | 28 | | 0.9 | 8.8 | 319.8 | |
| Azerbaijan | .. | 18 | 20 | 25 | | 0.8 | 9.9 | 23.7 | |
| United Kingdom | .. | 14 | 20 | 17 | | 0.5 | 47.9 | -16.7 | |
| Turkmenistan | .. | 5 | 6 | 16 | | 0.5 | 19.8 | 146.1 | |
| Armenia | .. | 1 | 1 | 10 | | 0.3 | 27.6 | 985.9 | |
| Belarus | .. | 9 | 2 | 7 | | 0.2 | -74.8 | 205.9 | |
| Italy | .. | 5 | 5 | 7 | | 0.2 | 18.0 | 20.4 | |
| Rep Moldova | .. | 1 | 2 | 6 | | 0.2 | 192.1 | 209.2 | |
| Netherlands | .. | 3 | 5 | 5 | | 0.2 | 38.9 | 10.9 | |
| France | .. | 2 | 3 | 4 | | 0.1 | 32.1 | 22.1 | |
| Israel | .. | 2 | 2 | 3 | | 0.1 | 3.3 | 25.2 | |
| Georgia | .. | 2 | 2 | 3 | | 0.1 | 9.7 | 59.1 | |
| Poland | .. | 1 | 2 | 3 | | 0.1 | 42.5 | 35.7 | |
| Hungary | .. | 3 | 2 | 1 | | 0.0 | -30.4 | -21.2 | |
| Austria | .. | 1 | 1 | 1 | | 0.0 | 11.6 | 20.8 | |
| Lithuania | .. | 0 | 1 | 1 | | 0.0 | 35.2 | 112.4 | |
| Switzerland | .. | 1 | 1 | 1 | | 0.0 | -6.3 | 2.8 | |
| Romania | .. | 0 | 1 | 1 | | 0.0 | 104.7 | 15.5 | |
| Spain | .. | 1 | 1 | 1 | | 0.0 | 37.4 | 28.7 | |
| Other intraregional | .. | 9 | 10 | 10 | | 0.3 | 9.7 | -0.8 | |
| *From other regions* | .. | *102* | *108* | *119* | | *3.7* | *5.7* | *10.6* | |
| China | .. | 41 | 48 | 57 | | 1.8 | 17.5 | 18.1 | |
| United States | .. | 14 | 20 | 19 | | 0.6 | 42.9 | -6.7 | |
| Iran | .. | 4 | 6 | 10 | | 0.3 | 39.4 | 65.7 | |
| Korea, Republic of | .. | 5 | 6 | 7 | | 0.2 | 11.2 | 14.5 | |
| India | .. | 4 | 4 | 5 | | 0.1 | 16.1 | 14.1 | |
| Canada | .. | 3 | 4 | 4 | | 0.1 | 29.0 | 0.1 | |
| Japan | .. | 3 | 3 | 3 | | 0.1 | -11.5 | 20.4 | |
| Mongolia | .. | 10 | 3 | 3 | | 0.1 | -69.3 | -3.0 | |
| Pakistan | .. | 1 | 1 | 2 | | 0.1 | 8.7 | 40.5 | |
| Australia | .. | 6 | 1 | 1 | | 0.0 | -77.8 | 8.8 | |
| Afghanistan | .. | 0 | 0 | 1 | | 0.0 | -4.9 | 40.5 | |
| Philippines | .. | 1 | 1 | 1 | | 0.0 | 36.5 | -30.0 | |
| Untd Arab Emirates | .. | 0 | 0 | 1 | | 0.0 | 91.8 | 46.9 | |
| Lebanon | .. | 0 | 1 | 1 | | 0.0 | 97.0 | -19.1 | |
| Saudi Arabia | .. | 0 | 0 | 0 | | 0.0 | 118.5 | 23.8 | |
| Malaysia | .. | 0 | 0 | 0 | | 0.0 | 83.1 | 28.0 | |
| Other interregional | .. | 8 | 7 | 5 | | 0.1 | -4.2 | -37.5 | |
| *Other World/Not specified* | .. | *6* | *1* | *5* | | *0.2* | *-83.5* | *437.1* | |

Source: World Tourism Organization (WTO) © (Data as collected by WTO December 2004)

# III.3.10 Kyrgyzstan Central and Eastern Europe

## Profile

# Kyrgyzstan

| | |
|---|---|
| Capital | Bishkek |
| Year of entry in WTO | 1993 |
| Area (1000 km²) | 200 |
| Population (2003, million) | 5.0 |
| Gross Domestic Product (GDP) (2003, euro million) | 1,877 |
| GDP per capita (2003, euro) | 370 |
| GDP growth (real, %) | |
| '-> 2002: 0.0; 2003: 6.7; 2004*: 5.5; 2005*: 4.9 | |

**Europe**
**Central and Eastern Europe**

| | 2001 | 2002 | 2003* | 2002/2001 | 2003*/2002 |
|---|---|---|---|---|---|
| **International Arrivals** | | | | | |
| Visitors (1000) | 199 | 183 | .. | -8.0 | |
| Tourists (overnight visitors) (1000) | 99 | 140 | .. | 41.6 | |
| - per 100 of inhabitants | 2 | 3 | .. | | |
| **Tourism accommodation** | | | | | |
| Number of rooms | 2,172 | 1,974 | .. | -9.1 | |
| **Outbound Tourism** | | | | | |
| Trips abroad (1000) | 46 | 45 | .. | -2.2 | |
| - per 100 of inhabitants | 1 | 1 | .. | | |
| **Receipts and Expenditure for International Tourism** | | | | | |
| International Tourism Receipts (euro million) | 26 | 40 | 51 | 54.7 | 26.3 |
| - per Tourist Arrival (euro) | 264 | 288 | .. | 9.2 | |
| - per Visitor Arrival (euro) | 131 | 220 | .. | 68.2 | |
| - per capita (euro) | 5 | 8 | 10 | | |
| International Fare Receipts (euro million) | 9 | 19 | 18 | 119.1 | -5.3 |
| International Tourism Expenditure (euro million) | 13 | 11 | 18 | -14.1 | 61.0 |
| - per trip (euro) | 282 | 248 | .. | -12.2 | |
| - per capita (euro) | 3 | 2 | 4 | | |
| International Fare Expenditure (euro million) | 10 | 15 | 14 | 49.0 | -5.3 |
| △ International Tourism Balance (euro million) | 13 | 29 | 33 | | |
| △ International Fare Balance (euro million) | -1 | 4 | 4 | | |

Source: World Tourism Organization (WTO) (Data as collected by WTO December 2004)

See annex for methodological notes and reference of external sources used.

# International Tourism by Origin

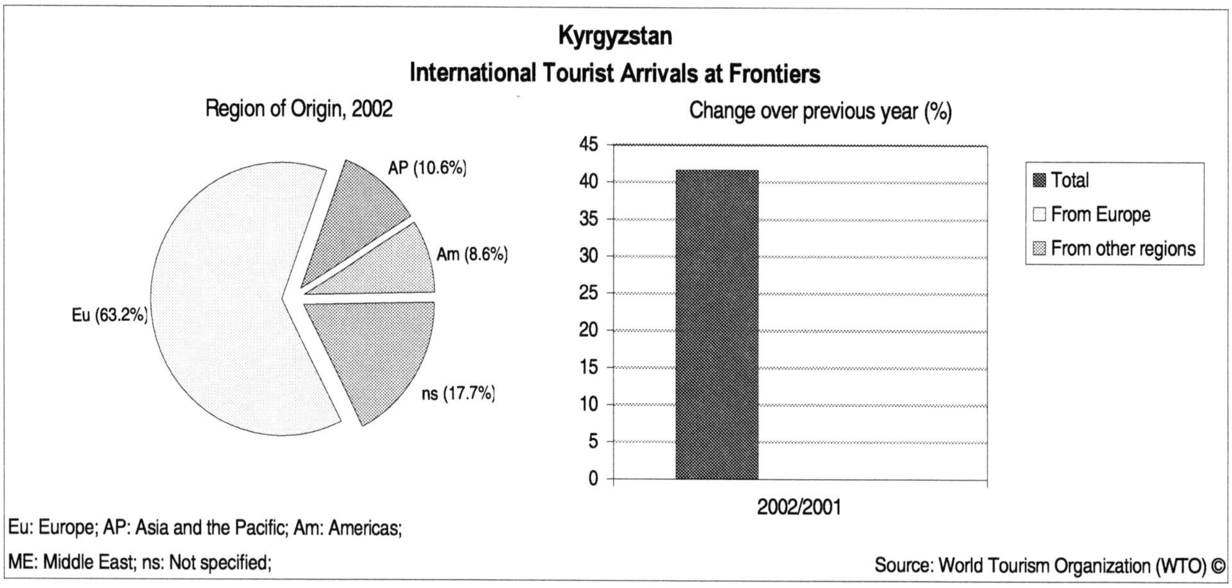

**Kyrgyzstan**

**International Tourist Arrivals at Frontiers (by residence)**

| | | | | (thousand) | Market share (%) | | Growth rate (%) | | Average per year (%) |
|---|---|---|---|---|---|---|---|---|---|
| | 1995 | 2000 | 2001 | 2002 | 1995 | 2002 | 2001/00 | 2002/01 | 1995-2002 |
| **Total** | **36** | **..** | **99** | **140** | **100** | **100** | | **41.6** | **21.2** |
| *From Europe* | *26* | *..* | *45* | *88* | *70.6* | *63.1* | | *97.1* | *19.2* |
| Commonwealth Indep. States | 26 | .. | 30 | 59 | 70.6 | 42.4 | | 95.3 | 12.6 |
| Germany | .. | .. | 3 | 7 | | 4.9 | | 124.4 | |
| Turkey | .. | .. | 3 | 6 | | 4.2 | | 79.8 | |
| France | .. | .. | 1 | 4 | | 3.2 | | 303.4 | |
| United Kingdom | .. | .. | 2 | 3 | | 2.1 | | 56.7 | |
| Spain | .. | .. | 0 | 2 | | 1.1 | | 421.3 | |
| Netherlands | .. | .. | 1 | 1 | | 0.8 | | 75.5 | |
| Switzerland | .. | .. | 1 | 1 | | 0.7 | | -6.5 | |
| Norway | .. | .. | 0 | 1 | | 0.7 | | 666.7 | |
| Denmark | .. | .. | 0 | 1 | | 0.6 | | 260.0 | |
| Italy | .. | .. | 1 | 1 | | 0.5 | | 16.3 | |
| Israel | .. | .. | 0 | 1 | | 0.4 | | 42.5 | |
| Austria | .. | .. | 0 | 0 | | 0.3 | | 10.7 | |
| Poland | .. | .. | 0 | 0 | | 0.2 | | 78.4 | |
| Sweden | .. | .. | 0 | 0 | | 0.2 | | -18.9 | |
| Belgium | .. | .. | 0 | 0 | | 0.2 | | -12.2 | |
| Finland | .. | .. | 0 | 0 | | 0.1 | | 131.1 | |
| Czech Rep | .. | .. | 0 | 0 | | 0.1 | | -16.2 | |
| Lithuania | .. | .. | 0 | 0 | | 0.1 | | 150.0 | |
| Ireland | .. | .. | 0 | 0 | | 0.1 | | 35.2 | |
| Hungary | .. | .. | 0 | 0 | | 0.1 | | 54.7 | |
| *From other regions* | *..* | *..* | *14* | *27* | | *19.1* | | *85.1* | |
| United States | .. | .. | 4 | 11 | | 7.8 | | 173.5 | |
| China | .. | .. | 5 | 7 | | 5.4 | | 43.0 | |
| Korea, Republic of | .. | .. | 1 | 2 | | 1.2 | | 60.4 | |
| India | .. | .. | 0 | 2 | | 1.1 | | 344.1 | |
| Japan | .. | .. | 2 | 1 | | 1.0 | | -12.7 | |
| Iran | .. | .. | 0 | 1 | | 0.8 | | 222.3 | |
| Canada | .. | .. | 0 | 1 | | 0.8 | | 157.5 | |
| Australia | .. | .. | 0 | 1 | | 0.4 | | 54.8 | |
| Pakistan | .. | .. | 0 | 1 | | 0.4 | | 15.0 | |
| Malaysia | .. | .. | 0 | 0 | | 0.1 | | 75.0 | |
| Afghanistan | .. | .. | 0 | 0 | | 0.1 | | -57.0 | |
| Saudi Arabia | .. | .. | 0 | 0 | | 0.0 | | -38.4 | |
| *Other World/Not specified* | *11* | *..* | *39* | *25* | *29.4* | *17.7* | | *-37.2* | *12.7* |

Source: World Tourism Organization (WTO) © (Data as collected by WTO December 2004)

# III.3.11 Latvia — Central and Eastern Europe

## Profile

# Latvia

Europe
Central and Eastern Europe

| | |
|---|---|
| Capital | Riga |
| Year of entry in WTO | 2005 |
| Area (1000 km²) | 65 |
| Population (2003, million) | 2.3 |
| Gross Domestic Product (GDP) (2003, euro million) | 11,700 |
| GDP per capita (2003, euro) | 4,988 |
| GDP growth (real, %) | |
| '-> 2002: 6.4; 2003: 7.5; 2004*: 6.5; 2005*: 6.0 | |

| | 2001 | 2002 | 2003* | 2002/2001 | 2003*/2002 |
|---|---|---|---|---|---|
| **International Arrivals** | | | | | |
| Visitors (1000) | 2,061 | 2,297 | 2,524 | 11.5 | 9.9 |
| Tourists (overnight visitors) (1000) | 591 | 848 | 971 | 43.5 | 14.5 |
| - per 100 of inhabitants | 25 | 36 | 42 | | |
| Same-day visitors (1000) | 1,448 | 1,425 | 1,499 | -1.6 | 5.2 |
| Cruise passengers (1000) | 26 | 76 | 79 | 192.3 | 3.9 |
| **Tourism accommodation** | | | | | |
| Number of rooms | 7,034 | 7,198 | 7,618 | 2.3 | 5.8 |
| *Nights spent in collective establishments (1000)* | 1,616 | 1,692 | 1,808 | 4.7 | 6.9 |
| by non-residents (inbound tourism) | 847 | 871 | 983 | 2.8 | 12.9 |
| by residents (domestic tourism) | 769 | 821 | 825 | 6.8 | 0.5 |
| *Nights spent in hotels and similar establishments (1000)* | 1,475 | 1,527 | 1,632 | 3.5 | 6.9 |
| by non-residents (inbound tourism) | 837 | 853 | 963 | 1.9 | 12.9 |
| by residents (domestic tourism) | 638 | 674 | 669 | 5.6 | -0.7 |
| **Outbound Tourism** | | | | | |
| Trips abroad (1000) | 2,697 | 2,306 | 2,286 | -14.5 | -0.9 |
| - per 100 of inhabitants | 114 | 99 | 98 | | |
| **Receipts and Expenditure for International Tourism** | | | | | |
| International Tourism Receipts (euro million) | 129 | 180 | 235 | 39.5 | 30.6 |
| - per Tourist Arrival (euro) | 218 | 212 | 242 | -2.8 | 14.1 |
| - per Visitor Arrival (euro) | 63 | 78 | 93 | 25.2 | 18.9 |
| - per capita (euro) | 55 | 77 | 101 | | |
| International Fare Receipts (euro million) | 37 | 44 | 52 | 18.3 | 19.0 |
| International Tourism Expenditure (euro million) | 243 | 257 | 347 | 5.9 | 35.1 |
| - per trip (euro) | 90 | 111 | 152 | 23.8 | 36.3 |
| - per capita (euro) | 103 | 110 | 149 | | |
| International Fare Expenditure (euro million) | 35 | 41 | 39 | 19.2 | -5.3 |
| △ International Tourism Balance (euro million) | -114 | -77 | -112 | | |
| △ International Fare Balance (euro million) | 2 | 2 | 13 | | |

Source: World Tourism Organization (WTO) (Data as collected by WTO December 2004)

See annex for methodological notes and reference of external sources used.

# Survey

Contributed by *Ministry of the Economy*
www.latviatourism.lv (promotional)
www.em.gov.lv (institutional/corporate)
www.csb.lv ; www.mfa.lv (research and data)

## Tourism development and outlook

**Overall evaluation of results**

In 2003, international arrivals in Latvia have reached the highest number in the last 10 years, reaching 2.5 billion on foreign travelers, experiencing an increase of 9.9 per cent as compared to 2002.
415 thousand arrivals in hotel and similar accommodation establishments, which led to 983 thousands overnight stays.
Total expenditure of international visitors: 124 millions LVL (+ 30% than in 2002).
Most important countries of origin are Lithuania (31%), Estonia (26%), Russia (8%), Finland (7%), Germany (8%) and Poland (4%).
Outgoing tourism: 2.3 million border crossings (-0,5% than in 2002);

**Supply**

Lack of hotels in capital city Riga in tourism season.

**External factors**

the European Union accessing country.
Visa-free regime with 60 countries.

**Tourism policy**

In 2003, the Cabinet of Ministers and Saeima (Parliament) decided to assign the responsibility for tourism state policy and its implementation to the Ministry of Economics (moved from the Ministry of Environmental Protection and Regional Development since the 1st March, 2003). With this tourism has been recognized as an important sector of the national economy.
Since May 2003 the Ministry of Economics has a Tourism Department, which is under the supervision of the Deputy State Secretary.
In 2003, the Ministry of Economics started to work on the Latvian Tourism Development Guidelines that will be the basic mid-term policy-planning document in the field of tourism.
To provide a state support and to increase the competitiveness of the industry Saeima adopted amendments to the Law on Value Added Tax, which determines reduction of VAT for tourism accommodation services to 9 per cent starting from 2003 instead of the 18 per cent and 5 per cent starting from the 1st May 2004.

**Marketing & promotion**

The main activities in 2003 within the country were: maximum modernisation and supplementation of the information basis, creation of common tourist information space, coordination of tourist information centres, creation of tourist road signs network; and abroad: participation in international tourism fairs, opening of tourist information bureaus, publishing of information materials about Latvia. In 2003, Latvian Tourist Bureau in Helsinki was maintained and Baltic Bureau in Munster (moving to Berlin in 2004) co-maintained, new Latvian Tourist Bureau was opened in London.

**Outlook 2004**

2004 is considered as the year of change in the field of tourism. Ministry of Economics managed to increase the state budget for 2004 for tourism by 2,3 times, which will allow to increase significantly marketing activities, e.g. increase number of brochures published, participate in more international tourism fairs, organize special promotional activities, open new tourism bureaus abroad. Will focus on more target markets.

For effective use of the potential of the tourism sector, it is planned to increase steadily the state budget for tourism sector in coming years and to work intensively on attraction of investment. Ministry of Economics is planning to increase the state budget from one million LS in 2004 up to 5.3 million LS in 2008. By realization of an active policy it is planned to reach significant growth in indicators: growth of tourism service exports by 10-15 per cent per year; tourism sector share in GDP up to 5-7 per cent in coming 4 years.

The public-private partnership will be strengthened in the field of tourism by establishing the Tourism Industry Expert Board in 2004.

In 2004, the Latvian Tourism Development Guidelines will be adopted by the Cabinet of Ministers and will determine mid-term priorities in the field of tourism. One of specific upcoming events in Latvia will be World Ice-Hockey Championship in 2006, that will attract world's attention and extra tourists.

## International Meetings Industry (MI)

**Characteristics of supply**

The main MICE destination is Riga. Its strengths:

- close distances;
- value for money;
- great accessibility internationally and locally.

Riga is one of the incoming MICE destination in Europe (according to ICCA).

**Organisation of promotion**

At the national level: Latvian Tourism Development Agency <www.tava.gov.lv>
Convention and destination marketing organization "Inspiration Riga": <www.inspirationriga.com>.

**Collection of statistics on the Meetings Industry?:** no.

**Description**

There are no official data on the Meetings Industry collected.

**Evolution MI**

It is estimated as a growing industry which gives an important contribution to the Latvian economy.

# International Tourism by Origin

**Latvia**

**International Tourist Arrivals in All Accommodation Establishments**

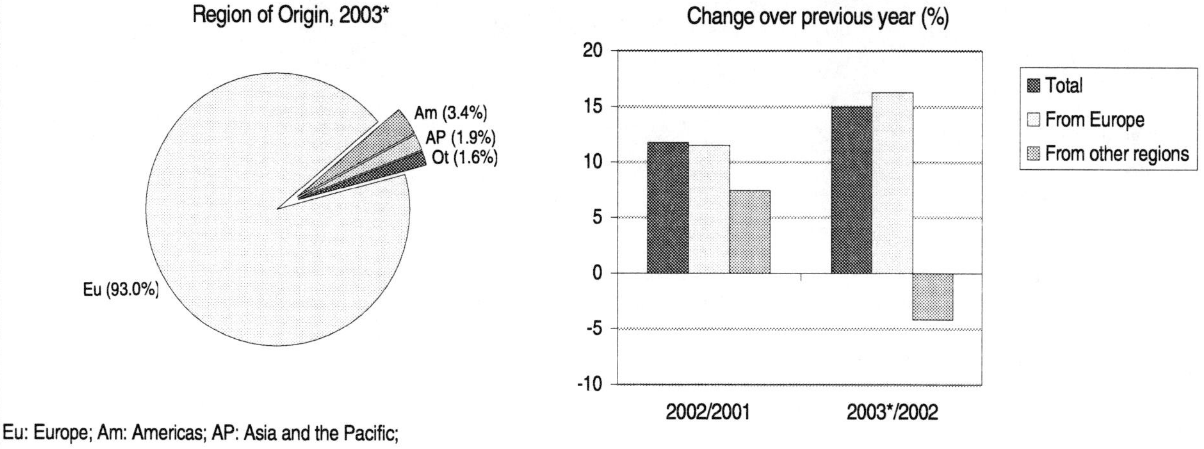


Eu: Europe; Am: Americas; AP: Asia and the Pacific;
Ot: Other;

Source: World Tourism Organization (WTO) ©

**Latvia**

**Nights of International Tourists in All Accommodation Establishments**

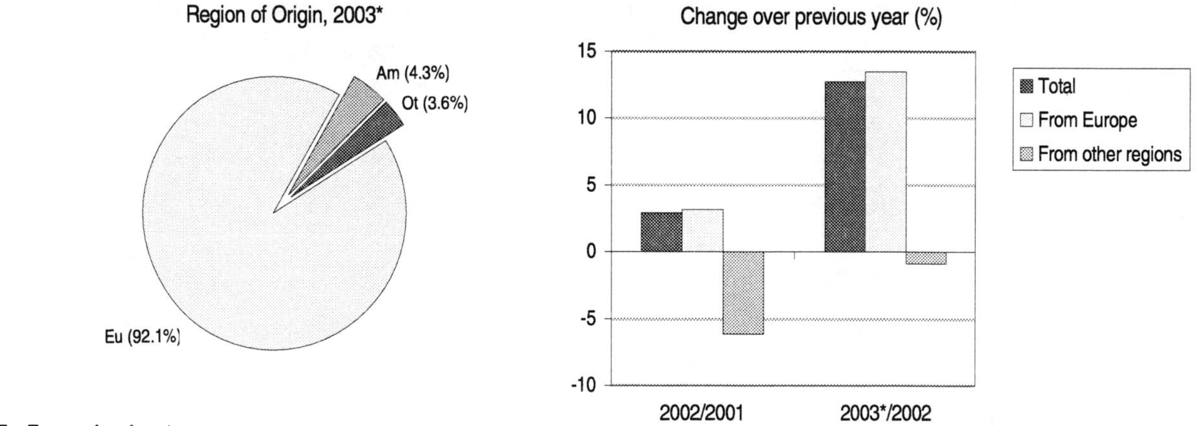


Eu: Europe; Am: Americas;
Ot: Other;

Source: World Tourism Organization (WTO) ©

**Latvia**

**International Tourist Arrivals in All Accommodation Establishments (by residence)**

| | | | | (thousand) | Market share (%) | | Growth rate (%) | | Average per year (%) |
|---|---|---|---|---|---|---|---|---|---|
| | 1995 | 2001 | 2002 | 2003* | 1995 | 2003* | 2002/01 | 2003*/02 | 1995-2003* |
| **Total** | **185** | **323** | **361** | **415** | **100** | **100** | **11.8** | **15.0** | **10.6** |
| *From Europe* | *161* | *298* | *332* | *386* | *87.1* | *93.0* | *11.5* | *16.2* | *11.6* |
| Germany | 26 | 48 | 49 | 63 | 14.2 | 15.1 | 1.8 | 29.1 | 11.5 |
| Finland | 14 | 50 | 56 | 62 | 7.5 | 14.8 | 10.4 | 10.4 | 20.4 |
| Commonwealth Indep. States | 42 | .. | .. | .. | 23.0 | | | | |
| Estonia | 8 | 31 | 35 | 39 | 4.3 | 9.5 | 12.5 | 11.7 | 22.2 |
| Russian Federation | .. | 29 | 36 | 37 | | 9.0 | 26.9 | 2.3 | |
| Lithuania | 13 | 24 | 28 | 31 | 7.2 | 7.4 | 18.5 | 8.6 | 11.1 |
| Sweden | 17 | 19 | 21 | 23 | 9.3 | 5.5 | 7.1 | 9.6 | 3.6 |
| United Kingdom | 8 | 16 | 16 | 21 | 4.4 | 5.0 | -1.5 | 33.6 | 12.6 |
| Poland | 3 | 9 | 12 | 15 | 1.4 | 3.6 | 34.5 | 25.8 | 24.2 |
| Norway | 4 | 10 | 12 | 13 | 2.1 | 3.2 | 10.9 | 13.9 | 16.6 |
| Denmark | 9 | 11 | 10 | 11 | 4.9 | 2.7 | -9.7 | 10.5 | 2.9 |
| Italy | 3 | 7 | 8 | 11 | 1.6 | 2.7 | 12.7 | 45.8 | 17.7 |
| Belarus | .. | 8 | 8 | 8 | | 2.0 | 7.1 | 1.3 | |
| France | 2 | 5 | 5 | 7 | 1.1 | 1.7 | 17.3 | 29.2 | 17.6 |
| Netherlands | .. | 4 | 5 | 6 | | 1.6 | 17.7 | 31.2 | |
| Czech Rep | .. | 3 | 4 | 5 | | 1.1 | 43.0 | 17.2 | |
| Ukraine | .. | 3 | 4 | 4 | | 1.0 | 7.7 | 19.9 | |
| Benelux | 4 | .. | .. | .. | 2.3 | | | | |
| Spain | 0 | 2 | 3 | 4 | 0.3 | 1.0 | 40.3 | 61.2 | 31.0 |
| Austria | 1 | 3 | 4 | 4 | 0.6 | 1.0 | 16.9 | 7.7 | 17.9 |
| Israel | 1 | 3 | 3 | 4 | 0.7 | 1.0 | 11.9 | 35.4 | 14.0 |
| Switzerland | 2 | 4 | 4 | 4 | 1.0 | 0.9 | 14.7 | -14.0 | 8.9 |
| Belgium | .. | 2 | 2 | 3 | | 0.7 | -3.4 | 17.3 | |
| Ireland | .. | 1 | 1 | 2 | | 0.4 | 31.0 | 30.7 | |
| Hungary | 1 | 1 | 1 | 1 | 0.3 | 0.3 | 18.5 | 11.7 | 8.2 |
| Other intraregional | 2 | 5 | 6 | 8 | 0.9 | 1.9 | 18.8 | 39.7 | 21.0 |
| *From other regions* | *11* | *22* | *23* | *22* | *5.8* | *5.4* | *7.4* | *-4.2* | *9.5* |
| United States | 8 | 11 | 13 | 12 | 4.5 | 3.0 | 12.1 | -3.1 | 5.3 |
| Japan | 1 | 6 | 6 | 6 | 0.4 | 1.4 | 2.5 | -1.2 | 27.7 |
| Canada | 1 | 2 | 2 | 1 | 0.4 | 0.3 | 13.7 | -30.1 | 8.6 |
| Australia | 1 | 1 | 1 | 1 | 0.4 | 0.3 | -9.5 | 7.8 | 7.7 |
| China | 0 | 0 | 0 | 0 | 0.1 | 0.0 | -10.6 | -16.8 | 3.0 |
| India | 0 | 0 | 0 | 0 | 0.1 | 0.0 | -16.6 | 13.2 | 6.5 |
| South Africa | .. | 0 | 0 | 0 | | 0.0 | 30.8 | 95.6 | |
| Philippines | .. | 0 | 0 | 0 | | 0.0 | 76.5 | 111.7 | |
| Brazil | .. | 0 | 0 | 0 | | 0.0 | -37.7 | 202.6 | |
| Korea, Republic of | .. | 0 | 0 | 0 | | 0.0 | -65.4 | 8.2 | |
| Korea, D P Rp | .. | 0 | 0 | 0 | | 0.0 | -72.9 | 507.7 | |
| Afghanistan | .. | 0 | 0 | 0 | | 0.0 | 142.4 | -65.9 | |
| Hong Kong (China) | .. | 0 | 0 | 0 | | 0.0 | 1480.0 | -11.4 | |
| Chile | .. | 0 | 0 | 0 | | 0.0 | 10.0 | -10.4 | |
| New Zealand | .. | 0 | 0 | 0 | | 0.0 | 47.5 | -26.4 | |
| Argentina | .. | 0 | 0 | 0 | | 0.0 | -43.2 | 18.0 | |
| Other interregional | 0 | 0 | 0 | 0 | 0.0 | 0.1 | 0.2 | -18.7 | 23.6 |
| *Other World/Not specified* | *13* | *3* | *6* | *7* | *7.1* | *1.6* | *63.9* | *18.0* | *-8.3* |

Source: World Tourism Organization (WTO) © (Data as collected by WTO December 2004)

**Latvia**

**Nights of International Tourists in All Accommodation Establishments (by residence)**

| | | | | (thousand) | Market share (%) | | Growth rate (%) | | Average per year (%) |
|---|---|---|---|---|---|---|---|---|---|
| | 1995 | 2001 | 2002 | 2003* | 1995 | 2003* | 2002/01 | 2003*/02 | 1995-2003* |
| **Total** | **668** | **847** | **871** | **983** | **100** | **100** | **2.9** | **12.8** | **4.9** |
| *From Europe* | *610* | *773* | *797* | *905* | *91.3* | *92.1* | *3.2* | *13.5* | *5.1* |
| Commonwealth Indep. States | 280 | .. | .. | .. | 41.9 | | | | |
| Germany | 72 | 110 | 103 | 129 | 10.7 | 13.1 | -6.2 | 25.4 | 7.7 |
| Finland | 44 | 100 | 108 | 121 | 6.6 | 12.3 | 7.9 | 12.2 | 13.5 |
| Russian Federation | .. | 103 | 106 | 110 | | 11.2 | 2.9 | 3.4 | |
| Belarus | .. | 96 | 97 | 94 | | 9.6 | 1.0 | -2.6 | |
| Estonia | 18 | 56 | 55 | 60 | 2.7 | 6.1 | -1.9 | 10.2 | 16.2 |
| United Kingdom | 24 | 37 | 39 | 54 | 3.6 | 5.5 | 4.9 | 37.3 | 10.5 |
| Sweden | 44 | 42 | 44 | 52 | 6.7 | 5.3 | 2.9 | 18.7 | 1.9 |
| Lithuania | 29 | 42 | 48 | 49 | 4.4 | 5.0 | 13.8 | 3.3 | 6.8 |
| Norway | 10 | 25 | 26 | 29 | 1.5 | 2.9 | 2.0 | 12.7 | 14.0 |
| Denmark | 29 | 24 | 22 | 25 | 4.3 | 2.5 | -7.0 | 12.9 | -1.8 |
| Italy | 9 | 16 | 17 | 25 | 1.3 | 2.5 | 7.5 | 46.3 | 14.3 |
| Israel | 11 | 18 | 18 | 24 | 1.7 | 2.4 | 2.2 | 30.8 | 9.8 |
| Poland | 8 | 16 | 22 | 23 | 1.2 | 2.3 | 36.8 | 3.2 | 14.4 |
| France | 5 | 13 | 13 | 15 | 0.8 | 1.6 | -0.8 | 16.0 | 13.8 |
| Netherlands | .. | 10 | 12 | 14 | | 1.5 | 12.2 | 25.2 | |
| Ukraine | .. | 10 | 9 | 11 | | 1.1 | -6.1 | 15.9 | |
| Benelux | 11 | .. | .. | .. | 1.6 | | | | |
| Czech Rep | .. | 5 | 7 | 9 | | 0.9 | 36.4 | 20.7 | |
| Spain | 1 | 5 | 6 | 9 | 0.2 | 0.9 | 12.6 | 53.2 | 27.5 |
| Austria | 4 | 7 | 8 | 9 | 0.6 | 0.9 | 2.2 | 12.9 | 10.9 |
| Switzerland | 5 | 9 | 10 | 8 | 0.7 | 0.8 | 11.6 | -18.6 | 7.2 |
| Belgium | .. | 6 | 6 | 7 | | 0.8 | 1.5 | 16.4 | |
| Ireland | .. | 3 | 3 | 4 | | 0.4 | 1.9 | 44.9 | |
| Greece | 0 | 1 | 2 | 3 | 0.1 | 0.3 | 57.9 | 60.9 | 25.4 |
| Other intraregional | 6 | 17 | 17 | 21 | 0.9 | 2.1 | 0.9 | 19.0 | 17.3 |
| *From other regions* | *36* | *66* | *62* | *61* | *5.3* | *6.2* | *-6.1* | *-0.9* | *7.1* |
| United States | 27 | 40 | 38 | 37 | 4.1 | 3.8 | -3.7 | -3.4 | 3.9 |
| Japan | 2 | 11 | 10 | 11 | 0.3 | 1.1 | -8.0 | 7.7 | 25.8 |
| Canada | 3 | 6 | 6 | 5 | 0.5 | 0.5 | 1.5 | -28.2 | 3.6 |
| Australia | 2 | 4 | 3 | 4 | 0.3 | 0.4 | -26.9 | 20.3 | 9.4 |
| China | 0 | 1 | 1 | 1 | 0.1 | 0.1 | -28.3 | 7.9 | 3.7 |
| South Africa | .. | 0 | 0 | 1 | | 0.1 | 51.1 | 141.8 | |
| Korea, Republic of | .. | 1 | 0 | 0 | | 0.0 | -80.7 | 220.8 | |
| Other interregional | 1 | 3 | 3 | 4 | 0.1 | 0.4 | 3.7 | 14.3 | 23.9 |
| *Other World/Not specified* | *22* | *8* | *12* | *16* | *3.3* | *1.6* | *57.8* | *33.8* | *-3.9* |

Source: World Tourism Organization (WTO) © (Data as collected by WTO December 2004)

# III.3.12 Lithuania Central and Eastern Europe

## Profile

# Lithuania

Europe
Central and Eastern Europe

| | |
|---|---|
| Capital | Vilnius |
| Year of entry in WTO | 2003 |
| Area (1000 km²) | 65 |
| Population (2003, million) | 3.6 |
| Gross Domestic Product (GDP) (2003, euro million) | 19,303 |
| GDP per capita (2003, euro) | 5,570 |
| GDP growth (real, %) | |

'-> 2002: 6.8; 2003: 9.0; 2004*: 7.0; 2005*: 7.0

| | 2001 | 2002 | 2003* | 2002/2001 | 2003*/2002 |
|---|---|---|---|---|---|
| **International Arrivals** | | | | | |
| Visitors (1000) | 4,195 | 3,999 | 3,635 | -4.7 | -9.1 |
| Tourists (overnight visitors) (1000) | 1,271 | 1,428 | 1,491 | 12.4 | 4.4 |
| - per 100 of inhabitants | 35 | 39 | 41 | | |
| Same-day visitors (1000) | 2,924 | 2,571 | 2,144 | -12.1 | -16.6 |
| Cruise passengers (1000) | 6 | 8 | 9 | 33.3 | 12.5 |
| **Tourism accommodation** | | | | | |
| Number of rooms | 6,430 | 6,545 | 7,694 | 1.8 | 17.6 |
| *Nights spent in collective establishments (1000)* | 3,077 | 2,851 | 2,811 | -7.3 | -1.4 |
| by non-residents (inbound tourism) | 1,073 | 1,149 | 1,170 | 7.1 | 1.8 |
| by residents (domestic tourism) | 2,004 | 1,702 | 1,641 | -15.1 | -3.6 |
| *Nights spent in hotels and similar establishments (1000)* | 937 | 1,029 | 1,069 | 9.8 | 3.9 |
| by non-residents (inbound tourism) | 656 | 708 | 745 | 7.9 | 5.2 |
| by residents (domestic tourism) | 281 | 321 | 324 | 14.2 | 0.9 |
| **Outbound Tourism** | | | | | |
| Trips abroad (1000) | 3,390 | 3,584 | 3,502 | 5.7 | -2.3 |
| - per 100 of inhabitants | 93 | 99 | 97 | | |
| **Receipts and Expenditure for International Tourism** | | | | | |
| International Tourism Receipts (euro million) | 415 | 564 | 675 | 36.0 | 19.7 |
| - per Tourist Arrival (euro) | 326 | 395 | 453 | 21.0 | 14.6 |
| - per Visitor Arrival (euro) | 99 | 141 | 186 | 42.6 | 31.6 |
| - per capita (euro) | 114 | 155 | 186 | | |
| International Fare Receipts (euro million) | 45 | 57 | 66 | 25.2 | 15.1 |
| International Tourism Expenditure (euro million) | 237 | 364 | 498 | 53.5 | 36.8 |
| - per trip (euro) | 70 | 102 | 142 | 45.2 | 40.1 |
| - per capita (euro) | 65 | 100 | 138 | | |
| International Fare Expenditure (euro million) | 9 | 8 | 5 | -9.8 | -32.3 |
| △ International Tourism Balance (euro million) | 178 | 200 | 177 | | |
| △ International Fare Balance (euro million) | 37 | 49 | 60 | | |

Source: World Tourism Organization (WTO) (Data as collected by WTO December 2004)

See annex for methodological notes and reference of external sources used.

# Survey

Contributed by *Lithuanian State Department of Tourism*
www.lithuaniantravel.com (promotional)
www.tourism.lt (institutional/corporate)
www.tourism.lt/statist/default.htm (research and data)

## Tourism development and outlook

**Overall evaluation of results**

The overall number of inbound tourists in 2003 was 1.5 million, 4.4 per cent more than in 2002.
The number of tourists from Russia was 417 thousand, 1.7 per cent less than in 2002, from other CIS countries 376 thousand, 6.1 per cent less, from Latvia 140 thousand, 18 per cent more than in 2002, from Estonia 91 thousand, 64 per cent more, from Germany 107 thousand, 27 per cent more.
From other European countries (excluding Poland) 224 thousand, 6.4 per cent more than in 2002.
It is evident that the Lithuanian tourism market is slowly changing from Eastern Europe to Western Europe.

**Supply**

The number of accommodation establishments in 2003 was 321, 16 per cent more than in 2002.
The total number of rooms in all accommodation establishments was 8 thousand, 17 per cent more; total number of beds 17 thousand, 17 per cent more.
The number of tour operators and travel agencies with small numbers of workers engaged in servicing of tourists (less than 10) in 2003 was 206, 11 per cent less than in 2002; number of medium and big tour operators and travel agencies in 2003 was 42 and 17 per cent greater.
The most popular routes are based on cultural tourism. In Vilnius the number of weekend tours has increased very quickly and there has been an overall increase of MICE activities in the whole country.
There are a lot of renovated hotels in the Druskininkai resort for spa and wellness.

**External factors**

The visa regime for visitors from Russia has influenced the number of same-day visitors from the Kaliningrad region.

**Tourism policy**

Amendments of the law on tourism came into force on 1st April last year and therefore the legislation database has changed a great deal.
The third National Tourism Development Programme was adopted for four years.
The accommodation service tax has been decreased from 18 per cent to 5 per cent.

**Marketing & promotion**

The marketing plan for 2003 was developed, which included fairs, workshops, tours for journalists and new publications. There were some workshops for foreign tour operators in Lithuania for the first time.

**Outlook 2004**

According to the Oxford Economic Forecasting report prepared for the World Travel and Tourism Council, Lithuania's travel and tourism industry is expected to generate 1.9 per cent of Gross Domestic Product (GDP) and 26 thousand jobs, while the broader travel and tourism economy is expected to total 10 per cent of GDP and 131 thousand jobs. The forecast for Travel and tourism demand is expected to total 9.3 per cent real growth in 2004, and 6.8 per cent real growth per annum between 2005 and 2014.

## International Meetings Industry (MI)

| | |
|---|---|
| **Characteristics of supply** | Exhibitions and fairs are concentrated in Vilnius.<br>There are possibilities to organize meetings and conferences in towns and rural areas.<br>Incentives are possible in towns and rural areas. |
| **Organisation of promotion** | Promotion of the industry is organised on national, regional and city levels. |

**Collection of statistics on the Meetings Industry?:** no.

| | |
|---|---|
| **Importance / size** | We are unable to provide an estimation. |
| **Evolution MI** | We estimate that the Meetings Industry will increase very soon. |

# International Tourism by Origin

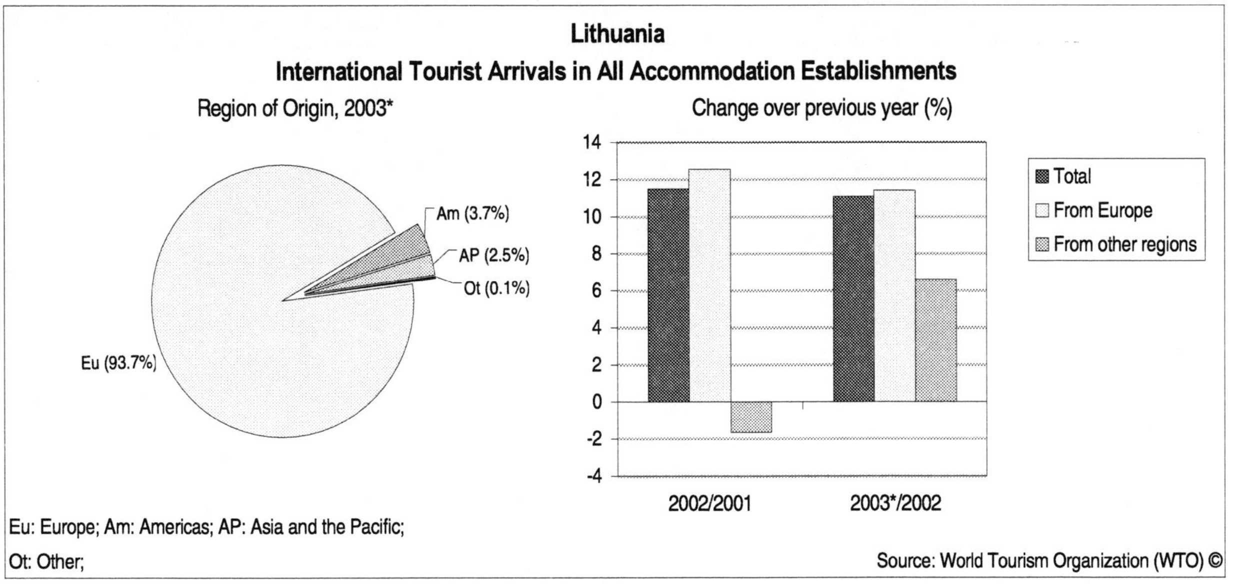


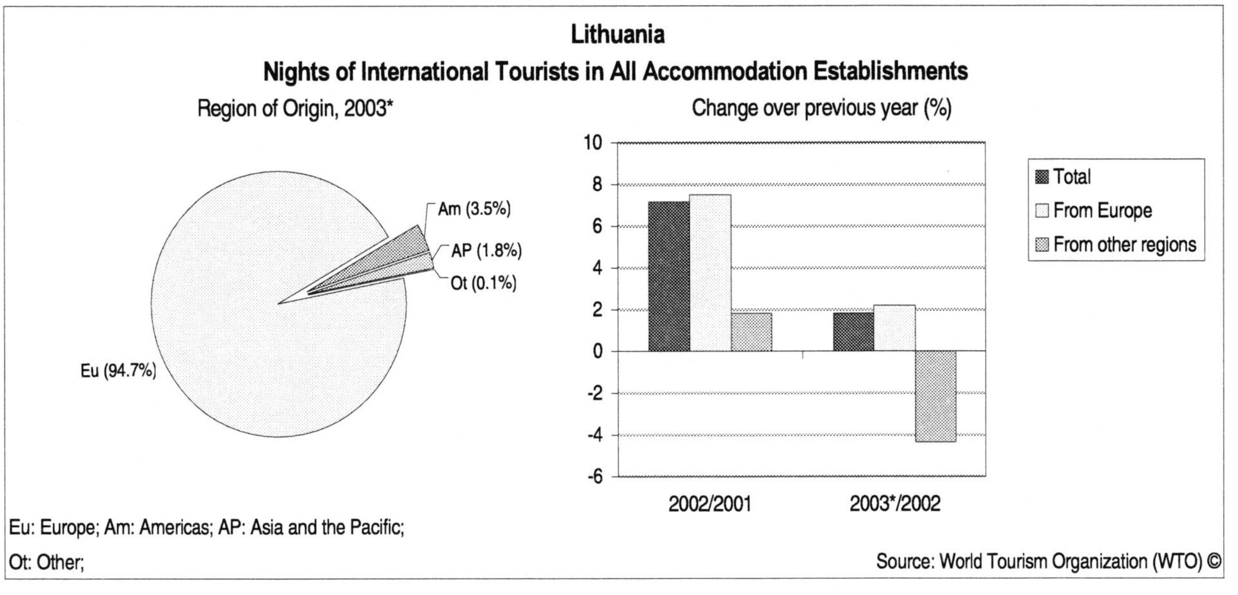

**Lithuania**

**International Tourist Arrivals in All Accommodation Establishments (by residence)**

| | | | | (thousand) | Market share (%) | | Growth rate (%) | | Average per year (%) |
|---|---|---|---|---|---|---|---|---|---|
| | 1995 | 2001 | 2002 | 2003* | 1995 | 2003* | 2002/01 | 2003*/02 | 1995-2003* |
| **Total** | **211** | **354** | **395** | **438** | **100** | **100** | **11.5** | **11.1** | **9.6** |
| *From Europe* | *195* | *328* | *369* | *411* | *92.6* | *93.7* | *12.5* | *11.4* | *9.7* |
| Germany | 35 | 56 | 68 | 79 | 16.8 | 18.1 | 21.2 | 16.3 | 10.6 |
| Poland | 27 | 46 | 60 | 60 | 12.9 | 13.6 | 30.2 | -0.4 | 10.3 |
| Russian Federation | 40 | 45 | 49 | 50 | 18.9 | 11.5 | 8.2 | 2.8 | 3.0 |
| Latvia | 11 | 27 | 26 | 28 | 5.0 | 6.4 | -5.6 | 8.4 | 13.0 |
| Belarus | 10 | 19 | 24 | 22 | 4.7 | 5.0 | 24.4 | -8.9 | 10.3 |
| Finland | .. | 21 | 19 | 21 | | 4.9 | -12.5 | 13.6 | |
| United Kingdom | 6 | 11 | 13 | 20 | 2.7 | 4.5 | 12.8 | 55.2 | 16.7 |
| Estonia | 8 | 14 | 15 | 19 | 3.6 | 4.4 | 3.8 | 30.1 | 12.3 |
| Sweden | .. | 14 | 14 | 15 | | 3.3 | -2.3 | 5.4 | |
| Italy | .. | 8 | 7 | 12 | | 2.6 | -4.4 | 57.7 | |
| Denmark | .. | 10 | 10 | 11 | | 2.5 | 3.2 | 5.3 | |
| Norway | .. | 8 | 8 | 9 | | 2.0 | 3.5 | 10.9 | |
| France | .. | 6 | 7 | 9 | | 1.9 | 6.7 | 28.3 | |
| All Southern Europe | 7 | .. | .. | .. | 3.1 | | | | |
| Netherlands | .. | 3 | 5 | 6 | | 1.4 | 31.2 | 32.2 | |
| Czech Rep | .. | 3 | 4 | 6 | | 1.3 | 52.5 | 35.1 | |
| Spain | .. | 2 | 3 | 5 | | 1.0 | 58.1 | 78.5 | |
| Israel | .. | 3 | 5 | 5 | | 1.0 | 35.4 | -0.4 | |
| Ukraine | .. | 5 | 6 | 4 | | 1.0 | 9.4 | -25.5 | |
| Belgium | .. | 2 | 3 | 3 | | 0.8 | 36.0 | 16.1 | |
| Austria | .. | 2 | 3 | 3 | | 0.7 | 32.5 | 6.2 | |
| Switzerland | .. | 3 | 3 | 3 | | 0.6 | -18.6 | 0.6 | |
| Ireland | .. | 1 | 1 | 2 | | 0.4 | 94.0 | 27.0 | |
| Hungary | .. | 4 | 1 | 2 | | 0.4 | -72.5 | 66.0 | |
| Portugal | .. | 1 | 1 | 1 | | 0.3 | 17.0 | 73.9 | |
| Other intraregional | 52 | 12 | 17 | 19 | 24.9 | 4.3 | 38.3 | 11.1 | -12.0 |
| *From other regions* | *16* | *26* | *26* | *27* | *7.4* | *6.3* | *-1.7* | *6.6* | *7.3* |
| United States | 10 | 13 | 14 | 14 | 4.6 | 3.2 | 0.8 | 3.7 | 4.8 |
| Japan | .. | 6 | 6 | 8 | | 1.8 | -9.3 | 33.8 | |
| All Asia | 4 | .. | .. | .. | 1.7 | | | | |
| All Oceania | 1 | 1 | 1 | 1 | 0.2 | 0.3 | -17.8 | 54.7 | 11.9 |
| Canada | 1 | 1 | 1 | 1 | 0.5 | 0.3 | 12.9 | -10.0 | 2.3 |
| All South America | 1 | 0 | 0 | 1 | 0.2 | 0.2 | 11.9 | 99.7 | 3.3 |
| China | .. | 0 | 1 | 1 | | 0.1 | 124.8 | -44.6 | |
| All Africa | 0 | 0 | 0 | 0 | 0.1 | 0.1 | -6.6 | 47.6 | 5.1 |
| Other North America | 0 | 0 | 0 | 0 | 0.0 | 0.0 | 44.5 | -67.2 | 13.9 |
| Other Asia | .. | 3 | 2 | 1 | | 0.3 | -21.5 | -37.5 | |

Source: World Tourism Organization (WTO) ©

(Data as collected by WTO December 2004)

**Lithuania**
**Nights of International Tourists in All Accommodation Establishments (by residence)**

| | | | | (thousand) | Market share (%) | | Growth rate (%) | | Average per year (%) |
|---|---|---|---|---|---|---|---|---|---|
| | 1995 | 2001 | 2002 | 2003* | 1995 | 2003* | 2002/01 | 2003*/02 | 1995-2003* |
| **Total** | **762** | **1,073** | **1,149** | **1,170** | **100** | **100** | **7.2** | **1.8** | **5.5** |
| *From Europe* | *714* | *1,009* | *1,084* | *1,108* | *93.7* | *94.7* | *7.5* | *2.2* | *5.6* |
| Germany | 99 | 143 | 175 | 196 | 13.0 | 16.8 | 22.0 | 12.2 | 8.9 |
| Poland | 262 | 193 | 219 | 189 | 34.4 | 16.2 | 13.5 | -13.7 | -4.0 |
| Belarus | 34 | 167 | 180 | 175 | 4.4 | 14.9 | 7.9 | -3.1 | 22.9 |
| Russian Federation | 98 | 109 | 104 | 108 | 12.9 | 9.3 | -4.1 | 4.1 | 1.2 |
| Latvia | 22 | 49 | 48 | 49 | 2.9 | 4.2 | -1.7 | 1.1 | 10.3 |
| United Kingdom | 19 | 28 | 34 | 47 | 2.5 | 4.0 | 24.3 | 35.3 | 11.9 |
| Finland | .. | 50 | 34 | 41 | | 3.5 | -30.4 | 20.3 | |
| Estonia | 16 | 27 | 28 | 33 | 2.1 | 2.9 | 3.9 | 17.9 | 10.0 |
| Sweden | .. | 31 | 29 | 30 | | 2.5 | -7.8 | 4.0 | |
| Denmark | .. | 23 | 24 | 24 | | 2.1 | 5.5 | 1.2 | |
| Italy | .. | 20 | 19 | 23 | | 2.0 | -6.5 | 24.0 | |
| Norway | .. | 21 | 20 | 20 | | 1.7 | -7.7 | -0.2 | |
| France | .. | 15 | 15 | 19 | | 1.6 | -1.0 | 23.4 | |
| Ukraine | .. | 24 | 28 | 19 | | 1.6 | 20.1 | -34.1 | |
| All Southern Europe | 18 | .. | .. | .. | 2.3 | | | | |
| Netherlands | .. | 8 | 11 | 13 | | 1.1 | 41.8 | 19.2 | |
| Israel | .. | 34 | 36 | 12 | | 1.0 | 4.9 | -66.3 | |
| Czech Rep | .. | 6 | 8 | 10 | | 0.8 | 34.3 | 28.5 | |
| Spain | .. | 4 | 6 | 9 | | 0.8 | 52.6 | 44.4 | |
| Belgium | .. | 5 | 7 | 7 | | 0.6 | 31.1 | -0.5 | |
| Austria | .. | 5 | 6 | 6 | | 0.5 | 33.5 | -0.4 | |
| Switzerland | .. | 6 | 5 | 5 | | 0.4 | -9.1 | -7.9 | |
| Ireland | .. | 2 | 3 | 4 | | 0.3 | 55.8 | 18.2 | |
| Hungary | .. | 9 | 2 | 4 | | 0.3 | -75.0 | 72.0 | |
| Greece | .. | 1 | 2 | 2 | | 0.2 | 25.4 | 39.6 | |
| Other intraregional | 147 | 29 | 39 | 63 | 19.3 | 5.4 | 35.1 | 60.4 | -10.0 |
| *From other regions* | *48* | *64* | *65* | *62* | *6.3* | *5.3* | *1.8* | *-4.3* | *3.4* |
| United States | 29 | 38 | 39 | 35 | 3.8 | 3.0 | 2.4 | -9.1 | 2.3 |
| Japan | .. | 12 | 11 | 14 | | 1.2 | -10.2 | 28.0 | |
| All Asia | 10 | .. | .. | .. | 1.3 | | | | |
| Canada | 3 | 3 | 4 | 3 | 0.5 | 0.3 | 8.9 | -10.9 | -0.9 |
| All Oceania | 1 | 2 | 2 | 3 | 0.2 | 0.2 | -2.2 | 31.8 | 9.5 |
| All South America | 1 | 1 | 1 | 2 | 0.2 | 0.2 | 29.8 | 85.6 | 3.5 |
| China | .. | 1 | 3 | 1 | | 0.1 | 178.3 | -57.7 | |
| All Africa | 2 | 1 | 1 | 1 | 0.3 | 0.1 | 18.6 | -0.2 | -9.5 |
| Other North America | 0 | 0 | 1 | 0 | 0.0 | 0.0 | 190.3 | -62.9 | 3.6 |
| Other Asia | .. | 6 | 4 | 3 | | 0.3 | -26.1 | -28.9 | |

Source: World Tourism Organization (WTO) © (Data as collected by WTO December 2004)

# III.3.13 Poland — Central and Eastern Europe

## Profile

# Poland

**Europe**
**Central and Eastern Europe**

| | |
|---|---|
| Capital | Warsaw |
| Year of entry in WTO | 1976 |
| Area (1000 km²) | 323 |
| Population (2003, million) | 38.6 |
| Gross Domestic Product (GDP) (2003, euro million) | 221,551 |
| GDP per capita (2003, euro) | 5,710 |
| GDP growth (real, %) | |

'-> 2002: 1.4; 2003: 3.8; 2004*: 5.8; 2005*: 5.1

| | 2001 | 2002 | 2003* | 2002/2001 | 2003*/2002 |
|---|---|---|---|---|---|
| **International Arrivals** | | | | | |
| Visitors (1000) | 61,431 | 50,735 | 52,130 | -17.4 | 2.7 |
| Tourists (overnight visitors) (1000) | 15,000 | 13,980 | 13,720 | -6.8 | -1.9 |
| - per 100 of inhabitants | 39 | 36 | 36 | | |
| Same-day visitors (1000) | 46,431 | 36,755 | 38,410 | -20.8 | 4.5 |
| **Tourism accommodation** | | | | | |
| Number of rooms | 60,658 | 65,658 | 68,588 | 8.2 | 4.5 |
| *Nights spent in collective establishments (1000)* | 45,947 | 44,212 | 45,348 | -3.8 | 2.6 |
| by non-residents (inbound tourism) | 6,991 | 7,085 | 7,828 | 1.3 | 10.5 |
| by residents (domestic tourism) | 38,956 | 37,127 | 37,520 | -4.7 | 1.1 |
| *Nights spent in hotels and similar establishments (1000)* | 13,215 | 13,381 | 14,263 | 1.3 | 6.6 |
| by non-residents (inbound tourism) | 4,918 | 4,999 | 5,450 | 1.6 | 9.0 |
| by residents (domestic tourism) | 8,297 | 8,382 | 8,813 | 1.0 | 5.1 |
| **Outbound Tourism** | | | | | |
| Trips abroad (1000) | 53,122 | 45,043 | 38,730 | -15.2 | -14.0 |
| - per 100 of inhabitants | 138 | 117 | 100 | | |
| **Receipts and Expenditure for International Tourism** | | | | | |
| International Tourism Receipts (euro million) | 5,030 | 4,817 | 4,303 | -4.2 | -10.7 |
| - per Tourist Arrival (euro) | 335 | 345 | 314 | 2.7 | -9.0 |
| - per Visitor Arrival (euro) | 82 | 95 | 83 | 15.9 | -13.1 |
| - per capita (euro) | 130 | 125 | 111 | | |
| International Fare Receipts (euro million) | 514 | 734 | 702 | 42.6 | -4.3 |
| International Tourism Expenditure (euro million) | 3,784 | 3,575 | 2,962 | -5.5 | -17.1 |
| - per trip (euro) | 71 | 79 | 76 | 11.4 | -3.6 |
| - per capita (euro) | 98 | 93 | 77 | | |
| International Fare Expenditure (euro million) | 107 | 181 | 213 | 68.7 | 17.5 |
| △ International Tourism Balance (euro million) | 1,246 | 1,242 | 1,341 | | |
| △ International Fare Balance (euro million) | 407 | 553 | 490 | | |

Source: World Tourism Organization (WTO) (Data as collected by WTO December 2004)

See annex for methodological notes and reference of external sources used.

## Survey

Contributed by *Ministry of Economy, Labour and Social Policy*
www.poland-tourism.pl (promotional)
www.mgpips.gov.pl (institutional/corporate)
www.intur.com.pl (research and data)

## Tourism development and outlook

**Overall evaluation of results**

*Inbound tourism:*
Exchange rates (strong euro) had a positive impact on the number of arrivals, but did not reflect positively on revenues.
The year 2003 was diversified in terms of the tourism business:
- The first half of the year was rather poor;
- During the summer season, there was a substantial improvement with more guests in hotels, more air-passengers and more tourists from the European Union;
- Last quarter: the East European markets went down (due to visas), there were more shopping visits from western and southern neighbors (due to weakening local currency) and the growth in air traffic still continued.

*Domestic tourism:*
In 2003, the tourism activity of Polish residents generally went down:
- The number of holiday trips decreased by 0.8 million (to 17.2 million), however the participation ratio did not change significantly;
- The number of short trips decreased sharply (this is probably due to growing popularity of short one-day visits to attractions);
- The number of trips abroad dropped too (unfavourable impact of exchange rates).

**External factors**

Exchange rates (strong euro).
Visas.
Good weather in the summer, however less hot than in Southern and Western Europe.

**Marketing & promotion**

Marketing activities were carried out in 2003 as set out in two documents, i.e. the "Programme of the Polish Tourist Organisation for the period 2001-2004" and "The Plan of activities for 2003" which was prepared in June 2002.
The Polish Tourist Organisation (PTO) used classic promotional tools in 2003, such as:
- A national stand in 87 international tourist fairs with almost one thousand polish exhibitors;
- 36 workshops for foreign and Polish tour operators;
- Study tours for 364 foreign journalist, 160 VIPs and 772 tour operators;
- Editing of 18 new brochures in 9 languages, altogether over 1.1 million copies.

One of the most important target markets for the PTO is Russia and the Ukraine. A branch office was opened in Moscow.
During the year 2003, regionalization of tourist promotion in Poland has continued. Five new regional tourist offices and over fifteen new local tourist promotion centres were established last year.
Work on the national tourism website were finished by the end of the year.
The PTO has twelve foreign offices which constitute main distribution channels. It is worth noting that promotional activities carried out by the PTO in the countries where there are no branch offices is performed by the Commercial Department of Polish Embassies. This cooperation was considerably enlarged in 2003.

**Outlook 2004**

Exchange rates do not seem to have changed substantially in 2004, so Poland is relatively inexpensive (except in high class hotels).
People are not afraid to fly to Poland, and generally tourists' opinion on safety in Poland have changed for the better (as our surveys show).
Entry into the European Union will be an advantage.
All of the above-mentioned items should improve the inbound tourism performance in 2004. We are particularly expecting more leisure and business visits.
The Polish Gross Domestic Product is growing considerably now, thus domestic and outbound tourism will possibly increase.

## International Meetings Industry (MI)

**Characteristics of supply**

Poland has recently experienced a rapid increase of 4 and 5 star hotels. In 2002, the number of hotels increased by 11 per cent and of this number over 13 per cent are 5 star hotels.
We have noted an increase in the number of organisers and orders in incentive travel.
There are new exhibition and fair centres in Warsaw and Poznan.

**Organisation of promotion**

The promotion of MICE is organised by the convention bureau of Poland, which is a part of the Polish Tourist Organisation. Promotion is also carried out by local convention bureaus in Warsaw <www.warsawtour.pl>, by Wroclaw in Cracow <www.convention.wroclaw.pl> and by local entities in Poznan.

**Collection of statistics on the Meetings Industry?:** no.

**Importance / size**

The Polish Tourist Organisation assesses that the MICE share in incoming tourism to Poland is about 40 per cent in quantitative and qualitative aspects.

**Evolution MI**

The MICE sector in Poland in 2003 increased by 25 per cent compared to 2002. We estimate that the increase in the next 3 years will reach 15-20 per cent per annum.

# International Tourism by Origin

**Poland**

**International Tourist Arrivals in All Accommodation Establishments**

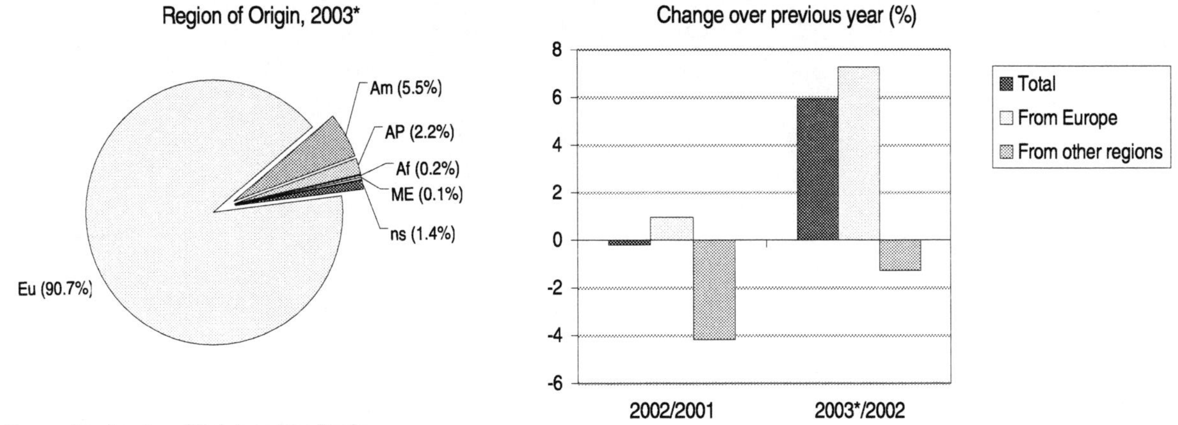


Eu: Europe; Am: Americas; AP: Asia and the Pacific;
Af: Africa; ME: Middle East; ns: not specified



**Poland**

**Nights of International Tourists in All Accommodation Establishments**

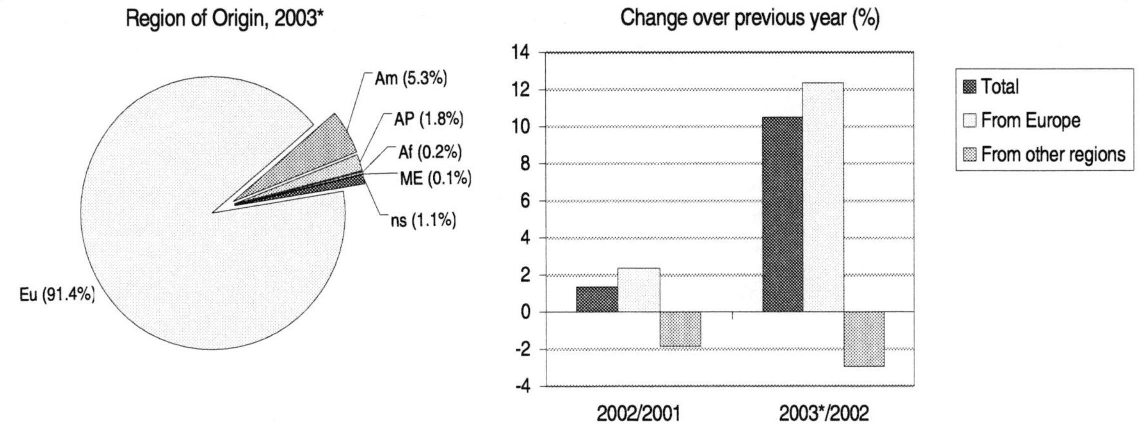


Eu: Europe; Am: Americas; AP: Asia and the Pacific;
Af: Africa; ME: Middle East; ns: not specified

**Poland**

**International Tourist Arrivals in All Accommodation Establishments (by residence)**

| | | | | (thousand) | Market share (%) | | Growth rate (%) | | Average per year (%) |
|---|---|---|---|---|---|---|---|---|---|
| | 1995 | 2001 | 2002 | 2003* | 1995 | 2003* | 2002/01 | 2003*/02 | 1995-2003* |
| **Total** | **3,590** | **3,152** | **3,145** | **3,332** | **100** | **100** | **-0.2** | **5.9** | **-0.9** |
| *From Europe* | *2,926* | *2,791* | *2,818* | *3,023* | *81.5* | *90.7* | *1.0* | *7.3* | *0.4* |
| Germany | 1,017 | 1,084 | 1,090 | 1,167 | 28.3 | 35.0 | 0.5 | 7.1 | 1.7 |
| Russian Federation | 425 | 141 | 163 | 171 | 11.8 | 5.1 | 15.9 | 4.5 | -10.8 |
| United Kingdom | 135 | 166 | 158 | 165 | 3.8 | 4.9 | -5.2 | 4.3 | 2.5 |
| Ukraine | 333 | 196 | 187 | 163 | 9.3 | 4.9 | -4.7 | -12.7 | -8.6 |
| France | 125 | 139 | 133 | 153 | 3.5 | 4.6 | -4.6 | 15.3 | 2.5 |
| Italy | 110 | 129 | 127 | 150 | 3.1 | 4.5 | -1.7 | 18.6 | 4.0 |
| Belarus | 86 | 105 | 111 | 103 | 2.4 | 3.1 | 5.0 | -6.9 | 2.3 |
| Netherlands | 131 | 89 | 91 | 97 | 3.7 | 2.9 | 2.4 | 6.2 | -3.8 |
| Israel | .. | 96 | 100 | 96 | | 2.9 | 4.6 | -3.9 | |
| Denmark | 119 | 70 | 74 | 89 | 3.3 | 2.7 | 6.0 | 19.7 | -3.6 |
| Sweden | 68 | 90 | 85 | 87 | 1.9 | 2.6 | -6.1 | 3.0 | 3.2 |
| Lithuania | 97 | 51 | 54 | 63 | 2.7 | 1.9 | 5.5 | 15.7 | -5.3 |
| Norway | 26 | 46 | 48 | 61 | 0.7 | 1.8 | 6.3 | 25.3 | 11.2 |
| Spain | 21 | 36 | 51 | 58 | 0.6 | 1.7 | 41.3 | 13.4 | 13.3 |
| Austria | 64 | 51 | 48 | 52 | 1.8 | 1.6 | -7.0 | 9.5 | -2.5 |
| Czech Rep | 30 | 44 | 45 | 50 | 0.8 | 1.5 | 0.7 | 12.4 | 6.5 |
| Belgium | 48 | 42 | 43 | 44 | 1.3 | 1.3 | 1.7 | 1.9 | -1.0 |
| Hungary | 20 | 25 | 26 | 37 | 0.6 | 1.1 | 6.3 | 40.6 | 8.0 |
| Finland | 18 | 31 | 29 | 33 | 0.5 | 1.0 | -5.2 | 13.2 | 7.7 |
| Switzerland | 34 | 33 | 28 | 29 | 1.0 | 0.9 | -12.9 | 3.7 | -2.0 |
| Estonia | .. | 23 | 22 | 23 | | 0.7 | -2.4 | 5.4 | |
| Slovakia | 11 | 16 | 18 | 22 | 0.3 | 0.7 | 13.0 | 18.0 | 9.3 |
| Latvia | .. | 9 | 12 | 19 | | 0.6 | 31.6 | 62.1 | |
| Romania | .. | 13 | 10 | 12 | | 0.3 | -25.4 | 19.3 | |
| Ireland | .. | 8 | 8 | 11 | | 0.3 | -2.6 | 33.6 | |
| Other intraregional | 6 | 58 | 58 | 69 | 0.2 | 2.1 | -0.1 | 20.1 | 37.2 |
| *From other regions* | *213* | *279* | *267* | *264* | *5.9* | *7.9* | *-4.2* | *-1.3* | *2.7* |
| United States | 176 | 179 | 161 | 157 | 4.9 | 4.7 | -9.9 | -2.2 | -1.4 |
| Japan | 20 | 29 | 29 | 31 | 0.5 | 0.9 | 1.0 | 9.0 | 6.2 |
| Canada | 17 | 13 | 16 | 15 | 0.5 | 0.4 | 21.4 | -8.6 | -1.7 |
| Korea, Republic of | .. | 9 | 9 | 13 | | 0.4 | 2.2 | 32.9 | |
| Australia | .. | 8 | 9 | 9 | | 0.3 | 6.0 | 6.4 | |
| China | .. | 4 | 5 | 4 | | 0.1 | 13.7 | -17.2 | |
| Mexico | .. | 2 | 2 | 3 | | 0.1 | 30.3 | 37.6 | |
| India | .. | 2 | 2 | 3 | | 0.1 | 2.1 | 47.3 | |
| Algeria | .. | 0 | 0 | 2 | | 0.1 | -24.6 | 389.3 | |
| New Zealand | .. | 1 | 1 | 2 | | 0.0 | -5.1 | 46.2 | |
| Taiwan (pr. of China) | .. | 3 | 2 | 1 | | 0.0 | -38.8 | -42.1 | |
| Argentina | .. | 2 | 1 | 1 | | 0.0 | -55.5 | 47.7 | |
| Vietnam | .. | 1 | 1 | 1 | | 0.0 | -16.2 | 67.9 | |
| Hong Kong (China) | .. | 1 | 1 | 1 | | 0.0 | -13.4 | -7.2 | |
| Korea, D P Rp | .. | 4 | 4 | 1 | | 0.0 | -8.9 | -76.6 | |
| Other interregional | .. | 20 | 24 | 20 | | 0.6 | 19.8 | -17.8 | |
| *Other World/Not specified* | *452* | *81* | *60* | *45* | *12.6* | *1.4* | *-26.1* | *-24.6* | *-25.0* |

Source: World Tourism Organization (WTO) © (Data as collected by WTO December 2004)

**Poland**

**Nights of International Tourists in All Accommodation Establishments (by residence)**

| | | | | (thousand) | Market share (%) | | Growth rate (%) | | Average per year (%) |
|---|---|---|---|---|---|---|---|---|---|
| | 1995 | 2001 | 2002 | 2003* | 1995 | 2003* | 2002/01 | 2003*/02 | 1995-2003* |
| **Total** | .. | **6,991** | **7,085** | **7,828** | | **100** | **1.4** | **10.5** | |
| *From Europe* | .. | *6,221* | *6,368* | *7,155* | | *91.4* | *2.4* | *12.4* | |
| Germany | .. | 2,852 | 3,016 | 3,460 | | 44.2 | 5.8 | 14.7 | |
| United Kingdom | .. | 365 | 350 | 351 | | 4.5 | -3.9 | 0.3 | |
| Ukraine | .. | 387 | 355 | 351 | | 4.5 | -8.1 | -1.3 | |
| Italy | .. | 260 | 266 | 316 | | 4.0 | 2.2 | 18.6 | |
| France | .. | 272 | 262 | 307 | | 3.9 | -3.6 | 17.4 | |
| Russian Federation | .. | 253 | 267 | 290 | | 3.7 | 5.4 | 8.8 | |
| Denmark | .. | 175 | 188 | 208 | | 2.7 | 7.9 | 10.5 | |
| Netherlands | .. | 174 | 179 | 192 | | 2.5 | 2.6 | 7.4 | |
| Israel | .. | 171 | 176 | 189 | | 2.4 | 2.9 | 7.4 | |
| Belarus | .. | 176 | 179 | 186 | | 2.4 | 1.5 | 4.2 | |
| Sweden | .. | 181 | 179 | 182 | | 2.3 | -1.1 | 1.4 | |
| Norway | .. | 89 | 97 | 124 | | 1.6 | 9.0 | 28.6 | |
| Spain | .. | 74 | 98 | 116 | | 1.5 | 33.1 | 18.2 | |
| Austria | .. | 95 | 85 | 99 | | 1.3 | -10.3 | 15.4 | |
| Czech Rep | .. | 89 | 85 | 96 | | 1.2 | -4.0 | 12.4 | |
| Lithuania | .. | 82 | 87 | 95 | | 1.2 | 5.3 | 9.3 | |
| Belgium | .. | 84 | 85 | 89 | | 1.1 | 1.3 | 3.8 | |
| Hungary | .. | 54 | 55 | 80 | | 1.0 | 1.5 | 46.4 | |
| Finland | .. | 64 | 60 | 70 | | 0.9 | -6.2 | 17.1 | |
| Switzerland | .. | 59 | 53 | 54 | | 0.7 | -8.8 | 1.3 | |
| Slovakia | .. | 35 | 34 | 38 | | 0.5 | -1.6 | 11.6 | |
| Latvia | .. | 14 | 18 | 30 | | 0.4 | 28.3 | 70.6 | |
| Estonia | .. | 27 | 25 | 29 | | 0.4 | -6.0 | 14.4 | |
| Portugal | .. | 25 | 22 | 25 | | 0.3 | -11.4 | 10.4 | |
| Ireland | .. | 18 | 17 | 24 | | 0.3 | -2.8 | 35.9 | |
| Other intraregional | .. | 147 | 127 | 153 | | 2.0 | -13.6 | 20.4 | |
| *From other regions* | .. | *617* | *605* | *588* | | *7.5* | *-1.8* | *-2.9* | |
| United States | .. | 409 | 377 | 353 | | 4.5 | -7.7 | -6.3 | |
| Japan | .. | 56 | 61 | 61 | | 0.8 | 10.0 | -0.2 | |
| Canada | .. | 33 | 38 | 40 | | 0.5 | 15.4 | 5.1 | |
| Australia | .. | 17 | 18 | 19 | | 0.2 | 3.8 | 8.3 | |
| Korea, Republic of | .. | 12 | 13 | 16 | | 0.2 | 5.6 | 24.4 | |
| China | .. | 11 | 12 | 9 | | 0.1 | 9.9 | -19.0 | |
| India | .. | 6 | 6 | 8 | | 0.1 | 0.1 | 38.7 | |
| Mexico | .. | 3 | 5 | 7 | | 0.1 | 35.6 | 55.8 | |
| Brazil | .. | 7 | 7 | 7 | | 0.1 | 0.8 | -11.2 | |
| New Zealand | .. | 2 | 2 | 3 | | 0.0 | 4.8 | 34.1 | |
| Egypt | .. | 2 | 2 | 3 | | 0.0 | -17.4 | 86.3 | |
| Taiwan (pr. of China) | .. | 4 | 3 | 3 | | 0.0 | -36.5 | 8.4 | |
| Argentina | .. | 3 | 2 | 3 | | 0.0 | -46.2 | 44.9 | |
| Vietnam | .. | 2 | 2 | 3 | | 0.0 | -29.4 | 59.3 | |
| South Africa | .. | 3 | 2 | 2 | | 0.0 | -43.0 | 16.8 | |
| Other interregional | .. | 45 | 56 | 49 | | 0.6 | 25.6 | -12.4 | |
| *Other World/Not specified* | .. | *152* | *111* | *86* | | *1.1* | *-26.8* | *-23.1* | |

Source: World Tourism Organization (WTO) © (Data as collected by WTO December 2004)

# III.3.14 Republic of Moldova — Central and Eastern Europe

## Profile

# Republic of Moldova

Europe
Central and Eastern Europe

| | |
|---|---|
| Capital | Chisinau |
| Year of entry in WTO | 1993 |
| Area (1000 km²) | 34 |
| Population (2003, million) | 4.4 |
| Gross Domestic Product (GDP) (2003, euro million) | 2,062 |
| GDP per capita (2003, euro) | 567 |
| GDP growth (real, %) | |
| '-> 2002: 7.8; 2003: 6.3; 2004*: 5.0; 2005*: 4.0 | |

| | 2001 | 2002 | 2003* | 2002/2001 | 2003*/2002 |
|---|---|---|---|---|---|
| **International Arrivals** | | | | | |
| Visitors (1000) | 16 | 20 | 24 | 28.5 | 17.0 |
| Tourists (overnight visitors) (1000) | 16 | 18 | 21 | 12.5 | 16.7 |
| - per 100 of inhabitants | 0 | 0 | 0 | | |
| Same-day visitors (1000) | 0 | 2 | 3 | 900.0 | 50.0 |
| **Tourism accommodation** | | | | | |
| Number of rooms | 2,905 | 2,806 | 2,559 | -3.4 | -8.8 |
| *Nights spent in collective establishments (1000)* | | | | | |
| by residents (domestic tourism) | 253 | 316 | 400 | 24.9 | 26.6 |
| *Nights spent in hotels and similar establishments (1000)* | | | | | |
| by non-residents (inbound tourism) | 64 | 76 | 84 | 18.8 | 10.5 |
| **Outbound Tourism** | | | | | |
| Trips abroad (1000) | 30 | 52 | 67 | 73.3 | 28.8 |
| - per 100 of inhabitants | 1 | 1 | 2 | | |
| **Receipts and Expenditure for International Tourism** | | | | | |
| International Tourism Receipts (euro million) | 42 | 56 | 61 | 32.2 | 9.9 |
| - per Tourist Arrival (euro) | 2,639 | 3,101 | 2,921 | 17.5 | -5.8 |
| - per Visitor Arrival (euro) | 2,691 | 2,769 | 2,599 | 2.9 | -6.1 |
| - per capita (euro) | 10 | 13 | 14 | | |
| International Fare Receipts (euro million) | 21 | 25 | 26 | 19.4 | 7.6 |
| International Tourism Expenditure (euro million) | 76 | 95 | 103 | 25.2 | 8.1 |
| - per trip (euro) | 2,526 | 1,825 | 1,531 | -27.8 | -16.1 |
| - per capita (euro) | 17 | 21 | 23 | | |
| International Fare Expenditure (euro million) | 16 | 16 | 20 | -3.8 | 28.5 |
| △ International Tourism Balance (euro million) | -34 | -39 | -41 | | |
| △ International Fare Balance (euro million) | 4 | 9 | 6 | | |

Source: World Tourism Organization (WTO) (Data as collected by WTO December 2004)

See annex for methodological notes and reference of external sources used.

# International Tourism by Origin

**Republic of Moldova**

**International Visitor Arrivals at Frontiers**

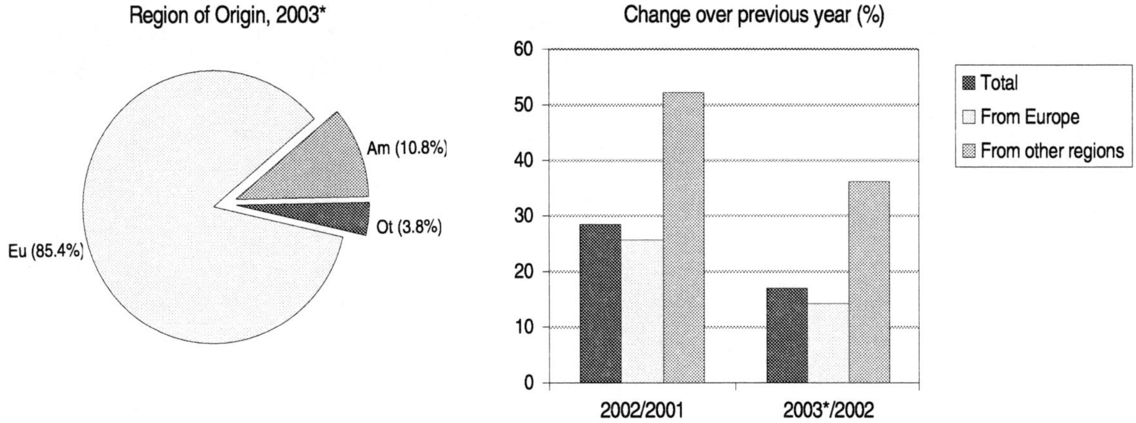


Eu: Europe; Am: Americas;
Ot: Other;

Source: World Tourism Organization (WTO) ©

**Republic of Moldova**
**International Visitor Arrivals at Frontiers (by nationality)**

| | | | | (thousand) | Market share (%) | | Growth rate (%) | | Average per year (%) |
|---|---|---|---|---|---|---|---|---|---|
| | 1995 | 2001 | 2002 | 2003* | 1995 | 2003* | 2002/01 | 2003*/02 | 1995-2003* |
| **Total** | **33** | **16** | **20** | **24** | **100** | **100** | **28.5** | **17.0** | **-4.0** |
| *From Europe* | *31* | *14* | *18* | *20* | *95.9* | *85.4* | *25.7* | *14.3* | *-5.4* |
| Turkey | 1 | 2 | 3 | 4 | 3.5 | 16.8 | 19.3 | 38.2 | 16.9 |
| Ukraine | 4 | 2 | 3 | 3 | 13.1 | 13.9 | 30.3 | 11.4 | -3.3 |
| Russian Federation | 11 | 2 | 4 | 3 | 34.0 | 13.9 | 59.2 | -13.0 | -14.2 |
| Romania | 6 | 2 | 2 | 2 | 18.3 | 10.1 | -7.1 | 23.4 | -10.9 |
| Belarus | 2 | 1 | 1 | 1 | 5.2 | 3.2 | 41.5 | 4.2 | -9.7 |
| Germany | 1 | 1 | 1 | 1 | 2.3 | 3.0 | 0.4 | 28.0 | -0.5 |
| Italy | 1 | 1 | 0 | 1 | 1.8 | 3.0 | -14.2 | 43.0 | 1.9 |
| Bulgaria | 2 | 0 | 0 | 1 | 5.1 | 2.6 | 10.5 | 91.7 | -11.7 |
| Netherlands | 0 | 0 | 0 | 1 | 0.3 | 2.2 | 28.8 | 228.6 | 24.8 |
| Austria | 0 | 0 | 0 | 0 | 0.2 | 1.9 | -40.0 | 615.9 | 26.2 |
| Israel | 0 | 0 | 0 | 0 | 1.2 | 1.7 | 43.0 | -2.9 | 0.8 |
| Switzerland | 0 | 0 | 0 | 0 | 0.1 | 1.5 | -30.6 | 1328.0 | 33.2 |
| Poland | 0 | 0 | 0 | 0 | 0.4 | 1.4 | 105.1 | -34.2 | 12.0 |
| France | 0 | 0 | 0 | 0 | 0.3 | 1.3 | -41.1 | 70.4 | 14.7 |
| Cyprus | 0 | 0 | 1 | 0 | 0.3 | 1.1 | 61.1 | -48.2 | 15.0 |
| Sweden | 0 | 0 | 0 | 0 | 0.2 | 1.1 | 30.0 | 60.9 | 19.1 |
| United Kingdom | 0 | 0 | 0 | 0 | 0.6 | 0.9 | 16.6 | 15.3 | 1.0 |
| Hungary | 0 | 0 | 0 | 0 | 0.8 | 0.7 | 25.0 | 6.9 | -5.8 |
| Serbia & Montenegro | .. | 0 | 0 | 0 | | 0.5 | -24.7 | 110.9 | |
| Lithuania | 0 | 0 | 0 | 0 | 0.7 | 0.5 | -34.1 | 38.6 | -7.9 |
| Greece | 0 | 0 | 0 | 0 | 0.8 | 0.4 | 21.2 | -14.2 | -11.5 |
| Czech Rep | 0 | 0 | 0 | 0 | 0.3 | 0.4 | 154.5 | -55.4 | 1.2 |
| Estonia | 0 | 0 | 0 | 0 | 0.1 | 0.3 | -49.1 | 177.8 | 13.1 |
| Norway | 0 | 0 | 0 | 0 | 0.2 | 0.3 | 10.0 | 56.8 | 1.1 |
| Spain | 0 | 0 | 0 | 0 | 0.1 | 0.2 | 107.0 | -50.8 | 3.8 |
| Other intraregional | 2 | 1 | 1 | 1 | 6.0 | 2.3 | 61.1 | -45.5 | -14.8 |
| *From other regions* | *1* | *2* | *3* | *3* | *4.1* | *14.6* | *52.2* | *36.2* | *12.5* |
| United States | 1 | 1 | 2 | 2 | 1.9 | 10.6 | 59.2 | 46.1 | 18.8 |
| Lebanon | 0 | 0 | 0 | 0 | 0.0 | 1.4 | 464.1 | 51.4 | 46.1 |
| Japan | 0 | 0 | 0 | 0 | 0.4 | 0.6 | 35.6 | 17.8 | -0.3 |
| Syrian Arab Republic | 0 | 0 | 0 | 0 | 0.1 | 0.4 | 280.0 | 352.6 | 16.7 |
| China | 0 | 0 | 0 | 0 | 0.2 | 0.4 | 22.9 | -65.6 | 2.3 |
| Canada | 0 | 0 | 0 | 0 | 0.1 | 0.2 | 23.8 | -5.8 | 4.3 |
| Jordan | 0 | 0 | 0 | 0 | 0.1 | 0.2 | 0.0 | 370.0 | -0.3 |
| Sierra Leone | .. | .. | 0 | .. | | | | | |
| Egypt | 0 | 0 | 0 | 0 | 0.0 | 0.1 | -28.6 | 420.0 | 11.4 |
| Australia | 0 | 0 | 0 | 0 | 0.0 | 0.1 | -40.0 | 216.7 | 3.9 |
| Korea, Republic of | 0 | 0 | 0 | 0 | 0.1 | 0.1 | 1300.0 | 35.7 | 0.0 |
| Saudi Arabia | .. | 0 | 0 | 0 | | 0.1 | 700.0 | 87.5 | |
| Taiwan (pr. of China) | .. | .. | 0 | 0 | | 0.1 | | 7.7 | |
| Sudan | .. | .. | 0 | 0 | | 0.1 | | 366.7 | |
| India | 0 | 0 | 0 | 0 | 0.1 | 0.1 | -76.0 | 100.0 | -12.8 |
| Costa Rica | .. | .. | 0 | .. | | | | | |
| Kuwait | .. | 0 | 0 | 0 | | 0.0 | 200.0 | 233.3 | |
| Other interregional | 0 | 0 | 0 | 0 | 0.9 | 0.4 | -61.5 | 35.5 | -14.6 |

Source: World Tourism Organization (WTO) © (Data as collected by WTO December 2004)

# III.3.15 Romania — Central and Eastern Europe

## Profile

# Romania

| | |
|---|---|
| Capital | Bucharest |
| Year of entry in WTO | 1975 |
| Area (1000 km²) | 238 |
| Population (2003, million) | 22.4 |
| Gross Domestic Product (GDP) (2003, euro million) | 60,228 |
| GDP per capita (2003, euro) | 2,700 |
| GDP growth (real, %) | |
| '-> 2002: 5.0; 2003: 4.9; 2004*: 5.0; 2005*: 5.0 | |

**Europe**
**Central and Eastern Europe**

| | 2001 | 2002 | 2003* | 2002/2001 | 2003*/2002 |
|---|---|---|---|---|---|
| **International Arrivals** | | | | | |
| Visitors (1000) | 4,938 | 4,794 | .. | -2.9 | |
| Tourists (overnight visitors) (1000) | 3,300 | 3,204 | 3,739 | -2.9 | 16.7 |
| - per 100 of inhabitants | 15 | 14 | 17 | | |
| Same-day visitors (1000) | 1,638 | 1,590 | .. | -2.9 | |
| **Tourism accommodation** | | | | | |
| Number of rooms | 95,226 | 95,062 | .. | -0.2 | |
| *Nights spent in collective establishments (1000)* | 18,122 | 17,277 | | -4.7 | |
| by non-residents (inbound tourism) | 2,391 | 2,534 | .. | 6.0 | |
| by residents (domestic tourism) | 15,731 | 14,743 | .. | -6.3 | |
| *Nights spent in hotels and similar establishments (1000)* | 16,372 | 15,840 | | -3.2 | |
| by non-residents (inbound tourism) | 2,301 | 2,471 | .. | 7.4 | |
| by residents (domestic tourism) | 14,071 | 13,369 | .. | -5.0 | |
| **Outbound Tourism** | | | | | |
| Trips abroad (1000) | 6,408 | 5,757 | .. | -10.2 | |
| - per 100 of inhabitants | 29 | 26 | .. | | |
| **Receipts and Expenditure for International Tourism** | | | | | |
| International Tourism Receipts (euro million) | 392 | 374 | 475 | -4.6 | 27.0 |
| - per Tourist Arrival (euro) | 119 | 117 | 127 | -1.7 | 8.8 |
| - per Visitor Arrival (euro) | 79 | 78 | .. | -1.7 | |
| - per capita (euro) | 17 | 17 | 21 | | |
| International Fare Receipts (euro million) | 62 | 73 | 78 | 17.6 | 7.8 |
| International Tourism Expenditure (euro million) | 488 | 439 | 506 | -10.0 | 15.2 |
| - per trip (euro) | 76 | 76 | .. | 0.2 | |
| - per capita (euro) | 22 | 20 | 23 | | |
| International Fare Expenditure (euro million) | 28 | 58 | 98 | 106.2 | 69.4 |
| △ International Tourism Balance (euro million) | -96 | -65 | -31 | | |
| △ International Fare Balance (euro million) | 34 | 15 | -20 | | |

Source: World Tourism Organization (WTO) (Data as collected by WTO December 2004)

See annex for methodological notes and reference of external sources used.

# Survey

Contributed by *Ministry of Tourism*
www.mtromania.ro ; www.discoveringromania.ro (promotional)
www. mtromania.ro (institutional/corporate)

## Tourism development and outlook

**Overall evaluation of results**

The number of foreign visitors in 2003 registered a growth of 17 per cent, compared to the previous year.
Domestic tourism increased by 2.7 per cent. The main determining factors were as follows:

- The completion of the privatisation program in 2002;
- The increasing quality in tourism services achieved by training in human resource programmes;
- Active promotion for the domestic market;
- The increasing number of entertainment at the seaside (a new aqua park with a capacity of 3 thousand people per day, aquatic sports, new clubs, restaurants and others);
- Enlargement of the winter season. 2002 was the first year when artificial snow was used on Romanian slopes.

**Supply**

The number of accommodation units has increased with 231 new establishments. The hotel bed capacity increased in 2003 by 0.5 per cent.

**Tourism policy**

Institutional organization.
Training courses.
Human resource development.
Romanian and foreign investment.
Public-Private partnership.

**Marketing & promotion**

The main activities in the Marketing and Promotion Plan are the following:

- Participating at major international tourism fairs;
- Permanently adapting the form and content of advertising material;
- Organizing documentary trips for mass-media representatives and tour operators;
- Creating special tourist areas of international standard;
- Creating special promotional events in diferent countries all over Europe;
- Development and modernization of the tourism base.

**Outlook 2004**

We expect an increase of approximately 10 per cent in international arrivals each year.
The main target countries where we are intensifying our efforts of promotion are the United States of America, Japan, Germany, Italy, Spain, France, the United Kingdom and China.
We shall intensify the organising of domestic cultural tourism events to better promote Romania. At the same time, we shall continue inviting foreign mass-media representatives to promote the different tourism regions of Romania.

## International Meetings Industry (MI)

**Characteristics of supply** The most important Romanian company for organising conventions is the "Romanian Convention Bureau" <www.conventionbureau.ro>.

**Collection of statistics on the Meetings Industry?:** yes.

# International Tourism by Origin

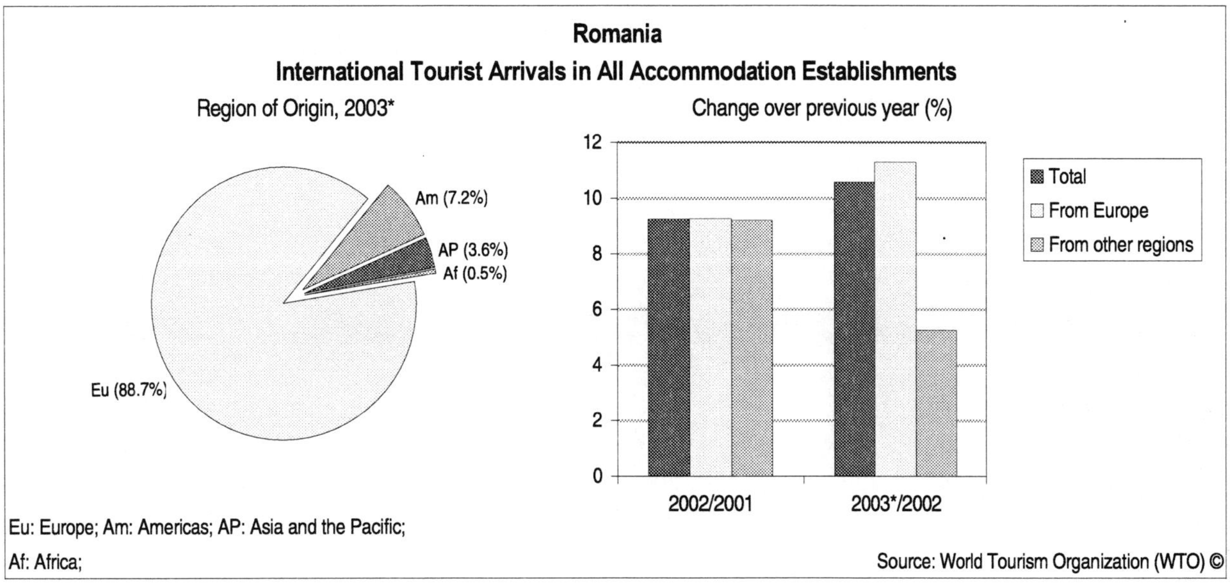


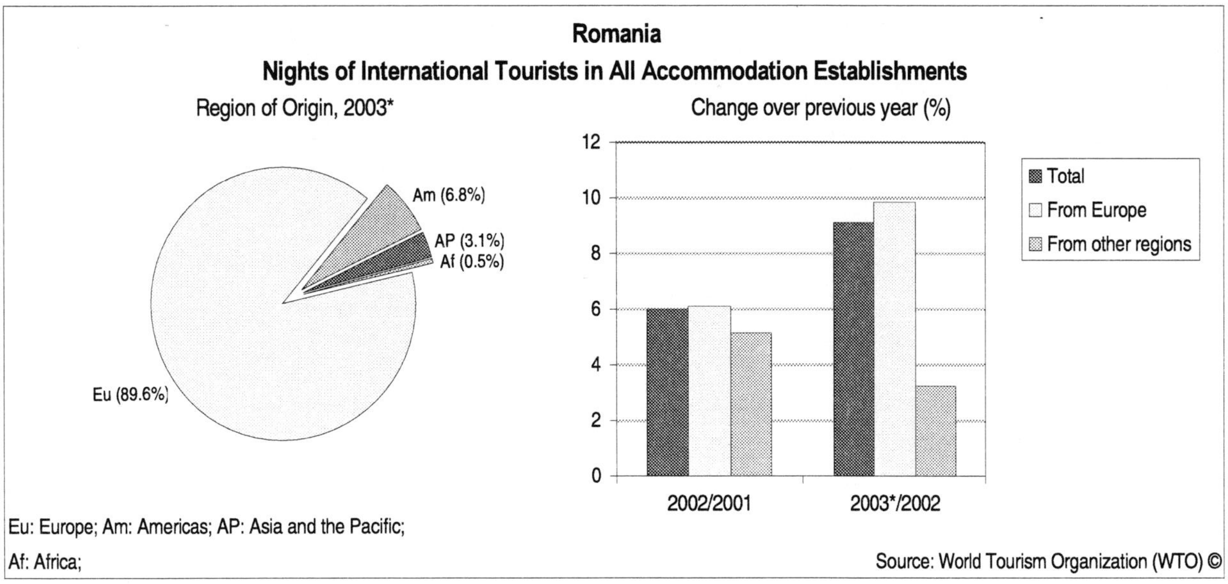

**Romania**

**International Tourist Arrivals in All Accommodation Establishments (by residence)**

| | | | | (thousand) | Market share (%) | | Growth rate (%) | | Average per year (%) |
|---|---|---|---|---|---|---|---|---|---|
| | 1995 | 2001 | 2002 | 2003* | 1995 | 2003* | 2002/01 | 2003*/02 | 1995-2003* |
| **Total** | **766** | **915** | **999** | **1,105** | **100** | **100** | **9.3** | **10.6** | **4.7** |
| *From Europe* | *675* | *806* | *881* | *980* | *88.1* | *88.7* | *9.3* | *11.3* | *4.8* |
| Italy | 77 | 124 | 140 | 161 | 10.0 | 14.6 | 13.0 | 15.0 | 9.7 |
| Germany | 86 | 122 | 135 | 154 | 11.2 | 14.0 | 10.5 | 14.3 | 7.6 |
| France | 52 | 71 | 84 | 93 | 6.8 | 8.4 | 19.3 | 10.2 | 7.4 |
| Hungary | 36 | 51 | 63 | 81 | 4.7 | 7.3 | 24.5 | 27.8 | 10.6 |
| United Kingdom | 35 | 48 | 54 | 66 | 4.6 | 6.0 | 13.9 | 22.4 | 8.3 |
| Israel | 56 | 75 | 69 | 63 | 7.3 | 5.7 | -8.6 | -7.8 | 1.5 |
| Austria | 25 | 34 | 35 | 41 | 3.2 | 3.7 | 4.5 | 15.6 | 6.5 |
| Netherlands | 19 | 30 | 33 | 32 | 2.4 | 2.9 | 8.1 | -1.6 | 7.0 |
| Spain | 22 | 24 | 29 | 31 | 2.9 | 2.8 | 21.3 | 9.0 | 4.6 |
| Rep Moldova | 79 | 30 | 30 | 29 | 10.3 | 2.7 | -2.2 | -0.5 | -11.6 |
| Turkey | 22 | 27 | 28 | 27 | 2.8 | 2.5 | 0.9 | -1.1 | 2.9 |
| Greece | 19 | 20 | 21 | 24 | 2.5 | 2.2 | 4.9 | 16.4 | 2.9 |
| Switzerland | 8 | 16 | 18 | 18 | 1.1 | 1.6 | 12.4 | -0.7 | 9.6 |
| Belgium | 12 | 15 | 16 | 16 | 1.5 | 1.4 | 11.6 | -3.9 | 3.6 |
| Poland | 5 | 9 | 10 | 14 | 0.7 | 1.2 | 12.7 | 32.5 | 13.1 |
| Russian Federation | 17 | 10 | 11 | 13 | 2.2 | 1.2 | 10.0 | 20.2 | -2.9 |
| Denmark | 8 | 11 | 12 | 13 | 1.0 | 1.2 | 8.8 | 6.2 | 7.1 |
| Sweden | 10 | 10 | 12 | 12 | 1.3 | 1.1 | 23.5 | 0.3 | 2.8 |
| Serbia & Montenegro | 11 | 16 | 10 | 11 | 1.4 | 1.0 | -40.0 | 14.7 | 0.3 |
| Bulgaria | 10 | 9 | 9 | 11 | 1.3 | 1.0 | 0.4 | 22.6 | 1.1 |
| Czech Rep | 5 | 7 | 9 | 10 | 0.7 | 0.9 | 21.0 | 20.3 | 8.7 |
| Norway | 8 | 8 | 7 | 9 | 1.0 | 0.8 | -5.5 | 21.7 | 2.4 |
| Ukraine | 18 | 8 | 9 | 9 | 2.3 | 0.8 | 19.4 | -2.5 | -8.5 |
| Ireland | 3 | 4 | 4 | 5 | 0.4 | 0.4 | 15.6 | 20.4 | 4.7 |
| Slovakia | 3 | 4 | 4 | 4 | 0.4 | 0.4 | 13.7 | -1.8 | 3.8 |
| Other intraregional | 31 | 26 | 30 | 32 | 4.0 | 2.9 | 13.6 | 9.7 | 0.7 |
| *From other regions* | *91* | *108* | *118* | *125* | *11.9* | *11.3* | *9.2* | *5.3* | *4.0* |
| United States | 38 | 55 | 58 | 67 | 5.0 | 6.1 | 6.1 | 14.7 | 7.3 |
| Japan | 7 | 15 | 18 | 18 | 1.0 | 1.7 | 22.0 | -0.3 | 12.1 |
| Canada | 5 | 6 | 8 | 8 | 0.6 | 0.7 | 33.8 | 0.8 | 6.4 |
| All Africa | 5 | 4 | 5 | 5 | 0.6 | 0.5 | 15.6 | 11.9 | 1.2 |
| China | 4 | 3 | 4 | 4 | 0.5 | 0.3 | 31.3 | -14.9 | -1.0 |
| All Oceania | 2 | 4 | 4 | 4 | 0.3 | 0.3 | -0.7 | -7.9 | 6.6 |
| All South America | 2 | 3 | 2 | 2 | 0.3 | 0.2 | -26.7 | -6.4 | -0.1 |
| All Central America | 2 | 2 | 2 | 2 | 0.2 | 0.2 | -4.1 | -11.7 | 1.9 |
| Other Asia | 26 | 16 | 16 | 15 | 3.4 | 1.3 | 4.0 | -9.7 | -7.0 |

Source: World Tourism Organization (WTO) © (Data as collected by WTO December 2004)

**Romania**

**Nights of International Tourists in All Accommodation Establishments (by residence)**

| | | | | (thousand) | Market share (%) | | Growth rate (%) | | Average per year (%) |
|---|---|---|---|---|---|---|---|---|---|
| | 1995 | 2001 | 2002 | 2003* | 1995 | 2003* | 2002/01 | 2003*/02 | 1995-2003* |
| **Total** | **2,381** | **2,391** | **2,534** | **2,766** | **100** | **100** | **6.0** | **9.1** | **1.9** |
| *From Europe* | *2,174* | *2,126* | *2,256* | *2,478* | *91.3* | *89.6* | *6.1* | *9.9* | *1.6* |
| Germany | 371 | 451 | 498 | 534 | 15.6 | 19.3 | 10.4 | 7.3 | 4.7 |
| Italy | 186 | 280 | 317 | 351 | 7.8 | 12.7 | 13.2 | 10.7 | 8.3 |
| France | 157 | 182 | 198 | 219 | 6.6 | 7.9 | 8.7 | 10.7 | 4.2 |
| Israel | 262 | 239 | 187 | 175 | 11.0 | 6.3 | -21.7 | -6.3 | -4.9 |
| Hungary | 84 | 118 | 126 | 169 | 3.5 | 6.1 | 6.9 | 34.3 | 9.2 |
| United Kingdom | 153 | 106 | 136 | 158 | 6.4 | 5.7 | 29.1 | 16.0 | 0.4 |
| Austria | 56 | 64 | 67 | 79 | 2.4 | 2.9 | 4.5 | 17.9 | 4.4 |
| Rep Moldova | 217 | 70 | 75 | 77 | 9.1 | 2.8 | 7.7 | 1.7 | -12.2 |
| Netherlands | 67 | 81 | 85 | 72 | 2.8 | 2.6 | 5.3 | -15.4 | 0.9 |
| Turkey | 45 | 64 | 59 | 62 | 1.9 | 2.2 | -7.9 | 4.9 | 4.1 |
| Spain | 45 | 40 | 52 | 57 | 1.9 | 2.0 | 28.0 | 9.3 | 3.0 |
| Russian Federation | 76 | 30 | 34 | 55 | 3.2 | 2.0 | 12.7 | 62.6 | -3.9 |
| Greece | 57 | 47 | 48 | 53 | 2.4 | 1.9 | 2.0 | 10.7 | -0.9 |
| Norway | 44 | 51 | 38 | 47 | 1.9 | 1.7 | -25.8 | 23.8 | 0.8 |
| Denmark | 31 | 35 | 38 | 41 | 1.3 | 1.5 | 6.7 | 8.7 | 3.5 |
| Belgium | 45 | 44 | 41 | 39 | 1.9 | 1.4 | -5.2 | -5.0 | -1.6 |
| Sweden | 46 | 26 | 38 | 38 | 1.9 | 1.4 | 48.1 | -0.3 | -2.3 |
| Poland | 10 | 18 | 20 | 36 | 0.4 | 1.3 | 10.4 | 82.7 | 16.9 |
| Switzerland | 20 | 25 | 29 | 32 | 0.9 | 1.2 | 13.6 | 11.7 | 5.8 |
| Serbia & Montenegro | 19 | 30 | 20 | 23 | 0.8 | 0.8 | -32.2 | 13.0 | 2.2 |
| Czech Rep | 29 | 14 | 18 | 22 | 1.2 | 0.8 | 27.0 | 25.2 | -3.2 |
| Bulgaria | 19 | 17 | 17 | 22 | 0.8 | 0.8 | -4.3 | 33.4 | 1.7 |
| Ukraine | 40 | 19 | 22 | 22 | 1.7 | 0.8 | 15.4 | 0.8 | -7.1 |
| Ireland | 8 | 8 | 9 | 11 | 0.3 | 0.4 | 8.1 | 28.9 | 4.5 |
| Slovakia | 13 | 7 | 10 | 10 | 0.5 | 0.4 | 32.8 | 7.6 | -2.7 |
| Other intraregional | 75 | 61 | 77 | 74 | 3.1 | 2.7 | 26.4 | -2.9 | -0.1 |
| *From other regions* | *206* | *264* | *278* | *287* | *8.7* | *10.4* | *5.1* | *3.2* | *4.2* |
| United States | 87 | 132 | 144 | 158 | 3.6 | 5.7 | 8.9 | 10.4 | 7.8 |
| Japan | 15 | 27 | 35 | 32 | 0.6 | 1.1 | 29.3 | -9.4 | 9.8 |
| Canada | 13 | 14 | 18 | 19 | 0.5 | 0.7 | 29.8 | 4.1 | 5.2 |
| All Africa | 13 | 16 | 12 | 15 | 0.5 | 0.5 | -25.8 | 21.7 | 2.0 |
| China | 10 | 7 | 8 | 7 | 0.4 | 0.3 | 11.5 | -14.5 | -4.6 |
| All Oceania | 4 | 8 | 7 | 7 | 0.2 | 0.2 | -7.5 | -5.4 | 6.8 |
| All South America | 5 | 9 | 5 | 5 | 0.2 | 0.2 | -40.8 | 5.5 | 0.8 |
| All Central America | 4 | 4 | 4 | 4 | 0.2 | 0.1 | -5.0 | -3.0 | 1.0 |
| Other Asia | 56 | 47 | 44 | 40 | 2.4 | 1.4 | -5.6 | -10.3 | -4.2 |

Source: World Tourism Organization (WTO) © (Data as collected by WTO December 2004)

# III.3.16 Russian Federation

## Central and Eastern Europe

## Profile

# Russian Federation

| | |
|---|---|
| Capital | Moscow |
| Year of entry in WTO | 1975 |
| Area (1000 km²) | 17,075 |
| Population (2003, million) | 145 |
| Gross Domestic Product (GDP) (2003, euro million) | 457,708 |
| GDP per capita (2003, euro) | 3,194 |
| GDP growth (real, %) | |
| '-> 2002: 4.7; 2003: 7.3; 2004*: 7.3; 2005*: 6.6 | |

**Europe**

**Central and Eastern Europe**

| | 2001 | 2002 | 2003* | 2002/2001 | 2003*/2002 |
|---|---|---|---|---|---|
| **International Arrivals** | | | | | |
| Visitors (1000) | 21,570 | 23,296 | .. | 8.0 | |
| Tourists (overnight visitors) (1000) | 7,400 | 7,943 | 8,015 | 7.3 | 0.9 |
| - per 100 of inhabitants | 5 | 5 | 6 | | |
| **Outbound Tourism** | | | | | |
| Trips abroad (1000) | 17,939 | 20,343 | .. | 13.4 | |
| - per 100 of inhabitants | 12 | 14 | .. | | |
| **Receipts and Expenditure for International Tourism** | | | | | |
| International Tourism Receipts (euro million) | 3,867 | 4,653 | 4,761 | 20.3 | 2.3 |
| - per Tourist Arrival (euro) | 523 | 586 | 594 | 12.1 | 1.4 |
| - per Visitor Arrival (euro) | 179 | 200 | .. | 11.4 | |
| - per capita (euro) | 26 | 32 | 33 | | |
| International Fare Receipts (euro million) | 1,249 | 1,408 | 1,456 | 12.7 | 3.4 |
| International Tourism Expenditure (euro million) | 10,053 | 12,599 | 13,621 | 25.3 | 8.1 |
| - per trip (euro) | 560 | 619 | .. | 10.5 | |
| - per capita (euro) | 69 | 87 | 94 | | |
| International Fare Expenditure (euro million) | 514 | 479 | 578 | -6.9 | 20.8 |
| △ International Tourism Balance (euro million) | -6,185 | -7,946 | -8,860 | | |
| △ International Fare Balance (euro million) | 735 | 929 | 878 | | |

Source: World Tourism Organization (WTO) (Data as collected by WTO December 2004)

See annex for methodological notes and reference of external sources used.

# Survey

Contributed by *Federal Agency for Physical Education, Sport and Tourism*
www.moscow-city.ru (promotional)
www.moshotel.com. (institutional/corporate)

## Tourism development and outlook

**Overall evaluation of results**

In general, incoming and domestic tourism has increased. This was assisted by advertising activities as well as by the development of tourism infrastructure and expansion of tourist destinations.

**Supply**

Tourists' accommodation facilities and the number of small hotels have grown. The volume of transport services for tourists has increased. The number of recreational sites and that of cultural and sports tourism has grown.

**External factors**

Last year, the following factors influenced tourism development in Russia: political stability, economic growth, development of infrastructure, and improvement of healthcare services.

**Tourism policy**

The Federal Agency for Physical Culture, Sports and Tourism of the Russian Federation, as the executive authority in the field of tourism, continues to actively develop international relations in tourism.
The Russian Federation consistently promotes participation in international tourist exhibitions as an efficient means of popularizing Russia as a destination.
In 2004, Russia was elected Chairman of the Executive Council of the World Tourism Organization (WTO) for the second time successively, which testifies to recognition of the international prestige of our country and its high position on the international tourist scene.
Russia in its capacity as a permanent member of the United Nations Security Council provides important support to transformation of the WTO into a United Nations specialized agency to raise the status and value of this Organization, which plays a significant role in the promotion of international cooperation in the field of tourism.
The afflux of foreign tourists into Russia grows year by year, which demonstrates the efficiency of the state policy in the field of tourism.

**Marketing & promotion**

Marketing plans in the field of tourism are being successfully implemented, advertising campaigns are being carried out and new technologies are being applied with the aim of creating resources to ensure the provision of information concerning tourism in Russia.

**Outlook 2004**

It is expected that domestic tourism, as well the number of tourist arrivals in the Russian Federation, will continue to grow. There are plans to step up exhibition activities and the organization of special advertising events abroad (conferences, seminars, workshops).

## International Meetings Industry (MI)

**Characteristics of supply**

The management of various activities aimed at promoting tourism is being improved and is now approaching European quality standards.

| | |
|---|---|
| **Organisation of promotion** | The Russian Federation actively participates in international tourist shows and provides for mass publication of advertising materials. |

**Collection of statistics on the Meetings Industry?:** no.

| | |
|---|---|
| **Description** | The Russian Federation does not keep statistics on tourist exhibitions, conferences, seminars, fairs, etc. |
| **Importance / size** | Since many activities (meetings, seminars, conferences, exhibitions, fairs) are carried out at the regional level, it is difficult to count the number of their participants and general size. |
| **Evolution MI** | There are continued improvements in the organization of tourist exhibitions, conferences, seminars, meetings, visits and other activities, and their number is expected to grow. |

## International Tourism by Origin

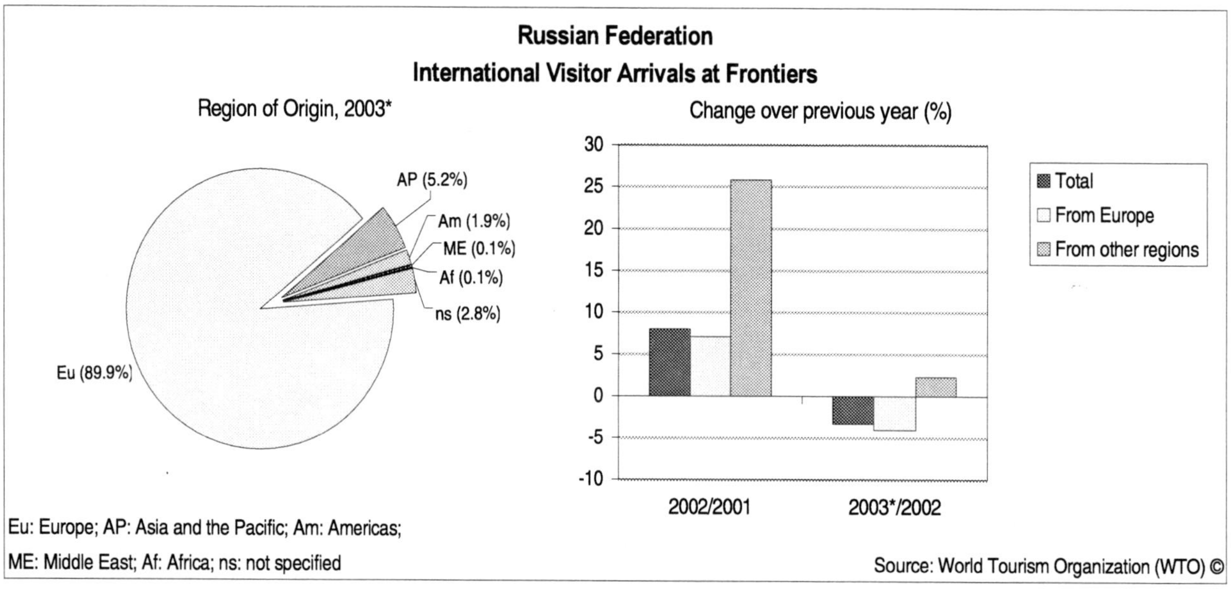

**Russian Federation**
**International Visitor Arrivals at Frontiers (by nationality)**

| | | | | (thousand) | Market share (%) | | Growth rate (%) | | Average per year (%) |
|---|---|---|---|---|---|---|---|---|---|
| | 1995 | 2001 | 2002 | 2003* | 1995 | 2003* | 2002/01 | 2003*/02 | 1995-2003* |
| **Total** | **10,290** | **21,570** | **23,296** | **22,521** | **100** | **100** | **8.0** | **-3.3** | **10.3** |
| *From Europe* | *9,143* | *19,704* | *21,097* | *20,239* | *88.8* | *89.9* | *7.1* | *-4.1* | *10.4* |
| Ukraine | 2,031 | 7,925 | 8,230 | 7,686 | 19.7 | 34.1 | 3.8 | -6.6 | 18.1 |
| Kazakhstan | 218 | 2,539 | 2,956 | 2,675 | 2.1 | 11.9 | 16.4 | -9.5 | 36.8 |
| Poland | 666 | 885 | 1,210 | 1,233 | 6.5 | 5.5 | 36.8 | 1.9 | 8.0 |
| Finland | 1,276 | 1,291 | 1,161 | 1,154 | 12.4 | 5.1 | -10.0 | -0.6 | -1.3 |
| Lithuania | 441 | 1,059 | 951 | 874 | 4.3 | 3.9 | -10.2 | -8.1 | 8.9 |
| Azerbaijan | 285 | 842 | 844 | 826 | 2.8 | 3.7 | 0.2 | -2.2 | 14.2 |
| Rep Moldova | 199 | 658 | 695 | 752 | 1.9 | 3.3 | 5.7 | 8.1 | 18.0 |
| Georgia | 521 | 975 | 988 | 738 | 5.1 | 3.3 | 1.4 | -25.3 | 4.4 |
| Uzbekistan | 73 | 497 | 507 | 554 | 0.7 | 2.5 | 2.0 | 9.3 | 28.8 |
| Germany | 323 | 415 | 493 | 516 | 3.1 | 2.3 | 18.9 | 4.7 | 6.0 |
| Estonia | 188 | 359 | 387 | 406 | 1.8 | 1.8 | 7.8 | 5.0 | 10.1 |
| Tajikistan | 59 | 332 | 358 | 367 | 0.6 | 1.6 | 7.9 | 2.4 | 25.6 |
| Latvia | 176 | 245 | 293 | 345 | 1.7 | 1.5 | 19.3 | 17.9 | 8.8 |
| Armenia | 330 | 317 | 309 | 332 | 3.2 | 1.5 | -2.4 | 7.4 | 0.1 |
| Kyrgyzstan | 39 | 223 | 308 | 272 | 0.4 | 1.2 | 38.2 | -11.6 | 27.6 |
| France | 106 | 107 | 147 | 189 | 1.0 | 0.8 | 36.4 | 29.0 | 7.5 |
| United Kingdom | 121 | 139 | 149 | 177 | 1.2 | 0.8 | 7.7 | 18.3 | 4.8 |
| Italy | 97 | 111 | 154 | 170 | 0.9 | 0.8 | 39.3 | 10.0 | 7.2 |
| Belarus | 1,178 | 189 | 197 | 149 | 11.4 | 0.7 | 4.6 | -24.6 | -22.8 |
| Turkey | 134 | 99 | 119 | 140 | 1.3 | 0.6 | 19.4 | 17.7 | 0.6 |
| Netherlands | 46 | 51 | 64 | 68 | 0.4 | 0.3 | 25.4 | 6.7 | 5.1 |
| Sweden | 79 | 43 | 56 | 63 | 0.8 | 0.3 | 28.1 | 13.8 | -2.6 |
| Israel | 39 | 47 | 58 | 60 | 0.4 | 0.3 | 23.0 | 3.0 | 5.5 |
| Spain | 27 | 33 | 59 | 52 | 0.3 | 0.2 | 78.2 | -10.8 | 8.5 |
| Austria | 33 | 31 | 38 | 47 | 0.3 | 0.2 | 23.1 | 24.0 | 4.5 |
| Other intraregional | 457 | 292 | 367 | 394 | 4.4 | 1.8 | 25.5 | 7.5 | -1.8 |
| *From other regions* | *1,134* | *1,280* | *1,611* | *1,647* | *11.0* | *7.3* | *25.8* | *2.3* | *4.8* |
| China | 390 | 461 | 726 | 680 | 3.8 | 3.0 | 57.4 | -6.4 | 7.2 |
| United States | 216 | 210 | 236 | 281 | 2.1 | 1.2 | 12.2 | 19.2 | 3.3 |
| Mongolia | 170 | 126 | 134 | 117 | 1.7 | 0.5 | 6.8 | -13.2 | -4.6 |
| Korea, Republic of | 42 | 117 | 96 | 95 | 0.4 | 0.4 | -17.9 | -1.5 | 10.5 |
| Japan | 57 | 71 | 74 | 87 | 0.6 | 0.4 | 4.2 | 17.7 | 5.3 |
| Bahamas | 2 | 31 | 32 | 62 | 0.0 | 0.3 | 3.5 | 91.2 | 50.1 |
| India | 26 | 28 | 34 | 33 | 0.3 | 0.1 | 21.6 | -1.8 | 3.0 |
| Canada | 25 | 22 | 30 | 30 | 0.2 | 0.1 | 38.1 | -1.8 | 2.3 |
| Philippines | 14 | 21 | 23 | 26 | 0.1 | 0.1 | 9.1 | 11.8 | 8.2 |
| Vietnam | 9 | 20 | 27 | 24 | 0.1 | 0.1 | 36.2 | -10.2 | 13.2 |
| Korea, D P Rp | 21 | 10 | 21 | 18 | 0.2 | 0.1 | 99.0 | -10.3 | -1.6 |
| Australia | 11 | 15 | 17 | 17 | 0.1 | 0.1 | 14.1 | 1.7 | 5.8 |
| Iran | 11 | 11 | 13 | 14 | 0.1 | 0.1 | 19.9 | 3.7 | 3.1 |
| Liberia | 1 | 19 | 8 | 11 | 0.0 | 0.0 | -59.6 | 42.2 | 34.7 |
| Panama | 4 | 9 | 13 | 10 | 0.0 | 0.0 | 39.4 | -17.3 | 13.0 |
| Syrian Arab Republic | 17 | 9 | 9 | 10 | 0.2 | 0.0 | -3.4 | 13.4 | -6.3 |
| Other interregional | 117 | 100 | 119 | 134 | 1.1 | 0.6 | 18.6 | 12.2 | 1.7 |
| *Other World/Not specified* | *13* | *586* | *588* | *635* | *0.1* | *2.8* | *0.3* | *7.9* | *62.0* |

Source: World Tourism Organization (WTO) © (Data as collected by WTO December 2004)

# III.3.17 Slovakia — Central and Eastern Europe

## Profile

# Slovakia

**Europe**
**Central and Eastern Europe**

| | |
|---|---|
| Capital | Bratislava |
| Year of entry in WTO | 1993 |
| Area (1000 km²) | 49 |
| Population (2003, million) | 5.4 |
| Gross Domestic Product (GDP) (2003, euro million) | 34,391 |
| GDP per capita (2003, euro) | 6,368 |
| GDP growth (real, %) | |
| '-> 2002: 4.4; 2003: 4.2; 2004*: 4.8; 2005*: 4.3 | |

| | 2001 | 2002 | 2003* | 2002/2001 | 2003*/2002 |
|---|---|---|---|---|---|
| **International Arrivals** | | | | | |
| Visitors (1000) | 27,761 | 26,450 | 24,985 | -4.7 | -5.5 |
| Tourists (overnight visitors) (1000) | 1,219 | 1,399 | 1,387 | 14.7 | -0.9 |
| - per 100 of inhabitants | 23 | 26 | 26 | | |
| **Tourism accommodation** | | | | | |
| Number of rooms | 31,655 | 34,619 | 35,853 | 9.4 | 3.6 |
| *Nights spent in collective establishments (1000)* | 11,320 | 12,306 | 12,059 | 8.7 | -2.0 |
| by non-residents (inbound tourism) | 4,378 | 5,043 | 4,964 | 15.2 | -1.6 |
| by residents (domestic tourism) | 6,942 | 7,263 | 7,095 | 4.6 | -2.3 |
| *Nights spent in hotels and similar establishments (1000)* | 7,387 | 8,967 | 8,778 | 21.4 | -2.1 |
| by non-residents (inbound tourism) | 3,550 | 4,050 | 3,989 | 14.1 | -1.5 |
| by residents (domestic tourism) | 3,837 | 4,917 | 4,789 | 28.1 | -2.6 |
| **Outbound Tourism** | | | | | |
| Trips abroad (1000) | 373 | 437 | 408 | 17.2 | -6.6 |
| - per 100 of inhabitants | 7 | 8 | 8 | | |
| **Receipts and Expenditure for International Tourism** | | | | | |
| International Tourism Receipts (euro million) | 694 | 822 | 915 | 18.4 | 11.3 |
| - per Tourist Arrival (euro) | 569 | 588 | 660 | 3.2 | 12.3 |
| - per Visitor Arrival (euro) | 25 | 31 | 37 | 24.3 | 17.8 |
| - per capita (euro) | 128 | 152 | 169 | | |
| International Fare Receipts (euro million) | 9 | 7 | 12 | -22.7 | 73.6 |
| International Tourism Expenditure (euro million) | 313 | 494 | 606 | 57.7 | 22.8 |
| - per trip (euro) | 839 | 1,129 | 1,485 | 34.6 | 31.5 |
| - per capita (euro) | 58 | 91 | 112 | | |
| International Fare Expenditure (euro million) | 55 | 71 | 94 | 29.4 | 31.7 |
| △ International Tourism Balance (euro million) | 381 | 328 | 309 | | |
| △ International Fare Balance (euro million) | -47 | -65 | -82 | | |

Source: World Tourism Organization (WTO) (Data as collected by WTO December 2004)

See annex for methodological notes and reference of external sources used.

# Survey

Contributed by *Ministry of Economy*
www.slovakiatourism.sk (promotional)
www.economy.gov.sk (institutional/corporate)
www.statistics.sk ; www.ustavturizmu.sk (will be inaugurated in the near future) (research and data)

## Tourism development and outlook

**Overall evaluation of results**

Tourism results in Slovakia during last year can be evaluated as being stagnated.

Positive factors:

- The increase in income from inbound tourism, US$ 863 million compared to US$ 724 million in 2002;
- The growth of average expenditure by foreign tourists per day and capita with more tourists coming from the most important feeder markets (the Czech Republic, Poland and Hungary).

Negative factors:

- A decrease of 5.5 per cent in total number of tourists and visitors;
- A decrease of 2 per cent of guests in accommodation facilities;
- A decrease of 0.6 per cent in the number of overnights of foreign guests;
- A decrease in the number of tourists from Germany, Austria and the Ukraine and a low share of new clients of only 7 per cent, etc.

Outbound tourism continues to grow 18.3 million trips (+3,9%).

The most frequent purposes for visiting Slovakia are business trips and study tours, visits to relations and friends, relaxation, shopping, sightseeing tours, winter sports and stays in spa resorts.

**Supply**

*Accommodation:*

Positive development both quantitative and qualitative. Total number of bed places recorded by the statistical office was 121 thousand beds, which is 2.6 per cent more compared to the year 2002. Hotels and other establishments of higher categories increased their share. Besides new facilities a lot of reconstruction and refurbishment of existing capacities was made in order to improve the standard and quality of service. Within accommodation facilities a lot of new leisure services were developed such as swimming pools, sauna, fitness, meeting rooms, etc.

*Travel agencies/Tour operators:*

More long-haul destination holidays are included in their offers for outbound tourism. Summer holidays on the sea coastal areas represent the majority of selling packages. Within outbound tourism some signs of specialisation in specific products can be seen.

*Transport capacity:*

Some new regular direct flights were opened from Bratislava to European cities (London, Paris, Brussels, Munich, Stuttgart, etc.). Transport capacity for winter sports was improved significantly by many new ski lifts and chairlifts (chairlifts are increasingly more popular than ski lifts in medium and large ski resorts).

*Attractions/Entertainment:*

The first big Aquapark based on thermal water was opened in the Liptov region between the High Tatras mountain and Low Tatras mountains.

*Specific products:*

Facilities for MICE are developing because of high domestic demand. Wellness and relax facilities are also growing. Plans have been made to promote the historical heritage for tourism development but implementation is still slow.

**External factors**

The most important external factors last year were:
- A more positive image of the country as a future member of the European Union;
- The growth of the Slovak economy and direct foreign investment reinforced development of business tourism;
- The duty on the entry visa for Russia and the Ukraine seems to be an obstacle;
- The exchange rate due to the stronger slovak crown at the end of the year;
- Unfavourable weather conditions during July impacted on summer holidays in Slovakia.

**Tourism policy**

The Ministry of Economy has finalised a Sectoral Operation Programme for Structural Funds (SF) of the European Union under the European Regional Development Fund (ERDF) and a Programme Complement for Industry and Services, of which one of the two priorities is devoted to the Tourism Sector for both private and public bodies. These documents are valid for the whole territory of Slovakia except the Bratislava region.

The Ministry of Construction and Regional Development has prepared a Single Programming Document for Objective 2 for SF EU (ERDF) which is valid for the Bratislava region. Tourism is one of the priorities.

The Ministry of Economy has ordered the elaboration of a document "Regionalisation of Tourism in the Slovak Republic“. Tourism regions and evaluation of tourism potential (within middle-term and long-term horizons) are defined and classified for particular tourist activities. The document will be used in many ways, e.g. as a basis for allocation of public funds, promotion, land planning, stimulating of private sector investments, motivation for regional cooperation, etc.

The Tourism Development Grant Scheme launched a call for proposals in September 2003. Within this grant scheme are supported projects of the Slovakian Ministry of Economy (SME), self-government and non-profit making bodies oriented to tourism suprastructure and infrastructure, planning, marketing, etc. The budget represents 5.5 million euro.

**Marketing & promotion**

"Marketing analysis of products and markets of the Slovakian Republic“ which was carried out by the National Tourism Office.

New promotional brochures focusing on caves and ecotourism were produced.

Completion of the edition of unified promotional brochures of particular regions.

New video cassettes promoted and presented culture as a basis for tourism products.

An information campaign was initiated at border crossings –providing information and promotional leaflets.

Participation in 31 international tourism fairs with the official stand of the Slovak Republic.

Ten workshops abroad were organised by the National Tourism Office which focussed mainly on the mountains and spa resorts.

Fifty-four presentations were made abroad, e.g. in Slovak embassies, international conferences, events, etc.

**Outlook 2004**

We expect that the positive trends in tourism development will continue with quality improvement, higher satisfaction of tourists and growth of tourist expenditure. The entry of Slovakkia into the European Union will attract the interest of tourists from member states (short-term wave of interest).

The continuing strength of the Slovak crown may negatively influence the tourist flow from Poland and only slightly from the Czech Republic (the Polish zloty is fixed to the United States dollar and the Czech crown to the euro).

Some problems of occupancy rate may occur in spa resorts because of the new approach of Social Insurance and Health Insurance in relation to stays in spas. It means that spa resorts will have to concentrate on new markets and clients.

The National Tourism Office has launched a promotional campaign to develop domestic tourism but the motivation to spend holidays abroad (preferably seaside holidays) is very strong.
Many new investments completed in 2003 and 2004 will enhance the attractiveness of Slovakia and its regions as a destination. The overall expectation for tourism development in 2004 is optimistic.

## International Meetings Industry (MI)

**Characteristics of supply**

The Meetings Industry in Slovakia has favourable conditions in the following places:

- Bratislava and other cities such as Kosice, Zilina, Nitra, Banska Bystrica and Trencin;
- Historical towns for small meetings such as Levoca, Banska Stiavnica and Bardejov;
- Spa resorts with suitable capacity and good atmosphere such as Piestany and Trencianske Teplice;
- Attractive mountain resorts mainly in the High Tatra, Low Tatra, Small Fatra and others;
- Certain specific places such as castles e.g. Smolenice, Mojmirovce, Budmerice, Moravany nad Vahom, etc.;
- The most suitable facilities for exhibitions and fairs are located in Bratislava, Nitra and Trencin. Smaller gatherings can be organised in Zilina, Banska Bystrica and Presov, etc.

Specialised travel agencies and tour operators for meetings, conferences and incentives are Satur, Hydrotour, Supravia, MSTT, MTT, etc.
Exhibition and Fair organisers include Incheba, Agrokomplex, Vystavnictvo, BB Expo, Vystavisko Trencin and others.

**Organisation of promotion**

A new department for MICE was created within the National Tourism Office. At present it prepares a catalogue of the facilities available for this kind of tourism in Slovakia. This department is the core of the future National Convention Bureau. It was set up by the Ministry of Economy in the year 1995 and it is still financed by this ministry with more than 90 per cent of the total budget of the National Tourism Office.
Travel Agencies and Tour Operators dealing with MICE established the "Slovak Association of Congress and Motivation of Tourism (SAKOM)" in the year 2001. This year SAKOM will participate in IMEX in Frankfurt.

**Collection of statistics on the Meetings Industry?:** no.

**Importance / size**

A very rough estimation would be approximately 2 per cent of hotel guests and 3-4 per cent of income of hotel establishments.

**Evolution MI**

The Meetings Industry has recorded rapid growth during recent years of the mainly small and medium-sized meetings and other gatherings. The main market is the domestic market. We expect this trend to continue because demand has not been saturated and economic growth generates new demand. In the near future, more international participation is expected but mainly in medium-sized events.

# International Tourism by Origin

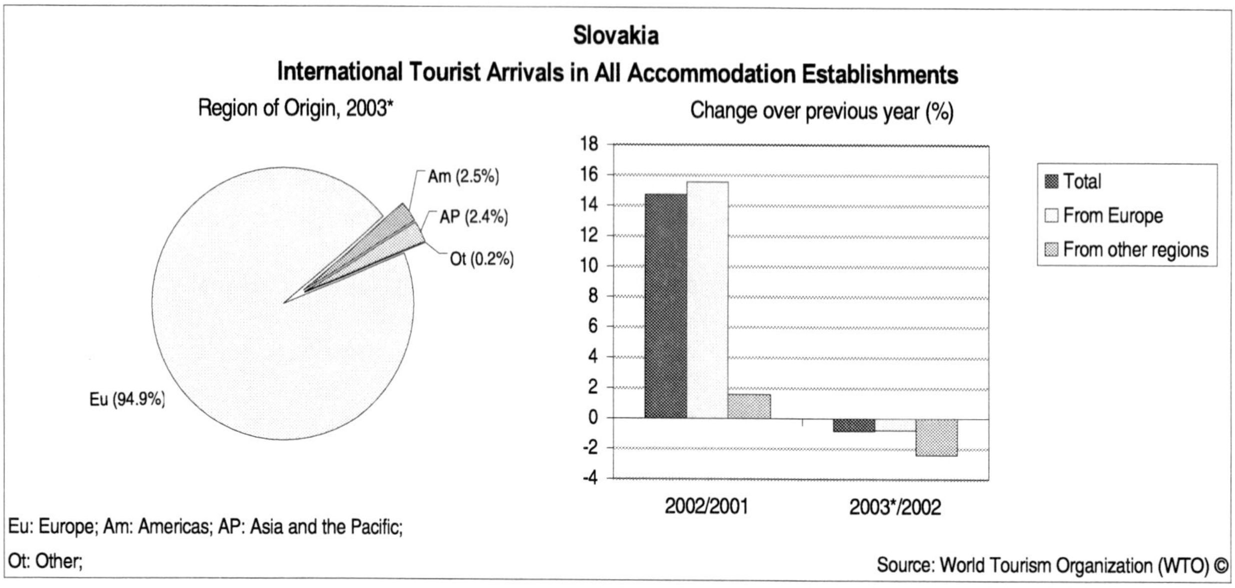


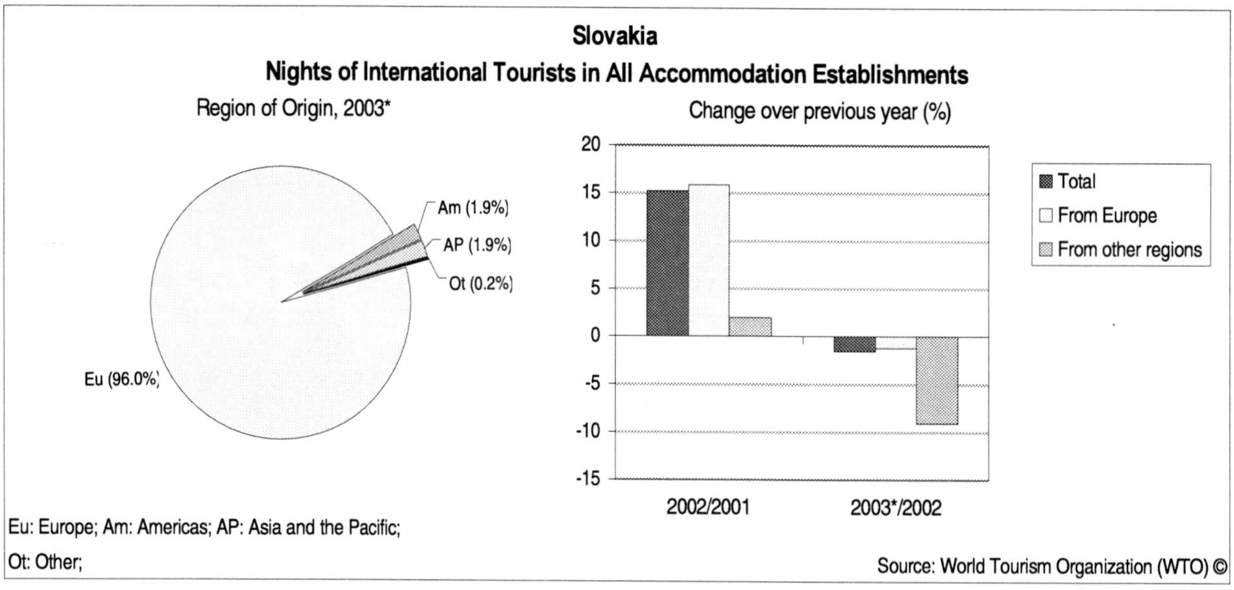

**Slovakia**

**International Tourist Arrivals in All Accommodation Establishments (by nationality)**

| | | | | (thousand) | Market share (%) | | Growth rate (%) | | Average per year (%) |
|---|---|---|---|---|---|---|---|---|---|
| | 1995 | 2001 | 2002 | 2003* | 1995 | 2003* | 2002/01 | 2003*/02 | 1995-2003* |
| **Total** | **903** | **1,219** | **1,399** | **1,387** | **100** | **100** | **14.7** | **-0.9** | **5.5** |
| *From Europe* | *854* | *1,148* | *1,326* | *1,316* | *94.6* | *94.9* | *15.6* | *-0.8* | *5.6* |
| Czech Rep | 215 | 328 | 448 | 470 | 23.8 | 33.9 | 36.7 | 4.9 | 10.3 |
| Poland | 114 | 265 | 267 | 215 | 12.6 | 15.5 | 0.9 | -19.3 | 8.3 |
| Germany | 161 | 172 | 189 | 176 | 17.8 | 12.7 | 9.4 | -6.9 | 1.1 |
| Hungary | 62 | 74 | 88 | 101 | 6.9 | 7.3 | 19.4 | 13.9 | 6.2 |
| Austria | 45 | 44 | 47 | 51 | 5.0 | 3.7 | 6.9 | 9.1 | 1.7 |
| Italy | 29 | 33 | 35 | 38 | 3.2 | 2.7 | 6.9 | 8.6 | 3.5 |
| France | 17 | 20 | 22 | 29 | 1.9 | 2.1 | 12.1 | 30.8 | 6.9 |
| United Kingdom | 16 | 22 | 28 | 26 | 1.8 | 1.9 | 29.9 | -7.2 | 6.5 |
| Netherlands | 26 | 22 | 24 | 24 | 2.9 | 1.8 | 8.5 | 2.3 | -0.8 |
| Russian Federation | 27 | 20 | 20 | 23 | 3.0 | 1.6 | 2.2 | 11.7 | -2.2 |
| Ukraine | 36 | 19 | 20 | 20 | 4.0 | 1.4 | 3.6 | 0.7 | -7.3 |
| Croatia | 9 | 9 | 9 | 11 | 1.0 | 0.8 | 5.7 | 21.2 | 3.0 |
| Belgium | 10 | 11 | 11 | 11 | 1.1 | 0.8 | 1.9 | -6.3 | 1.4 |
| Switzerland | 7 | 9 | 12 | 11 | 0.7 | 0.8 | 31.9 | -13.6 | 6.0 |
| Slovenia | 5 | 7 | 9 | 10 | 0.5 | 0.8 | 28.3 | 11.3 | 10.7 |
| Lithuania | .. | 10 | 9 | 10 | | 0.7 | -7.6 | 3.6 | |
| Finland | 2 | 4 | 7 | 8 | 0.2 | 0.6 | 72.5 | 7.4 | 19.8 |
| Israel | 8 | 9 | 7 | 8 | 0.8 | 0.6 | -28.1 | 21.7 | 0.6 |
| Denmark | 6 | 6 | 9 | 8 | 0.6 | 0.6 | 45.0 | -15.4 | 4.3 |
| Sweden | 4 | 7 | 7 | 7 | 0.4 | 0.5 | 3.8 | -4.7 | 6.5 |
| Romania | 8 | 9 | 5 | 6 | 0.9 | 0.4 | -42.7 | 12.7 | -3.8 |
| Spain | 3 | 5 | 5 | 5 | 0.4 | 0.4 | 9.6 | 0.0 | 6.6 |
| Serbia & Montenegro | 8 | 5 | 4 | 4 | 0.9 | 0.3 | -10.0 | 6.2 | -8.0 |
| Latvia | .. | 2 | 3 | 4 | | 0.3 | 52.8 | 21.1 | |
| Norway | 2 | 3 | 3 | 3 | 0.2 | 0.2 | 18.4 | 2.7 | 6.7 |
| Other intraregional | 36 | 34 | 36 | 38 | 4.0 | 2.7 | 5.1 | 5.4 | 0.6 |
| *From other regions* | *49* | *71* | *72* | *70* | *5.4* | *5.1* | *1.6* | *-2.4* | *4.6* |
| United States | 21 | 28 | 25 | 25 | 2.3 | 1.8 | -9.9 | 0.0 | 2.5 |
| Japan | 7 | 9 | 9 | 7 | 0.7 | 0.5 | 3.1 | -20.5 | 1.0 |
| Australia | .. | 4 | 5 | 7 | | 0.5 | 26.5 | 45.1 | |
| Canada | 3 | 5 | 5 | 6 | 0.3 | 0.4 | 4.6 | 11.8 | 9.5 |
| Australia, New Zealand | 2 | .. | .. | .. | 0.2 | | | | |
| All Africa | 2 | .. | .. | .. | 0.3 | | | | |
| India | .. | 2 | 1 | 1 | | 0.1 | -5.1 | -9.2 | |
| Korea, Republic of | .. | 1 | 1 | 1 | | 0.1 | -4.8 | 118.5 | |
| China | .. | 1 | 1 | 1 | | 0.0 | 41.8 | -12.3 | |
| New Zealand | .. | 0 | 0 | 1 | | 0.0 | 42.7 | 30.8 | |
| Thailand | .. | 0 | 0 | 0 | | 0.0 | -56.7 | 150.8 | |
| South Africa | .. | 1 | 0 | 0 | | 0.0 | -22.0 | -18.3 | |
| Brazil | .. | 0 | 0 | 0 | | 0.0 | 75.5 | -15.8 | |
| Other Africa | .. | 2 | 2 | 2 | | 0.2 | -1.4 | -8.7 | |
| Other Americas | 2 | 2 | 2 | 2 | 0.3 | 0.2 | -6.4 | 12.2 | -1.1 |
| Other Asia | 12 | 16 | 18 | 15 | 1.3 | 1.1 | 16.5 | -16.7 | 3.1 |
| Other interregional | .. | 1 | 1 | 1 | | 0.1 | -12.8 | -20.9 | |
| *Other World/Not specified* | .. | *0* | *0* | *0* | | *0.0* | *5.1* | *110.3* | |

Source: World Tourism Organization (WTO) © (Data as collected by WTO December 2004)

**Slovakia**
**Nights of International Tourists in All Accommodation Establishments (by nationality)**

| | | | | (thousand) | Market share (%) | | Growth rate (%) | | Average per year (%) |
|---|---|---|---|---|---|---|---|---|---|
| | 1995 | 2001 | 2002 | 2003* | 1995 | 2003* | 2002/01 | 2003*/02 | 1995-2003* |
| **Total** | **3,069** | **4,378** | **5,043** | **4,964** | **100** | **100** | **15.2** | **-1.6** | **6.2** |
| *From Europe* | *2,899* | *4,162* | *4,824* | *4,764* | *94.4* | *96.0* | *15.9* | *-1.2* | *6.4* |
| Czech Rep | 705 | 1,069 | 1,478 | 1,675 | 23.0 | 33.7 | 38.2 | 13.3 | 11.4 |
| Germany | 800 | 991 | 1,111 | 1,037 | 26.1 | 20.9 | 12.1 | -6.7 | 3.3 |
| Poland | 337 | 939 | 941 | 703 | 11.0 | 14.2 | 0.1 | -25.3 | 9.6 |
| Hungary | 219 | 233 | 268 | 296 | 7.1 | 6.0 | 14.9 | 10.3 | 3.8 |
| Austria | 151 | 146 | 160 | 176 | 4.9 | 3.5 | 9.8 | 9.8 | 1.9 |
| Russian Federation | 86 | 87 | 87 | 97 | 2.8 | 2.0 | 0.8 | 11.0 | 1.5 |
| Ukraine | 81 | 74 | 87 | 88 | 2.6 | 1.8 | 17.8 | 0.7 | 1.1 |
| Netherlands | 93 | 70 | 79 | 80 | 3.0 | 1.6 | 13.9 | 1.1 | -1.8 |
| Italy | 58 | 71 | 75 | 79 | 1.9 | 1.6 | 6.3 | 5.1 | 4.0 |
| United Kingdom | 39 | 53 | 68 | 63 | 1.3 | 1.3 | 28.6 | -7.9 | 6.0 |
| France | 38 | 43 | 49 | 59 | 1.2 | 1.2 | 14.1 | 20.6 | 5.9 |
| Israel | 37 | 58 | 48 | 48 | 1.2 | 1.0 | -16.7 | -0.6 | 3.4 |
| Croatia | 19 | 30 | 28 | 30 | 0.6 | 0.6 | -7.4 | 8.1 | 5.7 |
| Belgium | 33 | 31 | 32 | 29 | 1.1 | 0.6 | 6.3 | -11.8 | -1.8 |
| Switzerland | 17 | 21 | 30 | 25 | 0.5 | 0.5 | 44.3 | -15.8 | 5.4 |
| Lithuania | .. | 24 | 25 | 25 | | 0.5 | 3.9 | 0.2 | |
| Slovenia | 10 | 16 | 22 | 24 | 0.3 | 0.5 | 41.5 | 8.3 | 11.9 |
| Denmark | 16 | 18 | 32 | 22 | 0.5 | 0.5 | 75.8 | -30.0 | 4.5 |
| Finland | 4 | 11 | 19 | 22 | 0.1 | 0.4 | 73.1 | 15.7 | 23.4 |
| Romania | 13 | 22 | 15 | 15 | 0.4 | 0.3 | -30.4 | 0.7 | 1.7 |
| Sweden | 9 | 16 | 16 | 15 | 0.3 | 0.3 | 2.6 | -8.1 | 6.8 |
| Serbia & Montenegro | 18 | 14 | 12 | 14 | 0.6 | 0.3 | -11.8 | 8.8 | -3.8 |
| Belarus | .. | 6 | 9 | 12 | | 0.2 | 40.8 | 33.4 | |
| Spain | 8 | 13 | 14 | 12 | 0.3 | 0.2 | 9.9 | -15.5 | 4.4 |
| Latvia | .. | 7 | 8 | 9 | | 0.2 | 16.1 | 12.1 | |
| Other intraregional | 107 | 100 | 106 | 109 | 3.5 | 2.2 | 6.6 | 2.1 | 0.2 |
| *From other regions* | *171* | *215* | *219* | *199* | *5.6* | *4.0* | *2.0* | *-9.1* | *1.9* |
| United States | 63 | 82 | 75 | 69 | 2.1 | 1.4 | -8.8 | -7.4 | 1.1 |
| Canada | 10 | 12 | 15 | 16 | 0.3 | 0.3 | 23.5 | 1.2 | 6.3 |
| Australia | .. | 9 | 12 | 15 | | 0.3 | 30.8 | 31.4 | |
| Japan | 10 | 16 | 16 | 14 | 0.3 | 0.3 | -0.2 | -9.9 | 4.5 |
| All Africa | 8 | .. | .. | .. | 0.3 | | | | |
| Australia, New Zealand | 5 | .. | .. | .. | 0.2 | | | | |
| Korea, Republic of | .. | 1 | 2 | 4 | | 0.1 | 18.0 | 150.0 | |
| India | .. | 3 | 6 | 2 | | 0.0 | 139.0 | -67.3 | |
| Egypt | .. | 2 | 2 | 2 | | 0.0 | -5.7 | -5.8 | |
| Brazil | .. | 1 | 2 | 2 | | 0.0 | 126.3 | -24.9 | |
| China | .. | 2 | 2 | 1 | | 0.0 | -29.5 | -13.7 | |
| South Africa | .. | 2 | 1 | 1 | | 0.0 | -45.3 | 2.2 | |
| New Zealand | .. | 1 | 1 | 1 | | 0.0 | 56.0 | 15.6 | |
| Other Africa | .. | 8 | 8 | 8 | | 0.2 | 4.4 | -9.2 | |
| Other Americas | 7 | 9 | 8 | 8 | 0.2 | 0.2 | -9.4 | 5.4 | 3.1 |
| Other Asia | 68 | 63 | 67 | 53 | 2.2 | 1.1 | 5.1 | -20.1 | -3.1 |
| Other interregional | .. | 4 | 3 | 3 | | 0.1 | -12.8 | -21.8 | |
| *Other World/Not specified* | .. | *0* | *1* | *1* | | *0.0* | *22.1* | *89.9* | |

Source: World Tourism Organization (WTO) © (Data as collected by WTO December 2004)

# III.3.18 Tajikistan — Central and Eastern Europe

## Profile

**Tajikistan**

**Europe**
**Central and Eastern Europe**

| | |
|---|---|
| Capital | Dushanbe |
| Area (1000 km²) | 143 |
| Population (2003, million) | 6.9 |
| Gross Domestic Product (GDP) (2003, euro million) | 1,677 |
| GDP per capita (2003, euro) | 253 |
| GDP growth (real, %) | |
| 2002: 9.1; 2003: 10.2; 2004*: 10.0; 2005*: 8.0 | |

| | 2001 | 2002 | 2003* | 2002/2001 | 2003*/2002 |
|---|---|---|---|---|---|
| **International Arrivals** | | | | | |
| Visitors (1000) | 5 | .. | .. | | |
| Tourists (overnight visitors) (1000) | 4 | .. | .. | | |
| - per 100 of inhabitants | 0 | .. | .. | | |
| Same-day visitors (1000) | 2 | .. | .. | | |
| **Tourism accommodation** | | | | | |
| Number of rooms | 345 | .. | .. | | |
| **Outbound Tourism** | | | | | |
| Trips abroad (1000) | 3 | .. | .. | | |
| - per 100 of inhabitants | 0 | .. | .. | | |
| **Receipts and Expenditure for International Tourism** | | | | | |
| International Tourism Receipts (euro million) | .. | 2 | 2 | | -5.3 |
| - per capita (euro) | .. | 0 | 0 | | |
| International Fare Receipts (euro million) | .. | 3 | 5 | | 57.9 |
| International Tourism Expenditure (euro million) | .. | 2 | 2 | | -5.3 |
| - per capita (euro) | .. | 0 | 0 | | |

Source: World Tourism Organization (WTO) (Data as collected by WTO December 2004)

See annex for methodological notes and reference of external sources used.

## International Tourism by Origin

**Tajikistan**
**International Visitor Arrivals at Frontiers**

Region of Origin, 2001

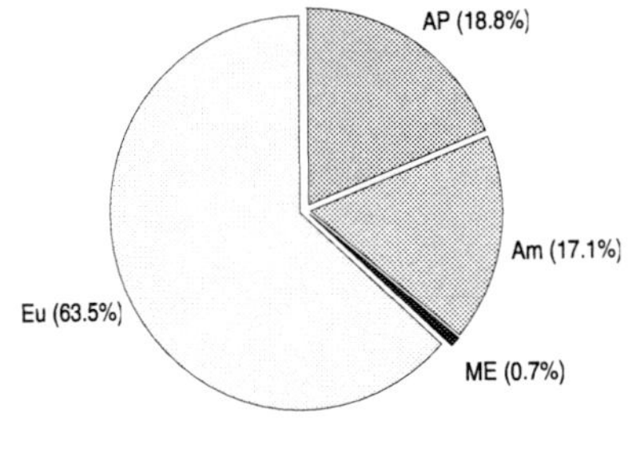


Eu: Europe; AP: Asia and the Pacific; Am: Americas;
ME: Middle East;

Source: World Tourism Organization (WTO) ©

**Tajikistan**
**International Visitor Arrivals at Frontiers (by residence)**

| | | | | (thousand) | Market share (%) | | Growth rate (%) | | Average per year (%) |
|---|---|---|---|---|---|---|---|---|---|
| | 1995 | 2000 | 2001 | 2002 | 1995 | 2002 | 2001/00 | 2002/01 | 1995-2002 |
| **Total** | .. | .. | **5** | .. | | | | | |
| *From Europe* | .. | .. | 3 | .. | | | | | |
| Russian Federation | .. | .. | 2 | .. | | | | | |
| France | .. | .. | 1 | .. | | | | | |
| Germany | .. | .. | 0 | .. | | | | | |
| United Kingdom | .. | .. | 0 | .. | | | | | |
| Switzerland | .. | .. | 0 | .. | | | | | |
| Turkey | .. | .. | 0 | .. | | | | | |
| Belgium | .. | .. | 0 | .. | | | | | |
| Italy | .. | .. | 0 | .. | | | | | |
| Netherlands | .. | .. | 0 | .. | | | | | |
| Bulgaria | .. | .. | 0 | .. | | | | | |
| Kyrgyzstan | .. | .. | 0 | .. | | | | | |
| Poland | .. | .. | 0 | .. | | | | | |
| Hungary | .. | .. | 0 | .. | | | | | |
| Austria | .. | .. | 0 | .. | | | | | |
| Greece | .. | .. | 0 | .. | | | | | |
| Kazakhstan | .. | .. | 0 | .. | | | | | |
| Israel | .. | .. | 0 | .. | | | | | |
| Denmark | .. | .. | 0 | .. | | | | | |
| Spain | .. | .. | 0 | .. | | | | | |
| Sweden | .. | .. | 0 | .. | | | | | |
| Finland | .. | .. | 0 | .. | | | | | |
| Other intraregional | .. | .. | 0 | .. | | | | | |
| *From other regions* | .. | .. | 2 | .. | | | | | |
| United States | .. | .. | 1 | .. | | | | | |
| Korea, D P Rp | .. | .. | 0 | .. | | | | | |
| Canada | .. | .. | 0 | .. | | | | | |
| Afghanistan | .. | .. | 0 | .. | | | | | |
| Iran | .. | .. | 0 | .. | | | | | |
| Japan | .. | .. | 0 | .. | | | | | |
| China | .. | .. | 0 | .. | | | | | |
| India | .. | .. | 0 | .. | | | | | |
| Pakistan | .. | .. | 0 | .. | | | | | |
| Libyan Arab Jamahiriya | .. | .. | 0 | .. | | | | | |
| Iraq | .. | .. | 0 | .. | | | | | |
| Untd Arab Emirates | .. | .. | 0 | .. | | | | | |
| Other interregional | .. | .. | 0 | .. | | | | | |

Source: World Tourism Organization (WTO) ©

(Data as collected by WTO December 2004)

# III.3.19 Turkmenistan Central and Eastern Europe

## Profile

| | | |
|---|---|---|
| **Turkmenistan** | Capital | Ashgabat |
| | Year of entry in WTO | 1993 |
| | Area (1000 km²) | 488 |
| | Population (2003, million) | 4.8 |
| | Gross Domestic Product (GDP) (2003, euro million) | 11,665 |
| | GDP per capita (2003, euro) | 2,397 |
| **Europe** | GDP growth (real, %) | |
| **Central and Eastern Europe** | • 2002: 19.8; 2003: 16.9; 2004*: 7.5; 2005*: 7.0 | |

Source: World Tourism Organization (WTO) (Data as collected by WTO December 2004)

See annex for methodological notes and reference of external sources used.

## Survey

Contributed by *The State Committee for Tourism and Sport*
www.tourism-sport.gov.tm (promotional)
www.tourism-sport.gov.tm (institutional/corporate)
www.tourism-sport.gov.tm (research and data)

### Tourism development and outlook

| | |
|---|---|
| **Supply** | Construction of a new hotel in the town of Turkmenbashi, in 2003. |
| **External factors** | Stabilisation of the economic situation.<br>Development of infrastructures. |
| **Marketing & promotion** | Participating at the exhibition "Ashgabat is white stone", in Ashgabat, every year. |
| **Outlook 2004** | Receiving more tourists.<br>The volume of tourism services in Turkmenistan is expected to grow. |

### International Meetings Industry (MI)

**Collection of statistics on the Meetings Industry?:** no.

| | |
|---|---|
| **Description** | We do not collect data on the Meetings Industry. |

# III.3.20 Ukraine — Central and Eastern Europe

## Profile

# Ukraine

Europe
Central and Eastern Europe

| | |
|---|---|
| Capital | Kiev |
| Year of entry in WTO | 1997 |
| Area (1000 km²) | 604 |
| Population (2003, million) | 48.1 |
| Gross Domestic Product (GDP) (2003, euro million) | 52,388 |
| GDP per capita (2003, euro) | 1,091 |
| GDP growth (real, %) | |

-> 2002: 5.3; 2003: 9.4; 2004*: 12.5; 2005*: 6.0

| | 2001 | 2002 | 2003* | 2002/2001 | 2003*/2002 |
|---|---|---|---|---|---|
| **International Arrivals** | | | | | |
| Visitors (1000) | 11,877 | 12,793 | .. | 7.7 | |
| Tourists (overnight visitors) (1000) | 5,791 | 6,326 | .. | 9.2 | |
| - per 100 of inhabitants | 12 | 13 | .. | | |
| Same-day visitors (1000) | 6,028 | 6,406 | .. | 6.3 | |
| Cruise passengers (1000) | 58 | 61 | .. | 5.2 | |
| **Tourism accommodation** | | | | | |
| Number of rooms | 43,487 | 35,139 | .. | -19.2 | |
| *Nights spent in collective establishments (1000)* | 45,306 | 43,708 | | -3.5 | |
| by non-residents (inbound tourism) | 5,177 | 4,757 | .. | -8.1 | |
| by residents (domestic tourism) | 40,129 | 38,951 | .. | -2.9 | |
| *Nights spent in hotels and similar establishments (1000)* | 9,369 | 9,851 | | 5.1 | |
| by non-residents (inbound tourism) | 1,070 | 1,453 | .. | 35.8 | |
| by residents (domestic tourism) | 8,299 | 8,398 | .. | 1.2 | |
| **Outbound Tourism** | | | | | |
| Trips abroad (1000) | 9,412 | 9,270 | .. | -1.5 | |
| - per 100 of inhabitants | 19 | 19 | .. | | |
| **Receipts and Expenditure for International Tourism** | | | | | |
| International Tourism Receipts (euro million) | 620 | 880 | 989 | 41.8 | 12.4 |
| - per Tourist Arrival (euro) | 107 | 139 | .. | 29.8 | |
| - per Visitor Arrival (euro) | 52 | 69 | .. | 31.7 | |
| - per capita (euro) | 13 | 18 | 21 | | |
| International Fare Receipts (euro million) | 201 | 238 | 284 | 18.1 | 19.6 |
| International Tourism Expenditure (euro million) | 613 | 734 | 834 | 19.7 | 13.7 |
| - per trip (euro) | 65 | 79 | .. | 21.5 | |
| - per capita (euro) | 13 | 15 | 17 | | |
| International Fare Expenditure (euro million) | 119 | 153 | 173 | 28.4 | 13.4 |
| △ International Tourism Balance (euro million) | 8 | 146 | 154 | | |
| △ International Fare Balance (euro million) | 82 | 85 | 111 | | |

Source: World Tourism Organization (WTO) (Data as collected by WTO December 2004)

See annex for methodological notes and reference of external sources used.

# Survey

Contributed by *State Commttee of Youth Policies, Sport and Tourism*
www.tourism.gov.ua (promotional)
www.tourism.gov.ua (institutional/corporate)

## Tourism development and outlook

**Overall evaluation of results**

As a result of the progressive development of international cooperation in the field of tourism, the number of foreign tourists who visit Ukraine is increasing each year. In 2002 they totalled 10.5 million people, an increase of 15 per cent during 2003 and 12.5 million foreign tourists visited Ukraine, which is 19 per cent, or 2 million, more than in the previous year. The main buyers of tourism products came from Russia, Moldova, Belarus, Poland and Hungary, together totalling more than 90 per cent of incoming tourism. The main tourism centres of Ukraine, receiving approximately 70 per cent of tourists supplied by tour operators, include the Autonomous Republic of the Crimea, the region near the capital (Kiev) and the western region of the Ukraine.
The volume of internal tourism is also gradually increasing. 7.6 million internal tourists travelled around Ukraine during 2003, which is 5.3 per cent more than in 2002 (7.2 million).
The number of sightseers and museum visitors in 2003 increased to 20.3 million people, which is 3.9 per cent more than in 2002 (19.5 million people).

**Supply**

On the first of January of 2004, there were 8342 businesses in the tourism and resort industry (3,864 travel agencies and tour operators; 1,218 hotels and other establishments for short-term accommodation and 3,260 health resorts and fitness institutions).
The volume of services provided by tourist and resort industries in 2003, totalled 4.1 billion UAH, which is 34 per cent more than in 2002.

**External factors**

The strict visa regime established for Ukrainian citizens by Europeans countries who are part of the Schengen Agreement is a problematic element in the cooperation between Ukraine and the European Union in the field of tourism. Inasmuch as the new members of the European Union must be automatically joined thereto, the first consequence of the European Union is the abolition of visa-free travel to Poland and Hungary and the introduction of stricter visa formalities with the European Union members countries. All this has a negative effect on the volume of tourists flows both into and out of Ukraine.
According to data from the leading tourism companies of Ukraine, the problematic aspects of cooperation with the consular establishments of foreign diplomatic representatives are as follows:

- The excessive list of formalities related to receiving accreditation as a tourist company with the consular establishments of foreign diplomatic representatives;
- The ungrounded introduction of visa quotas by foreign governments, limiting, in theory, the number of visas one tourism company may receive, (Czech Republic);
- The unreasonable increase in the lists of documents required by Ukrainian citizens in order to receive a visa (Europeans countries);
- The lack of reasoning given should a Ukrainian citizen not be granted a visa;
- The lack of opportunities to urgently register a tourist visa for European member countries.

**Tourism policy**

On the 18th November of 2003, the Supreme Soviet of Ukraine accepted Ukrainian Law Number 1282-IV "On Modifying the Ukrainian Law On Tourism".

The State Tourism Administration of Ukraine actively participated in the preparation of regulatory acts that were accepted in 2003:

- Ukrainian Law of 20.03.2003 "On Modifying the Decree of the Ukrainian Cabinet of Ministers of 20.05.1993 No 56-93 "On Local Taxes and Levies", abrogated by hotel takings;
- Ukrainian Law of 15.05.2003 No. 742-4 "On Individual Peasant Farming", in which the legal principles regarding the exploitation of rural tourism are defined;
- Ukrainian Law of 24.10.2002 No. 209 "On Modifying Article 3 of the Ukrainian Law "On Concessions", which will facilitate the introduction of investment into recreation and tourism by introducing concessions on the construction and exploitation of tourist sites;
- Ukrainian Presidential Decree of 11.03.2003 No 207 "On Measures for the Development of the Tourism and Recreational Resort Sphere of Ukraine", which envisages, in particular, the development of a set of measures intended to renew the resources of museums, cultural and historical reserves and cultural heritage sites;
- Resolution of the Cabinet of Ministers of Ukraine of 29.01.2003 No 133 "On Reinforcing the Programme to Develop the Crimea as an all-year-round recreational resort and tourist centre";
- Resolution of the Cabinet of Ministers of Ukraine of 19.03.2003 No 358 "On Modifying the List of Central Bodies of the Executive Authorities Responsible for the Technical Regulation of Specified Spheres of Activity and the Development of Technical Regulations", by which the State Administration for Tourism has been made responsible for technically regulating the activities of sites of the tourist industry and resort institutions (health resorts excluded) and the development of technical regulations, which provide the opportunity to improve the regulatory base that is called on to provide a unified approach to the assessment of the level of standards of hotel service provision, to introduce legality and provide safe stays in all types of accommodation.

New Ukrainian national standards DSTU 4268:2003 "Tourist Services, Accommodation, Main Requirements" and DSTU 4269:2003 "Tourist Services-Hotel Classification" have been developed by the State Administration for Tourism and the State Research Institute, Rules of Exploitation for hotels and similar forms of accommodation and for the provision of hotel services have also been developed.

Five international agreements on cooperation in the field of tourism have been signed in order to enlarge the contractual base for cooperation in tourism in 2003, (the total number of bilateral international, intergovernmental and interdepartmental agreements on cooperation in the field of tourism signed by Ukraine on 1.01.2004 was 34), including:

- Agreements between the Cabinet of Ministers of Ukraine and the Government of the Republic of Kazakhstan on cooperation in the field of tourism;
- Agreements between the Cabinet of Ministers of Ukraine and the Government of the Syrian Arab Republic on cooperation in the field of tourism;
- Agreements between the Cabinet of Ministers of Ukraine and the Government of the Lebanese Republic on cooperation in the field of tourism;
- Agreements between the Cabinet of Ministers of Ukraine and the Government of India on cooperation in the field of tourism;
- Agreements between the Cabinet of Ministers of Ukraine and the Council of Ministers of Serbia and Montenegro.

**Marketing & promotion**

The Scientific Centre for the Development of Tourism of the Ukrainian State Administration for Tourism has developed a concept of national tourist product image positioning on the tourist services market. Related research is being carried out into the main trends of development of national tourism and its progress on international markets.

About 50 press conferences were held in 2003 and in the first half of 2004 and cooperation with 30 or so media companies was fine-tuned. Permanent tourism columns have been developed for the newspapers Sevodnya, Pravitel'stvennii Courrier and Den', the weekly Zerkalo Nedeli and for national radio programmes, in cooperation with the Ukrainian State Administration for Tourism.

In order to provide operational information on its activities, the Ukrainian State Administration for Tourism opened a tourist information centre in 2003, which provides regular external publications containing reports on the events and processes presently taking place in the field of tourism.

The Ukrainian State Administration for Tourism organised 14 press tours during which the Ukrainian mass media was able to gather information on the present condition and the main development prospects of the tourist industry in Ukraine.

In its work, the Ukrainian State Administration for Tourism pays great attention to the organization of exhibitions as a priority marketing method for promoting national tourism products in the world market. In 2003 the Ukrainian State Administration for Tourism actively participated in 15 major tourism events abroad and 12 state and regional exhibitions in Ukraine and in the first half of 2004 it took part in 17 exhibitions abroad and 7 national exhibitions.

**Outlook 2004**

Considering the dynamics and the main development trends of the tourism and resort industry, forecasts for the number of foreign tourists visiting Ukraine in 2004, stand at 14 million, national tourists at 7.8 million and the volume of tourism consumption at 31.7 billion UAH (calculated as per WTO recommendations).

The forecast for the number of foreign tourists in 2008 stands at 21.6 million, the number of national tourists at 9 million and the volume of tourism consumption at 45.6 billion UAH.

Taking into consideration the fact that Ukraine will host the anniversary edition of the Eurovision 2005 competition, the following measures are to be carried out:

- A town tourism information centre and a network of sightseeing points are to be created;
- Construction work on hotels and hotel-office complexes is to be completed (hotel-office complexes Sofia Sheraton, Leiptsig and Teatral'nii and the Radison SAS hotel);
- Road upgrade work is to be completed in suburban and urban zones under the project for international transport corridors;
- Corresponding information signs for car parks, lay-bys and rest stops for tourist sightseeing transport are to be defined and developed;
- Work is to be organised to create and distribute printed advertising and informational material on tourism opportunities in Kiev;
- The publication of guidebooks, souvenir albums, cards, plans, booklets, posters, leaflets and other printed materials is to be organised for the beginning of the Eurovision 2005.

## International Meetings Industry (MI)

**Characteristics of supply**

To improve the State image, the following international events have been held in Ukraine: XII International Trade Fair, Crimea. Resorts and Tourism 2003 (February-March 2003, Yalta); IX International Exhibition of the UITT 2003, Ukraine, Travel and Tourism (April 2003, Kiev); III International Exhibition on Equipment and Technology for Hotels and Resorts, Equip Hotel Ukraine 2003 (April 2003, Kiev); III Kiev International Exhibition Sport and Relaxation. Spring KISS 2003 (April 2003, Kiev); I International Assembly of Tourist Companies (April 2003, Odessa); International Exhibition/Trade Fair on Industrial Technologies, Means of Production, Wares and Services from CIS Countries (May 2003, Kiev); II International Exhibition/Trade Fair on the European Tourist Centre, Transcarpathia 2003 (September 2003, Uzhgorod); X International Tourist Salon Ukraine 2003 (October 2003, Kiev), International Trade Fair-Festival, The Great Silk Route, Crimea 2003 (October 2003, Sudak); I International Conference and Exhibition, Hospitality Invest" (October 2003, Kiev).

Tourism exhibition events in Ukraine are becoming bigger and more popular every year.

**Organisation of promotion**

The State programme on the development of tourism for 2002-2010 is being carried out successfully, reinforcing the Resolution of the Cabinet of Ministers of the Ukraine of the 29th of April of 2002 Number 583.

The programme put in Policy the completion of measures along the following lines:

- State regulation of tourism;
- Development of material resources for tourism;
- The use of recreational resources and cultural heritage for the development of tourism;
- Professional and scientific provision for the tourism sector;
- Improvement of publicity and information activities in the tourist sector and improvement of Ukraine's image in the international arena;

Regulatory provision for the realisation of the programmes.

Programmes such as the development of tourism in different oblasts and individual towns in Ukraine are being carried out under the given general state programmes.

**Collection of statistics on the Meetings Industry?:** yes.

**Description**

Data collection, classification and analysis is carried out by the Ukrainian State Statistics Committee. The data produced includes:

- Statistical Bulletin "Company Activity by Service Area";
- Ukrainian Statistical Yearbook.

**Importance / size**

The tourist industry of Ukraine occupies a significant place in the national economic indicators and facilitates the following:

- Attraction of investment in the Ukrainian tourist industry by national and foreign companies;
- Regulation of the system for monetary circulation in the tourist sector, by strategic paths which re-orientate calculations for tourist services, work and goods onto a cashless basis;
- The establishment, allocation and stimulation of development to all tourist segments and concomitant sectors.

**Evolution MI**

The Ukrainian State Administration for Tourism positively assesses the development of exhibition activities, trade fairs, conferences and other events promoting national tourist products on international and target tourist markets.

# International Tourism by Origin

**Ukraine**

**International Tourist Arrivals at Frontiers**

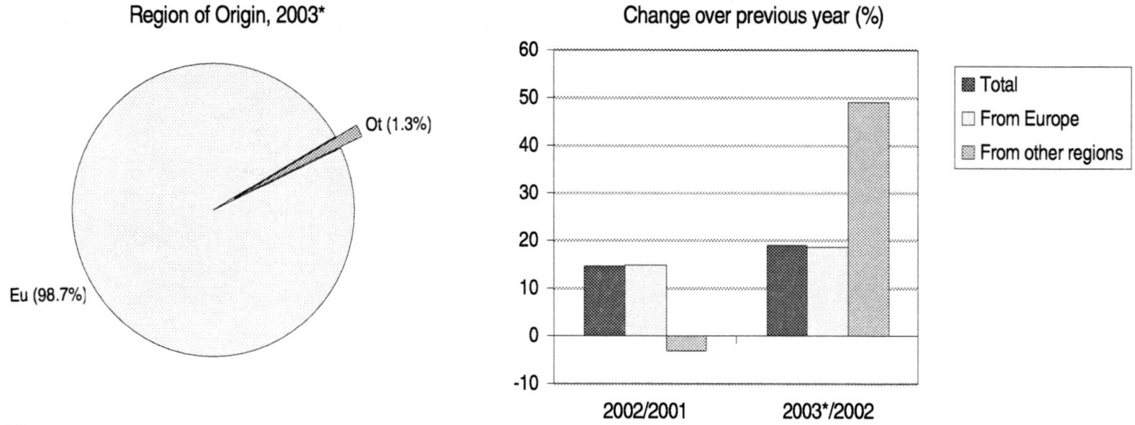


Eu: Europe;

Ot: Other;

Source: World Tourism Organization (WTO) ©

**Ukraine**
**International Tourist Arrivals at Frontiers (by residence)**

| | | | | (thousand) | Market share (%) | | Growth rate (%) | | Average per year (%) |
|---|---|---|---|---|---|---|---|---|---|
| | 1995 | 2001 | 2002 | 2003* | 1995 | 2003* | 2002/01 | 2003*/02 | 1995-2003* |
| **Total** | **3,716** | **9,174** | **10,517** | **12,514** | **100** | **100** | **14.6** | **19.0** | **16.4** |
| *From Europe* | *3,586* | *9,061* | *10,409* | *12,345* | *96.5* | *98.7* | *14.9* | *18.6* | *16.7* |
| Russian Federation | 434 | 4,858 | 5,170 | 5,026 | 11.7 | 40.2 | 6.4 | -2.8 | 35.8 |
| Rep Moldova | 390 | 2,194 | 2,259 | 2,557 | 10.5 | 20.4 | 3.0 | 13.2 | 26.5 |
| Belarus | 395 | 753 | 1,045 | 1,595 | 10.6 | 12.7 | 38.8 | 52.7 | 19.1 |
| Poland | 449 | 367 | 556 | 1,239 | 12.1 | 9.9 | 51.5 | 122.9 | 13.5 |
| Hungary | 390 | 357 | 776 | 1,182 | 10.5 | 9.4 | 117.3 | 52.3 | 14.9 |
| Germany | 69 | 78 | 95 | 119 | 1.9 | 0.9 | 21.9 | 24.8 | 7.0 |
| Slovakia | 190 | 43 | 43 | 105 | 5.1 | 0.8 | -1.0 | 147.0 | -7.1 |
| Romania | 186 | 54 | 43 | 68 | 5.0 | 0.5 | -19.6 | 57.7 | -11.8 |
| Israel | 28 | 57 | 81 | 40 | 0.8 | 0.3 | 40.7 | -50.5 | 4.6 |
| Turkey | 59 | 15 | 22 | 32 | 1.6 | 0.3 | 47.8 | 43.0 | -7.4 |
| Italy | 9 | 14 | 19 | 30 | 0.3 | 0.2 | 34.5 | 60.0 | 15.7 |
| Lithuania | 2 | 24 | 26 | 30 | 0.0 | 0.2 | 10.2 | 15.2 | 42.4 |
| United Kingdom | 18 | 30 | 35 | 29 | 0.5 | 0.2 | 15.5 | -16.1 | 6.2 |
| France | 16 | 16 | 17 | 25 | 0.4 | 0.2 | 3.1 | 52.7 | 6.0 |
| Armenia | 31 | 11 | 16 | 22 | 0.8 | 0.2 | 51.9 | 31.4 | -4.5 |
| Kazakhstan | 27 | 9 | 19 | 21 | 0.7 | 0.2 | 116.5 | 10.9 | -3.1 |
| Latvia | 1 | 24 | 24 | 19 | 0.0 | 0.2 | 1.1 | -18.4 | 54.1 |
| Uzbekistan | 36 | 19 | 13 | 19 | 1.0 | 0.2 | -29.9 | 41.6 | -7.7 |
| Georgia | 32 | 12 | 16 | 18 | 0.9 | 0.1 | 28.7 | 16.9 | -6.9 |
| Netherlands | 6 | 7 | 8 | 18 | 0.2 | 0.1 | 19.8 | 120.0 | 15.9 |
| Czech Rep | 12 | 18 | 16 | 18 | 0.3 | 0.1 | -14.1 | 12.3 | 4.9 |
| Azerbaijan | 18 | 10 | 10 | 14 | 0.5 | 0.1 | 1.0 | 29.3 | -3.2 |
| Bulgaria | 149 | 14 | 14 | 13 | 4.0 | 0.1 | -3.6 | -5.6 | -26.4 |
| Austria | 10 | 13 | 13 | 12 | 0.3 | 0.1 | 0.3 | -11.0 | 1.8 |
| Kyrgyzstan | 8 | 2 | 4 | 12 | 0.2 | 0.1 | 109.2 | 201.9 | 5.0 |
| Other intraregional | 623 | 62 | 68 | 82 | 16.8 | 0.7 | 9.3 | 20.9 | -22.4 |
| *From other regions* | *124* | *107* | *104* | *155* | *3.3* | *1.2* | *-3.1* | *49.0* | *2.9* |
| United States | 41 | 49 | 38 | 66 | 1.1 | 0.5 | -21.6 | 72.9 | 6.0 |
| Canada | 13 | 10 | 10 | 12 | 0.4 | 0.1 | -5.1 | 20.5 | -1.6 |
| China | 2 | 4 | 8 | 8 | 0.0 | 0.1 | 98.3 | -1.4 | 22.8 |
| India | 12 | 3 | 4 | 6 | 0.3 | 0.0 | 56.5 | 52.3 | -8.1 |
| Iran | 1 | 2 | 3 | 6 | 0.0 | 0.0 | 41.6 | 80.8 | 21.8 |
| Syrian Arab Republic | 9 | 4 | 4 | 5 | 0.2 | 0.0 | -17.7 | 47.8 | -6.6 |
| Japan | 1 | 2 | 2 | 5 | 0.0 | 0.0 | 22.3 | 114.6 | 22.4 |
| Lebanon | 1 | 3 | 3 | 4 | 0.0 | 0.0 | 22.6 | 36.5 | 25.0 |
| Korea, Republic of | 0 | 0 | 1 | 3 | 0.0 | 0.0 | 347.6 | 190.6 | 61.3 |
| Jordan | 2 | 3 | 3 | 3 | 0.0 | 0.0 | 8.1 | 5.8 | 7.3 |
| Rwanda | 0 | 0 | 0 | 3 | 0.0 | 0.0 | -33.3 | 47983.3 | 108.8 |
| Libyan Arab Jamahiriya | 0 | 1 | 1 | 2 | 0.0 | 0.0 | 27.5 | 71.4 | 42.0 |
| Angola | 0 | 0 | 0 | 2 | 0.0 | 0.0 | -9.3 | 2725.6 | 61.8 |
| Australia | 4 | 5 | 4 | 2 | 0.1 | 0.0 | -4.9 | -50.7 | -8.4 |
| Vietnam | 3 | 2 | 2 | 2 | 0.1 | 0.0 | -5.2 | -2.2 | -4.1 |
| Egypt | 3 | 1 | 2 | 2 | 0.1 | 0.0 | 44.5 | -7.4 | -6.5 |
| Other interregional | 30 | 18 | 17 | 22 | 0.8 | 0.2 | -4.1 | 30.6 | -3.7 |
| *Other World/Not specified* | *6* | *6* | *4* | *14* | *0.2* | *0.1* | *-30.9* | *237.9* | *9.9* |

Source: World Tourism Organization (WTO) © (Data as collected by WTO December 2004)

# III.3.21 Uzbekistan Central and Eastern Europe

## Profile

# Uzbekistan

**Europe**
**Central and Eastern Europe**

| | |
|---|---|
| Capital | Tashkent |
| Year of entry in WTO | 1993 |
| Area (1000 km²) | 447 |
| Population (2003, million) | 26.0 |
| Gross Domestic Product (GDP) (2003, euro million) | 9,230 |
| GDP per capita (2003, euro) | 361 |
| GDP growth (real, %) | |
| '-> 2002: 3.1; 2003: 1.5; 2004*: 2.5; 2005*: 2.5 | |

| | 2001 | 2002 | 2003* | 2002/2001 | 2003*/2002 |
|---|---|---|---|---|---|
| **International Arrivals** | | | | | |
| Tourists (overnight visitors) (1000) | 345 | 332 | 231 | -3.9 | -30.3 |
| - per 100 of inhabitants | 1 | 1 | 1 | | |
| **Tourism accommodation** | | | | | |
| Number of rooms | 7,332 | 7,332 | 7,332 | | |
| *Nights spent in collective establishments (1000)* | 2,639 | 2,566 | 2,190 | -2.8 | -14.7 |
| by non-residents (inbound tourism) | 1,082 | 1,069 | 935 | -1.2 | -12.5 |
| by residents (domestic tourism) | 1,557 | 1,497 | 1,255 | -3.9 | -16.2 |
| *Nights spent in hotels and similar establishments (1000)* | 1,311 | 1,260 | 733 | -3.9 | -41.8 |
| by non-residents (inbound tourism) | 699 | 672 | 249 | -3.9 | -62.9 |
| by residents (domestic tourism) | 612 | 588 | 484 | -3.9 | -17.7 |
| **Outbound Tourism** | | | | | |
| Trips abroad (1000) | 183 | 264 | 400 | 44.3 | 51.5 |
| - per 100 of inhabitants | 1 | 1 | 2 | | |
| **Receipts and Expenditure for International Tourism** | | | | | |
| International Tourism Receipts (euro million) | 78 | 76 | 51 | -2.6 | -33.1 |
| - per Tourist Arrival (euro) | 226 | 229 | 220 | 1.3 | -4.1 |
| - per capita (euro) | 3 | 3 | 2 | | |

Source: World Tourism Organization (WTO) (Data as collected by WTO December 2004)

See annex for methodological notes and reference of external sources used.

# International Tourism by Origin

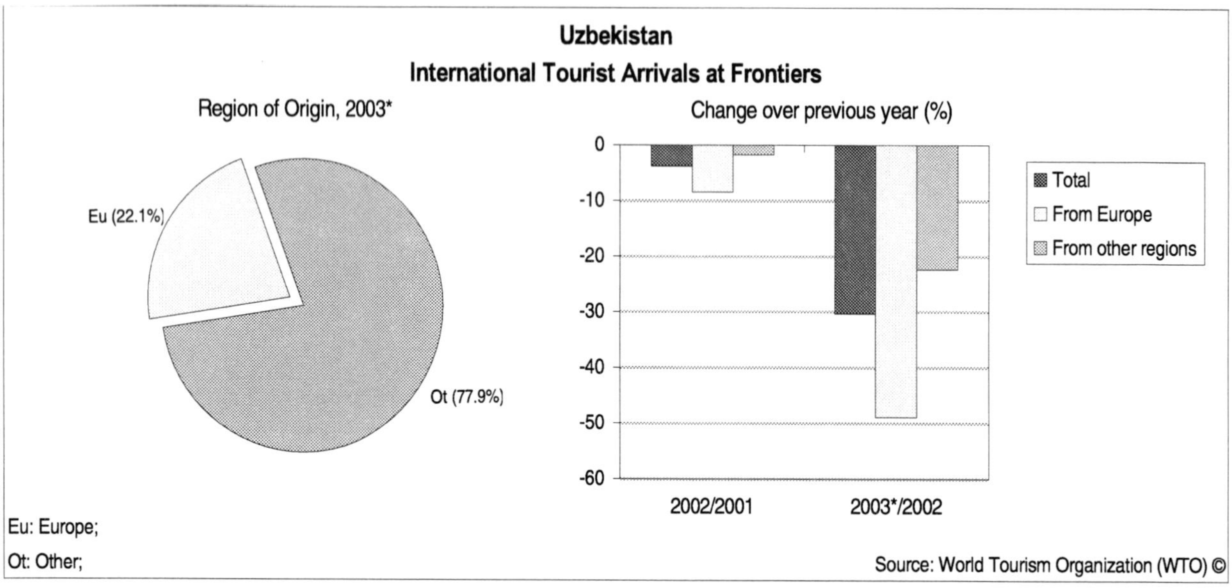


**Uzbekistan**
**International Tourist Arrivals at Frontiers (by residence)**

| | | | | (thousand) | Market share (%) | | Growth rate (%) | | Average per year (%) |
|---|---|---|---|---|---|---|---|---|---|
| | 1995 | 2001 | 2002 | 2003* | 1995 | 2003* | 2002/01 | 2003*/02 | 1995-2003* |
| **Total** | .. | **345** | **332** | **231** | | **100** | **-3.9** | **-30.3** | |
| *From Europe* | .. | *109* | *100* | *51* | | *22.1* | *-8.4* | *-48.9* | |
| All Europe | .. | 109 | 100 | 51 | | 22.1 | -8.4 | -48.9 | |
| *From other regions* | .. | *236* | *232* | *180* | | *77.9* | *-1.8* | *-22.3* | |
| All Asia | .. | 193 | 195 | 145 | | 62.8 | 1.1 | -25.7 | |
| All Middle East | .. | 24 | 24 | 24 | | 10.4 | -2.1 | 2.1 | |
| All South Asia | .. | 8 | 8 | 8 | | 3.5 | 0.0 | 0.0 | |
| All Americas | .. | 10 | 4 | 2 | | 0.9 | -59.0 | -51.2 | |
| All Africa | .. | 1 | 1 | 1 | | 0.4 | 0.0 | 0.0 | |

Source: World Tourism Organization (WTO) © (Data as collected by WTO December 2004)

# III.4 Southern Europe

## III.4.1 Albania Southern Europe

### Profile

**Albania**

| | |
|---|---|
| Capital | Tirana |
| Year of entry in WTO | 1993 |
| Area (1000 km²) | 29 |
| Population (2003, million) | 3.5 |
| Gross Domestic Product (GDP) (2003, euro million) | 6,494 |
| GDP per capita (2003, euro) | 1,859 |
| GDP growth (real, %) | |
| '-> 2002: 4.7; 2003: 6.0; 2004*: 6.2; 2005*: 6.0 | |

**Europe**
**Southern Europe**

| | 2001 | 2002 | 2003* | 2002/2001 | 2003*/2002 |
|---|---|---|---|---|---|
| **International Arrivals** | | | | | |
| Visitors (1000) | 354 | 470 | 557 | 32.8 | 18.5 |
| Tourists (overnight visitors) (1000) | 34 | 36 | 41 | 5.9 | 13.9 |
| - per 100 of inhabitants | 1 | 1 | 1 | | |
| **Tourism accommodation** | | | | | |
| Number of rooms | 3,881 | 4,107 | 4,161 | 5.8 | 1.3 |
| *Nights spent in hotels and similar establishments (1000)* | 394 | 533 | 547 | 35.3 | 2.6 |
| by non-residents (inbound tourism) | 91 | 143 | 137 | 57.1 | -4.2 |
| by residents (domestic tourism) | 303 | 390 | 410 | 28.7 | 5.1 |
| **Receipts and Expenditure for International Tourism** | | | | | |
| International Tourism Receipts (euro million) | 483 | 544 | 552 | 12.6 | 1.5 |
| - per Tourist Arrival (euro) | 14,203 | 15,104 | 13,465 | 6.3 | -10.9 |
| - per Visitor Arrival (euro) | 1,364 | 1,157 | 991 | -15.2 | -14.3 |
| - per capita (euro) | 138 | 155 | 157 | | |
| International Fare Receipts (euro million) | 5 | 6 | 16 | 3.1 | 184.2 |
| International Tourism Expenditure (euro million) | 278 | 408 | 517 | 46.5 | 26.9 |
| - per capita (euro) | 80 | 116 | 147 | | |
| International Fare Expenditure (euro million) | 13 | 23 | 19 | 80.5 | -18.8 |
| △ International Tourism Balance (euro million) | 205 | 136 | 35 | | |
| △ International Fare Balance (euro million) | -8 | -18 | -3 | | |

Source: World Tourism Organization (WTO) (Data as collected by WTO December 2004)

See annex for methodological notes and reference of external sources used.

# International Tourism by Origin

**Albania**

**International Visitor Arrivals at Frontiers**

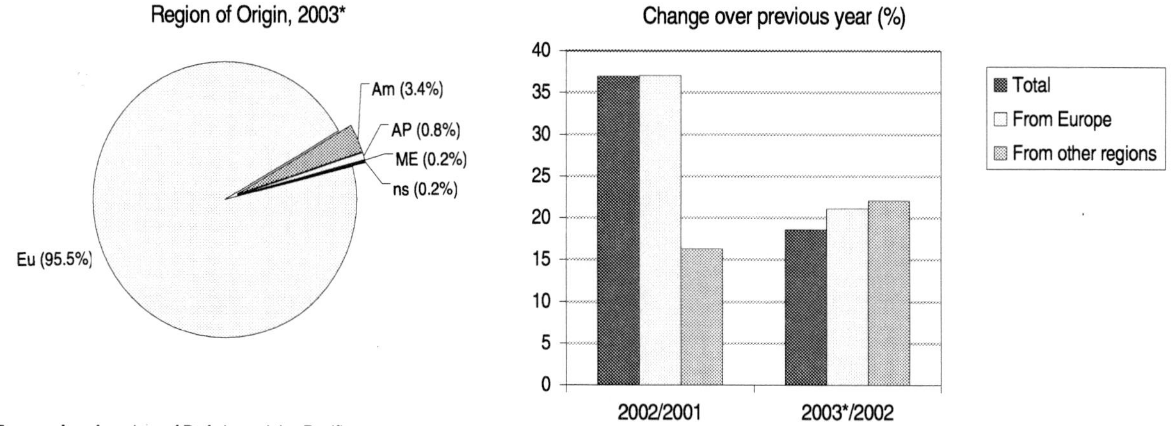


Eu: Europe; Am: Americas; AP: Asia and the Pacific;
ME: Middle East; Af: Africa; ns: not specified

Source: World Tourism Organization (WTO) ©

**Albania**
**International Visitor Arrivals at Frontiers (by nationality)**

| | | | | (thousand) | Market share (%) | | Growth rate (%) | | Average per year (%) |
|---|---|---|---|---|---|---|---|---|---|
| | 1995 | 2001 | 2002 | 2003* | 1995 | 2003* | 2002/01 | 2003*/02 | 1995-2003* |
| **Total** | .. | **343** | **470** | **557** | | **100** | **37.0** | **18.6** | |
| *From Europe* | .. | *320* | *439* | *532* | | *95.5* | *37.0* | *21.1* | |
| Serbia & Montenegro | .. | 109 | 199 | 272 | | 48.8 | 82.2 | 36.9 | |
| F.Yug.Rp.Macedonia | .. | 69 | 76 | 79 | | 14.2 | 10.2 | 4.3 | |
| Italy | .. | 47 | 52 | 50 | | 9.0 | 10.5 | -3.2 | |
| Greece | .. | 28 | 30 | 34 | | 6.1 | 8.2 | 13.0 | |
| United Kingdom | .. | 16 | 22 | 25 | | 4.5 | 38.7 | 16.8 | |
| Germany | .. | 13 | 15 | 15 | | 2.7 | 11.6 | 2.6 | |
| Turkey | .. | 9 | 10 | 10 | | 1.7 | 4.4 | -1.3 | |
| France | .. | 4 | 4 | 9 | | 1.7 | 20.0 | 113.2 | |
| Bulgaria | .. | 4 | 3 | 5 | | 0.9 | -15.7 | 49.6 | |
| Austria | .. | 3 | 3 | 4 | | 0.6 | 14.0 | 15.3 | |
| Switzerland | .. | 3 | 4 | 3 | | 0.6 | 22.4 | -2.6 | |
| Netherlands | .. | 3 | 4 | 3 | | 0.6 | 26.1 | -14.6 | |
| Belgium | .. | 2 | 3 | 2 | | 0.4 | 53.3 | -4.5 | |
| Sweden | .. | 1 | 2 | 2 | | 0.4 | 22.1 | 41.0 | |
| Croatia | .. | 1 | 2 | 2 | | 0.4 | 20.0 | 24.0 | |
| Norway | .. | 1 | 2 | 2 | | 0.3 | 9.2 | 12.0 | |
| Ireland | .. | 1 | 1 | 2 | | 0.3 | 50.3 | 37.0 | |
| Other intraregional | .. | 7 | 10 | 12 | | 2.1 | 43.0 | 20.6 | |
| *From other regions* | .. | *17* | *20* | *24* | | *4.4* | *16.3* | *22.1* | |
| United States | .. | 12 | 14 | 16 | | 3.0 | 14.7 | 17.5 | |
| Canada | .. | 1 | 1 | 2 | | 0.4 | 23.1 | 43.7 | |
| Australia | .. | 1 | 1 | 1 | | 0.2 | 26.6 | 13.9 | |
| Japan | .. | 0 | 0 | 1 | | 0.2 | 23.3 | 226.2 | |
| Other interregional | .. | 3 | 3 | 3 | | 0.6 | 16.4 | 17.5 | |
| *Other World/Not specified* | .. | *5* | *11* | *1* | | *0.2* | *99.4* | *-90.3* | |

Source: World Tourism Organization (WTO) © (Data as collected by WTO December 2004)

# III.4.2 Andorra Southern Europe

## Profile

**Andorra**

**Europe**
**Southern Europe**

| | |
|---|---|
| Capital | Andorra la Vella |
| Year of entry in WTO | 1995 |
| Area (10 km²) | 45 |
| Population (2003, 1000) | 69 |

| | 2001 | 2002 | 2003* | 2002/2001 | 2003*/2002 |
|---|---|---|---|---|---|
| **International Arrivals** | | | | | |
| Visitors (1000) | 11,351 | 11,507 | 11,601 | 1.4 | 0.8 |
| Tourists (overnight visitors) (1000) | 3,516 | 3,387 | 3,138 | -3.7 | -7.4 |
| - per 100 of inhabitants | 5,199 | 4,952 | 4,538 | | |
| Same-day visitors (1000) | 7,835 | 8,120 | 8,463 | 3.6 | 4.2 |
| **Tourism accommodation** | | | | | |
| Number of bed-places | .. | 34,522 | .. | | |
| *Nights spent in collective establishments (1000)* | | | | | |
| by non-residents (inbound tourism) | 9,809 | 9,737 | .. | -0.7 | |

Source: World Tourism Organization (WTO) (Data as collected by WTO December 2004)

See annex for methodological notes and reference of external sources used.

## Survey

Contributed by *Gobierno de Andorra*
www.andorra.ad (promotional)
www.andorra.ad (institutional/corporate)
www.andorra.ad (research and data)

## Tourism development and outlook

**Overall evaluation of results**

Tourism continues to be the engine of our economy. In 2003 we received 11.6 million visitors, 0.8 per cent more than in 2002. Of these 8.4 million were day-trippers (4.2% up on 2002) and 3.1 million were tourists (8.4 million overnight stays, 14% down on 2002).

**Supply**

Increase in the number of hotel places, mainly in four-star establishments.
Expansion of cultural tourism supply and initial measures to promote business tourism.
Ongoing heavy investment in mountain resorts (winter and summer) our visitors.

**External factors**

Decline in the purchasing power of our visitors.
Improvements in highway access to the Principality.

| | |
|---|---|
| **Tourism policy** | Public-private sector cooperation.<br>Joint planning of communication activities. |
| **Marketing & promotion** | Promotional campaigns more attuned to the various markets.<br>Improvements to our website <www.andorra.ad>.<br>More and better tourism promotion through sporting events.<br>For the ski sector, the trading association between the resorts of Pas de la Casa-Grau Roig and Soldeu el Tarter and the subsequent development of the GrandValira ski slope have raised considerable expectations. |
| **Outlook 2004** | The forecast is for a continuing decrease in overnight stays.<br>To counter this tendency special activities have been planned for certain markets (the United Kingdom, France and Spain).<br>Large-scale action will be taken to promote business tourism (meetings, conferences, incentive travel, seminars, etc.) |

## International Meetings Industry (MI)

| | |
|---|---|
| **Characteristics of supply** | We have some public centres that can host meetings or conferences.<br>Some 15 hotels specialized in business tourism, and there are many companies that organize conferences with services of all kinds. |
| **Organisation of promotion** | At present each conference centre carries out its own promotion.<br>Efforts are under way to set up a specialized body along the lines of a national convention bureau. |

**Collection of statistics on the Meetings Industry?:** no.

| | |
|---|---|
| **Importance / size** | This sector is expanding. |
| **Evolution MI** | Development is rapid, and we believe that the short-term prospects are favourable. |

# International Tourism by Origin

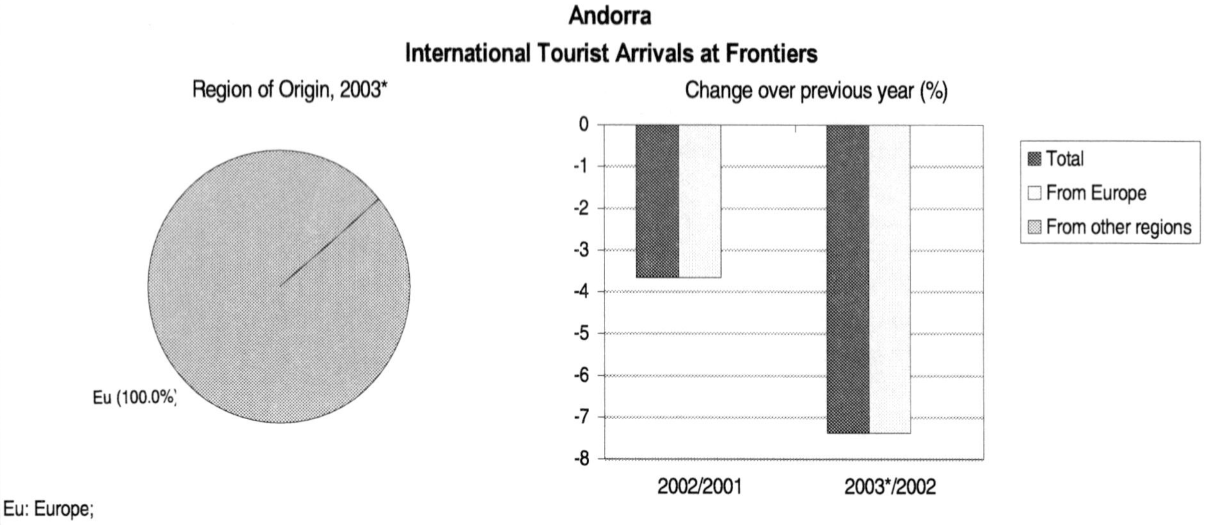


**Andorra**
**International Tourist Arrivals at Frontiers (by residence)**

| | | | | (thousand) | Market share (%) | | Growth rate (%) | | Average per year (%) |
|---|---|---|---|---|---|---|---|---|---|
| | 1995 | 2001 | 2002 | 2003* | 1995 | 2003* | 2002/01 | 2003*/02 | 1995-2003* |
| **Total** | .. | **3,516** | **3,388** | **3,138** | | **100** | **-3.7** | **-7.4** | |
| *From Europe* | *..* | *3,516* | *3,388* | *3,138* | | *100.0* | *-3.7* | *-7.4* | |
| Spain | .. | 2,517 | 2,334 | 2,266 | | 72.2 | -7.3 | -2.9 | |
| France | .. | 822 | 847 | 719 | | 22.9 | 3.0 | -15.1 | |
| Other Europe | .. | 177 | 207 | 153 | | 4.9 | 16.8 | -26.4 | |

Source: World Tourism Organization (WTO) © (Data as collected by WTO December 2004)

# III.4.3 Bosnia Herzegovina Southern Europe

## Profile

**Bosnia and Herzegovina**

**Europe**
**Southern Europe**

| | |
|---|---|
| Capital | Sarajevo |
| Year of entry in WTO | 1993 |
| Area (1000 km²) | 51 |
| Population (2003, million) | 4.0 |
| Gross Domestic Product (GDP) (2003, euro million) | 7,374 |
| GDP per capita (2003, euro) | 1,911 |
| GDP growth (real, %) | |
| '-> 2002: 5.5; 2003: 2.7; 2004*: 5.0; 2005*: 4.0 | |

| | 2001 | 2002 | 2003* | 2002/2001 | 2003*/2002 |
|---|---|---|---|---|---|
| **International Arrivals** | | | | | |
| Tourists (overnight visitors) (1000) | 139 | 160 | 165 | 15.3 | 3.6 |
| - per 100 of inhabitants | 4 | 4 | 4 | | |
| **Tourism accommodation** | | | | | |
| Number of rooms | 4,546 | .. | .. | | |
| *Nights spent in collective establishments (1000)* | 782 | 888 | 913 | 13.6 | 2.8 |
| by non-residents (inbound tourism) | 330 | 392 | 419 | 18.8 | 6.9 |
| by residents (domestic tourism) | 452 | 496 | 494 | 9.7 | -0.4 |
| **Receipts and Expenditure for International Tourism** | | | | | |
| International Tourism Receipts (euro million) | 189 | 214 | 249 | 13.1 | 15.9 |
| - per Tourist Arrival (euro) | 1,368 | 1,342 | 1,502 | -1.9 | 11.9 |
| - per capita (euro) | 48 | 54 | 62 | | |
| International Fare Receipts (euro million) | 15 | 21 | 24 | 40.0 | 14.7 |
| International Tourism Expenditure (euro million) | 42 | 55 | 62 | 29.6 | 14.0 |
| - per capita (euro) | 11 | 14 | 16 | | |
| International Fare Expenditure (euro million) | 24 | 30 | 41 | 26.6 | 36.8 |
| △ International Tourism Balance (euro million) | 147 | 160 | 186 | | |
| △ International Fare Balance (euro million) | -9 | -9 | -17 | | |

Source: World Tourism Organization (WTO) (Data as collected by WTO December 2004)

See annex for methodological notes and reference of external sources used.

# Survey

Contributed by *Ministry of Tourism and Trade*
www.bhtourism.ba (promotional)
www.mpv.gov.ba (institutional/corporate)

## Tourism development and outlook

**Overall evaluation of results**

The main result was the change of the image of the country through promotional activities. The Office of the High Representative in Bosnia and Herzegovina (OHR) coordinated projects:
- Some international projects concerning protected areas and sustainable tourism (JICA project, GEF project etc);
- Guidelines included in Bosnia and Herzegovian's Poverty Reduction Strategy Papers strategy (PRSP).

**External factors**

The entry formalities depend on visa regime.

**Tourism policy**

The major developments in the area of Tourism Policy last year were:
- Policy making and planning tourism law;
- Training seminar concerning protected areas (eg Azahar seminar, JICA seminar, etc).

**Marketing & promotion**

Special promotional campaign and activities, e.g. Paddy Achdown OHR promotional campaign in 5 world capital cities.

**Outlook 2004**

Cooperation in common promotion with ex-Yugoslavia countries.

## International Meetings Industry (MI)

**Organisation of promotion**

The international promotion of this industry is organised at the national level by the Ministry of Tourism.

**Collection of statistics on the Meetings Industry?:** no.

**Description**

No statistics are collected on the Meetings Industry.

# International Tourism by Origin

**Bosnia and Herzegovina**

**International Tourist Arrivals in All Accommodation Establishments**

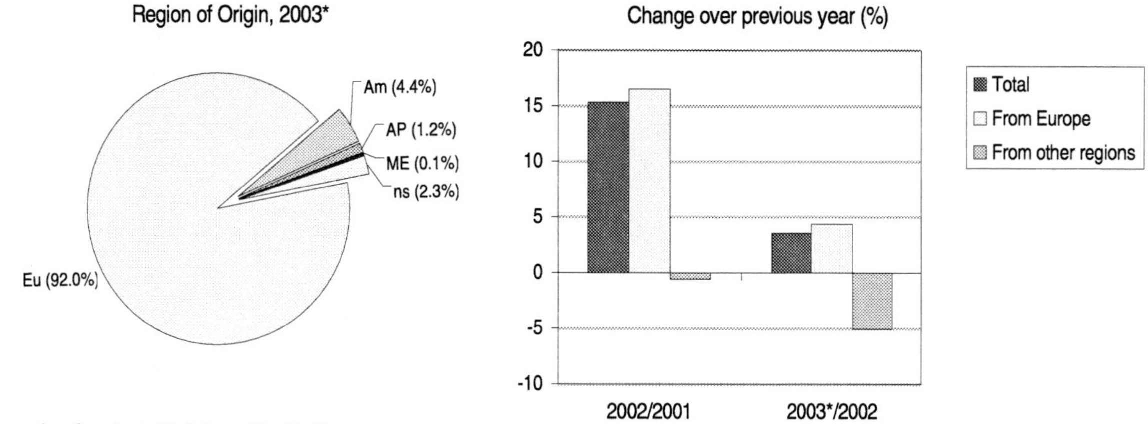


Eu: Europe; Am: Americas; AP: Asia and the Pacific;
ME: Middle East; ns: Not specified;

Source: World Tourism Organization (WTO) ©

**Bosnia and Herzegovina**

**Nights of International Tourists in All Accommodation Establishments**

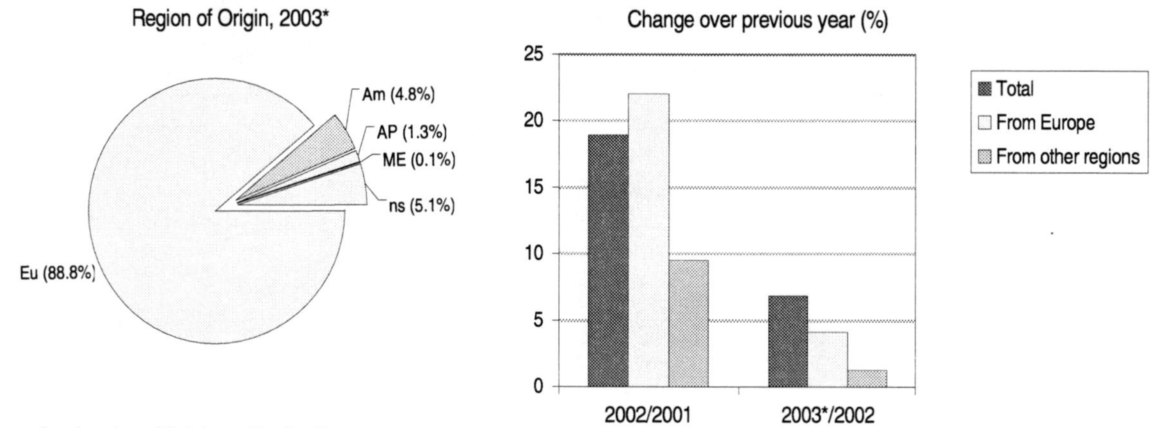


Eu: Europe; Am: Americas; AP: Asia and the Pacific;
ME: Middle East; ns: Not specified;

Source: World Tourism Organization (WTO) ©

**Bosnia and Herzegovina**
**International Tourist Arrivals in All Accommodation Establishments (by residence)**

| | | | | (thousand) | Market share (%) | | Growth rate (%) | | Average per year (%) |
|---|---|---|---|---|---|---|---|---|---|
| | 1995 | 2001 | 2002 | 2003* | 1995 | 2003* | 2002/01 | 2003*/02 | 1995-2003* |
| **Total** | .. | **139** | **160** | **165** | | **100** | **15.3** | **3.6** | |
| *From Europe* | .. | *125* | *146* | *152* | | *92.0* | *16.5* | *4.4* | |
| Serbia & Montenegro | .. | 42 | 45 | 40 | | 24.3 | 9.6 | -11.5 | |
| Croatia | .. | 22 | 24 | 28 | | 16.9 | 7.3 | 19.1 | |
| Slovenia | .. | 10 | 15 | 18 | | 10.8 | 49.7 | 16.8 | |
| Germany | .. | 7 | 8 | 8 | | 5.0 | 13.2 | 5.3 | |
| Italy | .. | 7 | 7 | 8 | | 4.6 | 5.0 | 4.5 | |
| Austria | .. | 3 | 4 | 6 | | 3.6 | 15.7 | 56.4 | |
| United Kingdom | .. | 4 | 4 | 5 | | 2.9 | 23.2 | 11.2 | |
| France | .. | 3 | 3 | 3 | | 1.9 | -13.8 | 27.5 | |
| Poland | .. | 2 | 4 | 3 | | 1.9 | 149.8 | -29.4 | |
| Czech Rep | .. | 2 | 3 | 3 | | 1.8 | 16.3 | 8.7 | |
| Hungary | .. | 2 | 2 | 3 | | 1.7 | 41.0 | 24.8 | |
| Sweden | .. | 2 | 2 | 3 | | 1.6 | 18.9 | 13.9 | |
| Turkey | .. | 2 | 2 | 3 | | 1.6 | -12.0 | 36.7 | |
| F.Yug.Rp.Macedonia | .. | 2 | 2 | 3 | | 1.6 | 44.5 | 15.0 | |
| Netherlands | .. | 2 | 2 | 2 | | 1.3 | 11.1 | 8.7 | |
| Spain | .. | 2 | 3 | 2 | | 1.0 | 15.9 | -41.4 | |
| Denmark | .. | 1 | 1 | 2 | | 1.0 | 3.2 | 39.3 | |
| Norway | .. | 1 | 1 | 1 | | 0.9 | 4.8 | 8.7 | |
| Slovakia | .. | 1 | 1 | 1 | | 0.8 | -16.7 | 92.9 | |
| Switzerland | .. | 1 | 1 | 1 | | 0.8 | 9.4 | 0.8 | |
| Iceland | .. | 0 | 0 | 1 | | 0.7 | -9.5 | 1286.0 | |
| Belgium | .. | 1 | 1 | 1 | | 0.6 | -2.5 | 51.7 | |
| Greece | .. | 1 | 1 | 1 | | 0.5 | 55.1 | -7.0 | |
| Ireland | .. | 1 | 1 | 1 | | 0.5 | 19.4 | 0.9 | |
| Russian Federation | .. | 1 | 1 | 1 | | 0.4 | 2.2 | -6.2 | |
| Other intraregional | .. | 5 | 7 | 5 | | 3.2 | 42.7 | -26.4 | |
| *From other regions* | .. | *10* | *10* | *9* | | *5.7* | *-0.6* | *-5.1* | |
| United States | .. | 7 | 7 | 7 | | 4.0 | -2.1 | -9.4 | |
| Japan | .. | 1 | 1 | 1 | | 0.6 | 8.5 | 52.5 | |
| Canada | .. | 1 | 1 | 1 | | 0.5 | 7.4 | -25.0 | |
| Australia | .. | 0 | 0 | 0 | | 0.3 | 77.7 | -9.4 | |
| China | .. | 0 | 0 | 0 | | 0.2 | 181.7 | 2.6 | |
| Iran | .. | 0 | 0 | 0 | | 0.1 | -66.8 | 54.9 | |
| New Zealand | .. | 0 | 0 | 0 | | 0.1 | -56.3 | 98.6 | |
| Egypt | .. | 0 | 0 | 0 | | 0.1 | -51.8 | 1.1 | |
| *Other World/Not specified* | .. | *3* | *4* | *4* | | *2.3* | *18.3* | *-4.0* | |

Source: World Tourism Organization (WTO) © (Data as collected by WTO December 2004)

**Bosnia and Herzegovina**
**Nights of International Tourists in All Accommodation Establishments (by residence)**

| | | | | (thousand) | Market share (%) | | Growth rate (%) | | Average per year (%) |
|---|---|---|---|---|---|---|---|---|---|
| | 1995 | 2001 | 2002 | 2003* | 1995 | 2003* | 2002/01 | 2003*/02 | 1995-2003* |
| **Total** | .. | **330** | **392** | **419** | | **100** | **19.0** | **6.9** | |
| *From Europe* | .. | *293* | *358* | *372* | | *88.8* | *22.1* | *4.1* | |
| Serbia & Montenegro | .. | 94 | 103 | 104 | | 24.8 | 9.7 | 1.3 | |
| Croatia | .. | 43 | 50 | 51 | | 12.2 | 17.2 | 2.3 | |
| Slovenia | .. | 21 | 44 | 49 | | 11.6 | 110.7 | 9.7 | |
| Poland | .. | 9 | 26 | 18 | | 4.2 | 194.2 | -33.5 | |
| Germany | .. | 15 | 15 | 17 | | 4.2 | 1.0 | 19.0 | |
| Italy | .. | 16 | 15 | 16 | | 3.8 | -7.2 | 6.0 | |
| Czech Rep | .. | 13 | 20 | 15 | | 3.7 | 58.5 | -23.1 | |
| Austria | .. | 6 | 7 | 12 | | 2.9 | 24.1 | 64.3 | |
| United Kingdom | .. | 8 | 11 | 11 | | 2.6 | 31.7 | 5.5 | |
| Hungary | .. | 5 | 6 | 8 | | 1.8 | 39.0 | 20.6 | |
| Turkey | .. | 6 | 4 | 7 | | 1.6 | -37.4 | 69.3 | |
| Sweden | .. | 5 | 5 | 7 | | 1.6 | -4.4 | 37.3 | |
| France | .. | 8 | 5 | 6 | | 1.5 | -30.0 | 23.0 | |
| Slovakia | .. | 5 | 2 | 6 | | 1.5 | -60.4 | 208.3 | |
| F.Yug.Rp.Macedonia | .. | 4 | 5 | 6 | | 1.4 | 51.0 | 8.4 | |
| Netherlands | .. | 4 | 4 | 5 | | 1.1 | 7.0 | 6.0 | |
| Denmark | .. | 3 | 2 | 4 | | 0.9 | -12.4 | 50.7 | |
| Spain | .. | 6 | 4 | 3 | | 0.8 | -27.1 | -17.9 | |
| Norway | .. | 3 | 3 | 3 | | 0.8 | 10.5 | 10.6 | |
| Switzerland | .. | 3 | 2 | 3 | | 0.7 | -5.1 | 21.0 | |
| Greece | .. | 1 | 1 | 2 | | 0.6 | 7.1 | 64.9 | |
| Belgium | .. | 2 | 2 | 2 | | 0.5 | -15.0 | 33.2 | |
| Ireland | .. | 1 | 2 | 2 | | 0.5 | 12.5 | 20.4 | |
| Russian Federation | .. | 2 | 3 | 2 | | 0.5 | 79.7 | -44.2 | |
| Bulgaria | .. | 3 | 2 | 1 | | 0.3 | -33.0 | -18.7 | |
| Other intraregional | .. | 10 | 12 | 11 | | 2.6 | 23.9 | -7.4 | |
| *From other regions* | .. | *23* | *25* | *26* | | *6.1* | *9.5* | *1.3* | |
| United States | .. | 17 | 19 | 18 | | 4.3 | 8.2 | -2.1 | |
| Japan | .. | 1 | 1 | 3 | | 0.7 | 2.1 | 121.8 | |
| Canada | .. | 2 | 3 | 2 | | 0.5 | 16.5 | -30.8 | |
| Australia | .. | 1 | 1 | 1 | | 0.2 | 74.5 | -14.4 | |
| China | .. | 0 | 1 | 1 | | 0.1 | 242.4 | -47.1 | |
| Iran | .. | 1 | 0 | 0 | | 0.1 | -56.2 | 107.9 | |
| New Zealand | .. | 0 | 0 | 0 | | 0.1 | -17.3 | 105.6 | |
| Egypt | .. | 1 | 0 | 0 | | 0.1 | -68.0 | 47.2 | |
| *Other World/Not specified* | .. | *14* | *9* | *21* | | *5.1* | *-31.5* | *125.9* | |

Source: World Tourism Organization (WTO) © (Data as collected by WTO December 2004)

# III.4.4 Croatia — Southern Europe

## Profile

# Croatia

| | |
|---|---|
| Capital | Zagreb |
| Year of entry in WTO | 1993 |
| Area (1000 km²) | 57 |
| Population (2003, million) | 4.5 |
| Gross Domestic Product (GDP) (2003, euro million) | 30,470 |
| GDP per capita (2003, euro) | 6,771 |
| GDP growth (real, %) | |
| '-> 2002: 5.2; 2003: 4.3; 2004*: 3.7; 2005*: 4.1 | |

**Europe**
**Southern Europe**

| | 2001 | 2002 | 2003* | 2002/2001 | 2003*/2002 |
|---|---|---|---|---|---|
| **International Arrivals** | | | | | |
| Visitors (1000) | 40,129 | 41,737 | 42,857 | 4.0 | 2.7 |
| Tourists (overnight visitors) (1000) | 6,544 | 6,944 | 7,409 | 6.1 | 6.7 |
| - per 100 of inhabitants | 147 | 155 | 165 | | |
| **Tourism accommodation** | | | | | |
| Number of rooms | 74,107 | 77,347 | 77,113 | 4.4 | -0.3 |
| *Nights spent in collective establishments (1000)* | 43,405 | 44,692 | 46,635 | 3.0 | 4.3 |
| by non-residents (inbound tourism) | 38,384 | 39,711 | 41,323 | 3.5 | 4.1 |
| by residents (domestic tourism) | 5,021 | 4,981 | 5,312 | -0.8 | 6.6 |
| *Nights spent in hotels and similar establishments (1000)* | 19,908 | 19,596 | 19,669 | -1.6 | 0.4 |
| by non-residents (inbound tourism) | 16,989 | 16,905 | 16,830 | -0.5 | -0.4 |
| by residents (domestic tourism) | 2,919 | 2,691 | 2,839 | -7.8 | 5.5 |
| **Receipts and Expenditure for International Tourism** | | | | | |
| International Tourism Receipts (euro million) | 3,611 | 4,255 | 6,743 | 17.8 | 58.5 |
| - per Tourist Arrival (euro) | 552 | 613 | 910 | 11.1 | 48.5 |
| - per Visitor Arrival (euro) | 90 | 102 | 157 | 13.3 | 54.3 |
| - per capita (euro) | 813 | 950 | 1,499 | | |
| International Fare Receipts (euro million) | 139 | 157 | 215 | 13.6 | 36.4 |
| International Tourism Expenditure (euro million) | 656 | 872 | 711 | 32.9 | -18.5 |
| - per capita (euro) | 148 | 195 | 158 | | |
| International Fare Expenditure (euro million) | 77 | 79 | 39 | 3.1 | -50.6 |
| △ International Tourism Balance (euro million) | 2,955 | 3,383 | 6,032 | | |
| △ International Fare Balance (euro million) | 62 | 78 | 176 | | |

Source: World Tourism Organization (WTO) (Data as collected by WTO December 2004)

See annex for methodological notes and reference of external sources used.

# Survey

Contributed by *Ministry of the Sea, Tourism, Transport and Development*
www.croatia.hr (promotional)
www.mmtpr.hr (institutional/corporate)
www.mmtpr.hr (research and data)

## Tourism development and outlook

**Overall evaluation of results**

In 2003, Croatia recorded a 7 per cent increase in total tourists arrivals and 4 per cent in tourist overnights. In National parks and Parks of Nature the increase was even higher, they recorded 9 per cent more visitors. High growth was recorded from the majority of markets (Germany, France, Great Britain, the Netherlands, etc.) which has helped Croatia even further recapture its 1990-2000 position. The recession in many generating markets did have some negative effects from previously flourishing markets (such as Poland), but these were not significant on the whole. Croatia recorded an exceptional growth in cruises as well (38% in number of trips and 45% in number of passengers).

**Supply**

*Accommodation:*
According to the new regulations based on high international standards adopted in 2002, 136 hotels obtained a higher category and an additional 113 are in the process of being assigned a higher category than before (most of them at least 3 star).
In 2003, some 300 million euro were invested in reconstruction, modernisation and refurbishing of accommodation facilities which resulted in upgrading hotel and other accommodation facilities standard and quality. It meant a considerable accommodation quality improvement which enabled setting and attaining higher prices and reaching competitiveness in the market place.
*Transport:*
Increased frequency and capacity of ferry and ship lines connecting the mainland with the islands. An increase in the number of transferred passengers/cars by 8 per cent.
The number of seats on national airliner's seasonal flights from the key generating markets (Germany, Great Britain, the Netherlands, Sweden and Denmark) increased by some 14 per cent.
The national airliner increased (14%) the number of charter flights.
The seasonal tourist trains introduced for passengers and cars from Prague to Split and the one from Bratislava continue operating.
Increased overall capacity for passengers and cars on trains.
*Attractions/entertainment:*
A large number of swimming pools were constructed, 18 additional beaches have been awarded «blue flags» and the number of restaurants, sports grounds and other entertainment and recreational offers have increased.

**External factors**

Croatia has been a completely peaceful and safe country.
Stable macroeconomic conditions (reasonably low price increase and inflation, acceptable level of interest rates, etc.).
A high safety level contributed to the continuation of successful tourism results and their permanent increase.
One hundred and ninety-one kilometres of new highways to the Adriatic coast were built and other roads repaired or reconstructed.
Weather conditions were exceptionally favourable.

**Marketing & promotion**

Continuance of the adopted «Strategic Marketing Plan of Croatian Tourism to the Year 2005». The Plan is being implemented by the National Tourist Organization (NTO) which in its annual plans sets the promotional and other campaigns, the most important being: study tours for journalists and agents, special presentations, presence at travel and tourism fairs, press conferences, different kinds of advertising (e.g. co-advertisements in the printed media, promotional spots on major TV channels), national evenings with presentation of national/regional cuisine and culture, etc.

**Outlook 2004**

If there are no major disruptions in the international market, foreign tourist traffic is forecasted to grow moderately in 2004 (by 3%-5%) and for the next few years. Further growth of traffic from all the West European generating markets, especially Germany, Italy, France, Great Britain and the Scandinavian countries is expected.
In all the important generating markets the NTO has been successfully running its planned activities such as presence at travel and tourism fairs, press conferences, special presentations, etc.

## International Meetings Industry (MI)

**Characteristics of supply**

The whole country is included in the MICE industry and the main destinations are:
- Central Croatia: Zagreb, the capital of the country, Pregrada, Varaždin;
- Slavonia: Osijek, Vinkovci;
- Istria: Brijuni, Porec, Pula, Rabac, Rovinj, Umag;
- Kvarner and Highlands: Crikvenica, Island Mali Lošinj, Lovran, Mošcenicka Draga, Opatija, Plitvice Lakes and Rijeka;
- Dalmatia, Zadar Region: Petrcane, Zadar;
- Dalmatia, Šibenik Region: Primošten, Šibenik;
- Dalmatia, Split Region: Island of Brac (Bol), Brela, Island of Hvar, Makarska, Split, Tucepi;
- Dalmatia, Dubrovnik Region: Cavtat, Dubrovnik, Island of Korcula, Island of Mljet, Ston.

Exhibitions and Fairs:
- 500.000 $m^2$ of the exhibition area;
- Zagreb Fair with a Congress Centre.

**Organisation of promotion**

The International promotion of the MICE industry is provided by the Croatian Convention and Incentive Bureau and Regional and City Convention Bureaux.
The main tasks of the Croatian Convention and Incentive Bureau are the following:
- Development and improvement of the existing offer;
- Forming the image of Croatia as a high-quality congress and incentive destination.

The services of the Croatian Convention and Incentive Bureau are:
- Site inspections are arranged;
- Help with familiarization tours and facility/contact information;
- Promotional assistance given, with press releases and programme covers supplied for printing;
- Supply of slide shows, promotional videos, brochures, maps and guides;
- Co-ordination of tours and activities for spouses;
- Help with planning special events, banquets, etc.;
- Co-ordination of pre-and post-convention tours;
- Help with organizing conventions and trade shows;
- Help with registration procedures;
- Most services are complimentary or provided at a minimal charge

<www.croatia.hr/activities/>.

**Collection of statistics on the Meetings Industry?:** yes.

**Description**

The Croatian Convention and Incentive Bureau is collecting information from regional convention bureaus and tourist boards, on the basis of a questionnaire of announced and held meetings.

**Importance / size**

According to our statistics which have not yet been completed, approximately one thousand meetings and incentives were organised in Croatia in the year 2003.

**Evolution MI**

The aims of Croatia's tourist policy until 2010 are as follows:

- To extend the tourist season, meetings and incentives;
- To improve quality and to activate new accommodation capacities;
- To improve Croatia's position in the international tourist market;
- To enhance supply with new facilities and products.

We are planning investments in so-called "smart centres", multi-purpose convention and exhibition centres in Zagreb with a capacity of four thousand seats and in Dubrovnik, Opatija, Istra with capacities of 1,500 seats.

Also, there will be development in the field of Destination Management Companies (DMC) and Professional Congress Organisers (PCO) in Zagreb, Dubrovnik, Opatija, Istra, and Dalmatia.

# International Tourism by Origin

**Croatia**

**International Tourist Arrivals in All Accommodation Establishments**

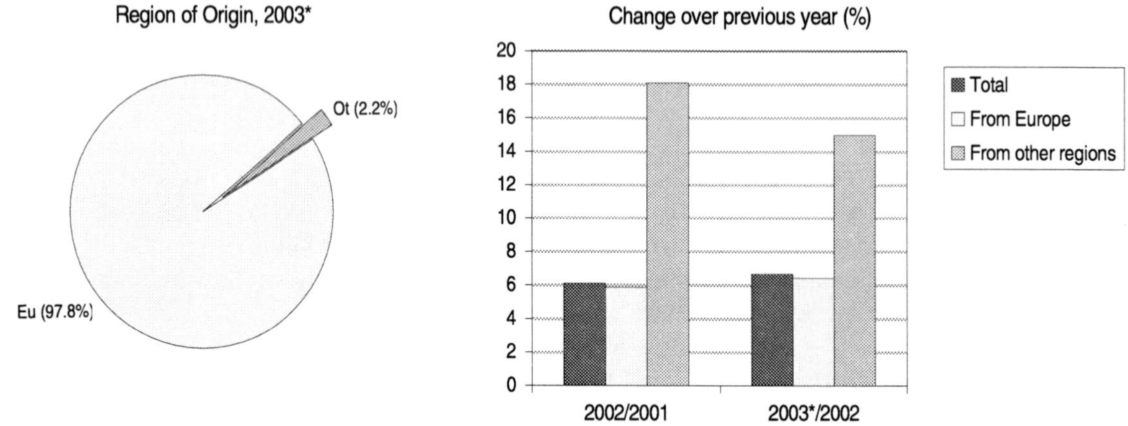


Eu: Europe;
Ot: Other;

Source: World Tourism Organization (WTO) ©

**Croatia**

**Nights of International Tourists in All Accommodation Establishments**

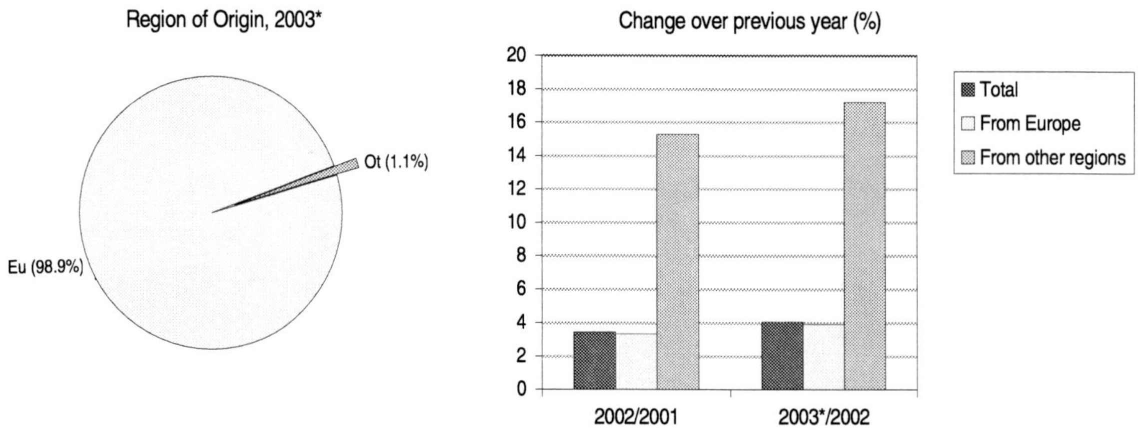


Eu: Europe;
Ot: Other;

Source: World Tourism Organization (WTO) ©

**Croatia**

**International Tourist Arrivals in All Accommodation Establishments (by residence)**

| | | | | (thousand) | Market share (%) | | Growth rate (%) | | Average per year (%) |
|---|---|---|---|---|---|---|---|---|---|
| | 1995 | 2001 | 2002 | 2003* | 1995 | 2003* | 2002/01 | 2003*/02 | 1995-2003* |
| **Total** | **1,485** | **6,544** | **6,944** | **7,409** | **100** | **100** | **6.1** | **6.7** | **22.3** |
| *From Europe* | *1,434* | *6,429* | *6,807* | *7,244* | *96.6* | *97.8* | *5.9* | *6.4* | *22.4* |
| Germany | 274 | 1,300 | 1,482 | 1,552 | 18.4 | 20.9 | 14.0 | 4.7 | 24.2 |
| Italy | 221 | 1,060 | 1,099 | 1,206 | 14.9 | 16.3 | 3.7 | 9.7 | 23.6 |
| Slovenia | 306 | 877 | 870 | 918 | 20.6 | 12.4 | -0.8 | 5.6 | 14.7 |
| Austria | 247 | 687 | 690 | 709 | 16.7 | 9.6 | 0.5 | 2.6 | 14.1 |
| Czech Rep | 119 | 742 | 698 | 699 | 8.0 | 9.4 | -6.0 | 0.2 | 24.8 |
| Hungary | 34 | 280 | 318 | 356 | 2.3 | 4.8 | 13.6 | 12.0 | 34.1 |
| Poland | 10 | 392 | 358 | 238 | 0.7 | 3.2 | -8.6 | -33.5 | 48.1 |
| France | 19 | 75 | 135 | 221 | 1.3 | 3.0 | 80.3 | 63.8 | 35.8 |
| Slovakia | 27 | 203 | 191 | 188 | 1.8 | 2.5 | -5.8 | -1.7 | 27.4 |
| Netherlands | 26 | 125 | 148 | 179 | 1.8 | 2.4 | 18.4 | 21.2 | 27.2 |
| Bosnia & Herzg | 46 | 172 | 173 | 178 | 3.1 | 2.4 | 0.4 | 2.6 | 18.3 |
| United Kingdom | 25 | 107 | 132 | 153 | 1.7 | 2.1 | 23.6 | 15.4 | 25.5 |
| Switzerland | 13 | 46 | 61 | 83 | 0.9 | 1.1 | 31.7 | 36.8 | 26.0 |
| Israel | 0 | 56 | 81 | 75 | 0.0 | 1.0 | 44.2 | -6.9 | 92.4 |
| Belgium | 12 | 48 | 60 | 73 | 0.8 | 1.0 | 26.6 | 21.3 | 25.0 |
| Russian Federation | 8 | 46 | 55 | 57 | 0.5 | 0.8 | 20.0 | 2.7 | 28.5 |
| Sweden | 6 | 27 | 35 | 53 | 0.4 | 0.7 | 27.1 | 53.7 | 31.1 |
| Spain | 5 | 20 | 26 | 44 | 0.4 | 0.6 | 32.1 | 68.3 | 30.4 |
| Denmark | 6 | 23 | 30 | 42 | 0.4 | 0.6 | 28.4 | 42.4 | 29.0 |
| Ireland | 2 | 10 | 19 | 29 | 0.1 | 0.4 | 88.6 | 55.0 | 42.6 |
| Norway | 4 | 14 | 12 | 24 | 0.3 | 0.3 | -12.4 | 92.1 | 23.5 |
| Serbia & Montenegro | .. | 9 | 13 | 23 | | 0.3 | 45.6 | 77.6 | |
| Bulgaria | 1 | 11 | 13 | 17 | 0.1 | 0.2 | 20.2 | 33.0 | 39.2 |
| Lithuania | 1 | 11 | 13 | 17 | 0.1 | 0.2 | 15.5 | 26.5 | 44.2 |
| Romania | 2 | 19 | 14 | 16 | 0.1 | 0.2 | -27.9 | 13.0 | 33.1 |
| Other intraregional | 20 | 68 | 80 | 95 | 1.3 | 1.3 | 17.0 | 18.6 | 21.7 |
| *From other regions* | *28* | *94* | *111* | *128* | *1.9* | *1.7* | *18.1* | *15.0* | *21.2* |
| United States | 17 | 52 | 59 | 65 | 1.2 | 0.9 | 11.6 | 11.8 | 18.0 |
| Australia | 2 | 10 | 16 | 20 | 0.1 | 0.3 | 51.1 | 29.8 | 32.0 |
| Canada | 6 | 15 | 16 | 19 | 0.4 | 0.3 | 10.3 | 16.0 | 15.3 |
| Japan | 1 | 13 | 15 | 16 | 0.1 | 0.2 | 22.1 | 4.6 | 39.0 |
| New Zealand | 1 | 4 | 5 | 7 | 0.0 | 0.1 | 35.4 | 34.1 | 35.2 |
| *Other World/Not specified* | *23* | *22* | *27* | *37* | *1.6* | *0.5* | *23.9* | *36.5* | *5.9* |

Source: World Tourism Organization (WTO) © (Data as collected by WTO December 2004)

**Croatia**

**Nights of International Tourists in All Accommodation Establishments (by residence)**

| | | | | (thousand) | Market | share (%) | Growth rate | (%) | Average per year (%) |
|---|---|---|---|---|---|---|---|---|---|
| | 1995 | 2001 | 2002 | 2003* | 1995 | 2003* | 2002/01 | 2003*/02 | 1995-2003* |
| **Total** | **8,763** | **38,384** | **39,711** | **41,323** | **100** | **100** | **3.5** | **4.1** | **21.4** |
| *From Europe* | *8,613* | *38,071* | *39,344* | *40,882* | *98.3* | *98.9* | *3.3* | *3.9* | *21.5* |
| Germany | 2,004 | 9,686 | 10,789 | 11,056 | 22.9 | 26.8 | 11.4 | 2.5 | 23.8 |
| Italy | 839 | 4,724 | 4,883 | 5,323 | 9.6 | 12.9 | 3.4 | 9.0 | 26.0 |
| Slovenia | 2,071 | 5,119 | 4,993 | 5,208 | 23.6 | 12.6 | -2.5 | 4.3 | 12.2 |
| Czech Rep | 889 | 4,921 | 4,560 | 4,554 | 10.2 | 11.0 | -7.3 | -0.1 | 22.6 |
| Austria | 1,346 | 3,601 | 3,543 | 3,585 | 15.4 | 8.7 | -1.6 | 1.2 | 13.0 |
| Hungary | 217 | 1,554 | 1,733 | 1,905 | 2.5 | 4.6 | 11.5 | 10.0 | 31.2 |
| Netherlands | 235 | 1,059 | 1,204 | 1,497 | 2.7 | 3.6 | 13.7 | 24.3 | 26.0 |
| Poland | 69 | 2,514 | 2,186 | 1,331 | 0.8 | 3.2 | -13.1 | -39.1 | 44.9 |
| Slovakia | 200 | 1,335 | 1,223 | 1,205 | 2.3 | 2.9 | -8.4 | -1.5 | 25.2 |
| Bosnia & Herzg | 206 | 802 | 787 | 848 | 2.4 | 2.1 | -1.8 | 7.8 | 19.3 |
| United Kingdom | 111 | 542 | 661 | 721 | 1.3 | 1.7 | 21.9 | 9.2 | 26.4 |
| France | 76 | 225 | 418 | 689 | 0.9 | 1.7 | 86.3 | 64.7 | 31.7 |
| Russian Federation | 38 | 407 | 504 | 510 | 0.4 | 1.2 | 23.9 | 1.2 | 38.4 |
| Belgium | 82 | 332 | 385 | 434 | 0.9 | 1.0 | 16.0 | 12.8 | 23.1 |
| Switzerland | 51 | 202 | 252 | 340 | 0.6 | 0.8 | 24.7 | 35.0 | 26.8 |
| Denmark | 27 | 145 | 196 | 302 | 0.3 | 0.7 | 35.4 | 54.3 | 35.0 |
| Sweden | 22 | 140 | 166 | 271 | 0.3 | 0.7 | 18.5 | 63.0 | 36.6 |
| Ireland | 7 | 37 | 80 | 152 | 0.1 | 0.4 | 116.1 | 89.9 | 47.4 |
| Israel | 2 | 141 | 188 | 151 | 0.0 | 0.4 | 33.7 | -19.9 | 74.5 |
| Norway | 14 | 70 | 49 | 110 | 0.2 | 0.3 | -31.0 | 126.5 | 29.2 |
| Spain | 18 | 62 | 72 | 101 | 0.2 | 0.2 | 17.2 | 40.1 | 23.8 |
| Serbia & Montenegro | .. | 31 | 43 | 84 | | 0.2 | 38.9 | 93.6 | |
| Romania | 4 | 82 | 53 | 63 | 0.0 | 0.2 | -35.2 | 17.3 | 40.5 |
| Ukraine | 11 | 35 | 48 | 61 | 0.1 | 0.1 | 38.2 | 27.4 | 24.4 |
| F.Yug.Rp.Macedonia | 14 | 63 | 61 | 61 | 0.2 | 0.1 | -2.6 | -1.1 | 20.0 |
| Other intraregional | 58 | 242 | 264 | 320 | 0.7 | 0.8 | 8.8 | 21.2 | 23.7 |
| *From other regions* | *82* | *243* | *280* | *328* | *0.9* | *0.8* | *15.3* | *17.2* | *18.9* |
| United States | 49 | 144 | 160 | 177 | 0.6 | 0.4 | 10.6 | 10.7 | 17.4 |
| Canada | 22 | 41 | 45 | 55 | 0.3 | 0.1 | 10.8 | 21.9 | 12.1 |
| Australia | 6 | 26 | 37 | 51 | 0.1 | 0.1 | 43.5 | 37.4 | 30.3 |
| Japan | 3 | 24 | 27 | 30 | 0.0 | 0.1 | 14.3 | 9.3 | 33.9 |
| New Zealand | 2 | 9 | 11 | 16 | 0.0 | 0.0 | 33.2 | 43.7 | 28.3 |
| *Other World/Not specified* | *68* | *70* | *88* | *113* | *0.8* | *0.3* | *24.5* | *29.2* | *6.6* |

Source: World Tourism Organization (WTO) © (Data as collected by WTO December 2004)

# III.4.5 Greece Southern Europe

## Profile

# Greece

| | |
|---|---|
| Capital | Athens |
| Year of entry in WTO | 1975 |
| Area (1000 km²) | 132 |
| Population (2003, million) | 10.6 |
| Gross Domestic Product (GDP) (2003, euro million) | 182,439 |
| GDP per capita (2003, euro) | 16,525 |
| GDP growth (real, %) | |
| '-> 2002: 3.9; 2003: 4.3; 2004*: 3.9; 2005*: 3.0 | |

**Europe**
**Southern Europe**

| | 2001 | 2002 | 2003* | 2002/2001 | 2003*/2002 |
|---|---|---|---|---|---|
| **International Arrivals** | | | | | |
| Visitors (1000) | 14,678 | 14,918 | .. | 1.6 | |
| Tourists (overnight visitors) (1000) | 14,057 | 14,180 | 13,969 | 0.9 | -1.5 |
| - per 100 of inhabitants | 133 | 134 | 131 | | |
| Cruise passengers (1000) | 621 | 738 | .. | 18.8 | |
| **Tourism accommodation** | | | | | |
| Number of rooms | 316,668 | 319,689 | 330,970 | 1.0 | 3.5 |
| *Nights spent in hotels and similar establishments (1000)* | 61,508 | | | | |
| by non-residents (inbound tourism) | 46,574 | .. | .. | | |
| by residents (domestic tourism) | 14,934 | .. | .. | | |
| **Receipts and Expenditure for International Tourism** | | | | | |
| International Tourism Receipts (euro million) | 10,259 | 10,858 | 11,317 | 5.8 | 4.2 |
| - per Tourist Arrival (euro) | 730 | 766 | 810 | 4.9 | 5.8 |
| - per Visitor Arrival (euro) | 699 | 728 | .. | 4.1 | |
| - per capita (euro) | 970 | 1,024 | 1,065 | | |
| International Fare Receipts (euro million) | 66 | 107 | 80 | 62.3 | -25.0 |
| International Tourism Expenditure (euro million) | 4,510 | 2,691 | 2,523 | -40.3 | -6.2 |
| - per capita (euro) | 426 | 254 | 237 | | |
| International Fare Expenditure (euro million) | 13 | 18 | 8 | 37.5 | -52.6 |
| △ International Tourism Balance (euro million) | 5,749 | 8,167 | 8,794 | | |
| △ International Fare Balance (euro million) | 53 | 89 | 72 | | |

Source: World Tourism Organization (WTO) (Data as collected by WTO December 2004)

See annex for methodological notes and reference of external sources used.

# Survey

Contributed by *Greek National Tourism Organization (GNTO)*
www.gnto.gr (promotional)
www.gnto.gr (institutional/corporate)
www.gnto.gr (research and data)

## Tourism development and outlook

| | |
|---|---|
| **Overall evaluation of results** | An overall estimation of the 2003 performance includes positive results for some Greek destinations, but also a relative stagnation in arrivals and a slight decrease in international and domestic overnight stays. |
| **Supply** | Improvement of transportation infrastructure (airports, highways, metro).<br>High-speed ferries to the islands.<br>Modernisation of accommodation facilities in Athens and other destinations, in view of the Athens 2004 Olympic Games.<br>New facilities for visitors (conference centres, marinas, etc). |
| **External factors** | The war in Iraq and the Severe Acute Respiratory Syndrome (SARS) outbreak had an impact on tourist flows during the first six months of the year.<br>The strong euro slowed the recovery from overseas origin countries.<br>Economic stagnation in some important generating markets resulted in decreased flows from some countries (Germany and Sweden). |
| **Tourism policy** | The Greek National Tourism Office (GNTO) has elaborated Master Plans for tourism development of the Greek Regions.<br>New legislation has been introduced for tourism education.<br>Incentives for private investment in order to modernize accommodation facilities.<br>Incentives for private investment in order to create new facilities (conference centres, marinas, spas, golf courses, etc). |
| **Outlook 2004** | The mega-event of the summer Olympic Games in Athens (13-29 August 2004) is expected to attract increased tourist flows during 2004, from traditional markets and also from overseas and emerging markets such as eastern European countries.<br>In successive years, an increase in tourism flows is expected, as a result of an expected improvement of economic conditions in generating markets, an improvement of tourist supply and infrastructure, the impact of the 2004 Olympic Games and an intensified promotional activity. The nomination of the city of Patras as cultural capital of Europe for 2006 will also have a positive impact, as will the possible nomination of Thessaloniki for the international "Expo 2008". |

## International Meetings Industry (MI)

| | |
|---|---|
| **Characteristics of supply** | There are fifteen conference centres throughout the country providing facilities for conventions and meetings. There are also modern conference facilities in two hundred hotels, with various capacities.<br>Important incentives (grants and tax alleviations) are provided to the private sector in order to create or increase capacity in new facilities, both in mainland Greece and in the islands.<br>The major tourism fair "Philoxenia" in Thessaloniki, along with other sectoral fairs and exhibitions in major cities contribute to enhancing tourist flows. |

**Organisation of promotion**
The Greek National Tourism Organization (GNTO) is promoting the MICE industry, specifically or integrated in various general promotion activities abroad. The GNTO has also recently created a specific Conference and Incentives Office based in London <www.greece-conferences.com>. There are also two Conventions and Visitors Bureaus, in Athens and Thessaloniki <www.tcvb.gr>. They were created by the private sector and are supported by public entities.

**Collection of statistics on the Meetings Industry?:** no.

**Importance / size**
Statistics are not available.

**Evolution MI**
The MICE sector is a growing market for Greek tourism. The increasing capacity, supported by public policies provides modern facilities, but is able to cover only part of the growing demand. In coming years, Greece is expected to become an important Meeting destination.

## International Tourism by Origin

**Greece**
**International Tourist Arrivals at Frontiers**

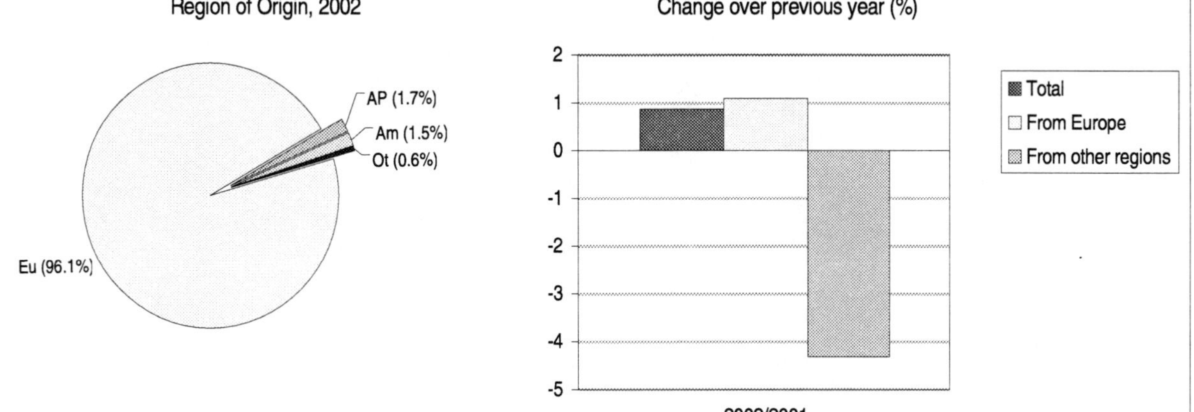


Eu: Europe; AP: Asia and the Pacific; Am: Americas;
Ot: Other;

Source: World Tourism Organization (WTO) ©

**Greece**

**International Tourist Arrivals at Frontiers (by nationality)**

| | | | | (thousand) | Market | share (%) | Growth rate | (%) | Average per year (%) |
|---|---|---|---|---|---|---|---|---|---|
| | 1995 | 2000 | 2001 | 2002 | 1995 | 2002 | 2001/00 | 2002/01 | 1995-2002 |
| **Total** | **10,130** | **..** | **14,057** | **14,180** | **100** | **100** | | **0.9** | **4.9** |
| *From Europe* | *9,467* | .. | *13,483* | *13,630* | *93.5* | *96.1* | | *1.1* | *5.3* |
| United Kingdom | 2,225 | .. | 2,932 | 2,858 | 22.0 | 20.2 | | -2.5 | 3.6 |
| Germany | 2,273 | .. | 2,345 | 2,511 | 22.4 | 17.7 | | 7.1 | 1.4 |
| Albania | 128 | .. | 1,038 | 1,256 | 1.3 | 8.9 | | 21.0 | 38.5 |
| Italy | 643 | .. | 890 | 805 | 6.4 | 5.7 | | -9.5 | 3.3 |
| France | 552 | .. | 727 | 736 | 5.4 | 5.2 | | 1.2 | 4.2 |
| Netherlands | 506 | .. | 716 | 721 | 5.0 | 5.1 | | 0.8 | 5.2 |
| Bulgaria | 137 | .. | 438 | 470 | 1.3 | 3.3 | | 7.3 | 19.3 |
| Sweden | 459 | .. | 517 | 466 | 4.5 | 3.3 | | -9.9 | 0.2 |
| Austria | 347 | .. | 496 | 462 | 3.4 | 3.3 | | -6.9 | 4.2 |
| Belgium/Luxembourg | 246 | .. | 393 | 358 | 2.4 | 2.5 | | -8.9 | 5.5 |
| Denmark | 324 | .. | 366 | 343 | 3.2 | 2.4 | | -6.3 | 0.8 |
| F.Yug.Rp.Macedonia | .. | .. | 282 | 310 | | 2.2 | | 9.8 | |
| Yugoslav SFR | 270 | .. | .. | .. | 2.7 | | | | |
| Poland | 50 | .. | 208 | 236 | 0.5 | 1.7 | | 13.2 | 24.9 |
| Switzerland | 259 | .. | 229 | 220 | 2.6 | 1.6 | | -3.9 | -2.3 |
| Serbia & Montenegro | .. | .. | 160 | 191 | | 1.3 | | 18.9 | |
| Norway | 142 | .. | 191 | 181 | 1.4 | 1.3 | | -5.0 | 3.6 |
| Spain | 95 | .. | 171 | 153 | 0.9 | 1.1 | | -10.7 | 7.1 |
| Finland | 103 | .. | 168 | 147 | 1.0 | 1.0 | | -12.5 | 5.3 |
| Hungary | 91 | .. | 159 | 145 | 0.9 | 1.0 | | -9.3 | 6.8 |
| Czech Rep | 108 | .. | 138 | 140 | 1.1 | 1.0 | | 1.2 | 3.8 |
| Cyprus | 98 | .. | 140 | 139 | 1.0 | 1.0 | | -0.6 | 5.1 |
| Turkey | 49 | .. | 114 | 139 | 0.5 | 1.0 | | 21.6 | 16.1 |
| Russian Federation | 129 | .. | 133 | 136 | 1.3 | 1.0 | | 2.1 | 0.7 |
| Romania | 39 | .. | 98 | 119 | 0.4 | 0.8 | | 20.7 | 17.3 |
| Other intraregional | 194 | .. | 430 | 389 | 1.9 | 2.7 | | -9.5 | 10.4 |
| *From other regions* | *663* | .. | *574* | *550* | *6.5* | *3.9* | | *-4.3* | *-2.6* |
| United States | 240 | .. | 165 | 147 | 2.4 | 1.0 | | -10.9 | -6.8 |
| Japan | 89 | .. | 73 | 70 | 0.9 | 0.5 | | -5.0 | -3.5 |
| Canada | 50 | .. | 49 | 56 | 0.5 | 0.4 | | 13.8 | 1.6 |
| Australia | 54 | .. | 63 | 55 | 0.5 | 0.4 | | -11.8 | 0.2 |
| Egypt | 21 | .. | 34 | 31 | 0.2 | 0.2 | | -9.3 | 5.2 |
| Lebanon | 16 | .. | 26 | 24 | 0.2 | 0.2 | | -5.6 | 6.5 |
| South Africa | 12 | .. | 13 | 12 | 0.1 | 0.1 | | -7.8 | 0.2 |
| Mexico | 5 | .. | 4 | 4 | 0.0 | 0.0 | | 11.6 | -0.3 |
| Iran | 6 | .. | 4 | 4 | 0.1 | 0.0 | | -3.9 | -4.7 |
| Brazil | 11 | .. | 3 | 3 | 0.1 | 0.0 | | -7.0 | -17.6 |
| Argentina | 10 | .. | 4 | 1 | 0.1 | 0.0 | | -61.0 | -23.7 |
| Other Africa | 15 | .. | 11 | 10 | 0.1 | 0.1 | | -10.0 | -5.7 |
| Other Americas | 9 | .. | 7 | 6 | 0.1 | 0.0 | | -16.8 | -5.8 |
| Other Middle East | 8 | .. | 11 | 9 | 0.1 | 0.1 | | -22.0 | 1.6 |
| Other Asia | 112 | .. | 98 | 109 | 1.1 | 0.8 | | 10.6 | -0.4 |
| Other Oceania | 6 | .. | 9 | 9 | 0.1 | 0.1 | | -5.6 | 6.4 |

Source: World Tourism Organization (WTO) © (Data as collected by WTO December 2004)

# III.4.6 Italy — Southern Europe

## Profile

# Italy

Europe

Southern Europe

| | |
|---|---|
| Capital | Rome |
| Year of entry in WTO | 1978 |
| Area (1000 km²) | 301 |
| Population (2003, million) | 58.0 |
| Gross Domestic Product (GDP) (2003, euro million) | 1,555,597 |
| GDP per capita (2003, euro) | 27,066 |
| GDP growth (real, %) | |
| '-> 2002: 0.4; 2003: 0.3; 2004*: 1.4; 2005*: 1.9 | |

| | 2001 | 2002 | 2003* | 2002/2001 | 2003*/2002 |
|---|---|---|---|---|---|
| **International Arrivals** | | | | | |
| Visitors (1000) | 60,960 | 63,561 | 63,026 | 4.3 | -0.8 |
| Tourists (overnight visitors) (1000) | 39,563 | 39,799 | 39,604 | 0.6 | -0.5 |
| - per 100 of inhabitants | 68 | 69 | 68 | | |
| Same-day visitors (1000) | 21,397 | 23,762 | 23,422 | 11.1 | -1.4 |
| **Tourism accommodation** | | | | | |
| Number of rooms | 975,601 | 986,326 | 999,722 | 1.1 | 1.4 |
| *Nights spent in collective establishments (1000)* | 350,323 | 345,247 | 344,413 | -1.4 | -0.2 |
| by non-residents (inbound tourism) | 146,672 | 145,560 | 139,653 | -0.8 | -4.1 |
| by residents (domestic tourism) | 203,651 | 199,687 | 204,760 | -1.9 | 2.5 |
| *Nights spent in hotels and similar establishments (1000)* | 238,881 | 231,132 | 229,152 | -3.2 | -0.9 |
| by non-residents (inbound tourism) | 100,322 | 97,837 | 93,935 | -2.5 | -4.0 |
| by residents (domestic tourism) | 138,559 | 133,295 | 135,217 | -3.8 | 1.4 |
| **Outbound Tourism** | | | | | |
| Trips abroad (1000) | 22,421 | 25,126 | 26,817 | 12.1 | 6.7 |
| - per 100 of inhabitants | 39 | 43 | 46 | | |
| **Receipts and Expenditure for International Tourism** | | | | | |
| International Tourism Receipts (euro million) | 27,958 | 30,005 | 33,019 | 7.3 | 10.0 |
| - per Tourist Arrival (euro) | 707 | 754 | 834 | 6.7 | 10.6 |
| - per Visitor Arrival (euro) | 459 | 472 | 524 | 2.9 | 11.0 |
| - per capita (euro) | 483 | 518 | 569 | | |
| International Fare Receipts (euro million) | 1,184 | 1,419 | 1,421 | 19.8 | 0.2 |
| International Tourism Expenditure (euro million) | 16,019 | 18,896 | 21,710 | 18.0 | 14.9 |
| - per trip (euro) | 714 | 752 | 810 | 5.3 | 7.6 |
| - per capita (euro) | 277 | 326 | 374 | | |
| International Fare Expenditure (euro million) | 2,384 | 3,127 | 3,380 | 31.2 | 8.1 |
| △ International Tourism Balance (euro million) | 11,939 | 11,108 | 11,310 | | |
| △ International Fare Balance (euro million) | -1,200 | -1,708 | -1,959 | | |

Source: World Tourism Organization (WTO) (Data as collected by WTO December 2004)

See annex for methodological notes and reference of external sources used.

# Survey

Contributed by *ENIT*
www.enit.it (promotional)
www.enit.it (institutional/corporate)
www.uic.it ;
www.istat.it (research and data)

## Tourism development and outlook

**Overall evaluation of results**

The events of 2003 are connected to other events of previous years, the most serious of these being the attack on the Twin Towers in 2001, for which we can say the panorama of the last three years has really been that of a seriously disruptive period for the prospects of development of the tourism industry.
Italy has successfully survived this very critical period, proving the vitality and solidity of its tourism organisation, which has been able to stand up not only the "exogenous" difficulties but also the "endogenous".
Considering these external factors, this dynamism in our hospitality industry gains even greater value. Italy has had to define its image so that it wouldn't be perceived as one of the countries "at risk", and protect the vitality of its touristic economy from numerous factors: euro system, the war in Iraq (scene of conflict which risked to involve a much wider area of the Middle East), the recessive tendencies of important economies, and lastly the SARS epidemic.
Accordingly to ISTAT (Istituto Nazionale di Statistica) provisional data, arrivals in terms of nationality confirm positive trends from France (+4%), the United Kingdom (+3,7%) and Switzerland (+1,1%) whereas there are a few worrying signs concerning the German and Japanese markets; there is also the reassurance that both are great lovers of Italy and are unlikely to go elsewhere on holiday, although they might experiment new destinations for a short period. This is demonstrated by the figures for arrivals and presence over the last three years 2000/2002, which are, on the whole, stable.
Italy found itself more exposed, on the other hand, to the above mentioned factors with regard to Americans and their concerns about security as well as a strong euro which has put Americans off coming to Europe.
On the other hand, an important indication of the markets from which Italy obtain customers concern the emerging countries. There are signs of growth in terms of arrivals almost throughout the three years 2000/2002 from Russia (+78 thousand), Korea (+8 thousand), Brazil (+15 thousand), New Zealand (+4 thousand), and Australia (+25 thousand).
The general trend has continued also into 2003.
The increase of tourists from emerging markets has in part compensated for the loss in our art cities. No country can fill the gap left by the Japanese, the German and the Americans, but there is no doubt that Italy, by aiming at new markets, can, to a great extent, increase its supply of foreign visitors.

**Supply**

*Infrastructure:*
The most recent trend in the Italian hotel industry is trading up.
The fall in the number of 1 and 2 star hotels and rooms has been particularly marked. The number of 3 and 4 hotels has risen considerably. Three-star hotels now predominate as they make up 44 per cent of hotels and 52 per cent of rooms.
A wide range of open-air accommodation is available which can satisfy the most varied tourist needs, whether in terms of organisation type or product, particularly when the overlapping market of rural tourism is taken into account.

*Transport:*
The Italian government's Annual Economic and Financial Programming Document, known as DPEF and other legislation delegates responsibility for infrastructure and strategic investments to the Italian government and reflects the priority of the General Transport Plan.
The main national strategic projects identified in GTP were, among others: the Frèjus tunnel, the Simpon rail tunnel, the Brenner rail tunnel, the Mo.Se project to save the Venice Lagoon, the Romea road link from Rome to Eastern Europe, the Rome integrated transport node, the Salerno Reggio Calabria Palermo Catania Siracusa Gela road rail link, the bridge over the straits of Messina.

**External factors**

A central policy in attracting tourist flows from emerging countries, was launched thank to a special law finalized to speed up the issuing of visas by the italian consular network.
The Government found ENIT to be the most appropriate instrument for this task, and thanks to the above law which has provided specific funds to pay for new employees to work in understaffed consular offices, ENIT was able to deal more effectively with the paperwork connected to visas in important countries, of which the first being Russia.
In 2003, in accordance with the law, ENIT has hired, in collaboration with diplomatic and consular offices, 28 new staff on fixed term contracts for Italian consulates in New Delhi, Mumbai, Moscow, St. Petersburg, Kiev, Beijing, Shanghai and Canton.

**Tourism policy**

Faced with the social and economic international situation, in 2003 ENIT has accomplished quite a feat in dealing rapidly with the needs of the world travel market.
In the first place it has had to equip itself to deal with unpredictable emergencies.
The first reaction to these events was to quickly establish "crisis units", dynamic structures that have monitored international movement and promote communication to spread a series of positive and persuasive images of Italy and its regions to counteract harmful description of the italian national heritage.
At the same time, ENIT has aimed its promotional strategies at the markets that are most vulnerable to the consequences of the various crisis, intensifying its activity to aid regions with specific programme agreements and special communication campaigns aimed mainly at promoting specific "products".
ENIT has also greatly pushed policies of coordination with the regions and the tourism industry putting into practice new courses of action, which include special mechanism of consultation with members of the tourism industry.
During the same year the Council of Ministers approved a bill for the internationalisation of business, aiming at reorganising the sector. It will create single information desks abroad, harmonise and coordinate promotional activities and provide for training of staff.
The single information desks will lead to greater efficiency abroad, by linking together activities carried out by commercial offices of the diplomatic-consular networks, ICE (Italian Commerce Institute), ENIT, Chambers of Commerce and the regional system.

**Marketing & promotion**

*Strategy for international promotion:*
In order to increase investment in the tourism and hotel sector, better management through local tourism system and new strategies for international promotion, in 2003, Italy has launched plans and strategies aimed at boosting tourism, especially in the South.
At present, projects concern Calabria, Sicily and Puglia, where 770 million euro will be invested in five new touristic areas; 7,770 rooms and 9 golf courses will be built, catering for 2,37 million tourists and creating 11,700 jobs.
On the basis of the provisions contained in the Framework Tourism Law, n. 135/2001, the Ministry of Productive Activities has co-financed 34 interregional/sovra-regional projects aimed to develop the Tourist Local Systems within the Italian regions.

*Culture and entertainment:*
Italy is the country that more than any other exerts an extraordinary appeal on a host of potential tourists from all over the world. For this reason, during 2003 ENIT has been working alongside with regions and tourism associations, to assess the best cultural opportunities to give added prestige to our international tourism promotion.
To this end, ENIT foreign offices provide assistance in organising "Italian events" that send out important messages of creativity, thereby allowing different sectors of the tourism system to reach a vaster audience than would be possible, for example in trade exhibitions.
Invited to participate in an Italian cultural event, which is not only a party but also an experience of discovery and knowledge, foreign operators and travel agents replied with exceptional enthusiasm to the numerous initiatives organized in the year.
The lion's share went to the United States of America, where italian destinations are traded by 45 per cent of the travel agencies and where tourists prime interest are art, Italian life-style, design, fashion, music and food.

**Outlook 2004**

An initial analysis of international tourism receipts in the period January-March 2004 reveals that receipts went up to 4,803 million euro, 11 per cent more than in the previous year, as a proof that travel confidence is improving after a strongly critic period.
The strategies pinpointed in the 2004/2006 three-years ENIT's promotion plan represent a valid solution to the problems now facing the tourism market. They should lead to:

- Rationalisation of promotional investments, increased effectiveness and efficiency;
- Strong unitary image of Italy backed by strong regional identity;
- Development of total quality through improvements in the accommodation system;
- Opening of new markets with innovative products in the sectors of cultural tourism, nature tourism and niche tourism;
- Introduction of new professions of freelance itinerants promoters, responsible for pin pointing new market niches;
- Improved capacity and capability of tourism promotion institutions;
- Reciprocal agreements among European national tourist boards and special marketing programmes overseas.

## International Meetings Industry (MI)

**Characteristics of supply**

Meetings and conferences are an important part of Italy's tourism industry. Both the major art and business cities, and the lake resorts and spas have a wide range of facilities. According to a recent survey for the Tourism Directorate of the Ministry of Productive Activities (Survey of Italy's congress business by a working group of Greta Econometrics, Cultura e Turismo & Congressi and Risposte Turismo), there are 2,830 congress centres in Italy. Most of these are attached to hotels (1,979). Another 560 are in historic buildings, 291 are in other locations, such as dedicated conference centres, trade fair buildings and theatres. There are 5,231 meeting rooms. Most (3,602) are in hotels. There are 736 in historic buildings and 893 in other types of facilities.
In addition, there are 2,072 congress organisers, 1,314 incentive firms of travel agencies specialising in incentive travel, 786 firms specialising in the necessary equipment (stands, etc.), 630 catering and banquet firms, 562 businesses providing technical and audiovisual services, 228 performing arts companies providing services for conferences and 338 interpretation and translation firms.

**Organisation of promotion**

The promotion of the Meetings Industry is organized at the regional level.

**Collection of statistics on the Meetings Industry?:** no.

**Description**

At the present congress tourism is not recorded separately by the Italian Statistics office, ISTAT.

**Evolution MI**

The industry has been expanding fast, given that there were only around 2,500 congress businesses (including congress organizers, service providers and facilities) a decade ago. The congress industry has a strong connection with primary tourism businesses (i.e. hotels). Thus, there is a case strong for considering that it is a fully fledged and major component of the tourism segment and a tourism product in its own right.

## International Tourism by Origin

**Italy**

**International Tourist Arrivals at Frontiers**

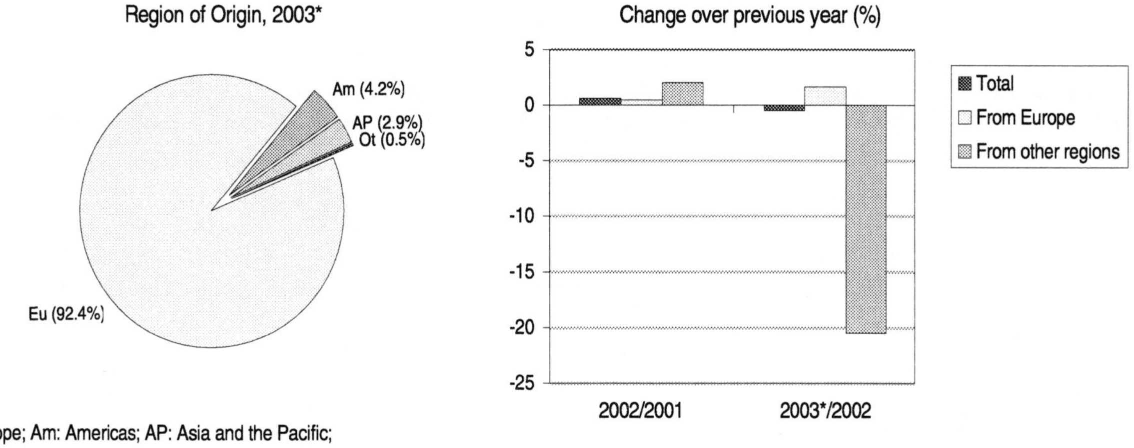


Eu: Europe; Am: Americas; AP: Asia and the Pacific;
Ot: Other;

Source: World Tourism Organization (WTO) ©

**Italy**

**Nights of International Tourists in All Accommodation Establishments**

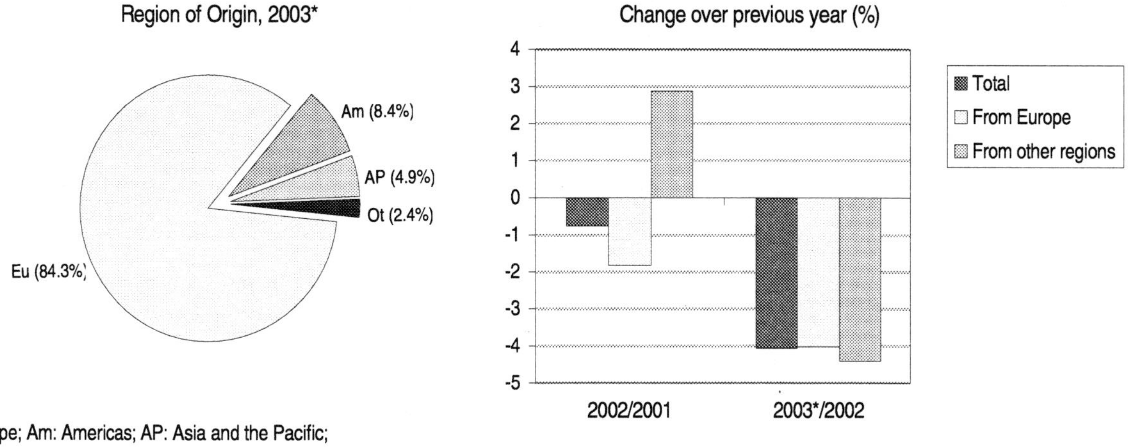


Eu: Europe; Am: Americas; AP: Asia and the Pacific;
Ot: Other;

Source: World Tourism Organization (WTO) ©

**Italy**
**International Tourist Arrivals at Frontiers (by nationality)**

| | | | | (thousand) | Market share (%) | | Growth rate (%) | | Average per year (%) |
|---|---|---|---|---|---|---|---|---|---|
| | 1995 | 2001 | 2002 | 2003* | 1995 | 2003* | 2002/01 | 2003*/02 | 1995-2003* |
| **Total** | .. | **39,563** | **39,799** | **39,604** | | **100** | **0.6** | **-0.5** | |
| *From Europe* | .. | *35,839* | *36,001* | *36,584* | | *92.4* | *0.5* | *1.6* | |
| Germany | .. | 12,460 | 11,800 | 11,536 | | 29.1 | -5.3 | -2.2 | |
| Austria | .. | 4,900 | 4,780 | 5,434 | | 13.7 | -2.4 | 13.7 | |
| France | .. | 4,859 | 5,431 | 5,141 | | 13.0 | 11.8 | -5.3 | |
| Switzerland | .. | 3,189 | 3,149 | 3,141 | | 7.9 | -1.3 | -0.3 | |
| United Kingdom | .. | 2,350 | 2,625 | 2,854 | | 7.2 | 11.7 | 8.7 | |
| Netherlands | .. | 1,431 | 1,529 | 1,491 | | 3.8 | 6.9 | -2.5 | |
| Spain | .. | 1,308 | 1,188 | 1,221 | | 3.1 | -9.2 | 2.8 | |
| Belgium | .. | 890 | 920 | 864 | | 2.2 | 3.3 | -6.0 | |
| Greece | .. | 637 | 689 | 826 | | 2.1 | 8.1 | 19.9 | |
| Poland | .. | 493 | 515 | 426 | | 1.1 | 4.5 | -17.3 | |
| Hungary | .. | 308 | 436 | 414 | | 1.0 | 41.7 | -5.1 | |
| Denmark | .. | 297 | 330 | 378 | | 1.0 | 11.3 | 14.4 | |
| Sweden | .. | 278 | 262 | 273 | | 0.7 | -5.5 | 3.9 | |
| Russian Federation | .. | 217 | 175 | 269 | | 0.7 | -19.6 | 53.8 | |
| Croatia | .. | 192 | 268 | 233 | | 0.6 | 40.0 | -13.0 | |
| Ireland | .. | 213 | 180 | 189 | | 0.5 | -15.4 | 5.0 | |
| Romania | .. | 41 | 156 | 185 | | 0.5 | 280.7 | 19.0 | |
| Turkey | .. | 132 | 125 | 165 | | 0.4 | -5.2 | 32.3 | |
| Norway | .. | 106 | 104 | 136 | | 0.3 | -2.7 | 31.7 | |
| Portugal | .. | 152 | 127 | 127 | | 0.3 | -16.5 | 0.0 | |
| Slovenia | .. | 161 | 159 | 126 | | 0.3 | -1.5 | -20.8 | |
| Finland | .. | 96 | 106 | 114 | | 0.3 | 10.4 | 7.5 | |
| Israel | .. | 61 | 62 | 76 | | 0.2 | 2.9 | 21.3 | |
| Luxembourg | .. | 45 | 30 | 43 | | 0.1 | -32.7 | 42.5 | |
| Serbia & Montenegro | .. | 17 | 27 | 25 | | 0.1 | 59.3 | -6.2 | |
| Other intraregional | .. | 1,003 | 826 | 896 | | 2.3 | -17.7 | 8.5 | |
| *From other regions* | .. | *3,723* | *3,798* | *3,020* | | *7.6* | *2.0* | *-20.5* | |
| United States | .. | 1,552 | 1,498 | 1,215 | | 3.1 | -3.5 | -18.9 | |
| Japan | .. | 738 | 850 | 612 | | 1.5 | 15.2 | -28.1 | |
| Canada | .. | 258 | 248 | 182 | | 0.5 | -3.8 | -26.4 | |
| Australia | .. | 154 | 164 | 164 | | 0.4 | 6.4 | -0.2 | |
| China | .. | 89 | 162 | 126 | | 0.3 | 81.6 | -22.6 | |
| Korea, Republic of | .. | 107 | 107 | 109 | | 0.3 | -0.1 | 1.6 | |
| Brazil | .. | 111 | 114 | 86 | | 0.2 | 3.0 | -24.6 | |
| Mexico | .. | 63 | 81 | 73 | | 0.2 | 29.1 | -10.0 | |
| Argentina | .. | 90 | 55 | 65 | | 0.2 | -38.7 | 17.2 | |
| India | .. | 49 | 66 | 49 | | 0.1 | 34.0 | -25.9 | |
| Tunisia | .. | 77 | 66 | 38 | | 0.1 | -15.2 | -42.1 | |
| Egypt | .. | 39 | 29 | 28 | | 0.1 | -25.0 | -3.9 | |
| Morocco | .. | 33 | 36 | 26 | | 0.1 | 10.1 | -27.6 | |
| South Africa | .. | 29 | 29 | 24 | | 0.1 | 3.1 | -19.3 | |
| All West Africa | .. | 30 | 28 | 20 | | 0.1 | -6.7 | -28.0 | |
| New Zealand | .. | 21 | 24 | 19 | | 0.0 | 18.1 | -21.4 | |
| Chile | .. | 19 | 14 | 14 | | 0.0 | -23.8 | -1.2 | |
| Other interregional | .. | 265 | 225 | 171 | | 0.4 | -15.3 | -23.8 | |

Source: World Tourism Organization (WTO) © (Data as collected by WTO December 2004)

**Italy**
**Nights of International Tourists in All Accommodation Establishments (by nationality)**

| | | | | (thousand) | Market share (%) | | Growth rate (%) | | Average per year (%) |
|---|---|---|---|---|---|---|---|---|---|
| | 1995 | 2001 | 2002 | 2003* | 1995 | 2003* | 2002/01 | 2003*/02 | 1995-2003* |
| **Total** | **113,001** | **146,672** | **145,560** | **139,653** | **100** | **100** | **-0.8** | **-4.1** | **2.7** |
| *From Europe* | *95,533* | *124,978* | *122,694* | *117,766* | *84.5* | *84.3* | *-1.8* | *-4.0* | *2.6* |
| Germany | 45,579 | 53,687 | 50,810 | 46,503 | 40.3 | 33.3 | -5.4 | -8.5 | 0.3 |
| United Kingdom | 6,890 | 10,675 | 10,696 | 11,145 | 6.1 | 8.0 | 0.2 | 4.2 | 6.2 |
| France | 7,146 | 9,704 | 8,780 | 9,175 | 6.3 | 6.6 | -9.5 | 4.5 | 3.2 |
| Austria | 7,709 | 8,551 | 8,296 | 7,748 | 6.8 | 5.5 | -3.0 | -6.6 | 0.1 |
| Netherlands | 3,853 | 7,404 | 7,547 | 7,595 | 3.4 | 5.4 | 1.9 | 0.6 | 8.9 |
| Switzerland | 5,870 | 6,846 | 6,827 | 6,975 | 5.2 | 5.0 | -0.3 | 2.2 | 2.2 |
| Belgium | 3,108 | 3,810 | 3,695 | 3,623 | 2.8 | 2.6 | -3.0 | -1.9 | 1.9 |
| Spain | 2,086 | 3,236 | 2,914 | 2,981 | 1.8 | 2.1 | -9.9 | 2.3 | 4.6 |
| Denmark | 1,336 | 2,488 | 2,256 | 2,152 | 1.2 | 1.5 | -9.3 | -4.6 | 6.1 |
| Czech Rep | .. | 2,033 | 1,929 | 1,912 | | 1.4 | -5.1 | -0.9 | |
| Poland | .. | 2,444 | 2,218 | 1,739 | | 1.2 | -9.2 | -21.6 | |
| Sweden | 1,129 | 1,766 | 1,676 | 1,626 | 1.0 | 1.2 | -5.1 | -3.0 | 4.7 |
| Russian Federation | .. | 1,343 | 1,330 | 1,426 | | 1.0 | -1.0 | 7.2 | |
| Hungary | .. | 1,218 | 1,273 | 1,370 | | 1.0 | 4.5 | 7.6 | |
| Former U.S.S.R. | 1,269 | .. | .. | .. | 1.1 | | | | |
| Yugoslav SFR | 1,126 | .. | .. | .. | 1.0 | | | | |
| Ireland | 286 | 854 | 942 | 1,024 | 0.3 | 0.7 | 10.2 | 8.7 | 17.3 |
| Norway | 373 | 722 | 742 | 798 | 0.3 | 0.6 | 2.8 | 7.6 | 10.0 |
| Israel | 488 | 711 | 768 | 710 | 0.4 | 0.5 | 8.1 | -7.6 | 4.8 |
| Greece | 599 | 799 | 771 | 709 | 0.5 | 0.5 | -3.5 | -8.0 | 2.1 |
| Croatia | .. | 638 | 592 | 597 | | 0.4 | -7.2 | 0.8 | |
| Finland | 389 | 694 | 548 | 577 | 0.3 | 0.4 | -21.0 | 5.2 | 5.0 |
| Slovenia | .. | 491 | 501 | 538 | | 0.4 | 2.0 | 7.5 | |
| Slovakia | .. | 605 | 516 | 505 | | 0.4 | -14.7 | -2.2 | |
| Portugal | 397 | 575 | 501 | 471 | 0.4 | 0.3 | -12.9 | -6.0 | 2.2 |
| Other intraregional | 5,899 | 3,685 | 6,567 | 5,867 | 5.2 | 4.2 | 78.2 | -10.7 | -0.1 |
| *From other regions* | *14,471* | *20,489* | *21,079* | *20,150* | *12.8* | *14.4* | *2.9* | *-4.4* | *4.2* |
| United States | 6,844 | 8,895 | 8,814 | 8,523 | 6.1 | 6.1 | -0.9 | -3.3 | 2.8 |
| Japan | 3,246 | 3,152 | 3,680 | 3,358 | 2.9 | 2.4 | 16.7 | -8.8 | 0.4 |
| Australia | 921 | 1,060 | 1,074 | 1,037 | 0.8 | 0.7 | 1.3 | -3.4 | 1.5 |
| Canada | 723 | 989 | 1,039 | 1,014 | 0.6 | 0.7 | 5.0 | -2.4 | 4.3 |
| China | .. | 695 | 992 | 920 | | 0.7 | 42.6 | -7.2 | |
| Brazil | 891 | 896 | 627 | 562 | 0.8 | 0.4 | -30.0 | -10.4 | -5.6 |
| Mexico | 153 | 440 | 491 | 438 | 0.1 | 0.3 | 11.6 | -10.7 | 14.0 |
| Argentina | 505 | 694 | 405 | 419 | 0.4 | 0.3 | -41.6 | 3.4 | -2.3 |
| Korea, Republic of | .. | 427 | 444 | 414 | | 0.3 | 4.0 | -6.8 | |
| New Zealand | .. | 190 | 194 | 201 | | 0.1 | 1.9 | 3.8 | |
| South Africa | 148 | 170 | 140 | 143 | 0.1 | 0.1 | -17.9 | 2.4 | -0.4 |
| Egypt | 89 | 128 | 113 | 114 | 0.1 | 0.1 | -11.9 | 0.4 | 3.1 |
| Venezuela | 83 | 154 | 126 | 100 | 0.1 | 0.1 | -18.0 | -20.6 | 2.4 |
| Other Africa | .. | 867 | 852 | 900 | | 0.6 | -1.8 | 5.7 | |
| Other South America | 504 | 601 | 715 | 652 | 0.4 | 0.5 | 18.9 | -8.8 | 3.3 |
| Other Middle East | 365 | 324 | 414 | 403 | 0.3 | 0.3 | 28.0 | -2.7 | 1.3 |
| Other Asia | .. | 807 | 960 | 951 | | 0.7 | 18.9 | -0.8 | |
| *Other World/Not specified* | *2,997* | *1,205* | *1,787* | *1,738* | *2.7* | *1.2* | *48.3* | *-2.7* | *-6.6* |

Source: World Tourism Organization (WTO) © (Data as collected by WTO December 2004)

# III.4.7 Malta — Southern Europe

## Profile

# Malta

Europe
Southern Europe

| | |
|---|---|
| Capital | Valletta |
| Year of entry in WTO | 1978 |
| Area (10 km²) | 32 |
| Population (2003, 1000) | 395 |
| Gross Domestic Product (GDP) (2003, euro million) | 4,754 |
| GDP per capita (2003, euro) | 12,201 |
| GDP growth (real, %) | |
| -> 2002: 1.2; 2003: -1.7; 2004*: 1.3; 2005*: 1.7 | |

| | 2001 | 2002 | 2003* | 2002/2001 | 2003*/2002 |
|---|---|---|---|---|---|
| **International Arrivals** | | | | | |
| Visitors (1000) | 1,439 | 1,483 | 1,516 | 3.1 | 2.2 |
| Tourists (overnight visitors) (1000) | 1,180 | 1,134 | 1,127 | -3.9 | -0.6 |
| - per 100 of inhabitants | 301 | 288 | 285 | | |
| Cruise passengers (1000) | 259 | 349 | 389 | 34.7 | 11.5 |
| **Tourism accommodation** | | | | | |
| Number of bed-places | 40,691 | .. | .. | | |
| *Nights spent in collective establishments (1000)* | | | | | |
| by non-residents (inbound tourism) | 11,067 | 10,599 | .. | -4.2 | |
| *Nights spent in hotels and similar establishments (1000)* | | | | | |
| by non-residents (inbound tourism) | 7,475 | 7,006 | .. | -6.3 | |
| **Outbound Tourism** | | | | | |
| Trips abroad (1000) | 179 | .. | .. | | |
| - per 100 of inhabitants | 46 | .. | .. | | |
| **Receipts and Expenditure for International Tourism** | | | | | |
| International Tourism Receipts (euro million) | 626 | 638 | 736 | 1.9 | 15.5 |
| - per Tourist Arrival (euro) | 530 | 562 | 653 | 6.0 | 16.2 |
| - per Visitor Arrival (euro) | 435 | 430 | 486 | -1.1 | 12.9 |
| - per capita (euro) | 1,597 | 1,620 | 1,863 | | |
| International Fare Receipts (euro million) | 155 | 160 | 169 | 3.1 | 6.0 |
| International Tourism Expenditure (euro million) | 195 | 171 | 227 | -12.3 | 32.8 |
| - per trip (euro) | 1,089 | .. | .. | | |
| - per capita (euro) | 497 | 434 | 574 | | |
| International Fare Expenditure (euro million) | 26 | 29 | 24 | 11.7 | -16.2 |
| △ International Tourism Balance (euro million) | 431 | 467 | 509 | | |
| △ International Fare Balance (euro million) | 129 | 131 | 145 | | |

Source: World Tourism Organization (WTO) (Data as collected by WTO December 2004)

See annex for methodological notes and reference of external sources used.

# Survey

Contributed by *Malta Tourism Authority'*
www.visitmalta.com (promotional)
www.mta.com.mt (institutional/corporate)
www.mtadigest.com.mt (research and data)

## Tourism development and outlook

**Overall evaluation of results**

Malta registered decreases from its main source markets (Germany, Italy, France, the Netherlands) with the exception of the United Kingdom where tourist arrivals increased by 3.4 per cent over 2002;
Secondary markets like Scandinavia, Austria and Switzerland registered increases in tourist volumes.
Factors of Malta's performance:
- Competition and accessibility by air;
- Diversification to a number of niche markets has helped to attract tourists from the various source markets.

**Supply**

Accommodation: Hotel beds in five star category increased by 1,302.
Transport capacity: A couple of airlines started operations to Malta.
Attractions/entertainment:
- In 2003 a Visitmalta bus service was set up to link tourist resorts with the more important visitor attractions;
- Improvements in some cultural sites were implemented.

**External factors**

In 2003 international tourism has been heavily influenced by the combination of an overall weak economy and a high level of uncertainty because of the struggle against terrorism and the looming Iraq conflict.
These sudden changes and continuous trends resulted:
- In shifts in demand towards trips to familiar and close to home destinations;
- Increased travel by car, train or coach as a substitute to a plane;
- Late bookings as a result of consumers' wait and see attitude.

All these factors influenced Malta directly, since the islands are mainly accessible by air.

**Tourism policy**

During the following and most intensive phase of preparation, the Ministry of Tourism, in close collaboration with the Malta Tourism Authority, has participated very actively in the preparation for the absorption of the European Union Structural and Cohesion Funds, which will amount to Lm90 million for the period 2004-2006.
This has been done through MoT/MTA's contribution in the National Development Plan (December 2001-July 2002), followed by the drafting of the Single Programming Document (SPD) and the Programme Complement (PC) (September 2002-March 2003).
These documents contain the details of proposed projects in all sectors of the economy which will directly benefit from the Structural and Cohesion Funds. The general descriptions of the approved projects are found in the SPD (www.ppcd.com.mt), while details of the projects' concrete objectives and indicators are developed in the Programme Complement.
Tourism has submitted proposals of a value of around 8 million euro in projects which have been identified and refined (through a wide ranging consultation process) during the last twenty four months.

There are four major areas of intervention, namely:

- Projects of assistance to tourism enterprises;
- Grading of Malta's cultural heritage (Hagar Qim/ Mnajdra Temples);
- Projects for the upgrading of tourism infrastructure (government projects);
- Upgrading of tourism human resources through projects for training and Human resources development.

**Marketing & promotion**

Marketing and promotion pursued its efforts to restructure the United Kingdom market while trying to recover the substantial losses from Germany and the Netherlands and achieve growth from other markets.

The long-term objective for each source market remained that of projecting the Malta brand image and increasing recognition, customer trust and loyalty based on added value. These programmes to increase visibility in the international market continued to be implemented during 2003.

The marketing and promotion plan for 2003, included the operation of an international network of offices and representatives, advertising campaigns, a public relations programme, tour operator support, the promotion of special incentive packages, participation in fairs and the promotion of the conference and incentive travel and special interest travel segments.

**Outlook 2004**

The indications look good from certain markets, such as Italy and Sweden and constant for other markets such as the United Kingdom, Germany and France. The current year should close up on a par with last year.

The situation is expected to improve in the next few years.

## International Meetings Industry (MI)

**Characteristics of supply**

Conference and meetings facilities of a very high standard in prime locations;
Dedicated and professional destination management companies;
A hospitable service on offer;
English-speaking country;
Proximity to originating countries;
Safety.

**Organisation of promotion**

The Malta Tourism Authority has a Conference & Incentive Travel Division. MTA's overseas network of offices actively promote Malta as a destination for conferences and incentives. MTA also regularly conducts market research on this market segment.

**Website(s)**

<www.maltaconferences.com>.

**Collection of statistics on the Meetings Industry?:** yes.

**Importance / size**

Business (including conference and incentive travel) is 8 per cent of total tourists. It is estimated that the conference & incentive travel market only accounts for 4 per cent.

**Evolution MI**

Following the events of 11$^{th}$ September, this market immediately suffered. However, in 2003 recovery started. Further investment and innovation in this segment should enable the destination to achieve growth in this market segment.

# International Tourism by Origin

**Malta**

**International Tourist Arrivals at Frontiers**

Region of Origin, 2003* — Change over previous year (%)

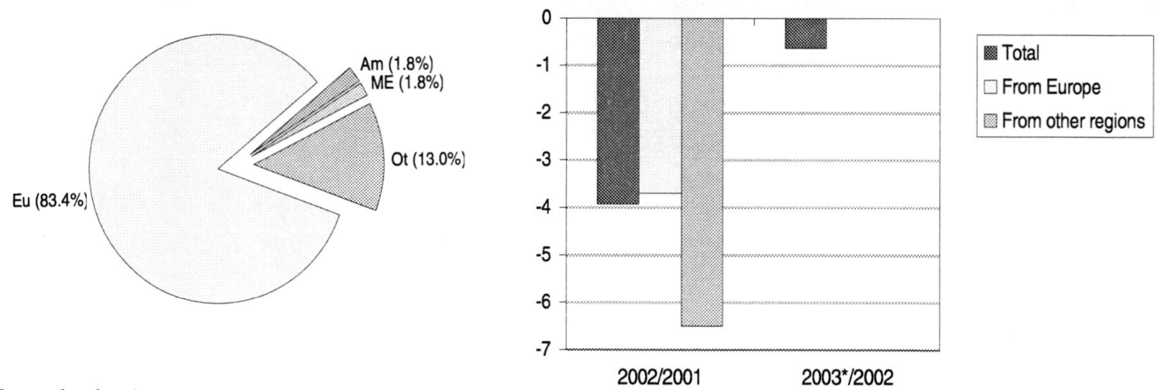


Eu: Europe; Am: Americas;

ME: Middle East; Ot: Other;

Source: World Tourism Organization (WTO) ©

**Malta**

**Nights of International Tourists in All Accommodation Establishments**

Region of Origin, 2003* — Change over previous year (%)

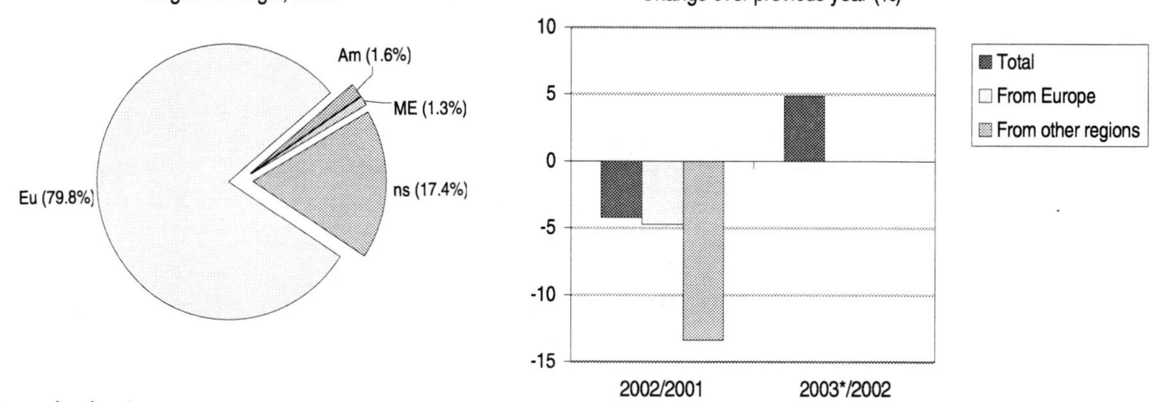


Eu: Europe; Am: Americas;

ME: Middle East; ns: Not specified;

Source: World Tourism Organization (WTO) ©

**Malta**
**International Tourist Arrivals at Frontiers (by nationality)**

| | | | | (thousand) | Market share (%) | | Growth rate (%) | | Average per year (%) |
|---|---|---|---|---|---|---|---|---|---|
| | 1995 | 2001 | 2002 | 2003* | 1995 | 2003* | 2002/01 | 2003*/02 | 1995-2003* |
| **Total** | **1,116** | **1,180** | **1,134** | **1,127** | **100** | **100** | **-3.9** | **-0.6** | **0.1** |
| *From Europe* | *1,036* | *1,080* | *1,040* | *940* | *92.8* | *83.4* | *-3.7* | *-9.6* | *-1.2* |
| United Kingdom | 461 | 452 | 444 | 460 | 41.3 | 40.8 | -1.6 | 3.4 | 0.0 |
| Germany | 188 | 160 | 142 | 126 | 16.8 | 11.2 | -11.3 | -11.5 | -4.9 |
| Italy | 97 | 94 | 101 | 94 | 8.7 | 8.4 | 7.8 | -6.6 | -0.4 |
| France | 73 | 83 | 80 | 76 | 6.5 | 6.8 | -3.1 | -4.6 | 0.6 |
| Netherlands | 46 | 51 | 44 | 41 | 4.1 | 3.6 | -12.5 | -8.1 | -1.4 |
| Austria | 20 | 28 | 24 | 28 | 1.8 | 2.5 | -11.6 | 16.2 | 4.4 |
| Belgium | 22 | 24 | 24 | 24 | 2.0 | 2.1 | 1.4 | -1.2 | 0.9 |
| Switzerland | 19 | 24 | 20 | 22 | 1.7 | 2.0 | -16.4 | 8.5 | 2.3 |
| Ireland | 14 | 22 | 21 | .. | 1.3 | | -2.5 | | |
| Russian Federation | 11 | 22 | 23 | 21 | 0.9 | 1.9 | 3.9 | -8.0 | 9.0 |
| Denmark | 18 | 18 | 17 | 18 | 1.6 | 1.6 | -4.2 | 1.8 | 0.2 |
| Spain | 8 | 9 | 13 | .. | 0.7 | | 41.7 | | |
| Sweden | 9 | 17 | 12 | 12 | 0.8 | 1.1 | -32.6 | 2.4 | 4.4 |
| Norway | 7 | 11 | 10 | 12 | 0.6 | 1.0 | -9.2 | 20.8 | 6.9 |
| Hungary | 6 | 8 | 8 | .. | 0.5 | | 6.6 | | |
| Greece | 3 | 8 | 7 | .. | 0.3 | | -14.1 | | |
| Poland | 3 | 8 | 7 | .. | 0.3 | | -13.8 | | |
| Finland | 6 | 6 | 4 | 6 | 0.5 | 0.5 | -27.5 | 42.0 | 1.2 |
| Czech Rep | 5 | 5 | 6 | .. | 0.4 | | 24.1 | | |
| Portugal | 9 | 5 | 4 | .. | 0.8 | | -15.6 | | |
| Turkey | 1 | 3 | 4 | .. | 0.1 | | 12.3 | | |
| Ukraine | .. | 3 | 4 | .. | | | 4.9 | | |
| Serbia & Montenegro | 2 | 3 | 3 | .. | 0.2 | | -10.8 | | |
| Cyprus | 1 | 2 | 3 | .. | 0.1 | | 53.9 | | |
| Slovenia | 4 | 2 | 2 | .. | 0.4 | | 55.2 | | |
| Other intraregional | 4 | 14 | 12 | .. | 0.4 | | -13.1 | | |
| *From other regions* | *73* | *94* | *88* | *41* | *6.5* | *3.6* | *-6.5* | *-53.6* | *-7.0* |
| United States | 11 | 20 | 20 | 21 | 1.0 | 1.8 | 0.5 | 2.9 | 8.3 |
| Libyan Arab Jamahiriya | 37 | 31 | 23 | 20 | 3.3 | 1.8 | -26.5 | -11.3 | -7.3 |
| Japan | 2 | 11 | 13 | .. | 0.2 | | 20.9 | | |
| Australia | 8 | 10 | 10 | .. | 0.7 | | -0.6 | | |
| Canada | 5 | 8 | 7 | .. | 0.5 | | -11.9 | | |
| Tunisia | 2 | 5 | 5 | .. | 0.1 | | -0.9 | | |
| Egypt | 2 | 2 | 2 | .. | 0.2 | | 28.8 | | |
| China | .. | 1 | 1 | .. | | | 45.3 | | |
| Morocco | 1 | 1 | 1 | .. | 0.1 | | -5.3 | | |
| New Zealand | 1 | 1 | 1 | .. | 0.0 | | 15.0 | | |
| India | 1 | 1 | 1 | .. | 0.1 | | 2.0 | | |
| South Africa | 0 | 1 | 1 | .. | 0.0 | | -5.9 | | |
| Algeria | 2 | 0 | 1 | .. | 0.2 | | 114.4 | | |
| Lebanon | 0 | 1 | 0 | .. | 0.0 | | -49.2 | | |
| Argentina | 0 | 0 | 0 | .. | 0.0 | | -33.3 | | |
| Syrian Arab Republic | 0 | 0 | 0 | .. | 0.0 | | -15.3 | | |
| Other interregional | 1 | 2 | 2 | .. | 0.1 | | -3.2 | | |
| *Other World/Not specified* | *7* | *6* | *6* | *146* | *0.7* | *13.0* | *-4.1* | *2430.9* | *45.2* |

Source: World Tourism Organization (WTO) © (Data as collected by WTO December 2004)

**Malta**

**Nights of International Tourists in All Accommodation Establishments (by nationality)**

| | (thousand) | | | | Market share (%) | | Growth rate (%) | | Average per year (%) |
|---|---|---|---|---|---|---|---|---|---|
| | 1995 | 2001 | 2002 | 2003* | 1995 | 2003* | 2002/01 | 2003*/02 | 1995-2003* |
| **Total** | **10,919** | **11,067** | **10,599** | **11,115** | **100** | **100** | **-4.2** | **4.9** | **0.2** |
| *From Europe* | *9,615* | *9,148* | *8,715* | *8,866* | *88.1* | *79.8* | *-4.7* | *1.7* | *-1.0* |
| United Kingdom | 5,116 | 4,636 | 4,600 | 5,165 | 46.9 | 46.5 | -0.8 | 12.3 | 0.1 |
| Germany | 1,812 | 1,513 | 1,324 | 1,183 | 16.6 | 10.6 | -12.5 | -10.6 | -5.2 |
| Italy | 711 | 709 | 739 | 627 | 6.5 | 5.6 | 4.3 | -15.2 | -1.6 |
| France | 600 | 660 | 629 | 624 | 5.5 | 5.6 | -4.6 | -0.9 | 0.5 |
| Netherlands | 445 | 459 | 380 | 357 | 4.1 | 3.2 | -17.4 | -5.9 | -2.7 |
| Belgium | 208 | 202 | 212 | 224 | 1.9 | 2.0 | 4.7 | 6.0 | 1.0 |
| Ireland | 152 | 209 | 205 | .. | 1.4 | | -2.0 | | |
| Austria | 162 | 228 | 189 | 198 | 1.5 | 1.8 | -17.3 | 5.2 | 2.5 |
| Switzerland | 150 | 218 | 193 | 193 | 1.4 | 1.7 | -11.2 | 0.0 | 3.2 |
| Denmark | 173 | 151 | 130 | 170 | 1.6 | 1.5 | -13.9 | 30.8 | -0.2 |
| Sweden | 87 | 163 | 115 | 123 | 0.8 | 1.1 | -29.3 | 6.9 | 4.5 |
| *From other regions* | *518* | *699* | *606* | *317* | *4.7* | *2.9* | *-13.4* | *-47.7* | *-6.0* |
| United States | 116 | 197 | 195 | 173 | 1.1 | 1.6 | -0.7 | -11.7 | 5.1 |
| Australia | 142 | 154 | 154 | .. | 1.3 | | 0.0 | | |
| Libyan Arab Jamahiriya | 185 | 261 | 177 | 144 | 1.7 | 1.3 | -32.3 | -18.4 | -3.0 |
| Canada | 76 | 87 | 79 | .. | 0.7 | | -8.8 | | |
| *Other World/Not specified* | *785* | *1,220* | *1,278* | *1,933* | *7.2* | *17.4* | *4.7* | *51.2* | *11.9* |

Source: World Tourism Organization (WTO) © (Data as collected by WTO December 2004)

# III.4.8 Portugal Southern Europe

## Profile

# Portugal

**Europe**
**Southern Europe**

| | |
|---|---|
| Capital | Lisbon |
| Year of entry in WTO | 1976 |
| Area (1000 km²) | 92 |
| Population (2003, million) | 10.5 |
| Gross Domestic Product (GDP) (2003, euro million) | 155,489 |
| GDP per capita (2003, euro) | 15,240 |
| GDP growth (real, %) | |
| -> 2002: 0.4; 2003: -1.2; 2004*: 1.4; 2005*: 2.2 | |

| | 2001 | 2002 | 2003* | 2002/2001 | 2003*/2002 |
|---|---|---|---|---|---|
| **International Arrivals** | | | | | |
| Visitors (1000) | 28,150 | 27,194 | 27,532 | -3.4 | 1.2 |
| Tourists (overnight visitors) (1000) | 12,167 | 11,644 | 11,707 | -4.3 | 0.5 |
| - per 100 of inhabitants | 117 | 112 | 112 | | |
| Same-day visitors (1000) | 15,814 | 15,389 | 15,535 | -2.7 | 0.9 |
| Cruise passengers (1000) | 169 | 161 | 290 | -4.7 | 80.1 |
| **Tourism accommodation** | | | | | |
| Number of rooms | 99,120 | 99,849 | 105,986 | 0.7 | 6.1 |
| *Nights spent in collective establishments (1000)* | 41,340 | 40,956 | 40,826 | -0.9 | -0.3 |
| by non-residents (inbound tourism) | 25,229 | 24,574 | 24,369 | -2.6 | -0.8 |
| by residents (domestic tourism) | 16,111 | 16,382 | 16,457 | 1.7 | 0.5 |
| *Nights spent in hotels and similar establishments (1000)* | 33,563 | 33,354 | 33,118 | -0.6 | -0.7 |
| by non-residents (inbound tourism) | 23,578 | 23,018 | 22,714 | -2.4 | -1.3 |
| by residents (domestic tourism) | 9,985 | 10,336 | 10,404 | 3.5 | 0.7 |
| **Receipts and Expenditure for International Tourism** | | | | | |
| International Tourism Receipts (euro million) | 5,922 | 6,432 | 7,336 | 8.6 | 14.1 |
| - per Tourist Arrival (euro) | 487 | 552 | 627 | 13.5 | 13.4 |
| - per Visitor Arrival (euro) | 210 | 237 | 266 | 12.4 | 12.7 |
| - per capita (euro) | 570 | 616 | 700 | | |
| International Fare Receipts (euro million) | 832 | 906 | 1,004 | 8.9 | 10.8 |
| International Tourism Expenditure (euro million) | 2,276 | 2,518 | 2,859 | 10.6 | 13.5 |
| - per capita (euro) | 219 | 241 | 273 | | |
| International Fare Expenditure (euro million) | 533 | 568 | 582 | 6.7 | 2.3 |
| △ International Tourism Balance (euro million) | 3,647 | 3,915 | 4,478 | | |
| △ International Fare Balance (euro million) | 299 | 337 | 422 | | |

Source: World Tourism Organization (WTO) (Data as collected by WTO December 2004)

See annex for methodological notes and reference of external sources used.

# Survey

Contributed by *Direcçao Geral de Turismo*
www.portugalinsite.pt (promotional)
www.dgturismo.pt (institutional/corporate)
www.portugalinsite.pt ;www.dgturismo.pt ; www.bportugal.pt ; www.ine.pt (research and data)

## Tourism development and outlook

**Overall evaluation of results**

In 2003, the total number of international visitor arrivals to Portugal amounted to 27,5 million, which represents an increase of 1.2 per cent over 2002. Of the total number of visitors, 43 per cent were tourists, 56 per cent same-day visitors and 1.1 per cent cruise passengers. 93 per cent of the overall international arrivals were originated from European countries, namely from six countries: Spain, the United Kingdom, Germany, France, the Netherlands and Italy were responsible for around 84 per cent of all tourist arrivals. Among these countries, Spain is to be noted, as it represents around 46 per cent of all arrivals. Spain is also the main source market in terms of same-day visitors, representing a share of 98 per cent. In 2003 the number of overnights stays in hotels and similar establishments amounted to 34 million, representing an increase of 0.5 per cent over the previous year. This growth was mainly determined by the 0.8 per cent rise in foreign overnight stays, as nationals' overnight stays decreased by 0.3 per cent. There was, however, a decrease in occupancy rates - room and bed occupancy rates, which in 2003, were of 56 per cent and 48 per cent, respectively, against 59 per cent and 50 per cent in 2002.
Tourism receipts amounted to 6.1 billion euro, according to the preliminary results by the Bank of Portugal, or 1.2 per cent more than in 2002. The net value of the tourism balance reached 3.7 billion euro, representing a growth of 1.8 per cent growth. Average expenditure tourist/day grew slightly to 120 euro, according to the survey developed by the Directorate General for Tourism, "Survey on non-residents expenditure". There is a trend of increase in the performance of this indicator in the period 1990-2003. Average expenditure visitor/day, though showing a more instable behaviour in the period 1990-2003, grew steadily as compared to 2002 (to 58 euro). As for domestic tourism, there was a slight decrease in the number of people travelling for holidays outside their usual place of residence. 52 per cent travelled for holidays, of which with 13 per cent abroad and 45 per cent within the country.

**Supply**

According to the National Institute of Statistics (INE), accommodation capacity amounted to 246 thousand beds in 2003, which represents an increase of 2.4 per cent over 2002. The latest available data (INE, 2002) regarding the Portuguese road network indicate that total road extension in the mainland reached 12.399 km, of which 1.835 km are high-way. Portugal has also 62 golf courses, 57 of which in the mainland. In 2003 there was a reinforcement of air capacity, in particular to Lisbon, Faro and Ponta Delgada, (the Azores), originating from some of the main generating markets to Portugal, such as the United Kingdom, France, Germany and Scandinavia.

**External factors**

The main negative factor affecting tourism in Portugal in 2003 was the national and international economic situation. Internationally the slower than expected recovery in the euro area and the strength of the euro against the US dollar determined some decrease in the competitive advantages of Portugal as compared to other destinations, such as the Central and Eastern European countries, North Africa and the Caribbean. There was also still some feeling of insecurity in travel. Internally, economy went through a difficult phase due to the needed restrained budgetary policy, which inevitably affected tourism. Tourism was also affected by the fires that occurred in several areas of the country during the summer months. As positive factors: the fact that Portugal was still perceived a safe destination within the geopolitical uncertainty and the political recognition of tourism as an important economic and social sector in the framework of the integration of the Portuguese Tourism Confederation in the Permanent Commission for Social Coordination. Tourism continued to benefit from a significant number of financial incentives schemes: the Programme of Incentives to the Modernization of the Economy and the National Training Programme "Better Tourism", both integrated in the III Community Support Framework, and the Programme of Interventions for the Qualification of Tourism.

**Tourism policy**

In 2003, in the framework of the tourism policy, the government approved the "Tourism Development Plan", which includes 40 measures in the areas of:

- Development of supply: revision of the law concerning the approval and Licensing of tourism accommodation establishments; creation of a Centre for the licensing of Strategic Tourism Projects; creation of the "Tourism Protected Areas"; creation of Centre for the evaluation, classification and qualification of tourism accommodation; elaboration of a "Strategic Training Plan" in the area of hotel management and tourism and the redefinition of the school network; reformulation of the tourist and road signage; revision of the legal set regarding the installation and functioning of restaurants and similar establishments;
- Development of demand: new model of coordination in terms of tourism promotion, based on an advisory and deliberative board encompassing public and private representatives; decentralized model of tourism promotion based upon the establishment of a contractual system between the central and the regional tourism boards for the implementation of tourism promotion activities; reinforcement of the tourism promotion budget abroad and in Portugal;
- Institutional reorganization: creation of the Portugal Tourism Institute, concentrating the competences of tourism promotion, financial support and investment; redefinition of the role of the Directorate General for Tourism; revision of the Basic Law regarding Regional Tourism Boards;
- Market Intelligence: redefinition of the system of collection and treatment of statistical information; incentive to the development of tourism studies and research; reformulation of the web portal;
- Other legislative measures: revision of the Travel Agencies Law; revision of the Basic Law on Thermal Activities; revision of the Hunting Law; legislation on electronic gambling; competitiveness of airport taxes.

**Marketing & promotion**

Strategic:
During 2003, and in the context of the Tourism Development Plan, a significant number of deep changes occurred in terms of tourism promotion. Such modifications were based in the attribution of new responsibilities to public and private regional agents, stimulating partnerships in the form of the "Regional Tourism Promotion Agencies". These organisations, acting in the framework of the regional brands/destinations, are responsible for defining the promotional plans for regional destinations and products in coordination with public and private stakeholders and with the central tourism board, which is responsible for the promotion on the brand "Portugal". The development of these regional promotion plans was made possible by central administration financing, supported in a 3 years contractual system. The activity of the central tourism board as been focused in the strategic coordination of the above mentioned plans and in the development of a promotional plan for the brand "Portugal". In this area, a deep study on the advantages and values associated with the destination took place, resulting in a new positioning for Portugal as a tourism destination. In this framework a coherent communication strategy (the Portuguese

Identity System) was designed and implemented in the basis of a new set of communication instruments.
Besides the creation of a new collection of promotional materials, two structural projects were set:
- A pan European contact centre, functioning since January 2004, and responsible for information requests from the main seven European generating markets to Portugal and for requests from Portugal. The coverage of the contact centre is expected to be expanded gradually to other European markets;
- A new Internet portal due to be active in October 2004.

Operational:
Having into account the recessive factors affecting world tourism, promotion was focused in a group of 14 generating markets among the 22 markets where Portugal develops a regular and active promotional activity, according to the following budget distribution:
- Spain (strategic market): 19 per cent;
- the United Kingdom and Germany (priority markets): 48 per cent;
- The Netherlands, France, Scandinavia, Italy, Ireland, Belgium, the United States of America and Brazil: 25 per cent;
- Other international markets: 8 per cent.

International Campaigns:
- Communication campaigns in the main markets during the first semester of 2003;
- Euro 2004 Football Cup promotional campaign during the fourth quarter of 2003.

International fairs: attendance of 63 international tourism fairs.
Promotion to new segments: promotional campaign aimed at the Portuguese residing abroad.
The promotional plan included also an intense set of activities for press (familiarisation trips) and trade (workshops) representations focused mainly in the priority markets and in high economic value products.
The overall evaluation of the promotional activity in 2003 was positive as it has allowed to contain some of the negative trends and to increase tourism receipts. Such activity has also contributed to the recovery felt in 2004, which was also stimulated by a number of events held in Portugal, which consolidated the positive image of the destination, in particular the promotion of Portugal in the framework of the Euro 2004 Football Cup.

**Outlook 2004**

In 2004 the Portuguese economy should benefit from a more favourable external context and from the expected European and world economic recovery. The national economy will also benefit from the political measures adopted internally to improve the competitiveness of the private sector and to consolidate the national budgetary situation. In the framework of an expected moderate economic recovery, exports of goods and services are likely to increase sector, which will profit from the effects of the Euro 2004 Football Cup held in Portugal in June 2004, and from other important events, such as the Rock-in-Rio Festival and the Laureus Awards Ceremony. In 2004 a new government was established, which includes, for the first time, a Ministry of Tourism, recognising thus the importance of the sector in the national economy. Prospects for 2004, and for the following years, will be influenced by the main objectives defined by the government, which are as follow for the area of tourism:
- Definition and revision of the legal framework for the tourism sector;
- Increase of foreign and domestic demand;
- Special oriented promotion aimed at priority generating markets, in particular Spain;
- Coordination with air and sea transport representatives aiming at the definition of targeted markets for promotion;
- Research and promotion activities to increase the competitive advantage of Portugal in the areas of airport operations and taxes;

- Development and consolidation of tourism itineraries;
- Incentive to the choice of Portugal as a destination for cultural and sports events with impact on tourism;
- Increase occupancy rates, decrease seasonality and regional concentration of demand;
- Incentive to leisure, sport and cultural activities aimed at low and medium season segments and products;
- Qualification of supply (quality and excellence);
- Institutional reorganization;
- Increase competitiveness and productivity.

## International Meetings Industry (MI)

**Characteristics of supply**

In recent years the facilities available for the Meetings Industry in Portugal have been growing in a sustained way. Simultaneously there has been an increase in the number and quality of accommodation (4 and 5 star hotels) and of specialized service providers in the main MICE destinations (Lisbon, Porto, Algarve and Madeira). Lisbon, the main national destination in terms of meetings and conventions, has an extraordinary flexibility in this segment, going from an excellent performance in terms of medium-size meetings (500 participants) to an growing capacity for bigger meetings, as proven by the organization of an increasing number of meetings with over five thousand participants.

As for incentive travel, national supply is mainly based, on one hand, in the diversity of experiences and landscapes Portugal can offer in a concentrated geographic area, and on the other hand, in the growing professionalism of specialized incentive travel enterprises and Convention Bureaux. The regulation and strict licensing of such enterprises has contributed to the quality of the services and to its recognition in the international market.

Still in this area, the organization of sports and cultural events in Portugal has gained special importance, with a particular note to events held in 2004, such as the Euro 2004 Football Cup and the "Rock in Rio Lisboa".

**Organisation of promotion**

MICE promotion is based, in the regional level, on the activity of the Convention Bureaux, namely the ones of Lisbon, Estoril and Sintra, Algarve and Porto. Their activity is coordinated with the Regional Agencies for Tourism Promotion and with the National Agency responsible for tourism promotion, the Portugal Tourism Institute.

**Collection of statistics on the Meetings Industry?:** no.

**Description**

Though there are no available statistics on the Meetings Industry, a study on the relative weight of tourism products in the overall tourism demand in Portugal, including MICE, was developed in 2000. A new research is set to be put in place in 2005.

**Importance / size**

As a reference, Lisbon which is the main national destination in the MICE segment, positioned 5$^{th}$ in the 2003 ranking of international destinations, with a volume of 63 meetings and a 20 per cent growth rate over 2002 (source: ICCA, )

**Evolution MI**

The number of programmed meetings to be held in Portugal and the reports available indicate that there will be a sustained growth in the sector. The on going research will allow, in the near future, to have a more consistent evaluation of the impact of the MICE in tourism and in the economy. Two factors are considered important to such sustained growth:

- a competitive tourism product (price / quality relation);
- the adaptation of the promotional structure.

# International Tourism by Origin

**Portugal**

**International Tourist Arrivals at Frontiers**

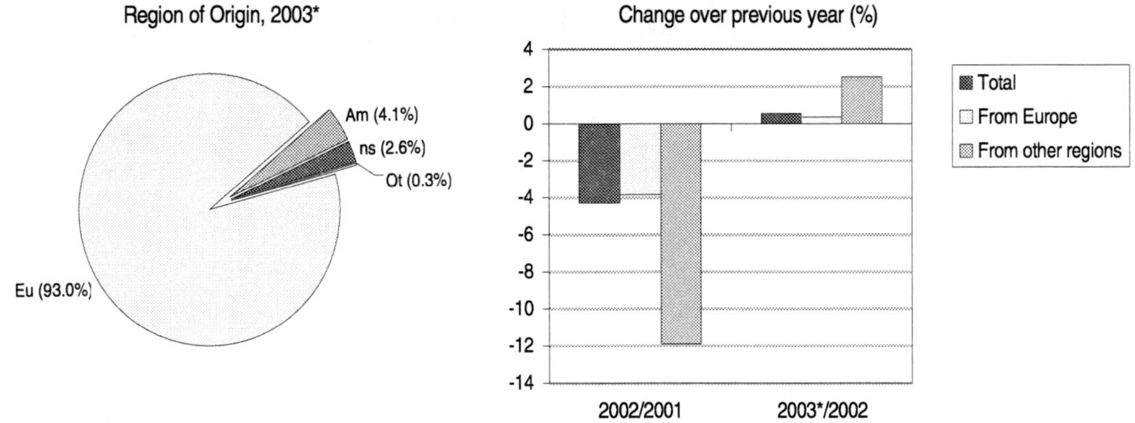


Eu: Europe; Am: Americas;
ns: Not specified; Ot: Other;

Source: World Tourism Organization (WTO) ©

**Portugal**

**Nights of International Tourists in All Accommodation Establishments**

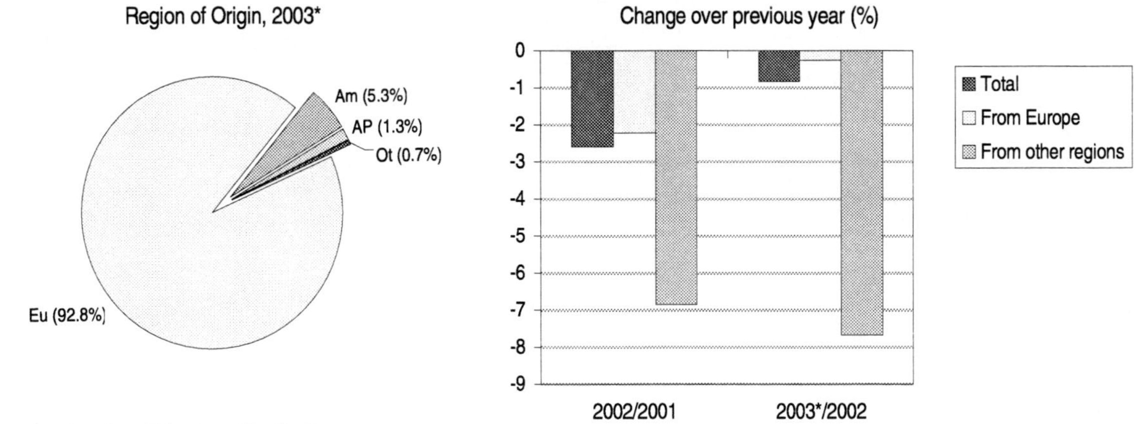


Eu: Europe; Am: Americas; AP: Asia and the Pacific;
Ot: Other;

Source: World Tourism Organization (WTO) ©

**Portugal**

**International Tourist Arrivals at Frontiers (by residence)**

| | | | | (thousand) | Market share (%) | | Growth rate (%) | | Average per year (%) |
|---|---|---|---|---|---|---|---|---|---|
| | 1995 | 2001 | 2002 | 2003* | 1995 | 2003* | 2002/01 | 2003*/02 | 1995-2003* |
| **Total** | .. | **12,167** | **11,644** | **11,707** | | **100** | **-4.3** | **0.5** | |
| *From Europe* | .. | *11,282* | *10,849* | *10,888* | | *93.0* | *-3.8* | *0.4* | |
| Spain | .. | 5,669 | 5,396 | 5,431 | | 46.4 | -4.8 | 0.6 | |
| United Kingdom | .. | 1,977 | 1,858 | 1,874 | | 16.0 | -6.0 | 0.9 | |
| Germany | .. | 909 | 852 | 848 | | 7.2 | -6.3 | -0.4 | |
| France | .. | 876 | 845 | 844 | | 7.2 | -3.5 | -0.1 | |
| Netherlands | .. | 495 | 483 | 479 | | 4.1 | -2.4 | -0.7 | |
| Italy | .. | 297 | 367 | 334 | | 2.9 | 23.5 | -9.1 | |
| Belgium | .. | 271 | 262 | 271 | | 2.3 | -3.2 | 3.4 | |
| Ireland | .. | 127 | 138 | 143 | | 1.2 | 8.6 | 3.3 | |
| Switzerland | .. | 152 | 139 | 137 | | 1.2 | -8.4 | -1.2 | |
| Sweden | .. | 139 | 132 | 130 | | 1.1 | -5.2 | -1.6 | |
| Denmark | .. | 127 | 122 | 126 | | 1.1 | -4.5 | 3.9 | |
| Finland | .. | 72 | 75 | 79 | | 0.7 | 3.0 | 5.4 | |
| Austria | .. | 63 | 58 | 62 | | 0.5 | -8.5 | 6.0 | |
| Norway | .. | 49 | 46 | 47 | | 0.4 | -7.7 | 2.1 | |
| Greece | .. | 23 | 39 | 44 | | 0.4 | 68.5 | 11.9 | |
| Luxembourg | .. | 34 | 37 | 39 | | 0.3 | 9.2 | 4.6 | |
| *From other regions* | .. | *576* | *508* | *521* | | *4.4* | *-11.9* | *2.5* | |
| United States | .. | 274 | 246 | 253 | | 2.2 | -10.3 | 2.6 | |
| Brazil | .. | 140 | 112 | 118 | | 1.0 | -20.0 | 5.5 | |
| Canada | .. | 122 | 106 | 110 | | 0.9 | -13.3 | 3.9 | |
| Japan | .. | 40 | 44 | 40 | | 0.3 | 9.8 | -8.9 | |
| *Other World/Not specified* | .. | *309* | *287* | *299* | | *2.6* | *-7.1* | *4.0* | |

Source: World Tourism Organization (WTO) © (Data as collected by WTO December 2004)

**Portugal**
**Nights of International Tourists in All Accommodation Establishments (by residence)**

| | | | | (thousand) | Market share (%) | | Growth rate (%) | | Average per year (%) |
|---|---|---|---|---|---|---|---|---|---|
| | 1995 | 2001 | 2002 | 2003* | 1995 | 2003* | 2002/01 | 2003*/02 | 1995-2003* |
| **Total** | **22,241** | **25,229** | **24,574** | **24,369** | **100** | **100** | **-2.6** | **-0.8** | **1.1** |
| *From Europe* | *20,716* | *23,175* | *22,661* | *22,603* | *93.1* | *92.8* | *-2.2* | *-0.3* | *1.1* |
| United Kingdom | 5,982 | 7,432 | 7,380 | 7,392 | 26.9 | 30.3 | -0.7 | 0.2 | 2.7 |
| Germany | 5,521 | 4,827 | 4,269 | 4,068 | 24.8 | 16.7 | -11.6 | -4.7 | -3.7 |
| Spain | 1,835 | 2,139 | 2,253 | 2,382 | 8.2 | 9.8 | 5.3 | 5.7 | 3.3 |
| Netherlands | 1,717 | 2,016 | 1,993 | 1,882 | 7.7 | 7.7 | -1.1 | -5.6 | 1.2 |
| France | 1,342 | 1,389 | 1,499 | 1,534 | 6.0 | 6.3 | 8.0 | 2.3 | 1.7 |
| Ireland | 611 | 775 | 938 | 1,073 | 2.7 | 4.4 | 21.0 | 14.5 | 7.3 |
| Italy | 735 | 857 | 820 | 769 | 3.3 | 3.2 | -4.3 | -6.3 | 0.6 |
| Belgium | 662 | 621 | 588 | 601 | 3.0 | 2.5 | -5.3 | 2.2 | -1.2 |
| Sweden | 426 | 722 | 676 | 584 | 1.9 | 2.4 | -6.3 | -13.6 | 4.0 |
| Norway | 186 | 434 | 387 | 434 | 0.8 | 1.8 | -10.8 | 12.2 | 11.2 |
| Finland | 244 | 318 | 349 | 371 | 1.1 | 1.5 | 9.8 | 6.2 | 5.4 |
| Denmark | 328 | 397 | 324 | 327 | 1.5 | 1.3 | -18.4 | 1.1 | 0.0 |
| Switzerland | 342 | 343 | 320 | 310 | 1.5 | 1.3 | -6.6 | -3.4 | -1.3 |
| Austria | 474 | 262 | 238 | 233 | 2.1 | 1.0 | -9.3 | -1.9 | -8.5 |
| Former U.S.S.R. | 48 | 142 | 135 | 130 | 0.2 | 0.5 | -4.3 | -4.1 | 13.1 |
| Poland | 29 | 91 | 109 | 102 | 0.1 | 0.4 | 20.0 | -6.3 | 16.9 |
| Iceland | 56 | 95 | 52 | 57 | 0.3 | 0.2 | -45.7 | 10.2 | 0.2 |
| Greece | 36 | 41 | 47 | 50 | 0.2 | 0.2 | 13.8 | 7.6 | 4.3 |
| Hungary | 21 | 38 | 38 | 44 | 0.1 | 0.2 | 0.7 | 15.5 | 9.6 |
| Luxembourg | 30 | 42 | 39 | 40 | 0.1 | 0.2 | -5.9 | 0.4 | 3.6 |
| Israel | .. | 37 | 28 | 30 | | 0.1 | -26.0 | 7.7 | |
| Romania | 7 | 13 | 19 | 20 | 0.0 | 0.1 | 48.8 | 1.9 | 13.5 |
| Turkey | 7 | 13 | 14 | 18 | 0.0 | 0.1 | 4.2 | 33.9 | 13.4 |
| Bulgaria | 6 | 9 | 12 | 11 | 0.0 | 0.0 | 37.0 | -10.7 | 9.0 |
| Other intraregional | 71 | 124 | 133 | 142 | 0.3 | 0.6 | 7.8 | 6.5 | 9.1 |
| *From other regions* | *1,525* | *2,053* | *1,913* | *1,766* | *6.9* | *7.2* | *-6.8* | *-7.7* | *1.9* |
| United States | 501 | 691 | 625 | 564 | 2.3 | 2.3 | -9.6 | -9.8 | 1.5 |
| Brazil | 266 | 358 | 331 | 309 | 1.2 | 1.3 | -7.6 | -6.5 | 1.9 |
| Canada | 221 | 384 | 309 | 302 | 1.0 | 1.2 | -19.6 | -2.2 | 4.0 |
| Japan | 125 | 137 | 169 | 145 | 0.6 | 0.6 | 23.5 | -14.3 | 1.9 |
| Australia | 47 | 64 | 72 | 66 | 0.2 | 0.3 | 12.7 | -8.2 | 4.4 |
| South Africa | 23 | 40 | 41 | 30 | 0.1 | 0.1 | 1.6 | -26.0 | 3.6 |
| Mexico | .. | 25 | 29 | 28 | | 0.1 | 17.8 | -2.7 | |
| China | .. | 23 | 24 | 24 | | 0.1 | 4.3 | -2.1 | |
| Argentina | .. | 36 | 21 | 23 | | 0.1 | -41.5 | 11.6 | |
| New Zealand | 11 | 21 | 20 | 17 | 0.1 | 0.1 | -1.5 | -14.1 | 5.7 |
| India | .. | 12 | 15 | 15 | | 0.1 | 21.0 | -0.9 | |
| Morocco | .. | 16 | 12 | 12 | | 0.0 | -20.8 | -4.4 | |
| Korea, Republic of | .. | 13 | 10 | 10 | | 0.0 | -23.4 | 2.1 | |
| Venezuela | .. | 18 | 20 | 10 | | 0.0 | 14.0 | -50.9 | |
| Chile | .. | 8 | 10 | 8 | | 0.0 | 17.4 | -16.2 | |
| Colombia | .. | 6 | 7 | 6 | | 0.0 | 17.5 | -18.8 | |
| Egypt | .. | 7 | 5 | 5 | | 0.0 | -25.3 | 7.4 | |
| Other interregional | 331 | 195 | 193 | 191 | 1.5 | 0.8 | -1.0 | -0.8 | -6.6 |

Source: World Tourism Organization (WTO) © (Data as collected by WTO December 2004)

# III.4.9 San Marino Southern Europe

## Profile

# San Marino

| | |
|---|---|
| Capital | San Marino |
| Year of entry in WTO | 1975 |
| Area (10 km²) | 6 |
| Population (2003, 1000) | 28 |

**Europe**
**Southern Europe**

| | 2001 | 2002 | 2003* | 2002/2001 | 2003*/2002 |
|---|---|---|---|---|---|
| **International Arrivals** | | | | | |
| Visitors (1000) | 3,036 | 3,102 | 2,882 | 2.2 | -7.1 |
| Tourists (overnight visitors) (1000) | 49 | 45 | 41 | -8.2 | -8.9 |
| - per 100 of inhabitants | 179 | 162 | 146 | | |
| **Tourism accommodation** | | | | | |
| Number of rooms | 486 | 500 | 683 | 2.9 | 36.6 |
| *Nights spent in hotels and similar establishments (1000)* | 75 | 70 | 64 | -6.7 | -8.6 |
| by non-residents (inbound tourism) | 15 | 14 | 12 | -6.7 | -14.3 |
| by residents (domestic tourism) | 60 | 56 | 52 | -6.7 | -7.1 |

Source: World Tourism Organization (WTO) (Data as collected by WTO December 2004)

See annex for methodological notes and reference of external sources used.

## Survey

Contributed by *Ufficio di Stato per il Turismo*
www.omniway.sm (promotional)
www.visitsanmarino.com (institutional/corporate)

## Tourism development and outlook

**Overall evaluation of results**

The tourism results achieved by San Marino in 2003 reveal a progressive decline in organized tours.

This is evident in the fewer arrivals by motorcoach in 2003, down by 2000 compared to the previous year.

This may be explained by:

- Slack demand for organized coach tours;
- Consolidation of new destinations offering more competitive rates;
- Economic conditions in Italy and Europe as a whole owing to the disorderly conversion to the euro;
- Unfavourable climatic conditions caused by the heat wave.

**Supply**

The main tourism products are:
*Conference tourism:*
- The recent opening of a conference centre in San Marino whose activity is at the development stage;
- Fairs, exhibitions and business travel,
- This important market accounts for 3,500 activities in San Marino.

*Cultural tourism:*
- Several important events are held each year;
- The main events in 2003 were: the feast of St Marinus and of the foundation of the Republic, the ceremonies for the investiture of the Captains Regent, the Libertatis Fundator cultural exhibition: the San Marino, the ethnic festival of San Marino, mediaeval events, St Sylvester night;
- Projects carried out in cooperation with tourism and business associations have served to attract many tourists, these include the illumination of San Marino's historic centre accompanied by street events.

*Sports tourism:*
- This sector is boosted by major sporting events, such as the Superbike Grand Prix, the San Marino Formula 1 Grand Prix, the Mille Miglia, the San Marino Underwater Hockey European Championships, the air show marking the centenary of motorized flight, the ATP international tennis tournament: the Challenger Tour;
- These sporting events have greatly stimulated group travel to San Marino, and to develop this type of tourism to the full, special tourism packages will be developed to cater for this demand.

**External factors**

The political and economic situation: the war and terrorism led to a 7.9 per cent decline in tourism.
Border formalities and security.
Construction and improvement of road infrastructure.
The meteorological conditions had a negative impact on the 2003 tourist season.

**Tourism policy**

The general tourism policy of the NTA is as follows:
- Development of sports tourism;
- Opening of the conference centre and relaunch of the Conference Tourism Master Plan;
- Institutional organization;
- Regulation and liberalization;
- Policy of restructuring tourist flows to increase holiday stays;
- Training and upgrading of human resources: information points, new summer service.

Measures of encouragement:
- Tax breaks;
- Public-private partnership;
- Partnership with the San Marino 2000 Hotel Consortium;
- Research.

**Marketing & promotion**

Marketing and promotion plans:
- Distribution of the marketing plan;
- New operational strategies and activities;
- Conferences on tourism;
- Establishment of contacts with French, British, Russian and German tour operators.

Main activities:
- Presence of San Marino at specialist tourism fairs on the internal markets of Italy,

Germany, Switzerland, Austria, France, England, Russia, Hungary, Czech Republic and Poland.

Main products:
- Distribution channels;
- Special promotional campaigns and activities;
- Development of websites;
- Regular events;
- New technologies.

**Outlook 2004**

Outlook for the next few years:
- Targeting the main markets with tourism events and promotional campaigns;
- Growth of the Russian market and that of eastern Europe as a whole. Growth of the Italian market is also forecast;Owing to its characteristics and geographical position at the centre of Italy, San Marino's tourists come mainly from Italy. It should be noted that it also attracts tourists from the eastern European countries, such as Poland and Hungary, that are Members of the European Union.

## International Meetings Industry (MI)

**Characteristics of supply**

Characteristics of supply:
- Meetings, conferences and congresses;
- Incentive travel;
- Few initiatives in this area; virtually total absence of exhibitions;
- Concentration on conference tourism.

**Organisation of promotion**

International promotion:
- Through a private company:In 2003 the company ACX managed the entire promotional activity for San Marino's conferences, in cooperation with the San Marino Tourism Office <www.acxcorporate.sm>;
- Through the Kursall Conference Centre <www.visitsanmarino.com>.

**Collection of statistics on the Meetings Industry?:** yes.

**Description**

The results are negative owing to the general downturn in tourism activity in 2003. There was however a sizeable increase in the number of overnight stays and days spent in San Marino.

**Importance / size**

Business tourism accounts for 30 per cent of San Marino's total tourism.

**Evolution MI**

Conference tourism is an important sector which the Government of San Marino is endeavouring to develop, setting a five-year target for achieving this.

# III.4.10 Serbia and Montenegro Southern Europe

## Profile

**Serbia and Montenegro**

**Europe**
**Southern Europe**

| | |
|---|---|
| Capital | Belgrade |
| Year of entry in WTO | 2001 |
| Area (1000 km²) | 102 |
| Population (2003, million) | 10.8 |
| Gross Domestic Product (GDP) (2003, euro million) | 21,957 |
| GDP per capita (2003, euro) | 2,635 |
| GDP growth (real, %) | |
| '-> 2002: 4.0; 2003: 3.0; 2004*: 4.4; 2005*: 4.5 | |

| | 2001 | 2002 | 2003* | 2002/2001 | 2003*/2002 |
|---|---|---|---|---|---|
| **Tourism accommodation** | | | | | |
| Number of rooms | 37,782 | 37,882 | 37,101 | 0.3 | -2.1 |
| *Nights spent in collective establishments (1000)* | 11,207 | 10,896 | 10,660 | -2.8 | -2.2 |
| by non-residents (inbound tourism) | 1,281 | 1,650 | 1,707 | 28.8 | 3.5 |
| by residents (domestic tourism) | 9,926 | 9,246 | 8,953 | -6.9 | -3.2 |
| *Nights spent in hotels and similar establishments (1000)* | 6,344 | 6,522 | 6,075 | 2.8 | -6.9 |
| by non-residents (inbound tourism) | 1,047 | 1,404 | 1,425 | 34.1 | 1.5 |
| by residents (domestic tourism) | 5,297 | 5,118 | 4,650 | -3.4 | -9.1 |

Source: World Tourism Organization (WTO) (Data as collected by WTO December 2004)

See annex for methodological notes and reference of external sources used.

## Survey

Contributed by *Ministry of Trade, Tourism and Services*
www.minttu.sr.gov.yu (promotional)
www.minttu.sr.gov.yu (institutional/corporate)

## Tourism development and outlook

**Overall evaluation of results**

Domestic tourism in 2003 accounts for 1.7 million tourists (-13 per cent and compared to 2002) and for 5.9 million overnights (-9%).

More than 34 per cent of domestic overnights were registered in spas destinations, in mountain centres (30%), in rural and small villages, including cities on the transit routes (18.5%) and in big cities (14%).

The fall in total domestic tourism was caused by the decrease of the number of visits for business and professional purposes to main cities like Belgrade mostly, while the best results in domestic tourism reached the spas and rural tourist resorts.

In spite of the decline in domestic tourism flows, international tourism continued its growth. The number of international tourists increased by 339 thousand and their overnights grew by 792 thousand which represents respectively increases of 9 and 7 per cent over 2002. Of these total figures, 64 per cent are registered in capital Belgrade and Novi Sad.

The main purpose of visit of international tourists was business and conferences. Nevertheless, the visitors number for the amusement, essentially youth, extremely increased, such as tourists number taking cruises in the Danube.
International tourists come from the TFYROM, Germany, Italy, the United Kingdom, Greece, Russia and Austria.

**Supply**

New accommodation inside the countries, especially in rural and transit tourism.
Development of new thematic products as wine tours, rafting and bicycles tours.
Ethno and music events, etc.
Increasing of the number of tours for youth and ship cruises along the Danube.

**Tourism policy**

Increase of public and private partnerships at the local level.
Growth of private investments in accommodation.
Special offers.

**Marketing & promotion**

Development promotional activities on the markets of the United Kingdom and Germany.
Research for the operational promotional activities on main foreign markets.

**Outlook 2004**

Forecasts for 2004 almost show similar tendencies in domestic and international tourism as in 2003, e.g. increase in international tourism and decrease in domestic tourism. Tourism receipts in 2004 are estimated to increase by 50 per cent over 2003.

## International Meetings Industry (MI)

**Characteristics of supply**

Congresses and Conferences.

**Organisation of promotion**

The Promotion of Meetings Industry is organised by the City Tourism Organization and by the City Convention Bureaux.

**Collection of statistics on the Meetings Industry?:** no.

**Importance / size**

About 14 thousand to 18 thousand visitors to Serbia and Montenegro come from the Meetings Industry.

**Evolution MI**

Accommodation represents the main problem for achieving big Meetings events. Nevertheless, in the 2005, Belgrade will host several important international conferences and sports events, which should draw more than 25 thousand participants.

# International Tourism by Origin

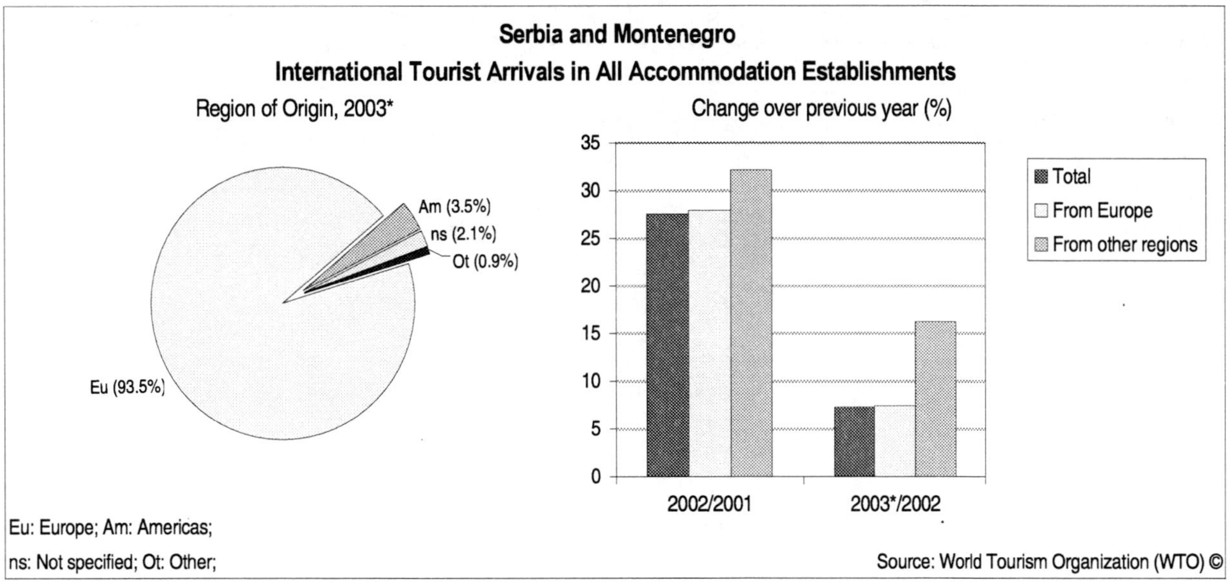


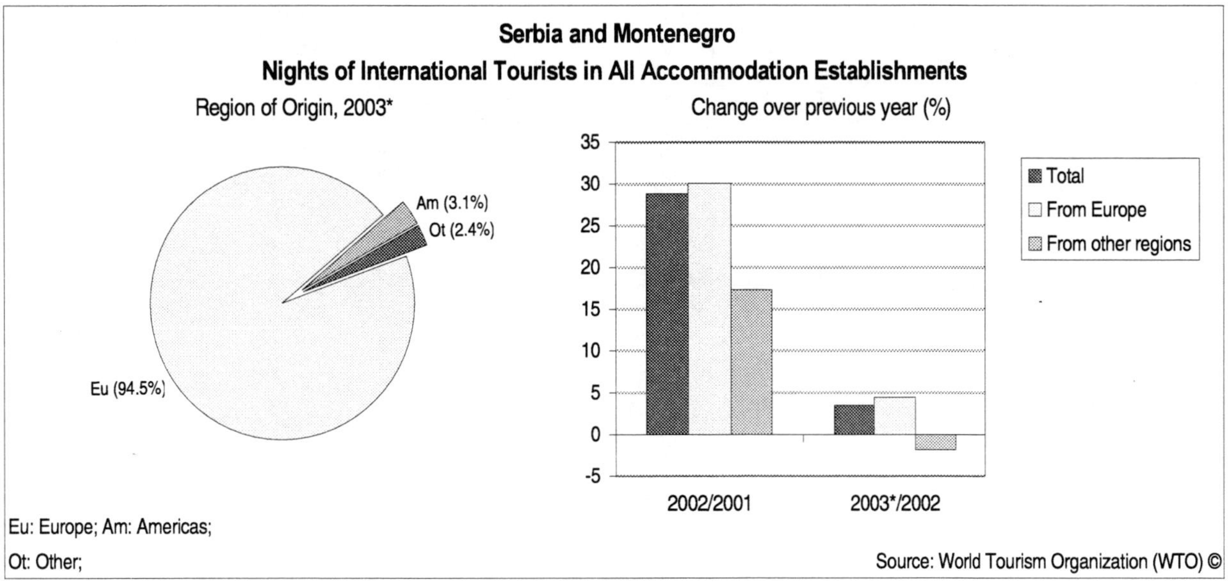

**Serbia and Montenegro**
**International Tourist Arrivals in All Accommodation Establishments (by nationality)**

| | | | | (thousand) | Market share (%) | | Growth rate (%) | | Average per year (%) |
|---|---|---|---|---|---|---|---|---|---|
| | 1995 | 2001 | 2002 | 2003* | 1995 | 2003* | 2002/01 | 2003*/02 | 1995-2003* |
| **Total** | **228** | **351** | **448** | **481** | **100** | **100** | **27.6** | **7.3** | **9.8** |
| *From Europe* | *218* | *327* | *419* | *450* | *96.0* | *93.5* | *27.9* | *7.5* | *9.5* |
| Bosnia & Herzg | 78 | 74 | 63 | 63 | 34.5 | 13.2 | -14.8 | 1.2 | -2.6 |
| Germany | 4 | 19 | 33 | 39 | 1.6 | 8.0 | 77.5 | 15.5 | 34.3 |
| Slovenia | 2 | 21 | 30 | 36 | 1.1 | 7.6 | 43.1 | 22.0 | 39.8 |
| Former Czechoslovakia | 2 | 21 | 41 | 34 | 0.8 | 7.1 | 92.2 | -15.7 | 44.9 |
| F.Yug.Rp.Macedonia | 34 | 26 | 32 | 32 | 14.9 | 6.7 | 24.4 | 0.0 | -0.7 |
| Italy | 8 | 17 | 23 | 25 | 3.4 | 5.2 | 39.2 | 5.9 | 15.9 |
| Croatia | 13 | 14 | 19 | 23 | 5.7 | 4.8 | 40.4 | 19.9 | 7.5 |
| Russian Federation | 15 | 18 | 21 | 19 | 6.7 | 3.9 | 13.6 | -11.0 | 2.5 |
| Bulgaria | 11 | 11 | 14 | 18 | 4.7 | 3.8 | 35.7 | 26.6 | 6.9 |
| Poland | 1 | 8 | 14 | 16 | 0.4 | 3.3 | 84.8 | 9.8 | 42.8 |
| Greece | 12 | 8 | 12 | 16 | 5.2 | 3.2 | 50.1 | 25.1 | 3.6 |
| Austria | 4 | 10 | 14 | 16 | 1.9 | 3.2 | 39.2 | 10.8 | 16.9 |
| Hungary | 3 | 10 | 14 | 14 | 1.4 | 3.0 | 45.8 | 1.0 | 20.2 |
| United Kingdom | 3 | 8 | 10 | 14 | 1.2 | 2.9 | 37.6 | 33.6 | 22.2 |
| Romania | 7 | 11 | 12 | 11 | 3.3 | 2.4 | 12.7 | -7.8 | 5.5 |
| France | 2 | 7 | 9 | 10 | 1.1 | 2.1 | 26.9 | 17.5 | 19.7 |
| Netherlands | 1 | 4 | 6 | 8 | 0.6 | 1.6 | 43.9 | 35.0 | 23.4 |
| Switzerland | 1 | 5 | 6 | 6 | 0.6 | 1.3 | 17.1 | 13.4 | 20.0 |
| Turkey | 2 | 4 | 6 | 6 | 0.7 | 1.3 | 28.1 | 5.1 | 18.7 |
| Sweden | 1 | 3 | 4 | 5 | 0.5 | 1.0 | 32.6 | 19.9 | 19.8 |
| Norway | 1 | 3 | 4 | 4 | 0.3 | 0.9 | 45.0 | 19.5 | 24.5 |
| Israel | 0 | 2 | 3 | 4 | 0.2 | 0.9 | 58.2 | 47.6 | 31.6 |
| Belgium | 2 | 3 | 4 | 4 | 0.8 | 0.9 | 58.1 | 3.9 | 11.5 |
| Spain | 0 | 2 | 2 | 3 | 0.2 | 0.6 | 18.5 | 29.1 | 29.3 |
| Denmark | 1 | 2 | 2 | 3 | 0.4 | 0.6 | 16.8 | 19.0 | 15.8 |
| Other intraregional | 9 | 19 | 19 | 20 | 3.8 | 4.2 | 0.0 | 4.7 | 10.9 |
| *From other regions* | *5* | *14* | *18* | *21* | *2.2* | *4.4* | *32.2* | *16.3* | *19.8* |
| United States | 3 | 9 | 12 | 14 | 1.4 | 2.9 | 35.8 | 15.2 | 20.6 |
| Canada | 1 | 2 | 2 | 3 | 0.3 | 0.6 | 51.4 | 15.2 | 18.9 |
| Australia | 0 | 1 | 1 | 2 | 0.2 | 0.4 | 17.5 | 40.1 | 20.9 |
| Japan | 1 | 2 | 2 | 2 | 0.3 | 0.4 | -0.6 | 5.5 | 13.8 |
| New Zealand | 0 | 0 | 0 | 0 | 0.0 | 0.1 | 110.5 | 13.2 | 33.2 |
| *Other World/Not specified* | *4* | *10* | *12* | *10* | *1.8* | *2.1* | *10.4* | *-11.7* | *11.8* |

Source: World Tourism Organization (WTO) © (Data as collected by WTO December 2004)

**Serbia and Montenegro**
**Nights of International Tourists in All Accommodation Establishments (by nationality)**

| | | | | (thousand) | Market share (%) | | Growth rate (%) | | Average per year (%) |
|---|---|---|---|---|---|---|---|---|---|
| | 1995 | 2001 | 2002 | 2003* | 1995 | 2003* | 2002/01 | 2003*/02 | 1995-2003* |
| **Total** | **805** | **1,281** | **1,650** | **1,707** | **100** | **100** | **28.8** | **3.5** | **9.9** |
| *From Europe* | *770* | *1,187* | *1,544* | *1,613* | *95.7* | *94.5* | *30.1* | *4.4* | *9.7* |
| Bosnia & Herzg | 330 | 332 | 244 | 270 | 41.0 | 15.8 | -26.4 | 10.6 | -2.5 |
| Former Czechoslovakia | 5 | 131 | 277 | 231 | 0.6 | 13.5 | 111.2 | -16.8 | 61.8 |
| Germany | 11 | 49 | 154 | 193 | 1.3 | 11.3 | 216.4 | 25.3 | 43.3 |
| Russian Federation | 77 | 111 | 133 | 116 | 9.5 | 6.8 | 19.9 | -12.8 | 5.3 |
| F.Yug.Rp.Macedonia | 105 | 68 | 83 | 94 | 13.0 | 5.5 | 22.9 | 12.6 | -1.4 |
| Slovenia | 5 | 64 | 79 | 86 | 0.7 | 5.0 | 23.2 | 8.1 | 41.2 |
| Italy | 24 | 43 | 60 | 60 | 3.0 | 3.5 | 38.4 | 0.3 | 12.0 |
| Croatia | 60 | 56 | 60 | 53 | 7.4 | 3.1 | 7.7 | -11.6 | -1.5 |
| Poland | 3 | 20 | 56 | 47 | 0.4 | 2.8 | 177.5 | -16.4 | 39.5 |
| United Kingdom | 12 | 25 | 33 | 46 | 1.4 | 2.7 | 33.7 | 38.9 | 18.8 |
| Hungary | 7 | 26 | 35 | 42 | 0.8 | 2.5 | 32.6 | 22.6 | 25.7 |
| Bulgaria | 20 | 22 | 29 | 38 | 2.5 | 2.2 | 27.7 | 34.0 | 8.6 |
| Norway | 3 | 18 | 33 | 37 | 0.4 | 2.2 | 84.2 | 12.6 | 36.6 |
| Greece | 28 | 19 | 28 | 33 | 3.5 | 1.9 | 48.3 | 15.6 | 1.9 |
| Austria | 7 | 21 | 29 | 31 | 0.9 | 1.8 | 41.9 | 6.4 | 20.2 |
| Netherlands | 5 | 11 | 20 | 30 | 0.6 | 1.7 | 75.0 | 50.5 | 26.3 |
| Romania | 17 | 26 | 26 | 27 | 2.1 | 1.6 | 1.2 | 5.2 | 6.2 |
| France | 8 | 19 | 23 | 26 | 1.0 | 1.5 | 23.8 | 10.3 | 15.5 |
| Switzerland | 3 | 13 | 16 | 16 | 0.4 | 1.0 | 24.1 | 3.3 | 22.1 |
| Belgium | 3 | 10 | 17 | 16 | 0.3 | 0.9 | 67.4 | -2.6 | 25.5 |
| Sweden | 5 | 10 | 12 | 14 | 0.6 | 0.8 | 24.1 | 11.3 | 14.5 |
| Turkey | 3 | 9 | 10 | 13 | 0.3 | 0.8 | 8.5 | 29.0 | 21.5 |
| Israel | 1 | 5 | 12 | 10 | 0.1 | 0.6 | 128.8 | -13.0 | 30.5 |
| Denmark | 5 | 5 | 7 | 8 | 0.6 | 0.4 | 38.2 | 11.3 | 6.4 |
| Spain | 1 | 6 | 6 | 7 | 0.2 | 0.4 | 1.8 | 19.6 | 25.0 |
| Other intraregional | 24 | 68 | 61 | 68 | 3.0 | 4.0 | -10.4 | 11.1 | 14.1 |
| *From other regions* | *21* | *55* | *65* | *64* | *2.6* | *3.7* | *17.3* | *-1.8* | *15.2* |
| United States | 13 | 42 | 47 | 44 | 1.6 | 2.6 | 11.6 | -6.2 | 16.4 |
| Canada | 4 | 5 | 8 | 9 | 0.4 | 0.5 | 62.9 | 7.1 | 12.1 |
| Australia | 1 | 3 | 4 | 6 | 0.2 | 0.3 | 20.0 | 39.0 | 19.2 |
| Japan | 2 | 4 | 5 | 4 | 0.3 | 0.2 | 11.6 | -10.7 | 7.9 |
| New Zealand | 0 | 0 | 1 | 1 | 0.0 | 0.0 | 85.4 | 13.4 | 24.8 |
| *Other World/Not specified* | *14* | *38* | *41* | *31* | *1.7* | *1.8* | *6.0* | *-25.0* | *10.2* |

Source: World Tourism Organization (WTO) © (Data as collected by WTO December 2004)

# III.4.11 Slovenia Southern Europe

## Profile

# Slovenia

Europe
Southern Europe

| | |
|---|---|
| Capital | Ljubljana |
| Year of entry in WTO | 1993 |
| Area (1000 km²) | 20 |
| Population (2003, million) | 2.0 |
| Gross Domestic Product (GDP) (2003, euro million) | 29,285 |
| GDP per capita (2003, euro) | 14,686 |
| GDP growth (real, %) | |
| '-> 2002: 3.4; 2003: 2.3; 2004*: 3.9; 2005*: 4.1 | |

| | 2001 | 2002 | 2003* | 2002/2001 | 2003*/2002 |
|---|---|---|---|---|---|
| **International Arrivals** | | | | | |
| Visitors (1000) | 61,878 | 60,031 | 59,388 | -3.0 | -1.1 |
| Tourists (overnight visitors) (1000) | 1,219 | 1,302 | 1,373 | 6.8 | 5.5 |
| - per 100 of inhabitants | 61 | 65 | 68 | | |
| **Tourism accommodation** | | | | | |
| Number of rooms | 14,970 | 15,056 | 15,534 | 0.6 | 3.2 |
| *Nights spent in collective establishments (1000)* | 6,890 | 7,057 | 7,228 | 2.4 | 2.4 |
| by non-residents (inbound tourism) | 3,653 | 3,847 | 4,009 | 5.3 | 4.2 |
| by residents (domestic tourism) | 3,237 | 3,210 | 3,219 | -0.8 | 0.3 |
| *Nights spent in hotels and similar establishments (1000)* | 4,594 | 4,763 | 4,891 | 3.7 | 2.7 |
| by non-residents (inbound tourism) | 2,879 | 3,049 | 3,166 | 5.9 | 3.8 |
| by residents (domestic tourism) | 1,715 | 1,714 | 1,725 | -0.1 | 0.6 |
| **Outbound Tourism** | | | | | |
| Trips abroad (1000) | 2,055 | 2,127 | 2,114 | 3.5 | -0.6 |
| - per 100 of inhabitants | 102 | 106 | 105 | | |
| **Receipts and Expenditure for International Tourism** | | | | | |
| International Tourism Receipts (euro million) | 1,068 | 1,212 | 1,419 | 13.5 | 17.1 |
| - per Tourist Arrival (euro) | 876 | 931 | 1,034 | 6.2 | 11.0 |
| - per Visitor Arrival (euro) | 17 | 20 | 24 | 17.0 | 18.4 |
| - per capita (euro) | 531 | 603 | 706 | | |
| International Fare Receipts (euro million) | 63 | 74 | 90 | 17.3 | 22.0 |
| International Tourism Expenditure (euro million) | 578 | 678 | 799 | 17.4 | 17.8 |
| - per trip (euro) | 281 | 319 | 378 | 13.4 | 18.5 |
| - per capita (euro) | 287 | 337 | 397 | | |
| International Fare Expenditure (euro million) | 35 | 44 | 56 | 25.7 | 28.7 |
| △ International Tourism Balance (euro million) | 490 | 534 | 620 | | |
| △ International Fare Balance (euro million) | 28 | 30 | 34 | | |

Source: World Tourism Organization (WTO) (Data as collected by WTO December 2004)

See annex for methodological notes and reference of external sources used.

# Survey

Contributed by *Slovenian Tourist Board*
www.slovenia-tourism.si (promotional)
www.slovenia-tourism.si/board (institutional/corporate)
www.slovenia-tourism.si/board (research and data)

## Tourism development and outlook

**Overall evaluation of results**

Existing markets: More than 59 per cent of overnight stays of foreign tourists were made by tourists from the following (main) four countries. Germany 20 per cent, Italy 17 per cent , Austria 16 per cent, Croatia 6 per cent.
Significant changes and emerging markets: More tourist arrivals were from Italy, the Netherlands, Austria, Israel, France, Hungary and Great Britain, but at German and other main Slovenian generating markets, ware noticed shorter average length of stay.
Emerging bigger markets by number of overnight stays of tourists (more than 30 thousand) were Ireland (+33%), the Netherlands and Israel (+30%), France (+20%).
Performance of different segments and products: Popularity increased especially among spa & wellness, active & touring holidays and city breaks in Slovenia in the year 2003.

**Supply**

Investments (Accommodation, Attractions): New investments in modern spas, thermal pools and wellness services, congress centres, 3 new authentically hostels, new merges in spa & wellness, in MICE and in ski resorts.
Marketing organisations: New marketing consortium SPOT (represents low cost airlines in Slovenia), new active Regional Tourist Board Julian Alps (represents one of the most important Slovenian tourist destination), new interesting Slovenian Tourist Information Centre in Ljubljana (capital of Slovenia), new cooperation between national and international tour operator.
Specific products: Wellness and congress tourism.

**External factors**

Slovenia was in the year 2003 among relatively safe countries, accessible from most important markets in a few hours, with almost no border control and new kilometers of highways.
Slovenia had endurable heat in summer and good snow conditions in winter 2003.
Slovenia was in the year 2003 very interesting destination according to European and global tourist trends as it was still a new attractive, short break, congress, wellness and active European tourist destination with no extreme seasons and with good relationship between quality and price.

**Tourism policy**

"The Tourism Policy for 2003 and its Orientations for 2004" contains the activities of the Ministry of the Economy which is based on strategic aims as defined in the "Slovenian Tourism Strategy 2002-2006". In order to implement the basic strategic aim in terms of the state and its role, the key areas of activities in the year 2003 were:

- Ensuring the systemic and organisational conditions for the development of tourism;
- Increasing the recognition on foreign markets of Slovenia as a tourist destination;
- Promoting start-up and implementation of the investment cycle within the planned scope (according to the Tourism Strategy);
- Promoting the development of Human Resources in tourism.

*Ensuring the systemic and organisational conditions for the development of tourism:*
In 2003, the Ministry of the Economy (ME) and its Tourism Section prepared a draft of a new Tourism Promotion Act and submitted it, in the latter part of 2003, to the Government of the Republic of Slovenia and the National Assembly of the Republic of Slovenia for adoption (it was adopted in December 2003 and is valid since January 2004). ME has also prepared changes to the Mountain Guides Act in order to harmonize it with the European Union regulation. In addition to the harmonisation of tourism legislation, ME has prepared also some other proposals for amendments of acts and regulations that create obstacles to entrepreneurship.
ME started with a process of implementation of the Tourism Satellite Accounts (TSA) methodology in the Republic of Slovenia in order to arrive at a more realistic evaluation of the impact of tourism and its importance in the national economy and to obtain internationally comparable data. The TSA methodology is recommended by the World Tourism Organization (WTO), EUROSTAT, and OECD and has become an important tool for creating and implementing the tourism development policy.
*Promotion and marketing of Slovene tourism:*
In the strategy, ME have foreseen the development of the marketing of Slovenian tourism towards a general, umbrella promotion of Slovenia as an integral tourist destination, by using the trademarks of Slovene tourism, and towards the marketing of integral tourist products by introducing modern methods and tools of market communication.
*Investment policy:*
ME tried to implement an investment cycle based on the quality renovation of existing and the construction of new tourist capacities with different measures:

- Strengthening the developmental potential of tourist destinations;
- Providing the conditions for investment activities by identifying and removing critical obstacles to planned investment projects;
- Improving the financial environment for investments in tourism.

*The development of human resources:*
The development of human resources and the improvement of the quality of intellectual capital are two key factors in the improvement of Slovene tourism competitiveness; ME therefore aims to put more emphasis on knowledge and to improve the educational qualifications of the employed in all areas.
*ME's measures in 2003 were the following:*

- Improving the quality and adaptability of educational and training programmes to the needs of the tourism industry and to the European Union standards;
- Improving the system of practical training within the above stated programmes by developing a network of hotels, catering establishments and tourist agencies used for practical training purposes;
- Encouraging tourist companies to undertake larger investments in the development of modern management of intellectual capital in companies;
- Promoting the development of a tourist culture among the population and the motivation of young people for employment in the tourist sector.

The most important activity in the years 2003 and 2004 was the implementation of the project: "Closing the gap" prepared on the initiative of ME in cooperation with the Ministry of Education, Science, and Sport, the Ministry of Labour, Family and Social Affairs and the Centre of the RS for vocational education, within a programme of bilateral assistance from the Netherlands. The project aims at the development, in cooperation with Dutch experts, of a flexible and practically oriented system of education and training for middle management and management of tourist destinations. The project is based on co-operation between the tourism industry and schools as well as other educational institutions in Slovenia and the Netherlands in the development of new educational and training programmes.

**Marketing & promotion**

Slovenian Tourist Board (STB) – 2003:

- STB performed the majority of promotion activities concentrated on the five key markets (Germany, Austria, Italy, Croatia and Slovenia) and executed additional partner promotion projects for entering prospective/emerging markets (Great Britain and Ireland, Scandinavia, Russian Federation, France and Israel);
- STB carried out an intensive improvement of the promotion campaign (for touring guests) "Byways are more attractive than highways - Next Exit" at the four main markets;
- STB started with the enhancing of the development of the wellness product and congress tourism;
- STB started a gradual implementing of creative solutions of the new system of trademarks into all tools of marketing communication;
- A preparation phase for advertising campaign in 2004 "Slovenia invigorates" started;
- A new attractive stand of the Slovenian tourism was used for the first time in WTM London;
- STB introduced a systematic provision of information on tourist operations, marketing trends, opportunities, competition, and development in Slovenian economy, which represent a support for strategic planning, and formation of annual politics of tourist and other subjects at all levels and fields of activity;
- STB started with acquiring information on possibilities of products' development in Slovenia, with acquiring information on developing and marketing of products in competitive countries, enhancing the marketing of products and development of new products;
- STB established the useful cooperation model with key and strategic partners;
- STB took care of the rise of the knowledge level and information level, in the area of development and marketing of tourism at all levels and for promotion of tourism as a strategic opportunity;
- STB introduced extensive market researches (surveys), statistical analysis and a balanced scorecards system into our operations;
- The STB developed and established the Slovenian Tourist Portal <www.slovenia-tourism.sl> and prepared the points for its improvement.

**Outlook 2004**

Estimated growth of tourist arrivals: Total +3%; Domestic 0%; Germany +2%; Austria +3%; Italy +3%; Croatia +3%; Great Britain +5%; Benelux +6%; Switzerland +6%; Hungary +5%; the United States of America and Canada +1%; Other perspective markets + 5%.

In the year 2004, STB is going to continue working according to the main guidelines and changes at main markets:

- An approach which is based on research (surveys on foreign tourists in the Republic of Slovenia, use of international and national statistical and other data);
- Concentration of marketing activities in cooperation with strategic partners;
- STB will continue with advertising campaign "Slovenia invigorates" at the entrance of Slovenia into the European Union (1st May 2004) on key markets (Germany, Italy and Austria);
- On perspective markets (Great Britain and Ireland, Benelux, Hungary, the United States of America and Canada, Switzerland, Scandinavia, Russian Federation, France, Israel) STB will stimulate partnership marketing (sales promotion, public fairs, other activities);
- STB will prepare certain activities in an individual market in the framework of regular, standard activities (e.g. trade fairs, public relations, image advertising, Slovenian Incomming Workshop), and ensure publications, execution of TIPS (Tourist Information and Promotion of Slovenia), ITIS (Integration Tourist Information System) project, and other promotion-informative elements as a support to market communication.

- Priority orientation towards the areas with the most developed Unique Selling Proposition (USP) (products: health resorts, casinos, MICE and new products – active holidays, and regions: Julian Alps (with National park), Coast and Carst, Ljubljana, Maribor with Pohorje);
- Partial transformation of the marketing communication tools' structure in favour of the electronic media, marketing, public relations and events (with a lesser emphasis on public fairs);
- More active participation in the actions of sales enhancing with main tour operators that include Slovenia in their programmes
- Further development of an information system (including national on-line reservation system);
- Consistent management of the general image and the system of trademarks in Slovene tourism;
- Linking of existing leading products and stimulating the formation of new ones;
- The development of strategic partnership with other branches of economy and areas of public life.

## International Meetings Industry (MI)

**Characteristics of supply** The Slovenian Meetings Industry has grown in terms of increasing the number of congresses and incentives as well as in building new congress infrastructure. The main congress destinations are: Portorož, Bled, Ljubljana, Maribor, Rogaška Slatina, Radenci, Nova Gorica.

**Organisation of promotion** Slovenia has established in 2004 its national convention bureau –congress cluster after 13 years of independence. This is going to be the top marketing and strategic organisation for the development of the Slovenian congress industry.

**Collection of statistics on the Meetings Industry?:** no.

**Description** Not yet. We are trying to do this in next years.

**Importance / size** No statistics

**Evolution MI** It is going to be one of the most important tourist trade.

# International Tourism by Origin

**Slovenia**

**International Tourist Arrivals in All Accommodation Establishments**

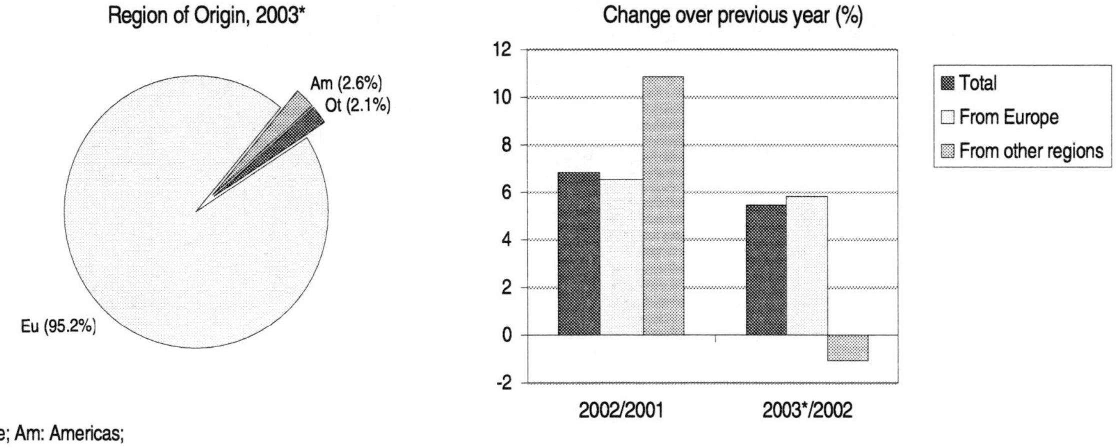


Eu: Europe; Am: Americas;
Ot: Other;

Source: World Tourism Organization (WTO) ©

**Slovenia**

**Nights of International Tourists in All Accommodation Establishments**

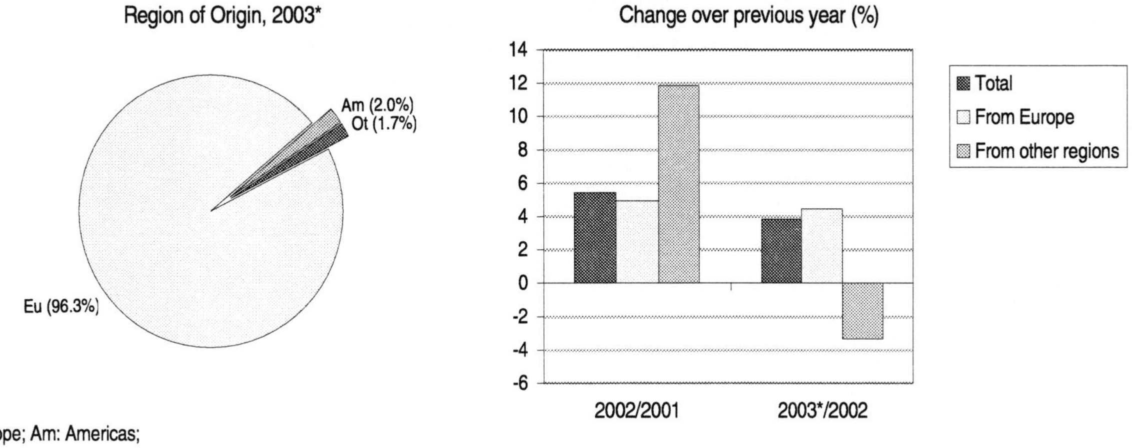


Eu: Europe; Am: Americas;
Ot: Other;

Source: World Tourism Organization (WTO) ©

**Slovenia**

**International Tourist Arrivals in All Accommodation Establishments (by nationality)**

| | | | | (thousand) | Market share (%) | | Growth rate (%) | | Average per year (%) |
|---|---|---|---|---|---|---|---|---|---|
| | 1995 | 2001 | 2002 | 2003* | 1995 | 2003* | 2002/01 | 2003*/02 | 1995-2003* |
| **Total** | **732** | **1,219** | **1,302** | **1,373** | **100** | **100** | **6.8** | **5.5** | **8.2** |
| *From Europe* | *704* | *1,160* | *1,236* | *1,308* | *96.2* | *95.2* | *6.6* | *5.8* | *8.0* |
| Italy | 160 | 269 | 275 | 289 | 21.9 | 21.0 | 2.0 | 5.0 | 7.6 |
| Germany | 136 | 234 | 229 | 229 | 18.6 | 16.7 | -2.1 | 0.1 | 6.7 |
| Austria | 117 | 174 | 193 | 201 | 16.0 | 14.7 | 10.9 | 4.1 | 7.0 |
| Croatia | 77 | 96 | 94 | 94 | 10.5 | 6.8 | -1.4 | -0.6 | 2.5 |
| United Kingdom | 14 | 40 | 46 | 50 | 1.9 | 3.7 | 14.1 | 8.9 | 17.4 |
| Netherlands | 18 | 35 | 39 | 47 | 2.5 | 3.4 | 11.1 | 20.9 | 12.4 |
| Israel | 1 | 14 | 32 | 40 | 0.1 | 2.9 | 122.5 | 24.6 | 57.0 |
| Hungary | 18 | 33 | 33 | 37 | 2.5 | 2.7 | 0.5 | 13.2 | 9.5 |
| France | 14 | 23 | 28 | 35 | 1.9 | 2.5 | 18.8 | 24.7 | 12.3 |
| Czech Rep | 16 | 29 | 30 | 31 | 2.1 | 2.3 | 3.7 | 4.3 | 9.1 |
| Bosnia & Herzg | 22 | 28 | 28 | 28 | 3.0 | 2.0 | -0.4 | -0.5 | 2.9 |
| Serbia & Montenegro | 11 | 15 | 20 | 25 | 1.5 | 1.8 | 29.2 | 28.2 | 11.1 |
| Belgium | 12 | 19 | 24 | 25 | 1.6 | 1.8 | 23.8 | 5.8 | 10.1 |
| Switzerland | 10 | 18 | 21 | 23 | 1.4 | 1.6 | 17.5 | 9.2 | 10.1 |
| Poland | 7 | 26 | 25 | 20 | 1.0 | 1.5 | -4.7 | -17.9 | 13.7 |
| Russian Federation | 15 | 16 | 15 | 16 | 2.0 | 1.2 | -0.9 | 4.3 | 1.1 |
| Spain | 2 | 7 | 10 | 13 | 0.3 | 0.9 | 44.4 | 31.3 | 23.5 |
| Sweden | 3 | 11 | 10 | 11 | 0.5 | 0.8 | -9.1 | 7.6 | 15.8 |
| Slovakia | 5 | 8 | 8 | 10 | 0.6 | 0.8 | -0.9 | 32.4 | 10.7 |
| Denmark | 2 | 9 | 9 | 10 | 0.3 | 0.7 | 1.4 | 11.8 | 18.8 |
| F.Yug.Rp.Macedonia | 15 | 9 | 10 | 9 | 2.0 | 0.7 | 15.5 | -10.3 | -5.8 |
| Ireland | 1 | 5 | 6 | 9 | 0.1 | 0.6 | 32.4 | 32.8 | 31.9 |
| Romania | 4 | 6 | 8 | 8 | 0.5 | 0.6 | 17.9 | 6.4 | 10.5 |
| Bulgaria | 2 | 7 | 8 | 8 | 0.3 | 0.6 | 8.6 | 1.1 | 17.5 |
| Finland | 1 | 3 | 4 | 6 | 0.2 | 0.4 | 24.5 | 44.8 | 18.7 |
| Other intraregional | 20 | 25 | 32 | 35 | 2.8 | 2.5 | 27.3 | 7.4 | 6.9 |
| *From other regions* | *19* | *48* | *54* | *53* | *2.7* | *3.9* | *10.9* | *-1.1* | *13.3* |
| United States | 12 | 28 | 30 | 30 | 1.6 | 2.2 | 6.5 | -1.5 | 12.1 |
| Australia | 2 | 7 | 8 | 8 | 0.2 | 0.6 | 25.8 | -1.6 | 21.1 |
| Japan | 2 | 7 | 7 | 7 | 0.2 | 0.5 | 2.2 | -5.5 | 17.4 |
| Canada | 3 | 5 | 6 | 6 | 0.5 | 0.5 | 20.4 | 2.8 | 7.8 |
| New Zealand | 1 | 2 | 2 | 2 | 0.1 | 0.2 | 30.5 | 11.5 | 20.0 |
| *Other World/Not specified* | *8* | *10* | *13* | *12* | *1.1* | *0.9* | *19.6* | *-1.8* | *4.9* |

Source: World Tourism Organization (WTO) © (Data as collected by WTO December 2004)

**Slovenia**

**Nights of International Tourists in All Accommodation Establishments (by nationality)**

| | | | | (thousand) | Market share (%) | | Growth rate (%) | | Average per year (%) |
|---|---|---|---|---|---|---|---|---|---|
| | 1995 | 2001 | 2002 | 2003* | 1995 | 2003* | 2002/01 | 2003*/02 | 1995-2003* |
| **Total** | **2,435** | **3,813** | **4,021** | **4,175** | **100** | **100** | **5.4** | **3.8** | **7.0** |
| *From Europe* | *2,359* | *3,666* | *3,848* | *4,020* | *96.9* | *96.3* | *4.9* | *4.5* | *6.9* |
| Germany | 572 | 878 | 848 | 813 | 23.5 | 19.5 | -3.3 | -4.1 | 4.5 |
| Italy | 388 | 688 | 718 | 729 | 15.9 | 17.5 | 4.4 | 1.5 | 8.2 |
| Austria | 441 | 620 | 677 | 691 | 18.1 | 16.5 | 9.2 | 2.0 | 5.8 |
| Croatia | 213 | 260 | 256 | 265 | 8.7 | 6.3 | -1.6 | 3.4 | 2.8 |
| United Kingdom | 66 | 191 | 194 | 202 | 2.7 | 4.8 | 1.8 | 4.2 | 15.1 |
| Netherlands | 83 | 139 | 150 | 195 | 3.4 | 4.7 | 7.9 | 29.9 | 11.2 |
| Hungary | 58 | 90 | 91 | 103 | 2.4 | 2.5 | 1.4 | 12.8 | 7.4 |
| Russian Federation | 85 | 93 | 93 | 101 | 3.5 | 2.4 | -0.1 | 8.8 | 2.2 |
| Bosnia & Herzg | 83 | 76 | 80 | 99 | 3.4 | 2.4 | 5.7 | 23.0 | 2.2 |
| Belgium | 50 | 74 | 95 | 94 | 2.0 | 2.3 | 28.7 | -1.2 | 8.3 |
| Israel | 4 | 37 | 64 | 83 | 0.2 | 2.0 | 73.7 | 29.9 | 44.9 |
| France | 39 | 56 | 63 | 76 | 1.6 | 1.8 | 13.9 | 19.5 | 8.7 |
| Serbia & Montenegro | 44 | 44 | 58 | 67 | 1.8 | 1.6 | 31.7 | 14.8 | 5.3 |
| Czech Rep | 39 | 61 | 62 | 65 | 1.6 | 1.6 | 2.5 | 3.9 | 6.7 |
| Switzerland | 31 | 48 | 58 | 62 | 1.3 | 1.5 | 20.0 | 7.3 | 9.1 |
| Poland | 26 | 58 | 56 | 50 | 1.1 | 1.2 | -3.0 | -10.1 | 8.8 |
| Slovakia | 18 | 17 | 22 | 37 | 0.8 | 0.9 | 31.1 | 63.8 | 9.1 |
| Ireland | 3 | 18 | 23 | 31 | 0.1 | 0.7 | 28.2 | 32.8 | 36.2 |
| Spain | 5 | 16 | 21 | 29 | 0.2 | 0.7 | 33.4 | 39.2 | 23.9 |
| Denmark | 7 | 25 | 25 | 29 | 0.3 | 0.7 | 2.4 | 15.4 | 20.3 |
| Sweden | 9 | 31 | 26 | 28 | 0.4 | 0.7 | -16.9 | 7.1 | 15.2 |
| Ukraine | 13 | 22 | 24 | 27 | 0.5 | 0.7 | 7.3 | 13.7 | 10.1 |
| F.Yug.Rp.Macedonia | 33 | 22 | 23 | 20 | 1.3 | 0.5 | 3.1 | -10.5 | -5.8 |
| Romania | 7 | 15 | 17 | 19 | 0.3 | 0.5 | 17.1 | 9.8 | 13.1 |
| Finland | 4 | 8 | 9 | 15 | 0.1 | 0.4 | 10.7 | 62.9 | 19.6 |
| Other intraregional | 41 | 79 | 91 | 89 | 1.7 | 2.1 | 14.4 | -2.3 | 10.2 |
| *From other regions* | *52* | *112* | *126* | *121* | *2.1* | *2.9* | *11.9* | *-3.3* | *11.2* |
| United States | 32 | 68 | 70 | 68 | 1.3 | 1.6 | 3.1 | -3.0 | 9.8 |
| Australia | 4 | 15 | 22 | 20 | 0.2 | 0.5 | 49.1 | -7.6 | 21.0 |
| Canada | 10 | 13 | 16 | 17 | 0.4 | 0.4 | 22.7 | 4.4 | 6.6 |
| Japan | 4 | 14 | 14 | 13 | 0.2 | 0.3 | -0.8 | -9.3 | 14.0 |
| New Zealand | 1 | 3 | 4 | 4 | 0.1 | 0.1 | 39.5 | 3.8 | 16.3 |
| *Other World/Not specified* | *24* | *35* | *47* | *34* | *1.0* | *0.8* | *36.1* | *-27.5* | *4.5* |

Source: World Tourism Organization (WTO) © (Data as collected by WTO December 2004)

Note: Including private accommodation

# III.4.12 Spain — Southern Europe

## Profile

# Spain

**Europe**
**Southern Europe**

| | |
|---|---|
| Capital | Madrid |
| Year of entry in WTO | 1975 |
| Area (1000 km²) | 506 |
| Population (2003, million) | 40.2 |
| Gross Domestic Product (GDP) (2003, euro million) | 890,548 |
| GDP per capita (2003, euro) | 21,787 |
| GDP growth (real, %) | |
| '-> 2002: 2.2; 2003: 2.5; 2004*: 2.6; 2005*: 2.9 | |

| | 2001 | 2002 | 2003* | 2002/2001 | 2003*/2002 |
|---|---|---|---|---|---|
| **International Arrivals** | | | | | |
| Visitors (1000) | 75,678 | 80,024 | 82,592 | 5.7 | 3.2 |
| Tourists (overnight visitors) (1000) | 50,094 | 52,327 | 51,830 | 4.5 | -1.0 |
| - per 100 of inhabitants | 125 | 130 | 129 | | |
| Same-day visitors (1000) | 25,585 | 27,697 | 30,114 | 8.3 | 8.7 |
| **Tourism accommodation** | | | | | |
| Number of rooms | .. | 713,481 | 740,747 | | 3.8 |
| *Nights spent in collective establishments (1000)* | 348,589 | 338,886 | 342,541 | -2.8 | 1.1 |
| .by non-residents (inbound tourism) | 232,035 | 220,707 | 217,852 | -4.9 | -1.3 |
| by residents (domestic tourism) | 116,554 | 118,179 | 124,689 | 1.4 | 5.5 |
| *Nights spent in hotels and similar establishments (1000)* | 228,682 | 222,554 | 228,160 | -2.7 | 2.5 |
| by non-residents (inbound tourism) | 143,421 | 135,836 | 136,865 | -5.3 | 0.8 |
| by residents (domestic tourism) | 85,261 | 86,718 | 91,295 | 1.7 | 5.3 |
| **Outbound Tourism** | | | | | |
| Trips abroad (1000) | 4,139 | 3,871 | 4,094 | -6.5 | 5.8 |
| - per 100 of inhabitants | 10 | 10 | 10 | | |
| **Receipts and Expenditure for International Tourism** | | | | | |
| International Tourism Receipts (euro million) | 35,395 | 37,720 | 44,174 | 6.6 | 17.1 |
| - per Tourist Arrival (euro) | 707 | 721 | 852 | 2.0 | 18.2 |
| - per Visitor Arrival (euro) | 468 | 471 | 535 | 0.8 | 13.5 |
| - per capita (euro) | 883 | 939 | 1,098 | | |
| International Fare Receipts (euro million) | 3,550 | 4,006 | 4,439 | 12.8 | 10.8 |
| International Tourism Expenditure (euro million) | 6,453 | 7,438 | 8,762 | 15.3 | 17.8 |
| - per trip (euro) | 1,559 | 1,922 | 2,140 | 23.3 | 11.4 |
| - per capita (euro) | 161 | 185 | 218 | | |
| International Fare Expenditure (euro million) | 2,097 | 2,312 | 2,389 | 10.3 | 3.3 |
| △ International Tourism Balance (euro million) | 28,942 | 30,281 | 35,412 | | |
| △ International Fare Balance (euro million) | 1,453 | 1,694 | 2,050 | | |

Source: World Tourism Organization (WTO) (Data as collected by WTO December 2004)

See annex for methodological notes and reference of external sources used.

# Survey

Contributed by *Secretaría de Estado de Comercio y Turismo*
www.spain.info (promotional)
www.iet.tourspain.es (research and data)

## Tourism development and outlook

**Overall evaluation of results**

The overall evaluation is positive, with Spain receiving 52.4 million tourists in 2003 (0.3%), thus consolidating its position as the world's number two tourism destination. In 2003, international tourism receipts amounted to 36.8 billion euro, representing an increase of 3.7 per cent over 2002, which places Spain as the second biggest destination in the world in terms of receipts as well.

Spain has become the favourite destination of Britons, and is recapturing other markets that were heavily affected by 11th September 2001 such as the U.S. market, or by the economic downturn, such as the German market. Spain has become the number one destination for Germans in terms of volume of expenditure.

The high level of satisfaction of tourists who come to Spain is evidenced by their high degree of loyalty to the destination. 82 per cent of foreign tourists who visited the country in 2003 had already visited Spain on a previous occasion, and out of these, most had visited the country four or more times previously (75%).

Tourism contributed to the national economy to the tune of 12 per cent of the GDP in 2002. According to the figures in the 2003 Balance of Payments, tourism covers more than 77 per cent of the country's trade deficit.

Tourism characteristic activities generate more than 1.5 million jobs, representing nearly 10 per cent of total employment in Spain.

As for outbound tourism, in the period from January to September 2003 (latest official figures), Spaniards made 38.3 million tourism trips, 3.8 per cent more than in the same period the previous year. Out of these, 3.2 million were international trips, 5.2 per cent more than in 2002.

One of the most notable developments has been the growth of independent tourism to Spain, along with the decline in demand for organized trips. In 2003, for the second consecutive year, individual tourism surpassed organized tourism, accounting for 53 per cent. This increase in independent tourism is closely linked to the rise in the use of the Internet for making travel arrangements, as well as the increasing use of low-cost airlines and the abundance of last-minute offers.

There has been substantial growth in the use of the Internet for researching, booking or purchasing services related to trips to Spain. In 2003, over 18 million tourists carried out travel-related research online, 51 per cent more than in the previous year. More than 7.4 million make a booking, representing an inter-annual increase of 72 per cent, but the largest jump was seen in the number of tourists who make some kind of payment via the Internet, which in 2003 amounted to double the figure for the preceding year, with an increase of 109 per cent for a total of 7.6 million.

In 2003, 6.4 million tourists used low-cost airlines to travel to Spain, 45 per cent more than the previous year, which had already posted growth of 42 per cent. The use of this type of transport favours an increase in the number of short-haul trips, as this sector's business model is based on flights of up to 3 hours.

In addition, there has been a fragmentation of holidays with a rise in the number of trips and a reduction in the average length of stay, as a result of the diversification of the purpose of travel (business, health and well-being, shopping, visits to exhibits or cultural events, practicing sports, etc.) which in turn leads to a diversification of tourism products demanded by consumers.

**Supply**

Especially notable is the diversification of Spain's tourism offerings over the past few years, leading to the development of tourism products that not only provide an alternative to the country's traditional sun-and-sand attractions, but also serve to complement and enrich them.

Spain's cultural tourism offerings are becoming richer, and a good example is the inauguration of the Picasso Museum in Málaga or the Es Baluard contemporary art museum in Palma de Mallorca. In 2004, four big cultural events are being held in Spain: the Universal Forum of Cultures in Barcelona, the commemoration of the Centenary of Salvador Dalí's birth, the fifth centenary of the death of Queen Isabella the Catholic, the celebration of the Xacobeo Holy Year and the expansion of three important museums in Madrid. Nature and sports tourism is one of the products with the greatest potential for growth, especially in mature European markets where Spain is successfully positioning itself as a tourism destination for enjoying nature, practicing sports (golf, watersports, skiing) and health and well-being tourism.

Health tourism is on the rise. Products include traditional hot spring establishments that have adapted and modernized themselves in terms of hotel infrastructure and treatment techniques, as well as establishments with health, spa and thalassatherapy centres. This development is due partly to government efforts to promote the use of hot springs as a tourism resource and subsidies for the improvement of facilities.

Sports tourism offerings are increasing as Spain is becoming a venue for major sporting events. Golf tourism is one of the country's most prominent, traditional and widely offered tourism products, and has a leading position in the European market with a market share of 35 per cent of the European market and a business turnover of nearly one billion euro.

Watersports tourism is gradually establishing itself as a tourism segment in its own right. In Spain there are 18 watersports resorts and some 300 recreational marinas with a capacity of 80 thousand slip spaces.

**External factors**

The international situation of uncertainty that existed at the beginning of 2003, and especially the economic difficulties experienced during the past year by some of Spain's major tourism generating markets determined the results for the year. Despite this, Spanish tourism has demonstrated its solidity and capacity to adapt to prevailing circumstances. The increase of 0.3 per cent in the number of tourists visiting Spain was above the growth of world tourism, which experienced a decline of 1.2 per cent, and that of other countries in Eastern Europe and the Mediterranean.

Spain undertook intense efforts to greatly improve its transport infrastructure, as reflected in the 2000-2006 Infrastructure Plan, to improve the accessibility of its tourism destinations, to cut travel times and to improve services and facilities in Spanish ports and airports. The more then 18 billion euro invested in the construction and improvement of roads in 2000-2006, the nearly 12 billion euro earmarked for new high-speed railway lines and the 2 billion spent on airport infrastructure have resulted in enhanced mobility to and from Spanish destinations.

A great effort has also been dedicated to investment in environmental sustainability directly related to tourism. Investments in tourism-environmental policy will surpass 5.1 billion euro over the period 2000-2006. These investments are to be applied to destination sustainability actions (repair and clean-up of waterways, regeneration of seaside areas and construction of beach promenades), improvement and maintenance of beaches, equipment of natural areas for tourism use (Red Natura 2000, construction of visitor centres at parks, or the Vías Verdes programme) and other awareness-raising and training programmes.

Aside from these factors, high temperatures in the summer months in Europe led to a reduction in the number of international trips among many Europeans, with the resulting effect on Spanish destinations; at the same time, fires in the south of France, temporarily impeded road traffic to Spain, which is especially intense in the summer season.

**Tourism policy**

The Spanish tourism administration is developing policies that allow the tourism sector to obtain instruments that can make it possible to adapt better to new market demands, in the conviction that the profound and rapid trend changes constitute an opportunity for Spanish tourism. The design and implementation of these policies are guided by the principle of cooperation among the public administrations with competencies in tourism, and of collaboration with the private sector.

The objective is to increase the competitiveness of the supply by controlling costs and increasing management efficiency through technological innovation of tourism enterprises and to continue efforts to enhance the quality of destinations and products.

The need to go further in the application of technological advances in production processes and in the management of tourism enterprises has led the tourism administration to create last year a state agency for the technological development of tourism, the Sociedad Estatal para el Desarrollo Tecnológico del Turismo (SEDETTUR), as the administration's response to the concerns of the Spanish tourism sector in the face of the opportunities offered by developments in new technologies and their importance as a factor for cost control and for product diversification. The fields of action include, among others, the optimization of energy use, relationships with the environment, architectural design, and the use of new construction materials, communication and information technologies, safety and security, health and quality.

New steps are being take, which go beyond traditional planning instruments in existing destinations, complemented by actions that are ambitious geographically speaking as well as in terms of the types of action, through integrated renovation plans for tourism areas, which make it possible for established tourism areas to be recovered and adapted to the principle of sustainability.

The administration is working in close collaboration with the private sector on the Spanish Tourism Quality System, a quality assurance system in which more than 3000 enterprises are voluntarily participating. The system, managed by the Instituto de Calidad Turística Española, grants the "Q" quality label to enterprises that make quality their number one management objective, which is recognized by international operators as a symbol of excellence.

**Marketing & promotion**

The main objectives of the 2003 Marketing Plan, in the framework of the Spanish Tourism Quality Integrated Plan, are:

- Consolidate Spain's world leadership in holiday tourism through a strategy of differentiating Spain's tourism offerings in international markets based on the concept of Spanish tourism quality;
- Position Spain as a first-class cultural tourism destination;
- Increase international tourism demand for Spain based on meetings, incentives, conventions and exhibits, sports and nature tourism, as well as tourism derived from other motivations in order to allow the Spanish tourism sector to grow based on product diversification and thus geographic and temporal de-concentration;
- Enhance Spain's brand image in order to provide added value to the promotion of Spain's different tourism products, based on the concepts of quality and innovation;
- Lead tourism promotion based on growing use of new information and communication technologies. For the international promotion of tourism brands, routes or itineraries (St. James Way, Silver Route, World Heritage Cities, España Verde and the Pyrenees) 5 supra-regional agreements were signed. Furthermore, another 6 agreements with Autonomous Communities were signed for carrying out joint advertising campaigns.

**Outlook 2004** The results of the first several months of 2004 allow us to be moderately optimistic about the future, albeit with the logical caveat of the uncertainty in the international situation.

## International Meetings Industry (MI)

**Characteristics of supply** Spain is the number two destination in the world in terms of international meetings, according to the International Congress & Conference Association (ICCA). This is due, among other factors, to the substantial transformation and modernization of this sector in Spain. Today, there are over 40 Spanish cities with more than 50 convention centres and 4 or 5-star hotels. There is a specialized body for the promotion and management of meetings tourism. Convention bureaus have represented a qualitative and quantitative leap in the perception of the international attractiveness of this product.

A Spanish city will host, starting in 2004, the EIBTM fair, which is the main European event in the meetings and incentives sector.

**Organisation of promotion** Spain's national tourism promotion body (Turespaña) has a specialized department in charge of marketing actions abroad, with 31 Spanish Tourism Offices (OETs) around the world.

Turespaña coordinates with the joint actions carried out with Autonomous Communities, and with convention bureaus through the collaboration agreement signed in 2002 with the Spain Convention Bureau, which lays down the general guidelines for actions in the meetings and incentives sector, as well as specific international promotional actions.

**Website(s)** <www.spain.info> and <www.scb.es>.

**Collection of statistics on the Meetings Industry?:** yes.

**Description** Turespaña has an Observatory for meetings tourism in charge of laying the foundations of the Study on Meetings Tourism in Spain (METURE), which has been published annually since 2000.

**Statistics included** The latest data available (2003) show that Spain was the venue of 17 thousand meetings that comply with the requirements established in the methodology of the observatory, with attendance of over 3 million participants and a direct economic impact for Spain of over 3 billion euro.

**Importance / size** This is a sector with good growth prospects for the coming years. Currently, this activity accounts for some 10 per cent of all tourism in Spain.

**Evolution MI** This sector has experienced sustained growth over the past few years. Spain is a leading destination in the international meetings tourism circuit.

# International Tourism by Origin

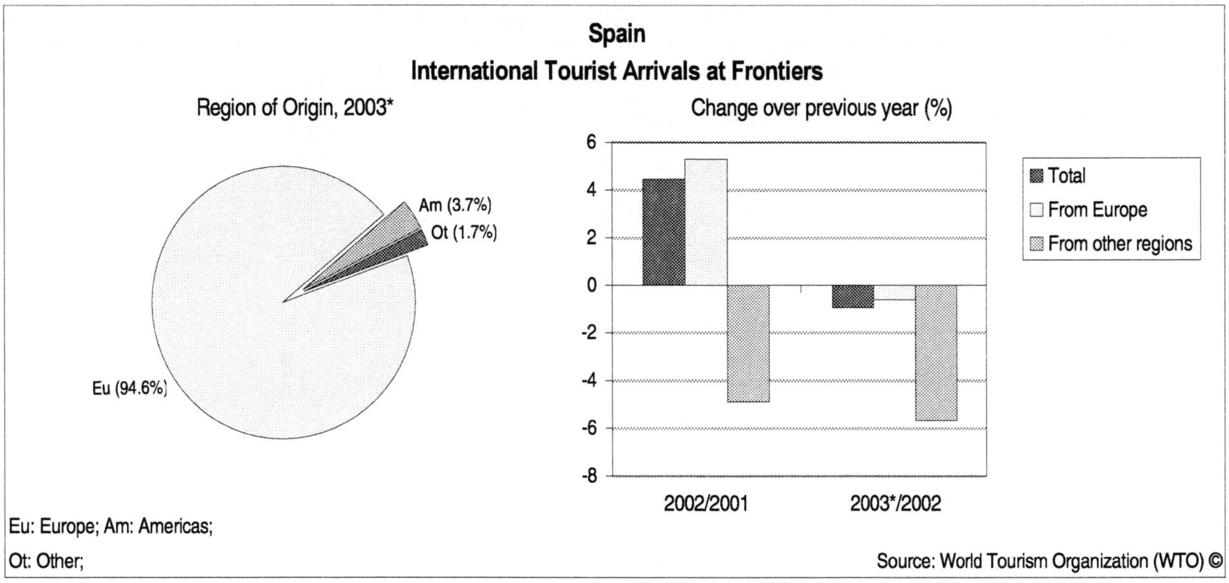


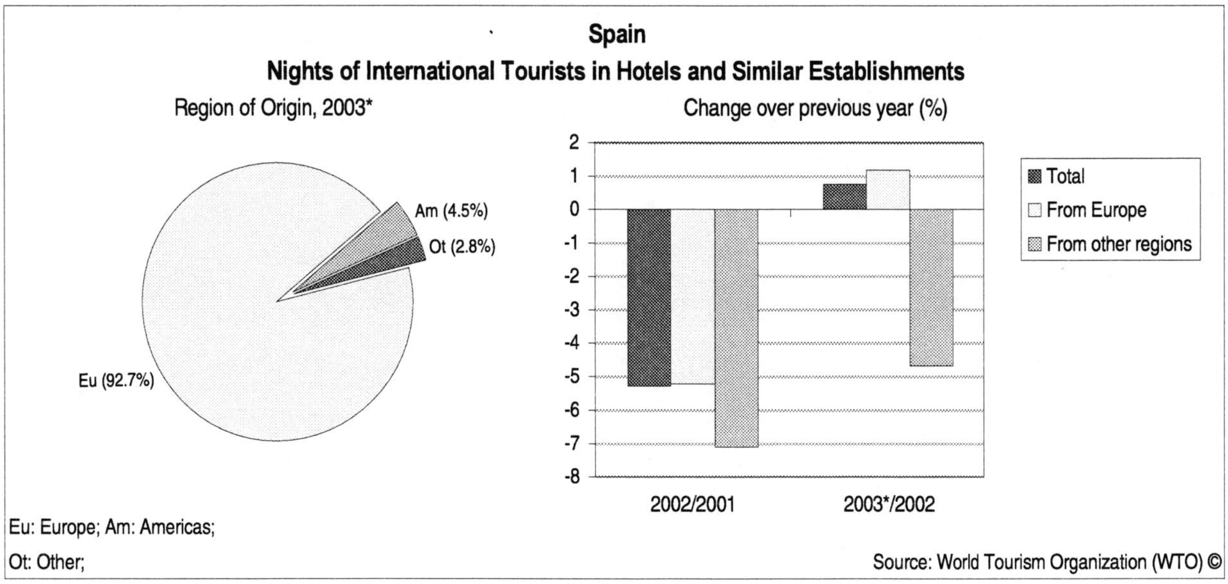

**Spain**
**International Tourist Arrivals at Frontiers (by residence)**

| | | | | (thousand) | Market share (%) | | Growth rate (%) | | Average per year (%) |
|---|---|---|---|---|---|---|---|---|---|
| | 1995 | 2001 | 2002 | 2003* | 1995 | 2003* | 2002/01 | 2003*/02 | 1995-2003* |
| **Total** | **34,920** | **50,094** | **52,327** | **51,830** | **100** | **100** | **4.5** | **-1.0** | **5.1** |
| *From Europe* | *..* | *46,827* | *49,304* | *49,005* | | *94.6* | *5.3* | *-0.6* | |
| United Kingdom | .. | 14,011 | 14,697 | 15,925 | | 30.7 | 4.9 | 8.4 | |
| Germany | .. | 10,783 | 10,211 | 9,754 | | 18.8 | -5.3 | -4.5 | |
| France | .. | 6,713 | 8,143 | 7,654 | | 14.8 | 21.3 | -6.0 | |
| Italy | .. | 2,412 | 2,532 | 2,367 | | 4.6 | 5.0 | -6.5 | |
| Netherlands | .. | 2,148 | 2,415 | 2,362 | | 4.6 | 12.4 | -2.2 | |
| Belgium | .. | 1,717 | 1,775 | 1,766 | | 3.4 | 3.4 | -0.5 | |
| Portugal | .. | 1,632 | 1,762 | 1,680 | | 3.2 | 7.9 | -4.6 | |
| Ireland | .. | 791 | 1,129 | 1,361 | | 2.6 | 42.7 | 20.5 | |
| Switzerland | .. | 1,234 | 1,223 | 1,044 | | 2.0 | -0.8 | -14.7 | |
| Sweden | .. | 1,184 | 1,138 | 1,001 | | 1.9 | -3.8 | -12.1 | |
| Norway | .. | 747 | 771 | 788 | | 1.5 | 3.2 | 2.2 | |
| Denmark | .. | 670 | 639 | 660 | | 1.3 | -4.7 | 3.2 | |
| Austria | .. | 421 | 461 | 435 | | 0.8 | 9.5 | -5.7 | |
| Finland | .. | 437 | 431 | 399 | | 0.8 | -1.2 | -7.5 | |
| Russian Federation | .. | 299 | 270 | 216 | | 0.4 | -9.6 | -20.0 | |
| Luxembourg | .. | 106 | 185 | 144 | | 0.3 | 75.3 | -22.3 | |
| Greece | .. | 67 | 155 | 103 | | 0.2 | 130.6 | -33.1 | |
| Other Europe | .. | 1,455 | 1,364 | 1,345 | | 2.6 | -6.2 | -1.4 | |
| *From other regions* | *..* | *2,439* | *2,320* | *2,189* | | *4.2* | *-4.9* | *-5.7* | |
| United States | .. | 1,136 | 940 | 929 | | 1.8 | -17.3 | -1.2 | |
| Japan | .. | 265 | 241 | 248 | | 0.5 | -9.2 | 3.1 | |
| Mexico | .. | 173 | 213 | 190 | | 0.4 | 23.3 | -11.1 | |
| Argentina | .. | 179 | 166 | 185 | | 0.4 | -6.9 | 11.3 | |
| Canada | .. | 144 | 155 | 129 | | 0.2 | 7.3 | -17.1 | |
| Brazil | .. | 165 | 146 | 100 | | 0.2 | -11.5 | -31.2 | |
| Venezuela | .. | 137 | 133 | 96 | | 0.2 | -2.8 | -28.0 | |
| Chile | .. | 66 | 62 | 59 | | 0.1 | -6.6 | -4.3 | |
| Other Americas | .. | 174 | 264 | 253 | | 0.5 | 51.9 | -4.2 | |
| *Other World/Not specified* | *34,920* | *827* | *703* | *636* | *100.0* | *1.2* | *-15.0* | *-9.5* | *-39.4* |

Source: World Tourism Organization (WTO) © (Data as collected by WTO December 2004)

**Spain**

**Nights of International Tourists in Hotels and Similar Establishments (by residence)**

| | | | | (thousand) | Market share (%) | | Growth rate (%) | | Average per year (%) |
|---|---|---|---|---|---|---|---|---|---|
| | 1995 | 2001 | 2002 | 2003* | 1995 | 2003* | 2002/01 | 2003*/02 | 1995-2003* |
| **Total** | **101,182** | **143,421** | **135,836** | **136,865** | **100** | **100** | **-5.3** | **0.8** | **3.8** |
| *From Europe* | *95,082* | *132,247* | *125,352* | *126,840* | *94.0* | *92.7* | *-5.2* | *1.2* | *3.7* |
| United Kingdom | 28,666 | 42,952 | 43,662 | 44,404 | 28.3 | 32.4 | 1.7 | 1.7 | 5.6 |
| Germany | 34,854 | 44,562 | 37,207 | 38,161 | 34.4 | 27.9 | -16.5 | 2.6 | 1.1 |
| France | 6,750 | 8,750 | 9,004 | 9,175 | 6.7 | 6.7 | 2.9 | 1.9 | 3.9 |
| Italy | 5,309 | 6,398 | 6,791 | 6,608 | 5.2 | 4.8 | 6.1 | -2.7 | 2.8 |
| Belgium | 4,959 | 5,730 | 5,533 | 5,615 | 4.9 | 4.1 | -3.4 | 1.5 | 1.6 |
| Netherlands | 4,075 | 5,407 | 5,538 | 5,379 | 4.0 | 3.9 | 2.4 | -2.9 | 3.5 |
| Portugal | 1,114 | 2,282 | 2,559 | 2,606 | 1.1 | 1.9 | 12.1 | 1.9 | 11.2 |
| Switzerland | 1,522 | 2,567 | 2,180 | 2,095 | 1.5 | 1.5 | -15.1 | -3.9 | 4.1 |
| Sweden | 1,204 | 2,685 | 2,315 | 2,061 | 1.2 | 1.5 | -13.8 | -11.0 | 6.9 |
| Ireland | 675 | 1,248 | 1,483 | 1,736 | 0.7 | 1.3 | 18.9 | 17.0 | 12.5 |
| Russian Federation | .. | 1,885 | 1,507 | 1,337 | | 1.0 | -20.1 | -11.3 | |
| Norway | 601 | 1,242 | 1,205 | 1,125 | 0.6 | 0.8 | -3.0 | -6.7 | 8.2 |
| Austria | 1,091 | 938 | 849 | 1,039 | 1.1 | 0.8 | -9.4 | 22.4 | -0.6 |
| Denmark | 761 | 949 | 967 | 988 | 0.8 | 0.7 | 1.8 | 2.2 | 3.3 |
| Czech Rep | .. | 925 | 920 | 873 | | 0.6 | -0.6 | -5.1 | |
| Finland | 390 | 695 | 646 | 623 | 0.4 | 0.5 | -7.0 | -3.6 | 6.0 |
| Poland | .. | 760 | 638 | 482 | | 0.4 | -16.0 | -24.4 | |
| Luxembourg | 331 | 409 | 381 | 419 | 0.3 | 0.3 | -6.8 | 9.8 | 3.0 |
| Greece | 169 | 189 | 224 | 217 | 0.2 | 0.2 | 18.6 | -3.0 | 3.2 |
| Hungary | .. | 217 | 202 | 200 | | 0.1 | -6.7 | -1.0 | |
| Slovakia | .. | 173 | 139 | 169 | | 0.1 | -19.3 | 21.4 | |
| Iceland | .. | 105 | 90 | 152 | | 0.1 | -13.9 | 68.3 | |
| Turkey | .. | 86 | 83 | 92 | | 0.1 | -3.5 | 10.6 | |
| Other Europe | 2,610 | 1,092 | 1,228 | 1,284 | 2.6 | 0.9 | 12.4 | 4.6 | -8.5 |
| *From other regions* | *4,093* | *9,735* | *9,044* | *8,621* | *4.0* | *6.3* | *-7.1* | *-4.7* | *9.8* |
| United States | 1,788 | 3,605 | 3,278 | 3,150 | 1.8 | 2.3 | -9.1 | -3.9 | 7.3 |
| Japan | 814 | 955 | 986 | 964 | 0.8 | 0.7 | 3.2 | -2.3 | 2.1 |
| All Africa | .. | 761 | 723 | 694 | | 0.5 | -5.1 | -3.9 | |
| Mexico | 158 | 544 | 632 | 582 | 0.2 | 0.4 | 16.2 | -7.9 | 17.6 |
| Argentina | 383 | 933 | 571 | 525 | 0.4 | 0.4 | -38.8 | -8.1 | 4.0 |
| Canada | 176 | 423 | 453 | 501 | 0.2 | 0.4 | 6.9 | 10.6 | 14.0 |
| Brazil | .. | 378 | 358 | 318 | | 0.2 | -5.3 | -11.3 | |
| Australia | .. | 242 | 255 | 268 | | 0.2 | 5.2 | 5.1 | |
| Venezuela | 74 | 173 | 173 | 151 | 0.1 | 0.1 | -0.5 | -12.4 | 9.4 |
| New Zealand | .. | 45 | 49 | 56 | | 0.0 | 7.0 | 14.5 | |
| Other Americas | 699 | 1,165 | 1,061 | 922 | 0.7 | 0.7 | -8.9 | -13.1 | 3.5 |
| Other Asia | .. | 510 | 506 | 492 | | 0.4 | -0.7 | -2.8 | |
| *Other World/Not specified* | *2,007* | *1,438* | *1,441* | *1,405* | *2.0* | *1.0* | *0.2* | *-2.5* | *-4.4* |

Source: World Tourism Organization (WTO) © (Data as collected by WTO December 2004)

# III.4.13 The Former Yugoslav Republic of Macedonia

Southern Europe

## Profile

# Former Yugoslav Republic of Macedonia

Europe
Southern Europe

| | |
|---|---|
| Capital | Skopje |
| Year of entry in WTO | 1995 |
| Area (1000 km²) | 26 |
| Population (2003, million) | 2.0 |
| Gross Domestic Product (GDP) (2003, euro million) | 4,903 |
| GDP per capita (2003, euro) | 2,384 |
| GDP growth (real, %) | |

'-> 2002: 0.9; 2003: 3.1; 2004*: 4.0; 2005*: 4.5

| | 2001 | 2002 | 2003* | 2002/2001 | 2003*/2002 |
|---|---|---|---|---|---|
| **International Arrivals** | | | | | |
| Visitors (1000) | 1,730 | 2,079 | 2,183 | 20.2 | 5.0 |
| Tourists (overnight visitors) (1000) | 99 | 123 | 158 | 24.2 | 28.3 |
| - per 100 of inhabitants | 5 | 6 | 8 | | |
| **Tourism accommodation** | | | | | |
| Number of rooms | 6,726 | 6,813 | 6,825 | 1.3 | 0.2 |
| *Nights spent in collective establishments (1000)* | 1,255 | 1,851 | 2,007 | 47.5 | 8.4 |
| by non-residents (inbound tourism) | 213 | 275 | 346 | 29.1 | 25.8 |
| by residents (domestic tourism) | 1,042 | 1,576 | 1,661 | 51.2 | 5.4 |
| *Nights spent in hotels and similar establishments (1000)* | 463 | 615 | 668 | 32.8 | 8.6 |
| by non-residents (inbound tourism) | 197 | 249 | 321 | 26.4 | 28.9 |
| by residents (domestic tourism) | 266 | 366 | 347 | 37.6 | -5.2 |
| **Receipts and Expenditure for International Tourism** | | | | | |
| International Tourism Receipts (euro million) | 28 | 44 | 60 | 54.7 | 38.4 |
| - per Tourist Arrival (euro) | 285 | 354 | 382 | 24.6 | 7.9 |
| - per Visitor Arrival (euro) | 16 | 21 | 28 | 28.7 | 31.8 |
| - per capita (euro) | 14 | 21 | 30 | | |
| International Fare Receipts (euro million) | 25 | 18 | 8 | -28.3 | -52.6 |
| International Tourism Expenditure (euro million) | 42 | 50 | 51 | 19.0 | 1.0 |
| - per capita (euro) | 21 | 25 | 25 | | |
| International Fare Expenditure (euro million) | 23 | 18 | 24 | -21.4 | 36.2 |
| △ International Tourism Balance (euro million) | -14 | -7 | 10 | | |
| △ International Fare Balance (euro million) | 2 | | -16 | | |

Source: World Tourism Organization (WTO) (Data as collected by WTO December 2004)

See annex for methodological notes and reference of external sources used.

# Survey

Contributed by *Ministry of Economy*
www.economy.gov.mk/tourism (promotional)
www.economy.gov.mk/tourism (institutional/corporate)
www.stat.gov.mk (research and data)

## Tourism development and outlook

**Overall evaluation of results**

Positive factors:
- Increased foreign demand for niche tourism supply and meetings facilities due to the business reasons combined with complementary offer;
- Increased number of cultural events and attractions;
- Segmentation of product on cultural events;
- Specialised tourism offer in village facilities.

Negative factor:
- Influence of the political situation.

**Supply**

Positive factors:
- Investments in transport capacities;
- Main transit corridor;
- Improving frequency on the border crossings;
- Quality of tourism services improved by tourism licencing in the new legislation;
- Specific product development on cultural tourism, eco and rural tourism.

Negative factor:
- Insufficient commercial presence of the tourist agencies on foreign markets.

**External factors**

Positive factors:
- Increased domestic tourism demand;
- Foreign flow increased due to business reasons;
- Increased number of cultural events and attractions;
- Facilitating of entry formalities;
- New infrastructure in the first half of 2004.

Negative factor:
- Influence of politics.

**Tourism policy**

Regulation of tourism and catering law in procedure;
Directives of European Union to be included in the forthcoming tourism and Catering Law;
Master plan proposals for further better organization and investment in tourism;
Public private partnership by governmental participating in the general promotion of the country.

**Marketing & promotion**

General Promotion Program with two following activities: publication of brochures and other materials, participation on targeted tourism fairs, visits of journalists, tourism promotion of cultural events, etc.

**Outlook 2004**

Promotional activities for the current and next year to be directed to neighbouring countries and major generating markets towards the Republic of Macedonia (the Netherlands, the United Kingdom, Germany);
Promotional campaigns by the visit of journalists and Tour-operators specialised in specific products.

## International Meetings Industry (MI)

| | |
|---|---|
| **Characteristics of supply** | Meetings, conferences. |
| **Organisation of promotion** | On the national level financed by the budget, with attendance of regional representatives and representatives of the tourism industry. |

**Collection of statistics on the Meetings Industry?:** no.

| | |
|---|---|
| **Importance / size** | official data not available.<br>Estimation of approximately 90 per cent of the foreign nights in the capital Skopje. |
| **Evolution MI** | Growing fast, especially in main tourism resort Ohrid lake, due to the investments made in meetings facilities in hotels, mainly in the existing hotel capacities. |

# International Tourism by Origin

**Former Yugoslav Republic of Macedonia**
**International Tourist Arrivals in All Accommodation Establishments**

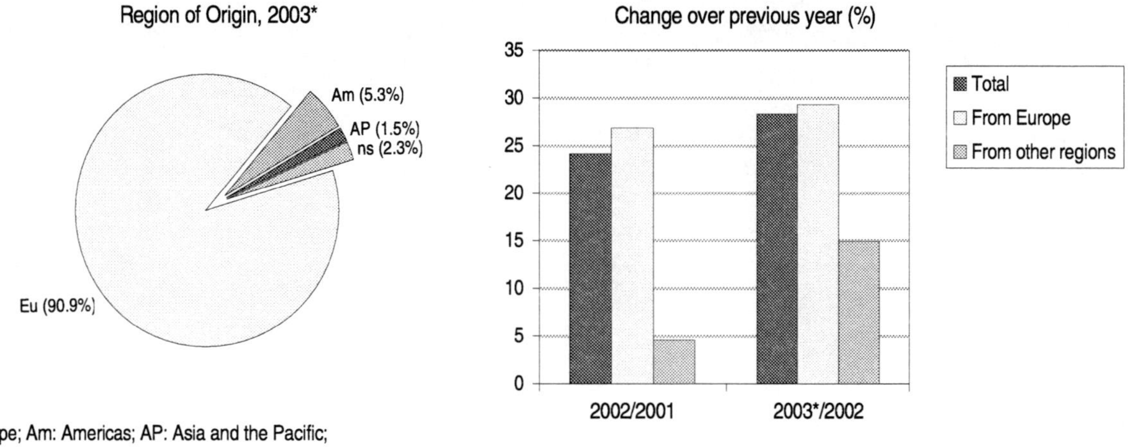


Eu: Europe; Am: Americas; AP: Asia and the Pacific;
ns: Not specified;

Source: World Tourism Organization (WTO) ©

**Former Yugoslav Republic of Macedonia**
**Nights of International Tourists in All Accommodation Establishments**

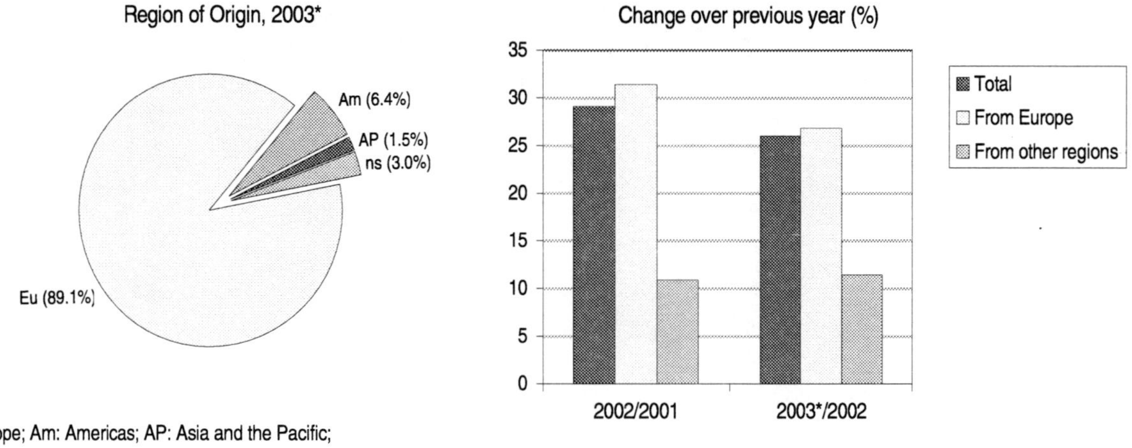


Eu: Europe; Am: Americas; AP: Asia and the Pacific;
ns: Not specified;

Source: World Tourism Organization (WTO) ©

**Former Yugoslav Republic of Macedonia**
**International Tourist Arrivals in All Accommodation Establishments (by nationality)**

| | | | | (thousand) | Market share (%) | | Growth rate (%) | | Average per year (%) |
|---|---|---|---|---|---|---|---|---|---|
| | 1995 | 2001 | 2002 | 2003* | 1995 | 2003* | 2002/01 | 2003*/02 | 1995-2003* |
| **Total** | **147** | **99** | **123** | **158** | **100** | **100** | **24.2** | **28.3** | **0.9** |
| *From Europe* | *141* | *87* | *111* | *143* | *95.9* | *90.9* | *26.9* | *29.3* | *0.2* |
| Serbia & Montenegro | 48 | 16 | 23 | 27 | 32.9 | 17.3 | 41.5 | 17.6 | -6.9 |
| Greece | 3 | 11 | 15 | 27 | 2.3 | 17.1 | 38.0 | 84.2 | 29.5 |
| Bulgaria | 22 | 8 | 12 | 14 | 15.0 | 9.0 | 37.9 | 20.9 | -5.4 |
| Albania | 8 | 6 | 9 | 12 | 5.4 | 7.7 | 41.5 | 33.0 | 5.3 |
| Germany | 8 | 5 | 6 | 6 | 5.4 | 4.0 | 25.2 | 3.8 | -2.8 |
| Turkey | 6 | 3 | 5 | 6 | 4.2 | 3.6 | 67.0 | 11.1 | -0.8 |
| Croatia | 6 | 3 | 4 | 5 | 4.4 | 3.5 | 57.0 | 33.4 | -2.1 |
| Slovenia | 8 | 3 | 4 | 5 | 5.4 | 2.9 | 44.4 | 19.3 | -6.7 |
| United Kingdom | 1 | 4 | 4 | 5 | 1.0 | 2.9 | -10.1 | 15.3 | 14.8 |
| Italy | 4 | 3 | 3 | 4 | 2.5 | 2.3 | 22.5 | 17.9 | -0.2 |
| France | 2 | 2 | 3 | 4 | 1.3 | 2.2 | 9.9 | 38.2 | 7.5 |
| Bosnia & Herzg | 2 | 1 | 2 | 3 | 1.3 | 1.7 | 36.9 | 42.5 | 4.7 |
| Austria | 3 | 1 | 2 | 3 | 1.9 | 1.6 | 47.6 | 33.6 | -0.8 |
| Netherlands | 2 | 2 | 2 | 2 | 1.3 | 1.6 | 28.9 | 22.5 | 2.9 |
| Hungary | 1 | 2 | 2 | 2 | 0.5 | 1.4 | -6.8 | 9.5 | 13.7 |
| Sweden | 1 | 1 | 1 | 2 | 0.5 | 1.0 | 12.5 | 38.9 | 8.6 |
| Switzerland | 3 | 1 | 1 | 1 | 1.9 | 0.9 | 3.3 | 53.9 | -7.6 |
| Spain | 0 | 1 | 1 | 1 | 0.2 | 0.9 | -4.2 | 64.6 | 21.3 |
| Russian Federation | 5 | 2 | 1 | 1 | 3.4 | 0.9 | -24.3 | 8.5 | -15.2 |
| Romania | 1 | 1 | 1 | 1 | 0.9 | 0.8 | 14.0 | 6.0 | 0.7 |
| Belgium | 1 | 1 | 1 | 1 | 0.6 | 0.8 | 19.2 | 28.1 | 3.4 |
| Czech Rep | 1 | 1 | 1 | 1 | 0.4 | 0.7 | 65.5 | 24.6 | 9.0 |
| Norway | 0 | 1 | 1 | 1 | 0.2 | 0.7 | 19.7 | 4.6 | 18.0 |
| Denmark | 0 | 1 | 1 | 1 | 0.3 | 0.7 | 11.6 | 33.3 | 10.9 |
| Poland | 1 | 1 | 1 | 1 | 0.4 | 0.7 | 51.0 | -6.0 | 7.4 |
| Other intraregional | 3 | 7 | 5 | 6 | 2.2 | 4.1 | -27.3 | 19.8 | 9.2 |
| *From other regions* | *5* | *9* | *9* | *11* | *3.2* | *6.8* | *4.6* | *14.9* | *10.8* |
| United States | 3 | 7 | 7 | 7 | 2.2 | 4.7 | -1.4 | 5.8 | 10.7 |
| Australia | 0 | 1 | 1 | 1 | 0.3 | 0.8 | 44.0 | 40.6 | 13.7 |
| Japan | 1 | 0 | 1 | 1 | 0.4 | 0.7 | 41.8 | 81.1 | 8.6 |
| Canada | 0 | 1 | 1 | 1 | 0.3 | 0.6 | 3.9 | 25.0 | 11.3 |
| New Zealand | 0 | 0 | 0 | 0 | 0.0 | 0.1 | 66.2 | -22.7 | 8.4 |
| *Other World/Not specified* | *1* | *3* | *3* | *4* | *0.9* | *2.3* | *0.8* | *35.0* | *13.9* |

Source: World Tourism Organization (WTO) © (Data as collected by WTO December 2004)

**Former Yugoslav Republic of Macedonia**
**Nights of International Tourists in All Accommodation Establishments (by nationality)**

| | | | | (thousand) | Market share (%) | | Growth rate (%) | | Average per year (%) |
|---|---|---|---|---|---|---|---|---|---|
| | 1995 | 2001 | 2002 | 2003* | 1995 | 2003* | 2002/01 | 2003*/02 | 1995-2003* |
| **Total** | **276** | **213** | **275** | **346** | **100** | **100** | **29.1** | **26.0** | **2.9** |
| *From Europe* | *259* | *185* | *243* | *308* | *94.0* | *89.1* | *31.5* | *26.8* | *2.2* |
| Serbia & Montenegro | 83 | 32 | 50 | 59 | 30.0 | 17.0 | 58.1 | 16.4 | -4.2 |
| Greece | 6 | 20 | 31 | 53 | 2.0 | 15.4 | 54.7 | 73.9 | 32.7 |
| Bulgaria | 47 | 17 | 24 | 29 | 17.1 | 8.3 | 42.1 | 17.9 | -6.0 |
| Albania | 12 | 12 | 21 | 24 | 4.3 | 7.0 | 79.5 | 16.6 | 9.2 |
| Germany | 14 | 12 | 15 | 16 | 5.2 | 4.7 | 28.0 | 10.4 | 1.6 |
| Croatia | 12 | 5 | 9 | 11 | 4.3 | 3.3 | 64.9 | 32.5 | -0.7 |
| Turkey | 11 | 6 | 11 | 11 | 4.0 | 3.2 | 73.9 | 6.0 | 0.2 |
| United Kingdom | 3 | 12 | 9 | 11 | 1.2 | 3.1 | -25.3 | 15.5 | 15.4 |
| France | 3 | 5 | 6 | 10 | 1.3 | 2.9 | 18.5 | 69.0 | 14.2 |
| Slovenia | 15 | 5 | 8 | 9 | 5.3 | 2.7 | 57.1 | 22.7 | -5.6 |
| Italy | 7 | 6 | 7 | 8 | 2.5 | 2.3 | 18.6 | 21.3 | 2.0 |
| Netherlands | 3 | 4 | 5 | 7 | 1.2 | 2.0 | 26.2 | 41.0 | 9.1 |
| Bosnia & Herzg | 3 | 2 | 4 | 5 | 1.2 | 1.6 | 69.4 | 34.3 | 6.8 |
| Austria | 4 | 3 | 4 | 5 | 1.4 | 1.4 | 28.9 | 26.6 | 2.3 |
| Hungary | 1 | 4 | 4 | 4 | 0.3 | 1.2 | -7.9 | 4.9 | 19.6 |
| Russian Federation | 12 | 5 | 3 | 4 | 4.3 | 1.1 | -32.1 | 12.8 | -13.0 |
| Switzerland | 3 | 2 | 2 | 4 | 1.2 | 1.0 | 5.2 | 80.1 | 0.7 |
| Poland | 1 | 2 | 4 | 4 | 0.5 | 1.0 | 49.9 | -1.6 | 11.7 |
| Sweden | 2 | 2 | 2 | 3 | 0.6 | 1.0 | 15.2 | 42.2 | 9.0 |
| Czech Rep | 1 | 2 | 3 | 3 | 0.4 | 0.9 | 66.3 | 19.2 | 14.3 |
| Romania | 2 | 3 | 3 | 3 | 0.8 | 0.9 | 10.7 | 10.2 | 4.6 |
| Norway | 1 | 2 | 2 | 3 | 0.3 | 0.8 | 24.0 | 27.6 | 17.9 |
| Belgium | 2 | 2 | 2 | 3 | 0.6 | 0.8 | 15.2 | 48.4 | 7.6 |
| Spain | 0 | 2 | 2 | 3 | 0.2 | 0.8 | -4.2 | 78.5 | 24.0 |
| Denmark | 1 | 1 | 1 | 2 | 0.3 | 0.7 | 4.6 | 68.4 | 13.5 |
| Other intraregional | 9 | 18 | 13 | 13 | 3.3 | 3.9 | -30.1 | 5.2 | 5.1 |
| *From other regions* | *13* | *22* | *25* | *28* | *4.6* | *8.0* | *10.9* | *11.5* | *10.2* |
| United States | 9 | 18 | 19 | 20 | 3.3 | 5.8 | 7.3 | 3.4 | 10.3 |
| Australia | 1 | 1 | 2 | 3 | 0.3 | 0.8 | 37.6 | 35.2 | 15.5 |
| Japan | 1 | 1 | 1 | 2 | 0.5 | 0.7 | 25.0 | 92.4 | 7.5 |
| Canada | 1 | 2 | 2 | 2 | 0.4 | 0.6 | 14.7 | 25.0 | 7.9 |
| New Zealand | 0 | 0 | 0 | 0 | 0.1 | 0.0 | 37.4 | -39.9 | 2.5 |
| *Other World/Not specified* | *4* | *5* | *7* | *10* | *1.4* | *3.0* | *24.6* | *50.0* | *13.3* |

Source: World Tourism Organization (WTO) © (Data as collected by WTO December 2004)

# III.5 East Mediterranean Europe

## III.5.1 Cyprus East Mediterranean Europe

### Profile

# Cyprus

**Europe**
**East Mediterranean Europe**

| | |
|---|---|
| Capital | Nicosia |
| Year of entry in WTO | 1975 |
| Area (100 km²) | 93 |
| Population (2003, 1000) | 772 |
| Gross Domestic Product (GDP) (2003, euro million) | 13,519 |
| GDP per capita (2003, euro) | 16,987 |
| GDP growth (real, %) | |
| '-> 2002: 2.0; 2003: 2.0; 2004*: 3.0; 2005*: 3.5 | |

| | 2001 | 2002 | 2003* | 2002/2001 | 2003*/2002 |
|---|---|---|---|---|---|
| **International Arrivals** | | | | | |
| Visitors (1000) | 2,841 | 2,495 | 2,416 | -12.2 | -3.2 |
| Tourists (overnight visitors) (1000) | 2,697 | 2,418 | 2,303 | -10.3 | -4.8 |
| - per 100 of inhabitants | 354 | 315 | 298 | | |
| Same-day visitors (1000) | 144 | 77 | 113 | -46.5 | 46.8 |
| Cruise passengers (1000) | 106 | 59 | 93 | -44.3 | 57.6 |
| **Tourism accommodation** | | | | | |
| Number of rooms | 45,060 | 46,220 | 46,706 | 2.6 | 1.1 |
| *Nights spent in collective establishments (1000)* | 18,832 | 16,159 | 14,458 | -14.2 | -10.5 |
| by non-residents (inbound tourism) | 18,093 | 15,289 | 13,490 | -15.5 | -11.8 |
| by residents (domestic tourism) | 739 | 870 | 968 | 17.7 | 11.3 |
| *Nights spent in hotels and similar establishments (1000)* | 18,799 | 16,104 | 14,381 | -14.3 | -10.7 |
| by non-residents (inbound tourism) | 18,070 | 15,236 | 13,424 | -15.7 | -11.9 |
| by residents (domestic tourism) | 729 | 868 | 957 | 19.1 | 10.3 |
| **Outbound Tourism** | | | | | |
| Trips abroad (1000) | 589 | 645 | 629 | 9.5 | -2.5 |
| - per 100 of inhabitants | 77 | 84 | 82 | | |
| **Receipts and Expenditure for International Tourism** | | | | | |
| International Tourism Receipts (euro million) | 2,158 | 2,152 | 2,132 | -0.3 | -0.9 |
| - per Tourist Arrival (euro) | 800 | 890 | 926 | 11.2 | 4.0 |
| - per Visitor Arrival (euro) | 760 | 862 | 882 | 13.5 | 2.3 |
| - per capita (euro) | 2,828 | 2,804 | 2,763 | | |
| International Fare Receipts (euro million) | 227 | 245 | 241 | 7.5 | -1.4 |
| International Tourism Expenditure (euro million) | 463 | 576 | 668 | 24.3 | 16.0 |
| - per trip (euro) | 787 | 893 | 1,063 | 13.5 | 19.0 |
| - per capita (euro) | 607 | 751 | 866 | | |
| International Fare Expenditure (euro million) | 152 | 80 | 95 | -47.0 | 18.4 |
| △ International Tourism Balance (euro million) | 1,694 | 1,575 | 1,464 | | |
| △ International Fare Balance (euro million) | 76 | 164 | 146 | | |

Source: World Tourism Organization (WTO) (Data as collected by WTO December 2004)

See annex for methodological notes and reference of external sources used.

# Survey

Contributed by *Cyprus Tourism Organization*
www.visitcyprus.org (promotional)
www.visitcyprus.org (institutional/corporate)

## Tourism development and outlook

**Overall evaluation of results**

The total number of visitor arrivals in 2003 as compared to 2002 recorded a decrease of 3.2 per cent.
The average length of stay of tourists in Cyprus was estimated at 10.9 days.
Revenue from tourism in 2003 recorded a decrease of 10 per cent in relation to the corresponding figure for 2002. By far the largest market share of tourist arrivals was captured yet again by Europe, which accounted for 95 per cent of total arrivals in 2003.

**Supply**

*Travel agencies/tour operators:*
There are approximately 449 licensed Travel Agencies (by the Cyprus Tourism Organisation), plus 161 branches, in operation throughout the island, many of which are IATA members (December 2003).
*Cyprus Domestic Transportation Services:*
One can travel around Cyprus either by bus or by taxi. There are no trains in Cyprus.
*Attractions/Entertainment:*
Numerous special interest products need to be developed to attract each targeted segment. These include themed routes and thematic parks based on the island's rich cultural and natural heritage, information and interpretation centres, state-of-the-art museums, conference and incentive facilities, cycling routes/centres and facilities and services for cyclists, routes/trails and facilities and services for hikers, facilities and services for the development of sports tourism, marinas, water sports centres and other nautical tourism and cruise tourism facilities and services, golf courses and other facilities and services for golfers, events, exhibitions and workshops, wellness and pampering facilities and services etc.
Aiming to encourage the development of the special interest products specified in the Strategic Plan, the Government is currently revising the incentive scheme for ancillary tourism projects, upgrading the incentives offered to investors for the creation of the priority products. The Government is also examining the potential of developing casinos in Cyprus.
*Special interest products:*
- Themed routes (e.g. wine route) and thematic parks;
- Information and interpretation centres;
- State-of-the-art museums;
- Conference and incentive facilities;
- Wellness and pampering facilities and services, spas;
- Cycling routes/centres and facilities and services for cyclists;
- Routes/trails and facilities and services for hikers;
- Facilities and services for the development of sports tourism;
- Golf courses and other facilities and services for golfers;
- Events, exhibitions and workshops;
- Marinas, water sports centres and other nautical tourism and cruise tourism facilities and services;
- Casinos.

**External factors**

*Political and economic situation:*
The war in Iraq has negatively affected tourist traffic to Cyprus and the global recession has also played a vital role in the decrease in tourist traffic.
*Facilitation of entry formalities:*
Since 2003 Cyprus has facilitated entry formalities for Russia and the CIS countries with the operation of consular offices in the above countries.
*New or improved infrastructure:*
- Airports: Visitors arriving in Cyprus by air, may still only enter the Republic through the International Airports of Larnaka and Pafos.
- Ports: Cyprus has become the cruise line hub of the region. Within easy reach of Greece and the Greek islands, Egypt, Lebanon and Syria, Cyprus can be enjoyed as part of an appealing multi-destination vacation. All cruise lines are served by the multipurpose ports of Lemesos (Limassol) and Larnaka on the south coast of the country.

*Stimulating factor:*
The entry of Cyprus into the European Union will lead to an increase of tourist traffic mainly from the European region (liberization of airlines).
*Constraint:*
The tax regulation that will come into force during 2004 due to the entry of Cyprus into the European Union will cause more constraints in the competitive position of Cyprus.

**Tourism policy**

Recognizing the need to face the great challenges that lie ahead in a strategic and well-planned fashion, a long-term strategy to the year 2010 has been drafted. The Strategy aims to ensure the sustainability and quality of tourism development on the island, reinforce the destination's ability to compete successfully in a European environment and enable it to grasp all opportunities springing from the accession to the European Union.
According to the Strategic Plan, Cyprus' accession to the European Union is an excellent opportunity to intervene decisively at the destination and its target markets/segments to position it as a sustainable, quality destination, a bridge of civilizations between Europe and its neighboring continents, a rich micro-world with an impressively diverse cultural and natural environment to which our markets can relate.
The tourism sector in Cyprus has been preparing for accession to the European Union, expending considerable effort to harmonize with the Acquis Communautaire.
In addition, ample opportunities for investment exist in the hotel and catering industry. Apart from the development of hotel and catering establishments in the priority categories, there are many investment opportunities in training and organisational development, information technology and systems, quality and environmental certification schemes for the industry etc.
Cyprus will also be investing heavily in the training and development of its human resources, in the promotion of quality and environmental systems in the industry, and the modernisation and technological advancement of its tourist enterprises which are mainly small to medium enterprises (SMEs).

**Marketing & promotion**

The Organisation revised and updated its declared 10 year Strategic Plan for tourism, the implementation of which began in 2000, in line with new conditions and trends evolving in the international tourist market. Consequently, the overall Marketing Strategy has also been modified.
Within the framework of the Strategic Plan, the Cyprus Tourism Organisation (CTO) is implementing an integral communication strategy for the promotion of the Cyprus tourist product, based on the systematic promotion of a single and unique image of Cyprus. This Communication Strategy comprises a wide spectrum of activities that directly promote the Cyprus tourist product. They include generic advertising campaigns, organisation of promotional activities, hosting in Cyprus of tourist

professionals, journalists and other personalities and participation in tourist fairs. The Organisation places high emphasis on the development and maintenance of excellent relations with tourism professionals and the media, in all source countries. The Organisation activities are backed by the appropriate printed, audio-visual and electronic promotional tools.

Furthermore, the Organisation is indirectly promoting the Cyprus tourist product by supporting the activities of tour operators, tourist professionals and other parties. The CTO promotional activities are geared towards the consumer, the travel trade and organised groups dealing within the special interest market segments, as these have been determined in the modified Marketing Strategy.

**Outlook 2004**

After the decision taken in Copenhagen in December 2002, the accession of Cyprus to the European Union has become a long-awaited reality. On 1st May 2004, Cyprus became a full EU member. It is worth noting that the overwhelming majority of the island's visitors (about 83%) source from the enlarged European Union.

Expectations in major markets: As a result of our entrance in the European Union lower airfares will stimulate tourism in the majority of the European source markets. The operation in 2004 of two new CTO Offices one in Dubai and one in Finland will further stimulate the tourist traffic from these countries to Cyprus.

Promotional campaigns: From January through March 2003 the Organisation executed its planned summer advertising campaign using the logo "Cyprus the island for four seasons" extending to 14 tourist source markets. The campaign was subsequently boosted with additional funds, to further attract consumer interest for Cyprus and encourage bookings to Cyprus. Thus, originally the summer campaign eventually was extended to July 2003, whilst at the same time a campaign was executed in six additional tourist source markets. The summer campaign included predominantly press and outdoor advertising. Television advertising was realized in the markets of the United Kingdom and Germany. In support of the advertising campaign a parallel campaign was scheduled with the international television networks CNN International and Eurosport. This campaign was of special importance for markets for which limited or no advertising funds were available.

During 2004 a series of mega-events (concerts, ballet and opera etc.) will take place.

In the light of the Olympic Games 2004 and within the framework of the development of sports tourism, the Organisation entered into an agreement with the British Olympic Association in order to highlight the fact that Britain selected Cyprus as the destination in order to carry out their Olympics preparation training. Furthermore, the Organisation provided hospitality for the Olympic and Para-Olympic Committee from Ireland.

The Organisation also supported the promotion of the Cyprus World Rally set for the 13th-16th May 2004 in Europe, the Middle East, and the Gulf Countries.

## International Meetings Industry (MI)

**Characteristics of supply**

The Cyprus International Conference Centre "Lefkosia" offers 2,916 square metres for international conferences, product launchers, exhibitions and television shows and easily accommodates functions of up to 1,600 delegates.

The Cyprus State Fairs Authority (CSFA) organizes the annual Cyprus International Fair and other specialised exhibitions, aiming at the promotion of products and services of Cypriot and foreign exhibitors in Cyprus and the neighboring countries.

Alongside the exhibitions the CSFA organizes associated conferences, establishing a significant platform for seeing and discussing the latest developments.

**Organisation of promotion**

International promotion is organised in a specialised area within the structure of the National/Regional Tourism Organization.

**Collection of statistics on the Meetings Industry?:** no.

| | |
|---|---|
| **Description** | The CTO has carried out research and the results are currently being examined. |
| **Importance / size** | Data is not available at the present time. |
| **Evolution MI** | Cyprus has already gained a reputation as an international conference venue thanks to its location, facilities, trained personnel and a first class communication system which links the island with the outside world. The proximity of Cyprus to the Middle East markets makes it an ideal regional center too. More and more businesses and international organisations choose the island for their meetings. This presupposes significant investments in product development and marketing and partnerships between organisations in the private and public sectors. Numerous special interest products need to be developed to attract each targeted segment.<br>At the same time the destination will invest in the enhancement of the quality of the services offered, the improvement of the quality-value relationship and the strengthening of the tourist industry's ability to compete effectively in a European, open-market, modern and technologically-advanced environment.<br>We expect these interventions to be undertaken using both public and private funds and the building of partnerships. Operating in a free market economy, the Government of Cyprus is focussing on the creation of a favourable entrepreneurial climate and the provision of incentives to encourage investment by the European Union residents and other investors in the priority areas specified in our Strategy. We also expect a number of the planned projects to attract the European Union funding from the European Union programmes and structural funds. |

## International Tourism by Origin

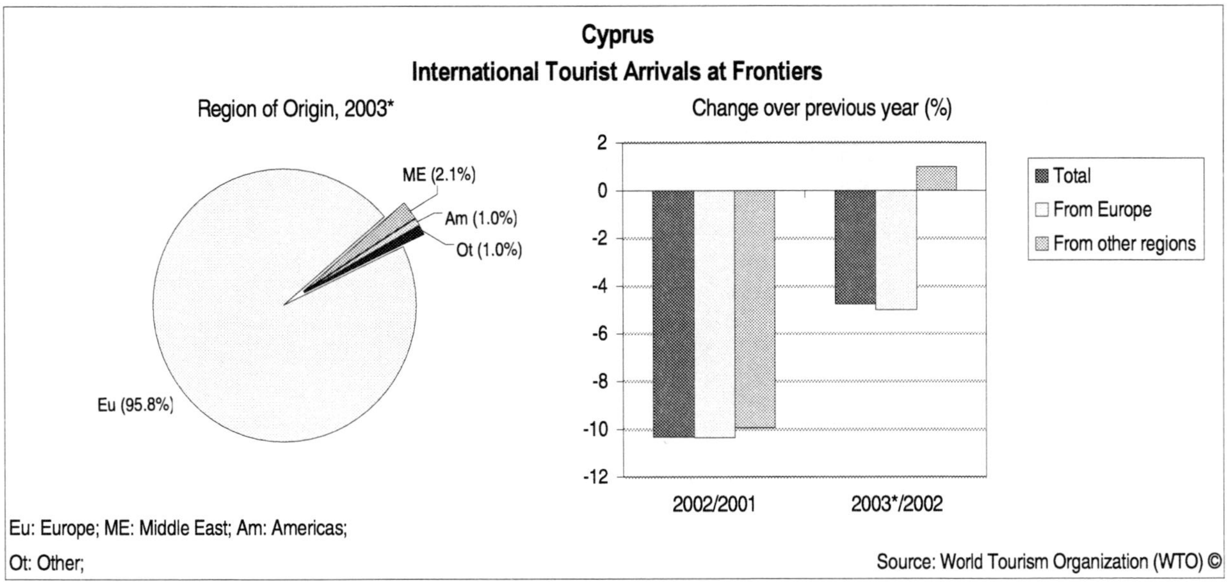

**Cyprus**

**International Tourist Arrivals at Frontiers (by residence)**

| | | | | (thousand) | Market share (%) | | Growth rate (%) | | Average per year (%) |
|---|---|---|---|---|---|---|---|---|---|
| | 1995 | 2001 | 2002 | 2003* | 1995 | 2003* | 2002/01 | 2003*/02 | 1995-2003* |
| **Total** | **2,100** | **2,697** | **2,418** | **2,303** | **100** | **100** | **-10.3** | **-4.8** | **1.2** |
| *From Europe* | *1,840* | *2,592* | *2,324* | *2,207* | *87.6* | *95.8* | *-10.3* | *-5.0* | *2.3* |
| United Kingdom | 850 | 1,487 | 1,338 | 1,347 | 40.5 | 58.5 | -10.0 | 0.7 | 5.9 |
| Scandinavia | 230 | .. | .. | .. | 11.0 | | | | |
| Germany | 235 | 214 | 174 | 129 | 11.2 | 5.6 | -18.9 | -25.7 | -7.2 |
| Greece | 65 | 90 | 93 | 110 | 3.1 | 4.8 | 3.9 | 18.2 | 6.8 |
| Russian Federation | 95 | 116 | 109 | 105 | 4.5 | 4.6 | -6.6 | -3.5 | 1.3 |
| Sweden | .. | 127 | 100 | 87 | | 3.8 | -21.7 | -13.0 | |
| Ireland | 16 | 52 | 57 | 62 | 0.8 | 2.7 | 9.2 | 8.7 | 18.3 |
| Norway | .. | 62 | 58 | 56 | | 2.4 | -6.4 | -2.8 | |
| Switzerland | 110 | 77 | 65 | 38 | 5.2 | 1.6 | -15.7 | -41.9 | -12.6 |
| Netherlands | 58 | 51 | 40 | 32 | 2.8 | 1.4 | -21.6 | -19.6 | -7.2 |
| France | 46 | 33 | 30 | 31 | 2.2 | 1.4 | -10.0 | 6.3 | -4.7 |
| Finland | .. | 49 | 45 | 29 | | 1.3 | -6.8 | -36.5 | |
| Denmark | .. | 33 | 32 | 29 | | 1.2 | -3.7 | -10.3 | |
| Israel | 33 | 37 | 40 | 27 | 1.6 | 1.2 | 8.9 | -31.9 | -2.4 |
| Austria | 43 | 31 | 29 | 26 | 2.0 | 1.1 | -6.4 | -10.9 | -6.1 |
| Belgium/Luxembourg | 38 | 31 | 24 | 21 | 1.8 | 0.9 | -21.9 | -14.9 | -7.4 |
| Italy | 21 | 22 | 12 | 13 | 1.0 | 0.6 | -44.4 | 9.8 | -5.5 |
| Czech Rep | .. | 10 | 14 | 13 | | 0.6 | 39.7 | -5.4 | |
| Poland | .. | 25 | 20 | 12 | | 0.5 | -22.4 | -39.7 | |
| Hungary | .. | 9 | 8 | 9 | | 0.4 | -5.2 | 8.4 | |
| Ukraine | .. | 7 | 9 | 7 | | 0.3 | 19.8 | -22.0 | |
| Slovakia | .. | 2 | 4 | 4 | | 0.2 | 118.3 | -5.6 | |
| Romania | .. | 3 | 3 | 4 | | 0.2 | -4.0 | 11.6 | |
| Bulgaria | .. | 3 | 3 | 3 | | 0.1 | 1.2 | 31.6 | |
| Serbia & Montenegro | .. | 6 | 5 | 3 | | 0.1 | -10.5 | -40.1 | |
| Other intraregional | .. | 17 | 15 | 12 | | 0.5 | -12.9 | -17.0 | |
| *From other regions* | *105* | *104* | *94* | *95* | *5.0* | *4.1* | *-9.9* | *1.0* | *-1.3* |
| All Middle East | 105 | .. | .. | .. | 5.0 | | | | |
| United States | .. | 23 | 21 | 18 | | 0.8 | -11.7 | -12.0 | |
| Lebanon | .. | 14 | 15 | 17 | | 0.7 | 6.5 | 11.8 | |
| Australia | .. | 8 | 8 | 8 | | 0.3 | -2.9 | -4.5 | |
| Jordan | .. | 5 | 5 | 6 | | 0.3 | -6.5 | 42.0 | |
| Untd Arab Emirates | .. | 6 | 6 | 6 | | 0.3 | -5.2 | 6.1 | |
| South Africa | .. | 6 | 6 | 5 | | 0.2 | -2.0 | -1.6 | |
| Egypt | .. | 7 | 6 | 5 | | 0.2 | -11.6 | -12.2 | |
| Saudi Arabia | .. | 5 | 5 | 5 | | 0.2 | -8.2 | -0.1 | |
| Canada | .. | 6 | 5 | 4 | | 0.2 | -8.8 | -16.6 | |
| Kuwait | .. | 3 | 3 | 3 | | 0.1 | 9.4 | 1.9 | |
| Other interregional | .. | 21 | 15 | 16 | | 0.7 | -28.6 | 9.1 | |
| *Other World/Not specified* | *155* | *1* | *1* | *1* | *7.4* | *0.0* | *-16.2* | *26.4* | *-46.7* |

Source: World Tourism Organization (WTO) © (Data as collected by WTO December 2004)

# III.5.2 Israel East Mediterranean Europe

## Profile

# Israel

**Europe**
**East Mediterranean Europe**

| | |
|---|---|
| Year of entry in WTO | 1975 |
| Area (1000 km²) | 21 |
| Population (2003, million) | 6.1 |
| Gross Domestic Product (GDP) (2003, euro million) | 115,224 |
| GDP per capita (2003, euro) | 17,884 |
| GDP growth (real, %) | |
| -> 2002: -0.7; 2003: 1.3; 2004*: 3.6; 2005*: 3.5 | |

| | 2001 | 2002 | 2003* | 2002/2001 | 2003*/2002 |
|---|---|---|---|---|---|
| **International Arrivals** | | | | | |
| Visitors (1000) | 1,219 | 862 | .. | -29.3 | |
| Tourists (overnight visitors) (1000) | 1,196 | 862 | 1,063 | -27.9 | 23.4 |
| - per 100 of inhabitants | 20 | 14 | 17 | | |
| Cruise passengers (1000) | 23 | 0 | .. | -98.7 | |
| **Tourism accommodation** | | | | | |
| Number of rooms | 46,143 | 46,545 | 46,368 | 0.9 | -0.4 |
| *Nights spent in collective establishments (1000)* | 18,305 | 16,770 | 17,293 | -8.4 | 3.1 |
| by non-residents (inbound tourism) | 4,637 | 2,745 | 3,438 | -40.8 | 25.2 |
| by residents (domestic tourism) | 13,668 | 14,025 | 13,855 | 2.6 | -1.2 |
| *Nights spent in hotels and similar establishments (1000)* | 15,114 | 14,606 | 15,095 | -3.4 | 3.3 |
| by non-residents (inbound tourism) | 3,826 | 2,628 | 3,285 | -31.3 | 25.0 |
| by residents (domestic tourism) | 11,288 | 11,978 | 11,810 | 6.1 | -1.4 |
| **Outbound Tourism** | | | | | |
| Trips abroad (1000) | 3,561 | 3,273 | 3,299 | -8.1 | 0.8 |
| - per 100 of inhabitants | 60 | 54 | 54 | | |
| **Receipts and Expenditure for International Tourism** | | | | | |
| International Tourism Receipts (euro million) | 2,667 | 2,277 | 2,156 | -14.6 | -5.3 |
| - per Tourist Arrival (euro) | 2,230 | 2,641 | 2,028 | 18.5 | -23.2 |
| - per Visitor Arrival (euro) | 2,188 | 2,641 | .. | 20.7 | |
| - per capita (euro) | 449 | 378 | 353 | | |
| International Fare Receipts (euro million) | 318 | 314 | 360 | -1.4 | 14.6 |
| International Tourism Expenditure (euro million) | 3,189 | 2,839 | 2,697 | -11.0 | -5.0 |
| - per trip (euro) | 895 | 868 | 818 | -3.1 | -5.8 |
| - per capita (euro) | 537 | 471 | 441 | | |
| International Fare Expenditure (euro million) | 1,020 | 871 | 838 | -14.6 | -3.8 |
| △ International Tourism Balance (euro million) | -522 | -563 | -541 | | |
| △ International Fare Balance (euro million) | -702 | -557 | -478 | | |

Source: World Tourism Organization (WTO) (Data as collected by WTO December 2004)

See annex for methodological notes and reference of external sources used.

## Survey

Contributed by *Ministry of Tourism*
www.tourism.gov.il (institutional/corporate)
www.tourism.gov.il (research and data)

## Tourism development and outlook

| | |
|---|---|
| **Overall evaluation of results** | An increase of 23 per cent in inbound tourism, a slight decrease of one per cent in domestic tourism. |
| **Supply** | Accommodation: no change.<br>Travel agencies/tour operators: a decrease of 6 per cent.<br>Transport capacity: a small decrease.<br>Attractions/entertainment: no change.<br>Specific products: a small decrease. |
| **External factors** | An improvement in the security situation but no change in all the other conditions. |
| **Tourism policy** | We have continued the policy of the last two years. |
| **Marketing & promotion** | We are continuing with the same policy as in the last two years.<br>Promotion on the special niche segments. |
| **Outlook 2004** | We hope that the positive trend will continue and that inbound tourism as well as domestic tourism will increase. |

## International Meetings Industry (MI)

| | |
|---|---|
| **Organisation of promotion** | Promotion is organised by the National Convention Bureau and Regional Convention Bureaux. |

**Collection of statistics on the Meetings Industry?:** yes.

| | |
|---|---|
| **Description** | We do collect data on the Meetings Industry by two methods:<br>- As part of the Ministry's on-going survey of incoming tourists (a sample survey), there are several questions regarding conferences/conventions;<br>- The Ministry requests data on the meetings conducted in Israel from professional congress organizers, tour operators, educational and health institutions, hotels, conventions centers and other organizations which we know conduct periodic conferences. Our annual statistical report includes a summary table of the data. |
| **Importance / size** | The Meetings Industry represents somewhere between 2-3 per cent of incoming tourism. |

**Evolution MI**

The Meetings Industry was growing significantly and respectably until October 2000 when the security situation in the country changed. The situation was aggravated further by the growing tension in the Persian Gulf. In the present situation we do not expect any major growth in this area.
However during this period (2001-2004) there have been a few international conferences initiated by local organizing committees which have managed to attract small numbers of professionals from abroad (30-80 participants from abroad). We believe that with an improvement in the security situation in the country, the Meetings Industry will return to robust activity over a period of time.

## International Tourism by Origin

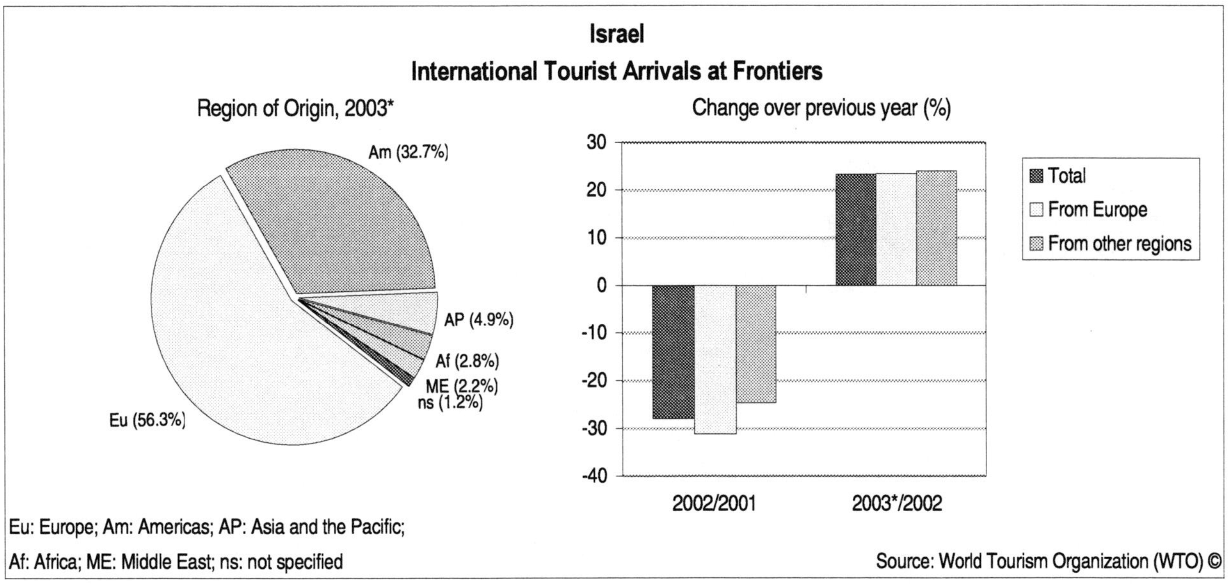


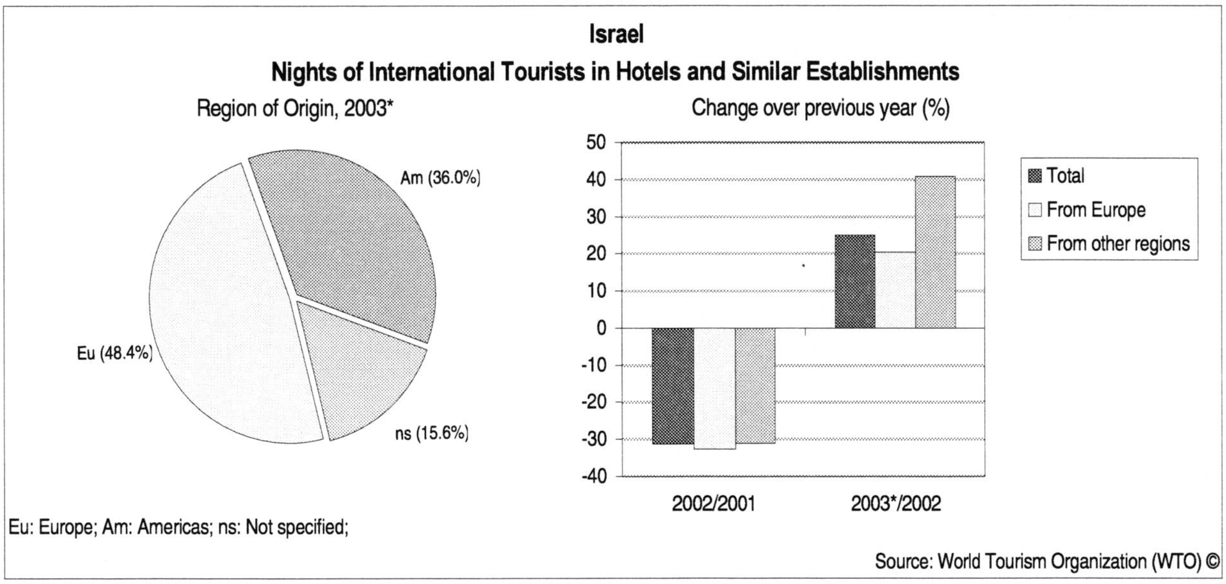

**Israel**
**International Tourist Arrivals at Frontiers (by residence)**

| | | | | (thousand) | Market share (%) | | Growth rate (%) | | Average per year (%) |
|---|---|---|---|---|---|---|---|---|---|
| | 1995 | 2001 | 2002 | 2003* | 1995 | 2003* | 2002/01 | 2003*/02 | 1995-2003* |
| **Total** | **2,215** | **1,196** | **862** | **1,063** | **100** | **100** | **-27.9** | **23.4** | **-8.8** |
| *From Europe* | *1,289* | *704* | *484* | *598* | *58.2* | *56.3* | *-31.2* | *23.5* | *-9.2* |
| France | 178 | 129 | 118 | 174 | 8.1 | 16.4 | -8.8 | 47.9 | -0.3 |
| United Kingdom | 217 | 140 | 97 | 104 | 9.8 | 9.8 | -30.6 | 7.1 | -8.8 |
| Germany | 219 | 65 | 39 | 49 | 9.9 | 4.6 | -40.7 | 26.3 | -17.1 |
| Russian Federation | 62 | 56 | 25 | 32 | 2.8 | 3.0 | -54.4 | 27.2 | -7.7 |
| Netherlands | 76 | 43 | 23 | 27 | 3.4 | 2.6 | -47.3 | 19.6 | -11.9 |
| Italy | 83 | 25 | 17 | 26 | 3.7 | 2.4 | -32.6 | 54.3 | -13.5 |
| Ukraine | 18 | 34 | 18 | 19 | 0.8 | 1.8 | -45.1 | 4.7 | 1.0 |
| Belgium | 47 | 22 | 15 | 18 | 2.1 | 1.7 | -28.8 | 15.8 | -11.4 |
| Switzerland | 54 | 20 | 14 | 17 | 2.4 | 1.6 | -29.2 | 22.2 | -13.4 |
| Spain | 33 | 12 | 9 | 16 | 1.5 | 1.5 | -27.2 | 85.1 | -8.6 |
| Turkey | 12 | 15 | 12 | 13 | 0.5 | 1.2 | -20.8 | 9.3 | 1.3 |
| Former U.S.S.R. | .. | .. | 11 | 9 | | 0.8 | | -21.7 | |
| Sweden | 37 | 11 | 7 | 9 | 1.7 | 0.8 | -37.9 | 27.8 | -16.7 |
| Austria | 40 | 10 | 8 | 8 | 1.8 | 0.8 | -21.4 | 9.1 | -18.0 |
| Former Czechoslovakia | 7 | .. | .. | .. | 0.3 | | | | |
| Denmark | 26 | 10 | 6 | 7 | 1.2 | 0.7 | -36.5 | 14.4 | -15.4 |
| Romania | 8 | 10 | 6 | 7 | 0.4 | 0.6 | -38.1 | 13.0 | -2.8 |
| Greece | 22 | 8 | 5 | 6 | 1.0 | 0.6 | -38.5 | 28.0 | -14.6 |
| Poland | 15 | 13 | 5 | 6 | 0.7 | 0.6 | -59.5 | 15.8 | -10.6 |
| Hungary | 15 | 8 | 5 | 5 | 0.7 | 0.5 | -37.5 | 2.2 | -12.2 |
| Cyprus | 10 | 5 | 4 | 5 | 0.5 | 0.4 | -19.1 | 18.2 | -9.6 |
| Norway | 18 | 6 | 4 | 4 | 0.8 | 0.4 | -35.3 | 5.3 | -16.4 |
| Belarus | 4 | 6 | 4 | 4 | 0.2 | 0.4 | -34.0 | 4.1 | 1.3 |
| Finland | 26 | 11 | 4 | 4 | 1.2 | 0.4 | -68.1 | 14.7 | -20.4 |
| Czech Rep | 3 | 5 | 3 | 3 | 0.1 | 0.3 | -40.7 | -4.6 | 2.4 |
| Other intraregional | 61 | 40 | 25 | 25 | 2.7 | 2.3 | -37.1 | -2.1 | -10.6 |
| *From other regions* | *903* | *484* | *365* | *453* | *40.7* | *42.6* | *-24.6* | *24.0* | *-8.3* |
| United States | 453 | 266 | 206 | 272 | 20.4 | 25.6 | -22.6 | 32.0 | -6.2 |
| Canada | 46 | 34 | 25 | 31 | 2.1 | 2.9 | -26.6 | 24.5 | -4.8 |
| Jordan | 84 | 25 | 24 | 18 | 3.8 | 1.7 | -0.6 | -25.0 | -17.4 |
| Nigeria | 13 | 9 | 13 | 12 | 0.6 | 1.1 | 51.3 | -8.6 | -1.6 |
| Argentina | 18 | 11 | 7 | 10 | 0.8 | 0.9 | -30.4 | 36.3 | -7.0 |
| Australia | 25 | 10 | 8 | 10 | 1.1 | 0.9 | -21.7 | 20.9 | -10.8 |
| South Africa | 34 | 13 | 9 | 10 | 1.5 | 0.9 | -32.2 | 8.0 | -14.5 |
| India | 8 | 12 | 9 | 8 | 0.4 | 0.8 | -22.3 | -9.6 | 0.1 |
| Mexico | 7 | 10 | 4 | 8 | 0.3 | 0.8 | -55.4 | 94.1 | 1.4 |
| Korea, Republic of | 20 | 11 | 8 | 8 | 0.9 | 0.8 | -27.7 | 1.6 | -10.4 |
| Brazil | 28 | 9 | 5 | 8 | 1.3 | 0.7 | -38.2 | 43.7 | -14.9 |
| Japan | 16 | 7 | 4 | 5 | 0.7 | 0.4 | -42.0 | 15.5 | -13.9 |
| Philippines | 5 | 7 | 5 | 5 | 0.2 | 0.4 | -29.0 | -8.8 | -1.8 |
| Colombia | 8 | 5 | 3 | 4 | 0.4 | 0.4 | -39.9 | 28.3 | -8.1 |
| Morocco | 3 | 2 | 2 | 3 | 0.1 | 0.3 | -10.3 | 31.6 | 0.8 |
| Egypt | 28 | 5 | 3 | 3 | 1.3 | 0.3 | -40.4 | -11.3 | -25.0 |
| Other interregional | 105 | 48 | 27 | 38 | 4.8 | 3.6 | -42.8 | 39.5 | -11.9 |
| *Other World/Not specified* | *23* | *8* | *12* | *12* | *1.0* | *1.2* | *60.3* | *-0.2* | *-7.7* |

Source: World Tourism Organization (WTO) © (Data as collected by WTO December 2004)

**Israel**

**Nights of International Tourists in Hotels and Similar Establishments (by residence)**

| | | | | (thousand) | Market share (%) | | Growth rate (%) | | Average per year (%) |
|---|---|---|---|---|---|---|---|---|---|
| | **1995** | **2001** | **2002** | **2003*** | **1995** | **2003*** | **2002/01** | **2003*/02** | **1995-2003*** |
| **Total** | **9,496** | **3,826** | **2,629** | **3,285** | **100** | **100** | **-31.3** | **24.9** | **-12.4** |
| *From Europe* | *5,686* | *1,961* | *1,320* | *1,589* | *59.9* | *48.4* | *-32.7* | *20.4* | *-14.7* |
| All Europe | 5,686 | 1,961 | 1,320 | 1,589 | 59.9 | 48.4 | -32.7 | 20.4 | -14.7 |
| *From other regions* | *2,391* | *1,219* | *840* | *1,183* | *25.2* | *36.0* | *-31.1* | *40.9* | *-8.4* |
| All North America | 2,198 | 1,130 | 789 | 1,110 | 23.1 | 33.8 | -30.2 | 40.7 | -8.2 |
| All South America | 193 | 88 | 51 | 74 | 2.0 | 2.2 | -42.0 | 43.8 | -11.3 |
| *Other World/Not specified* | *1,419* | *646* | *469* | *513* | *14.9* | *15.6* | *-27.4* | *9.3* | *-12.0* |

Source: World Tourism Organization (WTO) © (Data as collected by WTO December 2004)

# III.5.3 Turkey — East Mediterranean Europe

## Profile

# Turkey

**Europe**
**East Mediterranean Europe**

| | |
|---|---|
| Capital | Ankara |
| Year of entry in WTO | 1975 |
| Area (1000 km²) | 775 |
| Population (2003, million) | 68.1 |
| Gross Domestic Product (GDP) (2003, euro million) | 253,626 |
| GDP per capita (2003, euro) | 3,650 |
| GDP growth (real, %) | |

'-> 2002: 7.9; 2003: 5.8; 2004*: 7.0; 2005*: 5.0

| | 2001 | 2002 | 2003* | 2002/2001 | 2003*/2002 |
|---|---|---|---|---|---|
| **International Arrivals** | | | | | |
| Visitors (1000) | 11,619 | 13,256 | 14,030 | 14.1 | 5.8 |
| Tourists (overnight visitors) (1000) | 10,783 | 12,790 | 13,341 | 18.6 | 4.3 |
| - per 100 of inhabitants | 16 | 19 | 20 | | |
| Same-day visitors (1000) | 836 | 466 | 689 | -44.3 | 47.9 |
| **Tourism accommodation** | | | | | |
| Number of rooms | 176,635 | 189,528 | 201,510 | 7.3 | 6.3 |
| *Nights spent in collective establishments (1000)* | 50,546 | 58,514 | 57,100 | 15.8 | -2.4 |
| by non-residents (inbound tourism) | 36,368 | 43,312 | 40,866 | 19.1 | -5.6 |
| by residents (domestic tourism) | 14,178 | 15,202 | 16,234 | 7.2 | 6.8 |
| *Nights spent in hotels and similar establishments (1000)* | 50,454 | 58,377 | 57,018 | 15.7 | -2.3 |
| by non-residents (inbound tourism) | 36,307 | 43,225 | 40,819 | 19.1 | -5.6 |
| by residents (domestic tourism) | 14,147 | 15,152 | 16,199 | 7.1 | 6.9 |
| **Outbound Tourism** | | | | | |
| Trips abroad (1000) | 4,856 | 5,131 | 5,928 | 5.7 | 15.5 |
| - per 100 of inhabitants | 7 | 8 | 9 | | |
| **Receipts and Expenditure for International Tourism** | | | | | |
| International Tourism Receipts (euro million) | 10,900 | 13,288 | 13,963 | 21.9 | 5.1 |
| - per Tourist Arrival (euro) | 1,011 | 1,039 | 1,047 | 2.8 | 0.7 |
| - per Visitor Arrival (euro) | 938 | 1,002 | 995 | 6.9 | -0.7 |
| - per capita (euro) | 164 | 197 | 205 | | |
| International Tourism Expenditure (euro million) | 1,882 | 2,100 | 2,235 | 11.6 | 6.4 |
| - per trip (euro) | 388 | 409 | 377 | 5.6 | -7.9 |
| - per capita (euro) | 28 | 31 | 33 | | |
| △ International Tourism Balance (euro million) | 9,018 | 11,188 | 11,728 | | |

Source: World Tourism Organization (WTO) (Data as collected by WTO December 2004)

See annex for methodological notes and reference of external sources used.

# Survey

Contributed by *Ministry of Culture and Tourism*
www.goturkey.com (promotional)
www.kulturturizm.gov.tr (institutional/corporate)
www.kulturturizm.gov.tr (research and data)

## Tourism development and outlook

**Overall evaluation of results**

Turkish Tourism has been negatively affected by the following world events in 2003:

- The currency exchange in Europe (overtaking euro);
- SARS epidemic occurred in Asia-Pacific;
- Iraq War;
- Economic stagnation in the world and in Europe.

The positive events for turkish tourism have been the low exchange rates in USD and euro, considerable decrease in the inflation rate, comparative price advantages, stable economy and not being involved in the Iraq war.
The number of foreign visitors reached 14 million in 2003 (+5.8%). The number of turkish citizens going abroad amounted 6 million (+16%) in 2003.
A decrease of 3.8 per cent was observed in the number of visitors coming from the Organisation for Economic Co-operation and Development (OECD) while a 28 per cent increase occurred in foreign visitors from the Commonwealth of Independent States (CIS), summing 56 per cent of the total visitors in 2003.
Tourism receipts in 2003 amounted US$ 13.2 billion with an increase of 11 per cent. The share in the Gross National Product increased by 28 per cent. Tourism expenditure during the same period reached US$ 2.1 billion (+12%).

**Supply**

The number of accommodation establishments and their bed capacity increased by 5.5 per cent and 6.2 per cent respectively when compared to the previous year.
The number of travel agencies increased by 1.5 per cent in 2003 when compared to 2002.

**Marketing & promotion**

In 2003, the Ministry of Culture and Tourism spent US$ 47 million in the promotion of Turkey with promotional campaigns in over 50 countries through press, media, open-air, cinemas, internet, VCD/DVD production, bulletins, posters, brochures.
Our promotional campaigns are now destination oriented trying to promote tourism alternatives being offered in Turkey other than mass (sun-sea) tourism. Turkey has great tourism potential spread over 12 months and we are trying to obtain sustainability in tourism through marketing and promotion campaigns. Promotion leads in Germany, Australia, Poland, France, Belgium, Spain, Portugal, England, Ireland, the Netherlands, Italia, Scandinavia, Russia, United States of America, Canada, Austria, New Zealand, South Africa, Japan, China, Taiwan (province of China), United Arab Emirates, Saudi Arabia, Kuwait, Israel, Jordan markets. We have widen our promotion campaigns through Iran, Syria and Egypt.

**Outlook 2004**

Compared to the previous year, we have obtained in 2004 a 31 per cent increase in the number of visitors coming to Turkey between January and August. The number of visitors is 11.8 million in the first 8 months of the year. There is a 29 per cent increase in the number of OECD visitors (62% of the total number visitors) and 35 per cent increase in the number of visitors coming from East European countries (28% of total number visitors).

The number of visitors according to their nationalities during this first two quarters of the year is as follows:
Germany: 2,550,919 (+21,6%)
Russia: 1,171,730 (+10%)
England: 953,151 (+8%)
The Netherlands, Bulgaria, France, Iran, Austria, Belgium, Greece, Italia, Israel, Azerbaijan, Ukraine and Sweden follow up too these countries. We expect to obtain 14 million visitors at the end of the year, which means over 20 per cent increase in the number of visitors. Turkey as a tourism country with unbelievable potential will be one of the leading countries in Europe. We do forecast to achieve also over 20 per cent increase in the number of visitors through next year. With our unique location, historical and cultural treasure and besides these modern facilities and quality service we will carry on our promotional campaigns through our markets trying to achieve destination management and sustainability in tourism.

## International Meetings Industry (MI)

**Characteristics of supply**

Turkey, a treasure-house of history and culture, is a gateway into a world of exciting possibilities. Located at the juncture of Europe and Asia, Turkey is a superb venue for motivational meetings and conventions. Turkey offers a wealth of first-class hotel accommodation and conference facilities, easy access to major cities worldwide, beautiful settings, unique historical sightseeing attractions and wonderful weather. From Europe, Turkey is an ideal destination being both exotic and conveniently close. Only in a few hours one can reach Turkey from Europe. Turkish Airlines provides an important network of domestic flights from the international airports of Istanbul, Ankara, Izmir, Adana, Trabzon, Dalaman and Antalya to all of the major cities. Sightseeing and entertainment programs can be fully packaged. Istanbul is among the world's greatest tourism destinations with unrivalled setting and wealth of architectural treasures. The opening of Lutfi Kirdar Istanbul International Conference Centre doubled the capacity of congress facilities in the city. Izmir, a city of palm tresses and ancient ruins is the gateway to the Aegean region. The natural wonder of Pamukkale as well as charming seaside resorts such as Kusadasi, Çesme, Marmaris, Fethiye, Bodrum are good choices for the Meetings Industry. Antalya, Side, Kemer, Alanya, Mersin, Antakya and the other Mediterranean coastal resorts beckon visitors year-round to enjoy the sun, the beautiful sandy beaches and its ancient sites. Turkey's capital city, Ankara, boasts sophisticated hotels and restaurants, along with easy access to fabled Cappadocia. Bursa, the first Ottoman capital, offers a picturesque setting as well as hotels with thermal baths, excellent skiing on Uludag. Turkey today well-equipped to handle meetings, incentives and conferences of all sorts and sizes in comfort and style. This year important international events such as Eurovision Song Contest, NATO Summit have been successfully held in Turkey. Turkey, especially Istanbul and Antalya, have recently developed in the area of meetings, congresses, conferences and conventions, incentives, exhibitions and fairs.

**Organisation of promotion**

We promote this industry under our Marketing and Promotional campaigns; through press, media, Internet, VCD/DVD production, and brochures.
Istanbul Convention Visitors Bureau <http://www.icvb.org>;
The Istanbul Convention & Exhibition Centre (ICEC) <http://www.icec.org/index.asp>;
Antalya Convention Bureau <http://www.antalyaconvention.org>;

**Collection of statistics on the Meetings Industry?:** no.

**Importance / size**

The Meetings Industry has been one of the most important tourism products of Turkey in recent years. With modern facilities, Istanbul and Antalya are the main destinations for meetings and congress. 5,5 per cent of Turkeys' GDP consist of Tourism revenues and that shows the importance of tourism for the economy. According to the State Institute of Statistics, approximately 10 per cent of the foreign visitors come to Turkey for the meetings, congresses, seminars, fairs and exhibitions. Recent events held very successfully in Turkey such as NATO Summit, Eurovision Song Contest etc. will be good references for future events.

**Evolution MI**

Turkey with its 3,301 touristic licensed facilities, approximately one million bed capacity, 4,498 agencies, 42 airports and 28,952 seat capacity, 33 marinas with 12,300 yacht capacity and total US$ 35 billion tourism investment is hoping to be one of the worlds' leading tourism destinations. We believe that with a wealth of first-class hotel accommodation, conference facilities, easy access to major cities worldwide, beautiful settings, unique historical sightseeing attractions and wonderful weather Turkey, especially Istanbul and Antalya will be the meetings centre within the next few years.

## International Tourism by Origin

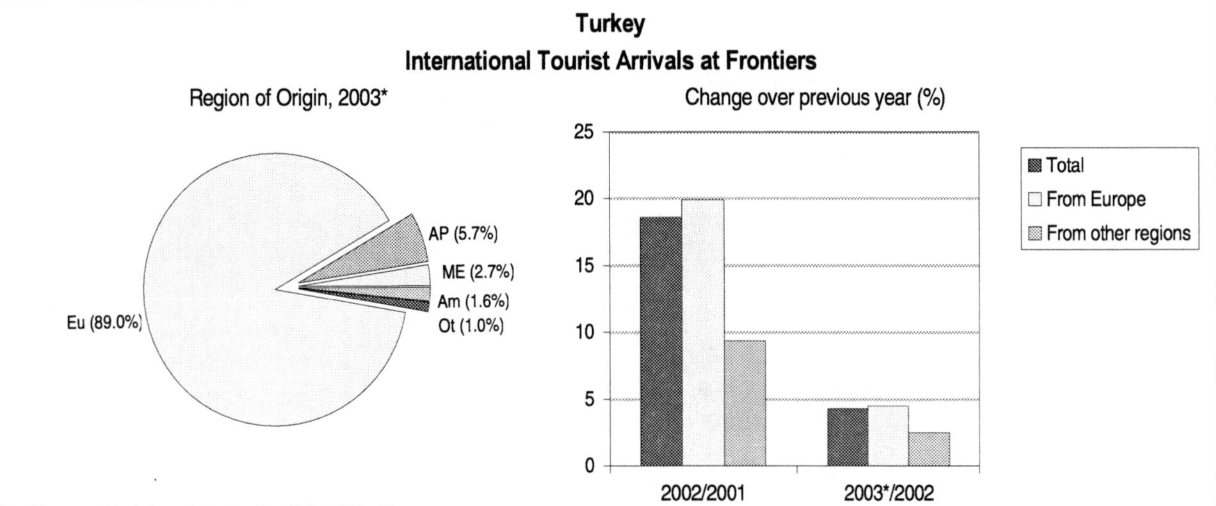


Eu: Europe; AP: Asia and the Pacific; ME: Middle East;
Am: Americas; Ot: Other;

Source: World Tourism Organization (WTO) ©

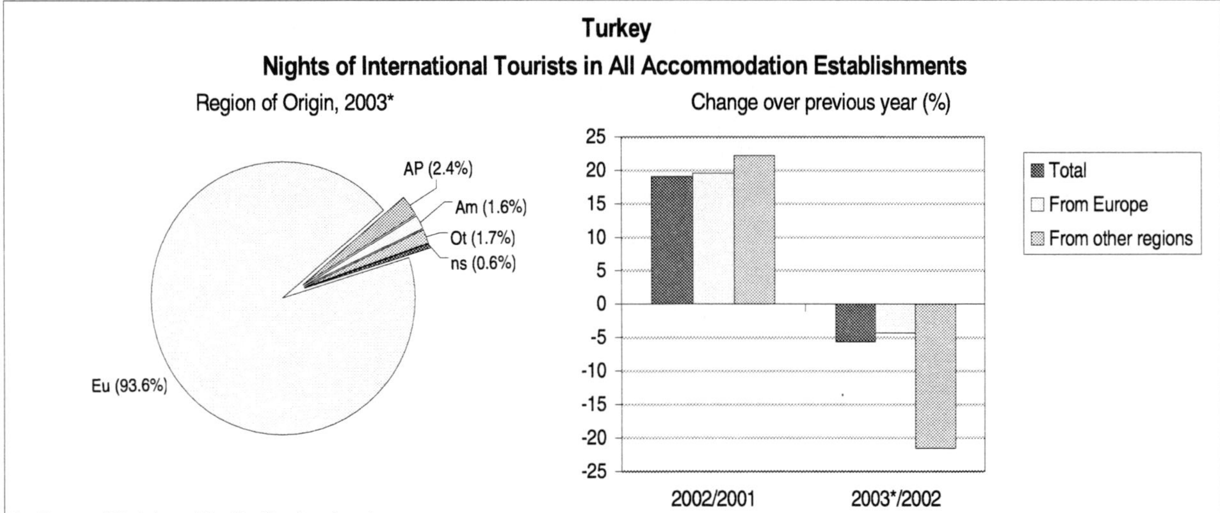


Eu: Europe; AP: Asia and the Pacific; Am: Americas;
Ot: Other; ns: not specified

Source: World Tourism Organization (WTO) ©

**Turkey**

**International Tourist Arrivals at Frontiers (by nationality)**

| | | | | (thousand) | Market share (%) | | Growth rate (%) | | Average per year (%) |
|---|---|---|---|---|---|---|---|---|---|
| | 1995 | 2001 | 2002 | 2003* | 1995 | 2003* | 2002/01 | 2003*/02 | 1995-2003* |
| **Total** | **7,083** | **10,783** | **12,790** | **13,341** | **100** | **100** | **18.6** | **4.3** | **8.2** |
| *From Europe* | *5,980* | *9,473* | *11,359* | *11,872* | *84.4* | *89.0* | *19.9* | *4.5* | *9.0* |
| Germany | 1,584 | 2,819 | 3,421 | 3,231 | 22.4 | 24.2 | 21.4 | -5.6 | 9.3 |
| Commonwealth Indep. States | 1,277 | .. | .. | .. | 18.0 | | | | |
| Russian Federation | .. | 750 | 937 | 1,272 | | 9.5 | 24.9 | 35.7 | |
| Bulgaria | 159 | 539 | 832 | 1,006 | 2.2 | 7.5 | 54.3 | 20.8 | 25.9 |
| United Kingdom | 667 | 684 | 918 | 936 | 9.4 | 7.0 | 34.2 | 1.9 | 4.3 |
| Netherlands | 192 | 616 | 849 | 922 | 2.7 | 6.9 | 37.8 | 8.6 | 21.6 |
| France | 231 | 489 | 510 | 444 | 3.3 | 3.3 | 4.3 | -13.0 | 8.5 |
| Austria | 176 | 351 | 370 | 370 | 2.5 | 2.8 | 5.3 | 0.1 | 9.8 |
| Greece | 124 | 173 | 256 | 365 | 1.8 | 2.7 | 47.7 | 42.5 | 14.4 |
| Israel | 283 | 283 | 264 | 303 | 4.0 | 2.3 | -6.6 | 14.8 | 0.8 |
| Belgium | 101 | 302 | 307 | 300 | 1.4 | 2.2 | 1.6 | -2.4 | 14.5 |
| Yugoslav SFR | 70 | .. | .. | .. | 1.0 | | | | |
| Ukraine | .. | 163 | 175 | 224 | | 1.7 | 7.8 | 27.6 | |
| Sweden | 122 | 190 | 197 | 195 | 1.7 | 1.5 | 3.9 | -1.2 | 6.0 |
| Azerbaijan | .. | 177 | 163 | 193 | | 1.4 | -8.3 | 18.6 | |
| Serbia & Montenegro | .. | 125 | 188 | 186 | | 1.4 | 50.0 | -1.1 | |
| Romania | 281 | 179 | 177 | 184 | 4.0 | 1.4 | -1.1 | 3.9 | -5.1 |
| Switzerland | 57 | 116 | 140 | 179 | 0.8 | 1.3 | 19.9 | 28.1 | 15.4 |
| Georgia | .. | 163 | 161 | 168 | | 1.3 | -1.3 | 4.0 | |
| Denmark | 98 | 118 | 160 | 148 | 1.4 | 1.1 | 35.6 | -7.6 | 5.2 |
| Italy | 87 | 216 | 194 | 144 | 1.2 | 1.1 | -10.2 | -25.6 | 6.5 |
| F.Yug.Rp.Macedonia | .. | 114 | 121 | 119 | | 0.9 | 6.5 | -1.4 | |
| Cyprus | 97 | 91 | 94 | 104 | 1.4 | 0.8 | 3.5 | 11.0 | 1.0 |
| Poland | 33 | 149 | 149 | 101 | 0.5 | 0.8 | 0.2 | -32.5 | 14.8 |
| Norway | 48 | 79 | 86 | 82 | 0.7 | 0.6 | 9.1 | -4.8 | 6.8 |
| Other intraregional | 292 | 587 | 691 | 698 | 4.1 | 5.2 | 17.8 | 1.0 | 11.5 |
| *From other regions* | *1,095* | *1,298* | *1,420* | *1,456* | *15.5* | *10.9* | *9.4* | *2.5* | *3.6* |
| Iran | 361 | 327 | 432 | 497 | 5.1 | 3.7 | 32.2 | 15.1 | 4.1 |
| United States | 152 | 255 | 197 | 162 | 2.1 | 1.2 | -22.7 | -17.8 | 0.8 |
| Syrian Arab Republic | 111 | 109 | 126 | 154 | 1.6 | 1.2 | 15.5 | 22.3 | 4.1 |
| Japan | 61 | 84 | 91 | 65 | 0.9 | 0.5 | 9.1 | -29.1 | 0.8 |
| Tunisia | 26 | 45 | 51 | 47 | 0.4 | 0.3 | 14.2 | -8.9 | 7.4 |
| Korea, Republic of | 12 | 29 | 42 | 46 | 0.2 | 0.3 | 47.3 | 9.1 | 18.9 |
| Australia | 36 | 49 | 53 | 45 | 0.5 | 0.3 | 8.1 | -13.8 | 2.8 |
| Algeria | 45 | 38 | 39 | 40 | 0.6 | 0.3 | 4.7 | 1.2 | -1.6 |
| Jordan | 25 | 27 | 33 | 37 | 0.3 | 0.3 | 23.1 | 12.9 | 5.4 |
| Lebanon | 28 | 22 | 31 | 35 | 0.4 | 0.3 | 43.0 | 12.3 | 2.9 |
| Egypt | 19 | 22 | 21 | 30 | 0.3 | 0.2 | -3.6 | 40.2 | 5.9 |
| Libyan Arab Jamahiriya | 7 | 31 | 30 | 28 | 0.1 | 0.2 | -4.8 | -6.9 | 18.7 |
| Canada | 23 | 35 | 29 | 28 | 0.3 | 0.2 | -18.7 | -3.3 | 2.5 |
| China | 10 | 24 | 32 | 27 | 0.1 | 0.2 | 29.7 | -16.2 | 13.2 |
| Iraq | 14 | 16 | 14 | 25 | 0.2 | 0.2 | -12.9 | 73.4 | 7.0 |
| Saudi Arabia | 24 | 20 | 26 | 23 | 0.3 | 0.2 | 25.1 | -9.2 | -0.5 |
| Other interregional | 141 | 165 | 173 | 168 | 2.0 | 1.3 | 4.7 | -2.7 | 2.2 |
| *Other World/Not specified* | *9* | *11* | *11* | *14* | *0.1* | *0.1* | *-7.7* | *29.4* | *5.8* |

Source: World Tourism Organization (WTO) © (Data as collected by WTO December 2004)

**Turkey**
**Nights of International Tourists in All Accommodation Establishments (by nationality)**

| | | | | (thousand) | Market share (%) | | Growth rate (%) | | Average per year (%) |
|---|---|---|---|---|---|---|---|---|---|
| | 1995 | 2001 | 2002 | 2003* | 1995 | 2003* | 2002/01 | 2003*/02 | 1995-2003* |
| **Total** | **18,477** | **36,369** | **43,312** | **40,866** | **100** | **100** | **19.1** | **-5.6** | **10.4** |
| *From Europe* | *15,029* | *33,442* | *39,985* | *38,267* | *81.3* | *93.6* | *19.6* | *-4.3* | *12.4* |
| Germany | 7,232 | 15,335 | 17,831 | 16,301 | 39.1 | 39.9 | 16.3 | -8.6 | 10.7 |
| Commonwealth Indep. States | .. | 3,657 | 5,247 | 6,638 | | 16.2 | 43.5 | 26.5 | |
| Benelux | 979 | 3,972 | 4,887 | 5,163 | 5.3 | 12.6 | 23.0 | 5.6 | 23.1 |
| United Kingdom | 1,429 | 2,402 | 2,316 | 2,240 | 7.7 | 5.5 | -3.6 | -3.3 | 5.8 |
| Former U.S.S.R. | 1,924 | .. | .. | .. | 10.4 | | | | |
| France | 1,231 | 2,248 | 2,375 | 1,520 | 6.7 | 3.7 | 5.7 | -36.0 | 2.7 |
| Austria | 805 | 1,167 | 1,691 | 1,428 | 4.4 | 3.5 | 44.9 | -15.6 | 7.4 |
| Israel | .. | 631 | 705 | 740 | | 1.8 | 11.7 | 5.1 | |
| Scandinavia | 460 | 648 | 934 | 678 | 2.5 | 1.7 | 44.0 | -27.3 | 5.0 |
| Switzerland | 97 | 397 | 685 | 624 | 0.5 | 1.5 | 72.4 | -8.9 | 26.1 |
| Italy | 341 | 878 | 823 | 483 | 1.8 | 1.2 | -6.3 | -41.4 | 4.4 |
| Yugoslav SFR | 53 | 159 | 412 | 460 | 0.3 | 1.1 | 159.6 | 11.6 | 30.9 |
| Spain | 118 | 368 | 415 | 386 | 0.6 | 0.9 | 12.7 | -6.8 | 15.9 |
| Greece | 111 | 161 | 238 | 293 | 0.6 | 0.7 | 47.8 | 23.0 | 12.9 |
| Ireland | .. | 195 | 189 | 281 | | 0.7 | -3.4 | 48.9 | |
| Poland | 60 | 282 | 328 | 257 | 0.3 | 0.6 | 16.2 | -21.6 | 19.9 |
| Czech Rep | .. | 90 | 223 | 185 | | 0.5 | 147.1 | -17.3 | |
| Romania | 92 | 139 | 184 | 174 | 0.5 | 0.4 | 31.8 | -5.6 | 8.2 |
| Bulgaria | 55 | 92 | 188 | 163 | 0.3 | 0.4 | 105.6 | -13.5 | 14.4 |
| Hungary | 40 | 43 | 116 | 96 | 0.2 | 0.2 | 171.7 | -17.2 | 11.6 |
| Cyprus | .. | 34 | 38 | 47 | | 0.1 | 12.3 | 23.6 | |
| Albania | .. | 19 | 31 | 42 | | 0.1 | 68.5 | 33.6 | |
| Portugal | .. | 61 | 40 | 27 | | 0.1 | -35.2 | -33.3 | |
| Other Europe | .. | 461 | 85 | 40 | | 0.1 | -81.5 | -53.6 | |
| Other intraregional | .. | 3 | 6 | 4 | | 0.0 | 129.7 | -36.2 | |
| *From other regions* | *1,435* | *2,448* | *2,991* | *2,347* | *7.8* | *5.7* | *22.2* | *-21.5* | *6.3* |
| United States | 556 | 853 | 813 | 586 | 3.0 | 1.4 | -4.7 | -27.9 | 0.7 |
| Japan | 336 | 503 | 461 | 334 | 1.8 | 0.8 | -8.3 | -27.5 | -0.1 |
| Iran | 69 | 247 | 313 | 279 | 0.4 | 0.7 | 26.7 | -10.9 | 19.1 |
| Australia | 45 | 128 | 248 | 141 | 0.2 | 0.3 | 94.4 | -43.0 | 15.4 |
| Saudi Arabia | 93 | 72 | 135 | 120 | 0.5 | 0.3 | 87.5 | -11.2 | 3.2 |
| Korea, Republic of | .. | 56 | 99 | 113 | | 0.3 | 77.8 | 13.9 | |
| Lebanon | 48 | 51 | 98 | 88 | 0.3 | 0.2 | 91.1 | -9.6 | 7.9 |
| Syrian Arab Republic | 60 | 66 | 85 | 80 | 0.3 | 0.2 | 30.0 | -7.0 | 3.6 |
| Jordan | 43 | 37 | 57 | 66 | 0.2 | 0.2 | 55.1 | 14.6 | 5.5 |
| Egypt | 39 | 50 | 59 | 65 | 0.2 | 0.2 | 17.1 | 9.9 | 6.6 |
| Untd Arab Emirates | .. | 11 | 33 | 65 | | 0.2 | 189.1 | 97.1 | |
| Iraq | 29 | 24 | 40 | 48 | 0.2 | 0.1 | 66.7 | 18.9 | 6.5 |
| China | .. | 30 | 46 | 43 | | 0.1 | 53.5 | -7.2 | |
| Canada | 41 | 55 | 83 | 36 | 0.2 | 0.1 | 49.9 | -56.3 | -1.7 |
| Libyan Arab Jamahiriya | 13 | 53 | 46 | 32 | 0.1 | 0.1 | -13.7 | -29.6 | 12.0 |
| Kuwait | 45 | 15 | 21 | 25 | 0.2 | 0.1 | 42.0 | 18.4 | -7.1 |
| Tunisia | .. | 23 | 23 | 24 | | 0.1 | -3.8 | 6.9 | |
| India | .. | 5 | 18 | 21 | | 0.1 | 248.7 | 18.4 | |
| Other interregional | 18 | 167 | 312 | 181 | 0.1 | 0.4 | 86.6 | -42.2 | 33.9 |
| *Other World/Not specified* | *2,013* | *479* | *337* | *252* | *10.9* | *0.6* | *-29.7* | *-25.2* | *-22.9* |

Source: World Tourism Organization (WTO) © (Data as collected by WTO December 2004)

# Annex

# 1. International Tourist Arrivals

**International Tourist Arrivals, 1950-2003***

| | World | Africa | Americas | Asia and the Pacific | Europe | Middle East | World | Africa | Americas | Asia and the Pacific | Europe | Middle East |
|---|---|---|---|---|---|---|---|---|---|---|---|---|
| | International Tourist Arrivals (million) | | | | | | Change over previous year (%)[1] | | | | | |
| **1950** | 25.3 | 0.5 | 7.5 | 0.2 | 16.8 | 0.2 | | | | | | |
| **1960** | 69.3 | 0.8 | 16.7 | 0.9 | 50.4 | 0.6 | | | | | | |
| **1965** | 112.9 | 1.4 | 23.2 | 2.1 | 83.7 | 2.4 | | | | | | |
| **1970** | 165.8 | 2.4 | 42.3 | 6.2 | 113.0 | 1.9 | | | | | | |
| **1975** | 222.3 | 4.7 | 50.0 | 10.2 | 153.9 | 3.5 | | | | | | |
| **1980** | 278.2 | 7.3 | 62.3 | 23.6 | 177.7 | 7.3 | | | | | | |
| **1981** | 278.8 | 8.1 | 62.5 | 25.4 | 175.0 | 7.8 | 0.2 | 11.1 | 0.3 | 7.7 | -1.5 | 5.9 |
| **1982** | 277.5 | 7.5 | 59.7 | 26.6 | 175.4 | 8.3 | -0.4 | -6.6 | -4.5 | 4.8 | 0.2 | 6.8 |
| **1983** | 283.2 | 8.2 | 59.9 | 27.1 | 180.4 | 7.6 | 2.0 | 8.6 | 0.4 | 2.0 | 2.8 | -8.3 |
| **1984** | 308.6 | 8.8 | 67.4 | 30.1 | 194.4 | 7.9 | 9.0 | 7.4 | 12.5 | 11.0 | 7.7 | 4.2 |
| **1985** | 322.1 | 9.6 | 65.1 | 33.6 | 205.6 | 8.2 | 4.4 | 9.3 | -3.4 | 11.6 | 5.8 | 3.9 |
| **1986** | 332.8 | 9.3 | 70.9 | 37.6 | 207.8 | 7.1 | 3.3 | -3.2 | 8.9 | 12.1 | 1.1 | -13.4 |
| **1987** | 362.4 | 9.8 | 76.6 | 43.1 | 225.6 | 7.3 | 8.9 | 5.2 | 8.0 | 14.6 | 8.6 | 2.4 |
| **1988** | 388.2 | 12.5 | 83.0 | 50.1 | 233.5 | 9.1 | 7.1 | 28.3 | 8.4 | 16.1 | 3.5 | 23.9 |
| **1989** | 414.0 | 13.8 | 86.9 | 50.8 | 253.2 | 9.2 | 6.6 | 10.4 | 4.7 | 1.4 | 8.4 | 1.6 |
| **1990** | 445.8 | 15.2 | 92.8 | 57.7 | 270.4 | 9.8 | 7.7 | 9.6 | 6.8 | 13.7 | 6.8 | 6.0 |
| **1991** | 449.2 | 16.0 | 95.3 | 59.7 | 269.0 | 9.2 | 0.7 | 5.4 | 2.7 | 3.4 | -0.5 | -5.9 |
| **1992** | 486.7 | 18.3 | 102.2 | 67.8 | 287.0 | 11.5 | 8.4 | 14.3 | 7.3 | 13.5 | 6.7 | 24.5 |
| **1993** | 501.4 | 18.7 | 102.2 | 74.5 | 294.4 | 11.6 | 3.0 | 2.5 | 0.0 | 9.9 | 2.6 | 1.0 |
| **1994** | 526.6 | 19.1 | 105.1 | 82.2 | 307.9 | 12.3 | 5.0 | 2.3 | 2.9 | 10.3 | 4.6 | 5.9 |
| **1995** | 544.9 | 20.7 | 109.0 | 85.0 | 316.4 | 13.8 | 3.5 | 8.2 | 3.7 | 3.5 | 2.8 | 12.4 |
| **1996** | 575.3 | 22.4 | 114.5 | 94.0 | 328.8 | 15.6 | 5.6 | 8.0 | 5.1 | 10.6 | 3.9 | 12.9 |
| **1997** | 597.8 | 23.4 | 116.3 | 93.0 | 348.4 | 16.7 | 3.9 | 4.6 | 1.5 | -1.1 | 6.0 | 7.4 |
| **1998** | 617.4 | 25.9 | 119.2 | 92.4 | 362.0 | 18.0 | 3.3 | 10.5 | 2.5 | -0.7 | 3.9 | 7.6 |
| **1999** | 641.1 | 27.3 | 122.0 | 102.3 | 368.1 | 21.5 | 3.8 | 5.4 | 2.3 | 10.8 | 1.7 | 19.5 |
| **2000** | 685.5 | 28.6 | 128.2 | 114.9 | 389.6 | 24.3 | 6.9 | 4.9 | 5.1 | 12.3 | 5.8 | 13.0 |
| **2001** | 683.8 | 29.2 | 122.2 | 120.5 | 387.8 | 24.0 | -0.3 | 2.3 | -4.7 | 4.9 | -0.5 | -1.0 |
| **2002** | 702.8 | 29.9 | 116.6 | 131.1 | 397.3 | 27.9 | 2.8 | 2.2 | -4.5 | 8.8 | 2.4 | 16.1 |
| **2003*** | 690.9 | 30.8 | 113.0 | 119.3 | 399.0 | 28.8 | -1.7 | 3.1 | -3.1 | -9.0 | 0.4 | 3.4 |

| Average annual growth (%) | World | Africa | Americas | Asia and the Pacific | Europe | Middle East |
|---|---|---|---|---|---|---|
| **1950-2000** | 6.8 | 8.3 | 5.8 | 13.2 | 6.5 | 10.1 |
| **1950-2003*** | 6.4 | 8.0 | 5.3 | 12.5 | 6.2 | 9.9 |
| **1950-1960** | 10.6 | 3.7 | 8.4 | 14.1 | 11.6 | 12.3 |
| **1960-1970** | 9.1 | 12.4 | 9.7 | 21.6 | 8.4 | 11.5 |
| **1970-1980** | 5.3 | 11.7 | 4.0 | 14.2 | 4.6 | 14.7 |
| **1980-1990** | 4.8 | 7.6 | 4.1 | 9.4 | 4.3 | 2.9 |
| **1980-1985** | 3.0 | 5.7 | 0.9 | 7.3 | 3.0 | 2.4 |
| **1985-1990** | 6.7 | 9.6 | 7.3 | 11.5 | 5.6 | 3.4 |
| **1990-2000** | 4.4 | 6.6 | 3.3 | 7.1 | 3.7 | 9.5 |
| **1990-1995** | 4.1 | 6.4 | 3.3 | 8.0 | 3.2 | 7.1 |
| **1995-2000** | 4.7 | 6.7 | 3.3 | 6.2 | 4.2 | 12.0 |
| **2000-2003*** | 0.3 | 2.5 | -4.1 | 1.3 | 0.8 | 5.9 |

Source: World Tourism Organization (WTO) © (Data as collected by WTO December 2004)

[1] Before 1995, data are simple aggregates of country results and are not corrected for changes in series, so changes on previous year might not be in all cases correct.

**International Tourist Arrivals by Country of Destination**

| | | International Tourist Arrivals (1000) | | | | | | Market share in the region (%) | | Change (%) | | Average annual growth (%) | |
|---|---|---|---|---|---|---|---|---|---|---|---|---|---|
| | Series | 1990 | 1995 | 2000 | 2001 | 2002 | 2003* | 1995 | 2003* | 02/01 | 03*/02 | 90-95 | 95-00 |
| ***Africa*** | | ***15,160*** | ***20,718*** | ***28,598*** | ***29,248*** | ***29,902*** | ***30,834*** | ***100*** | ***100*** | ***2.2*** | ***3.1*** | ***6.4*** | ***6.7*** |
| **North Africa** | | **8,398** | **7,271** | **10,202** | **10,680** | **10,407** | **10,887** | **35.1** | **35.3** | **-2.6** | **4.6** | **-2.8** | **7.0** |
| Algeria | VF | 1,137 | 520 | 866 | 901 | 988 | 1,166 | 2.5 | 3.8 | 9.6 | 18.0 | -14.5 | 10.7 |
| Morocco | TF | 4,024 | 2,602 | 4,240 | 4,342 | 4,303 | 4,552 | 12.6 | 14.8 | -0.9 | 5.8 | -8.4 | 10.3 |
| Sudan | TF | 33 | 29 | 38 | 50 | 52 | .. | 0.1 | | 4.0 | | -2.6 | 5.6 |
| Tunisia | TF | 3,204 | 4,120 | 5,058 | 5,387 | 5,064 | 5,114 | 19.9 | 16.6 | -6.0 | 1.0 | 5.2 | 4.2 |
| **West Africa** | | **1,352** | **1,913** | **2,422** | **2,543** | **2,734** | **2,689** | **9.2** | **8.7** | **7.5** | **-1.6** | **7.2** | **4.8** |
| Benin | TF | 110 | 138 | 96 | 88 | 72 | .. | 0.7 | | -17.4 | | 4.6 | -7.0 |
| Burkina Faso | THS | 74 | 124 | 126 | 128 | 150 | 163 | 0.6 | 0.5 | 16.9 | 8.6 | 10.9 | 0.3 |
| Cape Verde | TF | 24 | 28 | 83 | 115 | 126 | 140 | 0.1 | 0.5 | 9.2 | 11.2 | 3.1 | 24.3 |
| Côte d'Ivoire | TF | 196 | 188 | .. | .. | .. | 180 | 0.9 | 0.6 | | | -0.8 | |
| Gambia | TF | 100 | 45 | 79 | 57 | 81 | 73 | 0.2 | 0.2 | 42.1 | -9.9 | -14.8 | 11.9 |
| Ghana | TF | 146 | 286 | 399 | 439 | 483 | 483 | 1.4 | 1.6 | 10.0 | -0.1 | 14.4 | 6.9 |
| Guinea | TF | .. | .. | 33 | 38 | 43 | 44 | | 0.1 | 12.8 | 3.4 | | |
| Guinea-Bissau | TF | .. | .. | .. | 8 | .. | .. | | | | | | |
| Mali | TF | 44 | 42 | 86 | 89 | 96 | 70 | 0.2 | 0.2 | 8.1 | -27.3 | -0.9 | 15.4 |
| Mauritania | TF | .. | .. | 30 | .. | .. | .. | | | | | | |
| Niger | TF | 21 | 35 | 50 | 53 | 58 | 55 | 0.2 | 0.2 | 9.4 | -4.6 | 10.8 | 7.4 |
| Nigeria | TF | 190 | 656 | 813 | 850 | 887 | .. | 3.2 | | 4.4 | | 28.1 | 4.4 |
| Senegal | THS | 246 | 280 | 389 | 396 | 427 | 354 | 1.4 | 1.1 | 7.7 | -17.2 | 2.6 | 6.8 |
| Sierra Leone | TF | 98 | 38 | 16 | 24 | 28 | 37 | 0.2 | 0.1 | 18.3 | 30.7 | -17.3 | -15.9 |
| Togo | THS | 103 | 53 | 60 | 57 | 58 | 61 | 0.3 | 0.2 | 1.6 | 5.3 | -12.4 | 2.5 |
| **Central Africa** | | **365** | **357** | **665** | **614** | **633** | **685** | **1.7** | **2.2** | **3.1** | **8.1** | **-0.4** | **13.3** |
| Angola | TF | 67 | 9 | 51 | 67 | 91 | 107 | 0.0 | 0.3 | 34.4 | 17.8 | -33.1 | 41.5 |
| Cameroon | THS | 89 | 100 | 277 | 221 | 226 | .. | 0.5 | | 2.3 | | 2.4 | 22.6 |
| Cent.Afr.Rep. | TF | .. | 26 | .. | .. | .. | .. | 0.1 | | | | | |
| Chad | THS | 9 | 19 | 43 | 57 | 32 | 21 | 0.1 | 0.1 | -43.1 | -35.2 | 16.1 | 17.7 |
| Congo | THS | 33 | 37 | 19 | 28 | .. | .. | 0.2 | | | | 2.3 | -12.5 |
| .Dem.R.Congo | TF | 55 | 35 | 103 | 55 | 28 | 35 | 0.2 | 0.1 | -48.6 | 24.7 | -8.6 | 24.1 |
| Gabon | TF | 109 | 125 | 155 | 169 | 208 | 222 | 0.6 | 0.7 | 23.1 | 6.7 | 2.8 | 4.4 |
| Sao Tome Prn | TF | 3 | 6 | 7 | 8 | 9 | 14 | 0.0 | 0.0 | 22.8 | 46.3 | 15.6 | 2.7 |
| **East Africa** | | **2,842** | **5,186** | **7,073** | **7,312** | **7,324** | **7,796** | **25.0** | **25.3** | **0.2** | **6.4** | **12.8** | **6.4** |
| Burundi | TF | 109 | 34 | 29 | 36 | .. | .. | 0.2 | | | | -20.8 | -3.1 |
| Comoros | TF | 8 | 23 | 24 | 19 | 19 | .. | 0.1 | | -2.2 | | 23.5 | 0.9 |
| Djibouti | TF | 33 | 21 | 20 | 22 | 23 | 23 | 0.1 | 0.1 | 4.2 | 3.1 | -8.6 | -0.9 |
| Eritrea | VF | .. | 315 | 70 | 113 | 101 | 80 | 1.5 | 0.3 | -10.8 | -20.6 | | -26.0 |
| Ethiopia | TF | 79 | 103 | 136 | 148 | 156 | 180 | 0.5 | 0.6 | 5.3 | 15.1 | 5.4 | 5.7 |
| Kenya | TF | 814 | 896 | 899 | 841 | 838 | 927 | 4.3 | 3.0 | -0.4 | 10.6 | 1.9 | 0.1 |
| Madagascar | TF | 53 | 75 | 160 | 170 | 62 | 139 | 0.4 | 0.5 | -63.8 | 125.8 | 7.2 | 16.4 |
| Malawi | TF | 130 | 192 | 228 | 266 | 383 | 421 | 0.9 | 1.4 | 43.7 | 10.0 | 8.1 | 3.5 |
| Mauritius | TF | 292 | 422 | 656 | 660 | 682 | 702 | 2.0 | 2.3 | 3.2 | 3.0 | 7.6 | 9.2 |
| Mozambique | | .. | .. | .. | .. | 943 | 900 | | 2.9 | | -4.6 | | |
| Reunion | TF | 200 | 304 | 430 | 424 | 426 | 432 | 1.5 | 1.4 | 0.5 | 1.4 | 8.7 | 7.2 |
| Rwanda | TF | .. | .. | 104 | 113 | .. | .. | | | | | | |
| Seychelles | TF | 104 | 121 | 130 | 130 | 132 | 122 | 0.6 | 0.4 | 1.9 | -7.7 | 3.1 | 1.4 |
| Tanzania | TF | .. | 285 | 459 | 501 | 550 | 552 | 1.4 | 1.8 | 9.8 | 0.4 | | 10.0 |
| Uganda | TF | 69 | 160 | 193 | 205 | 254 | 305 | 0.8 | 1.0 | 23.8 | 19.8 | 18.3 | 3.8 |
| Zambia | TF | 141 | 163 | 457 | 492 | 565 | 578 | 0.8 | 1.9 | 14.9 | 2.2 | 2.9 | 22.9 |
| Zimbabwe | VF | 636 | 1,416 | 1,967 | 2,217 | 2,041 | 2,256 | 6.8 | 7.3 | -7.9 | 10.5 | 17.4 | 6.8 |
| **Southern Africa** | | **2,203** | **5,991** | **8,235** | **8,099** | **8,804** | **8,778** | **28.9** | **28.5** | **8.7** | **-0.3** | **22.1** | **6.6** |
| Botswana | TF | 543 | 521 | 1,104 | 1,049 | 1,037 | 975 | 2.5 | 3.2 | -1.2 | -5.9 | -0.8 | 16.2 |
| Lesotho | TF | 171 | 87 | .. | .. | .. | .. | 0.4 | | | | -12.6 | |
| Namibia | TF | .. | 399 | .. | 670 | 757 | 695 | 1.9 | 2.3 | 12.9 | -8.2 | | |
| South Africa | VF | 1,029 | 4,684 | 6,001 | 5,908 | 6,550 | 6,640 | 22.6 | 21.5 | 10.9 | 1.4 | 35.4 | 5.1 |
| Swaziland | THS | 263 | 300 | 281 | 283 | 256 | .. | 1.4 | | -9.6 | | 2.7 | -1.3 |

Source: World Tourism Organization (WTO) ©

(Data as collected by WTO December 2004)

**International Tourist Arrivals by Country of Destination**

| | Series | International Tourist Arrivals (1000) | | | | | | Market share in the region (%) | | Change (%) | | Average annual growth (%) | |
|---|---|---|---|---|---|---|---|---|---|---|---|---|---|
| | | 1990 | 1995 | 2000 | 2001 | 2002 | 2003* | 1995 | 2003* | 02/01 | 03*/02 | 90-95 | 95-00 |
| ***Americas*** | | ***92,795*** | ***108,994*** | ***128,222*** | ***122,164*** | ***116,611*** | ***112,987*** | ***100*** | ***100*** | ***-4.5*** | ***-3.1*** | ***3.3*** | ***3.3*** |
| **North America** | | **71,743** | **80,663** | **91,487** | **86,396** | **83,249** | **77,411** | **74.0** | **68.5** | **-3.6** | **-7.0** | **2.4** | **2.6** |
| Canada | TF | 15,209 | 16,932 | 19,627 | 19,679 | 20,057 | 17,534 | 15.5 | 15.5 | 1.9 | -12.6 | 2.2 | 3.0 |
| Mexico | TF | 17,172 | 20,241 | 20,641 | 19,810 | 19,667 | 18,665 | 18.6 | 16.5 | -0.7 | -5.1 | 3.3 | 0.4 |
| United States | TF | 39,362 | 43,490 | 51,219 | 46,907 | 43,525 | 41,212 | 39.9 | 36.5 | -7.2 | -5.3 | 2.0 | 3.3 |
| **Caribbean** | | **11,384** | **14,024** | **17,179** | **16,885** | **16,066** | **17,061** | **12.9** | **15.1** | **-4.8** | **6.2** | **4.3** | **4.1** |
| Anguilla | TF | 31 | 39 | 44 | 48 | 44 | 47 | 0.0 | 0.0 | -8.3 | 6.7 | 4.7 | 2.4 |
| Antigua,Barb | TF | 206 | 220 | 230 | 215 | 218 | 234 | 0.2 | 0.2 | 1.7 | 7.3 | 1.3 | 0.9 |
| Aruba | TF | 433 | 619 | 721 | 691 | 643 | 642 | 0.6 | 0.6 | -7.1 | -0.1 | 7.4 | 3.1 |
| Bahamas | TF | 1,562 | 1,598 | 1,544 | 1,538 | 1,513 | 1,510 | 1.5 | 1.3 | -1.6 | -0.2 | 0.5 | -0.7 |
| Barbados | TF | 432 | 442 | 545 | 507 | 498 | 531 | 0.4 | 0.5 | -1.8 | 6.7 | 0.5 | 4.3 |
| Bermuda | TF | 435 | 387 | 332 | 278 | 284 | 257 | 0.4 | 0.2 | 2.1 | -9.7 | -2.3 | -3.0 |
| Bonaire | TF | 37 | 59 | 51 | 50 | 52 | 64 | 0.1 | 0.1 | 3.4 | 23.2 | 9.8 | -2.9 |
| Br.Virgin Is | TF | 160 | 219 | 281 | 296 | 285 | .. | 0.2 | | -3.7 | | 6.5 | 5.1 |
| Cayman Islands | TF | 253 | 361 | 354 | 334 | 303 | 294 | 0.3 | 0.3 | -9.4 | -2.9 | 7.4 | -0.4 |
| Cuba | TF | 327 | 742 | 1,741 | 1,736 | 1,656 | 1,847 | 0.7 | 1.6 | -4.6 | 11.5 | 17.8 | 18.6 |
| Curaçao | TF | 219 | 224 | 191 | 205 | 218 | 221 | 0.2 | 0.2 | 6.5 | 1.6 | 0.5 | -3.1 |
| Dominica | TF | 45 | 60 | 70 | 66 | 69 | 73 | 0.1 | 0.1 | 4.2 | 5.4 | 5.9 | 3.1 |
| Dominican Rp | TF | 1,305 | 1,776 | 2,978 | 2,882 | 2,811 | 3,282 | 1.6 | 2.9 | -2.5 | 16.8 | 6.4 | 10.9 |
| Grenada | TF | 76 | 108 | 129 | 123 | 132 | 142 | 0.1 | 0.1 | 7.3 | 7.5 | 7.3 | 3.6 |
| Guadeloupe | TCE | 331 | 640 | 603 | 521 | .. | 439 | 0.6 | 0.4 | | | 14.1 | -1.2 |
| Haiti | TF | 144 | 145 | 140 | 142 | .. | .. | 0.1 | | | | 0.1 | -0.7 |
| Jamaica | TF | 989 | 1,147 | 1,323 | 1,277 | 1,266 | 1,350 | 1.1 | 1.2 | -0.8 | 6.6 | 3.0 | 2.9 |
| Martinique | TF | 282 | 457 | 526 | 460 | 447 | 453 | 0.4 | 0.4 | -3.0 | 1.4 | 10.1 | 2.9 |
| Montserrat | TF | 13 | 19 | 10 | 10 | 10 | 8 | 0.0 | 0.0 | -1.8 | -12.6 | 7.9 | -11.5 |
| Puerto Rico | TF | 2,560 | 3,131 | 3,341 | 3,551 | 3,087 | 3,238 | 2.9 | 2.9 | -13.1 | 4.9 | 4.1 | 1.3 |
| Saba | TF | .. | 10 | 9 | 9 | 11 | 10 | 0.0 | 0.0 | 22.2 | -6.7 | | -1.9 |
| Saint Lucia | TF | 141 | 231 | 270 | 250 | 253 | 277 | 0.2 | 0.2 | 1.3 | 9.3 | 10.4 | 3.2 |
| St.Eustatius | TF | .. | 9 | 9 | 10 | 10 | 11 | 0.0 | 0.0 | 1.0 | 7.1 | | 0.7 |
| St.Kitts-Nev | TF | 73 | 79 | 73 | 71 | 68 | 89 | 0.1 | 0.1 | -4.3 | 31.8 | 1.6 | -1.6 |
| St.Maarten | TF | 545 | 449 | 432 | 403 | 381 | 428 | 0.4 | 0.4 | -5.4 | 12.3 | -3.8 | -0.8 |
| St.Vincent,Grenadines | TF | 54 | 60 | 73 | 71 | 78 | 79 | 0.1 | 0.1 | 9.8 | 1.2 | 2.1 | 4.0 |
| Trinidad Tbg | TF | 195 | 260 | 399 | 383 | 384 | 409 | 0.2 | 0.4 | 0.3 | 6.5 | 5.9 | 8.9 |
| Turks,Caicos | TF | 49 | 79 | 152 | 166 | 155 | 164 | 0.1 | 0.1 | -6.6 | 5.5 | 10.0 | 14.0 |
| US.Virgin Is | TF | 463 | 454 | 607 | 592 | 553 | 538 | 0.4 | 0.5 | -6.6 | -2.7 | -0.4 | 6.0 |
| **Central America** | | **1,945** | **2,611** | **4,346** | **4,417** | **4,703** | **4,900** | **2.4** | **4.3** | **6.5** | **4.2** | **6.1** | **10.7** |
| Belize | TF | 197 | 131 | 196 | 196 | 200 | 221 | 0.1 | 0.2 | 2.0 | 10.5 | -7.8 | 8.4 |
| Costa Rica | TF | 435 | 785 | 1,088 | 1,131 | 1,113 | 1,239 | 0.7 | 1.1 | -1.6 | 11.3 | 12.5 | 6.7 |
| El Salvador | TF | 194 | 235 | 795 | 735 | 951 | 857 | 0.2 | 0.8 | 29.4 | -9.8 | 3.9 | 27.6 |
| Guatemala | TF | 509 | 563 | 826 | 835 | 884 | 880 | 0.5 | 0.8 | 5.8 | -0.4 | 2.0 | 8.0 |
| Honduras | TF | 290 | 271 | 471 | 518 | 550 | 611 | 0.2 | 0.5 | 6.1 | 11.1 | -1.3 | 11.7 |
| Nicaragua | TF | 106 | 281 | 486 | 483 | 472 | 526 | 0.3 | 0.5 | -2.3 | 11.5 | 21.5 | 11.6 |
| Panama | TF | 214 | 345 | 484 | 519 | 534 | 566 | 0.3 | 0.5 | 2.9 | 6.0 | 10.0 | 7.0 |
| **South America** | | **7,722** | **11,696** | **15,211** | **14,466** | **12,593** | **13,616** | **10.7** | **12.1** | **-13.0** | **8.1** | **8.7** | **5.4** |
| Argentina | TF | 1,930 | 2,289 | 2,909 | 2,620 | 2,820 | 2,995 | 2.1 | 2.7 | 7.6 | 6.2 | 3.5 | 4.9 |
| Bolivia | TF | 254 | 284 | 306 | 322 | 334 | 352 | 0.3 | 0.3 | 3.7 | 5.4 | 2.3 | 1.5 |
| Brazil | TF | 1,091 | 1,991 | 5,313 | 4,773 | 3,783 | 4,091 | 1.8 | 3.6 | -20.7 | 8.1 | 12.8 | 21.7 |
| Chile | TF | 943 | 1,540 | 1,742 | 1,723 | 1,412 | 1,614 | 1.4 | 1.4 | -18.0 | 14.3 | 10.3 | 2.5 |
| Colombia | TF | 813 | 1,399 | 557 | 616 | 541 | 624 | 1.3 | 0.6 | -12.1 | 15.3 | 11.5 | -16.8 |
| Ecuador | VF | 362 | 440 | 627 | 641 | 683 | 761 | 0.4 | 0.7 | 6.6 | 11.4 | 4.0 | 7.3 |
| French Guiana | TF | .. | .. | .. | 65 | 65 | .. | | | 0.0 | | | |
| Guyana | TF | 64 | 106 | 105 | 99 | 104 | 101 | 0.1 | 0.1 | 5.1 | -3.3 | 10.6 | -0.2 |
| Paraguay | TF | 280 | 438 | 289 | 279 | 250 | 268 | 0.4 | 0.2 | -10.1 | 7.1 | 9.4 | -8.0 |
| Peru | TF | 317 | 444 | 796 | 797 | 862 | 931 | 0.4 | 0.8 | 8.2 | 8.0 | 7.0 | 12.4 |
| Suriname | TF | 46 | 43 | 58 | .. | .. | .. | 0.0 | | | | -1.3 | 6.2 |
| Uruguay | TF | .. | 2,022 | 1,968 | 1,892 | 1,258 | 1,420 | 1.9 | 1.3 | -33.5 | 12.9 | | -0.5 |
| Venezuela | TF | 525 | 700 | 469 | 584 | 432 | 337 | 0.6 | 0.3 | -26.1 | -21.9 | 5.9 | -7.7 |

Source: World Tourism Organization (WTO) © (Data as collected by WTO December 2004)

**International Tourist Arrivals by Country of Destination**

| | | International Tourist Arrivals (1000) | | | | | | Market share in the region (%) | | Change (%) | | Average annual growth (%) | |
|---|---|---|---|---|---|---|---|---|---|---|---|---|---|
| | Series | 1990 | 1995 | 2000 | 2001 | 2002 | 2003* | 1995 | 2003* | 02/01 | 03*/02 | 90-95 | 95-00 |
| ***Asia and the Pacific*** | | ***57,740*** | ***85,024*** | ***114,863*** | ***120,541*** | ***131,131*** | ***119,268*** | ***100*** | ***100*** | ***8.8*** | ***-9.0*** | ***8.0*** | ***6.2*** |
| **North-East Asia** | | **27,969** | **44,115** | **62,525** | **65,860** | **74,127** | **67,595** | **51.9** | **56.7** | **12.6** | **-8.8** | **9.5** | **7.2** |
| China | TF | 10,484 | 20,034 | 31,229 | 33,167 | 36,803 | 32,970 | 23.6 | 27.6 | 11.0 | -10.4 | 13.8 | 9.3 |
| Hong Kong (China) | VF | 6,581 | 10,200 | 13,059 | 13,725 | 16,566 | 15,537 | 12.0 | 13.0 | 20.7 | -6.2 | 9.2 | 5.1 |
| Japan | TF | 3,236 | 3,345 | 4,757 | 4,772 | 5,239 | 5,212 | 3.9 | 4.4 | 9.8 | -0.5 | 0.7 | 7.3 |
| Korea, D P Rp | * | 115 | .. | .. | .. | 400 | .. | | | | | | |
| Korea, Republic of | VF | 2,959 | 3,753 | 5,322 | 5,147 | 5,347 | 4,753 | 4.4 | 4.0 | 3.9 | -11.1 | 4.9 | 7.2 |
| Macao (China) | TF | 2,513 | 4,202 | 5,197 | 5,842 | 6,565 | 6,309 | 4.9 | 5.3 | 12.4 | -3.9 | 10.8 | 4.3 |
| Mongolia | TF | 147 | 108 | 137 | 166 | 229 | 201 | 0.1 | 0.2 | 37.9 | -12.1 | -6.0 | 4.9 |
| Taiwan (pr. of China) | VF | .. | 2,332 | 2,624 | 2,831 | 2,978 | 2,248 | 2.7 | 1.9 | 5.2 | -24.5 | | 2.4 |
| **South-East Asia** | | **21,469** | **28,592** | **37,006** | **39,809** | **42,038** | **36,273** | **33.6** | **30.4** | **5.6** | **-13.7** | **5.9** | **5.3** |
| Brunei Darussalam | VF | 377 | 498 | 984 | 840 | .. | .. | 0.6 | | | | 5.7 | 14.6 |
| Cambodia | TF | 17 | 220 | 466 | 408 | 787 | 701 | 0.3 | 0.6 | 92.6 | -10.9 | 66.9 | 16.2 |
| Indonesia | TF | 2,178 | 4,324 | 5,064 | 5,154 | 5,033 | 4,467 | 5.1 | 3.7 | -2.3 | -11.3 | 14.7 | 3.2 |
| Lao P.D.R. | TF | 14 | 60 | 191 | 173 | 215 | 196 | 0.1 | 0.2 | 24.3 | -8.8 | 33.8 | 26.1 |
| Malaysia | TF | 7,446 | 7,469 | 10,222 | 12,775 | 13,292 | 10,577 | 8.8 | 8.9 | 4.0 | -20.4 | 0.1 | 6.5 |
| Myanmar | TF | 21 | 117 | 208 | 205 | 217 | 206 | 0.1 | 0.2 | 6.0 | -5.3 | 41.0 | 12.2 |
| Philippines | TF | 1,025 | 1,760 | 1,992 | 1,797 | 1,933 | 1,907 | 2.1 | 1.6 | 7.6 | -1.3 | 11.4 | 2.5 |
| Singapore | TF | 4,842 | 6,422 | 6,917 | 6,725 | 6,997 | 5,705 | 7.6 | 4.8 | 4.0 | -18.5 | 5.8 | 1.5 |
| Thailand | TF | 5,299 | 6,952 | 9,579 | 10,133 | 10,873 | 10,082 | 8.2 | 8.5 | 7.3 | -7.3 | 5.6 | 6.6 |
| Vietnam | TF | 250 | .. | 1,383 | 1,599 | .. | .. | | | | | | |
| **Oceania** | | **5,152** | **8,085** | **9,247** | **9,061** | **9,133** | **9,042** | **9.5** | **7.6** | **0.8** | **-1.0** | **9.4** | **2.7** |
| American Samoa | TF | 26 | 34 | 44 | 36 | .. | .. | 0.0 | | | | 5.5 | 5.3 |
| Australia | VF/TF | 2,215 | 3,726 | 4,530 | 4,435 | 4,420 | 4,354 | 4.4 | 3.7 | -0.3 | -1.5 | 11.0 | 4.0 |
| Cook Is | TF | 34 | 48 | 73 | 75 | 73 | 78 | 0.1 | 0.1 | -2.4 | 7.6 | 7.1 | 8.7 |
| Fiji | TF | 279 | 318 | 294 | 348 | 398 | 431 | 0.4 | 0.4 | 14.3 | 8.3 | 2.7 | -1.6 |
| French Polynesia | TF | 132 | 172 | 252 | 228 | 189 | 213 | 0.2 | 0.2 | -16.9 | 12.5 | 5.4 | 7.9 |
| Guam | TF | 780 | 1,362 | 1,287 | 1,160 | 1,059 | 910 | 1.6 | 0.8 | -8.7 | -14.1 | 11.8 | -1.1 |
| Kiribati | TF | 3 | 4 | 5 | 5 | 5 | .. | 0.0 | | 17.4 | | 5.4 | 4.2 |
| Marshall Is | TF | 5 | 6 | 5 | 5 | 6 | 7 | 0.0 | 0.0 | 10.2 | 19.9 | 1.9 | -1.1 |
| Micronesia (Fed.St.of) | TF | .. | .. | 21 | 15 | 19 | 18 | | 0.0 | 24.8 | -4.6 | | |
| N.Mariana Is | TF | 426 | 669 | 517 | 438 | 466 | 452 | 0.8 | 0.4 | 6.4 | -3.0 | 9.4 | -5.0 |
| New Caledonia | TF | 87 | 86 | 110 | 101 | 104 | 102 | 0.1 | 0.1 | 3.4 | -1.9 | -0.2 | 5.0 |
| New Zealand | VF | 976 | 1,409 | 1,787 | 1,909 | 2,045 | 2,104 | 1.7 | 1.8 | 7.1 | 2.9 | 7.6 | 4.9 |
| Niue | TF | 1 | 2 | 2 | 1 | 2 | 3 | 0.0 | 0.0 | 48.1 | 29.9 | 17.1 | -6.2 |
| Palau | TF | 33 | 53 | 58 | 54 | 59 | 68 | 0.1 | 0.1 | 8.2 | 16.6 | 9.9 | 1.8 |
| Papua New Guinea | TF | 41 | 42 | 58 | 54 | 54 | 56 | 0.0 | 0.0 | -1.0 | 4.7 | 0.5 | 6.7 |
| Samoa | TF | 48 | 68 | 88 | 88 | 89 | 92 | 0.1 | 0.1 | 0.8 | 3.8 | 7.2 | 5.3 |
| Solomon Is | TF | 9 | 12 | .. | .. | .. | .. | 0.0 | | | | 5.9 | |
| Tonga | TF | 21 | 29 | 35 | 32 | 37 | 40 | 0.0 | 0.0 | 13.0 | 9.6 | 6.7 | 3.8 |
| Tuvalu | TF | 1 | 1 | 1 | 1 | 1 | 1 | 0.0 | 0.0 | 15.2 | 4.9 | -2.1 | 4.1 |
| Vanuatu | TF | 35 | 44 | 58 | 53 | 49 | 50 | 0.1 | 0.0 | -7.2 | 1.9 | 4.7 | 5.7 |
| **South Asia** | | **3,150** | **4,233** | **6,086** | **5,811** | **5,833** | **6,358** | **5.0** | **5.3** | **0.4** | **9.0** | **6.1** | **7.5** |
| Bangladesh | TF | 115 | 156 | 199 | 207 | 207 | 245 | 0.2 | 0.2 | 0.0 | 18.1 | 6.3 | 5.0 |
| Bhutan | TF | 2 | 5 | 8 | 6 | 6 | 6 | 0.0 | 0.0 | -12.6 | 12.5 | 19.1 | 9.6 |
| India | TF | 1,707 | 2,124 | 2,649 | 2,537 | 2,384 | 2,726 | 2.5 | 2.3 | -6.0 | 14.4 | 4.5 | 4.5 |
| Iran | TF | 154 | 489 | 1,342 | 1,402 | 1,585 | 1,500 | 0.6 | 1.3 | 13.0 | -5.4 | 26.0 | 22.4 |
| Maldives | TF | 195 | 315 | 467 | 461 | 485 | 564 | 0.4 | 0.5 | 5.1 | 16.3 | 10.1 | 8.2 |
| Nepal | TF | 255 | 363 | 464 | 361 | 275 | 338 | 0.4 | 0.3 | -23.7 | 22.7 | 7.3 | 5.0 |
| Pakistan | TF | 424 | 378 | 557 | 500 | 498 | 479 | 0.4 | 0.4 | -0.3 | -3.8 | -2.3 | 8.1 |
| Sri Lanka | TF | 298 | 403 | 400 | 337 | 393 | 501 | 0.5 | 0.4 | 16.7 | 27.3 | 6.2 | -0.1 |

Source: World Tourism Organization (WTO) © (Data as collected by WTO December 2004)

**International Tourist Arrivals by Country of Destination**

| | | International Tourist Arrivals (1000) | | | | | | Market share in the region (%) | | Change (%) | | Average annual growth (%) | |
|---|---|---|---|---|---|---|---|---|---|---|---|---|---|
| | Series | 1990 | 1995 | 2000 | 2001 | 2002 | 2003* | 1995 | 2003* | 02/01 | 03*/02 | 90-95 | 95-00 |
| ***Europe*** | | ***270,364*** | ***316,410*** | ***389,591*** | ***387,813*** | ***397,305*** | ***398,952*** | ***100*** | ***100*** | ***2.4*** | ***0.4*** | ***3.2*** | ***4.2*** |
| **Northern Europe** | | **31,955** | **41,554** | **46,880** | **44,855** | **46,405** | **47,368** | **13.1** | **11.9** | **3.5** | **2.1** | **5.4** | **2.4** |
| Denmark | TCE | .. | .. | 2,088 | 2,028 | 2,010 | 2,016 | | 0.5 | -0.9 | 0.3 | | |
| Finland | TF | .. | 1,779 | 2,714 | 2,826 | 2,875 | 2,601 | 0.6 | 0.7 | 1.7 | -9.5 | | 8.8 |
| Iceland | TCE | 142 | 190 | 634 | 672 | 705 | 771 | 0.1 | 0.2 | 4.8 | 9.5 | 6.0 | 27.3 |
| Ireland | TF | 3,666 | 4,818 | 6,313 | 5,990 | 6,065 | 6,369 | 1.5 | 1.6 | 1.2 | 5.0 | 5.6 | 5.6 |
| Norway | TCE | 1,955 | 2,880 | 3,104 | 3,073 | 3,111 | 3,269 | 0.9 | 0.8 | 1.2 | 5.1 | 8.1 | 1.5 |
| Sweden | TCE/TF | .. | 2,310 | 2,746 | 7,431 | 7,459 | 7,627 | 0.7 | 1.9 | 0.4 | 2.3 | | 3.5 |
| United Kingdom | VF | 18,013 | 23,537 | 25,209 | 22,835 | 24,180 | 24,715 | 7.4 | 6.2 | 5.9 | 2.2 | 5.5 | 1.4 |
| **Western Europe** | | **108,627** | **112,184** | **139,659** | **135,818** | **137,961** | **136,070** | **35.5** | **34.1** | **1.6** | **-1.4** | **0.6** | **4.5** |
| Austria | TCE | 19,011 | 17,173 | 17,982 | 18,180 | 18,611 | 19,078 | 5.4 | 4.8 | 2.4 | 2.5 | -2.0 | 0.9 |
| Belgium | TCE | .. | 5,560 | 6,457 | 6,452 | 6,720 | 6,690 | 1.8 | 1.7 | 4.2 | -0.4 | | 3.0 |
| France | TF | 52,497 | 60,033 | 77,190 | 75,202 | 77,012 | 75,048 | 19.0 | 18.8 | 2.4 | -2.6 | 2.7 | 5.2 |
| Germany | TCE | 17,045 | 14,838 | 18,992 | 17,860 | 17,959 | 18,392 | 4.7 | 4.6 | 0.6 | 2.4 | -2.7 | 5.1 |
| Liechtenstein | THS | 78 | 59 | 62 | 56 | 49 | 49 | 0.0 | 0.0 | -13.7 | 0.6 | -5.4 | 1.0 |
| Luxembourg | TCE | 820 | 768 | 852 | 843 | 885 | 867 | 0.2 | 0.2 | 5.0 | -2.0 | -1.3 | 2.1 |
| Monaco | THS | 245 | 233 | 300 | 270 | 263 | 235 | 0.1 | 0.1 | -2.7 | -10.5 | -1.0 | 5.2 |
| Netherlands | TCE | 5,795 | 6,574 | 10,003 | 9,500 | 9,595 | 9,181 | 2.1 | 2.3 | 1.0 | -4.3 | 2.6 | 8.8 |
| Switzerland | TC | 7,963 | 6,946 | 7,821 | 7,455 | 6,868 | 6,530 | 2.2 | 1.6 | -7.9 | -4.9 | -2.7 | 2.4 |
| **Central/Eastern Europe** | | **35,876** | **59,993** | **62,297** | **63,452** | **65,341** | **67,763** | **19.0** | **17.0** | **3.0** | **3.7** | **10.8** | **0.8** |
| Armenia | TCE | .. | 12 | 45 | 123 | 162 | 206 | 0.0 | 0.1 | 31.5 | 27.1 | | 30.3 |
| Azerbaijan | TF | .. | 93 | 681 | 767 | 834 | .. | 0.0 | | 8.8 | | | 48.9 |
| Belarus | TF | .. | 161 | 60 | 61 | .. | 64 | 0.1 | 0.0 | | | | -17.9 |
| Bulgaria | TF | .. | 3,466 | 2,785 | 3,186 | 3,433 | 4,048 | 1.1 | 1.0 | 7.8 | 17.9 | | -4.3 |
| Czech Rep | TCE | .. | 3,381 | 4,666 | 5,194 | 4,579 | 5,076 | 1.1 | 1.3 | -11.8 | 10.8 | | 6.7 |
| Estonia | TF | .. | 530 | 1,220 | 1,320 | 1,362 | 1,462 | 0.2 | 0.4 | 3.2 | 7.3 | | 18.1 |
| Former U.S.S.R. | TF | 2,286 | .. | .. | .. | .. | .. | | | | | | |
| Georgia | TF | .. | 85 | 387 | 302 | 298 | .. | 0.0 | | -1.2 | | | 35.4 |
| Hungary | VF/2 | 20,510 | 20,690 | 15,571 | 15,340 | 15,870 | 15,706 | 6.5 | 3.9 | 3.5 | -1.0 | 0.2 | -5.5 |
| Kazakhstan | TF | .. | .. | 1,471 | 1,845 | 2,832 | 2,410 | | 0.6 | 53.5 | -14.9 | | |
| Kyrgyzstan | TF | .. | 36 | 59 | 99 | 140 | .. | 0.0 | | 41.6 | | | 10.4 |
| Latvia | TF | .. | 539 | 509 | 591 | 848 | 971 | 0.2 | 0.2 | 43.5 | 14.5 | | -1.1 |
| Lithuania | TF | .. | 650 | 1,083 | 1,271 | 1,428 | 1,491 | 0.2 | 0.4 | 12.4 | 4.4 | | 10.7 |
| Poland | TF | .. | 19,215 | 17,400 | 15,000 | 13,980 | 13,720 | 6.1 | 3.4 | -6.8 | -1.9 | | -2.0 |
| Rep Moldova | TF | .. | 32 | 18 | 16 | 18 | 21 | 0.0 | 0.0 | 12.5 | 16.7 | | -10.9 |
| Romania | TF | 3,099 | 2,757 | 3,274 | 3,300 | 3,204 | 3,739 | 0.9 | 0.9 | -2.9 | 16.7 | -2.3 | 3.5 |
| Russian Federation | TF | .. | .. | 7,030 | 7,400 | 7,943 | 8,015 | | 2.0 | 7.3 | 0.9 | | |
| Slovakia | TCE | 822 | 903 | 1,053 | 1,219 | 1,399 | 1,387 | 0.3 | 0.3 | 14.7 | -0.9 | 1.9 | 3.1 |
| Tajikistan | TF | .. | .. | 4 | 4 | .. | .. | | | | | | |
| Turkmenistan | TF | .. | 218 | .. | .. | .. | .. | 0.1 | | | | | |
| Ukraine | TF | .. | 3,716 | 4,406 | 5,791 | 6,326 | .. | 1.2 | | 9.2 | | | 3.5 |
| Uzbekistan | TF | .. | 92 | 302 | 345 | 332 | 231 | 0.0 | 0.1 | -3.9 | -30.3 | | 26.8 |
| **Southern Europe** | | **86,484** | **91,280** | **126,067** | **129,011** | **131,529** | **131,043** | **28.8** | **32.8** | **2.0** | **-0.4** | **1.1** | **6.7** |
| Albania | THS | 30 | 40 | 32 | 34 | 36 | 41 | 0.0 | 0.0 | 5.9 | 13.9 | 5.9 | -4.4 |
| Andorra | TF | .. | .. | 2,949 | 3,516 | 3,387 | 3,138 | | | -3.7 | -7.4 | | |
| Bosnia & Herzg | TCE | .. | .. | 171 | 139 | 160 | 165 | | 0.0 | 15.3 | 3.6 | | |
| Croatia | TCE | .. | 1,485 | 5,831 | 6,544 | 6,944 | 7,409 | 0.5 | 1.9 | 6.1 | 6.7 | | 31.5 |
| F.Yug.Rp.Macedonia | TCE | .. | 147 | 224 | 99 | 123 | 158 | 0.0 | 0.0 | 24.2 | 28.3 | | 8.8 |
| Greece | TF | 8,873 | 10,130 | 13,096 | 14,057 | 14,180 | 13,969 | 3.2 | 3.5 | 0.9 | -1.5 | 2.7 | 5.3 |
| Italy | TF | 26,679 | 31,052 | 41,181 | 39,563 | 39,799 | 39,604 | 9.8 | 9.9 | 0.6 | -0.5 | 3.1 | 5.8 |
| Malta | TF | 872 | 1,116 | 1,216 | 1,180 | 1,134 | 1,127 | 0.4 | 0.3 | -3.9 | -0.6 | 5.1 | 1.7 |
| Portugal | TF | 8,020 | 9,511 | 12,097 | 12,167 | 11,644 | 11,707 | 3.0 | 2.9 | -4.3 | 0.5 | 3.5 | 4.9 |
| San Marino | THS | 45 | 28 | 43 | 49 | 45 | 41 | 0.0 | 0.0 | -8.2 | -8.9 | -9.1 | 9.0 |
| Serbia & Montenegro | TCE | .. | 228 | 239 | 351 | 448 | 481 | 0.1 | 0.1 | 27.6 | 7.4 | | 0.9 |
| Slovenia | TC | .. | 732 | 1,090 | 1,219 | 1,302 | 1,373 | 0.2 | 0.3 | 6.8 | 5.5 | | 8.3 |
| Spain | TF | 34,085 | 34,920 | 47,898 | 50,094 | 52,327 | 51,830 | 11.0 | 13.0 | 4.5 | -1.0 | | 6.5 |
| Yugoslav SFR | | 7,880 | .. | .. | .. | .. | .. | | | | | | |
| **East Mediterranean Eu.** | | **7,423** | **11,398** | **14,689** | **14,676** | **16,070** | **16,707** | **3.6** | **4.2** | **9.5** | **4.0** | **9.0** | **5.2** |
| Cyprus | TF | 1,561 | 2,100 | 2,686 | 2,697 | 2,418 | 2,303 | 0.7 | 0.6 | -10.3 | -4.8 | 6.1 | 5.0 |
| Israel | TF | 1,063 | 2,215 | 2,417 | 1,196 | 862 | 1,063 | 0.7 | 0.3 | -27.9 | 23.4 | 15.8 | 1.8 |
| Turkey | TF | 4,799 | 7,083 | 9,586 | 10,783 | 12,790 | 13,341 | 2.2 | 3.3 | 18.6 | 4.3 | 8.1 | 6.2 |

Source: World Tourism Organization (WTO) © (Data as collected by WTO December 2004)

**International Tourist Arrivals by Country of Destination**

| | Series | International Tourist Arrivals (1000) | | | | | | Market share in the region (%) | | Change (%) | | Average annual growth (%) | |
|---|---|---|---|---|---|---|---|---|---|---|---|---|---|
| | | 1990 | 1995 | 2000 | 2001 | 2002 | 2003* | 1995 | 2003* | 02/01 | 03*/02 | 90-95 | 95-00 |
| ***Middle East*** | | ***9,772*** | ***13,780*** | ***24,256*** | ***24,011*** | ***27,879*** | ***28,813*** | ***100*** | ***100*** | ***16.1*** | ***3.4*** | ***7.1*** | ***12.0*** |
| Bahrain | TF | 1,376 | 1,396 | 2,420 | 2,789 | 3,167 | 2,955 | 10.1 | 10.3 | 13.6 | -6.7 | 0.3 | 11.6 |
| Egypt | TF | 2,411 | 2,871 | 5,116 | 4,357 | 4,906 | 5,746 | 20.8 | 19.9 | 12.6 | 17.1 | 3.6 | 12.2 |
| Iraq | VF | 748 | 61 | 78 | 127 | .. | .. | 0.4 | | | | -39.4 | 5.0 |
| Jordan | TF | 572 | 1,074 | 1,427 | 1,478 | 1,622 | 1,573 | 7.8 | 5.5 | 9.8 | -3.0 | 13.4 | 5.8 |
| Kuwait | THS | 15 | 72 | 78 | 73 | .. | .. | 0.5 | | | | 36.9 | 1.6 |
| Lebanon | TF | .. | 450 | 742 | 837 | 956 | 1,015 | 3.3 | 3.5 | 14.3 | 6.1 | | 10.5 |
| Libyan Arab Jamahiriya | TF | 96 | 56 | 174 | 169 | 135 | 142 | 0.4 | 0.5 | -20.1 | 5.2 | -10.2 | 25.5 |
| Oman | THS/TF | 149 | 279 | 571 \| | 829 | 817 | .. | 2.0 | | -1.4 | | 13.4 | 15.4 |
| Palestine | TF | .. | .. | 330 | 49 | 40 | 40 | | 0.1 | -18.4 | 0.0 | | |
| Qatar | TF | 136 | 294 | 67 | 76 | .. | .. | 2.1 | | | | 16.7 | -25.6 |
| Saudi Arabia | TF | 2,209 | 3,325 \| | 6,585 | 6,736 | 7,512 | 7,332 | 24.1 | 25.4 | 11.5 | -2.4 | 8.5 | 14.6 |
| Syrian Arab Republic | TCE | 562 | 815 | 1,416 | 1,318 \| | 2,870 | 2,788 | 5.9 | 9.7 | | | 7.7 | 11.7 |
| Untd Arab Emirates | THS | 973 | 2,315 | 3,907 | 4,134 | 5,445 | 5,871 | 16.8 | 20.4 | 31.7 | 7.8 | 18.9 | 11.0 |
| Yemen | THS | 52 | 61 | 73 | 76 | 89 | 148 | 0.4 | 0.5 | 17.1 | 66.6 | 3.2 | 3.7 |

Source: World Tourism Organization (WTO) © (Data as collected by WTO December 2004)

| : change of series.

# 2. International Tourism Receipts

**International Tourism Receipts, World**

| | International Tourism Receipts (billion) | | | | | | Change current prices (%) | | | | Change constant prices (%) | | | |
|---|---|---|---|---|---|---|---|---|---|---|---|---|---|---|
| | 1990 | 1995 | 2000 | 2001 | 2002 | 2003* | 00/99 | 01/00 | 02/01 | 03*/02 | 00/99 | 01/00 | 02/01 | 03*/02 |
| **Local currencies** | | | | | | | 13.6 | 4.0 | 3.7 | 1.4 | 9.2 | -0.4 | 0.3 | -1.9 |
| **US$** | 272.9 | 410.8 | 476.4 | 464.4 | 482.3 | 524.2 | 3.7 | -2.5 | 3.9 | 8.7 | 0.2 | -5.2 | 2.2 | 6.2 |
| **Euro** | 214.3 | 314.1 | 515.8 | 518.5 | 510.0 | 463.4 | 19.6 | 0.5 | -1.6 | -9.1 | 17.3 | -1.8 | -3.8 | -11.0 |

Source: World Tourism Organization (WTO) © (Data as collected by WTO December 2004)

**International Tourism Receipts by (Sub)region**

| | Change Local currencies, constant prices (%) | | | | US$ (billion) | | US$ Receipts per arrival | euro (billion) | | euro Receipts per arrival | Market share (%) |
|---|---|---|---|---|---|---|---|---|---|---|---|
| | 00/99 | 01/00 | 02/01 | 03*/02 | 2002 | 2003* | 2003* | 2002 | 2003* | 2003* | 2003* |
| **World** | **9.2** | **-0.4** | **0.3** | **-1.9** | **482.3** | **524.2** | **759** | **510.0** | **463.4** | **671** | **100** |
| ***Africa*** | ***5.2*** | ***15.3*** | ***4.8*** | ***-3.5*** | ***12.1*** | ***14.3*** | ***462*** | ***12.8*** | ***12.6*** | ***409*** | ***2.7*** |
| North Africa | 8.0 | 21.3 | -5.1 | -6.8 | 4.4 | 4.7 | 433 | 4.7 | 4.2 | 383 | 0.9 |
| West Africa | 26.6 | 11.7 | 6.2 | -6.3 | 1.3 | 1.4 | 537 | 1.4 | 1.3 | 474 | 0.3 |
| Central Africa | 2.5 | 54.4 | 17.3 | -10.5 | 0.3 | 0.3 | 489 | 0.3 | 0.3 | 432 | 0.1 |
| East Africa | -3.6 | 6.3 | -2.6 | 3.1 | 2.5 | 2.8 | 353 | 2.6 | 2.4 | 312 | 0.5 |
| Southern Africa | 1.7 | 14.1 | 23.1 | -2.3 | 3.5 | 5.0 | 570 | 3.7 | 4.4 | 504 | 1.0 |
| ***Americas*** | ***6.1*** | ***-10.3*** | ***-6.0*** | ***-1.2*** | ***113.8*** | ***114.4*** | ***1,012*** | ***120.3*** | ***101.1*** | ***895*** | ***21.8*** |
| North America | 5.9 | -12.8 | -6.5 | -4.5 | 86.3 | 84.5 | 1,092 | 91.2 | 74.7 | 965 | 16.1 |
| Caribbean | 4.8 | -3.0 | -3.0 | 12.3 | 16.7 | 17.9 | 1,052 | 17.6 | 15.9 | 930 | 3.4 |
| Central America | 15.1 | -5.1 | 4.3 | 6.9 | 3.1 | 3.4 | 688 | 3.3 | 3.0 | 608 | 0.6 |
| South America | 8.0 | 1.6 | -9.1 | 4.1 | 7.7 | 8.5 | 625 | 8.1 | 7.5 | 553 | 1.6 |
| ***Asia and the Pacific*** | ***8.1*** | ***7.5*** | ***6.9*** | ***-9.3*** | ***100.4*** | ***96.6*** | ***810*** | ***106.1*** | ***85.4*** | ***716*** | ***18.4*** |
| North-East Asia | 5.3 | 9.2 | 12.4 | -10.3 | 51.9 | 47.7 | 706 | 54.9 | 42.2 | 624 | 9.1 |
| South-East Asia | 12.7 | 8.1 | -1.4 | -16.6 | 27.8 | 24.4 | 672 | 29.4 | 21.5 | 594 | 4.6 |
| Oceania | 10.0 | 1.7 | 4.0 | -2.4 | 15.4 | 17.9 | 1,985 | 16.3 | 15.9 | 1,755 | 3.4 |
| South Asia | 4.1 | 5.1 | 8.9 | 19.2 | 5.2 | 6.5 | 1,024 | 5.5 | 5.8 | 905 | 1.2 |
| ***Europe*** | ***9.4*** | ***-0.5*** | ***-1.8*** | ***-2.7*** | ***243.2*** | ***285.1*** | ***715*** | ***257.2*** | ***252.0*** | ***632*** | ***54.4*** |
| Northern Europe | 3.7 | -3.1 | 3.3 | -2.1 | 37.1 | 42.0 | 886 | 39.3 | 37.1 | 783 | 8.0 |
| Western Europe | 11.7 | -1.0 | -0.1 | -2.5 | 87.6 | 103.6 | 761 | 92.7 | 91.6 | 673 | 19.8 |
| Central/Eastern Europe | -2.4 | -8.2 | -5.7 | -4.1 | 20.2 | 22.3 | 329 | 21.4 | 19.7 | 291 | 4.3 |
| Southern Europe | 10.7 | 1.8 | -4.4 | -1.2 | 82.4 | 100.0 | 763 | 87.2 | 88.4 | 675 | 19.1 |
| East Mediterranean Eu. | 21.3 | 5.5 | -3.6 | -11.1 | 15.8 | 17.3 | 1,033 | 16.7 | 15.3 | 913 | 3.3 |
| ***Middle East*** | ***11.3*** | ***-0.9*** | ***4.7*** | ***16.1*** | ***12.9*** | ***13.9*** | ***482*** | ***13.6*** | ***12.3*** | ***426*** | ***2.7*** |

Source: World Tourism Organization (WTO) © (Data as collected by WTO December 2004)

**International Tourism Receipts, 1950-2003***

| | World | Africa | Americas | Asia and the Pacific | Europe | Middle East | World | Africa | Americas | Asia and the Pacific | Europe | Middle East |
|---|---|---|---|---|---|---|---|---|---|---|---|---|
| | International Tourism Receipts (US$, billion) | | | | | | International Tourism Receipts (euro/ECU, billion) | | | | | |
| **1950** | 2.1 | 0.1 | 1.1 | 0.04 | 0.9 | 0.03 | | | | | | |
| **1960** | 6.9 | 0.2 | 2.5 | 0.2 | 3.9 | 0.1 | | | | | | |
| **1965** | 11.6 | 0.3 | 3.4 | 0.5 | 7.2 | 0.3 | | | | | | |
| **1970** | 17.9 | 0.5 | 4.8 | 1.2 | 11.0 | 0.4 | | | | | | |
| **1975** | 40.7 | 1.3 | 10.2 | 2.5 | 25.9 | 0.9 | 32.8 | 1.0 | 8.2 | 2.0 | 20.8 | 0.7 |
| **1980** | 106.5 | 2.6 | 25.4 | 11.3 | 63.7 | 3.5 | 76.5 | 1.9 | 18.3 | 8.1 | 45.7 | 2.5 |
| **1981** | 108.8 | 2.9 | 29.2 | 13.2 | 59.4 | 4.1 | 97.4 | 2.6 | 26.2 | 11.8 | 53.2 | 3.7 |
| **1982** | 103.0 | 2.7 | 25.1 | 13.4 | 58.0 | 3.9 | 105.2 | 2.8 | 25.7 | 13.6 | 59.2 | 3.9 |
| **1983** | 102.5 | 2.7 | 24.7 | 14.1 | 56.7 | 4.3 | 115.1 | 3.0 | 27.7 | 15.8 | 63.7 | 4.9 |
| **1984** | 112.9 | 2.5 | 31.9 | 15.1 | 58.8 | 4.6 | 143.1 | 3.2 | 40.5 | 19.2 | 74.5 | 5.8 |
| **1985** | 120.2 | 2.5 | 33.3 | 16.3 | 63.9 | 4.2 | 157.5 | 3.3 | 43.6 | 21.3 | 83.7 | 5.5 |
| **1986** | 145.9 | 2.9 | 38.4 | 21.0 | 80.2 | 3.4 | 148.3 | 3.0 | 39.0 | 21.3 | 81.5 | 3.4 |
| **1987** | 180.3 | 3.8 | 43.0 | 28.0 | 101.0 | 4.5 | 156.2 | 3.3 | 37.3 | 24.2 | 87.5 | 3.9 |
| **1988** | 209.2 | 4.6 | 51.3 | 36.7 | 112.2 | 4.3 | 176.9 | 3.9 | 43.4 | 31.1 | 94.9 | 3.7 |
| **1989** | 229.2 | 4.8 | 60.2 | 41.0 | 118.1 | 5.1 | 208.0 | 4.4 | 54.6 | 37.2 | 107.2 | 4.6 |
| **1990** | 272.9 | 5.6 | 69.2 | 46.7 | 145.7 | 5.6 | 214.3 | 4.4 | 54.4 | 36.6 | 114.4 | 4.4 |
| **1991** | 285.8 | 5.3 | 76.3 | 48.0 | 150.3 | 5.8 | 230.6 | 4.3 | 61.6 | 38.8 | 121.3 | 4.7 |
| **1992** | 328.6 | 6.8 | 83.6 | 56.3 | 174.5 | 7.5 | 253.2 | 5.3 | 64.4 | 43.3 | 134.4 | 5.8 |
| **1993** | 335.3 | 6.9 | 89.1 | 62.1 | 169.3 | 7.8 | 286.3 | 5.9 | 76.1 | 53.0 | 144.6 | 6.7 |
| **1994** | 365.6 | 7.6 | 92.4 | 73.0 | 183.8 | 8.8 | 307.3 | 6.4 | 77.7 | 61.4 | 154.5 | 7.4 |
| **1995** | 410.8 | 8.5 | 98.4 | 81.9 | 212.2 | 9.8 | 314.1 | 6.5 | 75.2 | 62.7 | 162.2 | 7.5 |
| **1996** | 446.0 | 9.6 | 108.3 | 92.8 | 224.5 | 10.9 | 351.3 | 7.6 | 85.3 | 73.1 | 176.8 | 8.6 |
| **1997** | 451.0 | 9.5 | 114.4 | 90.8 | 224.7 | 11.6 | 397.6 | 8.3 | 100.9 | 80.0 | 198.2 | 10.2 |
| **1998** | 448.6 | 10.2 | 115.1 | 77.5 | 234.8 | 10.9 | 400.1 | 9.1 | 102.7 | 69.1 | 209.5 | 9.7 |
| **1999** | 459.7 | 10.9 | 119.9 | 82.8 | 234.2 | 12.0 | 431.3 | 10.3 | 112.5 | 77.7 | 219.7 | 11.2 |
| **2000** | 476.4 | 10.6 | 131.0 | 89.0 | 232.5 | 13.2 | 515.8 | 11.5 | 141.8 | 96.4 | 251.8 | 14.3 |
| **2001** | 464.4 | 11.6 | 120.0 | 91.8 | 228.3 | 12.7 | 518.5 | 12.9 | 134.0 | 102.5 | 254.9 | 14.2 |
| **2002** | 482.3 | 12.1 | 113.8 | 100.4 | 243.2 | 12.9 | 510.0 | 12.8 | 120.3 | 106.1 | 257.2 | 13.6 |
| **2003*** | 524.2 | 14.3 | 114.4 | 96.6 | 285.1 | 13.9 | 463.4 | 12.6 | 101.1 | 85.4 | 252.0 | 12.3 |

Source: World Tourism Organization (WTO) © (Data as collected by WTO December 2004)

[1] Receipts data are in current US$ and euro (based on the average annual exchange rate for euro or ECU to US$) and can be strongly influenced by exchange rate fluctuations.

See for tables in euro values pages Annex - 16 to Annex - 20

**International Tourism Receipts by Country of Destination**

| | International Tourism Receipts (US$ million) | | | | | | Market share in the region (%) | | Change (%) | | Average annual growth (%) | |
|---|---|---|---|---|---|---|---|---|---|---|---|---|
| | 1990 | 1995 | 2000 | 2001 | 2002 | 2003* | 1995 | 2003* | 02/01 | 03*/02 | 90-95 | 95-00 |
| ***Africa*** | ***5,568*** | ***8,480*** | ***10,643*** | ***11,556*** | ***12,064*** | ***14,253*** | ***100*** | ***100*** | ***4.4*** | ***18.1*** | ***8.8*** | ***4.6*** |
| **North Africa** | **2,333** | **2,867** | **3,822** | **4,437** | **4,410** | **4,718** | **33.8** | **33.1** | **-0.6** | **7.0** | **4.2** | **5.9** |
| Algeria | 105 | 33 | 96 | 100 | 133 | 161 | 0.4 | 1.1 | 33.7 | 21.1 | -20.8 | 24.0 |
| Morocco | 1,259 | 1,296 | 2,039 | 2,583 | 2,646 | 2,856 | 15.3 | 20.0 | 2.4 | 7.9 | 0.6 | 9.5 |
| Sudan | 21 | 8 | 5 | 3 | 108 | 118 | 0.1 | 0.8 | | 9.3 | -17.6 | -9.0 |
| Tunisia | 948 | 1,530 | 1,682 | 1,751 | 1,523 | 1,583 | 18.0 | 11.1 | -13.0 | 3.9 | 10.0 | 1.9 |
| **West Africa** | **604** | **579** | **1,079** | **1,220** | **1,343** | **1,443** | **6.8** | **10.1** | **10.1** | **7.5** | **-0.8** | **13.3** |
| Benin | 55 | 85 | 77 | 85 | .. | .. | 1.0 | | | | 9.1 | -2.0 |
| Burkina Faso | 11 | .. | 19 | 20 | .. | .. | | | | | | |
| Cape Verde | 6 | 10 | 41 | 54 | 65 | 85 | 0.1 | 0.6 | 20.4 | 30.8 | 10.8 | 32.6 |
| Côte d'Ivoire | 51 | 89 | 49 | 53 | 51 | 84 | 1.0 | 0.6 | -3.8 | 64.7 | 11.8 | -11.3 |
| Gambia | 26 | 28 | .. | .. | .. | .. | 0.3 | | | | 1.5 | |
| Ghana | 81 | 11 | 335 | 351 | 358 | 414 | 0.1 | 2.9 | 2.0 | 15.6 | -32.9 | 98.0 |
| Guinea | 30 | 1 | 2 | 0 | .. | .. | 0.0 | | | | -49.4 | 14.9 |
| Guinea-Bissau | .. | .. | .. | 3 | 2 | .. | | | -33.3 | | | |
| Mali | 47 | 25 | 40 | 88 | 104 | .. | 0.3 | | 18.2 | | -11.9 | 9.9 |
| Mauritania | 9 | 11 | .. | .. | .. | .. | 0.1 | | | | 4.1 | |
| Niger | 17 | 15 | 28 | 32 | 28 | .. | 0.2 | | -12.5 | | -2.5 | 13.3 |
| Nigeria | 25 | 54 | 200 | 232 | 263 | .. | 0.6 | | 13.4 | | 16.7 | 29.9 |
| Senegal | 167 | 168 | 144 | 174 | 190 | 184 | 2.0 | 1.3 | 9.2 | -3.2 | 0.1 | -3.0 |
| Sierra Leone | 19 | 57 | 10 | 14 | 38 | 60 | 0.7 | 0.4 | 171.4 | 57.9 | 24.6 | -29.4 |
| Togo | 58 | 13 | 8 | 11 | 13 | .. | 0.2 | | 18.2 | | -25.9 | -9.3 |
| **Central Africa** | **98** | **135** | **155** | **244** | **313** | **335** | **1.6** | **2.3** | **28.0** | **7.0** | **6.6** | **2.9** |
| Angola | 13 | 10 | 18 | 22 | 60 | 71 | 0.1 | 0.5 | 172.7 | 18.3 | -5.1 | 12.5 |
| Cameroon | 53 | 36 | .. | .. | .. | .. | 0.4 | | | | -7.4 | |
| Cent.Afr.Rep. | 3 | 4 | 5 | 5 | 3 | .. | 0.0 | | -40.0 | | 5.9 | 4.6 |
| Chad | 8 | 43 | 14 | 23 | 25 | .. | 0.5 | | 8.7 | | 40.0 | -20.1 |
| Congo | 8 | 14 | 12 | 22 | 25 | 20 | 0.2 | 0.1 | 13.6 | -20.0 | 11.8 | -3.0 |
| Dem.R.Congo | 7 | .. | .. | .. | .. | .. | | | | | | |
| Equatorial Guinea | 1 | 1 | 5 | 14 | .. | .. | 0.0 | | | | 0.0 | 38.0 |
| Gabon | 3 | 17 | .. | 17 | .. | .. | 0.2 | | | | 41.5 | |
| Sao Tome Prn | 2 | .. | 10 | 10 | 10 | .. | | | 0.0 | | | |
| **East Africa** | **1,292** | **2,258** | **2,376** | **2,498** | **2,502** | **2,751** | **26.6** | **19.3** | **0.2** | **10.0** | **11.8** | **1.0** |
| Burundi | 4 | 1 | 1 | 1 | 1 | 1 | 0.0 | 0.0 | 120.0 | -36.4 | -18.9 | -10.6 |
| Comoros | 2 | 21 | .. | .. | .. | .. | 0.2 | | | | 60.0 | |
| Djibouti | .. | 4 | .. | .. | .. | .. | 0.0 | | | | | |
| Eritrea | .. | 58 | 36 | 74 | 73 | .. | 0.7 | | -1.4 | | | -9.1 |
| Ethiopia | 25 | 16 | 57 | 51 | 72 | .. | 0.2 | | 41.2 | | -8.5 | 28.9 |
| Kenya | 443 | 486 | 283 | 309 | 276 | 339 | 5.7 | 2.4 | -10.7 | 22.8 | 1.9 | -10.3 |
| Madagascar | 40 | 58 | 121 | 115 | 36 | 76 | 0.7 | 0.5 | -68.7 | 111.1 | 7.7 | 15.8 |
| Malawi | 16 | 17 | 25 | 25 | 33 | 33 | 0.2 | 0.2 | 32.0 | 0.0 | 1.2 | 8.0 |
| Mauritius | 244 | 430 | 542 | 623 | 612 | 697 | 5.1 | 4.9 | -1.8 | 13.9 | 12.0 | 4.7 |
| Mozambique | .. | .. | 74 | 64 | 63 | 98 | | 0.7 | -1.1 | 55.2 | | |
| Reunion | .. | 216 | 276 | 272 | 302 | 311 | 2.5 | 2.2 | 11.0 | 3.0 | | 5.0 |
| Rwanda | 10 | 2 | 23 | 25 | 31 | .. | 0.0 | | 24.0 | | -27.5 | 63.0 |
| Seychelles | 126 | 129 | 139 | 146 | 164 | 171 | 1.5 | 1.2 | 12.4 | 4.4 | 0.5 | 1.5 |
| Tanzania | 65 | 502 | 377 | 413 | 439 | 450 | 5.9 | 3.2 | 6.3 | 2.5 | 50.5 | -5.6 |
| Uganda | 10 | 78 | 165 | 165 | 171 | 189 | 0.9 | 1.3 | 3.6 | 10.5 | 50.8 | 16.2 |
| Zambia | 41 | 47 | 111 | 117 | 134 | 149 | 0.6 | 1.0 | 14.5 | 11.2 | 2.8 | 18.8 |
| Zimbabwe | 60 | 145 | 125 | 81 | 76 | 44 | 1.7 | 0.3 | -6.2 | -42.1 | 19.3 | -2.9 |
| **Southern Africa** | **1,241** | **2,641** | **3,211** | **3,157** | **3,496** | **5,006** | **31.1** | **35.1** | **10.7** | **43.2** | **16.3** | **4.0** |
| Botswana | 117 | 162 | 313 | 300 | 309 | 356 | 1.9 | 2.5 | 3.0 | 15.2 | 6.7 | 14.1 |
| Lesotho | 17 | 27 | 24 | 23 | 20 | .. | 0.3 | | -13.0 | | 9.7 | -2.3 |
| Namibia | 85 | 278 | 160 | 236 | 218 | 333 | 3.3 | 2.3 | -7.6 | 52.8 | 26.7 | -10.5 |
| South Africa | 992 | 2,126 | 2,677 | 2,569 | 2,923 | 4,270 | 25.1 | 30.0 | 13.8 | 46.1 | 16.5 | 4.7 |
| Swaziland | 30 | 48 | 37 | 29 | 26 | .. | 0.6 | | -10.3 | | 9.9 | -5.1 |

Source: World Tourism Organization (WTO) ©  (Data as collected by WTO December 2004)

**International Tourism Receipts by Country of Destination**

| | International Tourism Receipts (US$ million) | | | | | | Market share in the region (%) | | Change (%) | | Average annual growth (%) | |
|---|---|---|---|---|---|---|---|---|---|---|---|---|
| | 1990 | 1995 | 2000 | 2001 | 2002 | 2003* | 1995 | 2003* | 02/01 | 03*/02 | 90-95 | 95-00 |
| ***Americas*** | ***69,241*** | ***98,423*** | ***130,974*** | ***120,035*** | ***113,760*** | ***114,374*** | ***100*** | ***100*** | ***-5.2*** | ***0.5*** | ***7.3*** | ***5.9*** |
| **North America** | **54,813** | **77,491** | **101,472** | **90,903** | **86,277** | **84,545** | **78.7** | **73.9** | **-5.1** | **-2.0** | **7.2** | **5.5** |
| Canada | 6,339 | 7,917 | 10,778 | 10,609 | 10,691 | 10,579 | 8.0 | 9.2 | 0.8 | -1.0 | 4.5 | 6.4 |
| Mexico | 5,467 | 6,179 | 8,294 | 8,401 | 8,858 | 9,457 | 6.3 | 8.3 | 5.4 | 6.8 | 2.5 | 6.1 |
| United States | 43,007 | 63,395 | 82,400 | 71,893 | 66,728 | 64,509 | 64.4 | 56.4 | -7.2 | -3.3 | 8.1 | 5.4 |
| **Caribbean** | **8,716** | **12,239** | **17,175** | **17,108** | **16,676** | **17,945** | **12.4** | **15.7** | **-2.5** | **7.6** | **7.0** | **7.0** |
| Anguilla | 35 | 50 | 56 | 63 | 57 | 62 | 0.1 | 0.1 | -9.5 | 8.8 | 7.4 | 2.3 |
| Antigua,Barb | 298 | 247 | 291 | 272 | 274 | 301 | 0.3 | 0.3 | 0.7 | 9.9 | -3.7 | 3.3 |
| Aruba | 350 | 521 | 814 | 824 | 831 | 852 | 0.5 | 0.7 | 0.8 | 2.5 | 8.3 | 9.3 |
| Bahamas | 1,324 | 1,346 | 1,738 | 1,648 | 1,762 | 1,782 | 1.4 | 1.6 | 6.9 | 1.1 | 0.3 | 5.2 |
| Barbados | 494 | 622 | 723 | 697 | 658 | 758 | 0.6 | 0.7 | -5.6 | 15.2 | 4.7 | 3.1 |
| Bermuda | 490 | 488 | 431 | 351 | 379 | 370 | 0.5 | 0.3 | 8.0 | -2.4 | -0.1 | -2.5 |
| Bonaire | 18 | 37 | 87 | 75 | 33 | 21 | 0.0 | 0.0 | -56.0 | -36.4 | 15.5 | 18.6 |
| Br.Virgin Is | 132 | 211 | 316 | 337 | 342 | .. | 0.2 | | 1.5 | | 9.8 | 8.4 |
| Cayman Islands | 236 | 394 | 559 | 585 | 607 | .. | 0.4 | | 3.8 | | 10.8 | 7.2 |
| Cuba | 243 | 963 | 1,737 | 1,692 | 1,633 | 1,846 | 1.0 | 1.6 | -3.5 | 13.0 | 31.7 | 12.5 |
| Curaçao | 120 | 175 | 227 | 253 | 273 | 284 | 0.2 | 0.2 | 7.9 | 4.0 | 7.8 | 5.3 |
| Dominica | 25 | 42 | 48 | 46 | 46 | 51 | 0.0 | 0.0 | 0.0 | 10.9 | 10.9 | 2.7 |
| Dominican Rp | 900 | 1,571 | 2,860 | 2,798 | 2,730 | 3,110 | 1.6 | 2.7 | -2.4 | 13.9 | 11.8 | 12.7 |
| Grenada | 38 | 76 | 93 | 83 | 91 | 104 | 0.1 | 0.1 | 9.6 | 14.3 | 14.9 | 4.1 |
| Guadeloupe | 197 | 458 | 418 | .. | .. | .. | 0.5 | | | | 18.4 | -1.8 |
| Haiti | 46 | 90 | 128 | 105 | 112 | 93 | 0.1 | 0.1 | 6.7 | -17.0 | 14.4 | 7.3 |
| Jamaica | 740 | 1,069 | 1,333 | 1,232 | 1,209 | 1,355 | 1.1 | 1.2 | -1.9 | 12.1 | 7.6 | 4.5 |
| Martinique | 240 | 384 | 302 | 245 | 237 | 247 | 0.4 | 0.2 | -3.3 | 4.2 | 9.9 | -4.7 |
| Montserrat | 7 | 17 | 9 | 8 | 9 | 7 | 0.0 | 0.0 | 12.5 | -22.2 | 19.4 | -11.9 |
| Neth. Antilles | .. | 561 | 765 | 751 | 771 | 846 | 0.6 | 0.7 | 2.7 | 9.7 | | 6.4 |
| Puerto Rico | 1,366 | 1,828 | 2,388 | 2,728 | 2,486 | 2,677 | 1.9 | 2.3 | -8.9 | 7.7 | 6.0 | 5.5 |
| Saint Lucia | 154 | 230 | 279 | 237 | 215 | 282 | 0.2 | 0.2 | -9.3 | 31.2 | 8.4 | 3.9 |
| St.Kitts-Nev | 58 | 63 | 58 | 62 | 56 | 61 | 0.1 | 0.1 | -9.7 | 8.9 | 1.7 | -1.6 |
| St.Maarten | 316 | 349 | 498 | 493 | .. | .. | 0.4 | | | | 2.0 | 7.4 |
| St.Vincent,Grenadines | 56 | 53 | 75 | 80 | 83 | 85 | 0.1 | 0.1 | 3.8 | 2.4 | -1.1 | 7.2 |
| Trinidad Tbg | 95 | 77 | 213 | 201 | 242 | .. | 0.1 | | 20.4 | | -4.1 | 22.6 |
| Turks,Caicos | 37 | 53 | 285 | 311 | 292 | .. | 0.1 | | -6.1 | | 7.5 | 40.0 |
| US.Virgin Is | 697 | 822 | 1,206 | 1,323 | 1,195 | 1,271 | 0.8 | 1.1 | -9.7 | 6.4 | 3.4 | 8.0 |
| **Central America** | **735** | **1,496** | **2,970** | **2,933** | **3,120** | **3,369** | **1.5** | **2.9** | **6.4** | **8.0** | **15.3** | **14.7** |
| Belize | 44 | 78 | 122 | 120 | 130 | 156 | 0.1 | 0.1 | 8.3 | 20.0 | 12.1 | 9.4 |
| Costa Rica | 275 | 681 | 1,302 | 1,173 | 1,161 | 1,293 | 0.7 | 1.1 | -1.0 | 11.4 | 19.9 | 13.8 |
| El Salvador | 18 | 85 | 217 | 201 | 245 | 226 | 0.1 | 0.2 | 21.9 | -7.8 | 36.4 | 20.6 |
| Guatemala | 185 | 213 | 482 | 562 | 620 | 621 | 0.2 | 0.5 | 10.3 | 0.2 | 2.9 | 17.7 |
| Honduras | 29 | 80 | 260 | 256 | 301 | 337 | 0.1 | 0.3 | 17.6 | 12.0 | 22.5 | 26.6 |
| Nicaragua | 12 | 50 | 129 | 135 | 135 | 151 | 0.1 | 0.1 | 0.0 | 11.9 | 33.0 | 20.9 |
| Panama | 172 | 309 | 458 | 486 | 528 | 585 | 0.3 | 0.5 | 8.6 | 10.8 | 12.4 | 8.2 |
| **South America** | **4,977** | **7,197** | **9,358** | **9,091** | **7,687** | **8,515** | **7.3** | **7.4** | **-15.4** | **10.8** | **7.7** | **5.4** |
| Argentina | 1,131 | 2,222 | 2,904 | 2,642 | 1,535 | 2,097 | 2.3 | 1.8 | -41.9 | 36.6 | 14.5 | 5.5 |
| Bolivia | 91 | 55 | 68 | 76 | 100 | 111 | 0.1 | 0.1 | 31.6 | 11.0 | -9.6 | 4.3 |
| Brazil | 1,492 | 972 | 1,810 | 1,731 | 1,998 | 2,479 | 1.0 | 2.2 | 15.5 | 24.1 | -8.2 | 13.2 |
| Chile | 540 | 911 | 819 | 799 | 898 | 860 | 0.9 | 0.8 | 12.4 | -4.2 | 11.0 | -2.1 |
| Colombia | 406 | 657 | 1,030 | 1,217 | 967 | 816 | 0.7 | 0.7 | -20.5 | -15.6 | 10.1 | 9.4 |
| Ecuador | 188 | 255 | 402 | 430 | 447 | 406 | 0.3 | 0.4 | 4.0 | -9.2 | 6.3 | 9.5 |
| French Guiana | .. | .. | .. | 42 | 45 | .. | | | 7.1 | | | |
| Guyana | 27 | 33 | 75 | 61 | 49 | 39 | 0.0 | 0.0 | -19.7 | -20.4 | 4.1 | 17.8 |
| Paraguay | 128 | 137 | 101 | 65 | 59 | 64 | 0.1 | 0.1 | -9.2 | 8.5 | 1.4 | -5.9 |
| Peru | 217 | 428 | 911 | 788 | 801 | 923 | 0.4 | 0.8 | 1.6 | 15.2 | 14.6 | 16.3 |
| Suriname | 1 | 21 | 16 | 14 | 3 | 4 | 0.0 | 0.0 | -78.6 | 33.3 | 83.8 | -5.3 |
| Uruguay | 238 | 611 | 713 | 611 | 351 | 345 | 0.6 | 0.3 | -42.6 | -1.7 | 20.8 | 3.1 |
| Venezuela | 496 | 849 | 423 | 615 | 434 | 323 | 0.9 | 0.3 | -29.4 | -25.6 | 11.3 | -13.0 |

Source: World Tourism Organization (WTO) ©

(Data as collected by WTO December 2004)

**International Tourism Receipts by Country of Destination**

| | International Tourism Receipts (US$ million) | | | | | | Market share in the region (%) | | Change (%) | | Average annual growth (%) | |
|---|---|---|---|---|---|---|---|---|---|---|---|---|
| | 1990 | 1995 | 2000 | 2001 | 2002 | 2003* | 1995 | 2003* | 02/01 | 03*/02 | 90-95 | 95-00 |
| ***Asia and the Pacific*** | ***46,669*** | ***81,948*** | ***89,042*** | ***91,811*** | ***100,369*** | ***96,557*** | ***100*** | ***100*** | ***9.3*** | ***-3.8*** | ***11.9*** | ***1.7*** |
| **North-East Asia** | **23,001** | **38,140** | **44,415** | **46,535** | **51,871** | **47,726** | **46.5** | **49.4** | **11.5** | **-8.0** | **10.6** | **3.1** |
| China | 2,218 | 8,730 | 16,231 | 17,792 | 20,385 | 17,406 | 10.7 | 18.0 | 14.6 | -14.6 | 31.5 | 13.2 |
| Hong Kong (China) | 5,032 | 9,604 | 5,872 | 5,905 | 7,503 | 7,657 | 11.7 | 7.9 | 27.1 | 2.1 | 13.8 | -9.4 |
| Japan | 3,578 | 3,224 | 3,373 | 3,306 | 3,497 | 8,848 | 3.9 | 9.2 | 5.8 | 153.0 | -2.1 | 0.9 |
| Korea, D P Rp | 29 | .. | .. | .. | 150 | .. | | | | | | |
| Korea, Republic of | 3,559 | 5,150 | 6,834 | 6,384 | 5,936 | 5,256 | 6.3 | 5.4 | -7.0 | -11.5 | 7.7 | 5.8 |
| Macao (China) | 1,473 | 3,233 | 3,205 | 3,745 | 4,440 | 5,303 | 3.9 | 5.5 | 18.6 | 19.4 | 17.0 | -0.2 |
| Mongolia | 5 | 21 | 36 | 39 | 130 | 143 | 0.0 | 0.1 | 233.3 | 10.0 | 33.2 | 11.4 |
| Taiwan (pr. of China) | 1,740 | 3,286 | 3,738 | 4,335 | 4,584 | 2,976 | 4.0 | 3.1 | 5.7 | -35.1 | 13.6 | 2.6 |
| **South-East Asia** | **14,478** | **26,698** | **25,949** | **26,735** | **27,846** | **24,370** | **32.6** | **25.2** | **4.2** | **-12.5** | **13.0** | **-0.6** |
| Cambodia | .. | 53 | 304 | 380 | 454 | 389 | 0.1 | 0.4 | 19.5 | -14.3 | | 41.8 |
| Indonesia | 2,105 | 5,229 | 4,975 | 5,276 | 5,285 | 4,037 | 6.4 | 4.2 | 0.2 | -23.6 | 20.0 | -1.0 |
| Lao P.D.R. | 3 | 51 | 114 | 104 | 113 | 87 | 0.1 | 0.1 | 8.7 | -23.0 | 76.2 | 17.5 |
| Malaysia | 1,667 | 3,969 | 5,011 | 6,863 | 7,118 | 5,901 | 4.8 | 6.1 | 3.7 | -17.1 | 18.9 | 4.8 |
| Myanmar | 9 | 151 | 162 | 109 | 102 | 58 | 0.2 | 0.1 | -6.4 | -43.1 | 75.8 | 1.4 |
| Philippines | 1,306 | 1,136 | 2,134 | 1,723 | 1,740 | 1,464 | 1.4 | 1.5 | 1.0 | -15.9 | -2.8 | 13.4 |
| Singapore | 4,937 | 7,646 | 5,229 | 4,617 | 4,463 | 3,998 | 9.3 | 4.1 | -3.3 | -10.4 | 9.1 | -7.3 |
| Thailand | 4,326 | 8,035 | 7,483 | 7,075 | 7,901 | 7,822 | 9.8 | 8.1 | 11.7 | -1.0 | 13.2 | -1.4 |
| Vietnam | 85 | .. | .. | .. | .. | .. | | | | | | |
| **Oceania** | **7,161** | **13,706** | **14,172** | **13,776** | **15,405** | **17,948** | **16.7** | **18.6** | **11.8** | **16.5** | **13.9** | **0.7** |
| American Samoa | 10 | .. | .. | .. | .. | .. | | | | | | |
| Australia | 4,088 | 7,857 | 8,482 | 8,062 | 8,578 | 10,318 | 9.6 | 10.7 | 6.4 | 20.3 | 14.0 | 1.5 |
| Cook Is | 16 | 28 | 36 | 38 | 46 | .. | 0.0 | | 21.1 | | 11.8 | 5.2 |
| Fiji | 202 | 291 | 181 | 217 | 261 | 349 | 0.4 | 0.4 | 20.3 | 33.7 | 7.6 | -9.1 |
| French Polynesia | 171 | 326 | .. | .. | .. | .. | 0.4 | | | | 13.8 | |
| Guam | 936 | .. | .. | .. | .. | .. | | | | | | |
| Kiribati | 1 | 2 | 3 | 3 | .. | .. | 0.0 | | | | 14.9 | 6.2 |
| Marshall Is | .. | 3 | 4 | 4 | 4 | .. | 0.0 | | 0.0 | | | 9.9 |
| Micronesia (Fed.St.of) | .. | .. | 15 | 15 | 17 | 17 | | 0.0 | 13.3 | 0.0 | | |
| N.Mariana Is | 455 | 655 | .. | .. | .. | .. | 0.8 | | | | 7.6 | |
| New Caledonia | 94 | 108 | 110 | 93 | 125 | .. | 0.1 | | 34.4 | | 2.8 | 0.4 |
| New Zealand | 1,030 | 2,318 | 2,267 | 2,360 | 3,006 | 3,974 | 2.8 | 4.1 | 27.4 | 32.2 | 17.6 | -0.4 |
| Niue | .. | 2 | .. | .. | .. | .. | 0.0 | | | | | |
| Palau | .. | .. | 53 | 59 | 59 | .. | | | 0.0 | | | |
| Papua New Guinea | 41 | 25 | 7 | 5 | .. | .. | 0.0 | | | | -9.4 | -22.5 |
| Samoa | 20 | 35 | 41 | 40 | 45 | 53 | 0.0 | 0.1 | 12.5 | 17.8 | 11.8 | 3.2 |
| Solomon Is | 7 | 16 | 4 | 5 | 1 | 2 | 0.0 | 0.0 | -80.0 | 100.0 | 18.0 | -24.2 |
| Tonga | 9 | 10 | 7 | 7 | 6 | .. | 0.0 | | -14.3 | | 2.1 | -6.9 |
| Vanuatu | 39 | 45 | 56 | 46 | .. | .. | 0.1 | | | | 2.9 | 4.5 |
| **South Asia** | **2,029** | **3,405** | **4,505** | **4,764** | **5,248** | **6,513** | **4.2** | **6.7** | **10.1** | **24.1** | **10.9** | **5.8** |
| Bangladesh | 11 | 25 | 50 | 48 | 57 | 57 | 0.0 | 0.1 | 18.8 | 0.0 | 17.8 | 14.9 |
| Bhutan | 2 | 5 | 10 | 9 | 8 | 8 | 0.0 | 0.0 | -11.3 | 4.3 | 20.1 | 14.9 |
| India | 1,513 | 2,582 | 3,168 | 3,042 | 2,923 | 3,522 | 3.2 | 3.6 | -3.9 | 20.5 | 11.3 | 4.2 |
| Iran | 61 | 67 | 467 | 891 | 1,357 | 1,777 | 0.1 | 1.8 | 52.3 | 31.0 | 1.9 | 47.5 |
| Maldives | 89 | 211 | 321 | 327 | 337 | 402 | 0.3 | 0.4 | 3.1 | 19.3 | 18.8 | 8.8 |
| Nepal | 64 | 177 | 158 | 144 | 103 | 199 | 0.2 | 0.2 | -28.5 | 93.2 | 22.6 | -2.2 |
| Pakistan | 156 | 110 | 81 | 88 | 97 | 120 | 0.1 | 0.1 | 10.2 | 23.7 | -6.7 | -5.9 |
| Sri Lanka | 132 | 226 | 248 | 213 | 363 | 424 | 0.3 | 0.4 | 70.4 | 16.8 | 11.4 | 1.9 |

Source: World Tourism Organization (WTO) © (Data as collected by WTO December 2004)

**International Tourism Receipts by Country of Destination**

| | International Tourism Receipts (US$ million) | | | | | | Market share in the region (%) | | Change (%) | | Average annual growth (%) | |
|---|---|---|---|---|---|---|---|---|---|---|---|---|
| | 1990 | 1995 | 2000 | 2001 | 2002 | 2003* | 1995 | 2003* | 02/01 | 03*/02 | 90-95 | 95-00 |
| ***Europe*** | ***145,741*** | ***212,187*** | ***232,541*** | ***228,254*** | ***243,235*** | ***285,108*** | ***100*** | ***100*** | ***6.6*** | ***17.2*** | ***7.8*** | ***1.8*** |
| **Northern Europe** | **26,261** | **33,981** | **35,818** | **33,547** | **37,121** | **41,951** | **16.0** | **14.7** | **10.7** | **13.0** | **5.3** | **1.1** |
| Denmark | 3,645 | 3,673 | 3,694 | 4,014 | 4,761 | 5,265 | 1.7 | 1.8 | 18.6 | 10.6 | 0.2 | 0.1 |
| Finland | 1,167 | 1,640 | 1,406 | 1,437 | 1,578 | 1,894 | 0.8 | 0.7 | 9.8 | 20.0 | 7.0 | -3.0 |
| Iceland | 139 | 186 | 227 | 232 | 256 | 319 | 0.1 | 0.1 | 10.3 | 24.6 | 6.0 | 4.1 |
| Ireland | 1,459 | 2,286 | 2,608 | 2,790 | 3,088 | 3,875 | 1.1 | 1.4 | 10.7 | 25.5 | 9.4 | 2.7 |
| Norway | 1,570 | 2,238 | 2,050 | 1,958 | 2,179 | 2,541 | 1.1 | 0.9 | 11.3 | 16.6 | 7.3 | -1.7 |
| Sweden | 2,906 | 3,471 | 4,064 | 4,253 | 4,710 | 5,304 | 1.6 | 1.9 | 10.7 | 12.6 | 3.6 | 3.2 |
| United Kingdom | 15,375 | 20,487 | 21,769 | 18,864 | 20,549 | 22,752 | 9.7 | 8.0 | 8.9 | 10.7 | 5.9 | 1.2 |
| **Western Europe** | **63,114** | **80,795** | **82,815** | **81,458** | **87,617** | **103,586** | **38.1** | **36.3** | **7.6** | **18.2** | **5.1** | **0.5** |
| Austria | 13,417 | 12,927 | 9,931 | 10,259 | 11,239 | 14,068 | 6.1 | 4.9 | 9.5 | 25.2 | -0.7 | -5.1 |
| Belgium | .. | 4,548 | 6,592 | 6,903 | 6,890 | 8,130 | 2.1 | 2.9 | -0.2 | 18.0 | | 7.7 |
| Belgium/Luxembourg | 3,702 | .. | .. | .. | .. | .. | | | | | | |
| France | 20,184 | 27,587 | 30,981 | 30,363 | 32,738 | 37,038 | 13.0 | 13.0 | 7.8 | 13.1 | 6.4 | 2.3 |
| Germany | 14,245 | 18,001 | 18,637 | 17,940 | 18,968 | 22,984 | 8.5 | 8.1 | 5.7 | 21.2 | 4.8 | 0.7 |
| Luxembourg | .. | 1,695 | 1,686 | 1,780 | 2,184 | 2,793 | 0.8 | 1.0 | 22.7 | 27.9 | | -0.1 |
| Netherlands | 4,155 | 6,578 | 7,197 | 6,708 | 7,710 | 9,249 | 3.1 | 3.2 | 14.9 | 20.0 | 9.6 | 1.8 |
| Switzerland | 7,411 | 9,459 | 7,791 | 7,505 | 7,888 | 9,325 | 4.5 | 3.3 | 5.1 | 18.2 | 5.0 | -3.8 |
| **Central/Eastern Europe** | **4,849** | **19,373** | **19,603** | **19,654** | **20,235** | **22,306** | **9.1** | **7.8** | **3.0** | **10.2** | **31.9** | **0.2** |
| Armenia | .. | 1 | 38 | 65 | 63 | 73 | 0.0 | 0.0 | -3.1 | 15.9 | | 107.0 |
| Azerbaijan | 228 | 70 | 63 | 43 | 51 | 58 | 0.0 | 0.0 | 18.6 | 13.7 | -21.0 | -2.1 |
| Belarus | .. | 23 | 93 | 171 | 234 | 267 | 0.0 | 0.1 | 36.8 | 14.1 | | 32.2 |
| Bulgaria | 320 | 473 | 1,074 | 963 | 1,154 | 1,658 | 0.2 | 0.6 | 19.8 | 43.7 | 8.1 | 17.8 |
| Czech Rep | 419 | 2,880 | 2,973 | 3,104 | 2,964 | 3,556 | 1.4 | 1.2 | -4.5 | 20.0 | 47.0 | 0.6 |
| Estonia | .. | 357 | 504 | 507 | 555 | 674 | 0.2 | 0.2 | 9.5 | 21.4 | | 7.1 |
| Georgia | .. | .. | 97 | 117 | 126 | 147 | | 0.1 | 7.7 | 16.7 | | |
| Hungary | 824 | 2,928 | 3,444 | 3,770 | 3,274 | 3,440 | 1.4 | 1.2 | -13.2 | 5.1 | 28.9 | 3.3 |
| Kazakhstan | .. | 122 | 356 | 452 | 622 | 564 | 0.1 | 0.2 | 37.6 | -9.3 | | 23.9 |
| Kyrgyzstan | .. | 5 | 15 | 24 | 36 | 48 | 0.0 | 0.0 | 50.0 | 33.3 | | 24.6 |
| Latvia | .. | 20 | 131 | 120 | 161 | 222 | 0.0 | 0.1 | 34.2 | 37.9 | | 45.6 |
| Lithuania | .. | 77 | 391 | 383 | 505 | 638 | 0.0 | 0.2 | 31.9 | 26.3 | | 38.4 |
| Poland | 358 | 6,614 | 5,677 | 4,646 | 4,314 | 4,069 | 3.1 | 1.4 | -7.1 | -5.7 | 79.2 | -3.0 |
| Rep Moldova | .. | 57 | 39 | 39 | 50 | 58 | 0.0 | 0.0 | 28.2 | 16.0 | | -7.3 |
| Romania | 106 | 590 | 359 | 362 | 335 | 449 | 0.3 | 0.2 | -7.5 | 34.0 | 41.0 | -9.5 |
| Russian Federation | .. | 4,312 | 3,430 | 3,572 | 4,167 | 4,502 | 2.0 | 1.6 | 16.7 | 8.0 | | -4.5 |
| Slovakia | 70 | 623 | 433 | 641 | 736 | 865 | 0.3 | 0.3 | 14.8 | 17.5 | 54.8 | -7.0 |
| Tajikistan | .. | .. | .. | .. | 2 | 2 | | 0.0 | | 0.0 | | |
| Ukraine | .. | 191 | 394 | 573 | 788 | 935 | 0.1 | 0.3 | 37.5 | 18.7 | | 15.6 |
| Uzbekistan | .. | .. | 63 | 72 | 68 | 48 | | 0.0 | -5.6 | -29.4 | | |
| **Southern Europe** | **44,467** | **66,492** | **77,885** | **79,059** | **82,425** | **100,008** | **31.3** | **35.1** | **4.3** | **21.3** | **8.4** | **3.2** |
| Albania | 4 | 65 | 389 | 446 | 487 | 522 | 0.0 | 0.2 | 9.2 | 7.2 | 74.7 | 43.0 |
| Bosnia & Herzg | .. | .. | 165 | 175 | 192 | 235 | | 0.1 | 9.7 | 22.4 | | |
| Croatia | .. | 1,349 | 2,758 | 3,335 | 3,811 | 6,376 | 0.6 | 2.2 | 14.3 | 67.3 | | 15.4 |
| F.Yug.Rp.Macedonia | .. | 19 | 38 | 26 | 39 | 57 | 0.0 | 0.0 | 50.0 | 46.2 | | 14.9 |
| Greece | 2,587 | 4,135 | 9,219 | 9,476 | 9,725 | 10,701 | 1.9 | 3.8 | 2.6 | 10.0 | 9.8 | 17.4 |
| Italy | 16,458 | 28,731 | 27,493 | 25,822 | 26,873 | 31,222 | 13.5 | 11.0 | 4.1 | 16.2 | 11.8 | -0.9 |
| Malta | 496 | 661 | 610 | 578 | 571 | 696 | 0.3 | 0.2 | -1.2 | 21.9 | 5.9 | -1.6 |
| Portugal | 3,555 | 4,831 | 5,243 | 5,470 | 5,761 | 6,937 | 2.3 | 2.4 | 5.3 | 20.4 | 6.3 | 1.7 |
| Serbia & Montenegro | .. | 42 | 30 | 54 | 97 | 150 | 0.0 | 0.1 | 79.6 | 54.6 | | -6.5 |
| Slovenia | .. | 1,084 | 961 | 987 | 1,086 | 1,342 | 0.5 | 0.5 | 10.0 | 23.6 | | -2.4 |
| Spain | 18,593 | 25,510 | 30,979 | 32,691 | 33,783 | 41,770 | 12.0 | 14.7 | 3.3 | 23.6 | 6.5 | 4.0 |
| Yugoslav SFR | 2,774 | .. | .. | .. | .. | .. | | | | | | |
| **East Mediterranean Eu.** | **7,050** | **11,546** | **16,420** | **14,536** | **15,837** | **17,257** | **5.4** | **6.1** | **9.0** | **9.0** | **10.4** | **7.3** |
| Cyprus | 1,258 | 1,797 | 1,938 | 2,006 | 1,897 | 2,015 | 0.8 | 0.7 | -5.4 | 6.2 | 7.4 | 1.5 |
| Israel | 1,396 | 2,993 | 4,074 | 2,463 | 2,039 | 2,039 | 1.4 | 0.7 | -17.2 | 0.0 | 16.5 | 6.4 |
| Turkey | 3,225 | 4,957 | 7,636 | 10,067 | 11,901 | 13,203 | 2.3 | 4.6 | 18.2 | 10.9 | 9.0 | 9.0 |

Source: World Tourism Organization (WTO) ©

(Data as collected by WTO December 2004)

**International Tourism Receipts by Country of Destination**

| | International Tourism Receipts (US$ million) | | | | | | Market share in the region (%) | | Change (%) | | Average annual growth (%) | |
|---|---|---|---|---|---|---|---|---|---|---|---|---|
| | 1990 | 1995 | 2000 | 2001 | 2002 | 2003* | 1995 | 2003* | 02/01 | 03*/02 | 90-95 | 95-00 |
| ***Middle East*** | ***5,645*** | ***9,786*** | ***13,239*** | ***12,702*** | ***12,858*** | ***13,897*** | ***100*** | ***100*** | ***1.2*** | ***8.1*** | ***11.6*** | ***6.2*** |
| Bahrain | 135 | 247 | 573 | 630 | 740 | 740 | 2.5 | 5.3 | 17.5 | 0.0 | 12.8 | 18.3 |
| Egypt | 1,100 | 2,684 | 4,345 | 3,800 | 3,764 | 4,584 | 27.4 | 33.0 | -0.9 | 21.8 | 19.5 | 10.1 |
| Jordan | 512 | 660 | 723 | 700 | 786 | 815 | 6.7 | 5.9 | 12.3 | 3.7 | 5.2 | 1.8 |
| Kuwait | 132 | 121 | 98 | 104 | 118 | 117 | 1.2 | 0.8 | 13.5 | -0.9 | -1.7 | -4.2 |
| Lebanon | .. | 710 | 742 | 837 | 956 | 1,016 | 7.3 | 7.3 | 14.2 | 6.3 | | 0.9 |
| Libyan Arab Jamahiriya | 6 | 2 | 97 | 94 | 75 | 79 | 0.0 | 0.6 | -20.2 | 5.3 | -19.7 | 117.3 |
| Oman | 69 | .. | 221 | 144 | 206 | 219 | | 1.6 | 43.1 | 6.3 | | |
| Palestine | .. | .. | 226 | 7 | 1 | 4 | | 0.0 | -85.7 | 300.0 | | |
| Saudi Arabia | .. | .. | .. | .. | 3,418 | .. | | | | | | |
| Syrian Arab Republic | 320 | 1,258 | 1,082 | 1,150\| | 1,424 | 1,408 | 12.9 | 10.1 | 23.8 | -1.1 | 31.5 | -3.0 |
| Untd Arab Emirates | 315 | 632 | 1,063 | 1,200 | 1,332 | 1,439 | 6.5 | 10.4 | 11.0 | 8.0 | 14.9 | 11.0 |
| Yemen | 20 | 50 | 73 | 38 | 38 | 139 | 0.5 | 1.0 | 0.0 | 265.8 | 20.1 | 7.9 |

Source: World Tourism Organization (WTO) © (Data as collected by WTO December 2004)

| : change of series.

See for tables in US$ values pages Annex - 11 to Annex - 15

**International Tourism Receipts by Country of Destination**

| | International Tourism Receipts (euro million) | | | | | | Market share in the region (%) | | Change (%) | | Average annual growth (%) | |
|---|---|---|---|---|---|---|---|---|---|---|---|---|
| | 1990 | 1995 | 2000 | 2001 | 2002 | 2003* | 1995 | 2003* | 02/01 | 03*/02 | 90-95 | 95-00 |
| ***Africa*** | ***4,373*** | ***6,483*** | ***11,523*** | ***12,903*** | ***12,758*** | ***12,600*** | ***100*** | ***100*** | ***-1.1*** | ***-1.2*** | ***8.2*** | ***12.2*** |
| **North Africa** | **1,832** | **2,192** | **4,138** | **4,953** | **4,664** | **4,171** | **33.8** | **33.1** | **-5.8** | **-10.6** | **3.6** | **13.6** |
| Algeria | 82 | 25 | 104 | 111 | 141 | 142 | 0.4 | 1.1 | 26.6 | 1.2 | -21.2 | 32.9 |
| Morocco | 989 | 991 | 2,208 | 2,884 | 2,798 | 2,525 | 15.3 | 20.0 | -3.0 | -9.8 | 0.0 | 17.4 |
| Sudan | 16 | 6 | 5 | 3 | 114 | 104 | 0.1 | 0.8 | | -8.7 | -18.0 | -2.4 |
| Tunisia | 744 | 1,170 | 1,821 | 1,955 | 1,611 | 1,399 | 18.0 | 11.1 | -17.6 | -13.1 | 9.5 | 9.3 |
| **West Africa** | **474** | **442** | **1,168** | **1,363** | **1,420** | **1,276** | **6.8** | **10.1** | **4.2** | **-10.2** | **-1.4** | **21.4** |
| Benin | 43 | 65 | 83 | 95 | .. | .. | 1.0 | | | | 8.5 | 5.1 |
| Burkina Faso | 9 | .. | 21 | 22 | .. | .. | | | | | | |
| Cape Verde | 5 | 8 | 44 | 60 | 69 | 75 | 0.1 | 0.6 | 14.0 | 9.3 | 10.2 | 42.2 |
| Côte d'Ivoire | 40 | 68 | 53 | 59 | 54 | 74 | 1.0 | 0.6 | -8.9 | 37.7 | 11.2 | -4.9 |
| Gambia | 20 | 21 | .. | .. | .. | .. | 0.3 | | | | 1.0 | |
| Ghana | 64 | 8 | 363 | 392 | 379 | 366 | 0.1 | 2.9 | -3.4 | -3.3 | -33.3 | 112.3 |
| Guinea | 24 | 1 | 2 | 0 | .. | .. | 0.0 | | | | -49.6 | 23.1 |
| Guinea-Bissau | .. | .. | .. | 3 | 2 | .. | | | -36.9 | | | |
| Mali | 37 | 19 | 43 | 98 | 110 | .. | 0.3 | | 11.9 | | -12.3 | 17.8 |
| Mauritania | 7 | 8 | .. | .. | .. | .. | 0.1 | | | | 3.5 | |
| Niger | 13 | 11 | 30 | 36 | 30 | .. | 0.2 | | -17.1 | | -3.0 | 21.5 |
| Nigeria | 20 | 41 | 217 | 259 | 278 | .. | 0.6 | | 7.4 | | 16.0 | 39.3 |
| Senegal | 131 | 128 | 156 | 194 | 201 | 163 | 2.0 | 1.3 | 3.4 | -19.0 | -0.4 | 4.0 |
| Sierra Leone | 15 | 44 | 11 | 16 | 40 | 53 | 0.7 | 0.4 | 157.1 | 32.0 | 23.9 | -24.3 |
| Togo | 46 | 10 | 9 | 12 | 14 | .. | 0.2 | | 11.9 | | -26.2 | -2.7 |
| **Central Africa** | **77** | **103** | **168** | **273** | **331** | **296** | **1.6** | **2.3** | **21.3** | **-10.6** | **6.1** | **10.3** |
| Angola | 10 | 8 | 19 | 25 | 63 | 63 | 0.1 | 0.5 | 158.3 | -1.1 | -5.6 | 20.6 |
| Cameroon | 42 | 28 | .. | .. | .. | .. | 0.4 | | | | -7.9 | |
| Cent.Afr.Rep. | 2 | 3 | 5 | 6 | 3 | .. | 0.0 | | -43.2 | | 5.4 | 12.1 |
| Chad | 6 | 33 | 15 | 26 | 26 | .. | 0.5 | | 3.0 | | 39.2 | -14.3 |
| Congo | 6 | 11 | 13 | 25 | 26 | 18 | 0.2 | 0.1 | 7.6 | -33.1 | 11.2 | 4.0 |
| Dem.R.Congo | 5 | .. | .. | .. | .. | .. | | | | | | |
| Equatorial Guinea | 1 | 1 | 5 | 16 | .. | .. | 0.0 | | | | -0.5 | 47.9 |
| Gabon | 2 | 13 | .. | 19 | .. | .. | 0.2 | | | | 40.7 | |
| Sao Tome Prn | 2 | .. | 11 | 11 | 11 | .. | | | -5.3 | | | |
| **East Africa** | **1,015** | **1,726** | **2,572** | **2,789** | **2,646** | **2,432** | **26.6** | **19.3** | **-5.1** | **-8.1** | **11.2** | **8.3** |
| Burundi | 3 | 1 | 1 | 1 | 1 | 1 | 0.0 | 0.0 | 108.4 | -46.8 | -19.4 | -4.1 |
| Comoros | 2 | 16 | .. | .. | .. | .. | 0.2 | | | | 59.2 | |
| Djibouti | .. | 3 | .. | .. | .. | .. | 0.0 | | | | | |
| Eritrea | .. | 44 | 39 | 83 | 77 | .. | 0.7 | | -6.6 | | | -2.5 |
| Ethiopia | 20 | 12 | 62 | 57 | 76 | .. | 0.2 | | 33.7 | | -9.0 | 38.2 |
| Kenya | 348 | 372 | 306 | 345 | 292 | 300 | 5.7 | 2.4 | -15.4 | 2.7 | 1.3 | -3.8 |
| Madagascar | 31 | 44 | 131 | 128 | 38 | 67 | 0.7 | 0.5 | -70.3 | 76.5 | 7.1 | 24.2 |
| Malawi | 13 | 13 | 27 | 28 | 35 | 29 | 0.2 | 0.2 | 25.0 | -16.4 | 0.7 | 15.8 |
| Mauritius | 192 | 329 | 587 | 696 | 647 | 616 | 5.1 | 4.9 | -7.0 | -4.8 | 11.4 | 12.3 |
| Mozambique | .. | .. | 80 | 71 | 67 | 86 | | 0.7 | -6.3 | 29.7 | | |
| Reunion | .. | 165 | 299 | 304 | 319 | 275 | 2.5 | 2.2 | 5.2 | -13.9 | | 12.6 |
| Rwanda | 8 | 2 | 25 | 28 | 33 | .. | 0.0 | | 17.5 | | -27.9 | 74.7 |
| Seychelles | 99 | 99 | 151 | 163 | 174 | 152 | 1.5 | 1.2 | 6.5 | -12.8 | -0.1 | 8.9 |
| Tanzania | 51 | 384 | 408 | 461 | 464 | 398 | 5.9 | 3.2 | 0.7 | -14.3 | 49.7 | 1.2 |
| Uganda | 8 | 60 | 179 | 184 | 181 | 167 | 0.9 | 1.3 | -1.8 | -7.6 | 50.0 | 24.5 |
| Zambia | 32 | 36 | 120 | 131 | 142 | 132 | 0.6 | 1.0 | 8.5 | -7.1 | 2.2 | 27.3 |
| Zimbabwe | 47 | 111 | 135 | 90 | 80 | 39 | 1.7 | 0.3 | -11.1 | -51.6 | 18.7 | 4.1 |
| **Southern Africa** | **975** | **2,019** | **3,477** | **3,525** | **3,697** | **4,425** | **31.1** | **35.1** | **4.9** | **19.7** | **15.7** | **11.5** |
| Botswana | 92 | 124 | 339 | 335 | 327 | 315 | 1.9 | 2.5 | -2.4 | -3.7 | 6.2 | 22.3 |
| Lesotho | 13 | 21 | 26 | 26 | 21 | .. | 0.3 | | -17.6 | | 9.1 | 4.7 |
| Namibia | 67 | 213 | 173 | 264 | 231 | 294 | 3.3 | 2.3 | -12.5 | 27.7 | 26.1 | -4.0 |
| South Africa | 779 | 1,625 | 2,898 | 2,868 | 3,091 | 3,775 | 25.1 | 30.0 | 7.8 | 22.1 | 15.8 | 12.3 |
| Swaziland | 24 | 37 | 40 | 32 | 27 | .. | 0.6 | | -15.1 | | 9.3 | 1.8 |

Source: World Tourism Organization (WTO) © (Data as collected by WTO December 2004)

**International Tourism Receipts by Country of Destination**

| | International Tourism Receipts (euro million) | | | | | | Market share in the region (%) | | Change (%) | | Average annual growth (%) | |
|---|---|---|---|---|---|---|---|---|---|---|---|---|
| | 1990 | 1995 | 2000 | 2001 | 2002 | 2003* | 1995 | 2003* | 02/01 | 03*/02 | 90-95 | 95-00 |
| ***Americas*** | ***54,373*** | ***75,246*** | ***141,806*** | ***134,023*** | ***120,308*** | ***101,109*** | ***100*** | ***100*** | ***-10.2*** | ***-16.0*** | ***6.7*** | ***13.5*** |
| **North America** | **43,044** | **59,243** | **109,864** | **101,496** | **91,243** | **74,739** | **78.7** | **73.9** | **-10.1** | **-18.1** | **6.6** | **13.1** |
| Canada | 4,978 | 6,053 | 11,669 | 11,845 | 11,306 | 9,352 | 8.0 | 9.2 | -4.5 | -17.3 | 4.0 | 14.0 |
| Mexico | 4,293 | 4,724 | 8,980 | 9,380 | 9,368 | 8,360 | 6.3 | 8.3 | -0.1 | -10.8 | 1.9 | 13.7 |
| United States | 33,773 | 48,467 | 89,215 | 80,271 | 70,569 | 57,027 | 64.4 | 56.4 | -12.1 | -19.2 | 7.5 | 13.0 |
| **Caribbean** | **6,844** | **9,357** | **18,595** | **19,102** | **17,636** | **15,863** | **12.4** | **15.7** | **-7.7** | **-10.1** | **6.5** | **14.7** |
| Anguilla | 27 | 38 | 61 | 70 | 60 | 55 | 0.1 | 0.1 | -14.3 | -9.1 | 6.8 | 9.7 |
| Antigua,Barb | 234 | 189 | 315 | 304 | 290 | 266 | 0.3 | 0.3 | -4.6 | -8.2 | -4.2 | 10.8 |
| Aruba | 275 | 398 | 881 | 920 | 879 | 753 | 0.5 | 0.7 | -4.5 | -14.3 | 7.7 | 17.2 |
| Bahamas | 1,040 | 1,029 | 1,882 | 1,840 | 1,864 | 1,575 | 1.4 | 1.6 | 1.3 | -15.5 | -0.2 | 12.8 |
| Barbados | 388 | 476 | 783 | 778 | 696 | 670 | 0.6 | 0.7 | -10.6 | -3.7 | 4.2 | 10.5 |
| Bermuda | 385 | 373 | 467 | 392 | 401 | 327 | 0.5 | 0.3 | 2.3 | -18.4 | -0.6 | 4.6 |
| Bonaire | 14 | 28 | 94 | 84 | 35 | 19 | 0.0 | 0.0 | -58.3 | -46.8 | 14.9 | 27.2 |
| Br.Virgin Is | 104 | 161 | 342 | 376 | 362 | .. | 0.2 | | -3.9 | | 9.2 | 16.2 |
| Cayman Islands | 185 | 301 | 605 | 653 | 642 | .. | 0.4 | | -1.7 | | 10.2 | 15.0 |
| Cuba | 191 | 736 | 1,881 | 1,889 | 1,727 | 1,632 | 1.0 | 1.6 | -8.6 | -5.5 | 31.0 | 20.6 |
| Curaçao | 94 | 134 | 246 | 282 | 289 | 251 | 0.2 | 0.2 | 2.2 | -13.0 | 7.3 | 12.9 |
| Dominica | 20 | 32 | 52 | 51 | 49 | 45 | 0.0 | 0.0 | -5.3 | -7.3 | 10.3 | 10.1 |
| Dominican Rp | 707 | 1,201 | 3,097 | 3,124 | 2,887 | 2,749 | 1.6 | 2.7 | -7.6 | -4.8 | 11.2 | 20.9 |
| Grenada | 30 | 58 | 101 | 93 | 96 | 92 | 0.1 | 0.1 | 3.8 | -4.5 | 14.3 | 11.6 |
| Guadeloupe | 155 | 350 | 453 | .. | .. | .. | 0.5 | | | | 17.7 | 5.3 |
| Haiti | 36 | 69 | 139 | 117 | 118 | 82 | 0.1 | 0.1 | 1.0 | -30.6 | 13.8 | 15.0 |
| Jamaica | 581 | 817 | 1,443 | 1,376 | 1,279 | 1,198 | 1.1 | 1.2 | -7.1 | -6.3 | 7.1 | 12.0 |
| Martinique | 188 | 294 | 327 | 274 | 251 | 218 | 0.4 | 0.2 | -8.4 | -12.9 | 9.3 | 2.2 |
| Montserrat | 5 | 13 | 10 | 9 | 10 | 6 | 0.0 | 0.0 | 6.6 | -35.0 | 18.8 | -5.6 |
| Neth. Antilles | .. | 429 | 828 | 838 | 815 | 747 | 0.6 | 0.7 | -2.7 | -8.3 | | 14.1 |
| Puerto Rico | 1,073 | 1,398 | 2,585 | 3,046 | 2,629 | 2,367 | 1.9 | 2.3 | -13.7 | -10.0 | 5.4 | 13.1 |
| Saint Lucia | 121 | 176 | 302 | 265 | 227 | 249 | 0.2 | 0.2 | -14.1 | 9.6 | 7.8 | 11.4 |
| St.Kitts-Nev | 46 | 48 | 63 | 69 | 59 | 54 | 0.1 | 0.1 | -14.4 | -8.9 | 1.1 | 5.4 |
| St.Maarten | 248 | 267 | 539 | 550 | .. | .. | 0.4 | | | | 1.5 | 15.1 |
| St.Vincent,Grenadines | 44 | 41 | 81 | 89 | 88 | 75 | 0.1 | 0.1 | -1.7 | -14.4 | -1.6 | 14.9 |
| Trinidad Tbg | 75 | 59 | 231 | 224 | 256 | .. | 0.1 | | 14.0 | | -4.6 | 31.4 |
| Turks,Caicos | 29 | 41 | 309 | 347 | 309 | .. | 0.1 | | -11.1 | | 6.9 | 50.1 |
| US.Virgin Is | 547 | 628 | 1,306 | 1,477 | 1,264 | 1,124 | 0.8 | 1.1 | -14.4 | -11.1 | 2.8 | 15.7 |
| **Central America** | **577** | **1,144** | **3,216** | **3,275** | **3,300** | **2,978** | **1.5** | **2.9** | **0.8** | **-9.7** | **14.7** | **23.0** |
| Belize | 35 | 60 | 132 | 134 | 137 | 138 | 0.1 | 0.1 | 2.6 | 0.3 | 11.5 | 17.2 |
| Costa Rica | 216 | 521 | 1,410 | 1,310 | 1,228 | 1,143 | 0.7 | 1.1 | -6.3 | -6.9 | 19.2 | 22.0 |
| El Salvador | 14 | 65 | 235 | 224 | 259 | 200 | 0.1 | 0.2 | 15.5 | -22.9 | 35.7 | 29.3 |
| Guatemala | 145 | 163 | 522 | 627 | 656 | 549 | 0.2 | 0.5 | 4.5 | -16.3 | 2.3 | 26.2 |
| Honduras | 23 | 61 | 282 | 286 | 318 | 298 | 0.1 | 0.3 | 11.4 | -6.4 | 21.8 | 35.7 |
| Nicaragua | 9 | 38 | 140 | 151 | 143 | 133 | 0.1 | 0.1 | -5.3 | -6.5 | 32.3 | 29.6 |
| Panama | 135 | 236 | 496 | 543 | 558 | 517 | 0.3 | 0.5 | 2.9 | -7.4 | 11.8 | 16.0 |
| **South America** | **3,908** | **5,502** | **10,132** | **10,150** | **8,129** | **7,528** | **7.3** | **7.4** | **-19.9** | **-7.4** | **7.1** | **13.0** |
| Argentina | 888 | 1,699 | 3,144 | 2,950 | 1,623 | 1,854 | 2.3 | 1.8 | -45.0 | 14.2 | 13.8 | 13.1 |
| Bolivia | 71 | 42 | 74 | 85 | 106 | 98 | 0.1 | 0.1 | 24.6 | -7.2 | -10.1 | 11.9 |
| Brazil | 1,172 | 743 | 1,960 | 1,932 | 2,113 | 2,191 | 1.0 | 2.2 | 9.4 | 3.7 | -8.7 | 21.4 |
| Chile | 424 | 696 | 887 | 892 | 950 | 760 | 0.9 | 0.8 | 6.5 | -19.9 | 10.4 | 4.9 |
| Colombia | 319 | 502 | 1,115 | 1,359 | 1,023 | 721 | 0.7 | 0.7 | -24.7 | -29.5 | 9.5 | 17.3 |
| Ecuador | 148 | 195 | 435 | 480 | 473 | 359 | 0.3 | 0.4 | -1.5 | -24.1 | 5.7 | 17.4 |
| French Guiana | .. | .. | .. | 47 | 48 | .. | | | 1.5 | | | |
| Guyana | 21 | 25 | 81 | 68 | 52 | 34 | 0.0 | 0.0 | -23.9 | -33.5 | 3.5 | 26.3 |
| Paraguay | 101 | 105 | 109 | 73 | 62 | 57 | 0.1 | 0.1 | -14.0 | -9.3 | 0.8 | 0.9 |
| Peru | 170 | 327 | 986 | 880 | 847 | 816 | 0.4 | 0.8 | -3.7 | -3.7 | 13.9 | 24.7 |
| Suriname | 1 | 16 | 17 | 16 | 3 | 4 | 0.0 | 0.0 | -79.7 | 11.5 | 82.9 | 1.5 |
| Uruguay | 187 | 467 | 772 | 682 | 371 | 305 | 0.6 | 0.3 | -45.6 | -17.8 | 20.1 | 10.6 |
| Venezuela | 389 | 649 | 458 | 687 | 459 | 286 | 0.9 | 0.3 | -33.2 | -37.8 | 10.8 | -6.7 |

Source: World Tourism Organization (WTO) ©

(Data as collected by WTO December 2004)

**International Tourism Receipts by Country of Destination**

| | International Tourism Receipts (euro million) | | | | | | Market share in the region (%) | | Change (%) | | Average annual growth (%) | |
|---|---|---|---|---|---|---|---|---|---|---|---|---|
| | 1990 | 1995 | 2000 | 2001 | 2002 | 2003* | 1995 | 2003* | 02/01 | 03*/02 | 90-95 | 95-00 |
| ***Asia and the Pacific*** | ***36,649*** | ***62,651*** | ***96,406*** | ***102,509*** | ***106,146*** | ***85,358*** | ***100*** | ***100*** | ***3.5*** | ***-19.6*** | ***11.3*** | ***9.0*** |
| **North-East Asia** | **18,062** | **29,159** | **48,089** | **51,958** | **54,856** | **42,190** | **46.5** | **49.4** | **5.6** | **-23.1** | **10.1** | **10.5** |
| China | 1,742 | 6,674 | 17,573 | 19,865 | 21,558 | 15,387 | 10.7 | 18.0 | 8.5 | -28.6 | 30.8 | 21.4 |
| Hong Kong (China) | 3,952 | 7,342 | 6,358 | 6,593 | 7,935 | 6,769 | 11.7 | 7.9 | 20.4 | -14.7 | 13.2 | -2.8 |
| Japan | 2,810 | 2,465 | 3,652 | 3,691 | 3,698 | 7,822 | 3.9 | 9.2 | 0.2 | 111.5 | -2.6 | 8.2 |
| Korea, D P Rp | 23 | .. | .. | .. | 159 | .. | | | | | | |
| Korea, Republic of | 2,795 | 3,937 | 7,399 | 7,128 | 6,278 | 4,646 | 6.3 | 5.4 | -11.9 | -26.0 | 7.1 | 13.4 |
| Macao (China) | 1,157 | 2,472 | 3,470 | 4,181 | 4,696 | 4,688 | 3.9 | 5.5 | 12.3 | -0.2 | 16.4 | 7.0 |
| Mongolia | 4 | 16 | 39 | 44 | 137 | 126 | 0.0 | 0.1 | 215.7 | -8.1 | 32.5 | 19.4 |
| Taiwan (pr. of China) | 1,366 | 2,512 | 4,047 | 4,840 | 4,848 | 2,631 | 4.0 | 3.1 | 0.2 | -45.7 | 13.0 | 10.0 |
| **South-East Asia** | **11,369** | **20,411** | **28,095** | **29,851** | **29,448** | **21,544** | **32.6** | **25.2** | **-1.3** | **-26.8** | **12.4** | **6.6** |
| Cambodia | .. | 41 | 329 | 424 | 480 | 344 | 0.1 | 0.4 | 13.2 | -28.4 | | 52.0 |
| Indonesia | 1,653 | 3,998 | 5,386 | 5,891 | 5,589 | 3,569 | 6.4 | 4.2 | -5.1 | -36.1 | 19.3 | 6.1 |
| Lao P.D.R. | 2 | 39 | 123 | 116 | 120 | 77 | 0.1 | 0.1 | 2.9 | -35.6 | 75.3 | 25.9 |
| Malaysia | 1,309 | 3,034 | 5,425 | 7,663 | 7,528 | 5,217 | 4.8 | 6.1 | -1.8 | -30.7 | 18.3 | 12.3 |
| Myanmar | 7 | 115 | 175 | 122 | 108 | 51 | 0.2 | 0.1 | -11.4 | -52.5 | 74.8 | 8.7 |
| Philippines | 1,026 | 868 | 2,310 | 1,924 | 1,840 | 1,294 | 1.4 | 1.5 | -4.3 | -29.7 | -3.3 | 21.6 |
| Singapore | 3,877 | 5,846 | 5,661 | 5,155 | 4,720 | 3,534 | 9.3 | 4.1 | -8.4 | -25.1 | 8.6 | -0.6 |
| Thailand | 3,397 | 6,143 | 8,102 | 7,899 | 8,356 | 6,915 | 9.8 | 8.1 | 5.8 | -17.2 | 12.6 | 5.7 |
| Vietnam | 67 | .. | .. | .. | .. | .. | | | | | | |
| **Oceania** | **5,624** | **10,478** | **15,344** | **15,381** | **16,292** | **15,867** | **16.7** | **18.6** | **5.9** | **-2.6** | **13.3** | **7.9** |
| American Samoa | 8 | .. | .. | .. | .. | .. | | | | | | |
| Australia | 3,210 | 6,007 | 9,183 | 9,002 | 9,072 | 9,121 | 9.6 | 10.7 | 0.8 | 0.5 | 13.4 | 8.9 |
| Cook Is | 13 | 21 | 39 | 42 | 49 | .. | 0.0 | | 14.7 | | 11.2 | 12.7 |
| Fiji | 159 | 222 | 196 | 242 | 276 | 309 | 0.4 | 0.4 | 13.9 | 11.8 | 7.0 | -2.5 |
| French Polynesia | 134 | 249 | .. | .. | .. | .. | 0.4 | | | | 13.2 | |
| Guam | 735 | .. | .. | .. | .. | .. | | | | | | |
| Kiribati | 1 | 2 | 3 | 4 | .. | .. | 0.0 | | | | 14.3 | 13.8 |
| Marshall Is | .. | 2 | 4 | 4 | 4 | .. | 0.0 | | -5.3 | | | 17.8 |
| Micronesia (Fed.St.of) | .. | .. | 16 | 17 | 18 | 15 | | 0.0 | 7.3 | -16.4 | | |
| N.Mariana Is | 357 | 501 | .. | .. | .. | .. | 0.8 | | | | 7.0 | |
| New Caledonia | 74 | 83 | 119 | 104 | 132 | .. | 0.1 | | 27.3 | | 2.3 | 7.6 |
| New Zealand | 809 | 1,772 | 2,454 | 2,635 | 3,179 | 3,513 | 2.8 | 4.1 | 20.6 | 10.5 | 17.0 | 6.7 |
| Niue | .. | 2 | .. | .. | .. | .. | 0.0 | | | | | |
| Palau | .. | .. | 57 | 66 | 62 | .. | | | -5.3 | | | |
| Papua New Guinea | 32 | 19 | 8 | 6 | .. | .. | 0.0 | | | | -9.9 | -16.9 |
| Samoa | 16 | 27 | 44 | 45 | 48 | 47 | 0.0 | 0.1 | 6.6 | -1.5 | 11.2 | 10.7 |
| Solomon Is | 5 | 12 | 4 | 6 | 1 | 2 | 0.0 | 0.0 | -81.1 | 67.2 | 17.3 | -18.8 |
| Tonga | 7 | 8 | 8 | 8 | 6 | .. | 0.0 | | -18.8 | | 1.6 | -0.2 |
| Vanuatu | 31 | 34 | 61 | 51 | .. | .. | 0.1 | | | | 2.4 | 12.0 |
| **South Asia** | **1,593** | **2,603** | **4,878** | **5,320** | **5,550** | **5,757** | **4.2** | **6.7** | **4.3** | **3.7** | **10.3** | **13.4** |
| Bangladesh | 9 | 19 | 54 | 54 | 60 | 50 | 0.0 | 0.1 | 12.5 | -16.4 | 17.2 | 23.1 |
| Bhutan | 2 | 4 | 11 | 10 | 8 | 7 | 0.0. | 0.0 | -16.0 | -12.8 | 19.5 | 23.1 |
| India | 1,188 | 1,974 | 3,430 | 3,396 | 3,091 | 3,114 | 3.2 | 3.6 | -9.0 | 0.7 | 10.7 | 11.7 |
| Iran | 48 | 51 | 506 | 995 | 1,435 | 1,571 | 0.1 | 1.8 | 44.3 | 9.5 | 1.3 | 58.1 |
| Maldives | 70 | 161 | 348 | 365 | 356 | 355 | 0.3 | 0.4 | -2.4 | -0.3 | 18.2 | 16.6 |
| Nepal | 50 | 135 | 171 | 161 | 109 | 176 | 0.2 | 0.2 | -32.3 | 61.5 | 21.9 | 4.8 |
| Pakistan | 123 | 84 | 88 | 98 | 103 | 106 | 0.1 | 0.1 | 4.4 | 3.4 | -7.2 | 0.8 |
| Sri Lanka | 104 | 173 | 269 | 238 | 384 | 375 | 0.3 | 0.4 | 61.4 | -2.4 | 10.8 | 9.2 |

Source: World Tourism Organization (WTO) ©

(Data as collected by WTO December 2004)

**International Tourism Receipts by Country of Destination**

| | International Tourism Receipts (euro million) | | | | | | Market share in the region (%) | | Change (%) | | Average annual growth (%) | |
|---|---|---|---|---|---|---|---|---|---|---|---|---|
| | 1990 | 1995 | 2000 | 2001 | 2002 | 2003* | 1995 | 2003* | 02/01 | 03*/02 | 90-95 | 95-00 |
| ***Europe*** | ***114,447*** | ***162,221*** | ***251,773*** | ***254,853*** | ***257,235*** | ***252,040*** | ***100*** | ***100*** | ***0.9*** | ***-2.0*** | ***7.2*** | ***9.2*** |
| **Northern Europe** | **20,622** | **25,979** | **38,780** | **37,457** | **39,258** | **37,085** | **16.0** | **14.7** | **4.8** | **-5.5** | **4.7** | **8.3** |
| Denmark | 2,862 | 2,808 | 3,999 | 4,481 | 5,035 | 4,655 | 1.7 | 1.8 | 12.4 | -7.6 | -0.4 | 7.3 |
| Finland | 916 | 1,254 | 1,522 | 1,604 | 1,669 | 1,674 | 0.8 | 0.7 | 4.0 | 0.3 | 6.5 | 4.0 |
| Iceland | 109 | 142 | 246 | 259 | 271 | 282 | 0.1 | 0.1 | 4.5 | 4.2 | 5.4 | 11.6 |
| Ireland | 1,146 | 1,748 | 2,824 | 3,115 | 3,266 | 3,426 | 1.1 | 1.4 | 4.8 | 4.9 | 8.8 | 10.1 |
| Norway | 1,233 | 1,711 | 2,220 | 2,186 | 2,304 | 2,246 | 1.1 | 0.9 | 5.4 | -2.5 | 6.8 | 5.3 |
| Sweden | 2,282 | 2,654 | 4,400 | 4,749 | 4,981 | 4,689 | 1.6 | 1.9 | 4.9 | -5.9 | 3.1 | 10.6 |
| United Kingdom | 12,074 | 15,663 | 23,569 | 21,062 | 21,732 | 20,113 | 9.7 | 8.0 | 3.2 | -7.4 | 5.3 | 8.5 |
| **Western Europe** | **49,562** | **61,769** | **89,664** | **90,951** | **92,660** | **91,572** | **38.1** | **36.3** | **1.9** | **-1.2** | **4.5** | **7.7** |
| Austria | 10,536 | 9,883 | 10,752 | 11,455 | 11,886 | 12,436 | 6.1 | 4.9 | 3.8 | 4.6 | -1.3 | 1.7 |
| Belgium | .. | 3,477 | 7,137 | 7,707 | 7,287 | 7,187 | 2.1 | 2.9 | -5.5 | -1.4 | | 15.5 |
| Belgium/Luxembourg | 2,907 | .. | .. | .. | .. | .. | | | | | | |
| France | 15,850 | 21,091 | 33,543 | 33,901 | 34,622 | 32,742 | 13.0 | 13.0 | 2.1 | -5.4 | 5.9 | 9.7 |
| Germany | 11,187 | 13,762 | 20,179 | 20,030 | 20,060 | 20,318 | 8.5 | 8.1 | 0.1 | 1.3 | 4.2 | 8.0 |
| Luxembourg | .. | 1,296 | 1,825 | 1,987 | 2,310 | 2,469 | 0.8 | 1.0 | 16.2 | 6.9 | | 7.1 |
| Netherlands | 3,263 | 5,029 | 7,792 | 7,490 | 8,154 | 8,176 | 3.1 | 3.2 | 8.9 | 0.3 | 9.0 | 9.2 |
| Switzerland | 5,820 | 7,232 | 8,435 | 8,380 | 8,342 | 8,243 | 4.5 | 3.3 | -0.4 | -1.2 | 4.4 | 3.1 |
| **Central/Eastern Europe** | **3,808** | **14,811** | **21,225** | **21,944** | **21,400** | **19,719** | **9.1** | **7.8** | **-2.5** | **-7.9** | **31.2** | **7.5** |
| Armenia | .. | 1 | 41 | 73 | 67 | 65 | 0.0 | 0.0 | -8.2 | -3.1 | | 121.9 |
| Azerbaijan | 179 | 54 | 68 | 48 | 54 | 51 | 0.0 | 0.0 | 12.3 | -4.9 | -21.5 | 5.0 |
| Belarus | .. | 18 | 101 | 191 | 247 | 236 | 0.0 | 0.1 | 29.6 | -4.6 | | 41.8 |
| Bulgaria | 251 | 362 | 1,163 | 1,075 | 1,220 | 1,466 | 0.2 | 0.6 | 13.5 | 20.1 | 7.6 | 26.3 |
| Czech Rep | 329 | 2,202 | 3,219 | 3,466 | 3,135 | 3,144 | 1.4 | 1.2 | -9.6 | 0.3 | 46.3 | 7.9 |
| Estonia | .. | 273 | 546 | 566 | 587 | 596 | 0.2 | 0.2 | 3.7 | 1.5 | | 14.9 |
| Georgia | .. | .. | 105 | 131 | 133 | 130 | | 0.1 | 2.0 | -2.5 | | |
| Hungary | 647 | 2,239 | 3,729 | 4,209 | 3,462 | 3,041 | 1.4 | 1.2 | -17.7 | -12.2 | 28.2 | 10.7 |
| Kazakhstan | .. | 93 | 385 | 505 | 658 | 499 | 0.1 | 0.2 | 30.3 | -24.2 | | 32.8 |
| Kyrgyzstan | .. | 4 | 16 | 27 | 38 | 42 | 0.0 | 0.0 | 42.1 | 11.5 | | 33.6 |
| Latvia | .. | 15 | 142 | 134 | 170 | 196 | 0.0 | 0.1 | 27.1 | 15.3 | | 56.1 |
| Lithuania | .. | 59 | 423 | 428 | 534 | 564 | 0.0 | 0.2 | 24.9 | 5.6 | | 48.4 |
| Poland | 281 | 5,057 | 6,147 | 5,187 | 4,562 | 3,597 | 3.1 | 1.4 | -12.1 | -21.2 | 78.2 | 4.0 |
| Rep Moldova | .. | 44 | 42 | 44 | 53 | 51 | 0.0 | 0.0 | 21.4 | -3.0 | | -0.6 |
| Romania | 83 | 451 | 389 | 404 | 354 | 397 | 0.3 | 0.2 | -12.3 | 12.0 | 40.2 | -2.9 |
| Russian Federation | .. | 3,297 | 3,714 | 3,988 | 4,407 | 3,980 | 2.0 | 1.6 | 10.5 | -9.7 | | 2.4 |
| Slovakia | 55 | 476 | 469 | 716 | 778 | 765 | 0.3 | 0.3 | 8.8 | -1.8 | 54.0 | -0.3 |
| Tajikistan | .. | .. | .. | .. | 2 | 2 | | 0.0 | | -16.4 | | |
| Ukraine | .. | 146 | 427 | 640 | 833 | 827 | 0.1 | 0.3 | 30.3 | -0.8 | | 23.9 |
| Uzbekistan | .. | .. | 68 | 80 | 72 | 42 | | 0.0 | -10.5 | -41.0 | | |
| **Southern Europe** | **34,919** | **50,834** | **84,326** | **88,272** | **87,169** | **88,409** | **31.3** | **35.1** | **-1.3** | **1.4** | **7.8** | **10.7** |
| Albania | 3 | 50 | 421 | 498 | 515 | 461 | 0.0 | 0.2 | 3.4 | -10.4 | 73.7 | 53.3 |
| Bosnia & Herzg | .. | .. | 179 | 195 | 203 | 208 | | 0.1 | 3.9 | 2.3 | | |
| Croatia | .. | 1,031 | 2,986 | 3,724 | 4,030 | 5,636 | 0.6 | 2.2 | 8.2 | 39.9 | | 23.7 |
| F.Yug.Rp.Macedonia | .. | 15 | 41 | 29 | 41 | 50 | 0.0 | 0.0 | 42.1 | 22.2 | | 23.1 |
| Greece | 2,032 | 3,161 | 9,981 | 10,580 | 10,285 | 9,460 | 1.9 | 3.8 | -2.8 | -8.0 | 9.2 | 25.9 |
| Italy | 12,924 | 21,965 | 29,767 | 28,831 | 28,420 | 27,601 | 13.5 | 11.0 | -1.4 | -2.9 | 11.2 | 6.3 |
| Malta | 389 | 505 | 660 | 645 | 604 | 615 | 0.3 | 0.2 | -6.4 | 1.9 | 5.3 | 5.5 |
| Portugal | 2,792 | 3,693 | 5,677 | 6,107 | 6,093 | 6,132 | 2.3 | 2.4 | -0.2 | 0.7 | 5.8 | 9.0 |
| Serbia & Montenegro | .. | 32 | 32 | 60 | 103 | 133 | 0.0 | 0.1 | 70.1 | 29.3 | | 0.2 |
| Slovenia | .. | 829 | 1,040 | 1,102 | 1,148 | 1,186 | 0.5 | 0.5 | 4.2 | 3.3 | | 4.7 |
| Spain | 14,601 | 19,503 | 33,541 | 36,501 | 35,728 | 36,925 | 12.0 | 14.7 | -2.1 | 3.4 | 6.0 | 11.5 |
| Yugoslav SFR | 2,178 | .. | .. | .. | .. | .. | | | | | | |
| **East Mediterranean Eu.** | **5,536** | **8,827** | **17,778** | **16,230** | **16,749** | **15,255** | **5.4** | **6.1** | **3.2** | **-8.9** | **9.8** | **15.0** |
| Cyprus | 988 | 1,374 | 2,098 | 2,240 | 2,006 | 1,781 | 0.8 | 0.7 | -10.4 | -11.2 | 6.8 | 8.8 |
| Israel | 1,096 | 2,288 | 4,411 | 2,750 | 2,156 | 1,803 | 1.4 | 0.7 | -21.6 | -16.4 | 15.9 | 14.0 |
| Turkey | 2,533 | 3,790 | 8,268 | 11,240 | 12,586 | 11,672 | 2.3 | 4.6 | 12.0 | -7.3 | 8.4 | 16.9 |

Source: World Tourism Organization (WTO) © (Data as collected by WTO December 2004)

**International Tourism Receipts by Country of Destination**

| | International Tourism Receipts (euro million) | | | | | | Market share in the region (%) | | Change (%) | | Average annual growth (%) | |
|---|---|---|---|---|---|---|---|---|---|---|---|---|
| | 1990 | 1995 | 2000 | 2001 | 2002 | 2003* | 1995 | 2003* | 02/01 | 03*/02 | 90-95 | 95-00 |
| ***Middle East*** | ***4,433*** | ***7,482*** | ***14,334*** | ***14,183*** | ***13,599*** | ***12,285*** | ***100*** | ***100*** | ***-4.1*** | ***-9.7*** | ***11.0*** | ***13.9*** |
| Bahrain | 106 | 189 | 620 | 703 | 783 | 654 | 2.5 | 5.3 | 11.3 | -16.4 | 12.2 | 26.9 |
| Egypt | 864 | 2,052 | 4,704 | 4,243 | 3,981 | 4,052 | 27.4 | 33.0 | -6.2 | 1.8 | 18.9 | 18.0 |
| Jordan | 402 | 505 | 783 | 782 | 831 | 720 | 6.7 | 5.9 | 6.4 | -13.3 | 4.6 | 9.2 |
| Kuwait | 104 | 93 | 106 | 117 | 125 | 104 | 1.2 | 0.8 | 7.5 | -17.1 | -2.3 | 2.7 |
| Lebanon | .. | 543 | 803 | 935 | 1,011 | 898 | 7.3 | 7.3 | 8.2 | -11.2 | | 8.2 |
| Libyan Arab Jamahiriya | 5 | 2 | 105 | 105 | 79 | 70 | 0.0 | 0.6 | -24.4 | -12.0 | -20.2 | 133.0 |
| Oman | 54 | .. | 239 | 161 | 218 | 194 | | 1.6 | 35.5 | -11.1 | | |
| Palestine | .. | .. | 245 | 8 | 1 | 4 | | 0.0 | -86.5 | 234.4 | | |
| Saudi Arabia | .. | .. | .. | .. | 3,615 | .. | | | | | | |
| Syrian Arab Republic | 251 | 962 | 1,171 | 1,284 \| | 1,506 | 1,245 | 12.9 | 10.1 | 17.3 | -17.3 | 30.8 | 4.0 |
| Untd Arab Emirates | 247 | 483 | 1,151 | 1,340 | 1,409 | 1,272 | 6.5 | 10.4 | 5.1 | -9.7 | 14.3 | 19.0 |
| Yemen | 16 | 38 | 79 | 42 | 40 | 123 | 0.5 | 1.0 | -5.3 | 205.8 | 19.5 | 15.6 |

Source: World Tourism Organization (WTO) © (Data as collected by WTO December 2004)

| : change of series.

# 3. Methodological Notes

## 3.1 Concepts and Definitions

According to the WTO/United Nations *Recommendations on Tourism Statistics*, Tourism comprises *the activities of persons travelling to and staying in places outside their usual environment for not more than one consecutive year for leisure, business and other purposes.*

This concept can be applied to different forms of tourism. Depending upon whether a person is travelling to, from or within a certain country the following forms can be distinguished:

- **Inbound Tourism**, involving the non-residents received by a destination country from the point of view of that destination;
- **Outbound Tourism**, involving residents travelling to another country from the point of view of the country of origin;
- **Domestic tourism**, involving residents of a given country travelling within that country.

All types of travellers engaged in tourism are described as visitors. Visitors can be distinguished as same-day visitors or tourists (overnight visitors).

There are various units of measure to quantify the volume of tourism. An overview is set out below:

| Unit of measurement | | | Comment |
|---|---|---|---|
| **Visitors** | *Arrivals* | *- at frontiers* | or at a specific place in case of domestic tourism |
| **Tourists** (overnight visitors) | *Arrivals* | *- at frontiers* | |
| | | *- at collective tourism establishments (e.g. hotels and other, such as campings etc.)*<br>*- at hotels and similar establishments* | - excludes tourism in private accommodation;<br>- arrivals are counted in every new accommodation visited |
| | *Nights* | *- at collective tourism establishments (e.g. hotels and other)*<br>*- at hotels and similar establishments* | |

### Inbound Tourism

Unless otherwise stated, this report concentrates on **International Tourism** as measured from an **Inbound Tourism** perspective, i.e. the tourism received by any given destination country (and in a few cases territories) from non-residents travelling to that destination.

The most common unit of measure used to quantify the volume of International Tourism for statistical purposes is the number of International Tourist Arrivals. For a proper understanding of this unit, two considerations should be taken into account:

- Data refer exclusively to tourists (overnight visitors): 'a visitor who stays at least one night in a collective or private accommodation in the country visited'. Same-day visitors are not included.
- Data refer to the number of arrivals and not to the number of persons. The same person who makes several trips to a given country during a given period will be counted as a new arrival each time, as well as a person who travels through several countries on one trip is counted as a new arrival each time.

Figures on the volume of international tourism presented in the regional and subregional tables, preferably relate to the concept of *international tourist arrivals at frontiers*. However, as not all countries are collecting data according to this concept, another series may be used instead. In the tables, the series are indicated as follows:

TF: International tourist arrivals at frontiers (excluding same-day visitors);
VF: International visitor arrivals at frontiers (including tourists and same-day visitors);
TCE: International tourist arrivals at collective tourism establishments;
THS: International tourist arrivals at hotels and similar establishments.

With respect to the inbound tourism volume, if available, in the Profile tables for individual countries in Chapter III, except for data on International Tourist Arrivals, furthermore, data is included on International Visitor Arrivals, Same-day Visitor Arrivals, Cruise passengers (considered as a special category of same-day visitors) and Nights spent in collective establishments or in hotels and similar establishments.

**Outbound Tourism**

Data on outbound tourism volume in this series of reports originate from two different sources and likewise relate to two dissimilar concepts:

- On one hand, many countries are reporting the number of outbound trips of their residents. Data availability and comparability, however, is still limited and it is often not clear whether the reported figures refer only to tourists or to visitors in general.
- On the other hand, data are synthesised from the data on inbound tourism to destination countries (an arrival received in a destination can also be taken as an arrival generated by the generating country). Data on arrivals to destinations broken down by region of origin are taken to estimate and aggregate the number of arrivals originating from each region. The unit of measurement is the number of international tourist arrivals generated by the region of origin concerned. For a proper understanding, it should be borne in mind that these figures do not correspond to the number of trips, as one trip taken might result in various arrivals in destinations.

**Domestic Tourism**

International comparable data on domestic tourism is unfortunately still rather scarce. If available for a certain country, this series is represented in the Profile tables for countries in Chapter III of the regional volumes in the form of the number of nights spent by residents at hotels and similar establishments or at all collective tourism establishments.

**Accommodation**

As a measure for the capacity of accommodation, data is included on the number of rooms or the number of bed places in the country. When expressed in bed places, the number of rooms roughly will be half, as rooms on average count two bed places. The actual capacity of a country might eventually be larger, as some countries exclude hotels below a certain category or less than a certain size.

**International Tourism Receipts and Expenditure**

***International Tourism Receipts*** are the receipts earned by a destination country from inbound tourism and cover all tourism receipts resulting from expenditure made by visitors from abroad, on for instance lodging, food and drinks, fuel, transport in the country, entertainment, shopping, etc. This concept includes receipts generated by overnight as well as by same-day trips, which can be substantial, as will be the case with countries where a lot of shopping for goods and services takes place by visitors from neighbouring countries. It excludes, however, the receipts related to international transport contracted by residents of other countries (for instance ticket receipts from foreigners travelling with a national company). These receipts are covered in the separate category ***International Fare***

***Receipts***, which for most recent years is estimated at about 18 per cent of total tourism and fare receipts.

**International Tourism Expenditure** is the expenditure on tourism outside their country of residence made by visitors (same-day visitors and tourists) from a given country of origin.

Data on receipts and expenditure related to international tourism are generally gathered in the framework of the Balance of Payments under the items 'Services, Travel, Credit and Debit' (International Tourism Receipts and Expenditure) and 'Transportation, Passenger Services, Credit and Debit' (International Fare Receipts and Expenditure). See the *Balance of Payments Statistics Yearbook, Part 2 and Part 3* of the International Monetary Fund (IMF) for details on methodologies, compilation practices and data sources.

The International Tourism Balance and International Fare Balance as included in the Profile tables in Chapter III of the regional volumes, correspond to the net receipts or expenditure of a given country on respectively international tourism or international fares, i.e. receipts less expenditure.

**Further information**

More detailed information on concepts, definitions, classifications, indicators, methods of compiling and units of measure can be obtained from:

- the *Basic References on Tourism Statistics* on the WTO website under the link <www.world-tourism.org/statistics/tsa_project/basic_references/index-en.htm> setting out the main components that make up the System of Tourism Statistics (STS);

or from the following WTO publications:

- *Recommendations on tourism statistics* (WTO 1994),
- *Technical Manual No. 1: Concepts Definitions, and Classifications for Tourism Statistics* (WTO 1995);
- *Technical Manual No. 2: Collection for Tourism Expenditure Statistics* (WTO 1995);
- *Technical Manual No. 3: Collection of Domestic Tourism Statistics* (WTO 1995);
- *Technical Manual No. 4: Collection and Compilation of Tourism Statistics* (WTO 1995);
- *Data Collection & Analysis for Tourism Management, Marketing & Planning* (WTO 2000).

## 3.2 Sources, Data Treatment and Acknowledgement

**General**

Quantitative tourism-related data in this report is based on a selection of data included in the WTO database on World Tourism Statistics. This database contains a variety of series for over 200 countries and territories covering data for most countries from the 1980's on. The database is maintained by the WTO Secretariat and is updated on a continuous base.

Except where otherwise indicated, statistical data has been collected by the WTO Secretariat from the official institutions of the countries and territories (WTO member as well as non-member countries) or from official international bodies, e.g. the Caribbean Tourism Organization (CTO), International Monetary Fund (IMF).

The data for individual countries corresponding to 2003 are based on full year results, or projections, as communicated to the WTO Secretariat by the authorities of the countries and territories or disseminated through a news release, publication or on the Internet. Data collection for this series of reports closed in December 2004. For many countries 2003 figures are still preliminary and subject to revision.

In the world and (sub)regional aggregates, estimates are included for countries and territories with data still missing based upon data available for a part of the year or the general trend for the region. In particular for the Middle East and Africa the regional and subregional aggregates for 2003 should be treated with caution as estimations are based on a relatively small number of countries and territories that supplied data for the entire year. In the tables, provisional figures are marked with an asterisk (*).

WTO tourism statistics generally refer to figures for a country as a whole. In the collection of statistics, however, except for independent states, there are also a number of dependencies or territories of special sovereignty included (for instance Hong Kong (China) or French Polynesia). These territories report tourism figures independently and are for the sake of tourism statistics considered as an entity in itself. Because of this, where reference is made to "countries" the term generally should be taken to mean "countries and territories". In a few other cases, dependencies are not separately listed but included in the total for the country they depend upon (for instance Guernsey, Jersey and the Isle of Man in United Kingdom).

In general WTO does not collect data on the level of regions, states, provinces or specific destinations within a country (Hawaii is one of the few exceptions made because of its relevance for Asian outbound travel; in the overview tables, however, Hawaii is included in the United States figure). Most countries will have a further regional breakdown available as well as other series not included in the WTO database on World Tourism Statistics. Please refer to national sources for this data.

The regional country groupings are according to the WTO regional commissions. See the tables by country in the annex for the countries and territories included in the various regions and subregions.

The World Tourism Organization is aware of the limitations of the available statistical information on tourism. Despite the considerable progress made in recent decades, international tourism statistics are often not uniform, because definitions and methods of data collection tend to differ. Every user of this information should bear in mind that the international comparability of statistical data is still not optimal.

The qualitative information in the country sections of the reports was gathered by means of the survey on tourism development in 2003, as completed in the first nine months of 2004 by the NTAs, NTOs or Statistical Offices of the various countries and territories. See Annex 5 for the questionnaire used.

The World Tourism Organization wishes to express its gratitude to the correspondents of the various countries and territories for their indispensable cooperation.

**Tourism series in this report**

The tourism data series in Chapter II and in the Profile tables of countries in Chapter III correspond to the basic indicators included in the WTO *Compendium of Tourism Statistics*. Please refer to the latest publication for additional series, methodological references and notes on the series for specific countries.

A number of derived series are included relating tourism volume to the size of the population or tourism receipts and expenditure to tourism volume. In the Profile tables in Chapter III, those series are marked with '-'. Ratios are based on simple divisions of the concept in question by the population or of the receipts or expenditure by the corresponding concepts:

*International Tourist Arrivals per 100 of inhabitants* = International Tourist Arrivals / population * 100.

*Trips abroad per 100 of inhabitants* = Trips abroad / population * 100.

*International Tourism Receipts per International Tourist Arrival* = International Tourism Receipts / International Tourist Arrivals.

*International Tourism Receipts per International Visitor Arrival* = International Tourism Receipts / International Visitor Arrivals.

*International Tourism Receipts per capita* = International Tourism Receipts / population.

*International Tourism Expenditure per trip abroad* = International Tourism Expenditure / Trips abroad.

*International Tourism Expenditure per capita* = International Tourism Expenditure / population.

Financial data is generally collected and kept in the WTO database in US$ values. In the cases where countries report in local currency, values are transferred by WTO into US$ applying the average exchange rate for the corresponding year. However, part of the tables are also published in euros. These euro values are in general derived from the US$ values using the corresponding average annual exchange rates for the two currencies. The following exchange rates have been applied:

**Exchange rates US$ versus euro (ECU for the years before 1999) annual averages**

| | €/ECU per US$ | Change (%) | US$ per €/ECU | Change (%) |
|---|---|---|---|---|
| 1995 | 0.76452 | | 1.30801 | |
| 1996 | 0.78756 | 3.0 | 1.26975 | -2.9 |
| 1997 | 0.88180 | 12.0 | 1.13404 | -10.7 |
| 1998 | 0.89199 | 1.2 | 1.12109 | -1.1 |
| 1999 | 0.93828 | 5.2 | 1.06578 | -4.9 |
| 2000 | 1.08270 | 15.4 | 0.92361 | -13.3 |
| 2001 | 1.11653 | 3.1 | 0.89563 | -3.0 |
| 2002 | 1.05756 | -5.3 | 0.94557 | 5.6 |
| 2003 | 0.88402 | -16.4 | 1.13120 | 19.6 |

Source : Eurostat, European Central Bank (ECB)

As exchange rates fluctuate substantially over time, the evolution of International Tourism Receipts was also estimated in (weighted) local currencies. For this, receipts in US$ are recomputed in local currencies using an exchange rate table provided by IMF. In order to take care of inflation, receipts are calculated in constant prices using country data on inflation from IMF as deflator.

The data in the tables on international tourist or visitor arrivals and nights of international tourists by country of origin included in Chapter III correspond to the series as included in the WTO *Yearbook of Tourism Statistics*. Please refer to the latter publication for additional series, metrological references and notes on the series for specific countries.

**Series from external sources**

Information included, but not referring to tourism indicators, are in general taken from specialised international organisations and not collected by the WTO Secretariat from the individual countries and territories. Data are meant as indicators, providing a context for tourism performance and do not necessarily coincide fully with national data. The following series are included:

### *Population*

Data refer to total midyear population as included in the International Database (IDB) of the International Programs Center (IPC) of the Population Division of the U.S. Bureau of the Census, <www.census.gov/ipc/www>. The IDB combines data from country sources (especially censuses and surveys) with IPC's estimates and projections to provide information dating back as far as 1950 and as far ahead as 2050. The IDB can be considered as a practically complete and consistent set of population data covering 227 countries and areas with 1998 populations of 5,000 or more.

### *Area*

Data on the dimension of the area of countries and territories are taken from the Statistical database of the Food and Agriculture Organization of the United Nations (FAO) <www.fao.org> and refer to the total area of the country, including area under inland water bodies for the year 2000. In the case of Belgium and Luxembourg data is taken from national sources.

### *Economic Indicators*

The series on Gross Domestic Product (GDP), Gross Domestic Product per capita and economic growth (annual per cent change of Real Gross Domestic Product) are based on the World Economic Outlook (WEO) Database of September 2004 of the International Monetary Fund (IMF). See <www.imf.org/external/pubs/ft/weo/2004/02/data/index.htm>.

# 4. Sources of Information

## *A.* WTO web site <www.world-tourism.org>

The WTO has a comprehensive website available with news and information on its programme activities, members, regional activities, publications, special projects etc. in English, French and Spanish with a growing section in Russian.

- A qualitative and quantitative overview of world tourism and selected statistical country data is available under the *Facts & Figures* link, including the most updated tourism trends and data in the *"WTO World Tourism Barometer"*
- Information on the activities of the WTO Market Intelligence and Promotion department can be found under the *Market Intelligence and Promotion* link
- An overview of available publications and electronic products with detailed information on each item including contents and sample chapters can be found in the WTO Infoshop at <www.world-tourism.org/infoshop> or the WTOelibrary at <www.wtoelibrary.org>.

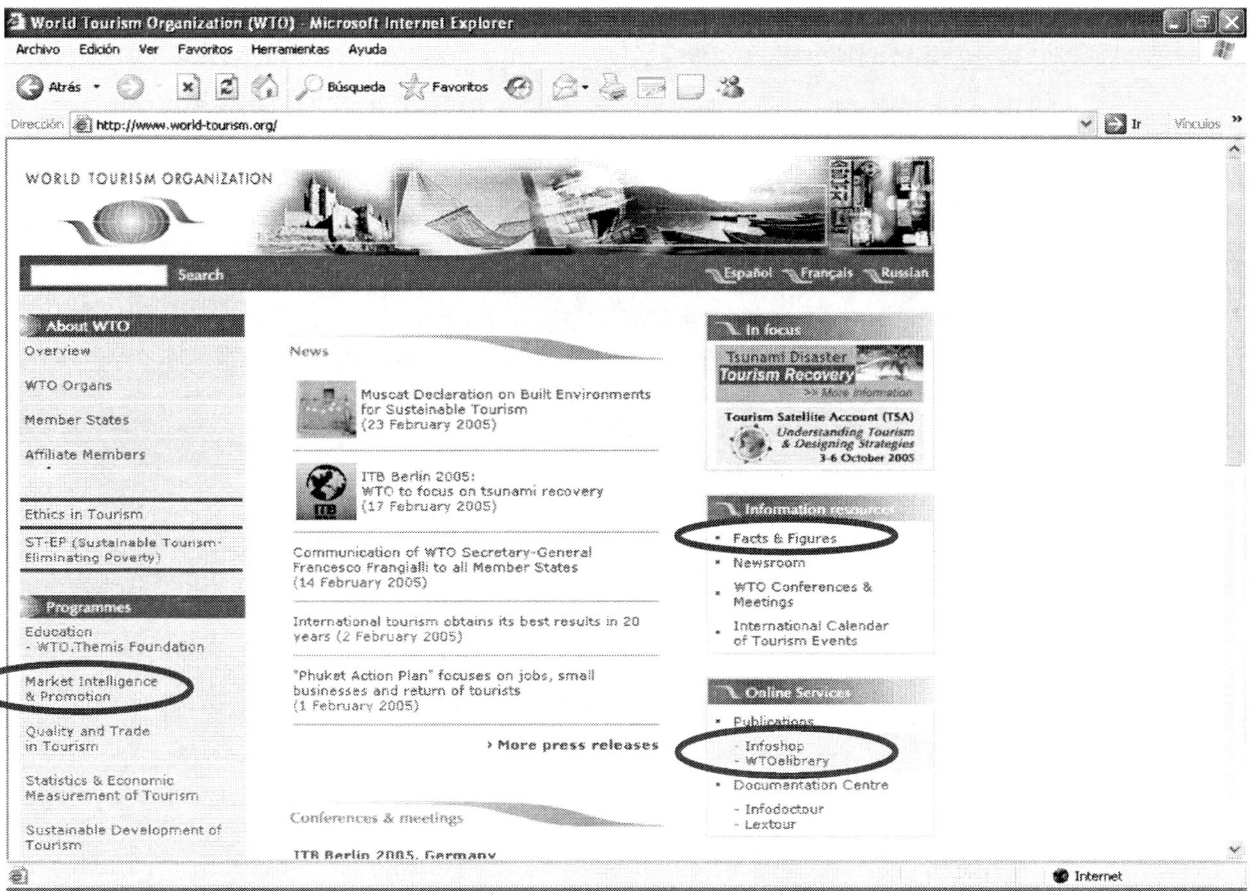

## B. *Related Publications of the World Tourism Organization*

### Inbound Tourism

This report is part of the *Tourism Market Trends, 2004 Edition* series consisting of 6 volumes published in English and partly in French and Spanish:

- World Overview and Tourism Topics (in English, French and Spanish)
- Africa (in English and French)
- Americas (in English and Spanish)
- Asia and the Pacific (in English)
- Europe (in English and French)
- Middle East (in English)

Excerpts of this series is included in:

- *Tourism Highlights 2004* (in English, French and Spanish). The electronic version can be downloaded free of charge from the Facts & Figures section of the WTO website at <http://www.world-tourism.org/facts/menu.html>

- *Special report No 23:* Inbound Tourism to the Middle East and North Africa (WTO 2003; in English)

### Outbound Tourism

- *Tourism Generating Markets: Overview and Country Profiles* (WTO 1999; in English, French and Spanish)
- *Special Reports* on specific markets:
    - No. 4: Outbound Tourism of Korea (WTO 2001; in English)
    - No. 5: Outbound Tourism of Australia (WTO 2001; in English)
    - No. 6: Outbound Tourism of Japan (WTO 2001; in English)
    - No. 7: Outbound Tourism of Belgium (WTO 2001; in English)
    - No. 8: Outbound Tourism of Spain (WTO 2001; in English and Spanish).
    - No. 9: Outbound Tourism of Japan & Korea, Results 2000 (WTO 2001; in English)
    - No. 21: Outbound Tourism of Scandinavia, Market Profile (WTO 2002; in English)
- Youth Outbound Travel of the Germans, the British & the French (WTO 2002, in English, French and Spanish)
- Chinese Outbound Tourism (WTO 2003; in English)
- Outbound Tourism from Saudi Arabia (WTO 2003; in English)

### Short-term Indicators

- *WTO World Tourism Barometer* (WTO, 3 times a year since June 2003; in electronic format (PDF) and print, in English, French and Spanish)

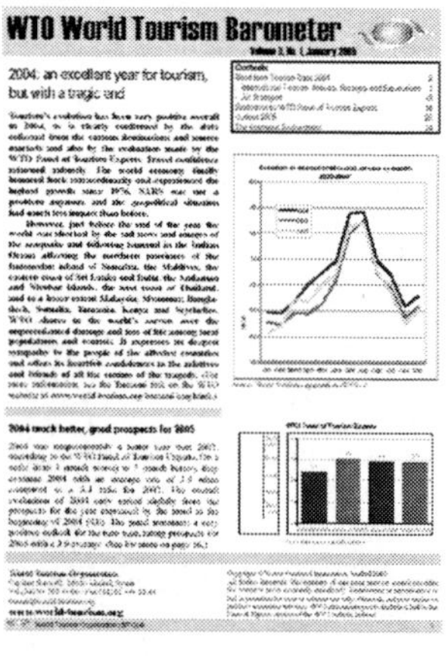


The WTO World Tourism Barometer monitors the short-term evolution of tourism and aims at providing adequate and timely information on the state of the sector. The Barometer is published three times a year (January, June, and October). It contains an overview of short-term tourism data from destination countries and tourism sectors such as air transport, a retrospective and prospective evaluation of tourism performance by the WTO Panel of Tourism Experts and selected economic data relevant for tourism.

*For more information see the "Facts & Figures" section of the WTO website www.world-tourism.org.*

**Forecasting**

WTO's long-term forecast *Tourism 2020 Vision* has been published in a series of 7 reports consisting of one summary volume and six regional volumes (WTO 2000, 2001):

- Global Forecasts and Profiles of Market Segments (in English, French and Spanish)
- Africa (in English and French)
- Americas (in English and Spanish)
- East Asia and the Pacific (in English)
- Europe (in English and French)
- Middle East (in English)
- South Asia (in English)

**Tourism Products**

- Tourism and Sport
  - *Sport and Tourism. 1st World Conference* (in English, French and Spanish; forthcoming). Excerpts of the presentations and the conference results of the World Conference on Sport and Tourism held February 2001 in Barcelona, Spain
  - *Introductory Report on Sport & Tourism* (WTO 2001);
  - *Sport Activities during the outbound holidays of the Germans, the Dutch and the French* (WTO 2001);
  - *Deporte Y Turismo: Destino América Latina* (WTO 2003; in Spanish)
- Ecotourism
  - Special report No. 10: The German Ecotourism Market (WTO 2001)
  - Special report No. 11: The British Ecotourism Market (WTO 2001)
  - Special report No. 12: The U.S. Ecotourism Market (WTO 2002)
  - Special report No. 13: The Italian Ecotourism Market (WTO 2002)
  - Special report No. 14: The Spanish Ecotourism Market (WTO 2002)
  - Special report No. 15: The Canadian Ecotourism Market (WTO 2002)
  - Special report No. 16: The French Ecotourism Market (WTO 2002)
- MICE
  - *MICE Outbound Tourism 2000* (WTO 2003;in English)
- Cruises
  - *Worldwide Cruise Ship Activity* (WTO 2003; in English, French and Spanish)
- Cultural Tourism
  - *City Tourism and Culture: The European Experience* (WTO 2005, in English)

**WTO Tourism Recovery Committee**

- Special report No. 17: *The impact of the attacks in the United States on international tourism: An initial analysis* (included in the Annex of Special report No. 18, not available separately)
- Special report No. 18: *Tourism after 11 September 2001:.Analysis, remedial actions and prospects* (WTO 2001; in English, French and Spanish)
- Special report No. 19: *Tourism Recovery Committee for the Mediterranean Region* (WTO 2002; in English, French and Spanish)
- Special report No. 20: *The impact of the September 11th attacks on tourism: The light at the end of the tunnel* (WTO 2002; in English, French and Spanish)
- Special report No. 21: 2002: Climbing Towards Recovery? (WTO 2002; in English)
- Special report No. 22: Fourth Meeting of the Tourism Recovery Committee - ITB Berlin 2003 (WTO 2003;in English)

**Basic Statistical Reference**

- *Compendium of Tourism Statistics* (WTO 2003; tri-lingual edition in English, French and Spanish and table descriptions in Arabic and Russian)
- *Yearbook of Tourism Statistics* (WTO 2003; tri-lingual edition in English, French and Spanish)

**Statistical Methodology**

- *Recommendations on Tourism Statistics* (WTO 1994; in English, French and Spanish)
- *Technical Manuals* (WTO 1995; in English, French and Spanish):
  - *No. 1: Concepts, Definitions and Classifications for Tourism Statistics*
  - *No. 2: Collection of Tourism Expenditure Statistics*
  - *No. 3: Collection of Domestic Tourism Statistics*
  - *No. 4: Collection and Compilation of Tourism Statistics*
- *Data Collection and Analysis for Tourism Management, Marketing and Planning* (WTO 2000; in English)

See for detailed information on concepts, definitions, classifications, indicators, methods of compiling and units of measure also the *Basic References on Tourism Statistics*, setting out the main components that make up the System of Tourism Statistics (STS), on the WTO website at: <www.world-tourism.org/statistics/tsa_project/basic_references/index-en.htm>.
See for documentation on the Tourism Satellite Account methodology the WTO website at: <www.world-tourism.org/frameset/frame_statistics.html>.

**Other**

- *Tourism in the Age of Alliances, Mergers and Acquisitions* (WTO 2002)
- *Apuntes de la Metodología de la Investigación en Turismo* (WTO 2001, only in Spanish)
- *Marketing Papers No.1* (WTO 2002)
- *Evaluating NTO Marketing Activities* (WTO 2003, English, French, Spanish)

## *C. References*

**International Organizations**

- United Nations; <www.un.org>
- United Nations Development Programme; <www.undp.org>
- International Monetary Fund (IMF); <www.imf.org>
- World Bank; <www.worldbank.org>
- Organisation for Economic Co-operation and Development (OECD); <www.oecd.org>
- World Trade Organization (WTO); <www.wto.org>

**Research Companies / Consultants**

- Tim Bartlett, TRI Hospitality Consulting Spain, <www.trihospitality.com>

**Country Sources**

References for information on the Internet of National Tourism Administrations (NTA), National Tourism Organisations (NTO) and / or web directions for research and data are included in the country contributions of Chapter III of the regional volumes of the *Tourism Market Trends 2004* series.

# 5. Questionnaire on Tourism Development 2003

| | | | |
|---|---|---|---|
| **Country:** | | | |
| **Institution:** | | | |
| **Department:** | | | |
| **Street:** | | **P.O. Box:** | |
| **City:** | | **Post/Zip Code:** | |
| **Tel:** | | **Fax:** | |
| **Contact person:** | | | |
| **Job title:** | | | |
| **Email:** | | | |

***A complimentary electronic copy of the Tourism Market Trends, 2004 Edition regional report will be automatically sent to all participants on this survey as a token of appreciation for their valuable contribution.***

| | |
|---|---|
| **Web site(s) for promotional use** (aimed at visitors to your country)**:** | |
| **Web site(s) for institutional/corporate use** (providing information on tourism policy, research, etc): | |
| **Web site(s) supplying research and data** (providing research and timely information on evolution of tourism, statistical data on tourism volume, receipts, etc): | |

**Please feel free to use as much space as necessary for your answers to the following questions (but try not to exceed 5 pages for the total of your reply to all questions).**

*if you wish you can use a separate document making reference to the number of the question*

*Please indicate the most decisive **positive** or **negative** factors for each of the following (when applicable).*

| **Evaluation of tourism results 2003** | |
|---|---|
| 1) How do you evaluate the overall tourism results in your country during last year and what have been the main determining factors of such performance?<br>For example: overall results (inbound and domestic tourism), significant changes in the performance of existing and/or emerging markets, niche markets, performance of different segments and products, etc. | |
| **2) Supply framework:** additions and changes in products, facilities, capacity and quality in for example the areas of:<br>▪ accommodation;<br>▪ travel agencies / tour operators<br>▪ transport capacity (routes and frequency)<br>▪ attractions / entertainment;<br>▪ specific products such as MICE; cultural tourism, wellness, sports tourism; etc | |
| **3) External factors you deem of relevance with respect to tourism development in your country last year**. For example:<br>▪ political and economic situation (eg exchange rates);<br>▪ facilitation of entry formalities (access constraints, security, etc.);<br>▪ new or improved infrastructures (roads, ports, airports, etc)<br>▪ health;<br>▪ weather conditions;<br>▪ any other stimulating factor or constraint. | |

| **Tourism Policy** | |
|---|---|
| **4) What have been the major developments in the area of Tourism Policy last year (Government / NTA)?**<br>For example: policy-making and planning, Tourism Master Plans, institutional organization, regulation and deregulation, training / human resource development, investment and tax incentives, public-private partnership, research, etc. | |
| **5) What have been the major developments in the area of Marketing and Promotion?**<br>For example: Marketing Plan (strategic and operational), main activities, targeted markets and segments, main products, distribution channels, special promotional campaigns and activities, events, use of new technologies, allocated resources, etc. | |

| **Short term outlook** | |
|---|---|
| **6) What are your prospects and forecasts for tourism in your country for the current year / next few years?**<br>Please include information on forecasts, expectations in major markets, upcoming special events, planned promotional campaigns, etc. | |

| **International Meetings Industry (MICE)** - *In this year's edition of the Tourism Market Trends we would like to pay special attention to the Meetings industry which encompasses the organization, promotion, sales and delivery of Corporate, Association or Government Meetings; Corporate Incentives; Seminars; Technical Visits; Congresses, Conferences and Conventions; Exhibitions and Fairs.* | |
|---|---|
| **7) What are the most important characteristics of supply for the Meetings industry in your country?**<br>For example facilities, organization, main destinations, in terms of:<br>▪ Meetings, Congresses, Conferences and Conventions<br>▪ Incentives<br>▪ Exhibitions and Fairs | |
| **8) How is the international promotion of this industry organised in your country?**<br>For example,<br>▪ at the national or at regional / city level;<br>▪ in a specialized area within the structure of the National / Regional Tourism Organization; or<br>▪ in specialized structures – e.g. National Convention Bureau / Regional Conventions Bureaux.<br>*(Please include the WebPages of the entities responsible for the international promotion of the Meetings industry)* | |
| **9) Does your country collect statistics on the Meetings industry?**<br>*If yes, please specify and provide a brief description of methodology, frequency and attach any data available on the subject* | yes [ ] / no [ ] |
| **10) Could you please provide an estimate of the importance / size of the Meetings industry in your country** (e.g. volume and/or percentage of visitors and/or receipts). | |
| **11) How do you assess the evolution of the Meetings industry in your country in recent years and as well as its future development.** | |

**Thank you very much for your reply to this questionnaire.**
**Please attach any information or document that you consider relevant for your reply of this questionnaire**